International Review of
Industrial
and Organizational
Psychology
1993   Volume 8

International Review of Industrial and Organizational Psychology 1993 Volume 8

Edited by

Cary L. Cooper
and
Ivan T. Robertson

*University of Manchester
Institute of Science & Technology, UK*

JOHN WILEY & SONS
Chichester · New York · Brisbane · Toronto · Singapore

International Review of Industrial and Organizational Psychology
ISSN 0886–1528

Published annually by John Wiley & Sons

The Library of Congress has cataloged this serial publication as follows:

International review of industrial and organizational psychology.
   —1986—Chichester; New York: Wiley, c1986—
   v.: ill.; 24 cm.
   Annual.
   ISSN 0886–1528 = International review of industrial and organizational psychology

   1.Psychology, Industrial—Periodicals. 2.Personnel management—Periodicals.
   [DNLM: 1.Organization and Administration—periodicals. 2.Psychology,
Industrial—periodicals.   W1IN832U]
HF5548.7.I57   158.7′05—dc19   86-643874
                          AACR 2 MARC-S
Library of Congress [8709]

British Library Cataloguing in Publication Data:

International review of industrial and organizational
   psychology 1993.
   1. Industrial psychology
   I. Cooper, Cary L. (C. Lynn), *1940–* II. Robertson,
   Ivan T.
   15877

ISBN 0-471-93634-0

Typeset in 10/12pt Plantin by Photo·graphics, Honiton, Devon
Printed and bound in Great Britain by Biddles Ltd, Guildford and King's Lynn

CONTENTS

CONTRIBUTORS

Cary L. Cooper
Editor

Manchester School of Management, University of Manchester Institute of Science & Technology, PO Box 88, Manchester M60 1QD, UK.

Ivan T. Robertson
Editor

Manchester School of Management, University of Manchester Institute of Science & Technology, PO Box 88, Manchester M60 1QD, UK.

Neil Anderson

Department of Psychology, University of Nottingham, University Park, Nottingham NG7 2RD, UK.

Linda Argote

Graduate School of Industrial Administration, Carnegie Mellon University, Pittsburgh, Pennsylvania 15213, USA.

Timothy T. Baldwin

School of Business, Indiana University, 10th and Fee Lane, Bloomington, Indiana 47405, USA.

Georgia T. Chao

Department of Psychology, Michigan State University, East Lansing, Michigan 48824-1117, USA.

James L. Farr

Department of Psychology, The Pennsylvania State University, University Park, Pennsylvania 16802, USA.

Adrian Furnham

Department of Psychology, University College London, Gower Street, London WC1E 6BT, UK.

Barrie Gunter

Department of Psychology, University College London, Gower Street, London WC1E 6BT, UK.

Jennifer Hedlund

Department of Psychology, Michigan State University, East Lansing, Michigan 48824-1117, USA.

Beryl Hesketh

School of Psychology, The University of New South Wales, PO Box 1, Kensington, New South Wales 2033, Australia.

David A. Hofmann   *Department of Psychology, The Pennsylvania State University, University Park, Pennsylvania 16802, USA.*

Diane Irvine   *Faculty of Management, University of Toronto, 246 Bloor Street West, Toronto, Ontario, Canada M5S 1V4.*

Nigel King   *University of Huddersfield, West Yorkshire HD1 3DH, UK.*

Steve W. J. Kozlowski   *Department of Psychology, Michigan State University, East Lansing, Michigan 48824-1117, USA.*

Gary P. Latham   *Faculty of Management, University of Toronto, 246 Bloor Street West, Toronto, Ontario, Canada M5S 1V4.*

Joseph E. McGrath   *Department of Psychology, University of Illinois, Champaign, Illinois 61820, USA.*

Margaret Y. Padgett   *College of Business Administration, Butler University, 4600 Sunset Avenue, Indianapolis, Indiana 46208, USA.*

Kathleen L. Ringenbach   *Department of Psychology, The Pennsylvania State University, University Park, Pennsylvania 16802, USA.*

Jacob P. Siegel   *Faculty of Management, University of Toronto, 246 Bloor Street West, Toronto, Ontario, Canada M5S 1V4.*

Daniel Skarlicki   *Faculty of Management, University of Toronto, 246 Bloor Street West, Toronto, Ontario, Canada M5S 1V4.*

Eleanor M. Smith   *Department of Psychology, Michigan State University, East Lansing, Michigan 48824-1117, USA.*

Töres Theorell   *National Institute of Psychosocial Factors and Health and Department of Occupational Medicine, Karolinska Hospital, PO Box 60210, 10401 Stockholm, Sweden.*

EDITORIAL FOREWORD

This is the eighth volume of the *International Review of Industrial and Organizational Psychology* and contains contributions from the United States, the United Kingdom, Australia, Sweden and Canada. As with previous volumes the chapters provide coverage of major topic areas within the I/O psychology field. Some of the chapters cover emerging issues or areas that are not the subject of regular review in the I/O psychology literature. Of necessity these chapters provide more in the way of background and orientating conceptual material than a state-of-the-art review might normally provide. The remaining chapters contain more focused reviews of recent literature. For all chapters, our authors were invited to supplement their review with some evaluative and critical analysis of the material covered.

This volume provides reviews on innovation in organizations, management development, performance appraisals, measurement issues, medical and psychological aspects of job interventions, goal orientation and action control theory, corporate culture, organizational downsizing and group processes in organizations.

Since the series began in 1986 we have published an increasing number of contributions from outside the United States and United Kingdom; with the last three volumes providing contributions from eight different countries. Despite this success we are keen to increase the representation of countries where English is not the first language and/or with which English-speaking I/O psychologists are less familiar. This is a difficult endeavour and we have commissioned many more contributions of this kind than we have eventually been able to publish. Our efforts here will continue.

We hope that this and future volumes will meet our objectives of providing regular, comprehensive and scholarly reviews of research and theory on major topics within I/O psychology.

CLC
IR
June, 1992

Chapter 1

INNOVATION IN ORGANIZATIONS

Neil Anderson
University of Nottingham, UK
Nigel King
University of Huddersfield, UK

INTRODUCTION

The process of innovation in organizations has become a salient topic for research amongst European and North American Industrial/Organizational (I/O) psychologists in recent years. At the fulcrum of developments in innovation research have been three national academic research centres: Sheffield in the UK, Leuven in Belgium, and Minnesota in the USA, all of which boasted teams of I/O psychologists and management scientists active in innovation research in the 1980s and early 1990s. The Sheffield group (including Nigel Nicholson, Michael West and the present authors), the Leuven team (principally Rene Bouwen, Jan de Visch, and Chris Steyaert), and the Minnesota centre (headed by Andrew Van de Ven, Harold Angle, and Marshall Scott Poole) have provided a focus for wider interests amongst I/O psychologists in innovation processes and outcomes. But it would be wrong to suggest that research has been restricted to these three centres; far from it. Interest amongst psychologists, both as academics and practitioners, has been extensive and international, grounded as it undoubtedly has been upon major shifts in business environments which have affected all developed, industrialized countries over the past two decades (see Kanter, 1983, 1990 and Peters and Waterman, 1982 for accessible debates of these changes).

DEFINING AND CHARACTERIZING INNOVATION

Innovation has proved to be an elusive term to define with any degree of specificity or general acceptance. A fundamental distinction can be drawn

International Review of Industrial and Organizational Psychology 1993 Volume 8
Edited by C. L. Cooper and I. T. Robertson. © 1993 John Wiley & Sons Ltd.

between definitions which conceive of innovation as a *product* or *outcome*, and those which envisage innovation as an emergent *process* in work settings (King, 1990; West and Farr, 1990). Numerous definitions in each perspective have been propounded but an example of each will suffice to illustrate the difference in emphasis:

> . . . any idea, practice, or material artifact perceived to be new by the relevant unit of adoption. (Zaltman; Duncan, and Holbek, 1973: p. 10)

> . . . innovation is the emergence, import or imposition of new ideas which are pursued towards implementation . . . through interpersonal discussions and successive re-mouldings of the original proposal over time. (Anderson, 1990: p. 3).

Part of the problem in attaining any degree of definitional specificity has been the confusion evident across many innovation studies over the level of analysis under investigation. Staw (1984), for instance, distinguishes between individual, group and organizational level innovations, a categorization which we adhere to in the review of the literature later in this chapter. Another intractable difficulty has been separating out innovation from wider processes of organizational change at the macro level of analysis and from individual creativity at the micro level. Amabile (1983, 1986) argues, however, that these difficulties are largely ones of categorization, and proposes instead that researchers adopt operational definitions of innovation which make sense to the individuals within organizations where innovation processes are being studied. This has been, in effect, precisely what researchers have done. Innovation has been operationalized in many different ways by researchers, often reflecting more the type of innovation under research than any grounded conceptualization of the distinctive qualities of innovations in organizations (see also Hosking and Anderson, 1992). Some headway has been made through researchers proposing a variety of typologies of innovations in organizations, and it is to these that we now turn to illustrate the range of operational definitions which have been adopted.

Typologies of Innovation

In this section we discuss some of the attempts which have been made to develop and apply typologies of innovation. A variety of typologies have been proposed which focus on differing aspects of innovations. Three main themes are evident, however, as illustrated in Figure 1.1. These are (i) the socio-technical systems approach, (ii) the innovation characteristics approach, and (iii) the sources of innovation approach.

Socio-technical systems approach

One innovation typology which has received considerable attention is the distinction between technical and administrative innovations. This is chiefly through the work of Fariborz Damanpour, William Even and Richard Daft (Damanpour and Evan, 1984; Daft, 1978; Damanpour, 1990). Technical innovations occur within the primary work activity of the organization; administrative innovations occur within the social system, and are concerned with the way that work is organized and the 'relationships between people who interact to accomplish a particular goal or task' (Damanpour and Evan, 1984).

Evan (1966) introduces the concept of 'organizational lag', the tendency for innovation in the administrative system of an organization to lag behind innovation in the technical system. Support for this concept came from Damanpour and Evan's (1984) study in American public libraries. They showed that the libraries tended to adopt technical innovations at a faster rate than administrative innovations and that administrative innovations tended to trigger technical innovations, but not vice versa. King and West (1992) also found a preponderance of technical over administrative innovations in a study of a hospital ward, and some evidence for the triggering of technical innovations by administrative innovations.

In a further examination of the data from the libraries study, Damanpour (1990) introduced a third category of innovation which he calls *ancilliary*: 'organizational-environment boundary innovations that go beyond the primary functional activities of the organization'. In the libraries these included the introduction of community services such as career development and adult education programmes. He showed that technical innovations were perceived as more effective than administrative or ancillary innovations, despite the fact that organizational performance was more strongly correlated with administrative than technical innovation. This may reflect the fact that innovations in technology tend to be highly visible, and have more status associated with their adoption than do administrative innovations (Rogers, 1983). Nelkin (1973) observes that organizations are commonly possessed by a 'technological fix'—placing unrealistic expectations on technological changes to solve organizational problems.

Innovation characteristics approach

An alternative to categorizing organizational innovations according to the system within which they occur is to focus on characteristics of the innovations themselves. This is the approach taken by Zaltman, Duncan and Holbek (1973) in their three-dimensional typology of innovations. The first dimension is *programmed–non programmed*. Programmed innovations are scheduled in advance; for instance, the development of larger jet engines following the invention of jumbo jets. Non-programmed innovations—those not scheduled

Author(s)	Damanpour (1987) Damanpour & Evan (1984)	Zaltman, Duncan & Holbeck (1973)	Peters & Waterman (1982) Kanter (1983)	Anderson (1990)	West & Anderson (1992)
Description of typology	Socio-technical systems typology of innovation	Interaction typology of innovation characteristics	Radicalness of innovation typology	Sources of innovation typology	Innovation characteristics and outcome effects of typology (Health Care Organizations)
Innovation types proposed	*Technical* Changes in production methods or products manufactured *Administrative* Changes in social relationships at work *Ancillary* Innovations which cross organization–environment boundaries	*Programmed–Non programmed* Innovations vary in the extent of pre-planning, scheduling and organizational programming undertaken *Instrumental–Ultimate* Instrumental innovations facilitate larger-scale ultimate innovations which can be self-contained change processes. *Radicalness* (a) Novelty—degree of new of the innovation (b) Risk—degree of risk involved in implementation	*Evolutionary–Revolutionary continuum* Evolutionary innovations as minor improvements on existing designs/systems. Revolutionary innovations as paradigm-breaking re-designs of existing designs/systems *See also* Kirton (1976, 1978) at the individual level of analysis who proposes an adaption-innovation continuum of creativity styles	*Emergent innovations* Novel, unproven ideas and proposals developed and implemented unique to a particular organization or organizational subunit *Adopted innovations* Systems/procedures already in use within comparator organizations which are replicated and adopted by other organizations *Imposed innovations* Where changes in environmental contingencies force the organization to develop innovative responses	*Magnitude* Size of innovation and the extent of likely consequences *Novelty* Relative newness of the innovation *Radicalness* Extent of likely change to the status quo *Effectiveness—patient care* Likely benefit to patient care *Effectiveness—staff well-being* Likely benefit to staff well-being *Effectiveness—hospital administration* Likely benefit to hospital administrative efficiency

in advance—are of two types: slack innovations, initiated in response to the availability of slack resources, and distress innovations, which occur when the organization perceives itself to be facing a crisis.

The second dimension distinguishes between *instrumental* and *ultimate* innovations, the former being innovations introduced to facilitate subsequent, more radical innovations, while the latter are innovations which can be considered ends in themselves. The third dimension is *radicalness*; the more risky and novel the innovation, the more radical it is.

Of Zaltman, Duncan and Holbek's dimensions, only radicalness has received much attention in the literature. The consensus is that more radical innovations will meet greater resistance than less radical innovations. Kelley (1976) argues that innovations therefore need to be presented to organizational elites as non-radical changes which fit their existing mind-sets. This may reduce initial resistance to innovations, but if it results in false expectations of the effects of innovation the tactic may harm the organization's future innovative potential (Kimberley, 1981). Radicalness by itself may not be a sufficient cause for resistance to innovation. In a longitudinal study of innovations introduced into a hospital ward, King and West (1992) showed that, in a climate favourable to change, innovation radicalness need not be associated with resistance.

The hospital ward study (King and West, 1992; King, 1992) also compared the innovation process for types on Zaltman, Duncan and Holbek's (1974) other two dimensions. Overall, it found the categorization system useful, in that it reflected real differences in the process between innovations. However, on the programmed–non-programmed dimension almost half of the innovations did not fit any of the existing categories. A third non-programmed category was introduced: *pro-active innovations*. These were innovations which represented attempts by individuals or groups to draw the organization's attention to areas where the possibility of change had not been recognized. Pro-active innovations were found to be abandoned or to meet serious obstacles to progress more often than other types of innovation; they were especially reliant on the power and influence of their initiator(s).

It is disappointing that there has not been a more systematic effort to test the applicability of Zaltman, Duncan and Holbek's (1973) typology, as it offers a good framework for investigating whether, and how, the innovation process and its outcomes differ for different types of innovation.

Another typology based on innovation characteristics is proposed by West and Anderson (1992). It is derived from their work on innovation in top management teams in the British National Health Service (see our discussion of the literature on 'the group as innovator'), though it is equally applicable to organizational-level innovation. They identify dimensions of *magnitude*, *novelty* and *radicalness*. In addition they categorize innovations in terms of *effectiveness* (for patient care, staff well-being, and hospital administrative efficiency).

Sources of innovation approach

A third approach to categorizing innovation types is by their source. Anderson (1990) distinguishes between *emergent, adopted* and *imposed* innovations. Emergent innovations are generated within the organization (or a subunit of it); they represent unique, unproven responses to the organization's particular challenges and problems. The creation within a nursing home of a staff rota to meet the needs of individual staff members would be considered an emergent innovation. Adopted innovations are imported from outside the organization—from other organizations in the same sector, from other sectors, from research institutions and so on. The adoption of Japanese management techniques within the British car industry is one example of this type of innovation. Imposed innovations are forced on the organization by external agencies; for instance, the imposition of new security procedures on airports following the Lockerbie bombing.

Sauer and Anderson (1992) have contrasted the development of imposed and emergent innovations in two British hospitals. The imposed innovations showed a considerably more complex pattern of development than the emergent innovations, with secondary innovations proliferating from it. However, participants tended to express stronger feelings about the emergent innovations and also to agree more often over what the key incidents in the process were.

Is a generalized approach to innovation justified?

Having looked at how researchers have developed typologies of innovation, and the relatively slight body of work which has attempted to apply these typologies in the field, we move on to the question of whether it makes sense to uphold a single, generalizable concept of innovation. There is certainly an argument to be made for rejecting the generalist approach. Different types of innovation have been shown to differ in complexity, in the reactions they provoke from organizational members, in who and where they originate from, in their perceived effectiveness. One response to the inconsistent findings of research searching for antecedents to innovation (Rogers, 1983; Downs and Mohr, 1976 and see our later discussion in this chapter) is to restrict the focus to facilitators and inhibitors associated with specific innovation types.

We would argue that it is unrealistic to expect precisely the same factors to facilitate or inhibit all innovations, or to expect the innovation process to develop in essentially the same way in all organizational settings. However, the maintenance of a unitary concept of innovation does serve a purpose. It enables us to step back from the details of particular innovations in particular organizations, and focus on understanding the psychology of how organizations, and the individuals within them, respond to and initiate change in their environments. Research therefore needs to operate at two levels; it needs to explore the distinctive characteristics of innovation types in specific organizational contexts, but it also needs to relate the understanding gained to our wider understanding of the psychology of innovation.

The purpose of the following sections is to provide a comprehensive but critical overview of developments in this research base. It should be noted, however, that extensive and detailed reviews of these three levels of analysis have been published elsewhere quite recently (see Angle, 1989; West and Farr, 1989; King, 1990; King and Anderson, 1990; Anderson, 1992). It is consequently not our purpose to replicate these individual reviews here, but to overview the field, and in so doing to draw attention and to challenge some of the inherent assumptions guiding the research agendas of I/O psychologists over the last two decades. Following Staw (1984) we sectionalize our review to cover:

(1) The organization as innovator.
(2) The work group as innovator.
(3) The individual as innovator.

THE ORGANIZATION AS INNOVATOR

Although research at the organizational level addresses a wide range of issues, for the purposes of this overview they can be summarized in three broad questions about innovation:

(1) What factors facilitate or inhibit the production, adoption and/or implementation of innovations by organizations?
(2) What is the nature of the innovation process and how can it best be managed?
(3) Are there consistent differences between different types of innovation?

These questions are not mutually exclusive; indeed all three need to be addressed in an attempt to provide a general theoretical framework for understanding organizational innovation. However, most empirical work focuses mainly or exclusively on one or other of the questions. We therefore examine how far I/O psychology has come in providing answers to each of the questions, and highlight the most promising areas for future development.

Facilitators and Inhibitors of Innovation

By far the largest proportion of research into the organization as innovator is concerned with identifying factors which help or hinder the introduction of innovations by organizations. The classic approach to this area, as in many other areas of I/O psychology, has been the use of attitude and other scale measures and self-completion questionnaires, in cross-sectional designs. This can lead to a rather simplistic input/output conception of organizational innovation which suggests that more of factor x and less of factor y will lead to higher or lower levels of innovation. The past decade has seen something of a shift in emphasis with a growing recognition of the need to study organizational innovation as a complete process over time (see our discussion below of research addressing the second underlying research question). As a result, some of the more valuable theoretical work has stressed the need to understand facilitators and inhibitors of innovation as they affect different stages of the process (Rogers, 1983; Van de Ven, 1986; West, 1990). In the following section we discuss the main groups of factors which have been suggested as helping or hindering organizational innovation.

People

In looking for factors which faciliate or inhibit innovation at the level of the organization, a considerable amount of attention has been given to the characteristics and behaviour of organizational members. Leader characteristics have long been a major focus, with researchers examining the relationship between leaders' values, motivation, tenure, educational level and professional allegiances on organizational innovativeness. Mohr (1969), for instance, found that public health health organizations whose leaders had liberal ideologies and who held an interactive view of their role tended to be more innovative than those with more conservative leaders who defined their role less interactively. The importance of leaders' values has also been stressed by other authors (e.g. Pierce and Delbecq, 1977; Patti, 1974; Hage and Dewar, 1973). In a study of US hospitals, Kimberly and Evanisko (1981) found that different leader characteristics were associated with innovativeness for hospital administrators than for chiefs of medicine.

No clear picture has emerged of leader characteristics which consistently faciliate innovation. It has become apparent though that the influence of leader characteristics is often secondary to, or mediated by, other variables: resource availability in Mohr's (1969) study; structural variables in Kimberly and Evanikos' (1981) study. It is therefore not surprising that in the last decade there has been a shift in emphasis away from leader characteristics and towards leadership style. The question regarding leadership and innovation therefore changes from 'What are innovative leaders like?' to 'What do innovative leaders do?' There is a strong consensus that a participative/collaborative leadership style is most likely to foster innovation in organizations (Kanter, 1983; Nystrom, 1979; Peters and Waterman, 1982; Farr and Ford, 1990). Equally, it is widely recognized that a key element of successful leadership for innovation is the leader's clear vision or sense of mission for his or her organization (West, 1990; Bennis, 1989; Kanter, 1983).

Dunphy and Stace (1988) have argued that a participative leadership style is not always the most effective for facilitating innovation. They propose a contingency model for planned organizational change, with the appropriate strategy for change depending on how 'out of fit' the organization is with its environment, whether time for participation is available, and whether there is support for radical innovation within the organization. Where the organization faces a turbulent, threatening environment, leaders may need to be dictatorial rather than participative in order to introduce necessary radical innovations.

Manz, Barstein, Hostager and Shapiro (1989) examined the influence of leadership styles on the development of seven major innovations studied longitudinally in the Minnesota Innovation Research Program (Van de Ven, Angle and Poole, 1989). They concluded that multiple leadership approaches were appropriate for different innovations and at different points in the innovation process, though rhetorical/visionary (Howell, 1982) and participative (Locke and Schweiger, 1979) styles were more often associated with successful innovation than was transactional leadership (Blau, 1964). Regardless of the leader's overall style, they found that six key issues needed to be addressed regarding the introduction of innovations: encouraging individual initiative; clarifying individual responsibilities; providing clear and complete performance evaluation feedback; maintaining a strong task orientation; emphasizing human resources; and demonstrating trust in organization members (p. 632). Anderson and King (1991) develop this point, arguing that effective leadership style is also contingent upon the stage of the process that a particular innovation has reached. Figure 1.2 illustrates their contingency model and suggests leadership styles most likely to prove effective at different stages in the innovation process. In addition to research focusing specifically on leaders in organizations, there is also a body of work examining the characteristics of other individuals with key roles in introducing innovations. These include organizational members who emerge as 'idea champions' (Bouwen and Fry, 1988), putting extraordinary efforts into the promotion of particular innovative ideas, and external change agents employed by organizations to guide innovation processes.

The tendency for innovation research to focus on leaders and other key actors and neglect the characteristics and behaviour of other organizational members has been criticized by several writers (Rogers and Agarwala-Roers, 1976; King, 1990). The influence of other organizational members is generally discussed in terms of resistance to change (Bedeian, 1980). There is a tendency to regard resistance as stemming from dispositional hostility to novelty, though the source of this hostility is rarely examined. The exceptions are Van de Ven's (1986) explanation in terms of individual cognition, that individuals have a physiologically determined limitation for perceiving novel and complex situations, and Gersick's (1988, 1989) model of routine habitualization within organizations.

Van de Ven (1986) is right to argue that we need to apply knowledge from cognitive and social psychology in order to understand reactions to innovation, rather than accepting assumptions about resistance to change which he

Figure 1.2 Contingency model of leadership of innovation
Source: based on Anderson and King (1991)

describes as 'folklore'. However, we also need to be aware of ideological reasons for the focus on resistance to change by organizational members subordinate to the decision-making higher management's agenda (Hosking and Anderson, 1992). From this perspective, the impact of subordinate organizational members is more likely to be noticed if it is negative than if it is positive. Equally, from higher management's perspective, opposition to an innovation may appear as irrational, whereas from the perspective of other organizational members opposition may be a rational response to an innovation which damages their interests.

Structure

The effect of organizations' structural characteristics on their adoption of innovations has been examined in numerous studies, especially during the 1960s and 1970s when this was arguably the dominant concern of organizational innovation research (e.g. Pierce and Delbecq, 1977; Zaltman, Duncan and Holbek, 1973; Shephard, 1967; Hage and Aiken, 1967). In the 1980s there was less interest in relating structural variables to innovativeness, largely because of the generally low correlations obtained and the inconsistency of findings (see Rogers, 1983; Downs and Mohr, 1976).

Zaltman, Duncan and Holbek's (1973) discussion of the influence of organizational structure on innovation has been highly influential and is still widely cited in the literature. Their focus is on three structural variables: *centralization*—the extent to which there is a concentration of decision-making power at the top of the hierarchy; *formalization*—the extent to which the organization emphasizes the following of rules and procedures; and *complexity*— the degree of task differentiation and occupational specialization in the organization. They argue that these variables tend to have opposite effects on the pre-and post-adoption stages of the innovation process (i.e. 'initiation' and 'implementation'), causing the 'innovation dilemma'. That is, innovation initiatives are facilitated by structures which exhibit low centralization and formalization, and high complexity. Implementation is expedited by highly centralized and formalized, non-complex structures.

Some evidence can be found for the effects of each of these variables on innovation initiation (Burns and Stalker, 1961; Hage and Aiken, 1967; Shephard, 1967; Gordon, Morse, Gordon, Kervasdoue, Kimberley et al, 1974) and implementation (Sapolsky, 1967; Radnor, Rubinstein and Bean, 1968; Neal and Radnor, 1973). However, there are three problems in evaluating the validity of Zaltman, Duncan and Holbek's model. Firstly, relatively few studies have focused on the implementation of innovations, as Kimberly (1981) points out. Secondly, the dominance of cross-sectional studies means that research has failed to examine the influence of organizational structure over the whole course of the innovation process. The third problem for Zaltman, Duncan and Holbek's proposals is that the authors do not make it clear how they expect the three structural variables to influence adoption decisions, yet the majority of studies in which organizational structure is related to innovativeness use adoption as the dependent variable. Thus it is hard to know what evidence constitutes support for the Zaltman, Duncan and Holbek studies showing centralization and formalization to be positively related to adoption (Evan and Black, 1967; Corwin, 1972) or those showing them to be negatively related (Rosner, 1968; Aiken and Hage, 1971).

Another structural characteristic which has received considerable attention is stratification—simply, the number of status levels within an organization, and the ease of mobility between levels. Pierce and Delbecq's (1977) review found a consensus that high stratification inhibits innovation, a conclusion with which Kanter (1983) concurs. Stratification leads to a preoccupation with status which discourages creative thinking and risk-taking, with the result that few innovations are initiated, and fewer still adopted and implemented. Kanter calls this 'the elevator mentality'.

As important as vertical relations within organizations are lateral relations. Structures encouraging lateral communications, with such matrix structures (Child, 1984), are more likely to facilitate innovation than those which are highly segmented, with relatively impermeable boundaries between subunits (Kanter, 1983). Matrix and similar structures allow multiple viewpoints to converge upon a problem, and encourage cross-fertilization of ideas, widely recognized as facilitative of innovation (Staw, 1990; Kanter, 1983; Peters and Waterman, 1982).

It is fair to say that by the mid-1980s organizational structure had become a rather stale topic within the innovation research literature. One of the few promising new directions for research into the organization structure/innovation relationship is Morgan's (1983, 1986) concept of the holographic organization. In a hologram, all elements of the whole are present in each part. Morgan argues that four principles need to be adhered to in creating a holographic, and thus innovative, organization:

(1) Redundancy of functions—the organization needs excess capacity in order to maximize its capacity for reorganization. An example is the autonomous work-group, with multiskilled members who can substitute for one another as required. At any one time, some of the skills of each member are redundant (in that they are not being used), but the potential for responding flexibly to changes in its environment is high.

(2) Requisite variety—the degree of complexity built into an organization should mirror the degree of complexity in the environment. Van de Ven (1986) argues that one way of achieving this is for all environmental scanning to be a responsibility of all organizational members, rather than for selected individuals in boundary roles. This ensures that perceptions of the environments are not reliant upon the perspectives of only a small number of people. Recruiting people with understanding of, and connections with, key stakeholders in the environment is also important.

(3) Minimum critical specification—for any organizational activity, only the minimum level of specification needed (i.e. in terms of rules, routines, and procedures) should be imposed.

(4) Learning to learn—the flexibility produced within an organization by the previous three principles could degenerate into a state of chaos. The active encouragement of the organization's learning capacities must therefore be a high priority in the holographic organization. This includes double loop learning, questioning the assumptions and evaluation criteria upon which organization activities are based.

Morgan's ideas are undoubtedly challenging, both conceptually and practically, but it is only through attempting to meet such challenges that the examination of organizational structure and its impact on innovation can progress.

Organization size and resources

There is some evidence to suggest a positive relationship between organization size and innovation (Soete, 1979; in Pavitt, 1991; Kimberly and Evanisko, 1981; Kaluzny, Veney and Gentry 1974). Pavitt (1991) highlights the contribution of large firms to innovation in the chemical, electical, aerospace and automobile sectors, and points out that large innovative firms have shown remarkable resilience and longevity in the twentieth century, despite successive waves of radical technological change. He identifies four key characteristics of such firms: the building-up of firm-specific competencies; high differentiation; high levels of collaboration between professional and functional specialist groups; and a high degree of uncertainty associated with innovative activity.

However, the evidence is not all supportive of the proposition that larger organizations are more innovative than smaller ones. A 1981 report from the US General Accounting Office (cited in Rogers, 1983) found that in the private sector, smaller organizations were more inventive than larger ones in producing new technological products. Utterback (1974) concluded from a review of innovation diffusion in industry that organization size was unassociated with speed of innovation adoption. Rogers (1983) argues that organization size may be no more than a surrogate for other variables, such as total and slack resources, and complexity of structure.

All innovations consume organizational resources—financial, human and material. Resource availability is therefore the bottom line for any innovation attempt. However, research suggests that there is far from a simple linear relationship between resources and innovation. The availabllity of resources for innovation can stimulate innovative activity, as Stocking (1985) argues in relation to the British National Health Service (NHS). One example was the development of regional secure units by Regional Health Authorities (RHAs), where the provision of funding from the centre was influential in an area in which the RHAs had previously shown little interest in acting. Mohr (1969) found that resource levels were a powerful mediating variable in the relationship between leadership characteristics of local health officers and innovative activity of their departments. Although innovation cannot occur without resources, the levels required may be surprisingly low. Stocking's (1985) study showed that many innovations were developed as far as a first pilot stage with very little need for new financial resources, through the imaginative use of existing personnel and materials. King and Coventry (1992) found examples of low-cost but highly effective innovative solutions to problems in communication between hospital doctors and general practitioners.

It is important to recognize that the concept of slack resources is as much psychological as it is financial (Rogers and Agarwala-Rogers, 1976). An organization may be aware that certain resources exist, but fail to recognize that they are available for the purpose of innovation, or lack the motivation to use them in such a way. Organizations must also be wary of 'short termism' in allocating resources to innovation development (Pavitt, 1991); that is the tendency to assess innovations' effectiveness—and thus worthiness of financial support—in terms of immediate payback.

Strategy

In examining the relationship between organizational strategy and innovation, a popular approach has been to identify and compare strategic types. Miles and Snow's (1978) typology of strategic types has been influential. They propose four types: 'Defenders' are primarily concerned with the efficiency of existing operations, seeking to dominate their niche in a stable market; 'Prospectors' are almost continually engaged in the development of new products and seeking of new markets; 'Analysers' operate in two types of product domain—stable and unstable—and therefore exhibit a dualistic structuring of activities; Finally, 'Reactors' may perceive change in their environment but are unable to respond to it effectively.

Meyer (1982) applied this typology to US hospitals and he found that strategic type was an important influence on whether innovation occurred in response to an 'environmental jolt' (a doctor's strike). Of those hospitals studied in depth, using ethnographic methods, the one identified by independent experts as a prospector-type viewed the crisis as a 'good experiment' and reacted innovatively. In contrast, the defender-type hospital responded by utilizing its considerable financial slack to 'weather the storm'—innovation was unnecessary. Nicholson, Rees and Brooks-Rooney (1990) also found that Miles and Snow's (1978) typology, in a somewhat modified version, was a useful tool for understanding differences in innovative activity between eight British wool-textile companies. They stress that there is no one 'ideal' strategy for maximizing organizational performance, but that all organizations do need to actively consider the appropriateness of their strategic outlook in relation to their environment.

Organizational climate and culture

The lessening of interest amongst innovation researchers in leader characteristics and structural variables has been matched over the last decade by a growing emphasis on the role of organizational climate and culture on facilitating or inhibiting innovation (Fischer and Farr, 1985; Morgan, 1986; West and Farr, 1989; Nystrom, 1990). There is no consensus regarding the precise dimensions of pro-innovation climates and cultures, and indeed, as with structure it would be unwise to expect one set of prescriptions to be effective in encouraging innovation in all organizational settings (Nicholson, Rees and Brooks-Rooney, 1990; Morgan, 1986). However, some aspects of climate and culture are commonly suggested as facilitative of innovation: support for ideas, and willingness to tolerate their failure; challenge, freedom and constructive controversy in climates; egalitarianism, risk-taking and norms for innovation in cultures.

The discussion of these factors within the innovation literature has largely been at a theoretical level, with a few empirical studies of climate (Duncan, 1972; Fischer and Farr, 1985) and fewer still of cultural variables. An exception is Nystrom's (1990) study of a large Swedish chemical manufacturing firm. Nystrom views innovation as a product of the interaction between organizational strategy and structure, with climate and culture as important intervening variables. Differences in climate and culture between the four divisions of the firm were associated with their orientation which Nystrom termed either 'positional' or 'innovative'. The most positional division was characterized by a climate that was low in challenge, risk-encouragement, playfulness and debates, and which emphasized the need for profit and survival, with security and discipline the dominant values. The most innovative division had a climate which strongly encouraged risk-taking and debate, and was high on challenge, idea support, playfulness and freedom. Its culture was dominated by a preoccupation with creativity and change, to the exclusion of other values such as customer orientation and profit. This division also exhibited a lack of harmony and trust, and high levels of conflict. This was in contrast to the second most innovative division, which had high levels of harmony and trust and very little conflict, but which fulfilled its creative potential less successfully. Nystrom argues that some conflict is probably needed if innovation is to be maximized; though if it is not kept within limits the resultant disharmony and mistrust may eventually be harmful.

Nystrom's (1990) study is an important step forward in examining expirically the role played by organizational climate and culture in the innovation process. It is limited by its cross-sectional design, as he himself acknowledges, and what is needed now is further research of this type, utilizing longitudinal designs.

Organizational environment

It has long been recognized that factors outside the organization, and the relationship between the organization and its environment, may infleunce the innovation process (Aiken and Alford, 1970; Balridge and Burnham, 1975). More than ten years ago, Kimberly (1981) called for more studies of the impact of environmental factors on organizational innovation. To date, the area remains underdeveloped. Some empirical studies have found a positive relationship between adoption of innovations and the size of the city or community within which the organization is sited (Mohr, 1969; Kimberly and Evanisko, 1981), while others have shown competition to stimulate innovation (Copper, 1984; Milo, 1971).

At least as important as objective features of organizational environments is how organizations perceive their environments (Morgan, 1986). One factor influencing this is the level of environmental 'scanning' for innovations carried out by organizations and their members (Kimberly, 1978). This has been associated with the existence of boundary-spanning roles within the organization (Tushman, 1977) and the degree of professionalization of organizational members (Daft, 1978). Nicholson, Rees and Brooks-Rooney (1990) argue that the type of environmental scanning carried out by organizations is dependent on their strategic types, as was evident in their own study. They also point out that scanning is not 'the sole prerogative of the successful'—indeed ailing organizations may scan very actively to search for a way out of their troubles, but without regard to improved performance as they lack strategies for coping with changes in their environment.

The Innovation Process

It has been recognized theoretically for many years that organizational innovation should be understood as a process or series of processes. For instance, Zaltman, Duncan and Holbek's (1973) concept of the innovation dilemma, mentioned earlier, predicts that structural factors which facilitate one stage of the innovation process ('initiation') will inhibit another ('implementation'). As mentioned earlier, the last decade has seen an increasing emphasis in the literature on the need to examine the process of innovation, rather than simply cataloguing its antecedents (Rogers, 1983; Schroeder, Van de Ven, Scudder and Polley, 1989).

Many authors have proposed descriptive models of the innovation process, for instance Harvey and Mills (1970), Hage and Aiken (1970), Kimberly (1981), Rogers (1983) and Staw (1990). Typically these depict the process as a linear sequence of discrete stages, with an explicit or implicit division between what happens up to the point where the organization adopts an innovation and what happens to the innovation after adoption. Disregarding differences which are mainly terminological—for example Harvey and Mills' (1970) 'issue perception', Zaltman, Duncan and Holbek's (1973) 'knowledge-awareness substage', Staw's (1990) 'presentation of problem'—the models chiefly vary in the extent to which they emphasize pre- or post-adoption phases of the process. Thus, the early models of Wilson (1986) and Harvey and Mills (1970) focus principally on events leading up to adoption, while Kimberly (1981), Rogers (1983) and Staw (1990) place at least as much emphasis on the post-adoption process. Despite these differences, it is possible to represent the conventional stage-based models with a single generic model, as shown in Figure 1.3.

The proliferation of innovation process models is not matched by an abundance of empirical research examining their validity. This is in part due to the fact that such research is difficult to conduct; the kind of simple cross-sectional design which has tended to dominate innovation research is entirely inadequate for examining how processes develop over time. Longitudinal or retrospective analyses of innovations are required, but they are more time-consuming and produce findings which can be difficult to interpret. Where such studies have been carried out they have offered at best only partial support to traditional stage-based models of the innovation process. Pelz (1983), in a study of urban innovations, found that for relatively simple, non-radical innovations there was some adherence to discrete developmental stages, but for more complex and radical innovations such stages in the process cannot be distinguished. Witte (1972) examined decision processes in the introduction of Electronic Data Processing (EDP) in 233 organizations, using retrospective

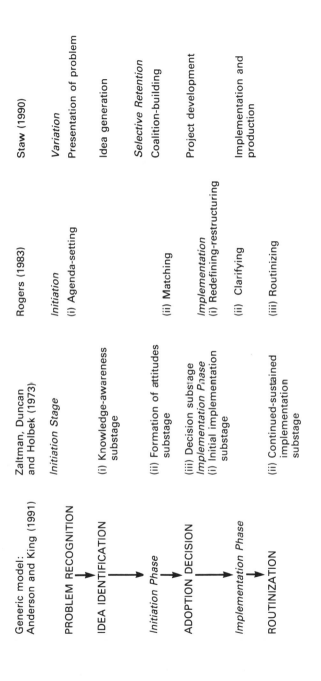

Figure 1.3 Stage-based models of the innovation process

Generic model: Anderson and King (1991)	Zaltman, Duncan and Holbek (1973)	Rogers (1983)	Staw (1990)
	Initiation Stage	*Initiation*	*Variation*
PROBLEM RECOGNITION		(i) Agenda-setting	Presentation of problem
IDEA IDENTIFICATION	(i) Knowledge-awareness substage		Idea generation
	(ii) Formation of attitudes substage		*Selective Retention*
Initiation Phase		(ii) Matching	Coalition-building
ADOPTION DECISION	(iii) Decision substage		
	Implementation Phase	*Implementation*	Project development
	(i) Initial implementation substage	(i) Redefining-restructuring	
Implementation Phase		(ii) Clarifying	Implementation and production
ROUTINIZATION	(ii) Continued-sustained implementation substage	(iii) Routinizing	

document analysis. There was no evidence of distinct phases, nor that the process was more efficient (in terms of speed, thoroughness, and absence of internal and external conflict) in those cases which approximated most closely to a sequence of discrete phases.

An important re-evaluation of how we should conceptualize the innovation process is presented by Schroeder et al. (1989). They criticize the common *a priori* assumption that the process progresses in a linear sequence of stages, arguing that in research such an assumption can easily become a self-fulfilling prophecy. Their own research uses longitudinal data on seven diverse major innovations, gathered as part of the Minnesota Innovation Research Program (MIRP: Van de Ven, Angle and Pool, 1989). On the basis of this they propose a model which depicts innovation as a much more fluid process than is suggested by most earlier models, centred on six common observations:

(1) innovation is stimulated by shocks, either internal or external to the organization;
(2) an initial idea tends to proliferate into several ideas during the innovation process;
(3) in managing an innovation effort, unpredictable setbacks and surprises are inevitable; learning occurs whenever the innovation continues to develop;
(4) as an innovation develops, the old and the new exist concurrently, and over time they are linked together;
(5) restructuring of the organization often occurs during the innovation process;
(6) hands-on top management involvement occurs throughout the innovation period.

King (1992) carried out an empirical comparison between Schroeder's model and a traditional stage-based model (Zaltman, Duncan and Holbek, 1973), using participant observation data from seven innovations introduced on a hospital ward. Interrater reliability was found to be higher for Schroeder et al.'s model, while overall support across raters was somewhat stronger for Zaltman, Duncan and Holbek's model. However, the latter finding was probably a product of the broad definitions of stages in the Zaltman, Duncan and Holbek model, which enable a wider range of events and actions to be interpreted as supportive than do the more narrow and precise definitions in Schroeder et al.'s model. In addition, support was not strong for the linear sequence of stages proposed in Zaltman, Duncan and Holbek's model, nor even for a clear-cut distinction between pre- and post-adoption activities. King concludes that the overall approach of Schroeder et al. offers more promise for the field than does the traditional stage-based approach, even if some of the individual observations in their model may be of limited generalizability.

A central failing of stage-based models of the innovation process is that they implicitly accept an image of organizations as unitary social worlds; there is no room for the notion that groups and individuals may differ in their perceptions and interpretations of events, nor that change processes might develop in different—perhaps conflicting—directions in different parts of the organization. Such an image is at odds with modern thinking about the nature of organizations and of processes of change within organizations (Morgan, 1986; Nicholson, 1990; Bouwen, Steyaert and De Visch, 1992). It is also contradicted by empirical evidence for the existence of differing social worlds within organizations. For instance, Aydin and Rice (1991) found that membership of occupational and departmental social worlds had a powerful influence on individual attitudes towards a major innovation in a hospital and on how the innovation was implemented, while King, Anderson and West (1991) identified different perceptions of the innovation process between managerial and non-managerial staff in two British homes for elderly people. Ramirez and Bartunek (1989) found that an action research programme to implement a management development project in a US hospital led to different values and attitudes surfacing between Medical, Nursing and Administrative managers, and as a result to increased political behaviour and intergroup conflict.

The recognition that diverse social worlds exist within organizations is not only of theoretical importance to innovation research. It also has major practical implementations for the management of the innovation process. Perhaps the most important of these is that managers and other change agents need to be aware from the start that different subunits have different professional values, expectations and experiences. These are likely to lead to differing perceptions of the purpose, impact and outcome of an innovation (Ramirez and Bartunek, 1989; Brown and Covey, 1987).

Given these differing perceptions of the innovation process within organizations, communication between groups or subunits, and between change agents and other organizational members becomes central concern for the management of innovation. Damanpour (1990) stresses the need for management to communicate their expectations of an innovation to organizational members, in order to create 'mutual expectancy of high performance' (p. 136). Similarly King, Anderson and West (1991) found that shared perceptions of influences on the innovation process were associated with good communications between management and care workers in the two residential homes examined in their study.

Recent research into the process of innovation above all highlights its complexity. Because of this, a key lesson for managers to learn is that the management of innovation must be actively attended to (Bouwen and Fry, 1988). Van de Ven (1986) recognizes the process problem of 'managing new ideas into good currency' as one of the central problems in the management of innovation. It is not enough to identify a good idea, adopt it within the organization, and then stand back to let it run its course. Managers must adopt strategies of realizing innovative ideas which take account of the differing perspectives of groups within the organization. Gaining support for the implementation of innovations requires political activity in the forming of alliances and power bases. A danger that managers must be particularly aware of is the tendency for rhetoric to replace action (Kimberly, 1981). This can lead to 'a facade of demonstrating progress'; which can only be seen through by managers maintaining 'hands-on' involvement with the innovation process.

THE WORK GROUP AS INNOVATOR

Of the three levels of analysis suggested by Staw (1984), substantially less research has been conducted into work group innovation in comparison with organizational and individual level research. The relative paucity of studies at this level of analysis noted, there has been sufficient research by I/O psychologists to permit two recent reviews of the extant research (King and Anderson, 1990; Anderson, 1992). Again, our aim here is to overview these empirical studies, drawing attention specifically to theoretical and methodological shortcomings in existing work, and therefore highlighting directions for future research at the group level of analysis.

Research into work group innovation can be categorized into three main areas:

(1) Studies into structural antecedent factors to innovation.
(2) Studies into climatic and psychological antecedent factors to innovation.
(3) Studies into innovation processes within work groups.

Structural Research

Several pragmatic questions have dominated research studies into the effects of group structure and composition upon innovativeness, most of which implicitly assume maximization of group innovativeness to be the ultimate objective. Perhaps this is not surprising given the potential benefits of group innovations for wider organizational profitability and the formal allotment of responsibilities for generating novel products to specific groups in organizations (e.g. Research and Development teams). Thus much research in this vein has taken a managerial perspective, or has focused upon those groups which possess formal responsibility to be innovative. The dilemma confronting this approach lies in attempting to advise senior managers how to initiate and direct innovation processes that are quintessentially emergent social processes and which, by their very nature, pose a threat to those in positions of managerial authority.

Payne (1990), for instance, reviews earlier work by Stankiewicz (1979) into the effects of cohesiveness upon the innovative productivity of 172 Swedish academic research groups. If groups were highly cohesive, larger groups tended to be more productive. If cohesiveness was low, however, groups with less than seven members performed better. Other researchers have argued cohesiveness to be a necessary but not sufficient condition for group innovation (e.g. Nystrom, 1979) but have been countered by others asserting that extremely high levels of cohesiveness may inhibit the development of novel and radical ideas (King and Anderson, 1990). Certainly, avoiding excessive homogeneity amongst group members in terms of their backgrounds and training and development has been advocated as one important requirement for securing a diversity of views and hence innovation (Geschka, 1983; Kanter, 1983). Popular models and methods of team building (Belbin, 1981) extend this argument to suggest that effective and innovative teams are comprised of individuals matching specific role types. It must be noted, however, that little published research supports the assertions of these models.

King (1990) reviews many of the studies into the effects of leadership style on innovation and concludes that the general consensus supports a democratic-participative style as being a facilitator of innovativeness in work groups (cf. Nystrom, 1979; Coopey, 1987; Wallace, 1987). Manz et al. (1989) advocate more of a contingency approach, arguing that multiple leadership approaches appear to be appropriate in varying innovation contexts and at different stages of the innovation process. Other pertinent elements of group structure including size, diversity and role relationships remain little researched and therefore it seems premature to speculate upon the effects of these variables on innovativeness.

A few studies have addressed the influence of group longevity upon innovativeness. Katz (1982) investigated the performance of 50 R & D teams over time. An inverse relationship between longevity and innovativeness was reported; the longer groups had been in existence the less innovative they became. Similarly, Nystrom (1979) argues for restricting the active lifespan of groups as a means for maximizing innovativeness. It is regrettable that research in this area has not built upon relevant social psychological literatures, including those on group development over time, creative problem-solving and decision-making, to elucidate the relation between the lifespan of the group and innovativeness.

Climate Research

The emergence of organizational climate and culture as concepts for research within the I/O psychological community has been striking over the last 10–15 years. Unfortunately, these developments appear to have gone almost unnoticed by researchers active in work group innovation. Group cohesiveness as a unidimensional facet of climate has constituted the primary focus for studies into innovation at this level.

West and Wallace (1991), for instance, found cohesiveness to be the principal discriminating variable between high and low innovative health care teams. More recently, however, research has considered the multifaceted composition of group climate. West (1990) proposes a four-factor model of climatic factors, comprising *vision, participative safety, norms for innovation*, and *climate for excellence*, to categorize influences upon group innovativeness. Longitudinal research to validate this model has shown significant correlations between this facet-specific climate model and management team innovation in UK health care settings (West and Anderson, 1992). However, research in this area is at an early stage of development and further studies are called for to elucidate the relationship between climate and innovativeness and, equally, the relationship between innovation processes and group climate over time.

Processual Research

Some recent work has examined how innovations develop from embryonic ideas into implemented changes within work groups, particularly in relation to group development over time. In initial experimental studies, Gersick (1989) presented groups of subjects with a simulated project task of one hour's duration, telling groups of this time constraint in advance of the experiment. Groups were videotaped with the knowledge and permission of subjects. The study revealed distinct changes in the interpersonal behaviours of subjects around the mid-point of the lifespan of the group, that is, after 30 minutes. Individuals reappraised their orientation to the group task, developed new ways of working, and proposed innovations in task objectives. Gersick argues that the groups showed a *punctuated equilibrium model* of group development. In other words that groups changed significantly at the mid-point of their lifespan, and conscious of the time limitation on the group task, instituted several innovations in work methods and procedures. A subsequent field study of this 'quantum leap effect' in organizational settings supports this model of innovation development in groups of limited longevity (Gersick, 1989), and hints at the possibility that earlier, simple linear models of innovation processes do not accurately reflect such group processes in real life (see our earlier discussion).

In this vein, West (1990) proposes a four-stage cyclical model of the innovation process—*recognition, initiation, implementation*, and *stabilization*. This model also differs from simple linear process models propounded at the individual and organizational level of analysis (e.g. Basadur et al., 1982; Amabile, 1983; Zaltman, Duncan and Holbek, 1973) in that it conceives innovation as an on-going and reiterative process; one innovation stimulating multiple peripheral innovations. McGrath (1985) refers to this as the cascading and amplifying effects that result from a major innovation triggering multiple peripheral innovations over time. West links the cyclical model to his four-factor theory of climate for innovation, hypothesizing that different climatic factors impinge upon innovation at each stage in the process (see West and

Farr, 1990: pp. 309–330). This model appears valuable, and remains to be validated through longitudinal studies across multiple organizational settings.

To summarize research at the level of the work group, we would argue that greater attention needs to be paid to this level of analysis in future research. Given the focal position of groups on many occasions for initiating and implementing innovations within organizations, it is surprising that relatively little research has focused upon the work group as a catalyst for innovation. Future research could usefully redress this imbalance by examining the influence of other structural and climatic variables upon group innovativeness, and by investigating the process of innovation in groups through testing the empirical validity of process models such as those proposed by Gersick (1989) and West (1990).

THE INDIVIDUAL AS INNOVATOR

In considering the nature of individual innovation within organizations, previous writers have been concerned to distinguish innovation from creativity (West, 19090; Farr and Ford, 1990). While there is not complete agreement on how this should be achieved, two principal distinctions are commonly made. Firstly, it is pointed out that creativity involves the generation of ideas which are novel to the individual. In contrast, innovation only requires ideas to be novel to the organization, work group or work role within which they are introduced and not necessarily to the individual introducing them. Secondly, while creativity requires only the production of novel and appropriate ideas, innovation demands their implementation or attempted implementation. Creativity is essentially a cognitive process, though influenced by social psychological factors (Amabile, 1983). Innovation is a social process (Pierce and Delbecq, 1977; Van de Ven, 1986) involving attempts to change the status quo within the organization and/or its subunits.

Although there is a real and important distinction to be made between the processes of innovation and creativity, at the level of the individual, they are so closely linked as to make some overlap between the literatures inevitable. We therefore begin by discussing Amabile's (1983) theory of the social psychology of creativity, and its implications for individual innovation in organizations and then we consider the literature on work role innovation.

Amabile's Social Psychology of Innovation

Amabile's (1983) theory of social psychology of creativity has been successful in raising awareness of the influence of social factors on individual creative performance. She proposes three components of creativity: task motivation, domain-relevant skills, and creativity-relevant skills. These influence the progress of the creative process, from task preparation, through presentation, idea generation, idea validation to outcome assessment. The central plank of the theory is what she calls 'the intrinsic motivation hypothesis of creativity', which predicts that a state of intrinsic motivation facilitates creativity, while a state of extrinsic motivation inhibits it. In experiments with children and adults, Amabile and her co-workers have found very strong support for this hypothesis (Hennessey and Amabile, 1988). The hypothesis has also been tested in R & D laboratories (Amabile and Gryskiewicz, 1988). Findings were that intrinsic factors were predominantly facilitating and external factors inhibiting creative performance, but there was some evidence for the motivating effects of certain external factors including 'pressure' and 'recognition' (Amabile, 1984). Similarly King and West (1987) found that amongst 27 managers and professionals interviewed about their experiences of innovation at work, 13 mentioned pressure as a facilitator of innovation. It is likely that in the complex environment of the workplace the differentiation between intrinsic and extrinsic motivating factors is less clear-cut, though the basic tenets of Amabile's theory remain applicable.

Amabile's theory is of direct relevance to innovation at work, suggesting that if organizations wish to facilitate the initiation of innovations, they need to create climates in which intrinsic motivation can flourish. Individuals need work tasks which are interesting and meaningful to them, and they need the freedom to approach these tasks in their own way (Burnside, 1990). Of course, facilitating innovation initiation does not ensure the successful adoption and implementation of innovations, as the organizational and group level literatures make clear (Zaltman, Duncan and Holbek, 1973; Rogers, 1983).

Work Role Innovation

Farr and Ford (1990) define work role innovation as: 'the intentional introduction within one's work role of new and useful ideas, processes, products, or procedures' (p. 63). They propose a model of work role innovation as a basis for understanding existing studies and informing future research. Four general factors are suggested as influencing the likelihood of an individual innovating in his or her work role: perceived need for change; perceived self-efficacy in implementing change; perceived payoff from change; and the ability to generate new and useful ideas. Each of these is in turn influenced by a range of subsidiary factors. To take the example of perceived self-efficacy (i.e. the individual's belief that he or she is capable of implementing change): this may be influenced by previous relevant job experiences, formal training and education, personal style in attributions of why innovations fail, and organizational support and information systems. It is a strength of the model that it balances the influence of individual, group and organizational factors, recognizing that work role innovation (like all innovation) is a social process.

Nicholson (1984) proposes a theory of work role transitions in which role innovation is one possible outcome. West and Rushton (1989) tested predictions from this theory in a study examining the effects of the transition into the low-discretion environment of student nursing. They found that subjects with high desire for control make more attempts to change their role than those with low desire for control, but also experience greater levels of frustration, surprise and personal change. The desire to role-innovate in an environment with minimal freedom to do so may thus be harmful to individual well-being and motivation at work.

INNOVATION RESEARCH IN CONTEXT

With the benefit of hindsight it is clear that the body of innovation literature and research has developed largely as a function of wider changes in organizational environments and business contexts. Pragmatic concerns have dominated the efforts of I/O psychologists and, importantly, it can be argued, those pragmatic concerns are most closely linked to managerial interests within organizations. To develop this argument it is necesary to place the growth of innovation research over the past two decades in the context of these changes in business and organizational environments. Many North American and European countries experiencd major political, social and economic changes throughout the 1970s and 1980s. The USA, however, serves as a particularly apposite case example, since the seminal practitioner texts on innovation and organization change originated from there during this period (e.g. Peters and Waterman, 1982; Kanter, 1983, 1990). Accounts of the environmental pressures upon US industry make compelling reading. Several sectors of manufacturing industry faced increasing competition in world markes, especially from the rapidly developing economies of the Far East (Bylinksy, 1981). According to Kanter, the USA lost 23% of its overall share of world markets in the 1970s alone; its share of major world product innovations resulting in USA patents fell from 80% of the total in the 1950s to 50% in the 1980s; and perhaps most acutely, business failures had reached record levels in the early 1980s, being even higher than insolvency levels recorded in the Great Depression of the 1930s (Kanter, 1983; pp. 39–41). The economies of the Far East (principally Japan, Hong Kong, Malaysia and Indonesia) were clearly perceived as posing a considerable threat to US corporations. Business competitiveness and profitability became the primary preoccupations amongst economic commentators, many of whom were already lamenting the demise of US industries and the declining market shares of US corporations (e.g. Lewis and Allison, 1982; *Wall Street Journal*, December 1981). Restoring corporate competitiveness and rejuvenating US industry thus became the economic and political issues of paramount concern.

That these trends in the business environment coincided with influential texts on espoused good practice in innovation and management was not just a serendipitous occurrence. Indeed, the two are inextricably entwined. These texts heralded innovation as the panacea for all ills bedevilling US industry. An organization's personnel were exalted as 'intrapreneurs' at the coal-face of corporate rejuvenation. Success and innovation became inseparable bedfellows: innovation *begat* success, success *demanded* innovation. Crucially, these writings were themselves symbolic of the prevalent value-system of that period. Their themes were the embodiment of widely exposued free-market entrepreneurial doctrines transmitted to the individual level of analysis to proclaim organizational advancement through individual 'intrapreneuring'. As Peters and Waterman (1982) enthuse:

> The excellent companies treat the rank and file as the root source of quality and productivity gain . . . [with] . . . every worker being seen as a source of ideas, not just a pair of hands. (Peters and Waterman, 1982: pp. 14–15)

Importantly, and again with the benefit of hindsight, it was not just the practitioner texts of this period which were singed by the rhetorical flames of the entrepreneurial fire. Much of the research conducted by I/O psychologists reviewed earlier in this chapter was fundamentally influenced by these prevailing social and managerial values, attitudes and beliefs. The research questions deemed worthy of investigation, methodologies utilized by researchers, and most importantly, the underlying assumptions over the objectives and purposes of innovation research, all bear testimony to this influence. Three highly practical objectives dominated research efforts:

(1) to evaluate relationships between variables at the individual, group, or organizational levels held to be antecedents of innovation;
(2) to devise methods of minimizing organizational blockages to innovation implementation; and thus
(3) to develop management techniques to maximize an organization's capacity for innovation.

Across much of the research these assumptions have been implicit rather than explicit, resulting in what Kimberly (1981) has described as a 'pro-innovation bias'. Examining this bias in greater detail, it is possible to discern two related beliefs—that innovations benefit all parties involved, and that innovating is an altruistic behaviour of individuals at work. Dealing with the assumption of multilevel and simultaneous benefit first, the belief appears to be that innovations are good for all—that they simultaneously benefit organizational performance (i.e. that they contribute to organizational profitability) and all members of the organization affected by the innovation (i.e. in terms of job security, job satisfaction, and psychological well-being). This assumption has received vociferous criticism of late (Nicholson, 1990; King and Anderson, 1990; Hosking and Anderson, 1992). The point at issue has been the predominance of unitarist and managerialist assumptions across much of the existing innovation research. Studies have tended to depict organizational and employee interests as necessarily coincident and congruent, and to assume that for all types of innovation, benefits will accrue to both the organization and the individual. Such assumptions are transparently naïve and, on many occasions, demonstrably inaccurate. One is forced to conclude that the predominant unitarist-managerialist stance has been adopted as a function of pragmatic convenience and theoretical hegemony rather than as a result of clearly thought-out notions of innovation processes.

The second assumption contributing to pro-innovation bias in many studies is that innovatory behaviour by employees is to be expected as a rational, purposive and altruistic attempt to contribute to organizational efficiency. The belief appears to be that employees conform to a sort of '*alruistic-creative model of man*', actively pursuing organizational goals as if they were their own and attempting to contribute new ideas and implement improved working practices in order to benefit organizational performance. Again, this assumption can be challenged as being somewhat naïve, especially, as several authors note, since any innovation poses a threat to the status quo and its thus likely to provoke conflict within an organization (West, 1990; Bouwen, Steyaert and De Visch, 1992).

To summarize the contextual managerial climate within which innovation research by I/O psychologists has flourished, it is apparent that innovation studies have been grounded in, and restricted by, the predominant managerialist and unitarist notions espoused by the seminal texts of the last two decades (in particular, Kanter, 1983, 1990; Peters and Waterman, 1982). This has circumscribed the range of research undertaken, the perspectives of innovation processes sought by researchers, and ultimately, any wider understanding of innovation processes and outcomes in organizations. In our concluding section, we consider briefly the range of potentially valuable directions for future research, arguing that six key themes need to be addressed by I/O psychologists in this area.

DIRECTIONS FOR FUTURE RESEARCH

Conclusions

(1) *To integrate and validate the findings of the mass of empirical studies at both the organizational and individual levels of analysis.*
Given the large number of separate studies into organizational innovation and into individual work role innovation and, more importantly, the variation in effect sizes across studies, future work is needed to summarize and codify effects of different antecedent variables upon innovation. The use of meta-analysis and validity generalization techniques (e.g. Hunter and Hirsh, 1987)

promises to meet this objective and thus to clarify the morass of findings at the organizational and individual levels of analysis as to which antecedent variables are important in determining innovativeness.

(2) *To focus research at the meso-analytical level of analysis of work group innovation, and the interfaces between individuals and groups, and between groups and organizations as mediums of innovation at work.*

Researchers have paid insufficient attention to work groups as a medium for instigating and implementing innovations (West, 1990; Hosking and Anderson, 1992). Moreover, even fewer studies have addressed the interface between individuals and groups, and between groups and organizations as their primary level of analysis. Given that many types of innovation span these multiple interfaces, future research should be directed at these meso-analytical levels of analysis.

(3) *To test and validate through controlled empirical research, models of innovation processes at the organization, group and individual levels of analysis.*

A striking feature of the innovation research as it currently stands is the number of process models of innovation at all levels of analysis, yet there is a paucity of empirical tests of these models by I/O psychologists. King (1992) is the exception, and it is our view that further tests of process models would make a valuable contribution to this area of innovation research.

(4) *To shift the predominant epistemological paradigm from naïve managerialist research toward pluralist and radical humanist research.*

Where is the humanist psychology in the existing psychology of innovation research? This is a telling question, since research by I/O psychologists has focused almost exclusively upon organizational and managerial issues. Research which incorporates a diversity of perspectives and which examines the meaning of innovation for those involved and affected by it is called for to redress the limitations placed upon our understanding of the psychology of innovation by the predominant managerialist paradigm.

(5) *To elucidate differences in the development process of different types of innovations.*

Further work is needed to extend understanding of the different types of innovation in organizations, including those suggested by the existing typologies reviewed in this chapter. As innovation research has developed, it has become increasingly apparent that the generic usage of the term 'innovation' is at best uninformative and at worst directly misleading. The diffuse range of innovation types in organizations needs to be more clearly understood and their processual dynamics chartered over time, again preferably from multiple psychological perspectives and vantage points.

(6)   *To include examination of the outcomes of innovations within studies of the innovation process.*

Finally, very little research has studied the outcomes of innovations in terms of their impact on the organization as a whole, its constituent units and individual members, or on individuals, groups and organizations in its environment. Yet assumptions about the positive effects of innovation at all these levels are commonly made in justifying innovation research. Innovation outcomes need to be studied empirically using longitudinal studies of particular innovations.

REFERENCES

Aiken, M. and Alford, R. (1970) Community structure and innovation: The case of urban renewal. *American Sociological Review*, **35**, 650–665.

Aiken, M. and Hage, J. (1971) The organic organization and innovation. *Sociology*, **5**, 63–82.

Amabile, T. M. (1983) *The Social Psychology of Creativity*. New York: Springer-Verlag.

Amabile, T. M. (1988) A model of creativity and innovation in organizations. *Research in Organizational Behaviour*, **10**, 123–167.

Amabile, T. M. and Gryskiewicz, S. S. (1988) Creative environment and personality: Innovation in the R&D lab. In R. L. Kuhn (ed.), *Handbook for Creative and Innovative Managers*. New York: McGraw-Hill.

Anderson, N. R. (1989) Work group innovation: Current research concerns and future directions. Paper presented at Fourth West European Congress on the Psychology of Work and Organization, Cambridge, April.

Anderson, N. R. (1992) Work group innovation: A state-of-the-art review. In D. M. Hosking and N. R. Anderson (eds), *Organizational Change and Innovation: Psychological Perspectives and Practices in Europe*. London: Routledge.

Anderson, N. R. and King, N. (1991) Managing innovation in organizations. *Leadership and Organizational Development Journal*, **12**, 17–21.

Angle, H. L. (1989) Psychology and organizational innovation. In A. H. Van de Ven, H. L. Angle, and M. S. Poole (eds), *Research on the Management of Innovation: The Minnesota Studies*. New York: Harper & Row.

Aydin, C. E. and Rice, R. E. (1991) Social worlds, individual differences, and implementation: Predicting attitudes toward a medical information system. *Information and Management*, **20**, 119–136.

Baldridge, J. V. and Burnham, R. A. (1975) Organizational innovation: Individual, organizational and environmental impacts. *Administrative Science Quarterly*, **20**, 165–176.

Basadur, M., Graen, G. B., and Green, G. (1982) Training in creative problem solving: Effects on ideation and problem finding and solving in an industrial research organization: *Organizational Behaviour and Human Performance*, **30**, 41–70.

Bedeian, A. G. (1980) *Organizations: Theory and Analysis*. Illinois: Dryden Press.

Belbin, M. (1981) *Why Management Teams Succeed or Fail*. London: Heinemann.

Bennis, W. G. (1989) Managing the dream: Leadership in the 21st century. *Journal of Organizational Change Management*, **2**, 6–10.

Blau, P. M. (1964) *Exchange and Power in Social Life*. New York: Wiley.

Bouwen, R. and Fry, R. (1988) An agenda for managing organizational innovation and development in the 1990s. In M. Lambrecht (ed.) *Corporate Revival*. Leuven, Belgium: Catholic University Press.

Bouwen; R., Steyaert, C., and De Visch, J. (1992) Organizational innovation. In D. M. Hosking and N. R. Anderson (eds), *Organizational Change and Innovation: Psychological Perspectives and Practices in Europe*. London: Routledge.

Brown, L. D. and Covey, J. G. (1987) Development organizations and organization development: Toward an expanded paradigm for organization development. In R. W. Woodman and W. A. Pasmore (eds), *Research in Organizational Change and Development*. Greenwich, CT: JAI Press.

Burns, T. and Stalker, G. M. (1961) *The Management of Innovation*. London: Tavistock.

Burnside, R. M. (1990) Improving corporate climates for creativity. In M. A. West and J. L. Farr (eds), *Innovation and Creativity at Work: Psychological and Organizational Strategies*. Chichester: Wiley.

Bylinsky, G. (1981) The Japanese score on a US fumble. *Fortune*, September, 68–72.

Child, J. (1984) *Organizations: A Guide to Problems and Practice*, 2nd edn. London: Harper & Row.

Cooper, R. G. (1984) The strategy-performance link in innovation. *R&D Management*, **14**, 247–267.

Coopey, J. (1987) Creativity in complex organizations. Paper presented at the Annual Occupational Psychology Conference of the British Psychological Society, University of Hull, January.

Corwin, R. G. (1972) Strategies for organizational innovation: An empirical comparison. *American Sociological Review*, **37**, 441–454.

Daft, R. L. (1978) A dual-core model of organizational innovation. *Academy of Management Journal*, **21**, 193–210.

Damanpour, F. (1987) The adoption of technological, administrative, and ancillary innovations: Impacts of organizational factors. *Journal of Management*, **13**, 4, 675–688.

Damanpour, F. (1990) Innovation effectiveness, adoption and organizational performance. In M. A. West and J. L. Far (eds), *Innovation and Creativity at Work: Psychological and Organizational Strategies*. Chichester: Wiley.

Damanpour, F. and Evan, W. M. (1984) Organizational innovation and performance: The problem of 'organizational lag'. *Administrative Science Quarterly*, **29**, 392–409.

Downs, G. W. J. and Mohr, L. B. (1976) Conceptual issues in the study of innovation. *Administrative Science Quarterly*, **21**, 700–714.

Duncan, R. (1972) Organizational climate and climate for change in three police departments: Some preliminary findings. *Urban Affairs Quarterly*, 17, 205–245.

Dunphy, D. C. and Stace, D. A. (1988) Transformational and coercive strategies for planned organizational change: Beyond the OD model. *Organizational Studies*, **9**, 317–334.

Evan, W. M. (1966) Organizational lag. *Human Organizations*, **25**, 51–53.

Evan, W. M. and Black, G. (1967) Innovation in business organizations: Some factors associated with success or failure of staff proposals. *Journal of Business*, **40**, 519–530.

Farr, J. L. and Ford, C. M. (1990) Individual innovation. In M. A. West and J. L. Farr (eds), *Innovation and Creativity at Work: Psychological and Organizational Strategies*. Chichester: Wiley.

Fischer, W. A. and Farr, C. M. (1985) Dimensions of innovative climate in Chinese R&D units. *R&D Management*, **15**, 183–190.

Gersick, C. J. G. (1988) Time and transition in work teams: Toward a new model of group development. *Academy of Management Journal*, **31**, 9–41.

Gersick, C. J. G. (1989) Marking time: Predictable transitions in task groups. *Academy of Management Journal*, **32**, 274–309.

Geschka, H. (1983) Creativity techniques in product planning and development: A view from West Germany. *R&D Management*, **16**, 169–183.

Gordon, G., Morse, E. V., Gordon, S. M., Kervasdoue, J. de, Kimberly, J. R.,

Moch, M., and Swartz, D. G. (1974) Organizational structure, environmental diversity, and hospital adoption of medical innovations. In A. D. Kaluzny, J. T Gentry, and J. E. Veney (eds), *Innovation in Health Care Organizations*. Chapel Hill, NC: Department of Health Administration.

Hage, J. and Aiken, M. (1967) Program change and organizational properties: A comparative analysis. *American Journal of Sociology*, 72, 503–519.

Hage, J. and Aiken, M. (1970) *Social Change in Complex Organizations*. New York: Random House.

Hage, J. and Dewar, R. (1973) Elite values versus organizational structure in predicting innovation. *Administrative Science Quarterly*, 18, 279–290.

Harvey, E. and Mills, R. (1970) Patterns of organizational adaptation: A political perspective. In M. N. Zald (ed.), *Power in Organizations*. Nashville: Vanderbilt University Press.

Hennessey, B. A. and Amabile, T. M. (1988) The conditions of creativity. In R. J. Sternberg (ed.), *The Nature of Creativity*. Cambridge: Cambridge University Press.

Hosking, D. M. and Anderson, N. R. (1992) *Organizational Change and Innovation: Psychological Perspectives and Practices in Europe*. London: Routledge.

Howell, W. S. (1982) *The Empathic Communicator*. Belmont, California: Wadsworth.

Hunter, J. E. and Hirsh, H. R. (1987) Applications of meta-analysis. In C. L. Cooper and I. T. Robertson (eds), *International Review of Industrial and Organizational Psychology*. Chichester: Wiley.

Kaluzny, A., Veney, J., and Gentry, J. (1974) Innovation of health services: A comparative study of hospitals and health departments. *Health and Society*, 15, 22–33.

Kanter, R. M. (1983) *The Change Masters*. New York: Simon & Schuster.

Kanter, R. M. (1990) *When Giants Learn to Dance: Mastering the Challenge of Strategy, Management and Careers in the 1990s*. New York: Routledge.

Katz, R. (1982) The effects of group longevity on project communication and performance. *Administrative Science Quarterly*, 27, 81–104.

Kelley, G. (1976) Seducing the elites: The politics of decision-making and innovation in organizational networks. *Academy of Management Review*, 1, 66–74.

Kimberly, J. R. (1978) Organizational size and the structuralist perspective: A review, critique, and proposal. *Administrative Science Quarterly*, 21, 571–597.

Kimberly, J. R. (1981) Managerial innovation. In P. C. Nystrom and W. H. Starbuck (eds), *Handbook of Organizational Design*. Oxford: Oxford University Press.

Kimberly, J. R. and Evanisko, M. J. (1981) Organizational innovation: The influence of individual, organizational and contextual factors on hospital adoption of technological and administrative innovations. *Academy of Management Journal*, 24, 689–713.

King, N. (1990) Innovation at work: The research literature. In M. A. West and J. L. Farr (eds), *Innovation and Creativity at Work: Psychological and Organizational Strategies*. Chichester: Wiley.

King, N. (1992) Modelling the innovation process: An empirical comparison of approaches. *Journal of Occupational and Organizational Psychology*, 65, 89–100.

King, N. and Anderson, N. R. (1990) Innovation in working groups. In M. A. West and J. L. Farr (eds), *Innovation and Creativity at Work: Psychological and Organizational Strategies*. Chichester: Wiley.

King, N. and Coventry, P. (1992) Past imperfect, future tense. *Health Service Journal*, 102, 24–25.

King, N. and West, M. A. (1987) Experiences of innovation at work. *Journal of Managerial Psychology*, 2, 6–10.

King, N. and West, M. A. (1992) Does the innovation process differ for different types of innovation? Working paper; Centre for Primary Care Research, Department of General Practice, University of Manchester.

King, N., Anderson, N. R., and West, M. A. (1991) Organizational innovation in the UK: A case study of perceptions and processes. *Work and Stress*, 5, 331–339.

Kirton, M. J. (1976) Adaptors and innovators: A description and measure. *Journal of Applied Psychology*, 6, 622–629.

Kirton, M. J. (1978) Have adaptors and innovators equal levels of creativity? *Psychological Reports*, 42, 695–698.

Lewis, H. and Allison, D. (1982) *The Real World War*. New York: Coward, McCann, & Geoghegan.

Locke, E. A. and Schweiger, D. M. (1979) Participation in decision-making: One more look. In L. Cummings and B. M. Staw (eds), *Research in Organizational Behaviour*. Greenwich, Connecticut: JAI.

Manz, C. C., Barstein, D. T., Hostager, T. J., and Shapiro, G. L. (1989) Leadership and innovation: A longitudinal process view: In A. Van de Ven, H. L. Angle, and M. S. Poole (eds), *Research on the Management of Innovation: The Minnesota Studies*. New York: Harper & Row.

McGrath, J. E. (1985) Groups and the innovation process. In R. L. Merritt and A. J. Merritt (eds), *Innovation in the Public Sector*. Beverly Hills: Sage.

Meyer, A. D. (1982) Adapting to environmental jolts. *Administrative Science Quarterly*, 27, 515–537.

Miles, R. E. and Snow, C. C. (1978) *Organisational Strategy, Structure and Process*. New York: McGraw-Hill.

Milo, N. (1971) Health care organizations and innovation. *Journal of Health and Social Behaviour*, 12, 163–173.

Mohr, L. B. (1969) Determinants of innovation in organizations. *American Political Science Review*, 63, 111–126.

Morgan, G. (1983) Action learning: A holographic metaphor for guiding social change. *Human Relations*, 37, 1–28.

Morgan, G. (1986) *Images of Organization*. Beverly Hills: Sage.

Neal, R. D. and Radnor, M. (1973) The relation between formal procedures for pursuing OR/MS activities and OR/MS group success. *Operations Research*, 40, 451–474.

Nelkin, D. (1973) *Methodone Maintenance: A Technological Fix*. New York: Braziller.

Nicholson, N. (1984) A theory of work role transitions. *Administrative Science Quarterly*, 29, 172–191.

Nicholson, N. (1990) Organizational innovation in context: Culture, interpretation and application. In M. A. West and J. L. Farr (eds), *Innovation and Creativity at Work: Psychological and Organizational Strategies*. Chichester: Wiley.

Nicholson, N., Rees, A., and Brooks-Rooney, A. (1990) Strategy, innovation and performance. *Journal of Management Studies*, 27, 511–534.

Nystrom, H. (1979) *Creativity and Innovation*. Chichester: Wiley.

Nystrom, H. (1990) Organizational innovation. In M. A. West and J. L. Farr (eds), *Innovation and Creativity at Work: Psychological and Organizational Strategies*. Chichester: Wiley.

Patti, R. J. (1974) Organizational resistance and change: The view from below. *Social Service Review*, 48, 367–383.

Pavitt, K. (1991) Key characteristics of the large innovating firm. *British Journal of Management*, 2, 41–50.

Payne, R. (1990) The effectiveness of research teams: A review. In M. A. West and J. L. Farr (eds), *Innovation and Creativity at Work: Psychological and Organizational Strategies*. Chichester: Wiley.

Pelz, D. C. (1983) Quantitative case histories of urban innovations: Are there innovation stages? *IEEE Transactions on Engineering Management*, 30, 60–67.

Peters, T. J. and Waterman, R. H. (1982) *In Search of Excellence*. New York: Harper & Row.

Pierce, J. L. and Delbecq, A. (1977) Organizational structure, individual attitude and innovation. *Academy of Management Review*, 2, 27–33.

Radnor, M., Rubinstein, A. H., and Bean, A. S. (1968) Integration and utilization of management-science activities in large US industrial corporations. *Operations Research*, **19**, 117–141.

Ramirez, I. L. and Bartunek, J. M. (1989) The multiple realities and experiences of internal organisation development consultation in health care. *Journal of Organizational Change Management*, 2, 40–57.

Rogers, E. M. and Agarwala-Rogers, R. (1976) *Communications in Organizations*. New York: Free Press.

Rogers, E. M. (1983) *Diffusion of Innovations*. 3rd edn. New York: Free Press.

Rosner, M. M. (1968) Administrative controls and innovation. *Behavioural Science*, **13**, 36–43.

Sapolsky, H. (1967) Organizational structure and innovation. *Journal of Business*, **40**, 497–510.

Sauer, J. and Anderson, N. R. (1992) Have we misread the psychology of innovation? A case study from two NHS hospitals. *Leadership and Organizational Development Journal*, **13**, 17–21.

Schroeder, R. G., Van de Ven, A., Scudder, G. D., and Polley, D. (1989) The development of innovation ideas. In A. Van de Ven, H. L. Angle, and M. S. Poole (eds), *Research on the Management of Innovation: The Minnesota Studies*. New York: Harper & Row.

Shephard, H. A. (1967) Innovation-resisting and innovation-producing organizations. *Journal of Business*, **40**, 470–477.

Soete, L. (1979) Firm size and inventive activity: The evidence reconsidered. *European Economics Review*, **12**, 319–340.

Stankiewicz, R. (1979) The size and age of Swedish academic research groups and their scientific performance. In F. M. Andrews (ed.), *Scientific Productivity*. Cambridge: Cambridge University Press.

Staw, B. M. (1984) Organizational behaviour: A review and reformulation of the field's outcome variables. *Annual Review of Psychology*, **35**, 627–666.

Staw, B. M. (1990) An evolutionary approach to creativity and innovation. In M. A. West and J. L. Farr (eds.), *Innovation and Creativity at Work: Psychological and Organizational Strategies*. Chichester: Wiley.

Stocking, B. (1985) *Initiative and Inertia: Case Studies in the NHS*. London: Nuffield Provincial Hospitals Trust.

Tushman, M. L. (1977) Special boundary roles in the innovation process. *Administrative Science Quarterly*, **22**, 587–605.

Utterback, J. M. (1974) Innovation in industry and the diffusion of technology. *Science*, **183**, 620–626.

Van de Ven, A. (1986) Central problems in the management of innovation. *Management Science*, **32**, 590–607.

Van de Ven, A., Angle, H. L., and Poole, M. S. (1989) *Research on the management of Innovation: The Minnesota Studies*. New York: Harper & Row.

Wallace, M. (1987) Innovation in primary health care teams. Unpublished MSC thesis, MRC/ESRC Social and Applied Psychology Unit, University of Sheffield, UK.

West; M. A. (1990) The social psychology of innovation in groups. In M. A. West and J. L. Farr (eds), *Innovation and Creativity at Work: Psychological and Organizational Strategies*. Chichester: Wiley.

West, M. A. and Anderson, N. R. (1992) Innovation, cultural values and the management of change in British hospital management. *Work and Stress*, **16**.

West, M. A. and Farr, J. L. (1989) Innovation at work: Psychological perspectives. *Social Behaviour*, **4**, 15–30.

West, M. A. and Farr, J. L. (1990) *Innovation and Creativity at Work: Psychological and Organizational Strategies*. Chichester: Wiley.

West, M. A. and Rushton, R. (1989) Mismatches in work-role transitions. *Journal of Occupational Psychology*, **62**, 271–286.

West, M. A. and Wallace, M. (1991) Innovation in health care teams. *European Journal of Social Psychology*, **21**, 303–315.

Wilson, J. Q. (1966) Innovation in organizations: Notes towards a theory. In J. D. Thompson (ed.), *Approaches to Organizational Design*. Pittsburgh: Pittsburgh University Press.

Witte, E. (1972) Field research on complex decision-making processes—the phase theorem. *International Studies of Management and Organisation*, 156–182.

Zaltman, G., Duncan, R., and Holbek, J. (1973) *Innovations and Organizations*. New York: Wiley.

Chapter 2

MANAGEMENT DEVELOPMENT: A REVIEW AND COMMENTARY

Timothy T. Baldwin
Indiana University, USA
Margaret Y. Padgett
Butler University, USA

Management development—the complex process by which individuals learn to perform effectively in managerial roles—has attracted increasing organisational and research interest. The growth in organisational interest is due in large part to an increasing recognition of the efficacy of management development as a strategy to improve firm performance (Hall & Foulkes, 1991; Ulrich, 1989; Fulmer, 1990). Indeed, management development is now a multi-billion dollar undertaking for organisations worldwide and recent survey evidence suggests that over 90% of firms engage in some form of development activities for managers (Loo, 1991; Constable, 1988; Saari, Johnson, McLaughlin, & Zimmerle, 1988). Increasing academic interest in management development is reflected in a burgeoning body of research articles and the emergence of several recent books on the subject (e.g. Bigelow, 1991; McCall, Lombardo & Morrison, 1988; Morgan, 1988; Whetten & Cameron, 1991).

This review focuses primarily on the scholarly literature on management development to appear in the last five years. Earlier reviews of the literature were reported by Wexley and Baldwin (1986) and Keys and Wolfe (1988). To uncover relevant literature, all scholarly journals known to include management development-related manuscripts were searched. In addition, a call for papers was included in newsletters of the Academy of Management (USA) and several outlets in the UK and Australia. We also directly solicited papers from over 100 authors in English-speaking countries who had previously published work in the area of management development.

As with earlier reviews, this one was intended to be comprehensive though certainly not exhaustive of the literature. We did not attempt to make a

International Review of Industrial and Organizational Psychology 1993 Volume 8
Edited by C. L. Cooper and I. T. Robertson. © 1993 John Wiley & Sons Ltd.

systematic review of the voluminous literature in practitioner-oriented publications nor of related, but distinct topical areas such as organisation development (Woodman & Passmore, 1987) or personnel training (Tannenbaum & Yukl, 1992; Noe & Ford, 1992). In addition, we did not include review of some methods of content delivery (e.g. management simulations, case studies, computer-based training) which have been subject to recent review elsewhere (Keys, 1989; Keys & Wolfe, 1990).

Based on the literature collected, the chapter is organised into three parts. Part one reviews recent work which has focused on the understanding and assessment of effective management. An underlying theme of much of this recent work is that the managerial role is changing and, therefore, new models of effective management and valid assessment technologies are required to adequately understand and develop successful managerial behaviour in the future. The literature suggests that many initiatives are underway to identify key competencies for specific organisations and managerial populations.

Part two reviews the current literature related to what we have called 'contexts' of managerial learning. Specifically, we have organised this literature into three such contexts: job assignments, relationships and formal training events. Although previous reviews have lamented the lack of attention devoted to on-the-job development (Kelleher, Finestone & Lowy, 1986; Wexley & Baldwin, 1986), our receipt of manuscripts suggests a significant increase in conceptual and empirical work related to managerial development which occurs in the course of job assignments, mentoring and coaching. The current literature on formal managerial training events indicates a greater emphasis on leadership, action learning and experiential approaches such as outdoor challenges.

In Part three we review and comment on three emerging issues in management development: (i) management development as a competitive advantage; (ii) self-directed management development; and (iii) management education in degree-granting institutions. Throughout the chapter we attempt to identify research gaps and highlight issues that need more attention. We conclude with some final comments on the state of management development research.

UNDERSTANDING AND ASSESSING EFFECTIVE MANAGEMENT

A considerable portion of recent work on management development continues to focus on issues related to the understanding and assessment of effective management. The research is reviewed under four categories: (i) general skill taxonomies; (ii) assessment instruments and strategies; (iii) the changing managerial environment; and (iv) specific managerial populations.

General Skill Taxonomies

Models of effective management have long been espoused in popular literature and taxonomies of important managerial skills are ubiquitous (cf. Campbell, Dunnette, Lawler & Weick, 1970; Margerison & Kakabadse, 1984; Katz, 1974; Mintzberg, 1973; Kotter, 1982; Wilson, 1978). Nonetheless, new studies of effective managers and new taxonomies of managerial competencies continue to attract both conceptual and empirical attention (Luthans, Hodgetts & Rosencrantz, 1988; McCall, Lombardo & Morrison, 1988; Powers, 1987; Whetten & Cameron, 1991; Yukl, 1989).

Perhaps the most widely publicised recent effort to systematically identify a taxonomy of managerial competencies is described by Powers (1987) who reports on a study commissioned by the American Management Association. The sample consisted of 2000 working managers in 41 different types of jobs in twelve different organisations. Using the Job Competence Assessment methodology pioneered by Boyatzis (1982), the research identified a group of managerial behaviours which were then grouped into 18 competencies and five larger clusters. The five clusters were: (i) goal and action management; (ii) directing subordinates; (ii) human resources management; (iv) leadership; and (v) focus on others. Specialised knowledge was also an important element in the model.

Another model of managerial effectiveness is presented in a popular text by Whetten and Cameron (1991). The authors identified and interviewed 402 highly effective managers in a variety of different firms and industries and extracted ten most frequently mentioned management skills. They ultimately condensed the list and linked management success to three *personal* skills: developing self-awareness, managing stress, and solving problems creatively, and four *interpersonal* skills: communicating supportively, gaining power and influence, motivating others, and managing conflict. They point out that the skill areas overlap such that managers must rely on parts of all skill areas in order to perform effectively in a managerial role.

A four-year observational study by Luthans, Hodgetts and Rosencrantz (1988) looked at how successful and effective managers differ from unsuccessful and less effective ones. Success was defined as speed of promotion within an organisation. Detailed observation of 44 managers from a variety of organisations indicated twelve behavioural categories associated with managerial success. The authors subsequently organised the behavioural categories into four managerial activities: communication; traditional management; networking; and human resource management. Data were then collected from 248 additional managers and the amount of recorded activity in each area was used to distinguish successful from unsuccessful managers. The largest differences occurred on networking activities such as external communications, socialising, and politicking.

After over a decade of research on many management groups, Yukl (1989) has created an integrated taxonomy that consists of eleven categories of behaviour (e.g. monitoring, networking, motivating, teambuilding). The main method used in his research was a questionnaire but it was also supplemented with diaries, interviews and integration of behaviour categories found in other work on managerial effectiveness. The behaviour categories in the taxonomy have been shown to be related to independent measures of managerial effectiveness (Yukl, Wall & Lepsinger, 1990; Yukl & Lepsinger, 1991).

Finally, a project initiated by the Center for Creative Leadership (McCall, Lombardo & Morrison, 1988) included in-depth interviews with 86 successful (success was defined as still in the running for the top job) executives in three corporations, and open-ended questionnaires from 100 high-performing managers in several additional corporations. Content analysis of this qualitative data resulted in 33 categories of managerial competence which have subsequently been condensed to 16 managerial skill categories (e.g. resourcefulness, being a quick study, acting with flexibility). In addition, a group (19) of top executives at three organisations provided descriptions of two people they knew well—an executive who succeeded and one who had recently derailed. Ten reasons for derailment were derived from these interviews.

In reviewing the recent taxonomic work, several observations can be made. First, though there are some notable differences, there continues to be considerable overlap in models of core managerial competencies. For example, most competency models include a dimension of dealing with subordinates which involves motivating, rewarding, delegating and developing. Each also encompasses familiar interpersonal skills such as managing conflict and building a team. Most models also emphasise the problem-solving aspect of managerial jobs.

Second, one of the criticisms which is commonly levelled at taxonomic work on managerial effectiveness is the failure to identify specific behaviours. Indeed, there is still a tendency for some work to fall prey to the type of imprecise trait labels and global behavioural descriptions which organisational scholars have long lamented (Campbell et al., 1970). However, despite some overlap and cases of hazy description, a significant contribution of recent taxonomic work has been the considerably more precise behavioural specification of managerial competencies.

For example, in the AMA model (Powers, 1987) the key issue is not possession of a competency but its use. An individual manager's command of the competency therefore involves three dimensions—its existence as an underlying characteristic, its expression, and the experience of others of its use in the managerial environment (Powers, 1987). Similarly, the model developed by researchers at the Center for Creative Leadership not only describes a behavioural dimension, but illustrates the dimension with even more specific sample items.

Third, far too much of prior taxonomic work has rested solely on opinion, anecdote and speculation. In contrast, several of the recent models (e.g. Yukl,

1989; McCall, Lombardo & Morrison, 1988) have been supported by some preliminary empirical evidence and refinement based on that evidence is ongoing. Nonetheless, much more needs to be learned and rigorous investigation by researchers *not* connected with model developers would be of particular value.

One recent example of an independent empirical test of core competencies was reported by Penley, Alexander, Jernigan and Henwood (1991). In that study, the authors explored the hypothesis that specific communication competencies are essential to effectiveness as a manager. The authors identified and assessed several specific communication competencies that have been conceptually associated with managerial performance (e.g. Luthans, Hodgetts & Rosencrantz, 1988) and gathered data from both male and female upper-level bank managers. Results indicated that though female managers provided lower self-reports of communication skills than male managers, there was a significant correlation between communications skills and managerial perform-ance for both genders.

Although more empirical tests of the link between demonstrated competencies and indices of managerial effectiveness are sorely needed, one caution is that many of the competency models continue to focus primarily on *frequency* of managerial behaviour with less regard to the level of expertise or *mastery* with which the behaviour is performed. In this regard, Shipper (1991) presented a study which suggested that an increase in frequency of managerial behaviour, with no increase in mastery, had little or no positive impact on performance. Rather, he found that managers of subunits high on morale and performance exhibited significantly higher levels of mastery of managerial behaviours. Higher frequency of some managerial behaviours was found to be associated with *low* performing subunits. Martinko and Gardner (1990) also found little support for the proposition that effective managers simply devote more time to specific managerial behaviours.

Clearly, the thrust of management development must be directed toward improving the mastery of skills and not just the frequency. Future research work that includes both the frequency of specific skills and the mastery or quality of the same skills is needed to further our understanding of this important distinction.

Finally, it should be noted that not all organisational scholars are convinced that the pursuit of competency models is even appropriate. For example, Vaill (1989) has seriously questioned whether a skills-list definition of competency can ever accurately reflect how effective managers function. Similarly, Stewart (1989a) suggests that improving the categorisation of behaviours and relating these to measures of effectiveness is less important than attempts to try and improve our understanding of the actions and thoughts of different managers over time. Taking a qualitative research perspective, she outlined eight specific suggestions for what she feels would be a more fruitful exploration of managerial jobs and behaviours.

Assessment Instruments and Strategies

Parallel to the development of models of effective management has been work on the assessment of managerial behaviour and skills. One emerging theme in the creation of assessment tools is an increased use of upward evaluations (input from subordinates and peers) and several thoughtful treatments of the process and validity of such upward feedback have appeared (Wohlers & London, 1989; London, Wohlers & Gallagher, 1990). One recent study even found that ratings by subordinates were better predictors of uncontaminated performance criteria in the short term than were full assessment centre rankings (McEvoy & Beatty, 1989). Consistent with such evidence, several recent assessment instruments embody upward evaluation along with self and superior assessment in what is known as a multiple perspective or '360-degree' feedback strategy (Van Velsor & Leslie, 1991).

For example, Yukl has used his taxonomic work to develop an assessment instrument known as Compass (aka, The Managerial Practices Survey). Compass is a set of three types of questionnaires used to provide managers with information about their managerial behaviour and developmental needs related to this behaviour (Yukl, Wall & Lepsinger, 1990; Yukl & Lepsinger, 1991). Subordinates and peers describe how much a manager uses each of several managerial practices, and they recommend whether the manager should do more, the same amount or less of each behaviour. Managers compare this feedback to their own self-assessment of behaviour and to norms for similar managers. Ratings of the importance of each type of behaviour for the manager's job provide additional information for selecting relevant training.

Another example of a needs assessment instrument stemming from competency identification work discussed above is Benchmarks (McCauley, Lombardo & Usher, 1989). Benchmarks is a rating form developed to measure relevant skills and traits identified in research on managerial experiences and managerial derailment. Self-ratings and ratings made by subordinates, peers and superiors are used to assess a manager's strengths and weaknesses and identify developmental needs.

Van Velsor and Leslie (1991) present an impressive compilation in which they use established criteria to compare 16 of the most frequently used multiple-perspective management assessment instruments (including Compass and Benchmarks). Each of the 16 measures is reviewed with respect to existing evidence on psychometric properties and utility for management development practice. The comparative information is useful for evaluating instruments as well as suggesting avenues for future research. Another useful collection of information regarding different assessment instruments is presented in a book edited by Clark and Clark, (1990).

With respect to other assessment approaches, Miner (1991) reports on a psychological assessment methodology he argues is particularly appropriate for diagnosing performance *problems*. The focus of the assessment is on the creation of test batteries for assessing ability and personality factors. Though Miner argues against a static or standard battery for assessment of all managerial problems, a central diagnostic is the author's 'Motivation to Manage' sentence completion instrument. Test batteries also typically include multiple measures of intelligence, risk taking, achievement motivation and locus of control.

It is now well documented that assessment centres are likely to be valid predictors of managerial performance in a variety of different organisations (Gaugler, Rosenthal, Thornton & Bentson, 1987; Munchus & McArthur, 1991). Furthermore, since the publication of Howard and Bray's (1988) long-term follow-up of the AT&T assessment centre project, there has been increased attention to the *developmental* applications of assessment centres (Hollenbeck, 1990).

Rayner and Goodge (1988) suggest that changing company attitudes and a growing body of research are progressively influencing the nature of assessment centres. More specifically, they discuss changes in traditional centre evaluation and feedback processes and describe how several of those changes have been incorporated by London Regional transport in their use of assessment centres. Goodge (1991) discusses guidelines and pitfalls of 'development centres', which he defines as an off-site process resulting in effective development actions that go beyond the feedback and assessment of a traditional assessment centre.

With respect to empirical research on centres, Noe and Steffy (1987) found that assessment centre ratings predicted career exploration behaviours. More precisely, participants who had received higher ratings were more accepting of those ratings and more likely to seek information about target jobs. Jones and Whitmore (1992) used data from a follow-up evaluation of a developmental assessment centre to address questions concerning the antecedents and consequences of feedback acceptance from the centre. Results indicated that participants' self-efficacy and perceived support of developmental activities had a significant impact on feedback acceptance. However, acceptance of feedback was not significantly related to managerial level attainment.

In an interesting longitudinal study, Fletcher (1990) explored individuals' reaction to assessment centres. He found that the experience of going through an assessment centre does have an impact on candidates, particularly with respect to variables such as self-esteem and need for achievement, though some of the effects tended to diminish over time.

Finally, Streufert, Pogash and Piasecki (1988) described research on assessment of managerial skills with two *compuer-based* simulations. The simulations were designed for a single individual (like an in-basket) rather than a group in order to regulate the information available to each participant. The authors contend that one significant advantage of this simulation methodology is that managerial behaviour and skills for handling crises can be assessed under standardised conditions.

Clearly, accurate assessment and feedback are keys to managerial effectiveness. Unfortunately, assessment prior to management development interventions continues to be an all too rare and haphazard activity (Saari et al., 1988). Part of the neglect may be attributed to the fact that traditional assessment instruments and methods have often been unreliable and not linked to any recognised theory of effective management. Recent work on assessment, however, includes several examples of empirically tested tools and certainly gives cause for optimism. Continued development and refinement of theoretically based and empirically validated measurement strategies is needed to stimulate more organisational attention to the assessment phase of the management development process.

Changing Managerial Environments

Traditional studies of core management competencies have generally focused on existing managerial positions and those who have already experienced success. Yet a pervasive theme in current organisational literature is that the world of the manager is rapidly changing. Unprecedented competitive pressures, increased technological complexity, globalisation of economies, changing social and cultural values, and a more diverse workforce are all frequently mentioned as relevant considerations for management development (Schein, 1989). With such changes in mind, a number of recent authors have suggested that while traditional core competencies may still be necessary for managerial success, they will not be sufficient in an increasingly turbulent world (Ames & Heide, 1991; Hunt, 1990; Morgan, 1988; Kleiner, 1991).

Predominant among the macro-competencies discussed as crucial for managing in the future are several variants of 'learning how to learn' (Argyris, 1991; Dechant, 1990). For example, Argyris (1991) contends that managerial jobs are increasingly taking on the contours of 'knowledge work' and, as such, a crucial managerial competency is what he has termed 'double loop learning'. In essence, this means that managers must learn how the way they go about defining and solving problems can be a source of problems in its own right. Effective managers in the future will be those who can reflect critically on their own behaviour, identify the ways they often inadvertently contribute to the organisation's problems, and then change how they act (Argyris, 1991).

In a similar vein, Streufert, Nogami, Swezey, Pogash and Piasecki (1988) argue that the majority of senior managers are already very well trained and often excel in many of the specific micro-competencies which are integral parts of most management development programmes. Based on that assumption, the authors argue that to enable managers to function well in changing and uncertain task environments, development interventions should focus not only on the specific content of managerial tasks (i.e. what managers should think or do in response to certain task demands) but also on structural components of managerial effectiveness (i.e. how managers think and function). The authors report on an initiative to develop such structural skills via a computer simulation methodology and results indicated that the inclusion of structural components generated considerable improvement in managerial performance.

Schein (1989) makes a compelling argument that the concept of *hierarchy* colours our most basic assumptions and beliefs about managerial work. He further contends that the advent of technological complexity will force the need to develop a new picture of what an effective manager should be. He suggests that hierarchical authority will probably play a much smaller role in that picture while *coordination skills* will play a much larger role. Morgan (1988) similarly contends that skills such as reading the environment and managing ambiguity and paradox will be essential for the effective manager of the future.

Kolb, Lublin, Spoth and Baker (1985) point out that much more is required of managers in a context of increased environmental complexity. They note that the days of classical organisation structures with limited spans of control, non-overlapping job definitions, single chains of command and formal authority matched to responsibility are already gone. As a result, the authors contend that greater competence is needed in four areas: *behavioural competence* in taking initiative under conditions of risk and uncertainty; *perceptual competence* in gathering and organising information and considering other perspectives; *affective competence* in empathising with others and resolving conflict; and *symbolic competence* to conceptualise the organisation as a system.

Keys and Case (1990) suggest that increasing team interdependence and widening spans of control are diminishing the effectiveness of formal authority and, therefore, authority must be replaced with influence. Using a critical incident approach and building on the work of Kotter (1982) and others, the authors conclude that influence in four directions—superiors, peers, outsiders and subordinates—will be among the most crucial future managerial competencies.

We interpret the literature on the changing management environment as suggesting that traditional core competencies are not wrong or invalid, but only incomplete. That is, because the managerial environment is changing so rapidly, the needed set of knowledge, skills and abilities is a moving target. Though we are beginning to learn how to do future-oriented job analysis to help focus some of our development initiatives (Schneider & Konz, 1989), it is clear that managers of the future will have to be strong self-learners not only to learn autonomously, but to have the capacity to learn about themselves. However, while the importance of skills such as sefl-awareness and knowing how to learn seems clear, there is a definite need to extend the range of human qualities which can be subjected to valid assessment (Raven, 1988). More research work aimed at conceptualising and operationalising the type of macro-competencies discussed in this section would be well directed.

Specific Managerial Populations

Nearly twenty years ago, Katz (1974) suggested that the degree to which managers need different skills is dependent on administrative level. According to Katz, technical skills are most needed at the lower level; conceptual skills are most needed at the executive level; and human skills are needed to about the same degree at all managerial levels. Yet, as the taxonomic work discussed earlier suggests, traditional research on managerial work has generally focused on the common denominators of management jobs. Moreover, a recent descriptive study of 155 organisations found that management development programmes do not significantly differentiate between managerial skill requirements according to hierarchical level (Blakely, Martinec & Lane, 1992).

Results of a study of the importance of managerial activities conducted by Kraut, Pedigo, McKenna and Dunnette (1989) were largely consistent with Katz's theory. A factor they labelled 'instructing subordinates', which contained several items about activities closely related to technical skills, was rated less important by senior managers than by middle- and lower-level managers. A factor they labelled 'monitoring the outside' which contained several items about activities closely related to conceptual skills, was rated more important by senior managers than by middle- and lower-level managers.

Other authors have focused strictly on the skill requirements of upper-level strategic managers (Cox & Cooper, 1989; Jonas, Fry & Srivasta, 1989; Stumpf, 1989): For example, Cox and Cooper (1989) studied 45 chief executives of successful British firms with over 1000 employees. Interviews were semi-structured and explored such aspects of the executives' lives as family background and childhood, education, career pattern, motivation and personality. Self-reported skill assessments indicated that the CEOs felt that decision-making, interpersonal skills and leadership skills, in that order, were most critical to their success. Other skills mentioned were moderate risk taking, ability to learn from failure, and a high work rate.

In an unconventional study of executive language, Jonas, Fry and Srivasta (1989) conducted in-depth interviews with 24 CEOs to determine the dimensions of executive experience. The authors concluded that there are two basic dimensions of executive experience: (i) the degree of their identification with the organisation; and (ii) their general degree of scepticism or optimism. Combining the two dimensions produces four types of executive experience (strategist, analyst, steward, artist) and each approach is expressed primarily through the particular language usage of the chief executive.

More generally, Stumpf (1989) summarised survey work on strategic thinking conducted at New York University which included the observation of several thousand managers. Based on that work he identified four factors that were associated with strategic manager effectiveness: (i) consistently applying a small number of key concepts, (ii) developing skills at thinking and acting strategically, (iii) knowing one's personal style and its impact on others; and

(iv) understanding the strategic management process. He further outlined a set of six crucial strategic thinking skills (e.g. manage subunit rivalry, find and overcome threats).

In an effort to facilitate the targeting of management development interventions for particular contexts, several recent authors have focused on identifying competencies within specific managerial populations. Included among these are secondary school principals (McCauley, 1990); utility and health care executives (Thareau, 1991; Johnson, 1991); team leaders (Komacki, Desselles & Bowman, 1989); global managers (Finney & Von Glinow, 1988; Sanders, 1988); engineers (Cobb & Gibbs, 1990); public sector management (Johnston & Dryssen, 1991); research and development managers (Pearson & McCauley, 1991); and women (Cotter, James, Lucas & Vinnicombe, 1991).

In addition, there has been a proliferation of recent study of important managerial competencies for managers in nearly every region of the world. Examples include the UK (Constable, 1988), Japan (Suzuki, 1989), Asia (Temporal, 1990), the Third World (Blunt & Jones, 1991), Singapore (Williams, 1991), Russia (McCarthy, 1991), Eastern Europe (Fogel, 1990), and Hong Kong (Yau & Sculli, 1990).

Finally, leaders of some progressive firms are stressing the importance of identifying managerial competencies crucial in their own organisations and are concerned with how abstract and general models might manifest themselves in particular firm settings (Kerr, 1990). Among reports of company initiatives to better understand managerial effectiveness within the context of the firm are General Electric (Hayes, 1988); British Airways (O'Neill, 1990); and Bell Canada, (Wilson, 1990).

Summary

In summary, a great deal of recent work has attempted to enhance our understanding of effective management by exploring personal qualities, environmental changes and a variety of different organisational and contextual variables. It should be abundantly clear from the diversity of research that it is incomplete to talk only about personal abilities leading to managerial success or only about the behaviours of good managers or only about the environments conducive to management success. Rather, managerial effectiveness is a function of complex interactions between ability, motivation and environmental variables and the nature of feedback, incentive and reward systems developed by organisational policies and practices. Managerial tasks and problems are highly interdependent, relatively unstandardised, highly susceptible to change, and often specific to situations rather than problems (Whitley, 1989).

Fortunately, recent research seems to be moving in a way that acknowledges this reality. The development of more precisely specified and empirically supported taxonomies facilities the mapping of characteristics of management jobs in different settings and the operationalisation of appropriate development objectives and strategies. Nonetheless, for research in specific contexts to have cumulative value and contribute to our understanding of effective management, rigorous work must continue to define, describe and measure the dimensions of jobs, cultures and organisations relevant to managerial success.

CONTEXTS OF MANAGERIAL DEVELOPMENT

In 1986, McCauley completed a review of the empirical literature examining experiences on the job that contribute to the development of managers. At that time, she noted that there was no systematic body of research which focused on what experiences or events might be significant in managerial careers. Indeed, the majority of traditional research examining management development has focused primarily on learning that takes place in structured training programmes. Yet, when managers are asked to describe their most significant learning experiences, they invariably describe on-the-job experiences as having contributed the most to their development (e.g. McCall, Lombardo & Morrison, 1988; Mumford, 1988; Davies & Easterby-Smith, 1984).

Recent literature suggests a rather dramatic increase in interest in on-the-job experiences and other learning contexts. Our review is organised around three contexts: job assignments, relationships, and formal training. Due to the relatively little attention that the first two contexts have received in the past, we focus our review there. However, several trends in the area of formal training that have received increased attention (e.g. outdoor challenge training and action learning) are reviewed as well.

Job Assignments

Job assignments have been frequently mentioned as an important context for the development of managers (e.g. McCall, Lombardo & Morrison, 1988; Lindsey, Homes & McCall, 1987; Lombardo, 1989). Research in this area has developed around two different but related ways of thinking about how job assignments contribute to development. Some research has focused on how job challenge enhances development. The intent has been to determine what essential or basic job elements contribute to the experience of job challenge (e.g. McCall, 1988; McCauley, Ohlott & Ruderman, 1989). The other approach focuses on identifying specific types of job assignments that contribute to development. The assumption is that these specific assignments provide managers with the opportunity to experience one or more of these challenging job elements (e.g. Lindsey, Homes & McCall, 1987; McCall, Lombardo & Morrison, 1988; Lombardo, 1989; Marsick; 1990; Mumford, 1991; Stumpf, 1989).

A third issue to be examined is the contribution that hardship experiences make to development. While hardship experiences are not a specific type of job assignment, these experiences typically occur within the context of a particular job and hence will be discussed with job assignments.

Sources of job challenge

Among the earliest research examining how job assignments contribute to management development were two studies (Berlew & Hall, 1966; Bray, Campbell & Grant, 1974) which suggested that early job challenge significantly enhances a manager's development. Subsequent research has added to our understanding of how challenging job experiences contribute to managerial learning. The experience of job challenge results from a gap between the skills and abilities of the individual and those required by the situation, which leads to the feeling of being 'stretched' by the job. Experiencing this gap motivates the manager to learn what is necessary to carry out the responsibilities of the job (McCauley, Ohlott & Ruderman, 1989; McCauley, Ruderman, Ohlott & Morrow, 1992). Akin (1987) describes this 'gap' as a 'sense of role' and considers it to be an important precondition for learning.

Until recently, our understanding of what exactly constituted a challenging job experience was limited. In the original studies at AT&T, job challenge involved four components: job stimulation and challenge, supervisory responsibility, degree of structure of assignments and degree to which the boss was an achievement model (Bray, Campbell & Grant, 1974; Bray & Howard, 1983). More recent research by McCall and his associates (e.g. McCall, 1988; McCall, Lombardo & Morrison, 1988) described eight key elements of job challenge that were derived from descriptions by executives of key developmental events. These fundamental challenges are: dealing with bosses; incompetence and resistance from subordinates; having to develop relationships with those whom he/she has never had to deal with before; playing for high stakes; business adversity; coping with scope and scale; missing trumps (i.e. entering a business situation at a disadvantage in some way); and starkness of transitions (i.e. degree of difference from what the manager has done before).

In a recent model of how job challenge contributes to on-the-job development, McCauley, Ohlott and Ruderman (1989) described two major categories of job challenges: job transitions and job demands. Job transitions included such things as changes in organisation level, a move to a new organisational unit or geographical location, and key first experiences, such as the first supervisory position. Four broad job demands were proposed in the model: creating change; performing in high stakes situations, dealing with uncertainty and experiencing supervisory pressure. According to their model, the experience of job challenge could lead to a variety of responses, such as seeking information, trying out new behaviours or building new relationships. These activities are expected to lead to learning, with learning being maximised under conditions where the manager receives feedback on his/her success and where the new behaviours are reinforced and supported. The model also proposes that individual differences, such as self-esteem, past experience and learning orientation, will influence how individuals react to the challenge and how much is learned from it. A preliminary test of the model revealed support for several of the hypothesised linkages.

Subsequent research has further refined our understanding of these fundamental job challenges. Researchers at the Center for Creative Leadership (USA) (McCauley, Ohlott & Ruderman, 1989; Ruderman, Ohlott & McCauley, 1990) have developed an instrument called the Job Challenge Profile (JCP) which is designed to measure the developmental aspects of managerial jobs. The content of the instrument was derived from the McCall, Lombardo and Morrison (1988) studies on executive learning and growth. Job incumbents rate the extent to which each item is seen as descriptive of their job.

In a comprehensive study examining the reliability and validity of the JCP (McCauley, Ruderman, Ohlott & Morrow, 1992), fourteen subscales were identified through factor analysis and grouped into five more general demand scales. The five demand scales were: dealing with scope and scale (including the high stakes, managing business diversity and job overload subscales); job transitions; creating change; coping with situations outside the chain of command (handling external pressure); and working without advice and support.

In addition to research examining challenges across jobs in general, there are a few studies which have focused on the challenges present in special types of jobs or organisations. For example, McCauley and Hughes (1991) examined the developmental opportunities present in the non-profit sector. Pearson and McCauley (1991) studied the challenges in research and development (R&D) jobs and found that, compared to other managers, R&D managers faced more job challenge from lack of top management support and more problemmatic relationships with their bosses and subordinates. However, they also reported learning less from their jobs.

Finally, Eichinger and Lombardo (1990) discussed the developmental potential of staff positions. In comparing line and staff positions on the key sources of developmental challenge described above, staff positions were lacking on all but two (influencing others without authority and involving significant intellectual, strategic or problem-solving challange with little or no guidance). They argued that over time, line managers will accumulate more developmental experiences than will staff managers. This is interesting since McCall, Lombardo and Morrison (1988) found that managers reported spending time in a staff position as a significant developmental experience. Perhaps spending a few years in a staff position is developmental although having a career in staff positions may not be. Eichinger and Lombardo (1990) suggest a variety of ways for maximising the developmental potential of staff positions.

The Job Challenge Profile, as it becomes more widely utilised, should contribute significantly not only to our understanding of how job challenge enhances growth and learning but also to our ability to use this knowledge to better develop managerial talent. One practical application for the instrument is to enable managers to obtain feedback on the developmental opportunities available to them in their current job. This feedback should facilitate career planning among managers. Further, the instrument could be used by organisations engaged in succession planning to periodically audit positions for their developmental potential. This could aid staffing decisions by enabling organisations to place individuals in positions where they would experience new job demands that would have value-added in terms of their growth and learning. This would be particularly valuable for those working in staff positions which, as described above, have fewer developmental opportunities within them (Eichinger & Lombardo, 1990). Being able to connect these challenging experiences with the specific skills, abilities or knowledges acquired would significantly add to our understanding of how job challenge contributes to managerial development.

Specific job assignments

Research examining specific job assignments is, for the most part, very sparse. Much anecdotal evidence exists for the value of serving on a project or task force, or for taking a staff position, but there is little evidence of an empirical nature. One notable exception is a study conducted by McCall, Lombardo and Morrison (1988) at the Center for Creative Leadership. They were interested in understanding what key events managers felt contributed to their development and what, specifically, they believed they had learned from these events. Based upon extensive interviews with 79 executives and survey information from 112 executives, they identified five specific types of job assignments that managers believed facilitated their development. These were: (i) project or task force assignments; (ii) fix-it assignments; (iii) assignments that involved starting something from scratch; (iv) line to staff switches; and (v) managing an operation of significant scope (see Lindsey, Homes & McCall, 1987; for more information concerning these assignments).

McCall, Lombardo and Morrison (1988) examined these five types of job assignments to determine what specific lessons managers learned from them that contributed to their development. A total of 34 lessons were identified by managers with the lessons being grouped into five categories: setting and implementing agendas, handling relationships, executive temperament, basic values and personal awareness.

It is clear that different lessons are learned from different job assignments. Generally speaking, however, job assignments are most likely to teach the lessons in the first three categories, with self-confidence being the lesson most likely to be learned. For example, project or task force assignments are most likely to teach self-confidence, external negotiation and management values. Fix-it assignments are most useful for learning about the directing and motivating of subordinates, lateral cooperation, how the business works and self-confidence. Starting something from scratch is most likely to teach lessons dealing with directing and motivating subordinates, standing alone and acting, and self-confidence. Line to staff switches teach technical knowledge, how business works, comfort with ambiguity and stress, how to work with executives, the organisation as a system and what executives are like. Finally, handling large-scope operations teaches directing and motivating subordinates, technical knowledge and self-confidence.

Bentz (1987) argues that being in jobs possessing scope and scale is an important determinant of the effectiveness of high-level executives. He defines scope in terms of breadth of management—the number of horizontal units included within a position. Scale refers to the internal complexity, diversity and ambiguity of functions within and across units managed, within and across varieties of personal relationships, and across decisions made. He discusses both specific job elements that contribute to the scope and scale of high-level positions and what kinds of experiences prepare managers to handle positions having significant scope and scale (i.e. high-level positions).

Temporal and Burnett (1990) and others (e.g. Beck, 1988) have argued for the use of strategic project assignments in an international setting to help develop international managers. One important example of such an assignment would be responsibility for developing and implementing market entry in a new country or region. An assignment such as this, which takes place in another country, can help to give high potential managers a solid general experience across financial, marketing, production, cultural and personal disciplines. The experience of working overseas, they note, is an essential component in the development of global managers.

Job rotation, while not a specific type of job assignment, has also been linked to managerial development (Wexley & Latham, 1991). Job rotation is believed to provide managers with a diversity of experiences which should, presumably, give them a broader perspective on the organisation. According to McCall and Lombardo (1983) having a wide range of different work experiences is one factor that differentiates between successful and derailed executives. Moreover, job rotation potentially exposes employees to new functional areas, helps them develop an appreciation for the inter-relationships between various parts of the company and assists them in developing a large network of contacts across the organisation.

Despite the widespread belief in the usefulness of job rotation for management development, few empirical studies exist. One exception is a study by London (1989) which evaluated the effectiveness of a job rotation programme for early career scientists and engineers. Results of the study indicated that those participating in the job rotation programme had a greater understanding of the importance of collaboration, the value of eliciting and comparing different problem solutions, and a stronger belief that work unit performance was rewarded and that mutual respect of other functions was important.

More recently, Campion, Cheraskin and Stevens (1991) examined the rewards and costs of job rotation for individuals and organisations. A survey study of 387 employees across a wide variety of occupations and organisational levels indicated that job rotation rates and promotion rates were positively correlated. Further, four categories of rewards were found (in order of importance): stimulating work, organisational integration (understanding of strategy, developing networks), awareness of self and of management styles and career (satisfaction and involvement in career and opportunities for promotion). Three categories of costs to job rotation were found (in order of importance): increased costs associated with the learning curve, increases in workload and decreases in productivity for the individual and his/her coworkers, and decreased satisfaction and motivation of coworkers.

Research by Gabarro (1987) also has some interesting implications for the practice of job rotation as a developmental strategy. Gabarro focused on how people adjust to new job assignments and the learning involved in making the adjustment. Based upon extensive study of 17 successions, he identified five stages in the process of taking charge: (i) taking hold; (ii) immersion; (iii) reshaping; (iv) consolidation; and (v) refinement. He argues that it is not until after the completion of the reshaping stage, where the manager typically makes significant changes based upon the learning acquired during the previous stage, that the manager has had the opportunity to learn enough to make the experience developmental. After the consolidation stage, little new learning occurs. Thus, from a developmental perspective, it appears that most of the value from experiencing job transitions may occur in the first three years (at which time the manager has reached the consolidation stage) and that little is to be gained by remaining in the assignment longer.

On the other hand, Gabarro cautions against moving managers too soon, before they have had time to fully understand the situation and to act upon their new understanding rather than upon their past experience. Others have suggested that the 'fast-track' developmental strategy employed by many organisations may not be beneficial to either the individual or the organisation (e.g. Thompson, Kirkhan & Dixon, 1985; Kovach, 1986).

Several authors have suggested that there may be individual differences in the ability of people to learn from experiences, such as job assignments (McCall, 1988; McCauley, Ohlott & Ruderman, 1989; Morrison & Brantner, 1991). Individual differences such as the manager's career history (McCall, Lombardo & Morrison, 1988), learning orientation (Dechant, 1990; Kelleher, Finestone & Lowy, 1986) and self-esteem (Brett, 1984) have been proposed.

Most of the recent research dealing with individual differences has focused on gender (e.g. Van Velsor & Hughes, 1990; Ohlott, Ruderman & McCauley, 1990; 1992). Ohlott, Ruderman and McCauley (1992) found evidence that women experience different demands from managerial jobs than do men in similar types of jobs at comparable levels. For example, women managers reported experiencing higher levels of job demands related to influencing without authority and lacking personal support. Furthermore, male managers were more likely to experience those demands generally believed to have important developmental opportunities (e.g. high stakes assignments) while women faced more problems involving the development of supportive relationships. Also of interest is the finding that, even when the effects of age, tenure and difference of current job from previous job are removed, women seem to learn more from the demands that they face. The authors suggest a variety of possible reasons for this, such as greater openness to learning by women in comparison to men. An earlier study by these authors (Ohlott, Ruderman & McCauley, 1990) supports some of these findings and further suggests that not only are female managers experiencing job demands to a greater extent than are males, but that they are also learning from a greater variety of sources than men.

Of course, job assignment-based development is not without its constraints and barriers. Hall and Foulkes (1991) argue that the barriers to cross-functional movement are greater now than in the past since line managers, faced with tighter headcount restrictions, may be reluctant to give up good people in a trade for an unknown individual. They also note that the trend in companies toward downsizing means that many of the 'key' high-visibility developmental jobs have been eliminated, while the movement toward delayering means that there are fewer promotional opportunities. Corporations may need to explore other forms of organisational movement, such as downward movement (Hall & Isabella, 1985), for their developmental opportunities.

There may also be resistance by bosses to the explicit use of job assignments for development since this necessarily results in placing individuals into positions where they do not currently have all the skills and abilities necessary to be successful. While this is necessary to stretch the individual so that learning occurs, resistance on the part of bosses might occur due to their reluctance to tolerate what they believe could be a longer learning and adjustment period by the individual. Staffing for development thus conflicts with the traditional selection approach which involves trying to achieve a good match between the person and the job, so that the individual hired is the individual whose present skills best match those required by the job (Ruderman, Ohlott & McCauley, 1990; McCauley et al., 1992).

Hardships

Until recently, the literature examining developmental experiences had little to say concerning the developmental potential of hardship experiences. Although some (e.g. Jennings, 1971; Gaylord & Simon, 1984) have suggested that these experiences provided the opportunity for growth and learning, most research has focused on the negative consequences rather than the potential positive outcomes. Recent research dealing with hardships focuses on three themes: identification of hardship experiences, the causes and consequences of experiencing hardships, and issues related to helping managers learn from these experiences.

The research of McCall, Lombardo and Morrison (1988) on key developmental events identified five types of hardship experiences that managers found to be significant in terms of their development as managers. These were: business mistakes and failures (which usually resulted from mistakes in dealing with key people, either superiors, subordinates or peers); demotions/missed promotions/lousy jobs; breaking a rut (i.e. changing careers); subordinate performance problems; and personal trauma (e.g. injury, illness, divorce).

Managers learned a variety of lessons from these experiences, but the most frequent lessons dealt with personal awareness. For example, from business mistakes and failures managers learned to recognise their personal limits, how to deal with people and about organisational politics. From demotions and lousy jobs managers learned to cope with situations outside their control and organisational politics, and they learned to recognise their personal limits.

Lombardo and McCauley (1988) have followed up on previous research examining executive *derailment* (e.g. McCall & Lombardo, 1983; Morrison, White & Van Velsor, 1987). Derailment occurs when a manager who has been judged to have the ability to go higher fails to live up to his/her full potential and is fired, demoted or plateaued below expected levels of achievement. Using supervisor ratings of over 300 middle- to upper-level managers in eight companies, six basic flaws that contribute to derailment were identified: (i) difficulty moulding a staff; (ii) difficulty making strategic transitions; (iii) lack of follow-through; (iv) problems with interpersonal relationships; (v) overdependence; and (vi) strategic differences with management. Additional reasons for derailment that occurred in a study examining derailment among female managers were poor image and narrow business experience (Morrison, White & Van Velsor, 1987).

The research by Lombardo and McCauley (1988) also indicated that managers who were rated by their bosses as having more flaws also had fewer strengths. Moreover, although the first three flaws have the strongest relationship to derailment, the flaws which contribute most to derailment seemed to vary somewhat across companies and across jobs. They concluded that some flaws which do not hinder performance in lower-level jobs become critical as the manager is moved into more challenging, higher-level jobs and this is consistent with previous research (e.g. McCall & Lombardo, 1983; Kovach, 1986). Finally, and perhaps most significantly, they concluded that derailment can be predicted in advance.

Kovach (1989) examined derailment from a somewhat different perspective. Rather than focusing on what causes derailment, she examined what happens to managers *after* they have been derailed. While derailment is possible for everyone, she suggests that it is likely to be particularly prevalent among those managers who are on the 'fast-track'. For example, being on the 'fast track' may produce an imbalance between the manager's work and personal life (Kofodimos, 1990). Fast-track managers may become so involved in their work (in an effort to continue the movement upward that is seen as a sign of success) that they neglect their personal life and eventually become ineffective at work.

Based upon her interviews with 17 managers who had been identified as fast-trackers, Kovach (1989) concluded that a career slowdown leads managers to a period of reflection about themselves and their relationship to others and that their reaction to the derailment and the learning which occurs while derailed can be significant factors in determining if they become mobile again. Derailment gives managers the opportunity to learn about themselves, about others, and about their organisation. From this reflection can develop a new understanding of their priorities and values.

Being able to learn from derailment and other hardship experiences requires a willingness on the part of the manager to examine him/herself and an ability to learn from their mistakes. Yet Argyris (1991) and others (e.g. Hall, 1986; Kaplan, Drath & Kofodimos, 1987) argue that this is very difficult for managers to do, primarily because they have been so successful all their lives. Having never experienced failure, they have an extremely difficult time learning from it. Managers tend to become defensive and find it difficult to admit that they may have inadvertently contributed to their mistakes.

Interestingly, the ability to accept responsibility for mistakes is one of the very characteristics that has been found to distinguish between successful and derailed executives (e.g. McCall & Lombardo, 1983; Kaplan, Drath & Kofodimos, 1987; Hall, 1986). Argyris (1991) describes a process used to help managers break out of what he calls the 'doom loop' of defensive reasoning. It requires getting managers to recognise the conflict between the theory of behaviour which they espouse and the theory which they actually use. Feedback from others can be a valuable source of information to help managers recognise their limitations.

Unfortunately, it appears that the higher managers advance, the more difficult it becomes for them to receive this feedback (Kaplan, Drath & Kofodimos 1987; Bartolome, 1989). A variety of factors, relating to the nature of the executive role, and his/her job and personal characteristics, combine to keep managers from obtaining this critical feedback both from other people and, through introspection, from themselves. For example, the executive's isolation and exaggerated perceptions of his/her impact may keep others from sharing this information with him/her. The many demands, pressures and requirements for action inherent in the job contribute to the problem by inhibiting managers from taking the time to reflect and examine themselves. Finally, the need to be competent may keep managers from being able to accept criticism from others.

Nonetheless, it has been argued that none of the identified barriers to learning are necessarily insurmountable. As noted by Kaplan, Drath and Kofodimos (1987), executives who really want to learn can do so and there are steps that organisations can take to make this process easier. For example, being more tolerant of mistakes and providing an environment where learning (and not just results) is valued can increase the willingness of managers to accept criticism (Kaplan, Drath & Kofodimos, 1987; Lombardo & McCauley, 1988). In addition, organisations can create developmental job assignments that follow a logical progression and build upon each other rather than the haphazard pattern often observed. Finally, organisations need to help managers make 'mental transitions' (p. 18) so they understand that the behaviours or qualities that were rewarded earlier in their careers may need to be modified to fit new situational demands (Lombardo & McCauley, 1988).

In examining the research on job assignments, several observations can be made. The first and most readily apparent is how little empirical research of an evaluative nature there is. We have very little conclusive evidence that these types of job assignments really are developmental. We concur with Noe and Ford's (1992) recommendations for the evaluation of job rotation programmes and argue that they need to be extended to other developmental job assignments as well. Specifically, a rigorous assessment of the value of these job assignments is necessary to determine if those who have them are actually more successful (using a variety of individual and organisational outcome measures) than those who do not. Thus far, almost all that we know concerning the value of different types of job assignments has been based on the opinions of executives/managers. While this is a valuable start, we now need to move beyond reaction and self-reported learning measures to more objective learning, behavioual change and results measures (e.g. London, 1989).

In addition to research evaluating the effectiveness of various job assignments, it would be valuable to learn more about how the specific assignments should be utilised to best enhance managerial development. For example, in order to maximise learning, should managers experience all of the different types of assignments or some subset? In what order should managers experience these assignments? Which should occur earlier in one's career and which later? Should managers experience some of these assignments more than once? McCall, Lombardo and Morrison (1988) have suggested that little additional learning comes from experiencing one type of assignment more than once but there is little empirical support for this contention.

Implicit in the research on specific types of job assignments is an assumption that the reason these assignments are developmental is because they provide an opportunity for the manager to be challenged. Thus, job challenge is assumed to mediate between specific assignments and learning outcomes. Surprisingly, though, research integrating these two streams of research is virtually non-existent. To further our understanding of how job assignments, job challenges and learning outcomes are related, it would be useful to know if certain types of assignments are most likely to provide certain basic elements of job challenge and also, which learning outcomes derive from these challenges.

Another direction for future research would be to determine what specific work experiences are most valuable for teaching which managerial competencies. While McCall, Lombardo and Morrison (1988) do identify the lessons learned from job assignments, most of the lessons do not relate to specific managerial competencies. An example of research which does this is Stumpf (1989) which identified specific work experiences that help to develop a manager's capacity for strategic thinking. Additional research of this nature would be extremely valuable.

Finally, research examining how to help managers actually learn from these informal learning experiences and what can be done to facilitate this process would be useful. As McCall, Lombardo and Morrison (1988) note, there is no guarantee that just because a manager experiences a developmental assignment he/she will learn from it. A variation on action learning, a developmental approach that is gaining popularity, has the potential to be very useful in terms of helping managers learn from their experiences (Marsick, 1990).

Relationships with Others

A growing body of recent literature supports the long-held belief that relationships play an important role in the development of managers, both as professionals and as individuals (McCall, Lombard & Morrison, 1988; Kram, 1985; Gabarro, 1987; Kovach, 1989; London & Mone, 1987). In this section we will review recent research examining how three different relationships (mentor, boss, peer) may contribute to managerial development.

Mentoring relationships

Perhaps the most frequently examined relationship in the context of management development is that of mentoring. The term 'mentor' is generally used to describe 'a relationship between a young adult and an older, more experienced adult that helps the younger individual to navigate in the adult world and the world of work' (Kram, 1985: p. 2). Recent research on mentoring has focused on three issues: the benefits of mentoring (for the protégé, the mentor and the organisation), dynamics within mentoring relationships, including issues related to the gender of the mentor and protégé, and structured mentoring programmes.

Prior research on mentoring relationships has identified two important functions which these relationships serve for the protégé: career and psycho-social (Kram, 1985). Career functions are those that enhance career advancement (e.g. exposure, visibility, coaching) while psycho-social functions enhance the protégé's sense of competence, identity and effectiveness in a professional role (e.g. role modelling, counselling and friendship).

Recently, some additional benefits of mentoring have also been reported. For example, Kram and Hall (1989) have found that mentor-protégé relationships may be a way to alleviate the stress that occurs during times of organisational change (e.g. corporate restructuring or downsizing). During these times, individuals reported a greater desire to serve as a mentor to others and were more likely to indicate both that mentoring was important and was not of sufficient quality in the organisation. Ostroff and Kozlowski (1992) reported that mentoring may influence the socialisation experiences of newcomers. Those newcomers with mentors were able to learn more about organisational issues and practices than newcomers without mentors. Interestingly, these two groups also differed in their information acquisition strategies. Newcomers with mentors relied on their mentor while newcomers without mentors relied more on their coworkers.

An important question is whether mentoring has any significant impact on the career outcomes of protégés. Yet beyond a study conducted a number of years ago (Roche, 1979) which found that executives who had sponsors earned more money at an earlier age, little research has emerged. One recent study, however, reported that individuals who had extensive experience in mentoring relationships (as the protégé) received more promotions, had higher incomes and were more satisfied with their pay and benefits than individuals who had experienced less extensive mentoring relationships (Dreher & Ash, 1990).

Recent work in this area has also begun to take into account benefits of relationships for the mentor and the organisation. For example, Smith (1990) argues that mentoring relationships foster the growth of mentors, give them satisfaction and increased motivation and help to develop their leadership skills.

Organisations are believed to benefit since younger employees have the opportunity to be guided by those with more experience, which should lead to more effective utilisation of human resources (Wright & Werther, 1991). The potential for mentoring relationships to aid in training and development is another important benefit to organisations (Zey, 1988), as is the ability to foster teamwork, shared values and improved communication (Smith, 1990).

In describing the nature of mentor/protégé relationships, Bushardt, Fretwell and Holdnak (1991) argue that mentors, regardless of their gender, utilise predominantly masculine sex-role behaviour. On the other hand, protégés, regardless of their gender, utilise predominantly feminine sex-role behaviour. Taking a socio-biological perspective, they draw parallels between the mentoring process and the mating process in terms of selection criteria, acquisition strategies and demographic characteristics of the relationship.

Several researchers have examined factors influencing the formation of mentor-protégé relationships and the reactions of the protégé and the mentor to those relationships. Olian, Carroll, Giannantonio and Feren (1988) studied the impact of both mentor characteristics and behaviours (gender, age, interpersonal competence, and integration into the organisation's decision-making network) and protégé characteristics (gender, age and previous work experience) on attraction to a mentoring relationship. Results of three laboratory studies involving a total of 675 participants found that the interpersonal competence of the mentor significantly increased protégé attraction to the mentoring relationship, that mentor integration into decision-making networks only increased protégé attraction to the relationship when mentor interpersonal competence was weak, and that protégé work experience and mentor age had no effect on protégé attraction. There was no consistent evidence that protégés are more attracted to same sex mentor-protégé relationships.

More recently, Olian, Carroll and Giannantonio (1992) examined several protégé factors (e.g. protégé performance, mentor-protégé gender similarity and protégé marital status) thought to influence mentor reactions to the mentoring relationship. Results revealed that protégé performance was positively related to mentor intentions to engage in mentoring behaviours and anticipated rewards from the relationship. Protégé marital status interacted with protégé sex such that mentors anticipated greater inclination to engage in career-enhancing behaviours and greater rewards to themselves when male protégés were married and when female protégés were single. Finally, mentors perceived somewhat greater drawbacks to mentoring single protégés.

Gender may be an important factor influencing the nature and formation of mentoring relationships. For example, it has been suggested that not only may mentoring relationships be more important to females seeking advancement but that they may be harder for women to obtain (Noe, 1988b; Ragins, 1989). Ragins (1989) describes some potential barriers for women in obtaining mentoring relationships. First, women may fail to recognise the importance of gaining sponsorship and may be less likely than men to seek mentors. Or, if they do realise the importance of having a mentor, they may not have the knowledge, skills or strategies necessary to obtain a mentor. A contributing factor is that mentors may be less willing to select female protégés.

Ragins and Cotton (1991a) examined some of these barriers empirically to determine if there actually are gender differences in barriers to gaining a mentor. The survey results obtained from 510 men and women indicated that women perceived more barriers than did men in gaining a mentor, even after controlling for experience as a protégé, age, rank and tenure. As noted by Ragins and Cotton (1991a), although this study is suggestive of greater barriers for women in mentoring, it focused entirely on *perceptions* of mentoring barriers which may or may not correspond to actual barriers. In fact, in a survey of 440 business school graduates, Dreher and Ash (1990) found little evidence that females were less likely than males to have mentors. Furthermore, there was no evidence that gender moderated the relationship between mentoring and career outcomes as was expected. It is conceivable that the perception of greater barriers by women may actually be a defense mechanism employed to rationalise their personal limitations, inability to obtain a mentor, or lack of advancement. Future research needs to examine more objective indices of mentoring barriers to resolve this issue.

Examining gender differences from the perspective of the mentor, Ragins and Cotton (1991b) found that although there was no difference between men and women in their willingness to serve as a mentor, women perceived more drawbacks and obstacles to becoming a mentor. Women were more likely than men to report that they did not feel qualified to be a mentor, that they did not want the risk of being made to look bad by their protégé's failure and that they lacked the time to be a mentor.

Another variation on the research examining gender differences in mentoring concerns cross-gender mentoring relationships. Cross-gender mentoring refers to a mentor-protégé relationship involving a male and female (Bushardt, Fretwell & Holdnak, 1991). There are special problems involved in these mentoring relationships due to latent and/or manifest sexual themes and these vary depending on whether the male or female is the mentor (Bushardt, Fretwell & Holdnak, 1991). Ragins and McFarlin (1990) compared protégé perceptions of mentor roles in both cross-gender and same-gender mentoring relationships. They found few differences between these types of relationships. However, cross-gender protégés reported that they were less likely than same-gender protégés to spend time in after-work social activities with their mentors. It is possible that sexual concerns may result in cross-gender relationships not being as close as same-gender relationships. Also of interest was the finding that female protégés with female mentors were more likely to report that their mentor served as a role model to them.

As described above, there are a number of benefits both to individuals and organisations from having mentoring relationships develop within the organisation. Yet it is clear that not everyone is able to establish such relationships. This has led some to suggest that organisations should establish formal mentoring programmes rather than relying on those relationships that develop naturally (e.g. Zey, 1988; Bernstein & Kaye, 1986). Indeed, a number of companies, (e.g. Johnson & Johnson, Motorolla, Honeywell) have already established such programmes.

It has been argued that formal mentoring programmes are somewhat risky because there is some question about whether appointed mentors will develop the 'favorable chemistry' (Wright & Werther, 1991: p. 27) with the protégé needed to make the relationship a success. There is a number of other possible problems with assigned mentors. There may be personality conflicts between the parties and a lack of true commitment to the relationship since it was not formed of their own volition (Kram, 1985; Kram & Bragar, in press). Furthermore, formal programmes might create expectations in those mentors of rapid career progress, which might lead to frustration or even turnover if those expectations are not met (Wright & Werther, 1991).

Thus far, most of the concerns raised about mentoring programmes are speculative in nature and there has been little empirical research examining actual mentoring programmes. One exception is a study by Noe (1988a) that examined determinants of successful assigned mentoring relationships. Results of this study suggest that organisations should not expect the same benefits to protégés from assigned mentoring relationships as those which arise naturally. More specifically, protégés in assigned relationships reported receiving valuable psychosocial outcomes from the mentoring relationships but limited career functions. Interaction between the mentor and the protégé appeared to be limited, which suggests the possible need to increase the accessibility of the mentor to the protégé, perhaps by requiring weekly meetings.

There appear to be a number of core components necessary to make planned mentoring programmes successful (Kram & Bragar, in press; Zey, 1988, 1989; Alleman, 1989). These include such things as specific objectives for the programme, a careful selection process that incorporates voluntary participation and an attempt to match mentors and protégés so that both will find value in the relationship, a monitoring and evaluation process, and a programme coordinator.

Smith (1990) describes an interesting variation on typical mentoring programmes that attempts to combine two developmental methods, mentoring and project work, to capitalise on the strengths of both. The programme, called 'mutual mentoring on projects', involves having managers identify real organisational problems that need to be solved but which they cannot solve on their own with their current skills and knowledge. A group of people who can contribute to solving the problem are identified and each member develops a learning contract that identifies what he/she intends to learn from the process as well as what he/she is responsible for teaching others. This process appears to have much in common with action learning programmes, which are reviewed later.

Other important relationships

In examining the research on relationships, it is clear that much more attention has been paid to mentoring than to other important relationships on the job. We know comparatively little about how bosses, peers and subordinates may help to contribute to the development of managers.

Given the large number of researchers and writers who have argued that bosses can play an important role in the development of managers (e.g. Kovach, 1989; London & Mone, 1987; Gabarro, 1987; McCall, Lombardo & Morrison, 1988), surprisingly little research of an empirical nature has been conducted. The importance of the relationship with one's boss can be seen in Gabarro's (1987) research examining the taking charge process. All of the failed successions examined were characterised by poor working relationships with their supervisor.

Clearly, ineffective relationships with bosses can negatively impact development. The research conducted by McCall and his colleagues (McCall, Lombardo & Morrison, 1988; Lindsey, Homes & McCall, 1987) examining key events in the development of managers identified two key events, both involving bosses, in which other people were the central feature. One type of key event was when the boss served as a role model. This event usually occurred over an extended period of time (from six months to three years). In contrast, the other event involving bosses (called 'values playing out') was typically a brief episode in which superiors (or sometimes the managers themselves) demonstrated their values by doing something either extremely bad or extremely good. The lessons learned from these two events were usually similar and they dealt mostly with values, either human, managerial or political. From observing the behaviour and seeing its impact on others, managers learned a great deal about not only their own values but also the values of the organisation.

Bosses can also aid in development by serving as a source of feedback to the manager about his/her strengths and weaknesses and as a source of advice and counselling (e.g. Hillman, Schwandt & Bartz, 1990). London and Mone (1987) described the various ways bosses can affect the career motivation (career resilience, insight and identity) of their employees. Career motivation is important because it has implications for how managers view their careers, how hard they work at them and how long they stay in them, all of which are important for management development. For example, career resilience should be strengthened by treating subordinates with respect, giving them challenging job assignments, allowing them to make their own mistakes, and encouraging them to use others as resources.

Since the pioneering work of Kram and Isabella (1985) examining peer relationships, the role of peers in the development of managers has been almost entirely ignored. Part of this inattention may be due to the belief that peer relationships will have less impact on development because peers do not typically have the knowledge and history of success that make true mentors such valuable career assets (Wright & Werther, 1991). This is a serious omission, given research by Gabarro (1987) which found that three out of four failed successions involved managers who had poor working relationships with two or more peers. Furthermore, peer relationships represent an alternative to mentoring, which, as noted earlier, may be less available to minorities and women (Ilgen & Youtz, 1986; Ragins, 1989; Noe, 1988b). These relationships may not only be more readily available but may also be more effective because the non-hierarchical nature of the relationship might make it easier to achieve communication, mutual support and collaboration.

One function that can be provided by peers that makes them an important developmental source is their ability to give the manager feedback of both a job-related and a personal nature (e.g. London & Mone, 1987). As noted earlier, feedback about his/her strengths and weaknesses is critical if the manager is to grow and develop and several studies have examined the use of feedback from both peers and subordinates to facilitate development (London & Wohlers, 1991; London, Wohlers & Gallagher, 1990). The 'mutual mentoring on projects' programme (Smith, 1990) described above represents another innovation in management development that relies heavily on lateral relationships and how peers learn from one another.

Research examining how significant relationships contribute to development - is in its infancy. We have made some progress in our understanding of mentoring relationships but much more needs to be done. For example, Noe (1988) suggested the need to study the types of functions provided by mentors at different career stages and specifically to determine if the functions desired differed by gender or other minority status. Empirical research examining the value of mentoring relationships to the mentors would also be beneficial. Finally, more research on the dynamics of mentoring relationships is needed since it is these dynamics which will most influence the success or failure of the relationship.

Our understanding of the role that bosses play in the development of managers would be enhanced by identifying the characteristics of bosses that make them effective coaches since it is unlikely that all bosses are equally effective at this. Clawson (1980), for example, found that bosses who were consistent in their behaviour, informal in their interactions, and willing to share information had more effective developmental relationships. Personality correlates of effectiveness in developing managers might include high self-esteem and high self-monitoring.

Research is also needed to determine how individual differences contribute to preferences for peer relationships versus mentoring relationships. It is possible that some people would learn more from the non-hierarchical peer relationships than from mentoring relationships (Kram & Isabella, 1985) . For example, highly authoritarian people might respond better to mentoring due to its hierarchical nature. Finally, we need a better understanding of the utility of lateral and upward feedback for management development. Valuable areas for future research include how managers interpret and apply the feedback data (regardless of whether it is upward or lateral feedback), how they interpret differences in ratings across people, and variables that influence their acceptance or denial of the results (London & Wohlers, 1991). The literature on feedback as a communication process (e.g. Ilgen, Fisher & Taylor, 1979) would be helpful in doing this.

Formal Training

Formal training programmes represent the third important context for management development. Formal programmes have always been an integral part of management development and have been the backbone of the management development efforts of most organisations (Mumford, 1991).

Traditionally, these formal development programmes have utilised lectures, discussions and case analyses to facilitate the development of managerial talent.

However, the growing recognition that managers (and adults in general) learn best by actually doing things that are of practical relevance to them, has led to changes in the content and process of formalised management development programmes (e.g. Braddick, 1988; Prideaux & Ford, 1988a; Knowles, 1984). In this section, we focus on three topics—outdoor challenge training, action learning and leadership training—that reflect this changing perspective and have received significant attention in the literature.

Outdoor challenge training

Outdoor challenge training is a rapidly growing innovation in formal training programmes. In a typical outdoor challenge programme, participants work as groups to complete a variety of outdoor activities that encompass an increasing level of challenge and risk, and that require greater trust in and dependence on group members. The focus of these programmes can be individual growth and change (e.g. Galagan, 1987) or leadership development and team building (e.g. Long, 1987). Two important components of outdoor challenge programmes are the development of action plans for transferring the learning of participants back to the workplace and follow-up on the success of these efforts by programme providers (Gall, 1987).

Descriptions of typical (e.g. Gall, 1987; Galagan, 1987; Long, 1987) and atypical (e.g. Blashford-Snell, 1991) outdoor learning programmes can be found in a variety of practioner-oriented journals. Unfortunately, despite the growing popularity of outdoor learning and its extensive use in many progressive organisations, little is known about how effective these programmes are at facilitating learning and bringing about changes in behaviour and attitudes. Some authors have argued that the extremely favourable anecdotal reports must be at least partially discounted given that participants almost uniformly experience a type of 'post-group euphoria' at the conclusion of novel outdoor experiential exercises (e.g. Baldwin, Wagner & Roland, 1991; Gall, 1987; Galagan, 1987; Long, 1987).

There is, however, some evidence that outdoor challenge programmes can produce changes in the attitudes and behaviour of participants (Galagan, 1987; Long, 1987; Marsh, Richards & Barnes, 1986, 1987; Baldwin, Wagner & Roland, 1991). For example, Marsh, Richards and Barnes (1986, 1987) found that participation in an adventure learning programme resulted in improvements in self-concept while Ewert (1988) found that trait anxiety declined for participants in the programme.

In one recent study of outdoor challenge training Baldwin, Wagner and Roland (1991) found some additional evidence for its effectiveness. They collected data from 343 programme participants, 115 non-participants and 13 team supervisors on a variety of individual and group measures. Results suggested that outdoor challenge training had a modest effect on some perceptions of group awareness and effectiveness as well as individual problem-solving measured three months after the training. However, no significant changes in trust or self-concept were observed. Group level analyses suggested that both the facilitator and the participation of intact work groups may be related to positive training outcomes.

Finally, in a study conducted at Federal Express, Inc. (USA), it was found that turnover dropped 10 percentage points in a group that had participated in an outdoor challenge learning programme and stayed the same in a group that had not (Gall, 1987).

Action learning

The growth of management development programmes based upon action learning principles represents a second important innovation in the area of management development (cf. Mumford, 1987). Action learning is most accurately thought of as a theory of adult learning rather than a training technique *per se* (Jones, 1990). It is based upon the idea that people learn best from their personal experience of doing something. It further assumes that managers can: (i) learn from experience; (ii) share that experience with others; (iii) have their colleagues criticise and advise them on possible actions; (iv) implement the advice; and (v) review the action taken and the lessons that are learned with those colleagues (Margerison, 1988).

All management development programmes utilising an action learning framework are project driven, meaning that participants work on solving real problems being faced by real organisations (often their own). In this way, the learning is practical and immediately relevant. While actual programme characteristics differ, other typical features include an emphasis on developing management competencies (rather than acquisition of knowledge), self-managed learning and learning from peers (Prideaux & Ford, 1988a,b).

Using the typology of management development formulated by Mumford (1991), action learning represents a 'middle ground' (Type 2) between the informal, unplanned, accidental (Type 1) learning processes described by the researchers at the Center for Creative Leadership (e.g. McCall, Lombardo & Morrison, 1988) and the formal, planned, deliberate (Type 3) management development practices that have been so heavily utilised by organisations in the past. These Type 2, 'opportunistic' learning processes share some characteristics with each type of learning process. Like Type 1 processes, they occur within the context of managerial activities and have task performance as an explicit goal. However, unlike Type 1 processes, development is also an explicit goal. In contrast, Type 3 learning processes occur outside the context of managerial activities and have development as the only explicit goal.

Essentially, action learning attempts to capitalise on the benefits of both the planned and unplanned learning processes that typically occur during the development of managers. Unfortunately, writings about action learning are not always clear about what, exactly, managers are expected to learn as a result of participating in these programmes. Very few descriptions of programmes have articulated much of a specific nature about programme outcomes. One exception is a study by Prideaux and Ford (1988b) which described seven major learnings reported by participants in their action learning programme: self-awareness and self-management, proactivity and vision, learning skills such as learning how to learn, staying power and emotional resilience, interactive skills, team skills, and analytical skills. Note the similarity of their list of learnings with the lists of management competencies described earlier.

Thus far, action learning programmes have been utilised most extensively in the UK and outside the United States. The literature provides examples of formal action learning programmes (both within companies, by external management development centres and within MBA programmes) as well as informal application of action learning principles in the UK (e.g. Mumford, 1991), Australia (e.g. Hubbard, 1990; Kable, 1989; Margerison, 1988; Prideaux & Ford, 1988a,b), Sweden (e.g. Marsick, 1990) and Africa (e.g. Safavi & Tweddell, 1990).

Though Marsick (1990) discusses some reasons why action learning has not been as popular in the United States, a few examples of applications exist (e.g. Lawrie, 1989; Noel & Charan, 1988). For example, Noel and Charan (1988) describe how General Electric changed their Business Management Course (part of their executive programme) at the Crotonville Management Development Institute to incorporate action learning principles.

Leadership development

Research on the development of leadership skills continues to receive a significant amount of attention in the management development literature and extensive reviews of leadership training programmes (Latham, 1988; Bass, 1990a,b) and leadership models (Yukl, 1989) have recently appeared. Our brief review of recent leadership literature is intended solely to give the reader a sense of the current research direction in this area.

Two research streams in the leadership area have been receiving a great deal of attention: (i) transformational leadership and the related concepts of charismatic leadership and inspirational leadership (e.g. Bass, 1990a,b; Bass & Avolio, 1991; Bennis & Nanus, 1985; Conger & Kanungo, 1988); and (ii) self-leadership (e.g. Manz, 1986; Neck & Manz, 1992; Gilbert-Smith, 1991). Current research in each of these areas will be briefly described.

According to Bass and his colleagues, an understanding of transformational leadership is necessary to account for the extraordinary efforts often exerted by followers. Transformational leaders, in contrast to transactional leaders, try to elevate follower needs to higher levels, try to develop followers into leaders and to bring about changes in the culture and strategies of the organisation. Recent research in this area has focused on gaining an understanding of how transformational leaders develop. Avolio and Gibson (1988) utilised a life-span approach to describe some of the factors that are believed to account for the development of transformational leaders and explored such variables as family factors, birth order, conflict and disappointments, previous leadership experience and mentors. From a somewhat different perspective, Bass and Avolio (1991) describe a workshop to develop transformational leadership and preliminary results of studies evaluating the effectiveness are promising.

Another major development in the leadership area is the emergence of self-leadership (e.g. Manz, 1986). Self-leadership is defined as 'the process of influencing oneself to establish the self-direction and self-motivation needed to perform' (Neck & Manz, 1992: p. 5). Neck and Manz (1992) discuss one aspect of self-leadership which involves controlling one's thoughts through the application of such cognitive strategies as self-dialogue and mental imagery.

The authors argue that self-leadership will lead to enhanced individual and organisational performance and suggest a number of propositions to guide future research in this area. The development of self-leadership skills is the first step toward becoming a superleader (Manz & Sims, 1991). Manz and Sims (1991) argue that leaders become superleaders by helping followers to develop their own leadership and self-leadership skills. Manz (1990) argued for the need to integrate the literature on self-managing teams with that on self-leadership, so that we can move beyond self-managing teams toward self-leading teams. Manz, Keating and Donnellon (1990) describe issues involved in preparing managers for their new role as facilitators of a self-managed work team.

Finally, research examining the application of established leadership models to the development of managers is ongoing. For example, research continues to be undertaken on path-goal (e.g. Neider & Schreisheim, 1988), the Vroom–Yetton model of participation in decision-making (e.g. Vroom & Jago, 1988; Maczynski, 1992), cognitive resources theory (e.g. Fiedler, in press), and an extension of the leader-member exchange model called leadership-making (e.g. Graen & Uhl-Bien, 1991a,b; Uhl-Bien & Graen, in press a). Other interesting developments in the area of leadership include a cross-cultural study examining how Japanese leadership techniques are utilised in US transplants (Graen & Wakabayashi, in press) and an attempt to enhance organisational effectiveness by linking leader requirements to the stage of the organisational life cycle (Hunt, Baiga & Peterson, 1988).

Recent developments in formal management programmes are exciting and have a great deal of intuitive appeal. Action learning programmes, in particular, seem uniquely suited for developing managers. It is difficult to argue with the logic of using actual work experiences as the basis for learning. It appears to be a strategy well suited to overcoming the difficulties of transferring learning back to the job when the learning was acquired in a very different context

(Baldwin & Ford, 1988). As noted by Kable (1989), the transfer problem occurs not only because the system often fails to reinforce the new behaviours, but because there is frequently direct pressure applied to individuals to keep their behaviour the same once they return to the job. This is much less likely to be a problem with action learning programmes because the projects that form the basis for the programme are of real concern to the organisation. In addition, action learning principles may help maximise the learning potential of the informal, unplanned experiences that occur naturally on the job.

Nevertheless, in our enthusiasm for new approaches to formal training we cannot overlook the need to carefully evaluate programmes to see how effective they truly are. As with all management development initiatives, we continue to lack evidence concerning the impact of these programmes on management behaviour and organisational effectiveness. To date, there have been few reported studies looking at the outcomes from either action learning or outdoor challenge programmes. In both cases, there are many positive testimonials but we know little about other outcomes.

Indeed, with respect to action learning, very little has even been said about *expected* outcomes. Future research similar to that of Prideaux and Ford (1988b) is necessary to determine what specific competencies managers acquire from participating in action learning programmes. One general concern is that, given the project-driven nature of these programmes, learning may be highly situation-specific and, therefore, not generalisable. On the other hand, given that the success of projects assigned to managers can be ascertained, action learning may lend itself to evaluation on objective outcome measures even more so than other development strategies.

Both action learning and adventure learning rely heavily on the use of teams for learning. For both types of programmes, it would also be valuable to know more about the characteristics that influence dynamics within the teams and how both team characteristics and team dynamics influence the success of programmes. Marsick (1990) has suggested that the action learning process is more effective when participants have different backgrounds (e.g. education, age, gender, ethnicity, experience and functional specialities), but research is needed which specifically examines this issue. Similarly, Marsick argues that participants should be from several different companies or organisations rather than just one (so that they will be working on a project outside their 'home environment' and presumably feel more free to ask questions), but there is also a pressing need for empirical evidence to support this contention.

Several team characteristics might be relevant to understanding the effectiveness of adventure learning. Baldwin, Wagner and Roland (1991) found preliminary evidence which suggests that more positive outcomes might be obtained when intact work teams are used rather than groups of strangers who come together only for purposes of participating in the training. Along similar lines, it is possible that newly formed teams in the earlier stages of development might be able to gain more than those who are further advanced because they have less 'history' to overcome. Other relevant team characteristics might include the size of the team and the extent of interdependence among team members on the job.

Summary

As this review of developmental contexts has shown, managers learn in a variety of ways from a variety of different experiences. As we attempt to make better use of the developmental opportunities present in day-to-day job experiences it would be valuable to have a better understanding of which individuals will benefit most from which experiences. Akin's (1987) learning themes might be useful in helping to differentiate between those who learn best from job assignments versus relationships with others versus formal developmental opportunities. Since legal constraints suggest that it may be difficult to differentially offer developmental experiences based upon learning style preferences, an understanding of these differences would enable human resource professionals to help managers maximise their own learning from each of the experiences they face.

EMERGING ISSUES IN MANAGEMENT DEVELOPMENT

Management Development as a Competitive Advantage

To gain competitive advantage, businesses have traditionally focused on technological, economic and strategic capabilities (Porter, 1985). However, a growing body of evidence supports the role of effective management on organisation and subunit performance (*Harvard Business Review*, 1987; Shipper, 1991; Day & Lord, 1988). Indeed Kotter (1988) argues that one thing that seems to distinguish excellent companies from the also rans is the amount of time and energy spent in the planning, designing and carrying out of development activities.

Such findings have prompted consideration of how organisations may treat development of managerial talent as a 'strategic weapon' (Ulrich, 1989; Hall & Foulkes, 1991; Fulmer, 1990). The traditional philosophy of development has often been that it should be aimed at benefiting the individual and, in some indirect way, would ultimately benefit the company. However, firms are now demanding development that is results oriented and aimed at implementing business strategy and corporate objectives (Bolt, 1987). More than ever before, organisations are stressing the importance of translating education into greater managerial effectiveness and responsiveness to a quickly changing business environment.

Ulrich reports on several case studies (e.g. Whirlpool, Borg-Warner) and presents eight transitions required to make executive development a competitive weapon. He presents a summary checklist of 24 key questions which he contends will focus development as a means of gaining competitiveness.

Hall and Foulkes (1991) make a similar case for the potential role of development as a competitive weapon. They debunk seven myths of existing executive development, present several corporate examples and emphasise the importance of organisation design, reward systems and CEO commitment for successful strategy-driven development to occur.

Rosow and Zager (1988) suggest that the evolution in training underway in organisations today is actually a movement towards a continuous learning philosophy. Pedler, Boydell and Burgoyne (1989) define the continuous learning organisation as one where learning is considered an everyday activity for all employees and the organisation continuously transforms itself. They argue that conditions for a learning organisation include extending the development to other significant shareholders and making the development strategy central to the business strategy so that learning becomes a major business activity. They further outline a set of nine guidelines for a firm to become a learning organisation.

In a widely acclaimed book, Senge (1990) identifies a number of specific organisational learning 'disabilities' and suggests that such disabilities cripple competitiveness. He argues that learning disabilities are eventually fatal in organisations and, because of them, few corporations live even half as long as a person. Senge identifies five disciplines (systems thinking, personal mastery, mental models, building shared visions, team learning) which he contends are key to the building of a learning organisation.

Of course, a shift to more strategic development is a complex process and several authors have discussed obstacles to the evolution of a continuous learning environment. For example, Culley (1989) discusses the factors that can cause resistance to development efforts and some key elements in overcoming such resistance. More specifically, he identified three factors that often conspire to work against a continuous learning environment: (i) executives are action-oriented and very sensitive to demands on time; (ii) bias against training and development activities and (iii) executives are preoccupied with what they left behind and what will be waiting upon return. To deal with this, Culley suggests that organisations need to be particularly sensitive to the organisation calendar, reinforce key learning, and use locations which symbolise the organisation's commitment to development efforts. Baldwin and Magjuka (1991) also make a case for the importance of management actions in signalling organisational commitment to development activities.

It seems clear that one key to long-term competitiveness in the years ahead is the ability of an organisation to continuously change and evolve in order to maintain leadership positions in quality, profitability and performance. Further, if management development is going to be a strategic weapon for achieving competitive advantage then firms must become increasingly self-renewing. The emerging, continuous learning paradigm of management development is a key driving force for building and sustaining this essential capacity. However, we still need a much better understanding of how organisations can stimulate continuous learning behaviours from their managers. Noe and Ford (1992) suggest that human resource strategies such as skill-based pay, reward for innovation and using learning as an evaluation dimension may be useful in this regard. In any case, more research devoted to the individual and organisational factors associated with continuous learning activities is clearly warranted.

Self-directed Management Development

Traditional research and writing on management development has generally reflected an implicit assumption that management development was something that was done *to* managers by some external force. However, the recent interest in continuous learning and experience-based development has prompted something of a revolution in thinking about management development.

The 'revolution' has involved a change in the assumed locus of control for learning. Responsibility for learning is shifting away from the trainer and toward the learner. The move toward becoming more learner centred is indicated by a growing literature on self-directed management development (e.g. Stewart, 1989b; Kaplan, Drath & Kofodimos, 1985; Manz & Manz, 1991; Knowles, 1984).

Manz and Manz (1991) outline a model of 'self-directed learning capacity' and propose four strategies that can be used to increase such a capacity. The authors assert that increases in the capacity for self-directed learning are a function of increases in an individual's self-efficacy and increases in self-leadership skills.

Spitzer (1991) attempts to more fully specify an operational definition of self-directed learning by describing it as a continuum in which the key defining attribute is choice (topic, timing, etc.). He further explores how principles of instructional design can help establish the conditions under which self-directed learning can be operationalised in a business setting.

Not surprisingly, the growth in interest in self-development has raised questions regarding the feasibility and utility of it for nurturing managerial talent. For example, several authors (e.g. Stewart, 1989b; Kinzie, 1990) express some reservations regarding the capability of learners to manage their own learning in an effective way (e.g. will they make good choices? will they be motivated to learn?). Kinzie (1990) reviewed the limited research relevant to this question and identified areas where more research is needed.

Stewart (1989b) argues that for self-development to be an effective strategy in organisational environments there must be an acceptance of the need to learn, a view of development as a continuous process, and the perspective that learning is something for which individual managers take a personal responsibility. Stewart questions whether these conditions typically exist in organisations and argues that the culture of a company will discourage or encourage the practice of individual development.

Finally, Kaplan, Drath and Kofodimos (1985) have suggested that high-level executives have trouble charting a self-development course because they are often isolated from criticism by their positional power, structurally detached by their executive suites and pressed by the staggering demands on their time.

Despite some significant challenges, the increased interest in self-development is consistent with the belief that the most significant managerial development occurs on the job (McCall, Lombardo & Morrison, 1988). Few would argue with the contention that self-development, in conjunction with constructive input from others (e.g. bosses, educators), is critical in a turbulent world. Moreover, learner self-control over training is becoming increasingly feasible with the advent of interactive training methods that allow individualised instruction and greater flexibility. Perhaps most importantly, the rapid globalisation of business is creating managerial tasks and roles that are so different from anything that we can imagine today that we cannot possibly develop stable development programmes which allow for all such contingencies (Schein, 1991). Thus, the role of self-directed learning will be even more crucial in the future and research aimed at making the linkage from theory to practice is sorely needed in this area.

Management Development in Degree-granting Institutions

A large body of recent literature continues to be devoted to management education in degree-granting institutions—most predominantly schools of management and business. Criticisms levelled at traditional business school education are pervasive in the literature and include claims that graduates are too analytical, lack interpersonal and communication skills, have unrealistic expectations about their first jobs after graduation, and do not work well in groups (Porter & McKibbin, 1988; Louis, 1990). In response to these criticisms, considerable effort has been centred around the design of business school curriculums in the United States (Bigelow, 1991), Europe (Porter, Muller & Rehder, 1991), Japan (Kimura & Yoshimori, 1989), and Australia (Hubbard, 1990). Much of this effort has focused on the development of skills or competency-based courses.

Perhaps the most visible effort in this regard is the outcome measurement project sponsored by the American Association of Collegiate Schools of Business (AACSB, 1987). Originally begun in 1976, the outcome measurement project sampled business school deans, consultants, corporate advisors and more than 2000 college students to identify clusters of skills and personal characteristics thought to comprise an effective business graduate. Skills and personal characteristics tests were created using assessment centre techniques (AACSB, 1987; Porter & McKibbon, 1989).

Boyatzis and colleagues (Boyatzis, Cowen and Kolb, 1991) report on a project undertaken at the Weatherhead School of Management at Case Western Reserve University. The objective of the project was to dramatically change the MBA programme to become distinctive as an outcome-oriented, competency-based, and value-added programme. In a study of 72 students participating in that programme, Boyatzis and Renio (1989) found significant improvement on six of the nineteen management skill variables assessed. The programme appeared to have a significant positive effect on students' abilities in areas of information collection and analysis, quantitative analysis, the management of technology, entrepreneurial and action skills. Unfortunately, the programme did not appear to have an impact on abilities that involve interaction with people.

McConnell and Seyboldt (1991) also argued for the usefulness of assessment centre technology in curriculum design and Mullin, Shaffer and Grelle (1991) present results of a study using that technology for teaching basic management skills. As predicted, students who participated in experimental assessment centre method classes demonstrated higher levels of competence on a target set of basic management skills with no loss of content knowledge. However, the difference between experimental assessment centre and traditional (lecture-intensive approaches) was of relatively small magnitude which the authors attributed to the limits of one course and lack of congruency with other courses in the business curriculum.

Other literature in the area of management education has focused on the changes in university-based executive programmes (Vicere, 1991). Until recently, it was possible to draw a distinct line between management training and education leading to academic qualifications (Wexley & Baldwin, 1986). However, this line is blurring with the growth of executive education and MBA schemes that are designed for a particular company or for a group of companies. Organisations are stressing more customised programmes, emphasising pragmatism in the programmes, and working more closely with universities (Bolt, 1987; Verlander, 1989). Moreover, organisations continue to increase their capacity to be their own educational provider as evidenced by the growth of corporate universities and campuses (Green & Lazarus, 1988).

Of particular note is the development of the International Management Centre from Buckingham (UK) which has adopted a decidedly client-based orientation. In designing curriculum, the Centre relies less on traditional content and more on the needs of the organisation footing the bill. As a result, the Centre is one of the fastest growing business schools in the UK and a leader in the provision of in-company action learning programmes (Lethbridge, 1989).

Of course, not all organisational scholars are enamoured with the growth of university-based executive education and some feel that it is nothing more than commercial activity with little academic credibility. However, Vicere (1988) argues that universities can add research capabilities, methodological expertise, and objectivity to the executive education process. Furthermore, a growing body of literature indicates that company-specific programmes may provide greater benefits to the organisation and are therefore more appropriate investments than traditional university programmes (Bolt, 1987; Armenakis, Flowers, Burdge, Kuerten, McCord & Arnold, 1989). For example, Armenakis et al. (1989) conclude that, while the instruction and research missions of universities will affect organisational competitiveness in the long run, tailored business extension programmes have greater potential for short-term impact.

Summary

As Keys and Wolfe (1988) point out, the competency movement and growing popularity of tailored executive education has prompted a soul searching on the part of organisations and academicians alike. With respect to the competency movement, we continue to need a better understanding of ways to integrate competency-based teaching within existing business school curricula and of how to motivate faculty to teach competencies (Wexley & Baldwin, 1986). With respect to executive education programming, research is needed which explores ways to identify the appropriate content and process for specific executive audiences and means to link those with institutional and organisational objectives.

CONCLUDING COMMENTS

Prior reviewers have often lamented the faddish and non-empirical nature of much management development literature and it is still prone to those tendencies (Wexley & Baldwin, 1986). However, we were pleasantly surprised by the volume and quality of the work that has appeared in the last five years and think it gives much cause for optimism.

For example, there has been a dramatic improvement in the behavioural specificity of models of effective management and a move toward more empirical work with generalisable samples. Although the efficacy of the billions of dollars spent on management development still remains largely an article of faith, and much more research is needed, at least some work documenting effects of development on criteria of organisational effectiveness is emerging. In addition, researchers have seemingly become far more cognisant of the distinction between management positions and the various contexts of managerial learning. That is, authors are now far less likely to treat 'management as management' or 'development as development', wherever they find it (Schein, 1989).

Research on the developmental value of job assignments and relationships such as mentoring and coaching is providing information with which to improve on-the-job learning of relevant skills and allow better integration of developmental experiences and formal training. Researchers at the Center for Creative Leadership have been at the forefront in examining how job assignments contribute to development.

In addition, conceptions of formal training have expanded to include consideration of both relevant content and issues related to the process of instruction which is appropriate for adult executive learners. Attention to exciting new approaches such as action learning and outdoor challenges reflect this expanded perspective. Finally, more than ever before, organisations are beginning to view management development as an integral component of competitive advantage and an activity that requires a great deal of self-directed effort and lifelong learning.

While the recent advances are encouraging, some concerns with the research and practice of management development persist. For example, there is still a paucity of research which illustrates attempts to systematically identify development objectives, choose an appropriate development strategy, and evaluate the outcomes to determine whether the objectives were met. Historically, most firms have not 'closed the loop' by evaluating their management development efforts and therefore have made subsequent decisions based on reactions, hunches or inertia (Tannenbaum & Woods, 1992).

In this regard, we would contend that it is time to move beyond research designed to show that a particular type of management development 'works'. Rather, we need to proceed to the more specific questions of why, when, and for whom a particular development strategy is effective. Furthermore, both practitioners and researchers need to do a better job of describing the nature and purpose of development initiatives. We need to be clear not only about the development strategy employed, but also about the basic content and purpose of the development. Making these distinctions should greatly enhance the ability to compare studies in future reviews of this type (Tannenbaum & Yukl, 1992).

The interest in continuous learning organisations has also prompted a need for renewed interest in learner motivation. As Campbell (1989) notes, everyone intuitively appreciates that motivational effects can completely swamp the potential benefits of a well-designed development initiative. We should therefore pay more attention to issues related to managers' goals and their correspondence with development goals, the reinforcement and punishment contingencies associated with development in organisations, and the socialisation and group processes that will influence managers' 'motivation for development'.

Finally, we need more published work on what progressive and successful companies are doing with respect to management development. An unfortunate paradox is that the more organisations truly believe that management development is a source of competitive advantage, the less inclined they are to share their secrets with the world. We hope that organisational scholars and corporate practitioners can be creative in finding mutually beneficial ways to share important concepts and data without violating proprietary concerns of progressive firms.

REFERENCES

AACSB (1987) *Outcome Measurement Project: Phase III report.* St. Louis: American Assembly of Collegiate Schools of Business.

Akin, G. (1987) Varieties of managerial learning. *Organizational Dynamics*, **16**, 36–48.

Alleman, E. (1989) Two planned mentoring programs that worked. *Mentoring International*, **3**, 6–12.

Ames, M. & Heide, D. (1991) The keys to successful management development in the 1990s. *Journal of Management Development*, **10**(2), 20–30.

Argyris, C. (1991) Teaching smart people how to learn. *Harvard Business Review*, **69**(3), 99–109.

Armenakis, A. A., Flowers, J. D., Burdge, H. B., Kuerten, K. M., McCord, S. O., & Arnold, H. D. (1989) The business schools' impact on US competitiveness. *Journal of Management Development*, **8**(1), 49–54.

Avolio, R. J. & Gibson, T. G. (1988) Developing transformational leaders: A lifespan approach. In J. Conger, R. Kanungo & Associates (eds), *Charismatic Leadership: The Elusive Factor in Organizational Effectiveness.* San Francisco, CA: Jossey-Bass.

Baldwin, T. T. & Ford, J. K. (1988) Transfer of training: A review and directions for future research. *Personnel Psychology*, **41**, 63–105.

Baldwin, T. T. & Magjuka, R. J. (1991) Organizational training and signals of importance: Linking pre-training perceptions to intentions to transfer. *Human Resource Development Quarterly*, **2**, 25–36.

Baldwin, T. T., Wagner, R. J., & Roland, C. C. (1991) Effects of outdoor challenge training on group and individual outcomes. Paper presented at the Annual Meeting of the Society for Industrial & Organizational Psychology (USA), St. Louis, MO.

Bartolome, F. (1989) Nobody trusts the boss completely—Now what? *Harvard Business Review*, **67**, 135–142.

Bass, B. M. (1988) The inspirational processes of leadership. *Journal of Management Development*, **7**, 21–31.

Bass, B. M. (1990a) *Handbook of Leadership: Theory, Research and Managerial Implications* (3rd edn.). New York: Free Press.

Bass, B. M. (1990b) From transactional to transformational leadership: Learning to share the vision. *Organizational Dynamics*, **18**, 19–36.

Bass, B. M. & Avolio, B. J. (1990) The implications of transactional and transformational leadership for individual, team and organizational development. In W. Pasmore & R. W. Woodman (eds), *Research on Organizational Change and Development*, **4**, 231–272. Greenwich, CT: JAI Press.

Bass, B. M. & Avolio, B. J. (1991) Developing transformational leadership: 1992 and beyond. *Journal of European Industrial Training*, **14**, 21–27.

Beck, J. E. (1988) Expatriate management development: Realizing the learning potential of overseas assignment. *Proceedings of the National Academy of Management (USA)*, pp. 112–116.

Bennis, W. & Nanus, B. (1985) *Leaders: The Strategies for Taking Charge.* New York: Harper & Row.

Bentz, V. J. (1987) Explorations of scope and scale: The critical determinant of high-level executive effectiveness. (Report No. 31.) Greensboro, NC: Center for Creative Leadership.

Berlew, D. E. & Hall, D. T. (1966) Teacher, tutor, colleague, coach. *Personnel Journal*, **65**(11), 44–51.

Bigelow, J. D. (1991) *Managerial Skills: Explorations in Practical Knowledge*. Newbury Park, CA: Sage.

Blakely, G. L., Martinec, C. L. & Lane, M. S. (1992) Management development programmes: The effects of management level and corporate strategy. Unpublished manuscript, Morgantown, WV: West Virginia University.

Blashford-Snell, J. (1991) Executive explorers. *Executive Development*, **4**, 15–17.

Blunt, P. & Jones, M. L. (1991) Management development in the third world. *Journal of Management Development* [Special Issue], **10**(6).

Bolt, J. F. (1987) Trends in management training and executive education: The revolution continues. *Journal of Management Development*, **6**(5), 5–15.

Boyatzis, R. E. (1982) *The Competent Manager: A Model for Effective Performance*. New York: Wiley.

Boyatzis, R. E. (1991) Developing the whole student: An MBA required course called managerial assessment and development. Paper presented at the National Academy of Management (USA), Miami, August.

Boyatzis, R. E., Cowen, S. S., & Kolb, D. A. (1991) Curricular innovation in higher education: The new Weatherhead MBA program. *Selections*, **8**(1), 27–37.

Boyatzis, R. E. & Renio, A. (1989) The impact of an MBA program on managerial abilities. *Journal of Management Development*, **8**(5), 66–77.

Braddick, W. (1988) How top managers really learn. *Journal of Management Development*, **7**, 55–62.

Bray, D. W., Campbell, R. J., & Grant, D. L. (1974) *Formative Years in Business*. New York: Wiley.

Bray, D. W. & Howard, A. (1983) The AT&T longitudinal studies of managers. In K. W. Shaie (ed.), *Longitudinal Studies of Adult Psychological Development* (pp. 266–312). New York: Guilford Press.

Brett, Jeanne M. (1984) Job transitions and personal and role development. In K. M. Rowland and G. R. Ferris (eds), *Research in Personnel and Human Resources Management*. Greenwich, CT: JAI Press.

Bushhardt, S. C., Fretwell, C. & Holdnak, B. J. (1991) The mentor/protégé relationship: A biological perspective. *Human Relations*, **44**, 619–635.

Campbell, J. P., Dunnette, M., Lawler, E. E., & Weick, K. E. Jr (1970) *Managerial Behavior, Performance and Effectiveness*. New York: McGraw-Hill.

Campbell, R. J. (1989) Human resource development strategies. In K. N. Wexley (ed.), *Developing Human Resources* (pp. 5/1–34), Washington, DC: Bureau of National Affairs.

Campion, M. A., Cheraskin, L., & Stevens, M. J. (1991) The rewards and costs of job rotation as a means of preparing for promotion. Paper presented at the Society for Industrial-Organizational Psychology, St. Louis, Missouri, April.

Clark, K. E. & Clark, M. B. (1990) *Measures of Leadership*. West Orange, NJ: Leadership Library of America.

Clawson, J. G. (1980) Mentoring in managerial careers. In C. B. Derr (ed.), *Work, Family and Career* (pp. 144–165). New York: Praeger.

Cobb, J. & Gibbs, J. (1990) A new competency-based, on-the-job programme for developing professional excellence in engineering. *Journal of Management Development*, **9**(3), 60–72.

Conger, J. A. & Kanungo, R. N. (1988) *Charismatic Leadership: The Elusive Factor in Organizational Effectiveness*. San Francisco: Jossey-Bass.

Constable, J. (1988) Developing the competent manager in a UK context. Report for the Manpower Services Commission, United Kingdom.

Cotter, S., James, K., Lucas, D. & Vinnicombe, S. (1991) Developing women managers at British Telecom. *Executive Development*, 4(2), 3–11.

Cox, C. J. & Cooper, C. L. (1989) The making of the British CEO: Childhood, work experience, personality and management style. *Academy of Management Executive*, 3, 241–245.

Culley, H. C. (1989) Overcoming resistance to management development. *Journal of Management Development*, 8(5), 4–10.

Davies, J. & Easterby-Smith, M. (1984) Learning and developing from managerial work experiences. *Journal of Management Studies*, 21(2), 169–183.

Day, D. V. & Lord, R. G. (1988) Executive leadership and organisational performance: Suggestions for a new theory and methodology. *Journal of Management*, 14, 453–464.

Dechant, K. (1990) Knowing how to learn: The 'neglected' management ability. *Journal of Management Development*, 9(4), 40–49.

Dreher, G. F. & Ash, R. A. (1990) A comparative study of mentoring among men and women in managerial, professional and technical positions. *Journal of Applied Psychology*, 75, 539–546.

Eichinger, R. W. & Lombardo, M. M. (1990) Twenty-two ways to develop leadership in staff managers. (Report No. 144.) Greensboro, NC: Center For Creative Leadership.

Ewert, A. (1988) Reduction of trait anxiety through participation in outward bound. *Leisure Sciences*, 10, 107–117.

Fiedler, F. E. (in press) The role and meaning of leadership experience. In K. E. Clark, M. B. Clark & D. Campbell (eds), *The Impact of Leadership*. Greensboro, NC: Center for Creative Leadership.

Finney, M. & Von Glinow, M. A. (1988) Integrating academic and organisational approaches to developing the international manager. *Journal of Management Development*, 7(2), 16–27.

Fletcher, C. (1990) Candidates' reactions to assessment centres and their outcomes: A longitudinal study. *Journal of Occupational Psychology*, 63, 117–127.

Fogel, D. S. (1990) Management education in central and eastern Europe and the Soviet Union. *Journal of Management Development*, 9(3), 14–19.

Fulmer, R. (1988) Corporate management development and education: The state of the art. *Journal of Management Development*, 7(2), 57–68.

Fulmer (1990) Executive learning as a strategic weapon. *Executive Development*, 3(3), 26–28.

Gabarro, J. J. (1987) *The Dynamics of Taking Charge*. Boston, MA: Harvard Business School Press.

Galagan, P. (1987) Between two trapezes. *Training and Development Journal*, 41(3), 40–53.

Gall, A. L. (1987) You can take the manager out of the woods, but . . . *Training and Development Journal*, 41(3), 54–61.

Gaugler, B. B., Rosenthal, D. B., Thornton, G. C. III, & Bentson, C. (1987) Meta-analysis of assessment center validity. *Journal of Applied Psychology*, 72, 493–511.

Gaylord, M. C. & Simon, E. B. (1984) Coping with job loss and job change. *Personnel*, 61(5), 70–75.

Gilbert-Smith, D. (1991) Training for leadership. *Executive Development*, 4, 25–27.

Goodge, P. (1991) Development centres: Guidelines for decision makers. *Journal of Management Development*, 10(3), 4–12.

Graen, G. B. & Uhl-Bien, M. (1991a) The transformation of professionals into self-managing and partially self-designing contributors: Toward a theory of leadership-making. *Journal of Management Systems*, 3, 33–48.

Graen, G. B. & Uhl-Bien, M. (1991b) Leadership-making applies equally well to sponsors, competence networks and teammates. *Journal of Management Systems*, **3**, 49–54.

Graen, G. B. & Wakabayashi, M. (in press) Adapting Japanese leadership techniques to their transplants in the United States: Focusing on manufacturing. *Research in International Business and International Relations*.

Green, W. A. & Lazarus, H. (1988) Corporate campuses: A growing phenomenon. *Journal of Management Development*, **7**(3), 56–67.

Hall, D. T. (1986) Dilemmas in linking succession planning to individual executive learning. *Human Resource Management*, **25**, 235–265.

Hall, D. T. (1989) How top management and the organization itself can block effective executive succession. *Human Resource Management*, **28**(1), 5–24.

Hall, D. T. & Foulkes, F. K. (1991) Senior executive development as a competitive advantage. *Advances in Applied Business Strategy*, **2**, 183–203. Greenwich, CT: JAI Press.

Hall, D. T. & Isabella, L. A. (1985) Downward movement and career development. *Organizational Dynamics*, **14**, 5–23.

Harvard Business Review (1987) Competitiveness survey; *Harvard Business Review* readers respond, **65**(5), 8–12.

Hayes, H. M. (1988) Internationalising the executive education curriculum at General Electric. *Journal of Management Development*, **7**(3), 5–12.

Hillman, L. W., Schwandt, D. R. & Bartz, D. E. (1990) Enhancing staff members' performance thru feedback and coaching. *Journal of Management Development*, **9**, 20–27.

Hollenbeck, G. P. (1990) The past, present, and future of assessment centers. *The Industrial-Organizational Psychologist*, **28**, 13–17.

Howard, A. & Bray, D. W. (1988) *Managerial Lives in Transition: Advancing Age and Changing Times*. New York: Guilford Publishing.

Hubbard, G. (1990) Changing trends in MBA education in Australia. *Journal of Management Development*, **9**(6), 41–49.

Hunt, J. G., Baiga, B. R. & Peterson, M. F. (1988) Strategic apex leader scripts and an organisational life cycle approach to leadership and excellence. *Journal of Management Development*, **7**, 61–83.

Hunt, J. W. (1990) Management development for the year 2000. *Journal of Management Development*, **9**(3), 4–13.

Ilgen, D. R., Fisher, C. D. & Taylor, M. S. (1979) Consequences of individual feedback on behavior in organizations. *Journal of Applied Psychology*, **64**, 349–371.

Ilgen, D. R. & Youtz, M. A. (1986) Factors influencing the evaluation and development of minorities. In K. Rowland & G. Ferris (eds), *Research in Personnel and Human Resource Management*, **4**, 307–337. Greenwich, CT: JAI Press.

Jennings, E. (1971) *Routes to the Executive Suite*. New York: McGraw-Hill.

Jonas, H. S. III, Fry, R. E. & Srivasta, S. (1989) The office of the CEO: Understanding the executive experience. *Academy of Management Executive*, **4**, 36–47.

Jones, M. L. (1990) Action learning as a new idea. *Journal of Management Development*, **9**, 29–34.

Jones, R. G. & Whitmore, M. D. (1992) When will developmental feedback from an assessment center make a difference in people's careers? Paper presented at the Annual Meeting of the Society for Industrial and Organizational Psychology (SIOP), Montreal.

Johnson, J. (1991) Health care management development. *Journal of Management Development* [Special Issue], **10**(4).

Johnston, A. & Dryssen, H. (1991) Co-operation in the development of public sector management skills: The SIDA experience. *Journal of Management Development*, **10**(6), 52–59.

Kable, J. (1989) Management development through action learning. *Journal of Management Development*, **8**, 77–80.

Kaplan, R. E., Drath, W. H. & Kofodimos, J. R. (1985) High hurdles: The challenge of executive self-development. (Technical Report No. 25). Greensboro, NC: Center for Creative Leadership.

Kaplan, R. E., Kofodimos, J. R. & Drath, W. H. (1987) Development at the top: A review and a prospect. In W. Pasmore & R. W. Woodman (eds), *Research on Organizational Change and Development*. Greenwich, CT: JAI Press.

Katz, R. L. (1974) Skills of an effective administrator. *Harvard Business Review*, **52**(1), 90–102.

Kelleher, D., Finestone, P. & Lowy, A. (1986) Managerial learning: First notes from an unstudied frontier. *Group and Organization Studies*, **11**, 169–202.

Kerr, S. (1990) British Telecom: On the right lines. *Executive Development*, **3**(2), 3–10.

Keys, B. (1989) Management development review. *Journal of Management Development* [Special Issue], **8**(2).

Keys, B. & Case, T. (1990) How to become an influential manager. *Academy of Management Executive*, **4**(4), 38–49.

Keys, B. & Wolfe, J. (1988) Management education and development: Current issues and emerging trends. *Journal of Management*, **14**, 205–229.

Keys, B. & Wolfe, J. (1990) The role of management games and simulations in education and research. *Journal of Management*, **16**, 307–336.

Kimura, Y. & Yoshimori, M. (1989) Japan imports American management methods through an MBA programme. *Journal of Management Development*, **8**(4), 22–31.

Kinzie, M. B. (1990) Requirements and benefits of effective interactive instruction: Learner control, self-regulation and continuing motivation. *Educational Technology Research & Development*, **38**, 1–21.

Kleiner, B. H. (1991) Developing managers for the 1990s. *Journal of Management Development*, **10**(2), 5–7.

Knowles, M. (1984) *The Adult Learner: A Neglected Species*. Houston: Gulf.

Kofodimos, J. (1990) Why executives lose their balance. *Organizational Dynamics*, **19**, 58–73.

Kolb, D., Lublin, S., Spoth, J. & Baker, R. (1985) Strategic management development: Using experiential learning theory to assess and develop managerial competencies. *Journal of Management Development*, **5**(3), 13–24.

Komacki, J. L., Desselles, M. L. & Bowman, E. D. (1989) Definitely not a breeze: Extending an operant model of effective supervision to teams. *Journal of Applied Psychology*, **74**, 522–529.

Kotter, J. P. (1982) *The General Managers*. New York: Free Press.

Kotter, J. P. (1988) *The Leadership Factor*. New York: Free Press.

Kovach, B. E. (1986) The derailment of fast-track managers. *Organizational Dynamics*, **15**, 41–48.

Kovach, B. E. (1989) Successful derailment: What fast-trackers can learn while they're off the track. *Organizational Dynamics*, **18**, 33–47.

Kram, K. E. (1985) *Mentoring at Work: Developmental Relationships in Organizational Life*. Glenview, IL: Scott, Foresman.

Kram, K. E. & Bragar, M. C. (in press) Development through mentoring: A strategic approach for the 1990s. In D. Montrose & C. Shinkman (eds), *Career Development in the '90s*.

Kram, K. E. & Hall, D. T. (1989) Mentoring as an antidote to stress during corporate trauma. *Human Resource Management*, **28**, 493–510.

Kram, K. E. & Isabella, L. A. (1985) Mentoring alternatives: The role of peer relationships in career development. *Academy of Management Journal*, **28**, 110–132.

Kraut, A. I., Pedigo, P. R., McKenna, D. D. & Dunnette, M. D. (1989) The role of the manager: What's really important in different managerial jobs. *Academy of Management Executive*, **3**, 286–93.

Latham, G. P. (1988) Human resource training and development. *Annual Review of Psychology*, **39**, 545–582.

Lawrie, J. (1989) Taking action to change performance. *Personnel Journal*, **68**, 59–69.

Lethbridge, D. (1989) University degrees for sale—the Buckingham experience. *Journal of Management Development*, **8**(3), 38–49.

Lindsey, E., Homes, V. & McCall, M. W., Jr (1987) Key events in executive lives. (Tech. Report No. 32.) Greensboro, NC: Center for Creative Leadership.

Lombardo, M. M. (1989) The road to the top is paved with good assignments. *Executive Development*, **2**, 4–7.

Lombardo, M. M. & McCauley, C. D. (1988) The dynamics of management derailment. (Tech. Report No. 134.) Greensboro, NC: Center for Creative Leadership.

London, M. (1989) *Managing the Training Enterprise*. San Francisco, CA: Jossey-Bass.

London, M. & Mone, E. M. (1987) *Career Management and Survival in the Workplace*. San Francisco, CA: Jossey-Bass.

London, M. & Wohlers, A. J. (1991) Agreement between subordinate and self-ratings in upward feedback. *Personnel Psychology*, **44**, 375–390.

London, M., Wohlers, A. J. & Gallagher, P. (1990) A feedback approach to management development. *Journal of Management Development*, **9**(6), 17–31.

Long, J. W. (1987) The wilderness lab comes of age. *Training and Development Journal*, **41**(3), 30–39.

Loo, R. (1991) Management training in Canadian organisations. *Journal of Management Development*, **10**(5), 60–72.

Louis, M. R. (1990) The gap in management education. *Selections*, **6**(3), 1–12.

Luthans, F., Hodgetts, R. M. & Rosencrantz, S. A. (1988) *Real Managers*. Cambridge, MA: Ballinger.

Maczynski, J. (1992) A cross-cultural comparison of decision-making based on the Vroom–Yetton model of leadership. (Tech. Report No. 23.) Wroclaw: Institute of Management.

Manz, C. C. (1986) Self leadership: Toward an expanded theory of self influence processes in organizations. *Academy of Management Review*, **11**, 585–600.

Manz, C. C. (1990) Beyond self-managing work teams: Toward self-leading teams in the workplace. In W. Pasmore & R. W. Woodman (eds), *Research on Organizational Change and Development*, **4**, 273–299. Greenwich, CT: JAI Press.

Manz, C. C., Keating, D. E. & Donnellon, A. (1990) Preparing for an organizational change to employee self-management: The managerial transition. *Organizational Dynamics*, **19**, 15–26.

Manz, C. C. & Manz, K. P. (1991) Strategies for facilitating self-directed learning: A process for enhancing human resource development. *Human Resource Development Quarterly*, **2**, 3–12.

Manz, C. C. & Neck, C. P. (1991) Inner leadership: Creating productive thought patterns. *Executive*, **5**, 87–95.

Manz, C. C. & Sims, H. P. (1991) SuperLeadership: Beyond the myth of heroic leadership. *Organizational Dynamics*, **20**, 18–35.

Margerison, C. J. (1988) Action learning and excellence in management development. *Journal of Management Development*, **7**, 43–54.

Margerison, C. J. & Kakabadse, A. (1984) *How American Chief Executives Succeed: Implications for Developing High Potential Employees*. New York: American Management Association.

Marsh, H. W., Richards, G. E. & Barnes, J. (1986) Multidimensional self-concepts: The effectors of participation in an Outward Bound program. *Journal of Personality and Social Psychology*, **50**, 195–204.

Marsh, H. W., Richards, G. E. & Barnes, J. (1987) A long-term follow-up of the effects of participation in an Outward Bound Program. *Personality and Social Psychology Bulletin*, **12**, 475–492.

Marsick, V. (1990) Experience-based learning: Executive learning outside the classroom. *Journal of Management Development*, **9**, 50–60.

Martinko, M. J. & Gardner, W. L. (1990) Structured observation of managerial work: A replication and synthesis. *Journal of Management Studies*, **27**, 329–357.

McCall, M. W. (1988) Developing executives through work experience. (Tech. Report No. 33.) Greensboro, NC: Center for Creative Leadership.

McCall, M. W. Jr & Lombardo, M. M. (1983) Off the track: Why and how successful executives get derailed. (Tech. Report No. 21.) Greensboro, NC: Center for Creative Leadership.

McCall, M. W., Lombardo, M. M. & Morrison, A. M. (1988) *The Lessons of Experience: How Successful Executives Develop on the Job*. Lexington, MA: Lexington Books.

McCarthy, D. J. (1991) Developing a programme for Soviet managers. *Journal of Management Development*, **10**(5), 26–31.

McCauley, C. D. (1986) Developmental experiences in managerial work: A literature review. (Tech. Report No. 26.) Greensboro, NC: Center for Creative Leadership.

McCauley, C. D. (1990) Effective school principals: Competencies for meeting the demands of educational reform. (Tech. Report No. 146.) Greensboro, NC: Center for Creative Leadership.

McCauley, C. D. & Hughes, M. W. (1991) Leadership challenges for human service administrators. *Nonprofit Management and Leadership*, **1**, 267–281.

McCauley, C. D., Lombardo, M. M. & Usher, C. J. (1989) Diagnosing management development needs: An instrument based on how managers develop. *Journal of Management*, **15**, 389–403.

McCauley, C. D., Ohlott, P. J. & Ruderman, M. N. (1989) On-the-job development: A conceptual model and preliminary investigation. *Journal of Managerial Issues*, **1**(2), 142–158.

McCauley, C. D., Ruderman, M. R., Ohlott, P. J. & Morrow, J. E. (1992) Assessing the developmental potential of managerial jobs. Unpublished manuscript: Center for Creative Leadership.

McConnell, R. V. & Seyboldt, J. W. (1991) Assessment center technology: One approach for integrating and assessing management skills in the business school curriculum. In J. Bigelow (ed.), *Managerial Skills: Explorations in Practical Knowledge* (pp. 105–115). Newbury Park, CA: Sage.

McEvoy, G. M. & Beatty, R. W. (1989) Assessment centers and subordinate appraisals of managers: A seven year examination of predictive validity. *Personnel Psychology*, **42**, 37–52.

Miner, J. B. (1991) Psychological assessment in a developmental context. In C. P. Hansen & K. A. Conrad (eds), *A Handbook of Psychological Assessment in Business* (pp. 226–237). New York: Quorum Books.

Mintzberg, H. (1973) *The Nature of Managerial Work*. New York: Harper-Row.

Morgan, G. (1988) *Riding the Waves of Change: Developing Managerial Competencies for a Turbulent World*. San Francisco, CA: Jossey Bass.

Morrison, A. M., White, R. P. & Van Velsor, E. (1987) *Breaking the Glass Ceiling: Can Women Reach the Top of America's Largest Corporations?* Reading, MA: Addison-Wesley.

Morrison, R. F. & Brantner, T. M. (1991) What affects how quickly a new job is learned? *Proceedings of the National Academy of Management*, 52–56.

Mullin, R. F., Shaffer, P. L. & Grelle, M. J. (1991) A study of the assessment center method of teaching basic management skills. In J. Bigelow (ed.), *Managerial Skills: Explorations in Practical Knowledge* (pp. 116–139). Newbury Park, CA: Sage.

Mumford, A. (1987) Action learning. *Journal of Management Development* [Special Issue], **6**(2), 1–70.

Mumford, A. (1988) *Developing Top Managers*. Aldershot: Gower.

Mumford, A. (1991) Developing the top team to meet organisational objectives. *Journal of Management Development*, **10**, 5–14.

Munchus, G. III & McArthur, B. (1991) Revisiting the historical use of the assessment center in management selection and development. *Journal of Management Development*, **10**(1), 5–13.

Neck, C. P. & Manz, C. C. (1992) Thought self-leadership: The influence of self-talk and mental imagery on performance. Unpublished manuscript: Arizona State University (USA).

Neider, L. L. & Schreisheim, C. A. (1988) Making leadership effective: A three-stage model. *Journal of Management Development*, **7**, 10–20.

Noe, R. A. (1988a) An investigation of the determinants of successful assigned mentoring relationships. *Personnel Psychology*, **41**, 457–79.

Noe, R. A. (1988b) Women and mentoring: A review and research agenda. *Academy of Management Review*, **13**, 65–78.

Noe, R. & Ford, J. K. (1992) Emerging issues and new directions for training research. In K. Rowland & G. Ferris (eds), *Research in Personnel and Human Resource Management*. Greenwich, CT: JAI Press.

Noe, R. A. & Steffy, B. D. (1987) The influence of individual characteristics and assessment center evaluation of career exploration behavior and job involvement. *Journal of Vocational Behavior*, **30**, 187–302.

Noel, J. L. & Charan, R. (1988) Leadership development at GE's Crotonville. *Human Resource Management*, **27**, 433–447.

Northcraft, G. B., Griffith, T. L. & Shalley, C. E. (1992) Building top management muscle in a slow growth environment: How different is better at Greyhound Financial Corporation. *Academy of Management Executive*, **6**(1), 32–41.

Ohlott, P. J., Ruderman, M. N. & McCauley, C. D. (1990) Women and men: Equal opportunity for development. Paper presented at the National Academy of Management (USA). San Francisco, CA: August.

Ohlott, P. J., Ruderman, M. N. & McCauley, C. D. (1992) Gender differences in managerial job demands and learning from experience. Unpublished manuscript: Center for Creative Leadership.

Olian, J. D., Carroll, S. J. & Giannantonio, C. M. (1992) Mentor reactions to protégés: An experiment with managers. Unpublished manuscript: University of Maryland (USA).

Olian, J. D., Carroll, S. J., Giannantonio, C. M. & Feren, D. B. (1988) What do protégés look for in a mentor? Results of three experimental studies. *Journal of Vocational Behavior*, **33**, 15–37.

O'Neill, B. (1990) The top-flight initiative at British Airways. *Executive Development*, **3**(2), 11–15.

Ostroff, C. & Kozlowski, S. (1992) The role of mentoring in the information gathering processes of newcomers during early organizational socialization. Unpublished manuscript: University of Minnesota (USA).

Pate, L. E. (1988) Developing leadership excellence. *Journal of Management Development* [Special Issue], **7**(5).

Pearson, A. W. & McCauley, C. D. (1991) Job demands and managerial learning in the research and development function. *Human Resource Development Quarterly*, **2**, 263–275.

Pedler, M., Boydell, T. & Burgoyne, J. (1989) Towards the learning company. *Management Education and Development*, **20**(1), 1–8.

Penley, L. E., Alexander, E. R., Jernigan, I. E. & Henwood, C. I. (1991) Communication abilities of managers: The relationship to performance. *Journal of Management*, **17**, 57–76.

Porter, J. L., Muller, H. J. & Rehder, R. R. (1991) Graduate management education in Europe. *Executive Development*, 4(2), 23–24.

Porter, L. W. & McKibbon, L. E. (1988) *Management Education and Development: Drift or Thrust into the 21st Century*. New York: McGraw-Hill.

Porter, M. (1985) *Competitive Advantage*. New York: Free Press.

Powers, E. A. (1987) Enhancing managerial competence: The American Management Association competency programme. *Journal of Management Development*, 6(4), 7–18.

Prideaux, G. & Ford, J. E. (1988a) Management development: Competencies, contracts, teams and work-based learning. *Journl of Management Development*, 7, 56–68.

Prideaux, G. & Ford, J. E. (1988b) Management development: Competencies, teams, learning contracts, and work experience based learning. *Journal of Management Development*, 7, 13–21.

Ragins, B. R. (1989) Barriers to mentoring: The female manager's dilemma. *Human Relations*, 42, 1–22.

Ragins, B. R. & Cotton, J. L. (1991a) Easier said than done: Gender differences in perceived barriers to gaining a mentor. *Academy of Management Journal*, 34, 939–951.

Ragins, B. R. & Cotton, J. L. (1991b) Gender differences in willingness to mentor. *Proceedings of the National Academy of Management* (USA), 57–61.

Ragins, B. R. & McFarlin, D. B. (1990) Perceptions of mentor roles in cross-gender mentoring relationships. *Journal of Vocational Behavior*, 37, 321–339.

Raven, J. (1988) Toward measures of high-level competencies: A re-examination of McClelland's distinction between needs and values. *Human Relations*, 41, 281–294.

Rayner, T. & Goodge, P. (1988) New techniques in assessment centres: LRT's experience. *Journal of Management Development*, 7(4), 21–30.

Revans, R. (1982) *The Origin and Growth of Action Learning*. Hunt, England: Chatwell Bratt, Bickley.

Roche, G. R. (1979) Much ado about mentors. *Harvard Business Review*, 57(1), 14–28.

Rosow, J. M. & Zager, R. (1988) *Training—The Competitive Edge*. San Francisco, CA: Jossey-Bass.

Ruderman, M. N., Ohlott, P. J. & McCauley, C. D. (1990) Assessing opportunities for leadership development. In K. E. Clark & M. B. Clark (eds), *Measures of Leadership* (pp. 547–562). West Orange, NJ: Leadership Library of America.

Saari, L. M., Johnson, T. R., McLaughlin, S. D. & Zimmerle, D. M. (1988) A survey of management training and education practices in US companies. *Personnel Psychology*, 41, 731–743.

Safavi, F. & Tweddell, C. E. (1990) Attributes of success in African management development programmes: Concepts and applications. *Journal of Management Development*, 9, 50–63.

Sanders, P. (1988) Global managers for global corporations. *Journal of Management Development*, 7(1), 33–44.

Schein, E. H. (1989) Reassessing the 'divine right' of managers. *Sloan Management Review*, 30(2), 63–68.

Schein, E. H. (1990) Career stress in changing times: Some final observations. In J. C. Quick, R. E. Hess, J. Hermalin & J. D. Quick (eds), *Career Stress in Changing Times: Prevention in Human Services*, 8(1), 251–261.

Schein, E. H. (1991) What are the pressing career issues of the 90s? Paper presented to the Annual Conference of Drake Beam Morin, Inc. San Francisco, CA.

Schneider, B. & Konz, A. M. (1989) Strategic job analysis. *Human Resource Management*, 28, 51–64.

Senge, P. M. (1990) *The Fifth Dimension: The Art and Practice of the Learning Organization*. New York: Doubleday.

Shipper, F. (1991) Mastery and frequency of managerial behaviours relative to subunit effectiveness. *Human Relations*, 44(4), 371–388.

Smith, B. (1990) Mutual mentoring on projects: A proposal to combine the advantages of several established management development methods. *Journal of Management Development*, **9**, 51–57.

Spitzer, D. R. (1991) Response to Manz and Manz's article on self-directed learning: An instructional design perspective. *Human Resource Development Quarterly*, **2**, 175–179.

Stewart, R. (1989a) Studies of managerial jobs and behaviour: The ways forward. *Journal of Management Studies*, **26**(1), 1–10.

Stewart, R. (1989b) Self-development. *Executive Development*, **2**(3), 15–16.

Streufert, S., Nogami, G. Y., Swezey, R. W., Pogash, R. M. & Piasecki, M. T. (1988) Computer assisted training of complex managerial performance. *Computers in Human Behavior*, **4**, 77–88.

Streufert, S., Pogash, R. & Piasecki, M. (1988) Simulation-based assessment of managerial competence: Reliability and validity. *Personnel Psychology*, **41**, 537–557.

Stumpf, S. A. (1989) Work experiences that stretch managers' capacities for strategic thinking. *Journal of Management Development*, **8**(5), 31–39.

Suzuki, N. (1989) Management development in Japan. *Journal of Management Development* [Special Issue], **8**(4).

Tanaka, T. (1989) Developing managers in the Hitachi Institute of management development. *Journal of Management Development*, **8**(4), 12–21.

Tannenbaum, S. I. & Woods, S. (in press) Determining a strategy for evaluating training: Operating within organizational constraints. *Human Resource Planning Journal*.

Tannenbaum, S. I. & Yukl, G. (1992) Human resource training and development. *Annual Review of Psychology*, **43**, 399–441.

Temporal, P. (1990) Management development in Asia. *Journal of Management Development* [Special Issue], **9**(5).

Temporal, P. & Burnett, K. (1990) Strategic corporate assignments and international management development. *Journal of Management Development*, **9** 58–64.

Thareau, P. (1991) Managers' training needs and preferred training strategies. *Journal of Management Development*, **10**(5), 46–59.

Thompson, P. H., Kirkham, K. L. & Dixon, J. (1985) Warning: The fast track may be hazardous to organizational health. *Organizational Dynamics*, **13**, 21–33.

Uhl-Bien, M. & Graen, G. B. (in press a) An empirical test of the leadership-making model in professional project teams. In K. E. Clark, M. B. Clark & D. Campbell (eds), *The Impact of Leadership*. Greensboro, NC: Center for Creative Leadership.

Uhl-Bien, M. & Graen, G. B. (in press b) Self-management and team-making in cross-functional work teams: Discovering the keys to becoming an integrated team. *Journal of High Technology Management*.

Ulrich, D. (1989) Executive development as a competitive weapon. *Journal of Management Development*, **8**(5), 11–22.

Vaill, P. (1989) *Managing as a Performing Art: New Ideas for a World of Chaotic Change*. San Francisco, CA: Jossey Bass.

Van Velsor, E. & Hughes, M. W. (1990) Gender differences in the development of managers: How women managers learn from experience. (Tech. Report No. 145.) Greensboro, NC: Center for Creative Leadership.

Van Velsor, E. & Leslie, J. B. (1991) *Feedback to Managers/Volume II: A Review and Comparison of Sixteen Multi-rater Feedback Instruments*. (Tech. Report No. 150.) Greensboro, NC: Center for Creative Leadership.

Vedder, J. (1992) How much can we learn from success? *Academy of Management Executive*, **6**(1), 56–66.

Verlander, E. G. (1989) Improving university executive programmes. *Journal of Management Development*, **8**(1), 5–19.

Vicere, A. A. (1988) University-based executive education: Impacts and implications. *Journal of Management Development*, 7(4), 5–13.

Vicere, A. A. (1991) The changing paradigm for executive development. *Journal of Management Development*, 10(3), 44–47.

Vroom, V. & Jago, A. G. (1988) Managing participation: A critical dimension of leadership. *Journal of Management Development*, 7, 32–42.

Wexley, K. N. & Baldwin, T. T. (1986) Management development. *Journal of Management*, 12, 277–294.

Wexley, K. N. & Latham, G. P. (1991) *Developing and Training Human Resources in Organizations*. New York: HarperCollins.

Whetten, D. A. & Cameron, K. S. (1991) *Developing Management Skills* (2nd edition). New York: HarperCollins.

Whitley, R. (1989) On the nature of managerial tasks and skills: Their distinguishing characteristics and organisation. *Journal of Management Studies*, 26(3), 209–224.

Williams, E. C. (1991) Management development programmes for the Asia Pacific Region maritime industry: The Singapore port institute. *Journal of Management Development*, 10(7), 66–69.

Wilson, C. L. (1978) The Wilson multi-level management surveys: Refinement and replication of the scales. JSAS: Catalog of selected documents in Psychology 8 (Ms. no 1707) American Psychological Association, Washington, DC.

Wilson, W. B. (1990) The changing bell(e) of the north. *Journal of Management Development*, 9(3), 35–41.

Wohlers, A. J. & London, M. (1989) Ratings of managerial characteristics: Evaluation difficulty, co-worker agreement and self-objectivity. *Personnel Psychology*, 42, 235–261.

Woodman, R. & Passmore, W. A. (1987) *Research in Organizational Change and Development*. Greenwich, CT: JAI Press.

Wright, R. G. & Werther, W. B. (1991) Mentors at work. *Journal of Management Development*, 10, 25–32.

Yau, W. S. L. & Sculli, D. (1990) Managerial traits and skills. *Journal of Management Development*, 9(6), 32–40.

Yukl, G. A. (1989) *Leadership in Organizations* (2nd edition). Englewood Cliffs, NJ: Prentice-Hall.

Yukl, G. & Lepsinger, R. (1991) An integrative taxonomy of managerial behavior: Implications for improving managerial effectiveness. In J. W. Jones, B. D. Steffy & D. W. Bray (eds), *Applying Psychology in Business* (pp. 563–572). Lexington, MA: Lexington Books.

Yukl, G., Wall, S. & Lepsinger, R. (1990) Preliminary report on validation of the managerial practices survey. In K. E. Clark & M. B. Clark (eds), *Measures of Leadership* (pp. 223–237). West Orange, NJ: Leadership Library of America.

Zey, M. G. (1988) A mentor for all reasons. *Personnel Journal*, 67, 46–51.

Zey, M. G. (1989) Building a successful mentor program. *Mentoring International*, 3, 48–51.

Chapter 3

THE INCREASING IMPORTANCE OF PERFORMANCE APPRAISALS TO EMPLOYEE EFFECTIVENESS IN ORGANIZATIONAL SETTINGS IN NORTH AMERICA

Gary P. Latham, Daniel Skarlicki, Diane Irvine and Jacob P. Siegel
University of Toronto, Canada

INTRODUCTION

This chapter reviews the scientific literature on performance appraisal published from 1986 through 1991. The chapter is organized into four areas. First, legal issues are reviewed because of the direct effect they have on the appraisal of employees in North America. Since the previous review on performance appraisal (Latham, 1986) there has been a strong shift in the legal climate in favor of the employer rather than the employee. Second, appraisal instruments are examined in terms of their ability to withstand legal scrutiny. Since 1986, however, there has been a gradual shift in research focus from psychometric issues to user reactions to different appraisal tools. Third, the relative advantages of different sources of appraisal are discussed. From 1986 to the present the literature has been more advocacy based rather than empirically driven with the advocates arguing the value of self-, peer, and subordinate appraisals. Fourth, cognitive psychology experiments designed to discover ways to overcome a rater's tendency to report general impressions rather than specific behaviors are reviewed. This research reflects the fact that raters have difficulty in distinguishing among discrete behaviors or dimensions on the appraisal instrument. Finally, advances in knowledge of how to effectively coach and develop employees are elaborated upon.

That organizations in North America are continuing to attach increasing

International Review of Industrial and Organizational Psychology 1993 Volume 8
Edited by C. L. Cooper and I. T. Robertson. © 1993 John Wiley & Sons Ltd.

importance to performance appraisals is evident from a recent survey by Locher and Teel (1988). Whereas 89% of organizations in the United States (US) conducted formal performance appraisals in 1977, this number had risen to 94% by 1988. The basis for the importance attached to appraisals can be seen in the myriad of purposes for which they are used (Cleveland, Murphy, & Williams, 1989; Lawler, 1988; Mallinger & Cummings, 1986) namely:

1. Ensuring mutual understanding of effective performance.
2. Building confidence between employer and employees.
3. Clarifying any misunderstandings regarding performance expectations.
4. Establishing developmental procedures.
5. Allocating rewards.
6. Sustaining and enhancing employee motivation.
7. Career planning.
8. Fostering communication and feedback.

This use of performance appraisals by companies for more than one purpose increased from 11% in 1977 to 30% in 1988 (Locher & Teel, 1988). This increase reflects the widespread recognition that performance appraisals if done effectively can increase employee productivity and decrease an organization's costs (Latham & Wexley, in press).

RESPONDING EFFECTIVELY TO LEGAL ISSUES IN NORTH AMERICA

Regardless of the uses for which appraisals are conducted, finding ways to minimize legal challenges to them continues to be a concern for employers in North America as a way of minimizing costs. This is especially true with regard to the outcomes of appraisals, namely, promotions, demotions, transfers, layoffs, and terminations (Martin, Bartol, & Levine, 1986). This is because of the increasing awareness by employees throughout the past decade of their civil and contractual rights. Moreover, employees in the 1970s and early 1980s found the US courts in more than half the states in the US to be more favorable in their rulings toward them than to their employers (Weiss, 1988). A study by the Rand Corporation Institute for Civil Justice (1988) revealed that employees are now three times more likely to sue their employers than they were in 1980. Because of the 1988 Free Trade Act between Canada and the US, which resulted in a large increase in the number of organizations employing people in both countries, and because Canadian equal employment laws tend to follow those in the US, these issues are important to most North American employers and employees.

Title VII of the 1964 Civil Rights Act in the US mandates that employment decisions are to be made without regard to a person's race, sex, religion, color, or national origin. This law has been amended over the years to extend protected class status to age, martial status, and disability. Similarly, Section 3 of the 1982 Canadian Human Rights Act states that race, national or ethnic origin, color, religion, sex, marital status, disability, and conviction for which pardon has been granted are prohibited grounds of discrimination. Section 5 states that in devising methods of assessing an individual's job performance, the employer must identify the essential tasks that make up the requirements of the job. Section 10 states that it is a discriminatory practice for an employer, trade union, employer or employee association and employment agencies to enter into an agreement affecting the promotion, training, apprenticeship or any other matter relating to employment that deprives or inhibits a group of individuals if it is based on prohibited grounds of discrimination.

The first US Supreme Court ruling regarding Title VII was *Griggs* v. *Duke Power* (1971). The Court made clear that the employer bears the burden of proof, in the face of apparent adverse impact, to prove the validity or job-relatedness of employment decisions. The Court stated that adverse impact can be demonstrated by simply showing that the proportion of blacks excluded from a job was significantly higher than the proportion of whites.

The Court also made clear that employers were to be blind as to the race of their employees when making employment decisions. *Wygant* v. *Jackson Board of Education* (1986) reaffirmed that stance by ruling against a collective bargaining agreement where the ratio of black to white schoolteachers was to be maintained during layoffs. Specifically, the US Supreme Court ruled that there must be strong evidence of prior discrimination within the organization before a voluntary plan can be put into effect that results in preferential treatment for members of a particular racial class. Thus only where an employer or labor union has engaged in persistent or egregious discrimination is such a voluntary plan acceptable (Redeker, 1986). Similarly, with regard to promotions, an organization may only take steps that are temporary in order to correct an imbalance in its workforce (*Johnson* v. *Transportation Agency of Santa Clara County, CA.*, 1987).

Barrett and Kernan (1987) have suggested that Title VII legislation of the 1964 Civil Rights Act does not apply to performance appraisal systems. But in *Watson* v. *Fort Worth Bank and Trust Company* (1988), the Supreme Court ruled that disparate impact analysis is as applicable to subjective employment criteria regarding promotion as it is to objective or standardized selection tests. The Court's position in this regard was supported by the American Psychological Association, which argued that subjective assessment devices should be evaluated against the same psychometric criteria as are so-called objective assessment devices (Bersoff, 1988). As Nathan and Cascio (1986) have noted, a performance appraisal is a test in that it is a predictor prior to a personnel decision (e.g. assessing who should be promoted); it is a criterion thereafter (e.g. being the basis for validating a selection or promotion decision). It is therefore subject to the same psychometric scrutiny as any other predictor or criterion.

What is noteworthy in the Watson case is that it began the shift in burden from the employer to the employee in the litigation of employment discrimination. This is because the Supreme Court now requires the employee to identify the specific employment practices that are allegedly responsible for any observed statistical disparity. Moreover, the employee's statistical evidence must be sufficiently substantial to prove that the practice in question has caused the exclusion of promotion-eligible employees because of their membership of a protected group.

The shift in the legal climate favoring employers rather than employees was further evident in *Price Waterhouse* v. *Hopkins* (1989). Written appraisals of Hopkins by her supervisors suggested strongly that the fact that she was female played a part in the decision to deny her a promotion to partner in the firm (Kandel, 1989). However, the court ruled that an employer may avoid a finding of liability by providing a preponderance of evidence that the organization would have made the same decision even if it had not taken the employee's gender into account (Blumrosen, 1989; Dwyer, 1989).

Ward's Cove v. *Antonio* (1989) went four steps further in creating a favorable legal climate for employers. First, the Court concluded that simply showing that an employer has a higher proportion of minorities in low-level than in high-level jobs is insufficient in itself for providing a prima facie case of employment discrimination. Thus comparative statistics within an organization or industry were ruled irrelevant. The proper comparison now is with the percentage of qualified women and minorities in the surrounding workforce. Thus it is not surprising that in *Cygnar* v. *Chicago* (1989), the 7th Circuit Court ruled against the city when a police official transferred most of the white males to another division and replaced them with blacks. The Court stated that the city's actions were based on the city official's perception of racial imbalance rather than on a comparison with the relevant labor pool. The City of Chicago was required to pay each transferred police officer $50 000.

Second, the Supreme Court ruled that the cumulative outcome of a company's multiple employment practices will not be examined. Instead, the employee must show the disparate impact of each employment procedure. This decision is consistent with Watson.

Third, the employer no longer has to defend an employment practice in terms of business necessity. Instead, an organization need only show a 'not insubstantial business reason'. Finally, the Court now requires the employee to show that there is an alternative employment practice which equally serves the employer's interest in productivity, and the employer then must subsequently refuse to use it before the employee can win a charge of employment discrimination.

In Canada there is as yet no jurisprudence by its Supreme Court regarding performance appraisal violations under the Canadian Human Rights Act. Lower court rulings have made it clear, however, that performance appraisals can be used as a basis for demotion and termination (e.g. *Trotter* v. *Chesley Town*, 1990).

To minimize successful legal challenges in both countries, at least eight steps should be taken (Burchett & DeMeuse, 1985; Goddard, 1989; Metz, 1988; Weiss, 1988). First, the race or sex of an employee should not be taken into account when promoting, transferring, laying off or terminating people unless there is an imbalance in the organization that needs to be corrected. This imbalance must be based on the percentage of women and members of minority groups in the organization versus those who are qualified in the local area labor market. Second, the organization should conduct a job analysis to determine those characteristics necessary for successful performance. For example, Ackerman, an equipment installer with asthma, filed suit against Western Electric after she was dismissed. The Court (*Ackerman* v. *Western Electric*, 1988) looked at how much time she spent on tasks which might affect her asthma and found that these tasks were required of her only about 12% of the time. Thus the Court ruled in her favor by concluding that these tasks were too insignificant and infrequent to be considered an essential function of her position. Third, the critical requirements for effective performance should be incorporated within a behaviorally based rating instrument. Fourth, appraisers should be trained to use the rating instrument. Fifth, the organization must insure that job-related performance and promotion standards are applied consistently. Sixth, the appraisals should be documented. The Ward's Cove case mandated employers to keep records that reflect the cumulative effect of their decisions, as well as the individual impact of their separate procedures. Failure to do so may be considered by the Court as an admission of guilt. Seventh, employees should be coached on ways for them to correct identified deficiencies in their performance. Finally, employers should develop and encourage the use of procedures within the organization that employees can use to challenge an appraisal they perceive to be unfair. These eight steps underlie the discussion in the remainder of this paper.

Conclusions

Subsequent to the previous literature review (Latham, 1986), the methods for rectifying employment discrimination practices in the US have changed dramatically in favor of the employer rather than the employee. The burden of proof is now on the plaintiff to show the discriminatory result of the employer's action, and that alternative means exist to correct it without harming the organization's concern for productivity. Affirmative action, defined as giving preferential treatment to members of protected classes through the use of quotas, can be carried out only on a temporary basis to correct an imbalance within the organization. The statistic for redressing the imbalance is the percentage of qualified minorities in the relevant labor market.

Unless Congress passes laws to overturn recent Supreme Court decisions, the number of employment discrimination lawsuits filed in the US is likely to decrease sharply in this decade. The opposite trend may occur in Canada. The Canadian Federal government is setting up a Royal Commission to examine the treatment of native people. The Ontario provincial government is funding grants to find ways to make people sensitive to racial differences. The Ontario premier has said that his government is going to fund a study on stereotyping, with the aim of determining which images will be approved for advertising. The people of Quebec continue to look for ways to form a distinct and separate society from the nine English-dominated provinces (Amiel, 1991).

THE APPRAISAL INSTRUMENT

The instrument that is used to appraise employees lies at the core of the appraisal system. It is the diagnostic tool which the appraiser uses to coach employees. It thus serves as the basis for setting goals which in turn directly affect an employee's motivation (Locke & Latham, 1990).

The North American courts do not wish to recommend a particular type of appraisal instrument, but rather require only that it be used in a manner free from bias and discrimination (Barrett & Kernan, 1987). Consequently industrial-organizational psychologists have focused on the psychometric properties of appraisals. In addition, user reactions to different types of appraisal forms have been studied, especially management by objectives (MBO) and behavioral criteria. This research emphasis on user reactions reflects the fact that the objective characteristics of an appraisal instrument affect perceptions of fairness and hence how well the appraisal is accepted (Lawler, 1967). Moreover, as Murphy has argued, 'an appraisal system that was moderately accurate, but which satisfied important organizational goals (e.g. motivating employees, providing useful feedback) would surely be preferable to one that provided completely accurate ratings at the expense of achieving important goals' (1991: p. 49).

Psychometric Issues

Bartlett (1983) obtained empirical support for the assertion that forced choice scales are an effective tool for minimizing illusory halo. However, Bownas and Bernardin (1991) showed that Bartlett's results were due to a methodological confound, namely the predictor and criterion were not independent in each of his 11 studies.

With regard to reliability and validity, a number of researchers have investigated ways of increasing appraisal accuracy independent of the appraisal scale that is used. For example, Jako and Murphy (1990) showed that breaking down an appraisal into a series of simple judgments increased interrater reliability.

Rothstein (1990) found a non-linear relationship between interrater reliability and length of exposure to the ratee. The relationship was strongest after the person had been on the job for 12 months. Thus the study points out the danger of appraising an employee too soon. An asymptotic correlation level for reliability was shown to persist over a 10- to 20-year period. Similarly, Hanges, Schneider, and Niles (1990) found that there is a transition stage where an employee settles into a new job. This is followed by a maintenance stage where automatic information processing begins and performance becomes stable over time.

Perhaps the most provocative finding regarding psychometric issues was obtained by Smither, Barry, and Reilly (1989). Their data showed that expert scores, unlike those from non-experts, correlated highly with performance output in terms of clerical activities completed, the resolution of problems in customer accounts, and number of sales made. In fact, the correlation between mean expert ratings and objective true scores on each performance dimension was very high ($r = 0.99$) even when the true intercorrelation among dimensions was zero. They concluded that true scores should be defined as the mean ratings of experts who have ample opportunity to observe performance.

Steiner and Rain (1989) also found that the mean of expert ratings correlated significantly with objective true scores. They concluded that expert ratings may indeed serve as valid estimates of true scores in appraisal research. On the other hand, Sulsky and Balzer (1988) pointed out that evidence of rating accuracy is not always a necessary criterion for evaluating an appraisal decision. Evidence of criterion-related validity is sufficient for evaluating promotion decisions.

User Reactions

With regard to user reactions, a survey by Bretz and Milkovich (1989) found that MBO is the preferred method of assessing performance by Fortune 100 companies. However, Kane and Freeman (1986) criticized MBO for its deleterious effect on the goal-setting process. This is because the goals employees set in an MBO process are generally short-term so as to spur them to achieve measurable results quickly. This emphasis on the bottom line often occurs at the expense of long-term planning. In addition, there is a tendency for employees to underperform in order to avoid the setting of future goals that are difficult for them to attain. Finally, differences in performance goals make comparisons among employees difficult (Kane and Freeman, 1987).

Daley (1987) summarized the results of Iowa state government employee reactions to MBO. Two-thirds of the respondents found the system to be of little help in planning for and receiving training and development activities. The dissatisfaction with the training aspect of the MBO process was so great that it eroded the employees' belief in the fairness of the entire appraisal process.

An alternative to bottom-line or cost-related measures is to use behavioral criteria. Not only are they largely under the control of the employee, but if based on a systematic job analysis they also make explicit what the person must do to improve the bottom line. Thus behavioral criteria facilitate self-management as well as coaching by employees' supervisors, peers, and subordinates because they make explicit what is expected of the individual.

Appraisal Scale Comparisons

In the past five years, several studies have compared different variations of behavioral criteria with other types of appraisal instruments against both psychometric and user criteria. With regard to psychometric criteria, Hughes and Prien (1986), in a study of government employees, evaluated three different scoring methods for Mixed Standard Scales (MSS). No significant differences between different scoring methods were found with regard to variance in score distribution, interrater reliability, or validity. Prien and Hughes (1987) did find that MSS can be used to identify and minimize rating errors.

Benson, Buckley, and Hall (1988) conducted two laboratory experiments where both undergraduate and MBA students evaluated supervisors on videotape, using either MSS or behaviorally anchored rating scales (BARS). The performance of the supervisors had been previously rated by 14 expert raters to determine a benchmark for which the accuracy of the two appraisal formats could be compared. In both experiments the ratings using BARS correlated significantly higher with the benchmarks than did the ratings from the MSS. Based on an earlier finding that raters prefer to use BARS rather than MSS (Dickinson & Zellinger, 1980), and the fact that MSS do not facilitate communication between supervisors and employees, further research in this area would appear to be unwarranted. This conclusion is underscored by a study (Dickinson & Glebocki, 1990) where modifications to the MSS were made in order to reduce halo and leniency errors. Specifically, raters were informed of the rating dimensions, and the raters were told that their ratings would be examined by others for the underlying logic. Again, no improvement in overcoming rating errors was found.

In a laboratory experiment where BARS were compared with trait scales, Krzystofiak, Cardy, and Newman (1988) found that the latter are more susceptible to implicit personality theories than are BARS in that even when ratee behavior was the only information available to the raters, they inferred personality characteristics that had an incremental influence on the rating beyond anything that was attributable to the ratee's behavior.

Murphy and Constans (1987) criticized BARS on the grounds that the behavioral anchors that make up the scale can bias the recall of performance in a laboratory setting, but this was later shown not to be an issue in the field (Murphy & Pardaffy, 1989). Gomez-Mejia (1988) compared the relative advantages of BARS with two other independent and less specific 'trait' or 'abstract global' rating scales. The study was conducted using technicians in the US, Australia, and New Zealand. BARS were not found to be superior to the other scales in terms of rating dispersion, halo effect, incremental utility, test-retest reliability, and criterion-related validity.

Miner (1988), in a study of mine and plant employees, integrated the use of behavioral rating scales with a ranking system. He found that this combination improves the validity of the performance appraisal system. His findings suggested that through the use of both systems, leniency, central tendency and range restriction errors were minimized because the ranking encouraged judgment discrimination. This procedure, however, is more useful for promotion than coaching/counseling purposes.

Focusing on user reactions to appraisal instruments is critical, as Dreher and Sackett (1983) have noted. In too many instances psychometrically sound instruments either are not used or are soon abandoned because of failure on the part of researchers to take user perceptions into account. Consequently, Wiersma and Latham (1986) examined the practicality of behavioral observation scales (BOS), BARS, and trait scales in terms of user preference. Managers and employees preferred BOS to BARS in all cases, and in all but two cases, BOS were preferred to trait scales. Attorneys who specialize in Title VII litigation preferred BOS to the two alternatives in terms of defensibility in the courtroom. Thus it is not surprising that organizations such as the US Drug Enforcement Administration (DEA) use BOS (Musicante, Pajer, & Goldstein, 1988).

Wiersma, van den Berg, and Latham (1992) replicated the American study (Wiersma & Latham, 1986) in the Netherlands. The data were collected from supervisors and peers who had appraised people using each of the three methods, namely, BOS, BARS, and trait scales. The results showed that BOS was preferred over the other two methods for providing feedback, differentiating among performers, determining training needs, setting goals, objectivity, and overall ease of use. The trait scale was viewed as good or slightly better than the BARS. Thus it would appear that the practicality of BOS is not culture-bound.

In a well-controlled laboratory experiment, Rothstein and Chooi (1990) examined the comparative benefits of feedback based on BARS and BOS on subsequent attitudes toward the appraisal process. College students were randomly assigned to either the BARS or BOS appraisal condition. The two appraisal instruments were those that had been developed for clerical employees in a public utility corporation. The performance dimensions which the two instruments evaluated were identical. The tasks which the students performed included an in-basket exercise and a group discussion. The appraisers were blind to the hypotheses of the study. The results showed that people who received feedback based on the BOS evaluated the appraisal more favorably than those who received feedback via BARS. Moreover, this was true regardless of whether the people were high, medium, or low performers. The authors concluded that the specificity of the feedback from BOS enables individuals to understand exactly what they need to do better to improve their performance. In addition, the feedback is relatively non-evaluative. If an employee receives a low score on the BOS it does not suggest that the individual is somehow inadequate, instead it indicates that specific behaviors are not being observed.

Tziner and Kopelman (1988) examined BOS and graphic rating scales on three goal-setting dimensions, namely, goal clarity, goal acceptance and goal commitment. The scores of employees on each of these dimensions were higher when BOS rather than the graphic rating scale was used. These results were due to the behavioral specificity provided by the BOS.

Tziner and Latham (1989), in a study of employees at the Israel Airport Authority, found that appraisals using BOS resulted in higher subsequent job satisfaction and organizational commitment than appraisals where graphic scales or no scales at all were used. The specificity of BOS strengthened the employees' feelings of control over their work, and dissipated feelings of ambiguity about expectations and requirements.

Job Analysis

The building block for any performance assessment instrument is a job analysis (Nathan & Cascio, 1986). Thus, regardless of the appraisal instrument that is used, its effectiveness is dependent upon the adequacy of the job analysis on which it is based. Mullins and Kimborough (1988) conducted a study of university patrol officers to determine if different groups of job incumbents would provide different job analysis outcomes. Job incumbents were divided into groups on the basis of seniority and educational level. All groups used the critical incident technique (Flanagan, 1954) to develop a job analysis for a university police department. The dependent variables were supervisor rank orderings and ratings of job performance by subject matter experts (SME) within each group. The results indicated that different groups produced different outcomes. However, this finding may reflect the difference in performance expectations by police officers versus dormitory supervisors.

In a similar study, Landy and Vasey (1991) explored the influence of demographic characteristics of SMEs on job analysis ratings. Approximately 400 incumbent police officers indicated the frequency with which tasks are performed. The results showed that sex and experience influenced the responses of the SMEs, but that sex was confounded with experience. The authors concluded, as did Mullins and Kimborough (1988), that the composition of SMEs should include varying levels of experience.

Fleishman and Mumford (1991) set forth general principles for establishing the construct validity of the descriptive information provided by a job analysis in order to establish the substantive meaningfulness of the proposed categories for organizing critical behavioral incidents. They argued that the propositional relationships implied by category status should be articulated and then validated through hypothesis testing. Hypotheses should be formulated concerning the outcomes expected after: (i) domain definition; (ii) measurement of behavioral properties; (iii) similarity assessment; and (iv) application of the decision rules for assigning behaviors to categories. Construct validity should also include the testing of expected relationships among the behaviors to be assigned to the categories and between the categories themselves. These tests constitute an evaluation of the internal validity of the job classification system.

Conclusions

Unlike the previous review (Latham, 1986), there has been a paucity of studies on the relative effectiveness of different job analysis techniques. Most studies used the critical incident technique (CIT) or a variant thereof. This finding supports the previous review (Latham, 1986) that the CIT is ideally suited for the development of an appraisal instrument, especially if an inductive rather than a deductive approach is used as was originally advocated by Flanagan (1954).

Several studies have looked at the composition of SMEs involved in job analysis. There is a growing body of evidence which suggests that they should be representative of the workforce in order to enhance the validity of the job analysis methodology.

Although the reliability and validity of behavioral criteria continue to be investigated, there has been a shift in emphasis to factors independent of any particular appraisal instrument. Perhaps this is in recognition of the fact that any instrument is subject to misuse. Thus it is not surprising that there has also been an increase in research emphasis on user reactions to different appraisal instruments. In this regard there is an emerging preference for the use of behavioral criteria over end-result measures and trait-based scales.

Regardless of the appraisal instrument employed or the job analysis methodology on which it is based, users need to be sensitive to the concept of what constitutes effective performance. If interpreted narrowly, this concept would be inconsistent with the 'Standards for Educational and Psychological Testing' (1985). Effective performance does not imply a dichotomous variable, rather the term embraces the notion of the additional value that higher levels of work behavior offer an organization. Similarly, the term job performance must be interpreted broadly to include behaviors such as attendance, trainability, and turnover.

Perhaps the most surprising finding in this area is that the research pendulum has swung back in favor of the use of experts for establishing true scores. Despite the warnings of Zedeck and Cascio (1984), the empirical evidence appears to suggest that this procedure can be acceptable in some instances because of the high correlation between expert-based true scores with objective performance measures.

SOURCES OF APPRAISAL

Once a reliable and valid appraisal instrument has been developed, attention must be given to who is qualified to use it. One way of determining the answer is to examine the various alternatives against Thorndike's (1949) four criteria: validity, reliability, freedom from bias, and practicality. The latter, as noted earlier, is usually evaluated in terms of user preference or acceptance.

The primary focus of research on the source of performance appraisals in the second half of the 1980s and early 1990s continues to be self- and peer appraisals. This is true despite the fact that Bretz and Milkovich (1989), in their survey of Fortune 100 companies, found that only two organizations reported using self-appraisals, less than 3% of the appraisals were conducted by peers, and no subordinate appraisal systems were reported. That this trend may be changing is evident in the popular press (e.g. *Fortune*, 19 June 1989: p. 201; Norman & Zawacki, 1991) where an increasing number of organizations are reportedly warming to the use of peer as well as subordinate appraisals.

Self-appraisals

The major portion of the research in the past five years on the appropriate source of a performance appraisal has focused on self. A survey of 1800 Minnesota Department of Transportation employees indicated that people want self-evaluations as part of their formal performance appraisal (Laumeyer & Beebe, 1988).

Meyer (1991) listed the following advantages of a self-review. First, it can enhance the subordinate's dignity and self-respect. Second, it places the manager in the role of a counselor rather than a judge. Third, it is likely to increase employee commitment to development plans or goals formulated in the discussion. Fourth, a discussion with a supervisor is more satisfying to employees than the traditional top-down appraisal.

Other advantages of self-appraisals include their potential for enhancing self-motivation (Baron, 1988; Lane & Herriot, 1990), and their tendency to reduce ratee defensiveness (Farh, Werbel, & Bedeian, 1988; Lawrie, 1989). Finally, self-evaluations can facilitate the integration of the evaluative and developmental purposes of performance appraisal. Since most organizations are inclined to use and to rely primarily on supervisory assessments, one relevant question that has been addressed in the literature is how do self-evaluations compare with supervisory assessments?

Harris and Schaubroeck (1988) conducted a meta-analysis based on empirical studies published in seven journals over the past 30 years. They found that despite correcting for statistical artifacts, self-ratings were more than half a standard deviation higher than supervisory ratings, and one quarter of a standard deviation higher than peer ratings. This was true more so for managerial/professional employees than for blue-collar/service employees. The authors suggested that this moderator may be due to the egocentric bias that is more likely to occur in ambiguous contexts such as professional work than in relatively well-defined jobs.

Restriction of range can also be a problem with using self-appraisals. Hoffman, Nathan, and Holden (1991) found less variation in self-appraisals than in supervisory-based appraisals. Thus only the latter predicted the field service productivity of maintenance employees.

Martin and Klimoski (1990), in a study of university employees, also found that self-ratings had higher positive leniency than did ratings produced by other sources. Relative to supervisory evaluations, the authors concluded that different information processing dynamics occur in self-appraisals. For example, when people appraised their own performance, poor results were attributed to external causes more so than when they appraised the performance of their subordinates. However, the lack of agreement between self- and supervisory ratings may be moderated by age. McFarlane Shore and Bleicken (1991) found that agreement is relatively high when the self-appraisals are done by older employees and relatively low when the self-appraisals are made by middle-age workers. The psychological correlate explaining this finding has yet to be determined.

In contrast to the above findings, two recent studies reported a high correlation between self-appraisals and supervisory assessments. Lane and Herriot (1990) conducted a field study of 40 British unit managers to compare the predictive validity of self- versus supervisory appraisals. Subsequent performance, as measured by gross profit and the number of customers served, was predicted equally well by the two sources of appraisal.

Fahr, Werbel, and Bedeian (1988), in a field study of faculty members and their chairpersons, investigated the effectiveness of a performance appraisal system that incorporated self-assessments with supervisory evaluations of faculty activity reports. The results revealed a high correlation between self- and chairpersons' ratings as well as criterion-related validity. Moreover, user acceptance was high, as indicated by ratings from both faculty and their chairpersons. A flaw in this study is that the chairpersons had access to the self-appraisals before making the appraisal. In practice, however, this is usually the case.

In explaining the differences that can occur between self- and supervisory appraisals, Campbell and Lee (1988) speculated that there are informational constraints in that many employees do not understand what is expected of the performance appraisal, that poorly conducted previous performance appraisals contribute to this ambiguity, and the excessive time length between appraisals reduces the potential for rating accuracy. Role clarification exercises, improved job descriptions, and thorough review sessions based on behavioral criteria may be ways of minimizing information distortions and cognitive constraints.

Another reason for the incongruence between self- and supervisory evaluation is the fact that different raters may focus on different facets of job performance (Fahr & Dobbins, 1989a). Ashford (1989) found that a person's early success experiences anchor them with specific beliefs about themselves. These beliefs filter subsequent information so that self-appraisal accuracy is reduced. However, self-assessments and criterion measures of behavior are more highly related for those people who are high in private self-awareness. Self-awareness is a function of one's ability to self-observe. Self-aware people compare their behavior against a goal or information relevant to their goals. It would appear that those who are self-aware are able to incorporate information from those comparisons into their self-evaluations, and ultimately into their behavior. Self-awareness also results in the incorporation of the assessments of others into one's self-evaluation. As a result self-aware people are more cognizant of how they are viewed by others which in turn results in relatively accurate self-assessments.

Culture is another moderator of self-supervisory agreement in appraisals. For example, negative leniency in self-ratings may be a cultural characteristic. In a study of 793 leader–subordinate dyads from nine organizations in Taiwan, Farh, Dobbins, and Cheng (1991) found that Chinese employees rated their job performance and organizational citizenship behavior less favorably than did their supervisors. This modesty bias held across gender, education levels and age groups. However, all raters in this study were told that the assessment was strictly for research purposes. An unanswered question is whether the results would change if the employees were told that their self-assessment would be used for promotion or salary purposes.

In North America, self-appraisals are subject to positive leniency bias. In a laboratory study that looked at the validity of self-estimates of ability and competence, Lowman and Williams (1987) found low correlations between self-ratings of ability and objective ratings such as the Seashore Measures of Musical Talent, Watson Glaser Critical Thinking Appraisal, and The Minnesota Paper Form Board.

At least five studies have addressed variables that influence the objectivity of self-appraisals. Farh and Werbel (1986) found that individuals who believed that self-reported information would be verified against other performance measures decreased positive leniency relative to people who did not believe that this would occur. Similarly, Fox and Dinur (1988) in an actual selection setting, found that informing raters that their evaluations would be checked against other indicators increased convergent validity. Thus the availability of comparative performance information appears to play a key role in removing positive leniency in self-ratings.

In a laboratory study of undergraduate university students, Farh and

Dobbins (1989b) used structural equation modeling and LISREL to examine the effects of the rater's self-esteem on positive leniency bias. On the basis of consistent theory (Korman, 1970), the authors found support for the hypothesis that high self-esteem self-raters exhibit more positive leniency than people with low self-esteem. One practical consequence of these findings is that high self-esteem individuals, whose performance evaluations include self-reports, may receive larger rewards than they deserve (Farh & Dobbins, 1989b).

Farh and Dobbins (1989a), in another laboratory study involving university undergraduates, found that the correlations between self-ratings and objective performance indicators were larger when the self-raters were presented with comparative performance information than when this was not done. They suggested that one reason for the lack of agreement between self- and supervisory ratings in field settings is that self-raters may lack the comparative performance information that is available to supervisors. This finding is consistent with earlier research (Farh, Werbel, & Bedeian, 1988) involving faculty members which showed that when self-raters and supervisors had comparable access to the same performance information, convergent validity increased.

Eder and Fedor (1989) conducted a field experiment to investigate the effects of rating purpose (i.e. promotion versus training) and judgment confidence on ratings generated by self-reports. They found that both effects tended to influence the assessments. They suggested that positive leniency in self-reports can be reduced by requiring employees to provide documentation for their appraisals.

In a field study, Somers and Birnbaum (1991) found no significant differences between staff nurse and supervisor performance ratings. These people had had at least two years experience with self-appraisal.

Conclusions

A problem with the use of self-appraisals is their lack of agreement with other sources, especially supervisors (Harris & Schaubroeck, 1988). This can be especially problematic with jobs that are ambiguous in nature and hence poorly defined. The solutions to the effective use of self-appraisals include conducting a job analysis to remove this ambiguity (Campbell & Lee, 1988), making appraisals against objective criteria (Lane & Herriot, 1990), making clear to the employee that the appraisal will be verified against other performance measures (Farh & Werbel, 1986; Fox & Dinur, 1988), providing the employee with comparative information (Farh & Dobbins, 1989a), requiring documentation in support of the appraisal (Eder & Fedor, 1989), and making certain that the employee has had ample experience of conducting self-appraisals before these are compared with alternative appraisal sources (Somers & Birnbaum, 1991).

Peer Appraisals

Validity coefficients are typically higher for peer assessments than for other sources such as supervisory ratings or even psychological tests (Fox, Ben-Nahum, & Yinon, 1989; Kremer, 1990; McEvoy & Buller, 1987). In a field study of an Israeli military training program, Fox, Ben-Nahum, and Yinon (1989) used peer assessments to forecast other group members' likelihood of success in the program. They found that raters who perceived peers as similar to them were more accurate than raters who perceived their peers as dissimilar. The authors also found that foreground similarity produced stronger peer rater accuracy than background similarity. This is because raters are better able to recall information about similar rather than dissimilar characteristics, they know more about similar others because they spend more time with them, and they compare themselves to similar others and hence take the opportunity to observe similar co-workers more than they do dissimilar co-workers.

McEvoy and Buller (1987) conducted a field study of food processing employees in which both managers and hourly employees rated their peers. The study revealed greater user acceptance for peer appraisals than previous research has done. An explanation offered by the authors is that the employees perceived that their peers would be easier on them than would their supervisors. Additionally, the authors found that employees were inclined to accept peer appraisals because they were being used for developmental rather than evaluative purposes such as promotion or salary increases. Finally, user acceptance was attributed to anonymity whereas other studies have used individually signed forms.

In a study of 226 employees, McEvoy, Buller, and Roghaar (1988) found that peer satisfaction with the appraisal process did not correlate with one's actual rating. In short, the employees valued an honest evaluation.

Kremer (1990), in a field study of university faculty members, found that the reliability of peer ratings was high for assessing teaching and research but it was only moderate for assessing service. This may reflect the fact that it is easier to establish objective criteria (e.g. number of publications; student ratings) for evaluating performance on the two former dimensions than it is on the latter.

A meta-analysis (Harris & Schaubroek, 1988) revealed moderate agreement between self–peer ($r = 0.36$), and self–supervisor ($r = 0.35$), and high peer–supervisor ($r = 0.62$) agreement. Moreover, job type did not affect the peer–supervisory correlation. Peer appraisals may be an especially useful process for withstanding legal scrutiny as it is in alignment with the North American judicial system, namely, a judgment by one's peers.

With regard to user reactions, Farh, Cannella, and Bedeian (1991) found that employees preferred peer appraisals for developmental rather than evaluative purposes. What is needed is a study of user preferences for evaluative appraisals from peers relative to alternative sources such as supervisors.

Subordinate Appraisals

Articles that have appeared in the literature in the past six years on subordinate appraisals have been primarily advocacy-driven rather than research-based. This may reflect the fact that few organizations use them. There are at least two reasons why they are rarely used (Bernardin & Beatty, 1987). First, a top-down approach is compatible with the management styles employed in most North American firms where the separation of management and non-management functions is still emphasized. Second, there is a fear that subordinate appraisals will undermine managerial power. Thus it is not surprising that little research on them exists beyond the findings of acceptable reliabilities and validities obtained in artificially created situations.

Bernardin and Beatty (1987) advocated three reasons why subordinate appraisals should be conducted. First, subordinates are in a position to observe managerial performance. Second, multiple assessments help eliminate one-rater-only biases. Third, a formal subordinate appraisal system is compatible with the employee 'commitment' and 'involvement' models that managers and academics alike are advocating as a way of increasing productivity.

Bernardin and Beatty argued that the keys to successful subordinate appraisals include a participative management style, rater anonymity, and making the items to be rated behaviorally specific. McEvoy (1988) advocated: (i) taking the steps necessary to ensure that subordinates are aware of the requirements of their supervisor's job; (ii) allowing subordinates to rate only those people-oriented dimensions of performance which they are in a position to observe; (iii) providing training in the observation and evaluation of behavior; and (iv) making certain that subordinate appraisals supplement, not replace, supervisory appraisals.

Levinson (1987) argued for the use of a consultant so as to avoid the risk of subordinates 'ganging up' on the boss. People are less likely to be angry and more likely to be specific in interviews with a consultant than when they confront the boss alone or with a group of colleagues. He advocated upward appraisals as a practical developmental tool for providing confidentiality and specific feedback, and for minimizing defensiveness on the part of the ratee due to the use of a consultant as a 'buffer'.

That the time is ripe for implementing and evaluating subordinate appraisals is evident from a survey administered to determine the likelihood of user acceptance of subordinate appraisals within eight organizations which were not using them (McEvoy, 1988). Two-thirds of the managers said that they would approve or strongly approve of subordinate appraisals. Only 17% said that they would disapprove or strongly disapprove of this process. Managerial receptivity toward subordinate appraisals was not moderated by age, gender, years with employer, salary, education level, self-rated performance, or satisfaction with the last performance appraisal.

To the question, 'If your subordinates were to evaluate your performance,

how valuable would you find such feedback for your personal development?',
three-quarters responded definitely or extremely valuable. Only 6% said that
it would be of limited or of no value to them, while 71% of the respondents
did not approve of subordinate appraisals counting as heavily as their
supervisor's appraisals for determining pay and promotions. This is because
managers fear retaliation for taking unpopular action (e.g. reprimanding an
employee), and they believe that their subordinates do not have full knowledge
of their job requirements. Thus, to be accepted, subordinate appraisals should
be restricted to 'people-oriented' as opposed to 'task-oriented' dimensions (e.g.
organizing, budgeting, and so on).

Conclusions

The choice of the appraiser is as critical, if not more critical, to the success
of an appraisal program as is the type of instrument used (Locher & Teel,
1988). If the appraiser fails to understand the objectives of the appraisal, how
to use the chosen system, or how to observe behavior objectively, the appraisal
will be ineffective in bringing about and sustaining high performance. Although
the supervisor continues to be the most commonly used source of performance
appraisals, the primary focus of research in the second half of the 1980s was
on self- and peer appraisals. In addition, there has been a growing number of
studies looking at subordinates as an additional source of appraisals.

Research is still needed on the outcome expectancies that affect self-
appraisals. If the outcome of an inflated rating is peer rejection, as appears to
be the case in Taiwan, then it is not surprising that self-appraisals are lower
than supervisory appraisals. If extrinsic rewards are tied directly or indirectly
to a positive appraisal, as is often the case in North America, then a positive
leniency bias should not be surprising when self-appraisals are conducted.

Appraisal instruments and documentation requirements that facilitate self-
monitoring are also in need of research. The latter may minimize information
distortion and cognitive biases. Research is needed on ways that organizations
can provide comparative information that will enable people to make accurate
self-assessments without violating the privacy of others.

Peer appraisal systems continue to present a curious paradox. It has long
been known by academicians that peer assessments are more stable than
supervisory ratings and are more likely to focus on performance than on the
effort one has exerted (Kane & Lawler, 1979); in fact they are among the
most accurate assessments of employee behavior (Wexley & Klimoski, 1984)
especially with regard to predicting future performance (Schmitt, Gooding,
Noe, & Kirsch, 1984). Yet only a handful of organizations are using them.
General Electric executives reportedly spend six days taking management
development classes based on the feedback they receive from both peer
and subordinate appraisals (Nelson-Horchler, 1988). Studies are needed to

systematically evaluate the long-term effect of this feedback on goal setting and subsequent behavior change.

Johnson and Johnson's divisional presidents are evaluated on how well they extract and act upon feedback from their subordinates (Nelson-Horchler, 1988). Peer and subordinate appraisals would appear critical to bringing about and sustaining what Lawler and his colleagues call a high-involvement organization (Lawler & Mohrman, 1989). This is because peer, subordinate, and self-appraisals help instill a culture where there is high value for teamwork and a participatory environment.

Edwards (1990) has proposed a TEAMS appraisal. TEAMS is an acronym for Team Evaluation and Management System. Appraisals are a joint function of team evaluation of employee merit and promotability and subsequent evaluation of the results by the supervisor. The employee participates in the selection of the team of evaluation and the selection of the criteria on which the evaluation will be made. Although psychometric and user acceptance information have yet to be collected, Edwards (1990) proposed that this approach is especially appropriate for project management teams and flat organizations.

For senior-level managers who wish to minimize the costs associated with litigation over an appraisal, attention should be given to the fact that feedback in which the employee has had appreciable input is perceived by the employee as more fair and more accurate than traditional top-down appraisals. Follow-up studies are needed on the frequency with which litigation involves supervisory appraisals versus alternative sources.

Research is also needed on the interaction effect of the appraisal instrument used and the person or persons using it on Thorndike's (1949) four criteria, namely, relevance, reliability, freedom from bias, and practicality. Appraisal instruments that emphasize trait or bottom-line outcomes may inhibit the commitment and involvement that can come from self-appraisals if employees cannot discern the actions needed to change and improve their performance. Thus such instruments may be appropriate only for those supervisors who are able to give employees this information.

There is a dearth of empirical research on client–customer–supplier appraisals. Nevertheless, Ivancevich and Stewart (1988) recommended that firms which are coping with mergers, acquisitions, and other traumatic changes use a four-tiered approach to appraisal, namely, peer, self, client/customer/supplier, and expert appraisals as a way of obtaining comprehensive data for making HRM decisions.

The use of outside experts as raters is also in need of empirical research. There are concerns that while experts may 'know' the job that they are evaluating, they often are not familiar enough with a particular organizational setting to appraise performance as satisfactory or unsatisfactory 'here'. However, as discussed earlier, Smither, Barry, & Reilly (1989) concluded that expert raters can provide accurate ratings with enhanced viewing opportunities. This may be due to their intensive knowledge of the job, as well as individual difference characteristics such as their intelligence (Smither & Reilly, 1987) and motivation (Salvemini, 1988). Intelligence and motivation, as discussed below, have been found to increase rating accuracy.

Further research on expert raters needs to address their reliability and validity in actual, as opposed to simulated, working conditions. In addition, the costs both in dollars and in employee non-participation need to be investigated. It is possible that appraisals by accepted experts will be perceived by ratees as objective and hence both accurate and fair.

APPRAISAL ACCURACY

Much of the research on performance appraisal from 1986 through 1991 has had as its focus, as was the case during the preceding five years (Latham, 1986), the identification and removal of rater biases. This has been done without regard to whether the rater is a superior, peer, subordinate, client, or outside expert. Specifically, the research has focused on rating error, and both rater and ratee characteristics that contribute to rating error. Several theories have been advanced as explanations of the appraisal outcomes, and research on training programs has been conducted to take some of these findings into account.

Rating Errors

Of all of the rating errors, halo continues to receive the most attention from academicians. For example, Nathan and Tippins (1990) investigated the consequences of halo error on appraisal accuracy in a study involving supervisors of clerical workers. True scores were operationalized as scores on a valid test battery of clerical abilities. Halo was operationalized as the standard deviation across dimensions. The authors found that halo can actually improve accuracy when an intercorrelation among dimensions is expected.

The need to distinguish between true halo, namely, the actual intercorrelation among performance dimensions, and illusory halo or halo error, namely, the inability to differentiate among conceptually distinct and potentially independent aspects of a ratee's behavior, has been emphasized by several researchers (e.g. Murphy & Jako, 1989; Nathan & Tippins, 1990; Pulakos, Schmitt, & Ostroff, 1986). Pulakos, Schmitt, and Ostroff (1986) identified the following methodological errors frequently made in the operationalization of halo error, namely: (i) an examination of the interdimension factor structure; (ii) use of a rater x ratee x dimension analysis of variance; (iii) calculation of interdimension correlations; and (iv) computation of a standard deviation for a given rater's ratings of a ratee across all performance dimensions. Fox, Bizman, and Hoffman (1989) have argued that these are not measures of halo error because these measures reflect the multidimensional characteristic of the construct that is being measured.

Pulakos, Schmitt, and Ostroff (1986) suggested three ways of identifying halo error, namely: (i) compute the average standard deviation or variance for each rater across standardized within-dimension scores; (ii) calculate a rater's average level of observed dimension intercorrelation; or (iii) calculate the average difference between the true and observed dimension intercorrelation for each rater. This third strategy implies that it is indeed possible to measure true halo. The resolution of this controversy is tied to the question of what constitutes an acceptable criterion against which to validate a performance appraisal tool. As noted throughout this paper, many researchers have employed the ratings of expert judges, who use the same rating tool as the subject raters, as a way of deriving true score estimates. The problem with this approach, as other investigators have noted (Kozlowski & Kirsch, 1987; Nathan & Tippins, 1990), is that such true scores are subject to any pervasive cognitive distortions. However, as noted earlier, Smither, Barry, and Reilly (1989) showed that expert rating scores correlate highly with actual performance output.

A second approach has been to use ability tests (Nathan & Tippins, 1990) and/or work sample tests (Vance, MacCallum, Coovert, & Hedge, 1988) as criteria against which the accuracy of performance appraisals can be evaluated. However, using criteria that in themselves have been used as predictors and have in turn been validated against performance measures, is circular reasoning. Further, work sample tests tend to measure maximum rather than typical performance (Borman & Hallam, 1991). In a study of supermarket cashiers, Sackett, Zedeck, and Fogli (1988) found that typical and maximum performance measures do not yield comparable data.

At least two studies have identified cognitive processes that contribute to halo error. Mount and Thompson (1987) found that the error occurred when the observed behaviors of a ratee are consistent with the categorization schema of the rater. Categorization schema was operationalized as subjects' responses to a questionnaire assessing perceived manager role congruence. In support of the categorization schema hypothesis, rating accuracy and halo were found to be higher when subordinates perceived the managers to be performing in a way that was consistent with their expectations. Moreover, this halo correlated positively with accuracy.

Kozlowski and Kirsch (1987) asked undergraduate students to rate the performance of baseball players three weeks after the end of the baseball season. The raters used a BOS. The objective true scores consisted of statistics of each player's actual performance in terms such as hitting averages or base hits. Halo error was defined as the difference between each respondent's average intercorrelation and the average true score intercorrelations. The subjects with low job knowledge, not surprisingly, showed more halo error than subjects with high job knowledge. Higher job knowledge resulted in a higher rating and true score covariation. The authors concluded that a systematic distortion process was operating such that the judgments of the subjects were influenced by the conceptual similarity among performance dimensions.

Murphy and Reynolds (1988) found that the actual effect of true halo on observed halo is small. They offered both a conceptual similarity hypothesis and regression towards the mean hypothesis as an explanation of halo effects. The latter was supported by the observation that subjects sometimes underestimate as well as overestimate true halo.

Similarly, Lance, Woehr, and Fiscaro (1991) argued that halo often represents valid variance and found that performance-based and non-performance-based aspects of raters' overall impressions can be distinguished. Moreover, their study showed that performance-based effects on ratings outweigh non-performance effects. Finally, the results revealed that 'raters are indeed capable of providing accurate ratings, but that situational characteristics sometimes reinforce deliberate rating distortions' (p. 16).

Underlying cognitive processes

Kozlowski and Kirsch (1987) found that the effects of conceptual similarity on rating accuracy varied as a function of the subject's job knowledge and familiarity of the ratees. Subjects with high job knowledge who rated highly familiar ratees, showed lower covariation between conceptual similarity and observed ratings than did subjects with low job knowledge. Ratee familiarity was shown by Rothstein (1990) to be associated with high interrater reliability among supervisors in a field setting.

Steiner and Rain (1989) conducted two studies investigating both the contrast/assimilation effect as well as the primacy/recency effect under conditions of immediate and delayed performance appraisal. Ratings were made on BOS with high reliability ($r = 0.80$). In each study, undergraduate students viewed four videotaped performances of a lecturer delivering three average and either one very good or one very poor performance. This viewing occurred either in one sitting (study 1) or over four consecutive days (study 2). An assimilation effect was found to be predominant in both studies; however, in the immediate viewing condition this effect was found only for the poor performance. Using cognitive schema theory to interpret their results, the authors suggested that subjects tended to view variable performance as consistent with the schema they had already developed of the instructor's performance. With regard to the recency effect that was found in both studies, the authors suggested that people pay attention to early information but pay less attention to later stimuli.

Smither, Reilly, and Buda (1988) obtained a within ratee contrast effect when raters had direct access to previous performance (via a videotape), and an assimilation effect when raters had indirect access to information about a ratee's previous performance through a written medium. In a second study, the contrast effect disappeared when subjects viewed the videotaped performance of a lecturer across one-week intervals. An implication of this study is that accuracy will improve when raters are given multiple opportunities to view the performance of ratees over extended time periods.

Maurer and Alexander (1991) obtained a between ratee contrast effect when student raters evaluated a lecturer's videotaped performance, using BOS. The experimental task was realistic in that the subjects were told that their ratings would influence the payment the instructor would receive for delivering the lecture; and the subjects were asked to indicate the key lecturer behaviors that triggered an evaluative response by pressing a button at their viewing station. This enabled an investigation of the information processing strategies the subjects used to arrive at their performance judgments. The contrast effect occurred as a result of the encoding of discrepant stimuli. The authors concluded that behaviors that are discrepant from a salient context attract attention and more effortful processing.

Several studies found support for Wherry's hypothesis that raters consciously introduce error into their performance ratings when anticipating the need to deliver face-to-face feedback (Wherry & Bartlett, 1982). For example Klimoski and Inks (1990) showed that anticipated feedback produced a leniency effect, while knowledge of the subordinate's self-assessment produced a bias in the direction of the subordinate's own rating. It would appear that a superior should independently complete a performance evaluation before having access to the subordinate's views.

Rothstein (1990) investigated the relationship between length of exposure to the ratee and interrater reliability of performance ratings made on first-line supervisors. The subjects were pooled across organizations, BARS which were developed from a job analysis was used by all raters, and the raters received instruction in the use of the scale. Rothstein (1990) found that the relationship between length of exposure and reliability was strongest for the first year of experience ($r = 0.82$ for ability, $r = 0.65$ for duty), and that reliability gradually tapered off after five years of experience ($r = 0.09$ for ability, $r = 0.25$ for duty). Interpretation of the leveling off of reliability after five years of observation was hindered by the fact that tenure was used as a surrogate for observation time. As suggested by Rothstein (1990), the leveling off of reliability among long-tenured employees could have been due to the fact that none of the employees was observed by the same rater pair for the entire observation period.

Ratee Characteristics

A literature review on the effects of non-verbal cues on the performance appraisal process (DeMeuse, 1987), concluded that demographic cues (gender, race, and age) have a consistent but small effect on performance appraisal;

and the magnitude of this effect is inflated in laboratory studies. However, in a subsequent laboratory experiment, Barnes-Farrell, L'Heureux-Barrett, and Conway (1991) found that employee gender did not affect the accuracy of performance ratings. In six field studies, the effect of gender on performance appraisal was found to be absent (Griffeth & Bedeian, 1989; McFarlane Shore & Thornton, 1986; Simpson, McCarrey, & Edwards, 1987), or of very small magnitude (Greenhaus, Parasuraman, & Wormley, 1990; Pulakos, White, Oppler, & Borman, 1989; Sackett, Dubois, & Wiggins Noe, 1991). The effect of race accounted for less than 1% of the variance in rating scores in one study (Pulakos et al., 1989), 3% of the variance in performance rating in a second study (Waldman & Avolio, 1991) and 4% of the variance in job performance evaluations in a third study (Greenhaus, Parasuraman, & Wormley, 1990). Waldman and Avolio (1991) found that when the effects of ability, education, and job experience were controlled, race of ratee generally did not contribute to the prediction of performance ratings. In a meta-analysis of two large data sets, Sackett and Dubois (1991) failed to find support for Kraiger and Ford's (1985) findings from an earlier meta-analysis that black raters rate blacks higher than they rate whites.

Stereotypical views explained in part the negative bias that does occur towards women in performance appraisals (Simpson, McCarrey, & Edwards, 1987). Being female and having dependents, however, can alter the direction of the bias in a woman's favor (Russell & Rush, 1987). Interestingly, having a history of a mental handicap (depression) can also promote a positive bias in favor of a disabled worker (Czajka & DeNisi, 1988). These results can be interpreted within an attribution framework. Raters are lenient in their appraisal of ratees who are exhibiting poor performance when the performance can be attributed to external factors (having to care for dependents) or to temporary causes not entirely under the control of the ratee (depression).

In a field study, Tsui and O'Reilly (1989) investigated the effect of the demographic characteristics of superior–subordinate dyads on supervisor performance ratings and affect toward the subordinate. Demographic variables accounted for only 6% of the variance in supervisory affect, and only 4% of the variance in effectiveness ratings. Of the relational demographic variables, there was weak support for the effect of race and age differences, and relatively strong support for the effect of gender differences on performance ratings. Subordinates in the mixed-gender dyads were rated as performing more poorly and were liked less well than subordinates in the same-gender dyads (Tsui & O'Reilly, 1989).

There seems to be little evidence that ratee age influences rater bias (Griffeth & Bedeian, 1989). In a meta-analysis of the literature, McEvoy and Cascio (1989) reported that the average correlation between ratee age and performance was 0.06. The only moderator that significantly altered the observed age–performance relationship was very young subjects; here the correlation between age and performance was 0.17.

There is growing research evidence that suggests that employees can influence their performance appraisal by creating a positive or negative impression on their supervisor. Klaas and DeNisi (1989) found that past employee grievance activity negatively influenced the performance appraisal ratings made by supervisors. Padgett and Ilgen (1989) found that consistency in the ratee's performance has a positive effect on raters. In a study of insurance agents, MacKenzie, Podsakoff, and Fetter (1991) found that the difference between an employee's actual sales performance and the manager's appraisal of that employee was accounted for by the fact that managers were affected as much by extra-role contributions by the employee as they were by in-role measures in making an appraisal. The former fall under the umbrella term, organizational citizenship behavior.

Wayne and Ferris (1990) found that impression management by a subordinate is particularly important initially when the appraiser is forming an impression of and categorizing the subordinate. This is because appraisers encode an employee's behaviors in terms of general trait concepts. Partially on the basis of these trait concepts, individuals form a general evaluative concept of the person as likable or unlikable. It is this evaluative concept that becomes the basis of the impression. Once this evaluative concept is formed, the employee's subsequent behaviors are interpreted in terms of this concept. When appraisers are asked to make a judgment of an employee, they search their memory for a general trait or an evaluative concept that specifically pertains to the judgment. After a period of time, impression management may become less important because the subordinate's performance maintains the appraiser's impression of the subordinate.

Rater Characteristics

Personal characteristics of the rater have also been shown to influence rater accuracy. A number of these studies have been conducted within a field setting (Borman & Hallam, 1991; Griffeth & Bedeian, 1989; Hogan, 1987; Huber, Neale, & Northcraft, 1987; Schoorman, 1988; Tsui & Barry, 1986). Unfortunately, only four of the studies reviewed employed a rating tool that was based on a job analysis (Borman & Hallam, 1991; Cardy & Dobbins, 1986; Huber, Neale, & Northcraft, 1987; Schoorman, 1988). Huber, Neale, and Northcraft (1987) found that female raters, more experienced raters, and raters who themselves had received higher ratings in the past, all recommended larger pay increases for good performers. Griffeth and Bedeian (1989) found that the rater's age accounted for 8% of the variance in performance ratings with younger raters giving lower ratings.

Smither and Reilly (1987) found that rater intelligence was significantly related to accuracy. Borman and Hallam (1991) also found that the past experience of raters and their cognitive ability influenced rating accuracy. The experienced raters not only closely monitored the performance of others, but they frequently found fault with it. Implicit in Borman's (Borman & Hallam, 1991) research is the notion that appraiser–appraisee characteristics that are not job-related must be studied before there is a complete understanding of what factors and cues raters use when they make evaluations.

Sinclair (1988) found that the rater's mood influenced accuracy. Undergraduate student raters, in the depressed mood condition, demonstrated less halo and more accuracy than subjects in the elated mood condition. Sinclair explained his findings by suggesting that 'depressed' subjects may be processing information in a more controlled manner than elated subjects, leading to more discrete judgments.

Caution should be exercised in generalizing these findings to the field setting. The subjects in Sinclair's (1988) study were students, who were in an experimentally induced mood state. An earlier study by Borman (1979) found that accurate raters were free from self-doubt, tended not to worry or become stressed, and tended to be detail-oriented in their approach to tasks. The attention to detail could have been the determinant of accuracy in both the Borman (1979) and Sinclair (1988) studies.

Cognitive Theories of Rating Errors

In a comprehensive review of cognitive theories of performance appraisal, DeNisi and Williams (1988) cited Bartlett (1932) as one of the first theorists to recognize that observers tend to remember events according to a generalized pattern or schema, and that reliance on a schemata leads observers to forget stimuli that are inconsistent with the schemata pattern. Bartlett's (cf. DeNisi & Williams, 1988) work influenced Wherry, whose theory of rating (Wherry & Bartlett, 1982) states that accuracy can be improved when the rater's attention is focused on the rating task, when a conscious effort to be objective is made, and when behavior is readily classified into specific categories, rather than overall schemata.

DeNisi and his colleagues (DeNisi, Cafferty, & Meglino, 1984; DeNisi & Williams, 1988) developed a model which emphasizes the information acquisition activities of the rater. They argued that factors such as the purpose for which the appraisal is conducted, prior impressions about ratees (i.e. expectations), and time constraints affect the way in which raters go about acquiring information. The model emphasizes the importance of patterns of information storage in memory. The data demonstrate empirically that accurate recall is greater when subjects are instructed to organize information in memory either by ratee (DeNisi, Robbins, & Cafferty, 1989) or by tasks (Williams, Cafferty, & DeNisi, 1990). DeNisi and Williams (1988) concluded their review with the following recommendations. First, imposing organization on performance data stored in memory (i.e. imposing appropriate behavioral schemata) increases accuracy. Second, training interventions that make the congruence between behavioral codes and impressionistic codes clear to raters should reduce bias resulting from impressionistic codes. Finally, performance diaries may result in the use of behavioral codes, in addition to, or in place of impressionistic codes. Research investigating the observational and attentional skills crucial to evaluation accuracy is needed.

Kozlowski and Ford (1991) conducted a laboratory study to investigate the active process of rater information acquisition. The study controlled for the amount of prior information that subjects had about ratees and the time raters took to acquire more information about the ratees. They found that when faced with a ratee showing poor performance, raters searched for more information when it was available. They suggested that raters may either spend extra time to document a low rating or they may be looking for a reason to change their ratings from a low to a high rating.

Hanges, Braverman, and Rentsch (1991) investigated how raters process new information, and found support for a catastrophe model of the effects of prior information on undergraduate students' performance ratings. Some subjects continuously adjusted their ratings over time as new performance data became available, whereas others changed their ratings discontinuously. Participants' attributions differentiated these two change patterns. Discontinuous change was more likely when participants made internal attributions, and continuous change was more likely when participants made external attributions.

Implicit personality theory is another framework that has guided empirical study into the cognitive processes that underlie rating errors. In a laboratory experiment comparing trait and BARS, Krzystofiak, Cardy, and Newman (1988) demonstrated that trait scales are more susceptaible to these implicit theories than are BARS.

Heneman, Greenberger, and Anonyuo (1989) investigated managers' attributions of subordinate performance in a field study. The study found that managers made attributions for effective performance to internal factors (ability & effort) for ingroup subordinates, and to external factors for outgroup subordinates. However, in another field study, Fedor and Rowland (1989) found that the affective relationship between the manager and subordinate was not associated with the direction of attribution made for employee control over performance. Similarly, Dobbins and Russell (1986) found that leaders made similar attributions for poor performance of liked and disliked subordinates, but they were more inclined to punish a disliked subordinate than a liked subordinate.

Duarte, Goodson, and Klich (1991) found that 'ingroup' employees in a telephone company were rated high on a trait scale regardless of their actual performance (e.g. time taken to complete a call) while employees who were in the 'outgroup' were rated relatively accurately. This is because raters have a well-developed categorization schema in terms of strong expectations about the performance of their ingroup members and as a result tend to give them high ratings consistent with their categorization of these people. In contrast, the actual performance of outgroup members is highly salient to supervisors, thus the evaluations tend to be accurate. The extent to which these findings would occur if BOS were used instead of a trait scale has yet to be explored.

Bernardin (1989) investigated attributions made towards self-performance and subordinate performance in a field setting involving middle managers and police sergeants. Managers and police sergeants were found to be more likely to attribute causes for ineffective performance to internal factors (ability and effort) when judging the performance of subordinates than when judging their own performance.

Rater Training

Studies of rating errors (Smither, Reilly, & Buda, 1988; Steiner & Rain, 1989) suggest the need for observation training to reduce both contrast and assimilation effects as well as primacy and recency effects. Training programs need to sensitize raters to the perils of premature judgment. While research is needed to better delineate the intellectual and perceptual skills important in performance appraisal, training programs are needed that can promote the development of these necessary cognitive and perceptual skills. The effect of the ratee's non-job-related behaviors on rater bias suggests the need for training programs that sensitize raters to their implicit steroetypes, and to the forms of impression management that can influence appraisal ratings. Last, there is a clear message from cognitive theorists (e.g. DeNisi & Williams, 1988) that training programs need to communicate to the rater the specific job performance standards on which observations should be based.

For the most part, training programs recognize the need to provide instruction on the behavioral standards that raters should observe and evaluate when formulating their appraisal rating. This is true for both observation training (e.g. Hedge & Kavanagh, 1988) and for frame of reference training (e.g. Athey & McIntyre, 1987).

Hedge and Kavanagh (1988) investigated the effectiveness of response set error training, observation training, and decision training, in a field setting. A reduction in accuracy was found among the raters in the response set error training group; but only the supervisors in the decision-making group showed a significant improvement in accuracy over pre-training scores.

Athey and McIntyre (1987) extended the work in frame of reference training by investigating the underlying theoretical mechanisms that explain its effectiveness. Two theoretical explanations were explored, namely levels of processing theory and social facilitation theory. Levels of processing theory defines memory of training content as a function of the depth of perceptual processing required. In performance appraisal training, raters must develop cognitive associations between rating dimensions and observed behavior. The benefit from frame of reference training is to enhance the pairing process by engaging raters in a relatively deep level of cognitive processing of the training information through the use of behavioral examples and feedback. Social facilitation theory suggests that memory is affected by the size of the training group in that the presence of others increases arousal and this in turn affects learning (Athey & McIntyre, 1987). Using a 3 × 3 factorial design they investigated the effect of three training methods (no information, information only, information and frame of reference training) and three group sizes (1, 6, and 12 members) on the accuracy of performance ratings. Ratings were done with a BOS, and target scores were based on the ratings of expert judges. The outcome measures included retention of training information, retention of pre-training information, rating accuracy (correlation and distance accuracy) and rating errors (halo, and leniency-severity). The study confirmed the effectiveness of frame of reference training over no information and information-only training. The authors concluded that levels of processing theory provides a better explanation for the effectiveness of this training than does social facilitation theory.

Conclusion

It has been shown repeatedly (Latham, 1986) that an employee's age, race, or sex has at most a marginal effect on a performance evaluation. What is needed is a research shift to investigations of organizational experiences that affect career outcomes of women and minorities. Impression management by employees is another avenue that should be explored (Huber, Latham, & Locke, 1989), especially in light of the growing research interest in organizational citizenship behavior (e.g. Karambayya, 1989; Organ, 1988) and its explanatory value regarding the difference between objective measures of performance and managerial appraisals of the employee's performance.

Rater characteristics such as past experience, gender, age, intelligence, cognitive abilities, and mood can affect a rater's accuracy. An avenue for further study is to examine to what extent rater training can compensate for the effects of gender, bias, intellect, and other cognitive ability differences which exist among raters. To reduce the potential biasing effect of mood on performance appraisal, it would appear advisable to conduct numerous appraisals, and to use the aggregate scores in performance reviews (Sinclair, 1988).

When job performance standards are clearly established through a job analysis, and when these are communicated to raters through a training program, there is less reliance on implicit categorization processes in performance appraisal. Providing raters with behavioral scales that are representative of the behaviors defined through the job analysis also improves rater accuracy by restructuring the processing task during memory-based judgments (DeNisi & Williams, 1988). Although an earlier study (Cardy, Bernardin, Abbott, Senderak, & Taylor, 1987) did not support this hypothesis, the experimental manipulation was weak in that there was limited exposure time to the BARS and there was no rater training.

Training programs are responding to the findings of cognitive theorists by focusing training on the development of appropriate behavioral observation sets. Decision-making training applies the principles of cognitive information processing to the performance appraisal situation (Hedge & Kavanagh, 1988). This would appear to be a fruitful area for future investigation, but research is still required to compare the effectiveness of decision-making training to observation training, as this training was first conceptualized by Latham, Wexley, and Pursell (1975), and to frame of reference training as it was conceptualized by Bernardin and Buckley (1981). Future research should also investigate the combined effectiveness of observation training and training in decision making.

Earlier (Latham, 1986) it has been argued that a parsimonious explanation for rater inaccuracy would be found in a study of raters' motives. Support for the conclusion is evident in a laboratory study by Greenberg (1991) who found that inflated ratings are due to a self-serving bias, mainly the desire to appear successful to oneself. Specifically, appraisers gave higher ratings of performance quantity and quality to people whom they had counseled about their work than to those with whom they had only social contact or no contact at all. This was true regardless of whether the appraiser was successful, unsuccessful, or had no effect on the worker's performance. Moreover, this self-serving bias was found only for rating dimensions that were discussed by the raters with their employees. Greenberg concluded that the developmental and evaluation functions of a supervisor's job need to be separated. This issue is addressed below. He also concluded that managers will not be motivated to evaluate their subordinates accurately unless they are explicitly rewarded for doing so. Research on this topic may result in the breakthroughs on rater accuracy that have eluded studies on cognitive processes thus far.

EMPLOYEE COACHING AND DEVELOPMENT

The primary purpose of performance appraisal is to coach and counsel people in a way that will lead to continuous improvement on the part of the employee (Latham & Wexley, in press). Yet performance reviews are frequently eschewed because of their adverse consequences such as negative feelings toward the appraiser (Meyer, 1991), or because they are perceived by supervisors as having outcomes that are neither positive nor negative for either them or their subordinates, regardless of whether the appraisal itself is positive or negative (Napier & Latham, 1986). To correct this situation, research has focused on the structure and the content of the appraisal.

Structural Characteristics

Research on structure has examined the frequency with which appraisals should be conducted as well as their evaluative and developmental aspects. With regard to frequency, a survey by Apt and Watkins (1989) found that performance reviews which occurred intermittently throughout the year resulted in employees feeling that they understood how to meet their job assignments, and that the appraisal system was fair. Fedor and Buckley (1988) argued that performance appraisals should be based on task cycles rather than on a calendar basis such as quarterly or annually. Nathan, Mohrman, and Milliman (1991) found that only a small amount of improvement in performance can be attributed to a once-a-year appraisal. Systematic research with proper experimental controls is still needed in this area.

The debate initiated by Meyer, Kay and French (1965) on the need to separate the evaluative from the developmental aspects of the appraisal interview continues a quarter of a century later. In support of this argument, Harackiewicz and Larson (1986) found that supervisors in a laboratory experiment provided less information about the person's competence when their role included administering rewards to the subordinate. And as noted above, Greenberg (1991) found that behavior which is coached receives an inflated evaluation regardless of actual performance. A survey by Deets and Tyler (1986) showed that an appraisal system which separated discussion of salary from the performance review was approved by 81% of the respondents.

In contrast, a survey involving multiple organizations (Prince & Lawler, 1986) found that including a discussion of salary in the performance review was particularly important to employees at lower hierarchical levels because it communicated the specific aspects of the person's performance that were valued. Moreover, the inclusion of salary in the discussion enhanced the information content of the appraisal by forcing managers to provide specific feedback to support the evaluation. Similarly, Dorfman, Stephan, and Loveland (1986), in a longitudinal study, showed that when prior performance is controlled, discussions of pay and advancement correlated significantly with employee satisfaction with the appraisal process.

Tying pay to performance would appear to be a necessary factor for increasing outcome expectancies of those who give and receive appraisals. Tying pay to performance accuracy has yet to be studied to determine its effect on those who give appraisals. Making appraisers comfortable in conducting the appraisal would appear to be especially important, hence the need to examine the content of an appraisal and ways to enhance the appraiser's credibility.

Appraisal Content

In a field study of nurses in Scotland, Anderson and Barnett (1987) found that when emphasis in the appraisal was placed on employee performance rather than personality, subordinates felt encouraged to improve their performance, and they perceived the appraisal as fair. The latter is especially important in a litigious society.

In a longitudinal study of 10 business units of a multinational corporation, Nathan, Mohrman, and Milliman (1991) found that the use of behavioral criteria as well as a discussion of the person's career correlated with subsequent improvement of the employee's performance. These two variables plus allowing the employee to participate in the appraisal process correlated significantly with subsequent job satisfaction.

The same study revealed that with regard to organizational satisfaction, a well-conducted appraisal compensated for a poor interpersonal relationship between the employee and the appraiser. Conversely, a good interpersonal relationship between a superior and subordinate compensated for a poor appraisal interview.

A laboratory experiment (Fedor, Eder, & Buckley, 1989) showed that the perceived intentions of the appraiser, the amount of personal support provided to the subordinate, and the sign of the feedback had a significant effect on subordinates' desire to improve their performance. For example, subordinates responded more favorably when the supervisor provided specific positive feedback than they did to negative feedback or when they perceived that the intentions of the appraiser were not constructive. As in the Nathan, Mohrman, and Milliman study (1991), this study found an interaction effect between perceived intentions and the sign of the feedback such that outcome discrepancies created by positive versus negative feedback decreased if the perceptions of the appraiser's intentions were that they were not constructive. Baron (1988) found that individuals who received constructive criticism reported higher subsequent self-efficacy than did individuals in a destructive criticism condition.

In a laboratory experiment, Podsakoff and Farh (1989) showed that the credibility of the appraiser influences acceptance of the feedback. Further, the more credible the feedback, the greater its effect on the subject's affective response to it, and the higher the likelihood of setting goals and subsequently improving performance. The reactions to the feedback were mediated by a self-evaluative mechanism. Those people who received negative feedback became more dissatisfied with their performance, set high performance goals, and performed at a higher level than did those who received either positive or no feedback.

In a survey of middle managers, Greenberg (1986) found that (i) the solicitation and use of employee input prior to evaluations, (ii) the use of two-way communication during the appraisal process, (iii) the opportunity to challenge or rebut the appraisal, (iv) the perceived degree of the appraiser's familiarity with the ratee's work, and (v) the consistent application of appraisal standards were the primary determinants of perceived fair performance evaluations. He also found (Greenberg, 1987a) that feedback from appraisers who kept observational diaries was perceived as more fair than feedback from appraisers who did not keep diaries because the existence of a diary was perceived as evidence of the rater's familiarity with the employee's work. In addition, perceptions of rating fairness were increased to the extent that the rater demonstrated sensitivity to the employee's self-image (Greenberg, 1988). Perceptions of fairness were not related to the actual rating received. In a litigious society, Greenberg's research on procedural and interactional justice may provide theoretical and practical insights to performance appraisal, especially with regard to taking into account the employee's perceived rights. In this regard, Leung and Li's (1990) findings suggested that if a superior intends to give a subordinate a negative evaluation, it would be beneficial to involve the person in the evaluation process. Merely increasing participation in the decision-making process, however, does not always enhance employee perceptions of fairness. It is also necessary to show people who will be affected by a negative appraisal that their views were considered before the final appraisal was made, and that the decision maker acted in good faith.

The effect that supervisory expectations alone can have on employee performance has been examined by Eden (1988) and his colleagues. For example, Eden and Shami (1982) found that trainees who were designated as having high command potential performed significantly higher than a control group on an objective achievement test. Eden and Ravid (1982) replicated these results and provided further insight into the nature of the Pygmalion effect. Specifically, these authors tested the influence of the Pygmalion effect when manipulated independently on the trainee as well as the trainer. Trainees in clerical courses in the Israeli Defense Force were randomly assigned to one of three conditions where the instructors were informed that trainees had either high potential for success, or regular potential for success, or that insufficient information prevented prediction of trainee success. The trainees in the insufficient information condition were then, unbeknown to the trainers, randomly assigned to two groups. Specifically, one group was told that they had high potential for success, while the other was told they had regular potential for success. Success in training was subsequently measured by instructor performance appraisal ratings as well as by an objective performance examination.

The results of this study demonstrated highly significant Pygmalion effects for both the instructor-expectancy and trainee-expectancy conditions. Instructor expectancy accounted for 52% of the variance in mean performance ratings; trainee expectancy (i.e. self-efficacy) accounted for 35% of the variance. As for the objective performance exam, instructor expectancy accounted for 27% of the variance in scores; trainee-expectancy accounted for 30% of the variance. Interestingly, these results persisted despite a change midway through the training course to instructors who were unaware of the Pygmalion manipulation. Thus, the effects of the initial expectancy induction 'carried over' to the relief instructors whose expectations had not been experimentally manipulated.

The results of this research demonstrated the powerful effect of supervisory beliefs alone on subordinates' beliefs and behavior. Supervisors who have high expectations of these people can communicate these expectations in a myriad of ways (e.g. attention, verbal persuasion). An employee who believes that others think highly of his or her capabilities develops a strong sense of self-efficacy and thus exhibits high performance.

SUMMARY IMPRESSIONS

As noted at the outset of this paper, it has been estimated that more than 90% of organizations in North America use some kind of performance evaluation system; however, fewer than 20% of these appraisals are conducted effectively (Longenecker & Gioia, 1988). What positive impressions stand out after reviewing the literature on performance appraisal from 1986–1991? And what recurring issues, problems, weaknesses and omissions are evident?

The most positive impression is that theories now exist to guide researchers in their search for ways to vastly improve the ability of employers and employees to use performance appraisal as a means to significantly increase the productivity of an organization's human resources. In a litigious society, Greenberg's theories of interactional and distributive justice suggest ways that employee terminations can be accomplished with 'class'. Despite the intriguing essay on punishment in organizations by Arvey and Ivancevich (1980) a decade ago, there is still little or no empirically conducted research on employee terminations. Viewing termination primarily from a psychological rather than a legal perspective may do much to lower both the organization's and the employee's costs in this area.

The inclusion of user reactions as a primary consideration in evaluating the appraisal instrument is consistent with Lawler's (1986) theory of high-involvement organizations. Similarly, the research on self-, peer, and subordinate appraisals can be guided by this work.

In this regard, it is interesting to note the serious challenge to the very use of performance appraisal posed by the engineer W. Edward Deming (1986). He has argued forcefully that performance appraisal is one of the seven deadly sins afflicting North American managers because it inappropriately attributes variation in performance to the individual employee rather than to problems with the system created by managers. The inappropriate assignment of variation in production to an individual employee rather than to the system leads managers to focus on wrong responses to production shortcomings, and concomitantly to create morale problems within the workforce. A shift from outcome measures to behavioral criteria as the basis for an appraisal, and the use of appraisal sources other than, or in addition to, the supervisor should provide dispensation for this sin. Research is needed to test this hypothesis.

Four areas remain troublesome. First, one has to question the payout relative to the cost and effort expended by organizational psychologists and their colleagues on cognitive processes. How much of the error variance in rating accuracy can now be removed as a result of the voluminous work in this area that has been conducted over the past quarter of a century? It is time to shift the research focus to other cognitive theories such as Bandura's (1986) self-efficacy and his concomitant work on outcome expectancies, and Greenberg's (1987b) work on due process. Ways need to be found to increase raters' conviction that they cannot only conduct appraisals accurately, but that the outcome of doing so will be seen as fair. The theory exists to guide this research. Parenthetically, it is interesting to note that no studies could be found that have tested N.R.F. Maier's (1958) seminal prescriptions for tell and sell, tell and listen, or problem-solving approaches to conducting formal performance appraisals.

In the introduction to this chapter, the research shift from psychometric issues to user reactions to appraisal instruments was noted. A similar shift is needed from the relative overemphasis on rater accuracy to that of ratee perceptions of fairness. As was the case in the previous literature review (Latham, 1986), a balance needs to be restored between the current emphasis on the appraisal system (e.g. instruments, psychometrics, accuracy) and the underemphasis on the appraisal process (e.g. coaching and developing people). As can be seen from the myriad of purposes for performance appraisal listed in this chapter's introduction, it would be difficult to enhance, let alone sustain employee motivation if appraisals were inaccurate or invalid. But it would be equally difficult, if not more so, to do this if appraisals were perceived by the workforce as unfair. Attention to issues involving organizational justice (Greenberg, 1987b) should not only increase perceptions of fairness, and hence facilitate coaching and developing of employees but it should also reduce involvement in legal issues that surround the appraisal system and process.

A second troublesome area is the recurring debate for a quarter of a century on the need to separate the evaluative from the developmental aspects of a formal performance appraisal. As Campbell and Stanley argued years ago:

> Whenever competent scientists advocate strongly divergent points of view, it seems likely on a priori grounds that both have observed something valid about the natural situation, and that both represent a part of the truth. The stronger the controversy, the more likely this is. (1963: p. 3)

It is our belief that this debate is misplaced. The focus should be on the value of ongoing informal feedback versus an annual or even a quarterly formal appraisal on subsequent job performance and satisfaction. The formal appraisal should serve as no more than a summarization of the ongoing feedback that has been given, and as an occasion for goal setting and goal commitment. It is our hypothesis that the formal appraisal is more effective if it includes both the evaluative and the developmental components than if it includes only one of these two components if and only if, it is preceded by informal ongoing feedback. And again, self-efficacy theory, along with Greenberg's research on interactional and distributive justice, provides the framework for developing the training appraisers need in this area.

Our third concern is the omission of context and system in appraisal research. The act of appraisal as reflected in the overwhelming majority of research operates in a relative vacuum, far removed from the rich contextual fabric and reality of organizational life. By and large, researchers have focused on methodology and technique, on one or several ratee-dependent behaviors or perceptions and/or individual characteristics of either rater or ratee (age, gender, race, confidence, inner directedness, and intelligence). Generally absent is consideration of the organizational context in which the appraisal process is imbedded.

That the systematic inattention to organizational contextual factors may be contributing to the low reported effective utilization of performance appraisal is the basis of intriguing empirical studies designed by Carson, Cardy, and Dobbins (1991). The results of their first study support Deming in that they showed that supervisors believe that variation in subordinate performance is produced almost exclusively by characteristics of the subordinates themselves. Subordinates, on the other hand, believe that much of the variation in their performance is produced by system level factors. In their second study, raters held subordinates accountable for observed variation despite available information concerning system constraints. These findings suggest that raters do not typically attend to and separate system variance in performance ratings. This has implications for the design and implementation of appraisal systems and the managerial actions and practices linked to appraisal outcomes. Research attention must be devoted to system or context factors, and training must be developed to teach managers how to deal with these contextual factors.

Our fourth and final concern is the almost universal neglect of new work designs in the examination of performance appraisal. The jobs being described appear in relative isolation of one another as if performance appraisal were the pooled performance of individual isolated workers. The organizational behavior literature is replete with studies of socio-technical systems, semi-autonomous work groups, project and product teams in matrix organizations and numerous other examples where the design of work involves a team of workers, managers, or professionals such as consultant teams or health care professionals, each involving interdependent job activities. Yet the research and literature on performance appraisal provides no recognition of the many interactive group designs of work.

ACKNOWLEDGEMENTS

The authors wish to thank Walter Borman for his critical comments on a draft of this chapter. Support for this article was provided by a grant from the Social Sciences and Humanities Research Council of Canada to the first author.

REFERENCES

Ackerman v. Western Electric Co., Inc. (1988) 860 F2d 1514.

Amiel, B. (1991, May) Through the lenses of gender and ethnicity. *Maclean's*, p. 15.

Anderson, G. C., & Barnett, J. G. (1987) Characteristics of effective appraisal interviews. *Personnel Review*, **16**, 18–25.

Apt, K. E., & Watkins, D. W. (1989) What one laboratory has learned about performance appraisal. *Research Technical Management*, July–August, 22–28.

Arvey, R. D., & Ivancevich, J. M. (1980) Punishment in organizations: A review, propositions, and research suggestions. *Academy of Management Review*, **5**, 123–132.

Ashford, S. (1989) Self assessments in organizations: A literature review and integration model. *Research in Organizational Behavior*, **11**, 33–174.

Athey, T. R., & McIntyre, R. M. (1987) Effect of rater training on rater accuracy: Levels-of-processing theory and social facilitation theory perspectives. *Journal of Applied Psychology*, **72**, 567–572.

Bandura, A. (1986) *Social Foundations of Thought and Action*. Englewood Cliffs, NJ: Prentice-Hall.

Barnes-Farrell, J. L., L'Heureux-Barrett, T. J., & Conway, J. M. (1991) Impact of gender related job features on the accurate evaluation of performance information. *Organizational Behavior & Human Decision Processes*, **48**, 23–35.

Baron, R. A. (1988) Negative effects of destructive criticism: Impact on conflict, self-efficacy, and task performance. *Journal of Psychology*, **73**, 199–207.

Barrett, G. V., & Kernan, M. C. (1987) Performance appraisal and terminations: A review of court decisions since *Brito v. Zia* with implications for personnel practices. *Personnel Psychology*, **40**, 489–501.

Bartlett, C. J. (1983) What's the difference between valid and invalid halo? Forced choice measurement. *Journal of Applied Psychology*, **68**, 218–226.

Bartlett, F. C. (1932) *Remembering*. Cambridge: Cambridge University Press.

Benson, P. G., Buckley, M. R., & Hall, S. (1988) The impact of rating scale format on rater accuracy: An evaluation of the mixed standard scale. *Journal of Management*, **14**, 415–423.

Bernardin, H. J. (1989) Increasing the accuracy of performance measurement: A proposed solution to erroneous attributions. *Human Resource Planning*, **12**, 239–249.

Bernardin, H. J., & Beatty, R. W. (1987) Can subordinate appraisals enhance managerial productivity? *Sloan Management Review*, Summer, 63–73.

Bernardin, H. J., & Buckley, M. R. (1981) Strategies in rater training. *Academy of Management Review*, **6**, 205–212.

Bersoff, D. N. (1988) Should subjective employment devices be scrutinized?—It's elementary, my dear Ms Watson. *American Psychologist*, **43**, 1016–1018.

Blumrosen, A. W. (1989) The 1989 Supreme Court ruling concerning employment discrimination and affirmative action: A minefield for employers and a gold mine for their lawyers. *Employee Relations Law Journal*, **15**, 175–186.

Borman, W. C. (1979) Individiual differences correlates of accuracy in evaluating others' performance effectiveness. *Applied Psychological Measurement*, **3**, 103–115.

Borman, W. C., & Hallam, G. L. (1991) Observation accuracy for assessors of work-sample performance: Consistency across task and individual-differences correlates. *Journal of Applied Psychology*, **76**, 11–18.

Bownas, D. A., & Bernardin, H. J. (1991) Suppressing illusory halo with forced-choice items. *Journal of Applied Psychology*, **76**, 592–594.

Bretz, R. D. Jr., & Milkovich, G. T. (1989) Performance appraisal in large organizations: Practice and research implications. (Working paper No. 89-17), Ithaca, NY: Cornell University, Center for Advanced Human Resource Studies (CAHRS).

Burchett, S. R., & DeMeuse, K. P. (1985) Performance appraisal and the law. *Personnel*, **62**, 29–37.

Campbell, D. J., & Lee, C. (1988) Self-appraisal in performance evaluation: Development versus evaluation. *Academy of Management Journal*, **13**, 302–314.

Campbell, D. T., & Stanley, J. C. (1963) Experimental and quasi-experimental designs for research. Chicago: Rand McNally.

Cardy, R. L., Bernardin, H. J., Abbott, J. G., Senderak, M. P., & Taylor, K. (1987) The effects of individual performance schemata and dimension familiarization on rating accuracy. *Journal of Occupational Psychology*, **60**, 197–205.

Cardy, R. L., & Dobbins, G. H. (1986) Affect and appraisal accuracy: Liking as an integral dimension in evaluating performance. *Journal of Applied Psychology*, **71**, 672–678.

Carson, K. P., Cardy, R. L., & Dobbins, G. H. (1991) Performance appraisal as effective management or deadly management disease. *Group and Organizational Studies*, **16**, 143–159.

Cleveland, J. N., Murphy, K. R., & Williams, R. E. (1989) Multiple uses of performance appraisal: Prevalence and correlates. *Journal of Applied Psychology*, **74**, 130–135.

Cygnar v. Chicago (1989) 865 U.S.F.2d 827.

Czajka, J. M., & DeNisi, A. S. (1988) Effects of emotional disability and clear performance standards on performance ratings. *Academy of Management Journal*, **31**, 394–404.

Daley, D. M. (1987) Performance appraisal and the creation of training and development expectations: A weak link in MBO-based appraisal systems. *Review of Public Personnel Administration*, **8**, 1–10.

Deets, N. R., & Tyler, D. T. (1986) How Xerox improved its perforamnce appraisals. *Personnel Journal*, April, 50–52.

DeMeuse, K. P. (1987) A review of the effects of non-verbal cues on the performance appraisal process. *Journal of Occupational Psychology*, **60**, 207–226.

Deming, W. E. (1982) Quality, productivity, and competitive position. Cambridge, MA: Massachusetts Institute of Technology.

Deming, W. E. (1986) Out of the crisis. Cambridge, MA: Massachusetts Institute of Technology.

DeNisi, A. S., Cafferty, T. A., & Meglino, B. M. (1984) A cognitive view of the performance appraisal process: A model and research propositions. *Organizational Behavior and Human Perforamnce*, **33**, 360–396.

DeNisi, A. S., Robbins, T., & Cafferty, T. P. (1989) Organization of information used for performance appraisals: Role of diary-keeping. *Journal of Applied Psychology*, **74**, 124–129.

DeNisi, A. S., & Williams, K. (1988) Cognitive approaches to performance appraisal. In G. Ferris, & K. Rowland (Eds), *Research in Personnel and Human Resource Management* (pp. 47–93). Greenwich, CT: JAI Press.

Dickinson, T. L., & Glebocki, G. G. (1990) Modification in the format of the mixed standard scale. *Organizational Behavior and Human Decision Processes*, **47**, 124–137.

Dickinson, T. L., & Zellinger, P. M. (1980) A comparison of the behaviorally anchored rating and mixed standard scale formats. *Journal of Applied Psychology*, **65**, 147–154.

Dobbins, G. H., & Russell, J. M. (1986) The biasing effects of subordinate likableness on leaders' responses to poor performers: A laboratory and a field study. *Personnel Psychology*, **39**, 759–777.

Dorfman, P. W., Stephan, W. G., & Loveland, J. (1986) Performance appraisal behaviors: Supervisors' perceptions and subordinate reactions. *Personnel Psychology*, **39**, 579–595.

Dreher, G. F., & Sackett, P. R. (Eds). (1983) *Perspectives on Employee Staffing and Selection*. Homewood, Ill.: Irwin.

Duarte, N. T., Goodson, J. R., & Klich, N. R. (1991) When time heals all ratings: The interactive effects of time on the supervisor-subordinate relationship on the accuracy of the performance appraisal. In J. L. Wall, & L. R. Jauch (eds), *Academy of Management Best Paper Proceedings* (pp. 262–266).

Dwyer, P. (1989, July) The blow to affirmative action may not hurt that much. *Business Week*, pp. 61–63.

Eden, D. (1988) Pygmalion, goal setting, and expectancy: Compatible ways to boost productivity. *Academy of Management Review*, **13**, 639–653.

Eden, D., & Ravid, G. (1982) Pygmalion v. self expectancies: Effects of instructor and self expectancy on trainee performance. *Organizational Behavior and Human Performance*, **30**, 351–364.

Eden, D., & Shami, A. B. (1982) Pygmalion goes to boot camp: Expectancy, leadership, and trainee performance. *Journal of Applied Psychology*, **67**, 194–199.

Eder, R. W., & Fedor, D. B. (1989) Priming performance self-evaluations: Moderating effects of rating purpose and judgment confidence. *Organizational Behavior & Human Decision Processes*, **44**, 474–493.

Edwards, M. R. (1990) A joint effort leads to accurate appraisals. *Personnel Journal*, **69**, 122–128.

Farh, J., Cannella, A. Jr, & Bedeian, A. (1991) The impact of purpose on rating quality and user acceptance. *Group and Organizational Studies*, **16**, 367–386.

Farh, J. L., & Dobbins, G. H. (1989a) Effects of self-esteem on leniency bias in self-reports of performance: A structural equation model analysis. *Personnel Psychology*, **42**, 835–850.

Farh, J. L., & Dobbins, G. H. (1989b) Effects of comparative performance information on the accuracy of self-ratings & agreement between self- & supervisor ratings. *Journal of Applied Psychology*, **74**, 606–610.

Fahr, J. L., Dobbins, G. H., & Cheng, B. S. (1991) Cultural relativity in action: A comparison of self-ratings made by Chinese and US workers. *Personnel Psychology*, **44**, 129–145.

Farh, J. L., & Werbel, J. D. (1986) Effects of purpose of the appraisal and expectation of validation on self-appraisal leniency. *Journal of Applied Psychology*, **71**, 527–529.

Farh, J. L., Werbel, J. D., & Bedeian, A. (1988) An empirical investigation of self-appraisal-based performance evaluation. *Personnel Psychology*, **41**, 141–156.

Fedor, D. B., & Buckley, M. R. (1988) Issues surrounding the need for more frequent monitoring of individual performance in organizations. *Public Personnel Management*, **17**, 435–442.

Fedor, D. B., Eder, R. W., & Buckley, M. R. (1989) The contributory effects of supervisor intentions on subordinate feedback responses. *Organizational Behavior and Human Decision Processes*, **44**, 396–414.

Fedor, D. B., & Rowland, K. M. (1989) Investigating supervisor attributions of subordinate performance. *Journal of Management*, **15**, 405–416.

Flanagan, J. C. (1954) The critical incident technique. *Psychological Bulletin*, **51**, 327–358.

Fleishman, E. A., & Mumford, M. D. (1991) Evaluation classifications of job behavior: A construct validation of the ability requirement scales. *Personnel Psychology*, **44**, 523–575.

Fox, S., Ben-Nahum, Z., & Yinon, Y. (1989) Perceived similarity and accuracy of peer ratings. *Journal of Applied Psychology*, **74**, 781–786.

Fox, S., Bizman, A. A., & Hoffman, M. (1989) The halo effect: It really isn't unitary: A rejoinder to Nathan (1986). *Journal of Occupational Psychology*, **62**, 183–188.

Fox, S., & Dinur, Y. (1988) Validity of self-assessment: A field evaluation. *Personnel Psychology*, **41**, 581–592.

Goddard, R. W. (1989) Is your appraisal system headed for court? *Personnel Journal*, **68**, 114–118.

Gomez-Mejia, L. R. (1988) Evaluating employee performance: Does the appraisal instrument make a difference? *Journal of Organizational Behavior Management*, **9**, 155–172.

Greenberg, J. (1986) Determinants of perceived fairness of performance evaluations. *Journal of Applied Psychology*, **71**, 340–342.

Greenberg, J. (1987a) Using diaries to promote procedural justice in performance appraisal. *Social Justice Research*, **1**, 219–234.

Greenberg, J. (1987b) A taxonomy of organizational justice theories. *Academy of Management Review*, **1**, 9–22.

Greenberg, J. (1988) Using explanations to manage impressions of performance appraisal fairness. In J. R. Greenberg, & R. Bies (Chairs), *Communicating Fairness in Organizations*. Symposium presented at the meeting of the Academy of Management, Anaheim, CA.

Greenberg, J. (1991) Motivation to inflate performance ratings: Perceptual bias or response bias? *Motivation and Emotion*, **15**, 81–97.

Greenhaus, J. H., Parasuraman, S., & Wormley, W. M. (1990) Effects of race on organizational experience, job performance evaluations, and career outcomes. *Academy of Management Journal*, **33**, 64–86.

Griffeth, R. W., & Bedeian, A. G. (1989) Employee performance evaluations: Effects of ratee age, rater age, and ratee gender. *Journal of Organizational Behavior*, **10**, 83–90.

Griggs v. *Duke Power Co.* (1971) 401 U.S. 424.

Hanges, P. J., Braverman, E. P., & Rentsch, J. R. (1991) Changes in raters' perceptions of subordinates: A catastrophe model. *Journal of Applied Psychology*, **76**, 878–888.

Hanges, P. J., Schneider, B., & Niles, K. (1990) Stability of performance: An interactionist perspective. *Journal of Applied Psychology*, **75**, 658–667.

Harackiewicz, J. M., & Larson, J. R., Jr., (1986) Managing motivation: The impact of supervisor feedback on subordinate task interest. *Journal of Personality and Social Psychology*, **51**, 547–556.

Harris, M. M., & Schaubroeck, J. (1988) A meta-analysis of self-supervisor, self-peer, and peer-supervisor ratings. *Personnel Psychology*, **41**, 43–62.

Hedge, J. W., & Kavanagh, M. J. (1988) Improving the accuracy of performance evaluations: Comparison of three methods of performance appraiser training. *Journal of Applied Psychology*, **73**, 68–73.

Heneman, R. L., Greenberger, D. B., & Anonyuo, C. (1989) Attributions & exchanges: The effects of interpersonal factors on the diagnosis of employee performance. *Academy of Management Journal*, **32**, 466–476.

Hoffman, C. C., Nathan, B. R., & Holden, L. M. (1991) A comparison of validation criteria: Objectives versus subjective performance measures and self- versus supervisor ratings. *Personnel Psychology*, **44**, 601–619.

Hogan, E. A. (1987) Effects of prior expectations on performance ratings: A longitudinal study. *Academy of Management Journal*, **30**, 354–368.

Huber, V., Latham, G. P., & Locke, E. A. (1989) The management of impressions through goal setting. In R. A. Giacalone and P. Rosenfeld (eds), *Impression Management in the Organization* (pp. 169–187). Hillsdale, NJ: Erlbaum.

Huber, V. L., Neale, M. A., & Northcraft, G. B. (1987) Judgment by heuristics: Effects of ratee and rater characteristics and performance standards on performance-related judgments. *Organizational Behavior and Human Decision Processes*, **40**, 149–169.

Hughes, G. L., & Prien, E. P. (1986) An evaluation of alternative scoring methods for the mixed standard scale. *Personnel Psychology*, **39**, 839–847.

Ivancevich, J. M., & Stewart, K. A. (1988) Appraising management talent in acquired organizations: A four-tiered recommendation. *Human Resource Planning*, **12**, 141–154.

Jako, R. A., & Murphy, K. R. (1990) Distributional ratings, judgement decomposition, and their impact on interrater agreement and rating accuracy. *Journal of Applied Psychology*, **75**, 500–505.

Johnson v. *Transportation Agency of Santa Clara County, CA.* (1987) 480 U.S. 616-632.

Kandel, W. (1989) Current developments in employment litigation. *Employee Relations Law Journal*, **15**, 101–113.

Kane, J. S., & Freeman, K. A. (1986) MBO and performance appraisal: A mixture that's not a solution, Part 1. *Personnel*, **63**, 26–36.

Kane, J. S., & Freeman, K. A. (1987) MBO and performance appraisal: A mixture that's not a solution, Part 2. *Personnel*, **64**, 26–32.

Kane, J. S., & Lawler, E. E. (1979) Performance appraisal effectiveness: Its assessment and determinants. *Research in Organizational Behavior*, **1**, 425–478.

Karambayya, R. (1989) Organizational citizenship behavior: Contextual predictors and organizational consequences. Unpublished doctoral dissertation, Northwestern University.

Klass, B. S., & DeNisi, A. S. (1989) Managerial reactions to employee dissent: The impact of grievance activity on performance ratings. *Academy of Management Journal*, **32**, 705–717.

Klimoski, R., & Inks, L. (1990) Accountability forces in performance appraisal. *Organizational Behavior and Human Decision Processes*, **45**, 194–208.

Korman, A. K. (1970) Toward a hypothesis of work behavior. *Journal of Applied Psychology*, **54**, 31–41.

Kozlowski, S. W. J., & Ford, J. K. (1991) Rater information acquisition processes: Tracing the effects of prior knowledge, performance level, search constraint, and memory demand. *Organizational Behavior and Human Decision Processes*, **49**, 282–301.

Kozlowski, S. W. J., & Kirsch, M. P. (1987) The systematic distortion hypothesis, halo, & accuracy: An individual-level analysis. *Journal of Applied Psychology*, **72**, 252–261.

Kraiger, K., & Ford, J. K. (1985) A meta-analysis of ratee race effects in performance ratings. *Journal of Applied Psychology*, **70**, 56–65.

Kremer, J. F. (1990) Construct validity of multiple measures in teaching, research and service and reliability of peer ratings. *Journal of Educational Psychology*, **82**, 213–218.

Krzystofiak, F., Cardy, R., & Newman, J. (1988) Implicit personality & performance appraisal: The influence of trait inferences on evaluations of behavior. *Journal of Applied Psychology*, **73**, 515–521.

Lance, C. E., Woehr, D. J., & Fiscaro, S. A. (1991) Cognitive categorization processes in performance evaluation: Confirmatory tests of two models. *Journal of Organizational Behavior*, **12**, 1–20.

Landy, F. J., & Vasey, J. (1991) Job analysis: The composition of SME samples. *Personnel Psychology*, **44**, 27–50.

Lane, J., & Herriot, P. (1990) Self-ratings, supervisor ratings, positions, & performance. *Journal of Occupational Psychology*, **63**, 77–88.

Latham, G. P. (1986) Job performance and appraisal. In C. Cooper & I. Robertson (eds), *Review of Industrial and Organizational Psychology* (pp. 117–155). Chichester, UK: Wiley.

Latham, G. P., & Wexley, K. N. (in press) *Increasing Productivity through Performance Appraisal*. Reading, MA.: Addison-Wesley.

Latham, G. P., Wexley, K. N., & Pursell, E. D. (1975) Training managers to minimize rating errors in the observation of behavior. *Journal of Applied Psychology*, **60**, 550–555.

Laumeyer, J., & Beebe, T. (1988) Employees and their appraisal. *Personnel Administrator*, **33**, 76–80.

Lawler, E. E. (1967) The multitrait-multimethod approach to measuring managerial job performance. *Journal of Applied Psychology*, **51**, 369–381.

Lawler, E. E. (1986) *High Involvement Management*. San Francisco, CA: Jossey-Bass.

Lawler, E. E., & Mohrman, S. A. (1989) With HR help, all managers can practice high involvement management. *Personnel*, **66**, 26–31.

Lawler, T. G. (1988) The objectives of performance appraisal—or 'Where can we go from here?' *Nursing Management*, **19**, 82–88.

Lawrie, J. W. (1989) Your performance: Appraise it yourself! *Personnel*, **66**, 21–23.

Leung, K., & Li, W. (1990) Psychological mechanisms of process-control effects. *Journal of Applied Psychology*, **75**, 613–620.

Levinson, D. (1987) Making employee performance evaluations work for you. *Nonprofit World*, **5**, 28–30.

Locher, A. H., & Teel, K. S. (1988) Assessment: Appraisal trends. *Personnel Journal*, September, 139–144.

Locke, E. A., & Latham, G. P. (1990) *A Theory of Goal Setting and Task Performance*. Englewood Cliffs, NJ: Prentice-Hall.

Longenecker, C. O., & Gioia, D. A. (1988) Please appraise me (performance appraisals for executives). *Across the Board*, **25**, 57–60.

Lowman, R. L., & Williams, R. E. (1987) Validity of self-ratings of abilities & competencies. *Journal of Vocational Behavior*, **31**, 1–13.

MacKenzie, S. B., Podaskoff, P. M., & Fetter, R. (1991) Organizational citizenship behavior and objective productivity as determinants of managerial evaluations of salespersons' performance. *Organizational Behavior and Human Decision Processes*, **50**, 123–150.

Maier, N. R. F. (1958) *The Appraisal Interview: Objectives, Methods and Skills*. New York: Wiley.

Mallinger, M. A., & Cummings, T. G. (1986) Improving the value of performance appraisals. *Advanced Management Journal*, **51**, 19–21.

Martin, D. C., Bartol, K. M., & Levine, M. J. (1986) The legal ramifications of performance appraisal. *Employee Relations Law Journal*, **12**, 370–395.

Martin, S. L., & Klimoski, R. J. (1990) Use of verbal protocols to trace cognitions associated with self- and supervisor evaluations of performance. *Organizational Behavior and Human Decision Processes*, **46**, 135–154.

Maurer, T. J., & Alexander, R. A. (1991) Contrast effects in behavioral measurement: An investigation of alternative process explanations. *Journal of Applied Psychology*, **76**, 3–10.

McEvoy, G. M. (1988) Evaluating the boss: Should subordinate appraisals of management be allowed? *Personnel Administrator*, **33**, 115–120.

McEvoy, G. M., & Buller, P. (1987) User acceptance of peer appraisals in an industrial setting. *Personnel Psychology*, **40**, 785–797.

McEvoy, G. M., Buller, P., & Roghaar, S. R. (1988) A jury of one's peers. *Personnel Administrator*, **33**, 94–101.

McEvoy, G. M., & Cascio, W. F. (1989) Cumulative evidence of the relationship between employee age and job performance. *Journal of Applied Psychology*, **74**, 11–17.

McFarlane Shore, L., & Bleicken, L. M. (1991) Effects of supervisor age on rating congruence. *Human Relations*, **44**, 1093–1105.

McFarlane Shore, L., & Thornton, G. C., III. (1986) Effects of gender on self and supervisory ratings. *Academy of Management Journal*, **29**, 115–129.

Metz, E. J. (1989) Designing legally defensible performance appraisal systems. *Training and Development Journal*, **42**, 47–51.

Meyer, H. H. (1991) A solution to the performance appraisal enigma. *Academy of Management Executive*, **5**, 68–75.

Meyer, H. H., Kay, E., & French, J. R. (1965) Split roles in performance appraisal. *Harvard Business Review*, **43**, 123–129.

Miner, J. B. (1988) Development and application of the rated ranking technique in performance appraisal. *Journal of Occupational Psychology*, **61**, 291–305.

Mount, M. K., & Thompson, D. E. (1987) Cognitive categorization and quality of performance ratings. *Journal of Applied Psychology*, **72**, 240–246.

Mullins, C. W., & Kimborough, W. W. (1988) Group composition as a determinant of job analysis outcomes. *Journal of Applied Psychology*, **73**, 657–664.

Murphy, K. R. (1991) Criterion issues in performance appraisal research: Behavioral accuracy versus classification accuracy. *Organizational Behavior and Human Decision Processes*, **50**, 45–50.

Murphy, K. R., & Constans, J. I. (1987) Behavioral anchors as a source of bias in rating. *Journal of Applied Psychology*, **72**, 573–577.

Murphy, K. R., & Jako, R. (1989) Under what conditions are observed intercorrelations greater or smaller than true intercorrelations? *Journal of Applied Psychology*, **74**, 827–830.

Murphy, K. R., & Pardaffy, V. A. (1989) Bias in behaviorally anchored rating scales: Global or scale-specific? *Journal of Applied Psychology*, **74**, 343–346.

Murphy, K. R., & Reynolds, D. H. (1988) Does true halo affect observed halo? *Journal of Applied Psychology*, **73**, 235–238.

Musicante, G. R., Pajer, R. G., & Goldstein, I. L. (1988) Design, implementation and evaluation of a behavioral observation scales-based appraisal system: Performance observation scales. Paper submitted to National Academy of Management Meeting. Anaheim, California.

Napier, N. K., & Latham, G. P. (1986) Outcome expectancies of people who conduct performance appraisals. *Personnel Psychology*, **39**, 827–837.

Nathan, B. R., & Cascio, W. F. (1986) Legal and technical standards for performance assessment. In R. A. Burk (ed.), *Performance Assessment: Methods and Applications* (pp. 1–50). Baltimore, Johns Hopkins University Press.

Nathan, B. R., Mohrman, A. H., Jr, & Milliman, J. (1991) Interpersonal relations as a context for the effects of appraisal interviews on performance and satisfaction: A longitudinal study. *Academy of Management Journal*, **34**, 352–369.

Nathan, B. R., & Tippins, N. (1990) The consequences of halo 'error' in performance ratings: A field study of the moderating effect of halo on test validation results. *Journal of Applied Psychology*, **75**, 290–296.

Nelson-Horchler, J. (1988, September) Performance appraisals. *Industry Week*, pp. 61–63.

Norman, C. A., & Zawacki, R. A. (1991) Team appraisals—team approach. *Personnel Journal*, **70**, 101–104.

Organ, D. W. (1988) *Organizational Citizenship Behavior: The Good Soldier Syndrome*. Lexington MA: D.C. Heath.

Padgett, M. Y., & Ilgen, D. R. (1989) The impact of ratee performance characteristics on rater cognitive processes and alternative measures of rater accuracy. *Organizational Behavior and Human Decision Processes*, **44**, 232–260.

Podsakoff, P. M., & Farh, J. L. (1989) Effects of feedback sign and credibility on goal setting and task performance. *Organizational Behavior and Human Decision Processes*, **44**, 45–67.

Price Waterhouse v. Hopkins (1989) 263 U.S. 321.

Prien, E. P., & Hughes, G. L. (1987) The effect of quality control revisions on mixed standard scale rating errors. *Personnel Psychology*, **40**, 815–823.

Prince, J. B., & Lawler, E. E. (1986) Does salary discussion hurt the developmental performance appraisal? *Organizational Behavior and Human Decision Processes*, **37**, 357–375.

Pulakos, R. D., Schmitt, N., & Ostroff, C. (1986) A warning about the use of a standard deviation across dimensions within ratees to measure halo. *Journal of Applied Psychology*, **71**, 29–32.

Pulakos, R. D., White, L. A., Oppler, S. H., & Borman, W. C. (1989) Examination of race and sex effects on performance ratings. *Journal of Applied Psychology*, **74**, 770–780.

Rand Corporation. (1988) *Annual Report—The Institute for Civil Justice*. Santa Monica, CA: Rand Corp.

Redeker, J. R. (1986) The supreme court on affirmative action: Conflicting opinions. *Personnel*, **63**, 8–14.

Rothstein, H. R. (1990) Interrater reliability of job performance ratings: Growth to asymptote level with increasing opportunity to observe. *Journal of Applied Psychology*, **75**, 322–327.

Rothstein, H. R., & Chooi, M. C. M. (1990) Evaluating the impact of behavioral performance appraisal procedures and feedback: An experimental analysis. Paper presented at the annual meeting of the Academy of Management, San Francisco, August.

Russell, J. E. A., & Rush, M. C. (1987) The effects of sex and marital/parental status on performance evaluations and attributions. *Sex Roles*, **17**, 221–236.

Sackett, P. R., & DuBois, C. L. Z. (1991) Rater-ratee effects on performance evaluation: Challenging meta-analytic conclusion. *Journal of Applied Psychology*, **76**, 873–877.

Sackett, P. R., DuBois, C. L. Z., & Wiggins Noe, A. (1991) Tokenism in performance evaluation: The effects of work group representation on male–female and white–black differences in performance ratings. *Journal of Applied Psychology*, **76**, 263–267.

Sackett, P. R., Zedeck, S., & Fogli, L. (1988) Relations between measures of typical and maximum job performance. *Journal of Applied Psychology*, **73**, 482–486.

Salvemini, N. J. (1988) The effects of rater rewards and prior ratee performance upon rating accuracy: An investigation of the motivational component in performance appraisal. Doctoral dissertation, Stevens Institute of Technology, NJ. *Dissertation Abstracts International*, **48**, 7A-1713.

Schmitt, N., Gooding, R. Z., Noe, R. A., & Kirsch, M. (1984) Meta-analyses of validity studies published between 1964 and 1982 and the investigation of study characteristics. *Personnel Psychology*, **37**, 407–422.

Schoorman, F. D. (1988) Escalation bias in performance appraisals: An unintended consequence of supervisor participation in hiring decisions. *Journal of Applied Psychology*, **73**, 58–62.

Simpson, S., McCarrey, M., & Edwards, H. P. (1987) Relationship of supervisors' sex role stereotypes to performance evaluation of male and female subordinates in non-traditional jobs. *Canadian Journal of Administrative Science*, **4**, 15–30.

Sinclair, R. C. (1988) Mood, categorization breadth, and performance appraisal: The effects of order of information acquisition and affective state on halo, information retrieval, and evaluations. *Organizational Behavior and Human Decision Processes*, **42**, 22–46.

Smither, J. W., Barry, S. R., & Reilly, R. R. (1989) An investigation of the validity of expert true score estimates in appraisal research. *Journal of Applied Psychology*, **74**, 143–151.

Smither, J. W., & Reilly, R. R. (1987) True intercorrelation among job components, time delay in rating, and rater intelligence as determinants of accuracy in performance ratings. *Organizational Behavior and Human Decision Processes*, **40**, 369–391.

Smither, J. W., Reilly, R. R., & Buda, R. (1988) Effect of prior performance information on ratings of present performance: Contrast versus assimilation revisited. *Journal of Applied Psychology*, **73**, 487–496.

Somers, M. J., & Birnbaum, D. (1991) Assessing self-appraisal of job performance as an evaluation device: Are the poor results a function of method or methodology? *Human Relations*, **44**, 1081–1091.

Standards for Educational and Psychological Testing (1985) American Educational Research Association, American Psychological Association (APA) and National Council on Measurement and Education, Washington, DC.

Steiner, D. D., & Rain, J. S. (1989) Immediate and delayed primacy and recency effects in performance evaluation. *Journal of Applied Psychology*, **74**, 136–142.

Sulsky, L. M., & Balzer, W. K. (1988) Meaning and measurement of performance rating accuracy: Some methodological and theoretical concerns. *Journal of Applied Psychology*, **73**, 497–506.

Thorndike, R. L. (1949) *Personnel Selection: Test and Measurement Techniques*. New York: Wiley.

Trotter v. *Chesley Town* (1990) T.L.W. 944-035 (Ontario District Court).

Tsui, A. A., & O'Reilly, C. A., III. (1989) Beyond simple demographic effects: The importance of relational demography in superior–subordinate dyads. *Academy of Management Journal*, **32**, 402–423.

Tsui, A. S., & Barry, B. (1986) Interpersonal affect and rating errors. *Academy of Management Journal*, **29**, 586–599.

Tziner, A., & Kopelman, R. (1988) Effects of rating format on goal-setting dimensions: A field experiment. *Journal of Applied Psychology*, **73**, 323–326.

Tziner, A., & Latham, G. P. (1989) The effects of appraisal instrument, feedback and goal setting on worker satisfaction and commitment. *Journal of Organizational Behavior*, **10**, 145–153.

Vance, R. J., MacCallum, R. C., Coovert, M. D., & Hedge, J. W. (1988) Construct validity of multiple performance measures using confirmatory factor analysis. *Journal of Applied Psychology*, **73**, 74–80.

Waldman, D. A., & Avolio, B. J. (1991) Race effects in performance evaluations: Controlling for ability, education, and experience. *Journal of Applied Psychology*, **76**, 897–901.

Ward's Cove v. *Antonio* (1989) 57 U.S.L.W. 4583.

Watson v. *Fort Worth Bank and Trust Company* (1988) 487 U.S. 108.

Wayne, S. J., & Ferris, G. R. (1990) Influence tactics, affect and exchange quality in supervisor–subordinate interactions: A laboratory experiment and field study. *Journal of Applied Psychology*, **75**, 487–499.

Weiss, D. H. (1988) The legal side of performance appraisals. *Management Solutions*, May, 27–31.

Wexley, K., & Klimoski, R. (1984) Performance appraisal: An update. In K. M. Rowland & G. D. Ferris (eds), *Research in Personnel & Human Resources Management* (pp. 35–79). Greenwich CT: JAI Press.

Wherry, R. J., Sr, & Bartlett, C. J. (1982) The control of bias in ratings: A theory of rating. *Personnel Psychology*, **35**, 521–551.

Wiersma, U., & Latham, G. P. (1986) The practicality of behavioral observation scales, behavioral expectation scales, and trait scales. *Personnel Psychology*, **39**, 619–628.

Wiersma, U., van den Berg, P. & Latham, G. P. (1992) Dutch reactions to behavioral observation expectation, and trait scales. Paper presented at the Third International Conference on Personnel and Human Resources Management. Hertfordshire, England, July.

Williams, K. J., Cafferty, T. P., & DeNisi, A. S. (1990) The effect of performance appraisal salience on recall and ratings. *Organizational Behavior and Human Decision Processes*, **46**, 217–239.

Wygant v. Jackson Board of Education (1986) 476 U.S. 267.

Zedeck, S., & Cascio, W. F. (1984) Psychological issues in personnel decisions. *Annual Review of Psychology*, **35**, 461–518.

Chapter 4

MEASUREMENT ISSUES IN INDUSTRIAL AND ORGANIZATIONAL PSYCHOLOGY

Beryl Hesketh
University of New South Wales, Australia

Expertise in measurement is the single most important skill that distinguishes industrial and organizational psychologists from other human resource and personnel professionals. A distinctive feature of psychological training relates to the development of statistical and measurement skills: measurement applied to human attributes, to situations, and to the resultant interactions between people and situations. The Minnesota Theory of Work Adjustment (Dawis & Lofquist, 1984) provides one way of illustrating the categories of domains to which measurement is applied in work contexts. This model, widely used within the vocational and rehabilitation fields of psychology, offers a framework for other areas of industrial and organizational psychology such as selection, career decision-making, training and ergonomic interventions. Its underlying assumption is that optimizing the fit between individuals and their work environments is good for individuals in terms of satisfaction and well-being and good for employers in terms of productive, effective and safe performance. Measurement is critical to optimizing fit. Even if one questions the classical view of person-environment fit models (see Edwards, 1991), the theory provides a useful framework in which to examine the domains of measurement relevant to industrial and organizational psychology.

The first section of the chapter provides a brief summary of the work adjustment framework, with comments about measurement relevant to tenure, job satisfaction, mental health and well-being. The second section of the chapter deals with general measurement issues and developments in Item Response Theory and generalizability theory, and with applications of Item Response Theory to adaptive testing and the reduction of bias. Applications of generalizability theory are outlined in relation to performance measurement in the third section of the chapter, which also contains a discussion of measurement issues in relation to other components of the work adjustment framework.

International Review of Industrial and Organizational Psychology 1993 Volume 8
Edited by C. L. Cooper and I. T. Robertson. © 1993 John Wiley & Sons Ltd.

MINNESOTA THEORY OF WORK ADJUSTMENT

The Minnesota Theory of Work Adjustment provides a structure for assessing both people and jobs and for evaluating the relationship between people and their work in terms of: (i) satisfaction, mental health and well-being; and (ii) satisfactory and safe performance. By way of introduction, a graphic presentation of the major components of the Work Adjustment Framework is provided in Figure 4.1. Each one of these components is discussed in turn below.

Tenure (Box 1)

The overall effectiveness of work adjustment is manifested in tenure, the length of time individuals keep interacting with their work or other environments (Box 1 in Figure 4.1). At one level tenure provides an opportunity for 'objective' measurement, as there can be little debate about the actual amount of time that someone has been employed. In practice, however,

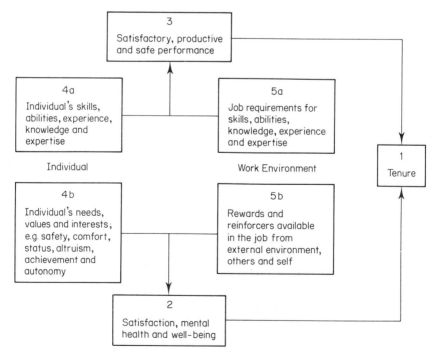

Figure 4.1 A diagrammatic representation of the Minnesota Theory of Work Adjustment

researchers often rely on self-reported tenure (e.g. Taber & Peters, 1991) which may be less objective. Furthermore, even a simple shift to a related concept, namely turnover, illustrates some of the measurement problems in industrial and organizational psychology. Turnover is a dichotomous variable, whereas tenure is not. It is also a dichotomous variable with a very skewed distribution sometimes requiring special analyses (Williams, 1990) and special consideration when making corrections in meta-analyses (Steel, Hendrix & Balogh, 1990; Bass & Ager, 1991; Steel, Shane & Kennedy, 1990).

Turnover as a topic has generated an enormous amount of research highlighting the importance of differentiating types of turnover (see Campion, 1991, for a discussion of five alternative turnover measures) and acknowledging that the consequences of turnover are not necessarily bad, nor equally costly. For example, Darman (1990) provides a framework for assessing the costs of various forms of turnover (e.g. voluntary, firing, promotion) among sales personnel. Unfortunately, personnel systems seldom keep sufficiently accurate records about different types of turnover to satisfy research requirements (Campion, 1991). In order to overcome these problems, many researchers have used turnover intentions as a proxy variable for turnover (Rosin & Korabik, 1991; Shore & Martin, 1989; Shore, Newton & Thornton, 1990; Hesketh, McLachlan & Gardner, 1992; see Steel & Ovalle, 1984, and Steel, Hendrix & Balogh, 1990, for meta-analyses) raising yet another interesting measurement issue, namely that of dealing with intention as an indicator of action. For example, Hinsz and Nelson (1990) tested four models of intention-action in the context of turnover and found the reasoned action model (Ajzen, 1991) to be the best (but see Evans, 1991, for a recent criticism of research on the reasoned action model).

In terms of the Minnesota Theory of Work Adjustment, tenure is a function of the well-being and satisfaction of the person (Box 2) and how effectively and safely they are performing in the environment (Box. 3). The more elaborate models of turnover that have been tested in recent years include variables like commitment and labour market conditions (Campion, 1991; Cotton & Tuttle, 1986; Gerhart, 1990; Hom & Griffeth, 1991), providing an area of research that requires careful thought about the independence of constructs in a model, and the need for multiple indicators of underlying constructs. These are themes that are central to measurement in industrial and organizational psychology.

Satisfaction, Mental Health and Well-being (Box 2)

There is a plethora of measures relevant to this domain of assessment (see for example Warr, 1990). A major measurement issue is the degree to which positive and negative affectivity (a generalized trait-like affective orientation, Watson & Pennebaker, 1989) or neuroticism, one of the 'big five' personality dimensions (Barrick & Mount, 1991), confounds attempts to tease out causal relationships among evaluative measures. The concern relates to the possibility that the trait-like nature of negative affectivity may colour responses to any evaluative questionnaires assessing well-being, mental health, job satisfaction and job perceptions, thereby giving rise to spurious relationships (Robbins, Spence & Clark, 1991; but see also Chen & Spector, 1991, and Levin & Stoker, 1989). The literature on mood congruence, memory and judgement (Forgas, 1990; Rothkopf & Blaney, 1991) may provide insight into the mechanisms by which mood influences responses to measures that may not even have been designed to tap affect.

The current debate in the literature about the stability of job satisfaction (Staw & Ross, 1985; Arvey, Bouchard, Segal, & Abraham, 1989) could benefit from a careful examination of whether the measures are tapping trait or state affective responses. This is a point highlighted by George (1991) who found that state measures of positive mood related to prosocial behaviours at work (which also related to sales performance) whereas trait measures (positive affectivity) did not. Given that individuals with trait-like predispositions, are more likely to experience state-like affective responses, it is difficult to tease out these distinctions, but the George (1991) study indicates the importance of doing so. It may be timely to develop trait and state measures of job satisfaction to accompany the trait and state measures available for anxiety and other affective domains. Longitudinal research such as that of Newton and Keenan (1991) may have benefited from the inclusion of both trait and state measures of generalized affect and possibly job satisfaction. Their longitudinal research involved an examination of change and stability among engineers in their early careers in an attempt to tease out situational and personal influences on affective responses. Newton and Keenan (1991) questioned assumptions of stability based on correlational analyses which do not take into account shifts that may occur in the absolute levels of dispositions, something that was evident in their data. The inclusion of trait and state measures of affect may have helped to clarify which components shifted over time, and whether the stability that was evident was primarily due to the trait-like aspects of negative or positive affectivity.

Satisfactory, Productive and Safe Performance (Box 3)

Satisfactory performance is related to tenure since it affects decisions to promote, retain, refer on, transfer or fire individuals in organizations or institutions. It also determines the likelihood of accidents, an area of renewed interest to industrial and organizational psychologists where methods such as goal setting can intervene to reduce unsafe behaviours (Cooper, Robertson, Duff & Phillips, 1992). As with turnover, the rarity of events renders actual accident statistics a difficult measure for research purposes, with the result that proxy variables are often used, particularly ones that avoid the use of 'all-or-nothing' measures (Cooper, Phillips, Robertson & Duff, 1991). The development of suitable outcome measures to evaluate accident intervention policies and approaches will become increasingly important.

The adequate measurement of performance and productivity (Campbell & Campbell, 1988; Pritchard, Jones, Roth, Stuebing & Ekeberg, 1988) is perhaps the most pressing problem facing industrial and organizational psychologists. For example, the weak link in most selection research is the criterion which, together with current interest in the work group as a unit of analysis (e.g. George, 1990; Guzzo et al., 1986), suggests the need for developments in the domain of performance assessment as it applies to groups. Comments relevant to the clarification of both conceptual and measurement issues relating to measures of performance and group productivity will be reviewed in a later section.

In terms of the Minnesota Theory of Work Adjustment, and selection models generally, satisfactory 'performance' is related to the extent to which the person's performance capabilities and limitations in perceptual, cognitive, physical and social domains match those required by the demands of the immediate, and increasingly, the changing work environment. This simple statement highlights the importance of assessment in industrial and organizational psychology; assessing what people do or do not know; what they can and cannot do and what the environment demands of them. Measurement is at the core of these activities.

The Individual (Box 4)

There are two broad classes of individual difference variables relevant to work adjustment. One set relates to *response capabilities* such as skills, knowledge and abilities (perceptual, cognitive, social and physical), many of which come from education and experience (Box 4a). The term competency assessment is often used in the education literature as an alternative for criterion-referenced testing. It too can provide a basis for assessing what the person can or cannot do (but see Barrett & Depinet, 1991, who argue that competency assessment of this type may be misguided in the context of selection).

The other set of individual difference variables covers the domains of *needs, interests, preferences, values, attitudes and temperamental factors* (Box 4b). Personality assessment, currently receiving increased attention in selection (Barrick & Mount, 1991; Hough, Eaton, Dunnette, Kamp, & McLoy, 1990; Robertson & Kinder, 1992; Tett, Jackson & Rothstein, 1991), probably fits into Box 4b, although some theorists argue that personality embraces intelligence (Hogan, 1982), which is more relevant to the assessment domain in Box 4a. It is possible that the more recently developed personality tests that assess 'work behaviours' measure applicants' social or practical intelligence (Cantor & Kihlstrom, 1987; Sternberg & Wagner, 1989), namely their knowledge about what they should do and be like on a job.

The Environment (Box 5)

There can be little point in understanding and measuring a person's capabilities and their preference orientations without having a detailed understanding of the environmental requirements and opportunities (Dawis, 1987). As is the case in describing the individual, there are two broad classes of environmental difference variables that map onto the individual difference variables. The first of these relates to *job requirements* for skills, knowledge, abilities (perceptual, cognitive, social and physical), education and experiences (Box 5a). The second relates to the *opportunities provided* in the environment as motivational incentives (Box 5b). For measurement to be useful in human resource functions, such as selection, career development and training, the environment must be described in terms similar to those used to assess individuals (Caplan, 1987; Edwards, 1991; Rice, Gentile & McFarlin, 1991; Rice, McFarlin & Bennett, 1989). Even though there is a long history of pleading for a common taxonomy (Owens & Schoenfeldt, 1979; Fleishman, 1982; Fleishman & Mumford, 1991) until very recently job analysis developments have tended to occur independently of developments in the domain of predictor assessment, and performance measurements have seldom related to either. Exceptions can be found in the work of Fleishman and Mumford (1991), the Army Selection and Classification Project (Campbell, 1990) and in that of Robertson and Kinder (1992) who make a conceptual link between performance measures and personality dimensions.

Even when the measurements of the person and the environment are made on common constructs, the issues remain of how best to determine an index of fit (Rounds, Dawis & Lofquist, 1987) and whether or not the concept of fit is redundant (Edwards, 1991; Rice, McFarlin & Bennett, 1989; Rice, Gentile & McFarlin, 1991). One section of this chapter will address developments in this area.

The Minnesota Theory of Work Adjustment has formally stated propositions about the relations among the various components in Figure 4.1, details of which are not relevant to this chapter, but can be obtained from Lofquist and Dawis (1969), Dawis and Lofquist (1984) or Hesketh and Dawis (1991). Since measurement should not be an end in itself (Thissen & Steinberg, 1988; Goldstein & Wood, 1989), one of the benefits of the Theory of Work Adjustment structure is that it prompts a complete review of the categories of factors that are typically assessed. Apart from the literature on Realistic Job Previews (Premack & Wanous, 1985; Wanous, 1989) and the social process view of selection (Herriot, 1988) much of the selection literature ignores the importance of assessments in the lower half of the diagram, while career assessments tend to ignore the upper half (Hesketh & Dawis, 1991; Hesketh, McLachlan & Gardner, 1992).

To summarize, assessment of the major components of the model of work adjustment can highlight where mismatches occur between job requirements and skills possessed, between interests, needs and values and rewards in the job. More directly, assessments are also useful in diagnosing performance and productivity deficits, or mental health and satisfaction difficulties. The major interventions that industrial psychologists have to offer employers to deal with these mismatches cover such areas as training (Andrews, 1991), ergonomic and job redesign (Wall & Davids, 1992; Adams, 1991), goal setting (Locke & Latham, 1990), and organizational career development (Driver, 1988). All of these 'interventions' are dependent upon sound measurement and assessment for initial diagnostic work needed to plan the appropriate interventions. Measurement is also an integral part of the evaluation of these interventions. Clearly measurement is critical to much of what industrial and organizational psychologists do.

GENERAL MEASUREMENT ISSUES

According to Ghiselli, Campbell and Zedeck (1981) the main reason for measurement in psychology is to describe individual differences. If these measurements are qualitative and categorical it is called classification, but where continuous scales are used it is called measurement. Determining the usefulness of quantitative scales gives rise to topics such as distributions, standardizing, correlation, regression, composites (differential weighting), classical reliability theory, validity, and more recently, generalizability theory (Cronbach, Gleser, Nanda & Rajaratnam, 1972; Shavelson, Webb & Rowley, 1989) and Item Response Theory (Hambleton, 1983; Hambleton & Swaminathan, 1985; McKinley, 1989).

Constructs and Measures, or Latent and Measured Variables

Measurement involves the use of numbers or values to provide quantitative descriptions of individual differences (or differences in environments). Variables are those characteristics or properties on which individuals or jobs differ. When the variable under examination is abstract, as is often the case in industrial and organizational psychology, it tends to be referred to as a construct. More recently, with the increased use of latent trait analyses, a related distinction is drawn between measured and latent variables. A latent variable is similar to the construct, whereas the measured component of the variable provides the link with operations or behaviours.

Measurement problems increase the further removed constructs become from the level of measurement (Schuler & Gulden, 1991). This is no doubt one of the reasons for the difficulties that are encountered in applying abstract personality dimensions to work contexts (Baker & Jackson, 1991). The more specific behavioural measures appear more successful (Robertson & Kinder, 1992). It is worth noting, however, the long tradition of better reliabilities for higher order personality constructs such as those identified in the 'big five' (Barrick and Mount, 1991).

Although it may be possible for every measured variable to have an associated latent variable, in practice this is often not sensible, with increased agreement about the need for multiple indicators or measured variables to explicate the latent underlying construct (Lawrence, 1989). Retaining the distinction between constructs and their measures (or latent and measured variables) is essential in industrial and organizational psychology. Too often faulty conclusions are drawn about the relationship among constructs based on observed relationships between measured variables that are not reliable or do not measure the construct adequately. A recent article by Landy, Rastegary, Thayer and Colvin (1991) on the construct and measurement of time urgency illustrates this dilemma well, and provides an example of a systematic approach to the development of more appropriate measures. The article is discussed because of the many relevant measurement issues it illustrates. Too often the response of researchers to disappointing results with a particular construct is to abandon the construct, rather than to question and examine the adequacy of the measures.

Landy et al. (1991), building on the work of Edwards, Baglioni and Cooper (1990) provide a healthy exception. They set out to develop more appropriate scales of time urgency using sound measurement principles. These principles included the careful analysis of the concept and its dimensionality, giving rise to the identification of several components of time urgency (e.g. competitiveness, speech pattern). Previous measures of time urgency were probably assessing different components which masked the multi-dimensionality of the construct. As is traditional in scale development, items were selected from existing measures of 'time urgency', factor analysed, and the resultant scales checked for internal consistency (alpha reliability) and stability (test re-test reliability) on several samples (note the importance of different estimates of reliability which could be reinterpreted within the framework of generalizability theory discussed below). In this example LISREL analysis was used to calculate the test-retest reliability (see p. 648 in Landy et al., 1991), illustrating one of the advances available to industrial and organizational psychologists in measurement methods. The LISREL analysis of reliability overcomes the traditional approach to test-retest reliabilities which requires an assumption of uncorrelated measurement errors across measurement occasions. Such an assumption is often unwarranted.

Landy et al. (1991) then used the well known Behaviorally Anchored Rating Scale (BARS) technique to develop an alternative set of Behaviorally Anchored Time Urgency Scales. Finally, a series of analyses were undertaken to determine the construct validity of the two different sets of measures. One interesting approach involved a multi-trait, multi-rater analysis (potentially interpretable within a generalizability framework), where the scales were completed by the person and his or her spouse. The Behaviorally Anchored Scales demonstrated higher trait variance and lower halo variance than is typically observed in studies examining convergent and discriminant validity. Note, however, that there was no discussion of the potential difficulty with BARS in the performance appraisal context where the anchors are taken too literally rather than as indicators of an underlying dimension.

Issues that remain relate to the value of retaining a superordinate construct such as time urgency for the cluster of dimensions that appear to define it. Landy et al. (1991) also point to the importance of measuring the environment in terms of the demands that it makes on time urgency. In doing so the various time urgency dimensions could become the basis for rating environments for these demands. The issue of commensurate measurement between people and environments is taken up again in the third section of this chapter where measurement of fit issues are covered.

Developments in Measurement Relevant to I/O Psychologists

Having discussed a specific example of the conceptual clarification and development of a measure, this section of the chapter will deal with general measurement issues, particularly as they relate to ideas arising from modern test theory. Although classical test theory approaches remain relevant to I/O psychologists, modern test theory has made available new approaches to item analysis (Item Response Theory) and reliability assessment (generalizability theory), both of which have wider implications. Other reviewers in this series have drawn attention to the relevance of modern test theory ideas (Murphy, 1988; Schuler & Guldin, 1991).

The development of Item Response Theory is important to industrial and organizational psychologists for two major reasons. First, it provides a basis for item analysis that, among other things, offers a more appropriate way of reducing bias at the item level (Wainer, 1989; Lim & Drasgow, 1990). Second, the combination of Item Response Theory and computerized testing makes possible the application of adaptive testing principles to increase the efficiency of assessment. Another relevant development, generalizability theory provides a means to increase the efficiency of measurement by ensuring that efforts to improve reliability are directed at changes that will have the most effect for the particular purpose of the measurement (Shavelson, Webb & Rowley, 1989; Marcoulides & Goldstein, 1990).

Although most research applying modern test theory has related to ability assessment, Item Response Theory and adaptive testing have also been used in relation to personality assessment (e.g. Reise & Waller, 1990; Lee & Smith, 1988; Waller & Reise, 1989), attitude measurement (Koch, Dodd & Fitzpatrick, 1990), market research (Balasubramanian & Kamakura, 1989) and the development of adaptive interviews for surveys (Singh, Howell & Rhoads, 1990). Generalizability theory has been used quite widely to achieve a better understanding of the sources of error variance in performance appraisals

(Shavelson, Webb & Rowley, 1989; Shavelson, Mayberry, Li & Webb, 1990; Marcoulides, 1989) and in increasing the efficiency of surveys (Johnson & Bell, 1985). In future, applications of all these developments are likely in the areas of biodata (Rothstein, Schmidt, Erwin, Owens & Sparks, 1990), assessment centres and structured selection interviewing.

Item Response Theory and Generalizability Theory

Traditional classical test theory tools that are available for item analysis are distractor analysis, item difficulty analysis and item discrimination analysis. Interactions among these features of items are also important (Murphy & Davidshofer, 1991). Distractor analysis aims to determine whether the 'distractor' items in a multiple choice type question are effective. Effective distractors reduce the payoff of guessing, and do so equally, such that incorrect responses are evenly distributed across the incorrect items.

From a classical test theory perspective, item difficulty is defined in terms of the number of people who correctly answer a particular test item. This is commonly expressed as a p value for the item which is simply the number of people who answered the item correctly divided by the total number taking the test. The disadvantage of the p value approach lies in its dependence upon the particular characteristics of the item and the sample taking the test rather than on the latent trait being measured. Because of this property the p value of items varies in groups with differing levels of the attribute in question. These are the features of difficulty analysis that Item Response Theory approaches (discussed below) attempt to overcome.

The final feature of item analysis traditionally available is item discrimination analysis which is used to establish how well each item measures the construct underlying the test as a whole (Murphy & Davidshofer, 1991). This can be determined from an item discrimination index, D (e.g. comparing the number of people who scored in the top 25% on the test as a whole, with those who scored in the bottom 25%), an item-total correlation or from an examination of the inter-item correlations. Examination of inter-item correlations may highlight reasons for low item discrimination which may be due to the multi-dimensionality of the underlying scale (e.g. the time urgency construct discussed above—Landy et al., 1991), reading problems or some other factors. Item analyses have been used in pruning tests and scales to develop ones that are reliable, valid and free from bias (Murphy & Davidshofer, 1991).

Item Response Theory

Item Response Theory is a new development in item analysis that attempts to describe and explain the relationship between characteristics of the individual (their level on a particular attribute such as intelligence) and their responses to individual items. Assumptions about the relationship between a person's ability (or other trait level) and the probability of responding correctly to an item form the basis of Item Characteristic Curves (ICCs, also called Item Response Functions, IRFs, or Item Response Characteristics, IRCs). Item Response Theory has advantages over traditional item analyses in determining difficulty levels and in distractor analysis. Unlike the p values derived from classical test theory approaches, the difficulty estimates obtained from Item Response Theory are not sample-dependent, a useful feature for detecting bias. Furthermore, the sophistication of distractor analysis available through Item Response Theory has aided the development of adaptive testing (Hambleton & Swaminathan, 1985; Weiss & Vale, 1987).

Item Characteristic Curves, which may be derived from a variety of models, make it possible to infer more accurately the actual latent trait (e.g. intelligence) from the measured behaviour or item response. Several sources can be consulted for a discussion about the mathematical assumptions concerning the relationship between the underlying trait and the probability of responding 'correctly'—assumptions that are used in developing Item Characteristic Curves (Hambleton & Swaminathan, 1985; Lord, 1980; Weiss & Vale, 1987). Item Characteristic Curves usually contain one, two or three parameters (sources of information). For example, they can contain a difficulty or location parameter, a discrimination or slope parameter and an item guessing or lower asymptote parameter. In the literature these are usually referred to as parameters a, b and c respectively. Rasch models of Item Response Theory focus on the difficulty or location parameter and hold slope constant, while also assuming that guessing is zero.

Item Response Theory is being used widely in educational and psychological testing (e.g. Carroll, 1990; Kane, 1987; Wainer, Sireci & Thissen, 1991) with several applications relevant to industrial and organizational psychology. For example, Frost and Orban (1990) used IRT to analyse the effect of inappropriate responding on the validity of the Personnel Selection Inventory. The concepts are also being applied to the measurement of job satisfaction (e.g. Roznowski, 1989; Ironson, Smith, Brannick & Gibson, et al., 1989), and personality assessment (Thissen & Steinberg, 1988).

Increasingly, computer packages and tools are available that will make it easier to calculate and produce ICCs. Mislevy and Stocking (1989) offer a user's guide to LOGIST and BILOG, two computer programs for estimating item response parameters. Applegate and LeBlanc (1990) describe SAS programs that use the output generated from commercially available packages such as LOGIST to produce graphical presentations of item and test characteristic curves and associated functions for visual inspection. Kingma and Taerum (1988) have written a program for non-parametric Item Response Theory model.

The plethora of new models that can be used for estimating ICCs in Item Response Theory is considerable (e.g. Bejar, 1990; Mislevy & Verhelst, 1990; Stout, 1990; Hoijtink, 1990—dichotomous data). For example Mislevy and

Verhelst (1990) present an Item Response Model that allows one to infer the strategy used for responding to items even though all that is known is the response itself. Such an approach may be potentially helpful in differentiating random guessers from serious responders. However, Goldstein and Wood (1989) in a thoughtful article question whether the development of the many different models has helped our understanding of how individuals actually respond to items. They refer to the developments as Item Response Models rather than Item Response Theories as these models are 'not about why people get things right or wrong, but about the supposed probabilistic nature of responses conditional on an assumed trait called ability' (p. 163). With respect to intelligence, for example, IRT has done little to help tease out the contributions of speed, accuracy and persistence, although White (1979, cited in Goldstein & Wood, 1989) has attempted to do so. Too many of the articles discuss IRT in the abstract without grounding the discussion in actual empirical data (other than simulation data) or even in particular domains of assessment. An exception is an excellent article in the *Psychological Bulletin* by Thissen and Steinberg (1988) that illustrates IRT in relation to actual items on personality and life satisfaction scales.

In support of their view that the large array of IRT models is not necessarily indicative of progress, Goldstein and Wood (1989) argue that a standard linear modelling framework captures most of what is available in these models. If this is indeed so it would be a welcome relief to industrial and organizational psychologists trying to use IRT even though guidelines are available about what to consider in choosing a particular item response model (e.g. Traub, 1983). In the present review two applications of Item Response Theory will be discussed, namely adaptive testing and reducing test bias at the item level.

Adaptive testing. The concept of adaptive or tailored testing is simply that of assessing the same underlying construct through non-identical items on a test, with the selection of items depending upon early estimates of an individual's standing on the construct or trait. Adaptive testing is not new. Ever since the Binet scales, several individually administered tests (e.g. WAIS and WAIS-R) have used different starting points depending upon responses to early items, and different termination points depending upon progress in the test. Some of these adaptive administrative procedures were built into early forms of computerized adaptive testing. However, the combination of computerized testing and Item Response Theory made available an extremely powerful testing technology that has resulted in significant advances in adaptive testing (Drasgow & Hulin, in press).

It is well known that traditional tests seldom assess equally precisely over the full range of the trait in question. Specifically, most tests tend to assess best for those people whose scores fall in the middle ranges, and worst (least accurately) for those who fall at the ends of the distribution. Item Characteristic Curves and computerized systems made it possible to retain a bank of items containing information about the precision with which each item measures at particular levels of the trait. This information about discrimination and difficulty can be used to select items that assess a person most precisely for their given level of the trait. Hence, each individucal is only administered those items that discriminate most effectively at their level of ability. By drawing on a bank of item information available with computerized testing, it is possible to make initial estimates of a candidate's level on a trait from responses to early questions, to subsequently select items that will best assess at this estimated level of the trait, to update the estimates of the candidate's ability based on responses to new questions, and then to continue selecting items that maximize the efficiency of assessment at the person's estimated level of the trait. Indeed the developments in Item Response Theory make it possible to use the responses to distractor items as a means of assessing ability, increasing the speed and accuracy with which early estimates of ability can be made. This is because Item Response Theory enables the construction of separate ICCs for each of the alternate responses in a multiple choice item. For example, an individual with a low level on a particular trait who makes a mistake may be likely to choose a different incorrect distractor from that chosen by an individual with higher score on that trait. Traditional distractor analysis has tended not to identify such information, particularly if the overall response rate to the different distractor items was approximately equal. In practice these developments mean that it is possible to reduce the number of items that are required for accurate assessment.

Computerized adaptive tests can also use the information contained in Item Characteristic Curves together with the responses of a candidate to determine the optimum point to terminate assessment given the level of precision required (Weiss & Vale, 1987). This is possible because the form of assessment yields individual standard errors of measurement or confidence bands. If highly accurate assessment is required over the whole range of an ability, then the assessment for every individual should continue until maximum precision is achieved. Alternatively, if selection or classification is all that is required, the aim should be to achieve maximum precision around the cut-off point, with less concern for precise assessment of individuals who clearly fall within one category or another (e.g. accept or reject). Weiss and Vale (1987) highlight how the use of individualized (or adaptive) termination rules based on individualized assessments of error of measurement can result in increased efficiency of classification to a pre-specified probability of error. Clearly these developments have implications for cost effectiveness of testing, although the complexity of explaining the procedures may act as a barrier to their use.

Reckase (1989) and Weiss and Vale (1987) both provide clear descriptions of the principles and stages involved in implementing a computerized adaptive testing procedure. There are several different methods that may be used to select items for adaptive testing. For example, likelihood functions can be calculated from the Item Characteristic Curves (see Weiss & Vale, 1987), and there are several different methods for calculating these functions (e.g. Bayesian or maximum-likelihood) which may have consequences for reducing bias in test items (see below). Computerized systems are available that help in setting up the data base needed for adaptive testing (e.g. Dodd, Koch & de Ayala, 1989) or in developing adaptive tests without having to program (Klieger, 1990). Unfortunately, off-the-shelf packages seldom meet all the requirements of a particular user.

The promise of adaptive testing has not yet been fully realized in practice. Although several examples of computerized adaptive assessment procedures have been described (see Kingsbury, 1990, for application of the MicroCAT adaptive testing system; Henly, Klebe, McBride & Cudeck, 1989, for a description of the computerized adaptive version of the Differential Aptitude Test; and Bartram, 1987, for an application to pilot selection), mainstream personnel selection and guidance work has not made widespread use of the procedures. No doubt one of the major reasons relates to the difficulty of mass testing with computerized systems. The other is probably a function of a lack of awareness of the relevance of these developments to the practice of assessment.

The broader concept of adaptive assessment can also be applied to job analysis systems and other forms of interviewing. This is already done where the level of specificity with which areas are explored depends upon answers to critical filter questions. These developments have not necessarily relied upon IRT.

Reducing bias at the item level. The issue of bias in tests has been and continues to be a controversial one with both theoretical and practical significance. Earlier debate about the difficulties of sex bias in interest inventories highlighted many of the issues, and foreshadowed some attempts to reduce bias at the item level. Briefly, the concern relates to measures such as Holland's Self Directed Search (see Holland, 1985) which yields a Holland interest profile (Realistic, Investigative, Artistic, Social, Enterprising and Conventional interests) based on raw scores. In general many more men than women have profiles with a high Realistic score, while many more women than men have high Social scores. These differences may reflect real differences in the interests of men and women, but there is concern that, when used in a counselling context, the Self Directed Search reinforces traditional career trajectories. Several approaches are available to overcome difficulties with sex bias in interest inventories (e.g. same sex norms, suppression of bias at the test or item level). A thoughtful discussion of the problem of sex bias in interest inventories is provided in the Strong Interest Inventory manual (Hansen & Campbell, 1985). As part of The American College Testing Program (1981) a sex-balanced interest inventory, UNIACT, was developed consisting of sex-balanced items. Critics of this approach argue that the removal of gender differences at any level reduces the predictive validity of instruments. The use of Item Response Theory provides a more powerful and effective method for dealing with the issues of bias.

Developments in the application of IRT technology to the reduction of bias have been strongest in the field of educational measurement (e.g. Young, 1991; Cohen, Kim & Subkoviak, 1991). Industrial psychologists have been slower to use these approaches. There is, however, considerable utility in using IRT to reduce any potential bias in tests used in the selection context.

Lim and Drasgow (1990) are critical of the use of the traditional p values of items for identifying subgroup differences, a procedure that has been employed by testing agencies in response to various legal cases. For example the 'Golden Rule' settlement, although not a legal precedent, has been used to suggest that tests should not contain items for which the differences in proportions correct between subgroups are larger than 5%. As discussed above, the p value approach, based on Classical Test Theory, confounds true subgroup differences with actual differences in the trait being measured. Under these circumstances both Type I errors (where p values show up differences that are not real) and Type II errors (where p values fail to detect items that do actually function differently between subgroups) can occur. Item Response Theory, which provides information about item discrimination, item difficulty and often about the lower asymptote (based on guessing), provides a much more accurate basis from which to make decisions about bias at the item level (Lim & Drasgow, 1990).

Wainer, Sireci and Thissen (1991) refer to the methods for detecting DIFferential functioning, or DIF functioning as it has become known, based on latent variables or on observed scores. The issues are complex, since the particular models used to estimate the parameters of item responses appear to matter (Lim & Drasgow, 1990), with the methods varying in terms of their power and robustness against violations of underlying assumptions such as that of uni-dimensionality (that a single latent trait underlies performance on an item). For example, in Monte Carlo simulation studies, Lim and Drasgow (1990) found that Bayes' model, and to some extent the marginal maximum-likelihood model of estimation, were more robust with respect to violations of the uni-dimensionality assumption and to sample size than was joint maximum-likelihood estimation. Even Goldstein and Wood (1989), who question the need for all the variants on the standard linear modelling approach, acknowledge the problem of violations of the assumption of uni-dimensionality.

Partly in response to these concerns, Wainer, Sireci and Thissen (1991) have suggested the idea of using the 'testlet' as a unit of analysis rather than the item, particularly with respect to identifying DIFferential functioning (one detects some humour about the level at which to suppress bias, item, testlet or test as a whole). A 'testlet' is the smallest unit of items that cluster together in a meaningful and uni-dimensional manner. In some circumstances DIF functioning at the item level may mean items cancel each other out at the 'testlet' level, thereby avoiding the Type I error. Equally, however, DIF functioning may be detected at the 'testlet' level that was missed at the item level because of insufficient power (cumulative effect of marginal amounts of bias in several items), thereby avoiding a Type II error. As with item level analysis, the analysis at the 'testlet' level will need to satisfy the uni-dimensionality assumption. Gitomer and Yamamoto (1991) offer an alternative approach to Item Response Theory, based on Latent Class Modelling, which may be useful where uni-dimensional constructs cannot be assumed. Applications of DIFferential function based on Latent Class Modelling are likely to appear in the literature soon.

An issue not unrelated to that of test bias involves the increasing need in a multi-cultural society to translate tests and measures into different languages. Item Response Theory technology offers a way of improving these translations (Ellis, Minsel & Becker, 1989; Ellis, 1989) by providing information about the measurement equivalence of translated assessment devices that may otherwise not have been available.

Obviously, the use of Item Response Theory information will become essential for test developers of the future, and test users will need to examine carefully whether the selection of the items in the tests they choose has been based on the best available technology. Issues that will require further development from the perspective of industrial and organizational psychologists include the influence of coaching and practice effects upon the appropriateness of IRT models (see Sackett, Burris & Ryan, 1989, for an excellent and informative discussion on practice effects). Generalizability theory, discussed below, is also relevant to problems arising from practice effects, since the reliabilities obtained on successive administrations of a test may not necessarily be the same (Shavelson, Webb & Rowley, 1989).

Generalizability theory

Generalizability theory is an extension of classical reliability theory particularly in dealing with multiple sources of error (Cronbach et al., 1972; Shavelson, Webb & Rowley, 1989). In classical test theory an observed score is made up of a true score and an error component, while reliability is defined as the ratio of the true score variance to the observed score variance. In generalizability theory it is recognized that error variance comes from a variety of sources, such as the lack of internal consistency of items, variability due to testing conditions, or time (traditional test-retest reliability) and so on. In the context of raters, error variance may be due to the raters, the context of the ratings, the domains to which the ratings apply and the interactions among these factors. Traditional reliability theory failed to distinguish between these different sources of error. By partitioning error variance, generalizability theory allows researchers and practitioners to be more precise about the reliability of the particular decisions made on the basis of assessments. In the context of selection, the prediction of interest involves generalizing from measurements obtained prior to appointment to criterion measures obtained subsequently, and hence test-retest reliability is important.

Even validity can be conceptualized within a generalizability framework (Kraiger & Teachout, 1990). To the extent that the predictors and criteria are measuring the same underlying construct, they can be thought of as alternative measures of it. The use of a generalizability theory framework allows one to partition the many alternative sources of error influencing both the predictor and criterion measurement, providing a better basis for assessing validity, the relationship between true scores (or universe scores in generalizability theory terminology). This is the approach that is taken in recent applications of LISREL analysis to test validation (Campbell, McHenry & Wise, 1990; Wise, McHenry & Campbell, 1990) and to understanding performance measures (Borman, White, Pulakos & Oppler, 1991).

The term 'universe score', used instead of the classical concept of true score, gives an indication of the key idea underlying generalizability theory, namely that an ideal measure would assess the person over the universe of occasions, contexts and relevant domains. To the extent that it does not, generalizing from the observed score is limited. Knowing exactly which dimensions are comparatively error-free provides a basis for knowing the certainty with which generalizations can be made in particular domains. Generalizability theory is most easily understood within an Analysis of Variance framework, and more recently through the use of structural equation modelling or LISREL analysis (Wise, McHenry & Campbell, 1990). The ANOVA framework provides ideas for the design of measures that allow one to estimate an overall generalizability coefficient (instead of a reliability coefficient) as well as specific generalizability coefficients for particular sources of variation.

Shavelson, Webb and Rowley (1989) provide an excellent tutorial discussion of generalizability theory, and also highlight how it distinguishes between reliability for relative decisions (relevant to norm-referenced assessment) and absolute decisions (relevant to criterion-referenced assessment). One of the examples given in their article relates to the estimation of the General Educational Development (GED) scale for the Dictionary of Occupational Titles, illustrating the application of generalizability principles to job analysis (Box 5a in Figure 4.1, in Dawis and Lofquist's 1984 model).

Performance appraisal ratings which lend themselves to generalizability analysis are discussed more fully in the next section, which also addresses the application of measurement issues to person-environment fit and the propensity for change.

APPLICATIONS OF MEASUREMENT TO THE DOMAINS OF I/O PSYCHOLOGY

The Minnesota Theory of Work Adjustment outlined in the introductory section to the chapter highlighted several major domains of assessment in industrial and organizational psychology. Space does not permit further comment about measurement issues in relation to each of these domains. However, the critical importance of improving criterion measures (Guion & Gibson, 1988; Schmitt & Robertson, 1990) and the potential use of generalizability theory ideas in doing so (Shavelson, Webb & Rowley, 1989), justifies attention to performance assessment. This is followed by a discussion of measurement and analysis issues associated with 'person-environment fit' and with understanding individual and organizational responses to change.

Measuring Productivity and Performance

Relevance of generalizability theory

Appraisal ratings collected routinely within organizations remain the most widely used indicator of performance, despite recognized problems associated with their reliability and validity. Some studies have approached performance appraisal research within a generalizability theory framework (Komaki, Zlotnick & Jensen, 1986; Marcoulides, 1989; Shavelson et al., 1990; Webb et al., 1989) although not all make explicit the relevance of generalizability theory to their research (Borman & Hallan, 1991; Hoffman, Nathan & Holden, 1991; Rothstein, 1990).

In particular, several laboratory studies examining the 'accuracy' of performance ratings (e.g. Sulsky & Balzar, 1988; Padgett & Ilgen, 1989; Murphy & Balzar, 1989) have used generalizability theory because it offers one way of teasing out sources of error that affect accuracy. Effort can then be directed to reducing the source of error that will detract most from the particular uses of the ratings. In support of the idea of allowing a purpose to direct measurement effort, Murphy (1991) suggests that the debate about whether to increase accuracy at the behavioural level (e.g. Murphy, Philbin & Adams, 1989) or at the trait or construct level (e.g. Padgett & Ilgen, 1989) can be resolved by examining the purpose of the performance appraisal rating (e.g. behavioural for feedback and trait for selection decisions).

In a laboratory study, Hauenstein and Alexander (1991) used a generalizability framework (within an ANOVA design involving multiple ratings on multiple dimensions provided by multiple raters) to examine the extent to which rater characteristics affected performance ratings. Laboratory studies, however, cannot easily capture the influence of contextual factors, power relations and the influence of time-based processes involved in observing behavioural incidents, encoding and storing them, and later retrieving them to provide a rating (Kozlowski & Ford, 1991).

Hoffman, Nathan and Holden (1991) provide an example of a field study that could have been interpreted within generalizability theory. Their validation study involved four criteria, two that were objective (production quantity and production quality) and two that were subjective (self- and supervisor ratings, on five behaviourally based rating scales and an overall effectiveness rating scale). The productivity measure consisted of a 12-month moving average of computer-generated productivity indices calculated from work orders. Data were available for previous years allowing for stability estimates. Quality data were based on blind inspection of 150 appliance repairs for each service worker collected during a year. Errors detected were weighted according to their severity. Quality data were also available from previous years. Five ability tests were administered as predictors. Although the field data were not fully crossed, as is possible in laboratory experiments, the multiple sources of criterion data made it feasible to estimate different types of reliability information, an idea implicit in generalizability theory. This study is mentioned not so much for the actual results, which were based on comparatively small sample sizes, but for the novelty of the use of multiple criterion data and the thoughtful discussion comments (outlined below) that took into account the influence of contextual factors on their criterion measures.

Variability in criteria. The data from Hoffman, Nathan and Holden (1991) indicated that both self- and supervisor ratings were highly skewed, although supervisors' ratings were more varied, probably accounting for the higher intercorrelations among the supervisor-rated dimensions than among the self-rated dimensions. Intercorrelations between supervisor and self-ratings were low, and self-ratings were not predicted by test scores (see also Lane & Herriot, 1990, for a study using both self- and supervisor ratings). The tests in the Hoffman, Nathan and Holden study did predict supervisor ratings and production quantity, but not production quality.

The authors drew attention to the lack of variance in the measure of quality which probably attenuated the validity of the tests when it was used as a criterion. The low variability in quality was attributed to the company policy of achieving a mastery level with respect to quality, a common approach in many organizations. It is interesting to note that Nathan and Alexander's (1988) meta-analytic study examining whether the validity generalization coefficients generalized equally to different criteria found that they did for supervisor ratings, supervisor rankings, production quantity and work samples but not for production quality.

The more general issue and important lesson from these studies relates to the danger of validating tests against a mastery-based criterion (competency standard) which, by definition, has reduced variability. Since organizations are increasingly trying to set standards and ensure that all their employees achieve these (an often unstated aim in the 'competency approach', Woodruffe, 1991), the implications for validation studies are important. Under these conditions a more appropriate criterion may be the time taken to achieve mastery rather than mastery itself.

The problem of lack of variability in a criterion such as quality relates to an important measurement issue relevant to selection, namely the effects on performance criteria of differential exposure to training and other opportunities to learn. The literature on dynamic criteria attempts to address changes in the criterion over time that might account for unstable validity coefficients (see Austin, Humphreys & Hulin, 1989; Deadrick & Madigan, 1990; Hanges, Schneider & Niles, 1990; Murphy, 1989). Few writers, however, have explored the mechanisms underlying unstable ability performance relationships where they do exist (see Murphy, 1989 and Fleishman & Mumford, 1989 for exceptions). The key to understanding such changes lies in the interaction between aptitude and experience or training and in the varying influences of ability on peformance at different levels of skill development (see Ackerman, 1987, and Kanfer & Ackerman, 1989, for a more fundamental discussion).

Hunter, Schmidt and Judiesch (1990) raise a related issue, namely that of the increase in performance variability as a function of job complexity. Levels of variability in performance that are a function of the nature of the work performed, amount or extensiveness of training or organizational policy may affect validity estimates.

Content and meaning of performance ratings

In line with the increased care in measurement issues associated with criteria more attention is being paid to the dimension content on which performance is assessed (McDonald, 1991). Clear definitions of dimensions not only improve rater accuracy, but if these dimensions are also related to job and organizational goals, they provide a structure for rational selection hypotheses leading to appropriate use of predictors (Landy, 1986). In a special issue of *Personnel Psychology*, Campbell (1990) summarizes the key features of 'The Army Selection and Classification Project'. Several of the articles in the special issue provide a blueprint for future selection research in terms of conceptual definition and measurement of predictor and criterion data. The project also offers an example of the uses of structural equation modelling (LISREL analyses) in the way suggested by Anderson and Gerbing (1988), namely, examining the measurement model before testing the structural model.

The shift in research in the last decade has been away from improving rating scales to trying to understand contextual and other influences on ratings (see Ilgen & Schneider, 1991, for a recent review). This shift is important in understanding the meaning underlying the numbers given in performance ratings. Depending on the contextual uses of performance appraisals supervisors may distort ratings to achieve an outcome they want (promotion for one of their staff, a pay increase, or non-attendance at a training course). Under circumstances such as this, which are not unusual, one cannot assume a common meaning underlying the same number on a rating scale in different organizations, nor even in different parts of one organization. As a minimum, performance scores should be standardized within organizations prior to examining relationships to other variables (Hesketh, McLachlan & Gardner, 1992).

Wall, Jackson and Davids (1992) illustrate the care needed in interpreting the meaning behind ostensibly objective measures of performance or productivity. The study, which examined the effects of increasing operator control on a robotics line, used the number of stoppages recorded on the system as a measure of operator performance in managing faults. In this particular study the authors controlled for a potential increase in stoppages resulting from an increase in 'uptime' arising out of the intervention. Failure to do so would have resulted in faulty conclusions. Furthermore, stoppages were divided into those of less than 15 minutes duration, those of 16–60 minutes duration, and stoppages of longer than 60 minutes duration. Stoppages of different lengths had very different meanings. Neither a simple count of stoppages, nor information about actual downtime would have conveyed the information needed to test their hypotheses. Short-duration stoppages tended to be indicative of preventive maintenance, since the equipment had to be stopped to make any contact. Increased operator control resulted in an increase in the incidence of short stoppages (which did not require specialist support). Preventive maintenance, indexed by an increase in short-duration stoppages, was associated with a reduction in stoppages of medium duration, but the incidence of large-scale system failures requiring specialist intervention remained the same. Overall, the 'uptime' of the machines improved as the result of increased operator control. Clearly, considerable insight was needed on the part of the researchers to understand the meaning of what superficially might have appeared to be simple numbers.

Group productivity measurement

Pritchard and his team (Pritchard & Roth, 1991; Pritchard et al., 1988, 1989) have developed an interesting approach to measurement (Productivity and Measurement Enhancement System—ProMES) that has the possibility of taking into account situation-specific meanings attached to various indicators. The development is also interesting because of its application to measuring group productivity. The ProMES system involves a creative combination of several ideas: goal setting at a group level; development of objective productivity indicators of effectiveness; establishment of the relative importance of these indicators; agreement on the amount of change in effectiveness to be gained from changes at different levels of the indicators (including the opportunity to capture non-linear relationships); monitoring of performance in relation to the agreed indicators; provision of graphic visual feedback to staff involved; the use of an interesting scaling procedure that makes it possible to calculate an overall measure of effectiveness across different types of indicators; and the use of the same scaling procedure to facilitate comparisons of productivity across different units in an organization.

The scaling procedure is based on the notion of an expected level of effectiveness (a goal), arbitrarily given a zero value, a maximum possible effectiveness level, and a minimum possible effectiveness level. Because the indicators are scaled psychologically to a common effectiveness scale (which is assumed to have a normal distribution), the effectiveness scale becomes the basis for comparison across different indicators and groups. Group discussion and management input is required to establish the expected levels of effectiveness for each indicator and the additional contingencies between indicators and effectiveness levels below and above the expected level. The contingencies are presented graphically with the indicators (e.g. number of units to be produced, or acceptable reject levels) along the x-axis and effectiveness on the y-axis. Important indicators have steeper slopes (the effectiveness increases more for a unit increase in the indicator, but note the difficulty of no common unit in the indicator). Non-linearities are built into the system such that effectiveness may increase more for a change at one level of an indicator than for a similar amount of change at a different level of the same indicator.

The ProMES metric is similar to that underlying Goal Attainment Scaling (GAS), an evaluation system used in the clinical field to obtain an overall measure of the effectiveness of interventions despite varied individual therapeutic goals (Kiresuk & Sherman, 1968; Kiresuk & Lund, 1982; Heavlin, Lee-Merrows & Lewis, 1982). The scaling metric in GAS involves an expected level of outcome with two 'better than expected' and two 'worse than expected' anchor points (a 5-point scale assumed to have the characteristics of z-score). Measurable indicators of outcome for each client are developed for at least three of the five points. In an evaluation context care must be taken to check that the indicators set are not 'rigged' to ensure successful outcomes. The same problem arises in relation to establishing contingencies for ProMES, although management input in the development phase helps overcome this.

Surprisingly, Goal Attainment Scaling, which would fit well with Management By Objective approaches (see Rodgers & Hunter, 1991 for meta-analysis of MBO effectiveness), has not filtered through to the industrial psychology literature. Although ProMES uses a similar idea, Pritchard et al. (1988, 1989) make no reference to GAS. An interesting feature of ProMES not available in GAS is the inclusion of non-linearities in the contingencies. Pritchard and Roth (1991) provide evidence of the added value in the non-linearities in increasing productivity, even though linear systems correlate well with the non-linear contingencies established.

One of the advantages of the ProMES system generally, and the non-linearities in particular, lies in its acceptability to users. As was found with behaviourally based measurement of performance ratings, the involvement of users in the development of the scaling procedure facilitates the acceptance and communicability of the measurement. In addition to satisfying sound psychometric principles, measurement in industrial and organizational psychology must be acceptable and easily communicated to users.

Assessment of People and Environments on Common Dimensions: The Measurement of FIT

Most of the measurement effort in mainstream psychology relates to the assessment of the person (Boxes 4a and 4b in Figure 4.1). The extension of measurement to assessing environmental differences is one of the major potential contributions made by industrial and organizational psychologists to psychology generally. Neuropsychologists, for example, make extensive predictions about the likely performance of head-injured patients in work and daily living situations based solely on assessing the person. Their predictions could benefit from assessing differential requirements of environments and from validating predictions against performance on the tasks or daily living situations (Hesketh, Adams & Allworth, 1991).

The components of work adjustment theory outlined in Figure 4.1 remind us that we need to assess what people can do as well as what they want to do, and that we need to think of environments in terms of the performance demands that will be made on individuals as well as the motivational features in the environment. In order to facilitate individual and organizational decision-making, assessments of the job, the person and performance should be on common dimensions. Similarly the measurement of what people are seeking (needs, interests, values) should be on the same dimensions as the measurement of what jobs have to offer. Furthermore, in order to test person-environment fit theories, facet satisfactions should also be measured on the same dimensions (Edwards, 1991), although only a few studies have done so (see Rice, Gentile & McFarlin 1991, and Hesketh, McLachlan & Gardner, 1992, for exceptions).

The first part of this section discusses fit issues in relation to the lower part of Figure 4.1 (Boxes 4b and 5b). The measurement and methodological issues raised in relation to these domains will then be applied to the match between skills and abilities and skill/ability requirements, the upper half of Figure 4.1.

Needs/values/interests and reinforcer match

Edwards (1991), who stressed the importance of measuring the person, the environment and satisfaction on the same dimensions even at an item level (e.g. Rice, McFarlin & Bennett, 1989; Rice, Gentile & McFarlin, 1991; Hesketh, McLachlan & Gardner, 1992), also argued for a different way of conceptualizing fit. Most studies derive an index of fit between the person and environment which is related to an outcome measure, namely satisfaction or mental health. Although a range of indices of fit have been used, Cronbach and Gleser's (1953) D'' index, which calculates fit on shape after removing both elevation and scatter, is considered the best (Rounds, Dawis & Lofquist, 1987; Hesketh, McLachlan & Gardner, 1992). Hesketh, McLachlan and Gardner (1992) used a computerized fuzzy rating scale to measure both preferences and job perceptions (see Figure 4.2). The D'' index of fit was calculated as well as a 'judged match' index based on the visual analysis of relationships between fuzzy preferences and fuzzy job perceptions. The 'judged match' index (the reliability was 0.8 between two judges) correlated significantly more strongly with satisfaction than did traditional indices (0.58 compared with 0.44). This higher correlation was derived partly as the result of using fuzzy ratings that incorporated flexibility, but also because judges were using different rules for different items. For example, to perceive one's job as having more friendly co-workers than one wishes does not necessarily result in dissatisfaction, while a job with more 'conventional' or clerical work than one wishes usually does. Many traditional indices of match do not take into account the need for different rules for different items (see Edwards, 1991, and Rice, McFarlin & Bennett, 1989; Rice, Gentile & McFarlin, 1991 for extremely thorough discussions of the issue). Similar issues may be relevant to personality profile matching in a selection context (see also Caldwell & O'Reilly, 1990, for an alternative approach to profile matching).

More importantly, according to Edwards (1991) some approaches to testing matching theories fail to control for the absolute level of either the person or the environmental component of the match. A more appropriate analysis involves the use of hierarchical regression, where the outcome measure (e.g. satisfaction) is regressed on the person component (e.g. preferences), the job component (e.g. job perceptions), possibly on both of these components squared to test for non-linearities, and on the interaction between the two. 'Fit' can only be considered important if the interaction between preferences and perceptions adds a significant amount of incremental variance over and

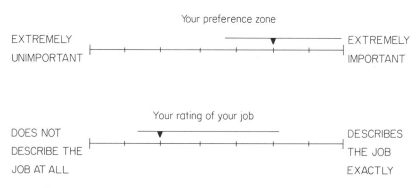

Figure 4.2 Example of a fuzzy preference and job perception rating

above that accounted for by the two independent components (and their squared functions). These analyses may need to be done at the item level (Rice, McFarlin & Bennett, 1989; Rice, Gentile & McFarlin, 1991). Invariably, the variance explained by 'fit' is less than appeared to be the case using traditional indices of match. The traditional approaches to deriving indices of match amount to doing a hierarchical regression analysis without entering the separate independent components first, a practice that has been severely criticized (Evans, 1991). However, despite the strong stand taken by Edwards (1991) and Evans (1991) with respect to testing for interactions, concern is still evident about the conservatism of hierarchical regression and the difficulty of detecting significant interactions in field research. When the effect is expected for only one particular combination of independent variables (as may be the case in stress research, Martin & Wall, 1989), subgroup analysis is suggested as an alternative approach (Bobko, 1986; Clegg & Wall, 1990).

Skills and abilities and the skill/ability requirement match

Edwards (1991) discusses fit primarily in relation to the domains highlighted in the lower half of Figure 4.1. The issues raised, however, are also relevant to the relationships embodied in the upper half of Figure 4.1, namely the fit between skills and abilities and skill and ability requirements, and the relationship of this fit to satisfactory performance.

Applying the Edwards' (1991) approach to testing a matching selection hypothesis requires three types of assessment information all based on common dimensions: (i) relevant ratings of the cognitive and other requirements of jobs or tasks; (ii) person assessments; and (iii) assessments of performance. For the analysis, performance should be regressed on the job ratings, person assessments as well as on the interaction between these (product term), an approach that is seldom used, perhaps because so many validation studies are carried out on a homogeneous group of jobs (see Prediger, 1989, for a comment about the validity of specific ability tests across different jobs), and because the job analysis approaches used traditionally did not relate specifically to the person dimensions being assessed (see Hogan, 1991, for an exception in relation to physical abilities and physical ability requirements). The lack of symmetry is particularly so for the relationship between cognitive ability requirements and cognitive ability. Traditional job analysis systems provide inadequate information about cognitive requirements because they tend to be 'input/output oriented rather than designed to capture what is occurring within the incumbent's mind' (Spector, Brannic & Coovert 1989: p. 290).

To date the moderating role of task requirements has not been tested using a variety of jobs or with job analyses that describe jobs in terms of cognitive demands rather than tasks or behaviours. It is not surprising that job requirements (Box 5a) fail to moderate the ability performance relationship in jobs that are essentially the same, or where the requirements (job analyses) are stated in 'behaviour description' rather than 'cognitive and ability requirement' terms (Schmidt, Hunter & Pearlman, 1981).

There is a problem, however, in obtaining information about the cognitive requirements of jobs. Although people in jobs can describe what tasks they do, they may not be well equipped to describe the skills and abilities required to perform the tasks, especially not in a terminology that is useful for linking job requirements to cognitive assessments of the person (Hesketh, McLachlan & Gardner, 1992; Hughes & Prien, 1989). This is so for two reasons. First, job incumbents may have automated or proceduralized their skills and hence they may no longer have sufficient verbal access to the skills that are required to perform a task. Such automation is in the nature of expertise (Andrews, 1991; Ackerman, 1987). Landy and Vasey (1991) found that 'subject matter experts' (SMEs) with more job experience provided very different task ratings when compared with SMEs with less experience. Although the authors suggest other possible explanations, it is quite likely that raters with more expertise had automated many of the skills they used and hence paid attention to different aspects of their job compared with those with less experience. The second reason for concern about using job incumbents as a source of information about the skills required in jobs is that they may not have a sufficiently detailed conceptual understanding of the constructs underlying ability assessments to provide suitable ratings. For this reason, judges with a relevant conceptual understanding are required to make the inferences of the cognitive and other requirements of the tasks involved.

The development of accurate methods of assessing the cognitive skills required in jobs is important for reasons other than the testing of selection hypotheses. The increased symbolic nature of work (Hesketh & Chandler, 1990), the ageing workforce (Warr, in press), and the demands of technical personnel for job analysis systems that capture the complexities and requirements of their jobs combine to create pressure for the development of a cognitive job analysis system. For example, in a study examining attitudes to job analysis systems, Taber and Peters (1991) found that people in technical and more complex jobs were the most negative and critical of job analysis systems, complaining that they were incomplete and did not apply to their work.

Through student project work at the University of New South Wales (Hesketh et al., 1992) Task Anchored Rating Scales (TARS) assessing the cognitive demands of jobs have been developed using a BARS procedure (similar to that used by Landy et al., 1991 for the time urgency construct discussed above). The idea is similar to that found in Mumford, Weeks, Harding and Fleishman's approach to measuring occupational difficulty (1988) and to Fleishman and Mumford's (1991) ability requirement scales. Ideas for dimensions were drawn from developments in describing the cognitive constructs underlying performance on ability and intelligence tests (e.g. Carroll, 1976). This approach offers one way of linking job analysis to ability testing, something that is essential to provide a fair test of the matching selection hypothesis.

The emphasis evident in this section on person-environment fit embodied in the Theory of Work Adjustment (Dawis & Lofquist, 1984) does not imply that people and organizations are static. Change is occurring constantly, and employees and organizations must adapt to these changes. The challenge is to develop appropriate measurement for dealing with change.

Dealing with Change

A major challenge facing industrial and organizational psychologists lies in the need to describe, understand, predict and ultimately manage the increased pace of change in jobs, organizations and in individuals' skill levels. The measurement challenges are considerable. In order to describe and understand change, one must know the state of both the individual and the organization before change takes place, during the transition and at some defined end point. A sensible approach to measuring change involves keeping a constant set of constructs and measures across the various time periods to simplify the analysis. Concerns remain, however, that the concepts and measures developed to assess individuals or environments at one time may cease to be appropriate, or may fail to fully capture the new state of events at a later stage. Furthermore, estimates of error variance relevant to reliability are not necessarily uniform across time (Shavelson, Webb & Rowley, 1989). Since the influential article by Cronbach and Furby (1970) the debate about the best way of measuring change has continued (e.g. Fischer, 1987; Willett, 1989; Sackett, 1991).

In moving from description and understanding of change to its prediction and management, it will be necessary to develop adequate measures of individuals' and organizations' flexibility, adaptability and propensity to change. There is a convergence among several theoretical models about two major styles of change, called active and reactive modes of adjustment in the Theory of Work Adjustment (Dawis & Lofquist, 1984), and shaping and adaptation by Sternberg (1985). Active modes of adjustment involve individuals changing the organization or managers of environments trying to change individuals, while reactive modes involve individuals adjusting to fit the organization and managers adjusting the situation for individuals.

A reactive mode of adjustment from an individual's perspective involves accommodating to the environment, by changing behaviour to fit the organizational and job culture. This is what Schein (1978) claims happens in the early stages of joining an organization. From an organizational perspective this reactive mode on the part of the individual is facilitated by the active use of various socialization techniques such as Realistic Job Previews (Premack & Wanous, 1985) and induction or other training.

However, individuals are not passive absorbers of what happens in organizations. They may actively change the situation to suit themselves, for example by shedding tasks they can no longer do (or no longer want to do) in favour of ones they feel better equipped to do or prefer to do (Warr & Conner, 1992). This process usually takes place after an individual has worked for some time in a job (Schein, 1978). From an organizational perspective job redesign is one way of responding reactively to accommodate the active demands of individuals. Warr and Conner (1992) highlight these processes as one of the ways in which people adjust and jobs get altered to cope with the changes associated with ageing. Other terms used to describe adjustment modes can be found in Nicholson's (1984) model of transitions and in Kirton's Adaptation-Innovation Index (Kirton, 1987).

In addition to measuring modes of adjustment, there is a need to assess an overall propensity for change on the part of individuals and environments. For example, particular environments may be more constrained and less flexible, limiting individuals' opportunities for active modes of adjustment. This idea relates to the notion of strong situations in which there is little scope for individual differences to count (Buss & Craik, 1983; Adler & Weiss, 1988; Kendrick & Funder, 1988). Alternatively, individuals will vary in terms of their flexibility, placing constraints on the extent to which environments can actively change them. Interestingly, one of the 'big five' personality dimensions has been defined as 'openness to experience' (Barrick & Mount, 1991), which was shown to relate to success in training. 'Openness to experience' may be relevant to understanding and measuring adaptability, flexibility and propensity for change. An associated idea is that of Brockner (1983) who found that individuals low in self-esteem were more susceptible to social influence. No doubt research in future will explore how self-esteem and openness to experience interact to determine the extent to which individuals do change.

Kirton and McCarthy (1988) have attempted to assess organizational climate in terms of the same constructs underlying the Kirton Adaptation-Innovation inventory, providing what could be considered a measure of an organization's propensity for change. There remains, however, an urgent need for further conceptual clarification and the development of suitable ways of measuring individual and organizational adjustment styles and openness to change.

Other Areas Where Measurement Issues Warrant Attention

Three somewhat unrelated issues are raised in this section because of the need for more careful attention to relevant measurement problems. The first deals with the reactivity of measures in the context of selection, the second with ability as a moderator of the validity and structure of other measures, and the third with a very practical issue, namely the psychometric adequacy of job evaluation systems.

Reactivity of measures

More attention should be paid to the reactivity of measures to the context in which they are administered, an issue relevant to concurrent and predictive validity and to differences in typical and maximal performance (Sackett, Zedeck & Fogli, 1988). An associated idea is the inappropriate reactivity of measures to the mood states of respondents (see earlier discussion on negative affectivity). Lane and Herriot (1990) provide insight into reactivity as it relates to self- and supervisor performance ratings. The reactivity of tests and ratings can be examined within a generalizability theory framework. What is needed is information about the reliability of tests performed under different demand conditions. Arvey, Strickland, Drauden and Marlin (1990) attempted to address this issue by developing a measure to assess the motivational component of test taking. Applicants did report higher effort and motivation when taking tests as part of a selection procedure than when doing so after being employed.

Tests of cognitive ability, with clear right and wrong answers, are less likely to be reactive than are non-cognitive tests. However, Hough et al. (1990) argue that reactivity of this sort is not an issue for personality assessment, and that one can generalize from validities established in a concurrent context to their use in a predictive sense. A thorough generalizability analysis of personality and cognitive tests which includes an examination of the extent to which these tests are reactive to the demand characteristics of the context of administration as well as to the influence of training and job experience is required. With respect to personality tests, it is probably important to distinguish reactivity to the demand characteristics of the administration context from the concept of social desirability (Walsh, 1990) and from a form of 'social intelligence' or 'practical intelligence' (Cantor & Kihlstrom, 1987; Sternberg & Wagner, 1989) which may be indicative of an applicant's capacity to know what is required and to respond appropriately to a test. Careful partitioning of the variance due to trait levels of personality, state mood affects, social desirability, socially intelligent responses to the demand characteristics of the situation, and random error will be needed in order to understand the nature of scores on non-cognitive tests. A clarification of these issues will be helpful in deciding whether these measures can be useful in a selection context.

Ability as a moderator of the adequacy of measurement of other variables

Another measurement issue that has received surprisingly little attention is the possibility of differential reliability and perhaps validity of a particular measure (e.g. personality tests and attitude scales) as the function of the trait level on another measure (e.g. intelligence). Apart from attention given to the reading level of testing material and questionnaires, few studies have addressed this question. A welcome exception is evident in the work of Stone, Stone and Guental (1990), who examined the influence of ability on questionnaire responses. Among other results they found higher levels of missing data in the lower ability respondents' questionnaires. Research is currently underway at the University of New South Wales examining the role of ability as a moderator of the structure of work values and interests. Significant findings will have implications for a wide array of measures used in organizational settings.

Job evaluation

The final issue relates to problems with job evaluation systems arising out of the inadequate measurement of the cognitive demands of jobs and the failure to apply appropriate psychometric principles to the systems. There is considerable dissatisfaction with traditional job evaluation systems on the part of technical staff who suspect that the systems fail to capture the cognitive requirements and complexity of their work (Taber & Peters, 1991). A disproportionate amount of attention in recent years has been directed toward capturing and remunerating the management requirements in jobs, with the resulting disparity in salaries paid to managerial and technical personnel (Hesketh, Gardner & Lissner, in press). These differences probably reflect the comparative lack of value placed on skills in countries such as the USA, UK and Australia, a value orientation that has infused the job evaluation systems. Cross-cultural research on job evaluation systems may demonstrate a different value orientation in countries such as Japan and Germany.

Job evaluation systems are in need of much closer psychometric scrutiny (Henderson, 1988; Sanchez & Levine, 1989). This is particularly so with respect to the number of dimensions that are needed both for validity and for acceptability (Taber & Peters, 1991), the uni-dimensionality and independence of these compensable dimensions, the explicit weightings given to the dimensions (Davis & Sauser, 1991), and the unintended weightings arising from a failure to standardize dimensions prior to combining factors.

SUMMARY

This chapter uses the Minnesota Theory of Work Adjustment (Dawis & Lofquist, 1984) as an organizing framework for examining measurement issues in industrial and organizational psychology. Modern test theory issues covered include Generalizability Theory and Item Response Theory, and the applications of IRT to detecting DIFferential item functioning and to the development of adaptive testing. The chapter illustrates the relevance of generalizability theory to developments in criterion measurement, and outlines measurement developments such as the group productivity measurement system ProMES (Pritchard et al., 1988). The importance of measuring individuals and environments on common dimensions to facilitate person-environment fit is outlined, while measurement issues associated with testing notions of fit are highlighted. Finally measurement issues are raised with respect to the reactivity of measurements particularly in selection contexts, ability as a moderator of the validity of other tests and questionnaires, and psychometric issues in job evaluation.

REFERENCES

Ackerman, P. L. (1987) Individual differences in skill learning: an integration of the psychometric and information processing perspective. *Psychological Bulletin*, **102**, 3–37.

Adams, A. (1991) Ergonomic interventions. In B. Hesketh and A. Adams (eds), *Psychological Perspectives on Occupational Health and Rehabilitation*. Marrickville: Harcourt Brace Jovanovich.

Adler, S. and Weiss, H. M. (1988) Recent developments in the study of personality and organizational behaviour. In C. L. Cooper and I. T. Robertson (eds), *International Review of Industrial and Organizational Psychology 1988*. Chichester: Wiley.

Ajzen, I. (1991) The theory of planned reasoned action. *Organizational Behavior and Human Decision Processes*, **50**, 179–211.

Anderson, J. C. and Gerbing, D. W. (1988) Structural equation modeling in practice: A review and recommended two-step approach. *Psychological Bulletin*, **103**, 411–423.

Andrews, S. (1991) Cognitive processes in skill acquisition: Implications for training. In B. Hesketh and A. Adams (eds), *Psychological Perspectives on Occupational Health and Rehabilitation*. Marrickville, NSW: Harcourt Brace Jovanovich.

Applegate, B. and LeBlanc, W. G. (1990) Creating item characteristic curves from LOGIST and BICAL output. *Educational and Psychological Measurement*, **50**, 581–584.

Arvey, R. D., Bouchard, T. J. Jr, Segal, N. L. and Abraham, L. M. (1989) Job satisfaction: Environmental and genetic components. *Journal of Applied Psychology*, **74**, 187–192.

Arvey, R. D., Strickland, W., Drauden, G. and Martin, C. (1990) Motivational components of test taking. *Personnel Psychology*, **43**, 695–716.

Austin, J. T., Humphreys, L. G. and Hulin, C. L. (1989) Another view of dynamic criteria: A critical reanalysis of Barrett, Caldwell and Alexander. *Personnel Psychology*, **42**, 583–596.

Baker, C. and Jackson, P. R. (1991) Validity of two personality inventories: A cautionary tale. *British Psychological Society*, **7**, 4–7.

Balasubramanian, S. K. and Kamakura, W. A. (1989) Measuring consumer attitudes toward the marketplace with tailored interviews. *Journal of Marketing Research*, **26**, 311–326.

Barrett, G. V. and Depinet, R. L. (1991) A reconsideration of testing for competence rather than for intelligence. *American Psychologist*, **46**, 1012–1024.

Barrick, M. R. and Mount, M. K. (1991) The big five personality dimensions and job performance: A meta-analysis. *Personnel Psychology*, **44**, 1–26.

Bartram, D. (1987) The development of an automated testing system for pilot selection. The MICROPAT project. *Applied Psychology: an International Review*, **36**, 279–298.

Bass, A. R. and Ager, J. (1991) Correcting point-biserial turnover correlations for comparative analysis. *Journal of Applied Psychology*, **76**, 595–598.

Bejar, I. I. (1990) A generative analysis of a three-dimensional spatial task. *Applied Psychological Measurement*, **14**, 237–245.

Bobko, P. (1986) A solution to some dilemmas when testing hypotheses about ordinal interactions. *Journal of Applied Psychology*, **71**, 323–326.

Borman, W. C. and Hallan, C. L. (1991) Observation accuracy for assessors of work sample performance: Consistency across task and individual difference correlates. *Journal of Applied Psychology*, **76**, 11–19.

Borman, W. C., White, L. A., Pulakos, E. D. and Oppler, S. H. (1991) Models of supervisory job performance ratings. *Journal of Applied Psychology*, **76**, 863–872.

Brockner, J. (1983) Low self esteem and behavioral plasticity. In L. Wheeler and P. Shaver (eds), *Review of Personality and Social Psychology* Vol. 4. Beverly Hills, CA: Sage.

Buss, D. and Craik, K. (1983) The act frequency approach to personality. *Journal of Personality and Social Psychology*, **90**, 105–216.

Caldwell, D. F. and O'Reilly, III, C. A. (1990) Measuring Person-Job fit with a profile comparison process. *Journal of Applied Psychology*, **73**, 648–657.

Campbell, J. P. (1990) An overview of The Army Selection and Classification Project (Project A). *Personnel Psychology*, **43**, 231–240.

Campbell, J. P. and Campbell, R. J. (1988) *Productivity in Organizations*. London: Jossey Bass.

Campbell, J. P., McHenry, J. J. and Wise, L. L. (1990) Modeling job performance in a population of jobs. *Personnel Psychology*, **43**, 313–333.

Campion, M. A. (1991) Meaning and measurement of turnover: Comparisons of alternative measures and recommendations for research. *Journal of Applied Psychology*, **76**, 199–212.

Cantor, N. and Kihlstrom, J. F. (1987) *Personality and Social Intelligence*. Englewood Cliffs, NJ: Prentice-Hall.

Caplan, R. D. (1987) Person-environment fit theory and organizations: Commensurate dimensions, time perspectives and mechanisms. *Journal of Vocational Behavior*, **31**, 248–267.

Carroll, J. B. (1976) Psychometric tests as cognitive tasks: a new 'structure of intellect'. In L. Resnick (ed.), *The Nature of Intelligence*. Hillsdale, NJ: Lawrence Erlbaum.

Carroll, J. B. (1990) Estimating item and ability parameters in homogeneous tests with the person characteristic function. *Applied Psychological Measurement*, **14**, 109–125.

Chen, P. Y. and Spector, P. E. (1991) Negative affectivity as the underlying cause of correlations between stressors and strains. *Journal of Applied Psychology*, **76**, 398–407.

Clegg, C. and Wall, T. (1990) The relationship between simplified jobs and mental health: A replication study. *Journal of Occupational Psychology*, **63**, 289–296.

Cohen, A. S., Kim, S. H. and Subkoviak, M. J. (1991) Influence of prior distribution on detection of DIF. *Journal of Educational Measurement*, **28**, 49–59.

Cooper, M. D., Phillips, R. A., Roberston, I. T. and Duff, A. R. (1991) Improving safety on construction sites by the utilization of psychologically based techniques: Alternative approaches to the measurement of safety behaviour. Paper presented at the Vth European Congress of the Psychology of Work and Organization, Rouen, France, 1991.

Cooper, M. D., Robertson, I. T., Duff, A. R. and Phillips, R. A. (1992) Assigned or participatively set goals: Do they make a difference? Paper presented at the BPS Occupational Psychology Conference, Liverpool, 1992.

Cotton, J. L. and Tuttle, J. M. (1986) Employee turnover: A meta-analysis and review with implications for research. *Academy of Management Review*, **11**, 55–70.

Cronbach, L. J. and Furby, L. (1970) How should we measure 'change'—or should we? *Psychological Bulletin*, **74**, 68–80.

Cronbach, L. J. and Gleser, G. C. (1953) Assessing similarity between profiles. *Psychological Bulletin*, **50**, 456–473.

Cronbach, L. J., Gleser, G. C., Nanda, H. and Rajaratnam, N. (1972) *The Dependability* of Behavioral Measurements: Theory of Generalizability for Scores and Profiles. New York: Wiley.

Darman, R. Y. (1990) Identifying sources of turnover costs: A segmental approach. Journal of Marketing, 54, 46–56.

Davis, K. R. and Sauser, W. I. (1991) Effects of alternative weighting methods in a policy-capturing approach to job evaluation: A review and empirical investigation. Personnel Psychology, 44, 85–127.

Dawis, R. V. (1987) Requirement, capability and opportunity. Canadian Journal of Guidance and Counselling, 3, 55–60.

Dawis, R. V. and Lofquist, L. H. (1984) A Psychological Theory of Work Adjustment. Minneapolis: University of Minnesota Press.

Deadrick, D. L. and Madigan, R. M. (1990) Dynamic criteria revisited: A longitudinal study of performance stability and predictive validity. Personnel Psychology, 43, 717–744.

Dodd, B. G., Koch, W. R. and de Ayala, R. J. (1989) Operational characteristics of adaptive testing procedures using the graded response model. Applied Psychological Measurement, 13, 129–143.

Drasgow, F. and Hulin, C. (1992) Item Response Theory. In M. D. Dunnette and L. Hough (eds), Handbook of Industrial and Organizational Psychology (2nd edn). Vol III. Palo Alto: Consulting Psychologists Press.

Driver, M. J. (1988) Careers: A review of personal and organizational research. In C. L. Cooper and I. Robertson (eds), International Review of Industrial and Organizational Psychology 1988. Chichester: Wiley.

Edwards, J. (1991) Person-job fit. In C. Cooper and I. Robertson (eds), International Review of Industrial and Organizational Psychology 1991. Chichester: Wiley.

Edwards, J. R., Baglioni, A. J., Jr and Cooper, C. L. (1990) Examining relationships among self-report measures of Type A behavior pattern: The effects of dimensionality, measurement error and differences in underlying constructs. Journal of Applied Psychology, 75, 440–454.

Ellis, B. B. (1989) Differential item functioning: Implications for test translations. Journal of Applied Psychology, 74, 912–921.

Ellis, B. B., Minsel, B. and Becker, P. (1989) Evaluation of attitude survey translations: An investigation using Item Response Theory. International Journal of Psychology, 24, 665–684.

Evans, M. G. (1991) The problem of analyzing multiplicative composites: Interactions revisited. American Psychologist, 46, 6–15.

Fischer, G. H. (1987) Applying the principles of specific objectivity and generalizability to the measurement of change. Psychometrica, 54, 565–587.

Fleishman, E. A. (1982) Systems for describing human tasks. American Psychologist, 37, 1–14.

Fleishman, E. A. and Mumford, M. D. (1989) Abilities as causes of individual differences at different stages of skill acquisition. Human Performance, 2, 201–222.

Fleishman, E. A. and Mumford, M. D. (1991) Evaluating classification of job behavior: A construct validation of the Ability Requirements Scales. Personnel Psychology, 44, 523–576.

Forgas, J. P. (1990) Affective influences on social perception and judgments. Psychologia, 9, 495–520.

Frost, A. G. and Orban, J. A. (1990) An examination of an appropriateness index and its effect on validity coefficients. Journal of Business and Psychology, 5, 23–36.

George, J. M. (1990) Personality, affect and behavior in groups. Journal of Applied Psychology, 75, 107–116.

George, J. M. (1991) State or trait: Effects of positive mood on prosocial behaviors at work. *Journal of Applied Psychology*, **76**, 299–307.

Gerhart, B. (1990) Voluntary turnover and alternative job opportunities. *Journal of Applied Psychology*, **75**, 467–476.

Ghiselli, E. E., Campbell, J. P. and Zedeck, S. (1981) *Measurement Theory for the Behavioral Sciences*. San Francisco: W. H. Freeman.

Gitomer, D. H. and Yamamoto, K. (1991) Performance modeling that integrates latent trait and class theory. *Journal of Educational Measurement*, **28**, 173–189.

Goldstein, H. and Wood, R. (1989) Five decades of item response modelling. *British Journal of Mathematical and Statistical Psychology*, **42**, 139–167.

Guion, R. M. and Gibson, W. M. (1988) Personnel selection and placement. *Annual Review of Psychology*, **39**, 349–374.

Guzzo, R. A. et al. (1986) Implicit theories and the evaluation of group processes and performance. *Journal of Organizational Behavior and Human Decision Processes*, **37**, 279–295.

Hambleton, R. K. (ed.) (1983) *Applications of Item Response Theory*. Vancouver, BC, Canada: Educational Research Institute of British Columbia.

Hambleton, R. K. and Swaminathan, H. (1985) *Item Response Theory: Principles and applications*. Boston: Kluwer-Nijhoff.

Hanges, P. J., Schneider, B. and Niles, K. (1990) Stability of performance: An interactionist perspective. *Journal of Applied Psychology*, **75**, 658–667.

Hansen, J. C. and Campbell, D. P. (1985) *Manual for the Strong–Campbell Interest Inventory*. Palo Alto, CA: Consulting Psychologists Press.

Hauenstein, N. M. A. and Alexander, R. A. (1991) Rating ability in performance judgements: The joint influence of implicit theories and intelligence. *Organizational Behavior and Human Decision Processes*, **50**, 300–323.

Heavlin, N. D., Lee-Merrow, S. W. and Lewis, V. M. (1982) The psychometric foundations of goal attainment scaling. *Community Mental Health Journal*, **18**, 230–241.

Henderson, R. I. (1988) Job evaluation, classification and pay. In S. Gael (ed.), *The Job Analysis Handbook for Business, Government and Industry* (pp. 90–118). New York: Wiley.

Henly, S. J., Klebe, K. J., McBride, J. R. and Cudeck, R. (1989) Adaptive and conventional versions of the DAT: The first complete test battery comparison. *Applied Psychological Measurement*, **13**, 363–371.

Herriot, P. (1988) Selection at a crossroads. *The Psychologist: Bulletin of the British Psychological Society*, **10**, 388–392.

Hesketh, B. et al. (1992) *The 'g' factor in job analysis: Do we need specific task ratings?* Special Report, School of Psychology, University of New South Wales, Sydney, Australia.

Hesketh, B., Adams, A. and Allworth, E. (1991) Ability, cognitive and physical requirements. In B. Hesketh and A. Adams (eds), *Psychological Perspectives on Occupational Health and Rehabilitation*. Marrickville, NSW: Harcourt Brace Jovanovich.

Hesketh, B. and Chandler, P. (1990) Training in the use of numerically controlled and computerized numerically controlled systems in industry. In U. E. Gattiker (ed.), *End User Training*. New York: Walter de Gruyter.

Hesketh, B. and Dawis, R. V. (1991) The Minnesota Theory of Work Adjustment: A conceptual framework. In B. Hesketh and A. Adams (eds), *Psychological Perspectives on Occupational Health and Rehabilitation*. Marrickville, NSW: Harcourt Brace Jovanovich.

Hesketh, B., Gardner, D. and Lissner, D. (in press) Technical and managerial career paths: an unresolved dilemma. *International Journal of Career Management*.

Hesketh, B., McLachlan, K. and Gardner, D. (1992) Work Adjustment Theory: An empirical test using a fuzzy rating scale. *Journal of Vocational Behavior*, to appear September.

Hinsz, V. B. and Nelson, L. C. (1990) Testing models of turnover intentions with university faculty. *Journal Applied Social Psychology*, **20**, 68–84.

Hoffman, C. C., Nathan, B. R. and Holden, L. M. (1991) A comparison of validation criteria: Objective versus subjective performance measures and self-versus supervisor ratings. *Personnel Psychology*, **44**, 601–619.

Hogan, J. (1991) Structure of physical performance in occupational tasks. *Journal of Applied Psychology*, **76**, 495–507.

Hogan, R. (1982) A socioanalytic theory of personality. In M. Page and R. Dienstbier (eds), *Nebraska Symposium on Motivation* (pp. 55–89). Lincoln, NE: University of Nebraska Press.

Hoijtink, H. (1990) A latent trait model for dichotomous choice data. *Psychometrika*, **55**, 641–656.

Holland, J. L. (1985) *Making Vocational Choices: A Theory of Vocational Personalities and Work Environments*. Englewood Cliffs, NJ: Prentice-Hall.

Hom, P. W. and Griffeth, R. W. (1991) Structural equation modelling test of a turnover theory: Cross sectional and longitudinal analyses. *Journal of Applied Psychology*, **76**, 350–366.

Hough, L. M., Eaton, N. K., Dunnette, M. D., Kamp, J. D. and McLoy, R. A. (1990) Criterion-related validities of personality constructs and the effect of response distortion on those validities. *Journal of Applied Psychology*, **75**, 581–595.

Hughes, G. L. and Prien, E. P. (1989) Evaluation of task and job skill linkages: judgments used to develop test specifications. *Personnel Psychology*, **42**, 284–292.

Hunter, J. E., Schmidt, F. L. and Judiesch, M. K. (1990) Individual differences in output variability as a function of job complexity. *Journal of Applied Psychology*, **75**, 28–42.

Ilgen, D. and Schneider, J. (1991) Performance measurement: A multi-discipline view. In C. L. Cooper and I. T. Robertson (eds), *International Review of Industrial and Organizational Psychology 1991*. Chichester: Wiley.

Ironson, G. H., Smith, P. C., Brannick, M. T., Gibson, W. M. et al. (1989) Construction of a Job in General scale: A comparison of global, composite and specific measures. *Journal of Applied Psychology*, **74**, 193–200.

Johnson, S. and Bell, J. F. (1985) Evaluating and predicting survey efficiency using generalizability theory. *Journal of Educational Measurement*, **22**, 107–119.

Kane, M. T. (1987) On the use of IRT models with judgmental standard setting procedures. *Journal of Educational Measurement*, **24**, 333–345.

Kanfer, R. and Ackerman, P. L. (1989) Motivation and cognitive abilities: An integrative/aptitude-treatment interaction approach to skill acquisition. *Journal of Applied Psychology*, **74**, 657–690.

Kendrick, D. R. and Funder, D. C. (1988) Profiting from controversy: Lessons from the person-situation debate. *American Psychologist*, **43**, 23–35.

Kingma, J. and Taerum, T. (1988) A FORTRAN 77 program for a nonparametric item response model: The Mokken scale analysis. *Behaviour Research Methods, Instruments and Computers*, **20**, 471–480.

Kingsbury, G. G. (1990) Adapting testing: Using the MicroCAT testing system in a local school district. *Educational Measurement Issues and Practice*, **9**, 3–6.

Kiresuk, T. J. and Lund, S. H. (1982) Goal attainment scaling: A medical–correctional application. *Medicine and Law*, **1**, 227–251.

Kiresuk, T. J. and Sherman, R. E. (1968) Goal attainment scaling: A general method for evaluating comprehensive community mental health programs. *Community Mental Health Journal*, **4**, 443–453.

Kirton, M. J. (1987) *Kirton Adaptation-Innovation Inventory (KAI)-Manual*, 2nd edn. Hatfield: Herts: Occupational Research Centre.

Kirton, M. J. and McCarthy, R. M. (1988) Cognitive climate and organizations. *Journal of Occupational Psychology*, **61**, 175–184.

Klieger, D. M. (1990) Flexible testing without programming. *Behavior Research Methods, Instruments and Computers*, **22**, 138–141.

Koch, W. R., Dodd, B. G. and Fitzpatrick, S. J. (1990) Computerized adaptive measurements of attitudes. *Measurement and Evaluation in Counseling and Development*, **23**, 20–30.

Komaki, J. L., Zlotnick, S. and Jensen, M. (1986) Development of an operant-based taxonomy and observational index of supervisory behavior. *Journal of Applied Psychology*, **71**, 260–269.

Kozlowski, S. W. J. and Ford, J. K. (1991) Rater information acquisition: Tracing the effects of prior knowledge, performance level, search constraint and memory demand. *Organizational Behavior and Human Decision Processes*, **49**, 282–301.

Kraiger, K. and Teachout, M. S. (1990) Generalizability theory as construct-related evidence of the validity of job performance ratings. *Human Performance*, **3**, 19–35.

Landy, F. J. (1986) Stamp collection versus science: Validation as hypothesis testing. *American Psychologist*, **41**, 1183–1192.

Landy, F. J., Rastegary, J., Thayer, J. and Colvin, C. (1991) Time urgency: The construct and its measurement. *Journal of Applied Psychology*, **76**, 644–657.

Landy, F. J. and Vasey, J. (1991) Job analysis: The composition of SME samples. *Personnel Psychology*, **44**, 27–50.

Lane, J. and Herriot, P. (1990) Self ratings, supervisor ratings, positions and performance. *Journal of Occupational Psychology*, **63**, 77–88.

Lawrence, R. J. (1989) Causal modelling in industrial and organizational psychology. In C. L. Cooper and I. T. Robertson (eds), *International Review of Industrial and Organizational Psychology 1989*. Chichester: Wiley.

Lee, C. W. and Smith, G. A. (1988) The efficiency of a tailored procedure in predicting CPI scale scores. *Australian Psychologist*, **23**, 25–30.

Levin, I. and Stoker, J. P. (1989) Dispositional approaches to job satisfaction: Role of negative affectivity. *Journal of Applied Psychology*, **74**, 725–758.

Lim, R. G. and Drasgow, F. (1990) Evaluation of two methods for estimating Item Response Theory parameters when assessing differential item functioning. *Journal of Applied Psychology*, **75**, 164–174.

Locke, E. A. and Latham, G. P. (1990) *A Theory of Goal Setting and Task Performance*. London: Prentice-Hall.

Lofquist, L. H. and Dawis, R. V. (1969) *Adjustment to Work*. New York: Appleton-Century-Crofts.

Lord, F. M. (1980) *Applications of Item Response Theory to Practical Testing Problems*. Hillsdale, NJ: Erlbaum.

Marcoulides, G. A. (1989) Performance appraisal: Issues of validity. *Performance Improvement Quarterly*, **2**, 3–12.

Marcoulides, G. A. and Goldstein, Z. (1990) The optimization of generalizability studies with resource constraints. *Educational and Psychological Measurement*, **50**, 761–768.

Martin, R. and Wall, T. D. (1989) Attentional demand and cost responsibility as stressors in shopfloor jobs. *Academy of Management Journal*, **1**, 69–86.

McDonald, T. (1991) The effect of dimension content on observation and rating of job performance. *Organizational Behavior and Human Decision Processes*, **48**, 252–271.

McKinley, R. L. (1989) An introduction to Item Response Theory. *Measurement and Evaluation in Counseling and Development*, **22**, 37–57.

Mislevy, R. J. and Stocking, M. L. (1989) A consumer's guide to LOGIST and BILOG. *Applied Psychological Measurement*, **13**, 57–75.

Mislevy, R. J. and Verhelst, N. (1990) Modeling item responses when different subjects employ different solution strategies. *Psychometrika*, **55**, 195–215.

Mumford, M. D., Weeks, J. L., Harding, F. D. and Fleishman, E. A. (1988) Measuring occupational difficulty: A construct validation against training criteria. *Journal of Applied Psychology*, **72**, 578–587.

Murphy, K. (1988) Psychological measurement: abilities and skills. In C. C. Cooper and I. T. Robertson (eds), *International Review of Industrial and Organizational Psychology 1988*. Chichester: Wiley.

Murphy, K. R. (1989) Is the relationship between cognitive ability and job performance stable over time? *Human Performance*, **2**, 183–200.

Murphy, K. R. (1991) Criterion issues in performance appraisal research: Behavioral accuracy versus classification accuracy. *Organizational Behavior and Human Decision Processes*, **50**, 45–50.

Murphy, K. R. and Balzar, W. K. (1989) Rater errors and rating accuracy. *Journal of Applied Psychology*, **74**, 619–624.

Murphy, K. R. and Davidshofer, C. O. (1991) *Psychological Testing: Principles and Applications*. Englewood Cliffs, NJ: Prentice-Hall.

Murphy, K. R., Philbin, T. A. and Adams, S. R. (1989) Effect of purpose of observation on accuracy of immediate and delayed performance ratings. *Organizational Behavior and Human Decision Processes*, **43**, 336–354.

Nathan, B. R. and Alexander, R. A. (1988) A comparison of criteria for test validation: A meta-analytic investigation. *Personnel Psychology*, **41**, 517–536.

Newton, T. and Keenan, T. (1991) Further analyses of the dispositional argument in organizational behavior. *Journal of Applied Psychology*, **76**, 781–787.

Nicholson, N. (1984) A theory of work role transitions. *Administrative Science Quarterly*, **29**, 172–191.

Owens, W. A. and Schoenfeldt, L. E. (1979) Towards a classification of persons. *Journal of Applied Psychology*, **68**, 570–607.

Padgett, M. Y. and Ilgen, D. R. (1989) The impact of ratee performance characteristics on rater cognitive processes and alternative measures of rater accuracy. *Organizational Behavior and Human Decision Processes*, **44**, 232–260.

Prediger, D. (1989) Ability differences across occupations: more than g. *Journal of Vocational Behavior*, **34**, 1–27.

Premack, S. and Wanous, J. P. (1985) A meta-analysis of realistic job preview experiments. *Journal of Applied Psychology*, **70**, 706–719.

Pritchard, R. D., Jones, S. D., Roth, P. L., Stuebing, K. K. and Ekebert, S. E. (1988) Effects of group feedback, goal setting and incentives on organizational productivity. *Journal of Applied Psychology*, **73**, 337–358.

Pritchard, R. D., Jones, S. D., Roth, P. L., Stuebing, K. K. and Ekebert, S. E. (1989) The evaluation of an integrated approach to measuring organizational productivity. *Personnel Psychology*, **42**, 69–115.

Pritchard, R. D. and Roth, O. G. (1991) Accounting for nonlinear utility functions in composite measures of productivity and performance. *Organizational Behavior and Human Decision Processes*, **50**, 341–359.

Reckase, M. D. (1989) Adaptive testing: The evolution of a good idea. Special Issue:

Computer applications to testing: Review of recent research and developments. *Educational Measurement Issues and Practice*, **8**, 11–15.

Reise, S. P. and Waller, N. G. (1990) Fitting the two-parameter model to personality data. *Applied Psychological Measurement*, **14**, 45–58.

Rice, R. W., Gentile, D. A. and McFarlin, D. B. (1991) Facet importance and job satisfaction. *Journal of Applied Psychology*, **76**, 31–29.

Rice, R. W., McFarlin, D. B. and Bennett, D. E. (1989) Standards of comparison in job satisfaction. *Journal of Applied Psychology*, **74**, 591–598.

Robbins, A. S., Spence, J. T. and Clark, H. (1991) Psychological determinants of health and performance: The tangled web of desirable and undesirable characteristics. *Journal of Personality and Social Psychology*, **61**, 755–765.

Robertson, I. T. and Kinder, A. (1992) The criterion related validity of personality variables: An hypothesis driven meta-analysis. Paper presented at the British Psychological Society Conference, Liverpool, 1992.

Rodgers, R. and Hunter, J. E. (1991) Impact of management by objectives on organizational productivity [Monograph]. *Journal of Applied Psychology*, **76**, 322–335.

Rosin, H. M. and Korabik, K. (1991) Workplace variables, affective responses and intention to leave among women managers *Journal of Occupational Psychlogy*, **64**, 317–330.

Rothkopt, J. S. and Blaney, P. H. (1991) Mood congruent memory: The role of affective focus and gender. *Cognition and Emotion*, **5**, 53–64.

Rothstein, H. R. (1990) Interrater reliability of job performance ratings: Growth to asymptote level with increasing opportunity to observe. *Journal of Applied Psychology*, **75**, 322–327.

Rothstein, H. R., Schmidt, F. L., Erwin, F. W., Owens, W. A. and Sparks, C. P. (1990) Biographical data in employment selection: Can validities be made generalizable? *Journal of Applied Psychology*, **75**, 175–184.

Rounds, J. B., Dawis, R. V. and Lofquist, L. H. (1987) Measurement of person-environment fit and prediction of satisfaction in the Theory of Work Adjustment. *Journal of Vocational Behavior*, **31**, 297–318.

Roznowski, M. (1989) Examination of the measurement properties of the Job Descriptive Index with experimental items. *Journal of Applied Psychology*, **74**, 805–814.

Sackett, P. R. (1991) On interpreting measures of change due to training or other interventions. A comment on Cascio (1989, 1991). *Journal of Applied Psychology*, **76**, 590–591.

Sackett, P. R., Burris, L. R. and Ryan, A. M. (1989) Coaching and practice effects in personnel selection. In C. Cooper and I. Robertson (eds), *International Review of Industrial and Organizational Psychology 1989*. Chichester: Wiley.

Sackett, P. R., Zedeck, S. and Fogli, L. (1988) Relations between measures of typical and maximum job performance. *Journal of Applied Psychology*, **73**, 482–486.

Sanchez, J. I. and Levine, E. L. (1989) Determining important tasks within jobs: A policy capturing approach. *Journal of Applied Psychology*, **74**, 336–342.

Schein, E. H. (1978) *Career Dynamics*. Reading, MA: Addison-Wesley.

Schmidt, F. L., Hunter, J. E. and Pearlman, K. (1981) Task differences as moderators of aptitude test validity in selection: A red herring. *Journal of Applied Psychology*, **66**, 166–185.

Schmitt, N. and Robertson, I. T. (1990) Personnel selection methods. *Annual Review of Psychology*, **41**, 289–319.

Schuler, H. and Guldin, A. (1991) Methodological issues in personnel selection research. In C. L. Cooper and I. T. Robertson (eds), *International Review of Industrial and Organizational Psychology 1991*. Chichester: Wiley.

Shavelson, R. J., Mayberry, P. W., Li, W. and Webb, N. M. (1990) Generalizability of job performance measurements: Marine Corps rifleman. *Military-Psychology*, **2**, 129–144.

Shavelson, R. J., Webb, N. M. and Rowley, G. L. (1989) Generalizability theory. *American Psychologist*, **44**, 922–932.

Shore, L. M. and Martin, J. J. (1989) Job satisfaction and organizational commitment in relation to work performance and turnover intentions. *Human Relations*, **42**, 625–638.

Shore, L. M., Newton, L. H. and Thornton, G. C. (1990) Job and organizational attitudes in relation to employee behavioral intention. *Journal of Organizational Behavior*, **11**, 57–67.

Singh, J., Howell, R. D. and Rhoads, G. K. (1990) Adaptive designs for Likert-type data: An approach for implementing marketing surveys. *Journal of Marketing Research*, **27**, 304–321.

Sparrow, J. (1989) The utility of the PAQ in relating job behaviours to traits. *Journal of Occupational Psychology*, **62**, 151–162.

Spector, P. E., Brannick, M. T. and Coovert, M. D. (1989) Job analysis. In C. L. Cooper and I. T. Robertson (eds), *International Review of Industrial and Organizational Psychology 1989*. Chichester: Wiley.

Staw, B. M. and Ross, J. (1985) Stability in the midst of change: A dispositional approach to job attitudes. *Journal of Applied Psychology*, **70**, 469–480.

Steel, P. P., Shane, G. S., Kennedy, K. A. (1990) Effects of social systems factors on absenteeism, turnover and job performance. *Journal of Business and Psychology*, **4**, 473–430.

Steel, R. P., Hendrix, W. H. and Balogh, S. P. (1990) Confounding effects of the turnover base rate on relations between time lag and turnover study outcomes: An extension of meta-analysis findings and conclusions. *Journal of Organizational Behavior*, **11**, 237–242.

Steel, R. P. and Ovalle, N. K. (1984) Review and meta-analysis of research on the relationship between behavioral intention and employee turnover. *Journal of Applied Psychology*, **69**, 637–686.

Sternberg, R. J. (1985) *Beyond IQ: A Triarchic Theory of Human Intelligence*. Cambridge: Cambridge University Press.

Sternberg, R. J. and Wagner, R. K. (eds) (1989) *Practical Intelligence: Nature and Origins of Competence in the Everyday World*. Cambridge: Cambridge University Press.

Stone, E. F., Stone, D. L. and Guental, H. G. (1990) Influence of cognitive ability on responses to questionnaire measures: Measurement precision and missing response problems. *Journal of Applied Psychology*, **75**, 418–427.

Stout, W. F. (1990) A new Item Response Theory modeling approach with applications to uni-dimensionality assessment and ability estimation. *Psychometrika*, **55**, 293–325.

Sulsky, L. M. and Balzar, W. K. (1988) Meaning and measurement of performance rating accuracy: Some methodological and theoretical concerns. *Journal of Applied Psychology*, **73**, 497–506.

Taber, T. D. and Peters, T. D. (1991) Assessing the completeness of a job analysis procedure. *Journal of Organizational Behavior*, **12**, 581–593.

Tett, R. P., Jackson, D. N. and Rothstein, M. (1991) Personality measures as predictors of job performance: A meta-analytic review. *Personnel Psychology*, **44**, 703–742.

The American College Testing Program (1981) Technical report for the Unisex edition of the ACT Interest Inventory (UNIACT). Iowa City, Iowa: ACT.

Thissen, D. and Steinberg, L. (1988) Data analysis using Item Response Theory. *Psychological Bulletin*, **104**, 385–395.

Traub, R. E. (1983) A priori considerations in choosing an item response model. In R. K. Hambleton (ed.), *Applications of Item Response Theory*. Vancouver, BC, Canada: Educational Research Institute of British Columbia.

Wainer, H. (1989) The future of item analysis. *Journal of Educational Measurement*, **26**, 191–208.

Wainer, H., Sireci, S. G. and Thissen, D. (1991) Differential testlet functioning: Definitions and detectors. *Journal of Educational Measurement*, **28**, 197–220.

Wall, T. D. and Davids, K. (1992) Shopfloor work organization and advanced manufacturing technology. In C. Cooper and I. T. Robertson (Eds.). *International Review of Industrial and Organizational Psychology 1992*. Chichester: Wiley.

Wall, T. D., Jackson, P. R. and Davids, K. (1992) Operator work design and robotics system performance: A serendipitous field study. *Journal of Applied Psychology*, **77**, 353–362.

Waller, N. G. and Reise, S. P. (1989) Computerized adaptive personality assessment: An illustration with the Absorption scale. *Journal of Personality and Social Psychology*, **57**, 1051–1058.

Walsh, J. A. (1990) Comment on social desirability. *American Psychologist*, **45**, 289–290.

Wanous, J. P. (1989) Installing a realistic job preview: Ten tough choices. *Personnel Psychology*, **42**, 117–133.

Warr, P. (1990) The measurement of well-being and other aspects of mental health. *Journal of Occupational Psychology*, **63**, 193–210.

Warr, P. B. (in press) Age and employment. In M. D. Dunnette (ed.), *Handbook of Industrial and Organizational Psychology* Vol. IV. Palo Alto: Consulting Psychologists Press.

Warr, P. and Conner, M. (1992) Job competence and cognition. In B. M. Staw and L. L. Cummings (eds), *Research in Organizational Behavior*, Vol. 12. Greenwich, Conn.: JAI Press.

Watson, D. and Pennebaker, J. W. (1989) Health complaints, stress and distress: Exploring the central role of negative affectivity. *Psychological Review*, **96**, 234–254.

Webb, N. M, Shavelson, R. J., Kim, K. and Chen, Z. (1989) Reliability (generalizability) of job performance measurements: Navy machinest mates. *Military Psychology*, **1**, 91–110.

Weiss, D. J. (ed.) (1983) *New Horizons in Testing: Latent Trait Theory and Computerized Adaptive Testing*. New York: Academic Press.

Weiss, D. J. and Vale, C. D. (1987) Adaptive testing. *Applied Psychology: An International Review*, **36**, 249–262.

White, P. O. (1979) A latent trait model for individual differences in speed, accuracy and persistence. In R. Wood (ed.), *Rehabilitating Psychometrics*. London: Social Sciences Research Council.

Willett, J. B. (1989) Some results on reliability for the longitudinal measurement of change. *Educational and Psychological Measurement*, **49**, 587–602.

Williams, C. R. (1990) Deciding when, how and if to correct turnover correlations. *Journal of Applied Psychology*, **75**, 736–737.

Wise, L. L., McHenry, J. and Campbell, J. P. (1990) Identifying optimal predictor composites and testing for generalizability across jobs and performance factors. *Personnel Psychology*, **43**, 355–366.

Woodruffe, C. (1991) Competent by any other name. *Personnel Management*, **23**, Sept, 30–33.

Young, J. W. (1991) Gender bias in predicting college academic performance: A new approach using Item Response Theory. *Journal of Educational Measurement*, **28**, 37–47.

Chapter 5

MEDICAL AND PHYSIOLOGICAL ASPECTS OF JOB INTERVENTIONS

Töres Theorell
Karolinska Hospital, Stockholm, Sweden

INTRODUCTION

Several recent publications support the hypothesis that work organization resulting in a poor psychosocial work environment may result in increased mortality, incidence of illness and sick leave. Efforts to improve the work organization according to theories based upon such findings, which will be labelled job interventions in the following text, have been a logical consequence. The question of whether and to what extent job interventions really lead to improved health has been the next scientific medical question in this field. A related research field is the use of physiological and medical methods in the monitoring of the change process itself. In the present review a medical perspective will be used. First of all there will be a general review of publications dealing with the relationship between different aspects of the psycho-social work environment on one hand and various medical conditions on the other hand. The second section will review physiological and medical monitoring of the job intervention process itself, while the third section will deal with medical consequences of job interventions aimed at improved psycho-social work conditions.

PSYCHO-SOCIAL WORK ENVIRONMENT AND MEDICAL CONDITIONS

A Clinical Example Illustrating the Impact of Work Problems on the Heart

Merely thinking about psychosocial job problems may have a dramatic physiological impact. One example in the literature (see de Faire and Theorell,

1984) was a conversation with a man who had recently suffered a myocardial infarction and who was a supervisor in a department store. The electrocardiogram that was continuously recorded during a conversation showed short bouts of ventricular tachycardia, a potentially life-endangering condition, during a discussion about a particular work problem (one of the subordinates was suspected of theft in the department where the patient was working). One other topic was also associated with similar bouts of ventricular tachycardia—the discussion about the horrifying experiences he had had during the onset and early course of his myocardial infarction. During other problematic parts of the conversation no electrocardiographic abnormalities were recorded. Thus the arrhythmias were not merely a consequence of conversation about non-specific troubling previous experiences—only certain kinds of topics were able to trigger them. This example illustrates the impact that a common work organization problem may have on an employee. In this case, we were dealing with a mixture of feelings of lack of control and lack of support from workmates.

Work Environment and Coronary Heart Disease

Does the psycho-social work environment really affect health? A common belief is that the work organization affects work satisfaction and other soft endpoints that may not be very important anyway. Most of the present article will therefore deal with somatic 'hard endpoints'. Research by our group and others has shown that 'job strain', a combination of excessive psychological demands and lack of decision latitude, is associated with increased risk of developing myocardial infarction before regular retirement age (for reviews see Kristensen, 1989, and Karasek and Theorell, 1990). American, Finnish and Swedish studies have indicated that the relative risk of developing a myocardial infarction in occupations characterized in aggregated analyses as 'strain occupations' is between 1.2 and 2.0. If self-reported descriptions of the jobs are used, the relative risks are in the order of 2.0 to 4.0. If lack of social support is added to job strain, the precision of the predictions is improved (Johnson and Hall, 1988). One way of summarizing this is to say that individual workers in the best 'iso-strain' quintile, who describe their jobs as not excessively demanding and with good decision latitude and good support avoid cardiovascular death for eight years longer than other workers (Johnson, Hall and Theorell, 1989). The original 'demand-control' model seems to work better for men in blue-collar jobs than for other strata of the working population. For women and for white-collar men interactions between social support and decision latitude seemed more important (Johnson and Hall, 1988). There have been considerable variations in methodology, outcomes and samples studied. Despite this, the findings on job strain and cardiovascular illness or mortality have been remarkably consistent. A prospective cohort study of middle-aged men in Hawaii showed no association between job strain and cardiovascular disease incidence (Reed, La Croix, Karasek, Miller and McLean, 1989), but this study of a sample that deviates culturally from other studied samples is the only one that has not shown any association at all.

Using another frame of reference, Siegrist and collaborators (Siegrist, Peter, Junge, Cremer and Seidel, 1990) have shown that 'lack of social reward' is significantly associated with increased risk of developing early myocardial infarction and that chronic exposure to adverse psycho-social job stressors (lack of promotion possibility, shift work and threat of unemployment) is associated with atherogenic risk factor patterns (Siegrist, Matschinger, Cremer and Seidel, 1988). Cooper and Marshall (1976) and Kahn (1974) have also pointed at relationships between occupational stressors and coronary heart disease risk indicators.

Work Environment, Life Style and Physiological Mechanisms

Although the terminology varies between different authors (Karasek and Theorell, 1990; Cooper and Payne, 1978; Katz and Kahn, 1966), there is general agreement that basic dimensions that have to do with work load, ability to influence decisions, opportunity to learn things and social interactions could be of importance to the amount of perceived stressors that the employee is exposed to in his work. And the amount of perceived job stressors may subsequently affect health.

Several mechanisms may underlie the association between job stressors and cardiovascular risk. One mechanism may be indirect—job stressors influencing lifestyle factors. It has been pointed out (Green, 1988; Tagliacozzo and Vaughn, 1982; Conway, Vickers, Ward and Rahe, 1981) that excessive smoking is more common among employees who work in high-pressure jobs than it is for other people. Any clear relationship between job strain and serum lipids has not been established, although there may be a relationship between chronic exposure to some kinds of job stressors and atherogenic serum lipoproteins (Siegrist et al., 1988; Lundberg, Fredrikson, Wallin, Melin and Franken-haeuser, 1989). In the case of blood pressure, there is evidence that blood pressure regulation is affected by job strain (Theorell, Knox, Svensson and Waller, 1985; Theorell, Perski, Åkerstedt, Sigala, Ahlberg-Hulten, Svensson and Eneroth, 1988; Theorell, de Faire, Johnson, Hall, Perski and Stewart, 1991a; Schnall, Pieper, Karasek, Schwartz, Schlussel, 1990) although the evidence is hard to interpret with conflicting findings in other studies (Chapman, Mandryk, Frommer, Edye and Ferguson, 1990; Winkleby, Ragland and Syme, 1988). The discrepancy in findings on hypertension may partly be due to underlying systematic distortions in self-reported job descriptions (Theorell, 1990a) in hypertensive-prone persons and in persons with early-stage asymptomatic hypertension. Both these groups have been described as less prone to report problems than other subjects. Conversely, in subjects who are aware that they are hypertensive the distortion may become reversed, leading to over-reporting of problems. Also, the way in which blood pressure has been measured is important. The most recent development is measuring blood pressure continuously by means of ambulatory equipment which provides more relevant data than the conventional blood pressure recordings.

It has been shown that variations in social support at work over time are associated with changes in systolic blood pressure—improving social support with decreasing systolic blood pressure during working hours (Theorell, 1990b) and vice versa. Furthermore, there is evidence that subjects who report poor social support at work have a higher habitual heart rate than others, possibly indicating a high level of sympatho-adrenal activity (Undén and Orth-Gomér, 1991). In summary, it is possible that part of the relationship between demand–control–support and cardiovascular disease is due to effects on established cardiovascular risk factors. On the other hand, several studies (see Karasek and Theorell, 1990) have shown that part of the association is independent of such risk factors. Catecholamines may be significant mediators, and it has been speculated that catecholamine effects on coagulation may be important (Markowe, Marmot, Shipley, Bulpitt, Meade and Stirling, 1985; Möller and Kristensen, 1991). Carbohydrate metabolism is also influenced by catecholamines, and studies have shown that glycated haemoglobin—which is influenced by carbohydrate metabolism—reacts slowly after several weeks of continuously high catecholamine excretion. Glycated haemoglobin (HbA_1C) may thus be a useful indicator of mediating link between job strain and cardiovascular risk (Kawakami, Hayashi and Matsumoto, 1989; Netterström and Sjöl, 1991).

Individual Psychological Characteristics and Work Environment

What about individual psychological characteristics? One criticism against the hypothesis that work organization has an aetiological role in cardiovascular disease is that subjects choose occupations on the basis of personal characteristics and that, accordingly, all the associations could be spurious. Studies have been made both with direct (self-reported) and indirect measures (group means) of the work environment, and parallel findings have been made. Several studies which include both measures of personal characteristics (mainly Type A behaviour) and work environment have been published, and they show that the association between job characteristics and cardiovascular illness risk holds even when adjustment for behaviour pattern has been made. Although individual behaviour pattern or personality, as far as we know, cannot explain the job strain–myocardial infarction association, it is likely, however, that such individual characteristics interact with job stressors. For instance, in the Framingham study (La Croix, 1984), the Type A pattern showed strong interaction with job strain—the coronary heart disease incidence was highest in subjects with both Type A behaviour and job strain. It has been shown in a longitudinal study that subjects with a family history of hypertension react with more blood pressure elevation, more decrease in testosterone levels and less cortisol and prolactin elevation than others when job strain increases (Theorell et al., 1988; Theorell, 1990b). Such results could be interpreted in a psycho-physiological perspective. It could be that hypertensive-prone persons do not appraise difficulties in stressful situations to the same extent that others do. Despite this, they react with a more pronounced sympatho-adrenal activation than others, and also show differences from other subjects in the normal population with regard to physiological reactivity to stressors.

Work Environment and Rehabilitation

Could the psycho-social work environment affect the subsequent course of a chronic disease? If so, this would have importance to rehabilitation as well. A recent study has indicated that men aged below 45 returning to a stressful job after a first myocardial infarction may run an elevated risk of dying from a new myocardial infarction during five years of follow-up (Theorell, Perski, Orth-Gomér, Hamsten and de Faire, 1991b). If this finding can be replicated on larger samples, it may indicate that job stressors are also important in cardiac rehabilitation. Physicians involved in rehabilitation after myocardial infarction should check not only the amount of physical demands that the worker is exposed to when he is sent back to work, but also what the psycho-social situation may be.

Other Illnesses

I have gone into some detail regarding cardiovascular risk because heart disease is a 'hard' endpoint, illustrating that job stressors could not only make employees seriously ill but also shorten their lives. However, the job stressors we have discussed may have relevance to other somatic illnesses as well, such as musculo-skeletal (Theorell, Harms-Ringdahl, Ahlberg-Hulten and Westin, 1991c; Johnson, 1985), gastro-intestinal symptoms (Nyhrén, 1985), and psychiatric conditions (Karasek, 1979; Broadbent, 1985; Alfredsson, Spetz and Theorell, 1985). Sick leave rates have been studied in the Danish slaughterhouse industry in a wide study by Kristensen (1991). This showed a strong relationship between job strain and a high sickness absence rate in these workers. In addition, House and his co-workers (House, 1981; House, Strecher, Metzner and Robbins, 1986) have shown that lack of social support at work is a powerful predictor of several indicators of poor health.

Theoretical Concepts and their Relationship to Work Organization

How do the three theoretical concepts—demand, decision latitude and social support—relate to work organization? All three dimensions are associated with the work organization. Qualitative and quantitative demands are possible to regulate through organizational change. Decision latitude, terminology introduced by Karasek (1979), has two main components, namely 'intellectual discretion' and 'authority over decisions'. *Intellectual discretion* refers to the opportunities that the work environment provides the individual to develop new skills (and possibly to cope with unexpected events at work). *Authority over decisions* refers to the direct possibility that the individual has to influence what should be done and how it should be done. The two components mostly constitute one element in factor analysis, although they could be dissociated, as in orchestral musicians—who have very low authority over decisions although intellectual discretion is relatively high—and also have different health correlates (Theorell, 1989). They are both affected by the work environment. Increased intellectual discretion corresponds to increased opportunities for the employees to develop skills at work, whereas increased authority over decisions corresponds to improved workplace democracy. The employer could increase the opportunities for workers to learn new things at work, although the opposite alternative has also been discussed (Berg, 1970). Increased intellectual discretion in the workplace might make workers more able and more motivated, but unless this increase in knowledge and engagement is coupled with opportunities for workers to participate in decisions, this will have no lasting beneficial effect on the company. In our own studies, the two single questions ('Do you learn new things at your work—yes or no?' and 'Is your work monotonous—yes or no?'), used for classifying jobs on the Swedish labour market, have been very successful in predicting which occupations are associated with increased risk of developing long-lasting illness, and are consequently associated with substantial financial losses for society (Karasek and Theorell, 1990; Alfredsson, Spetz and Theorell, 1985). General calculations regarding financial costs as a result of psycho-socially induced illness, although difficult to interpret, indicate the great potential financial importance of improved intellectual discretion. The interesting argument from the employer's point of view is 'what is good for the health of the employees is generally also good for productivity'.

On the basis of a study of spontaneous changes in job conditions in the Swedish working population, Karasek (1990) observed that change in general was associated with increased prevalance of health problems. However, a closer examination revealed that changes leading to increased decision latitude were associated with decreased prevalance of some health problems—it was among workers with decreased decision latitude that increased health problems were observed.

Social support at work is also associated with work organization (Johnson, 1991). An example of examining the working environment in a specific sector is a study of conditions in Swedish prisons. Several work dimensions, such as consensus in work goals, understimulation, decision latitude, management style, self-rated work performance and social climate were constructed on the basis of questionnaire responses. Data concerning sick leave rates, self-reported symptoms and plasma cortisol were collected. Averages were calculated for 67 prisons, and ecological analyses were performed. Several strong relationships were found among these variables (Härenstam, Palm and Theorell, 1988; Härenstam, 1989). As pointed out by Johnson (1991), decision latitude and social support may be closely inter-related. This will also be evident in the descriptions of the job interventions below.

USING PHYSIOLOGICAL MONITORING IN THE FOLLOW-UP OF ORGANIZATIONAL CHANGE

The Change Process

Once the decision has been made to initiate a change, it is important also to monitor the process itself. Change processes are frequently monitored by means of psycho-social questionnaires and observations. It is possible, however, that medical doctors could also contribute to the understanding of the change process by introducing physiological parameters that mirror important aspects of the change. It is important to know, for instance, whether employees perceive the process as something that induces feelings of uneasiness, whether there is a general feeling of powerlessness or the reverse, and whether the process is able to stimulate anabolism (restoration of bodily functions). It is clear that the change process itself could be described as a sequence of stages. In Figure 5.1 (see Karasek and Theorell, 1990), an effort has been made to describe the different stages. During the 'engagement' and 'search' phases there is mostly a neutral or positive feeling in relation to the change. During the 'change' phase, however, there could be serious conflicts and a multitude

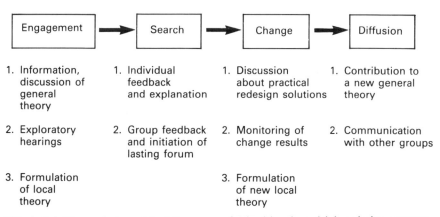

Figure 5.1 Theoretical model of the successful health-oriented job redesign process
Source: R. A. Karasek and T. Theorell, *Healthy Work. Stress, Productivity and the Reconstruction of Working Life*. New York: Basic Books, Figure 6.1. © 1990 Reproduced by permission of HarperCollins Publishers

of negative and positive feelings. This is where endocrinological observations could be helpful. During the 'diffusion' phase most of the turmoil has stopped. It is during this phase—which could occur many months and even years after the start of the intervention—that the enduring beneficial health effects, if any, could be observed.

An Endocrinological Description of the Change Phase

Research which may illustrate endocrine changes taking place during a psychosocial job change is a study of a job intervention (Eriksson, Orth-Gomér, Moser and Theorell, 1991; Theorell, Moser, Orth-Gomér, Undén and Eriksson, 1992) which took place in government offices in Sweden. The intervention, which lasted for several months, comprised a thorough exploration of psychosocial conditions and a follow-up with feedback and recommendations regarding work organization changes. It was followed-up after four months. Plasma samples were taken in the morning before, three times at regular intervals during and immediately after the intervention, and finally four months after the end of the intervention. Three endocrine factors were measured in plasma, namely cortisol, prolactin and testosterone. Cortisol elevation is probably an indicator of feelings of uneasiness in change (Frankenhaeuser, 1991), prolactin elevation—which is partly caused by decreased activity in the dopaminergic system in the brain—is probably an indicator of feelings of powerlessness in a crisis situation (Theorell, 1992), and testosterone may indicate a positive physical and psychological activation which may mirror increased anabolic activity (Theorell, Karasek and Eneroth, 1990). In the study of the job intervention, one of the work sites was described as much more active in organizational change than the other sites. This was reflected in marked differences in cortisol reaction (see Figure 5.2). During the end of the intervention, when feedback from superiors was reported to deteriorate in the relatively passive groups but to improve in the active group, cortisol levels were high in the passive and low in the active group, probably indicating feelings of uneasiness in the passive and feelings of joy in the active group. Prolactin changes differed significantly between men and women. In women, there was an increased prolactin level in the beginning of the intervention in both groups. In men, plasma prolactin even tended to decrease. This may indicate that there were different attitudes to the change in men and women respectively. Plasma testosterone increased in both groups, possibly indicating a general stimulation effect. The combined study of several endocrine factors may increase the understanding of the change process. Observed variations in endocrine variables are not vulnerable to bias in the same way as questionnaires, interviews and observations, although they have other sources of error. In most cases, we shall have to rely on the latter kinds of methodology, but endocrine and other physiological measures may facilitate a deeper understanding of the general conditions in changes of work organization.

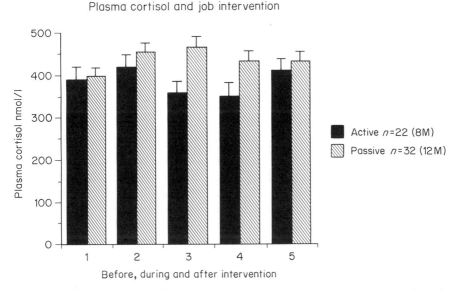

Figure 5.2 Morning levels of plasma cortisol in participants in a psycho-social job intervention on an 'organizationally active' work site (Active) and on three 'organizationally passive' sites (Passive). ANOVA group $p = 0.11$, time $p = 0.01$, interaction group time $p = 0.003$

CHANGES IN HEALTH AFTER JOB CHANGE

There is a wide range of measurable health outcomes, from sick leave measures which reflect a mixture of health and non-health-related outcomes, to the more specific cardiovascular mortality. There are measurement and interpretation problems in all of these outcomes. The ideal situation from a medical point of view is when objective physiological parameters have been used.

Lipoproteins

In the study described above, one of the aims was to improve individual lifestyle. In order to test whether real changes had taken place, plasma lipoproteins were measured before, immediately after intervention, and four months later. In the follow-up the lipoprotein patterns had changed, with a significantly improved ratio between the harmful LDL and the beneficial HDL in the intervention (active and passive groups together), but not in the control group. This could be a consequence of the individually oriented health education and stress management components of the programme. There has been substantial interest in the use of the workplace as a basis for individually oriented health promotion—which is an important activity (Fielding, 1989;

Kilbom, 1988), but not the topic of the present review. There is also a possibility, however, that a general improvement in the psycho-social work situation could increase the employees' willingness to follow health promotion advice, and that the improved psycho-social climate is associated with improved health *per se*. Accordingly, we could expect some beneficial spin-off effects on health after a successful work organization change. There are several examples of this.

Sick Leave

Most studies in this field have used sick leave data as the measure of health outcome. Job enrichment, job enlargement, responsibility for a complete product and feedback or group formation were the central components in the Quality of Working Life experiments. Kopelman's review (1985) of the results of Quality of Working Life experiments indicated that both quality and quantity of production increased and at the same time sick leave had decreased on average by 19% (in 16 studies with such data, reanalysis by Karasek and Theorell, 1990: p. 182). The central ideas in these experiments were very close to the job intervention strategies, which are logical consequences of the results we have discussed above. Sick leave is not a pure health outcome, since it is also influenced to some extent by non-work-related factors. In the examples that follow, the public sector has been in focus. Relatively few research findings are available from the private sector, and part of the reason for this may be business competition. There are exceptions to this rule, for instance, from the Volvo car factories in Sweden (Wallin and Wright, 1986). The occupational health care team at Volvo has been using a set of questionnaires in order to explore the psycho-social environment, which also contains questions about health. This is used for the monitoring of both psycho-social work environment and health changes during job intervention.

In a study of health care personnel, Jackson (1983) tried a job change intervention involving the training of all employees in problem-solving and a doubling or tripling of the number of scheduled staff meetings to two per month. The study group was a hospital outpatient facility, and randomly assigned experimental and control groups were used with a pre-test and a 6-month follow-up period. The results indicated that after 6 months there was a significant drop in two job stressors related to 'decision-making', 'role conflict and role ambiguity'. As a result, employees in the experimental group experienced significant reduction in emotional strain, job dissatisfaction, absenteeism and intention to leave their jobs.

Another example was the redesign tested on two floors of a nursing home (Arnetz, 1983). The primary goal of the intervention was to increase the social competence and active coping ability of the nursing home customers—the elderly. The idea was to bring about this change by finding out what the previous occupations and interests of the elderly had been, and on the basis of this information to constitute groups of elderly who met at frequent and regular intervals to jointly perform activities that they were interested in. The nursing personnel played an important role in this because they had to trigger the group activities. However, the nursing staff also received education in social support for the elderly, and they actually made some of the observations on the elderly people in the experiment.

The experiment involved two floors of the nursing home, one for the experiment and one for the control. In both groups, behavioural and endocrinological measurements were performed before, during and immediately after the intervention in the elderly. These measurements showed that the elderly in the experimental group, but not those in the control group, developed more active anabolism and improved carbohydrate metabolism, and became calmer and more socially active. The nursing staff met once every month to discuss the progress of this change and to find solutions for unexpected complications. One consequence of these meetings was that the nursing staff decided to start working in teams rather than to use an individual rotation scheme. One of the most important observations was that the sick leave rate among the personnel in the experimental group became half that of those in the control group. A trend of increasing sick leave was broken.

Lazes and co-workers (Lazes, 1978; Lazes, Wasilewski and Redd, 1977) have described a similar experiment in a diabetes-control outpatient clinic in New Jersey. The job design intervention in this case initially focused on correcting the health care assistants' clinical errors, reducing their dissatisfaction and absenteeism, and thus relieving the overloading of doctors' schedules. The old hierarchical structures were changed by means of the creation of new tasks for the underutilized health care workers who were assigned to teach classes to patients on diabetes control procedures such as self-administration of insulin,- diet maintenance and exercise. This redesign of work had the double effect of making the employees more involved in their work, and of making the patients more responsible for their own treatments. The result of this was an increase in the kept-appointment rate among patients from 52 to 71%, and a decrease in sick leave rate among nursing staff by 50%.

More Specific Health Outcomes

An experiment in the postal service was initiated by Wahlstedt (Wahlstedt and Edling, 1992) on 100 postal workers. The organizational change consisted of a 'flattening' of the work organization, with the deliberate intention of increasing the opportunities for the employees to influence decisions at work and the starting of regular staff meetings every week, with up-dated notice boards. In this case, specific questions were asked regarding symptoms of ill-health. A significantly improved intellectual discretion and authority over decisions was observed, and this change was correlated with a decrease in the level of psychosomatic complaints.

A large-scale experiment has recently been carried out in the home service in seven Swedish communities. As in many of the job redesign experiments already mentioned, an important element in this study was increasing the number of staff meetings and making them more structured. However, several other work organization change were made. The consequences were studied by means of questionnaires which were delivered before and after the intervention, both to the intervention and to the control groups. Several improvements in work climate were observed in the experimental, but not in the control group. Of particular interest, from the health perspective, was the fact that the number of subjects who had back problems decreased significantly in the experimental but not in the control group (Forster, Rönnberg, Skanse and Svensson, 1991). Svensson (1991) has had long experience in work organization changes and has emphasized the importance of a democratic perspective (not top-down but the other way) when changes are initiated. He has also effectively used employees who have already participated in a successful work organization change as messengers to other wards—employees in the unchanged and changed wards exchange jobs for a period (Svensson, 1991).

Work Content in Focus

Most changes in work organization have been initiated because of necessary changes in productivity. One interesting example from private industry was Almex, a factory producing mass-transit bus ticketing machines, a product that must be customized to the requirements of each city transit system. The job change process at Almex began with separate initiatives coming from the local labour union's interest in an engineering redesigning of the product lines to reduce component inventories and to increase design flexibility (Gardell and Svensson, 1981). The organizational change which was coupled to this engineering change consisted of the creation of assembly work groups, comprising 5 to 15 workers. They were given the responsibility for determining all aspects of coordinating the assembly of the complex ticketing apparatus. As a consequence of these changes the company's profitability increased, and management comments indicated that the job reorganization had resulted in fewer customer complaints and increased flexibility (Gardell, 1982). The autonomous groups were compared to other workers in the same factory (control group). The results indicated that feelings of 'psychological stress' and of 'being too tired at night to pursue hobbies or meet friends' were dramatically reduced among the workers in the autonomous groups compared to the control group. These lower reports of psychological strain and higher levels of job satisfaction existed in spite of the fact that the autonomous groups gave employees 'more work' and a higher level of perceived psychological demand.

In all of the examples given, the starting point in the work organization change has been the work itself, the work content and the job organization, not the health of the employees. However, as we have seen, improved health—somatic or psychological, sometimes observed as manifested decrease in sick leave—was a consequence of successful work organization change. An important element in all the interventions presented has been that regular meetings have been arranged or made more frequent or that work has been organized to improve communication. These processes could affect both social support and decision latitude.

Psychological Aspects of the Change Process

A problem which may arise in the change process is that of unexpected, undesired consequences. There is a need for those who initiate organizational change to plan for the whole process. In a longitudinal study of several work sites (Karasek and Theorell, 1990), psycho-social job information was collected for research purposes during a period extending over a year. Each participant was contacted four times, at 3-monthly intervals, with self-administered questionnaires being used on every occasion, and group interviews were performed on every work site. The information was used in scientific publications. However, the exploration itself also started a change process. Every subject received individual feedback regarding medical data. After the collection of individual data had been completed, every subject received a chart indicating his variations in psycho-social and medical data over the year of study. After this, group feedback was given—every work site was compared to other work sites with regard to psycho-social and medical-physiological data. The individual data collection and feedback resulted in some discussions regarding the work organization. After group feedback and meetings of the safety committees, however, such discussions among employees increased substantially (see Table 5.1; Karasek and Theorell, 1990). The questionnaires

Table 5.1 Percentage of participants reporting discussions of the psycho-social work environment

	At the end of data collection (N = 133) (%)	After feedback (N = 139) (%)
Symphony orchestra musicians	32	61
Air traffic controllers	33	61
Physicians	14	28
Freight handlers	35	41
Waiters	27	44
Airplane mechanics	21	29

Note: Percentages are based on two-thirds of the total number of participants. The remaining subjects were lost in the follow-up.
Source: R. A. Karasek and T. Theorell, *Healthy Work. Stress, Productivity and the Reconstruction of Working Life.* New York: Basic Books. ©1990 Reproduced by permission of HarperCollins Publishers.

indicated that awareness about psycho-social problems (such as conflicts and judgement that 'My boss cannot distribute jobs') increased substantially during the period of data collection and individual feedback. This illustrates that conflicts and problems may surface during the search phase. It was only after group feedback, however, that the psycho-social main dimensions changed beneficially—demands decreased and intellectual discretion increased significantly (see Table 5.2; Karasek and Theorell, 1990). This illustrates that work organization change may be a slow process. Resources must be allocated to the change process itself over a long period; in the examples presented the beneficial changes were observable only after many months.

Table 5.2 Changes in self-reported psycho-social job characteristics (Total group of men and women, including only those who participated in the follow-up after feedback, $N = 114$–135, differs between questions)

	First obs. Oct. 1984	Second obs. Feb. 1985	Third obs. May 1985	Fourth obs. Sept. 1985	After feedback
Role conflict[a] ('In order to satisfy one ... one has to disappoint another') (1–4)	1.44	1.46	1.53	1.65	1.73
High turnover of personnel[a] (1–4)	1.70	1.72	1.77	1.79	1.90
Boss cannot superivse and distribute job[a] (1–4)	1.72	1.63	1.70	1.75	1.99
Frequent conflicts with supervisors[a] (1–4)	1.16	1.20	1.24	1.33	1.41
Frequent conflicts in job[a] (1–4)	1.75	1.63	1.67	1.73	1.97
Demand index[a] (5–20)	13.7	13.6	13.6	13.1	12.7
Intellectual discretion index[a] (4–16)	11.8	11.9	11.8	11.7	13.3
Authority over decisions index[b] (2–8)	5.2	4.8	5.1	5.1	5.1

[a]Significant trend ($p < 0.05$), analysis of variance.
[b]No significant trend ($p > 0.05$), analysis of variance.
Source: R. A. Karasek and T. Theorell, *Health/Work. Stress, Productivity and the Reconstruction of Working Life*. New York: Basic Books. ©1990 Reproduced by permission of HarperCollins Publishers.

GENERAL DISCUSSION

There are many research questions that remain unanswered in this field. The most crucial psycho-social work environment factor combinations in relation to cardiovascular disease risk seem to vary in relation to age, social class and gender, and much more research that is specific to different strata of the working population is needed. To be even more specific, the findings on theoretical concept demands, decision latitude and support are too vague to be practically useful. They could be used in a general orientation phase of a change process (general theory according to Figure 5.1), but specific measures have to be constructed for each occupation or branch, as in the study of Swedish occupations, and to some extent even for each work site (local theory according to Figure 5.1). There may even be problems in the measurement of decision latitude when special occupations are studied, since the variance in decision latitude is determined to a great extent by occupation. Karasek (1991), in a theoretical analysis of possible strategies for job redesign, has pointed out that these problems should be attacked in widely different ways among different strata of the working population (managers, professionals, craftsmen, mid-level professionals and administrators, manual labourers, bureaucratized impersonal service workers and commercialized service delivery workers).

The problem in measuring psychological work demands is different from that of measuring decision latitude. Psychological demands have a strong subjective component, and it has been pointed out that occupation explains very little of the variance in this variable (Karasek and Theorell, 1990). In longitudinal studies of individuals, it is the demand component in job strain that shows the strongest variation and also the strongest association with physiological variables (Theorell et al., 1988).

From a medical standpoint, the most crucial combinations of psycho-social work environment factors, seem to vary with outcome as well. Studies of sick leave rates have the advantage that a financially relevant outcome is used. Another advantage is that many illnesses are 'collected' in the same outcome. The disadvantage is that the amount of admixture of 'non-work-caused' sick leave and 'coping' sick leave is unknown, and could differ between different study populations. Studies of well-defined medical diagnoses, on the other hand, have the advantage that they are more objective and less vulnerable to recall bias. But they may be uncommon and of less financial relevance to the company.

The descriptions of job interventions reveal that most interventions have been dealing with the way in which employees communicate with one another and with management. Sometimes social support and sometimes various aspects of decision latitude, intellectual discretion or authority over decisions have been in focus. Sometimes more profound job interventions are needed, which may require technological innovations and advanced new computer systems, as in the case of Almex described above. On the other hand, technological changes do not suffice by themselves, as has been shown in the case of car factories, which have been organized for increased job rotation and team work. In some cases, these changes have not had a lasting beneficial effect on the work climate. Part of the reason for this may simply be that financial constraints have made optimal use of the new factory impossible (Edgren, 1991).

It is important that continued research on medical aspects of job interventions takes place. In the studies of health outcome in relation to job intervention, most data have been on sick leave and we need more objective data. In the study of more specific outcomes, very large samples may be needed, which is the case in the study of myocardial infarction risk. Furthermore, many of the studies published suffer from design problems—only a few of them have used control groups, for instance. An additional problem is that follow-up periods have been relatively short and longer periods are needed in future work.

Very few studies of health outcome in relation to job interventions in the private sector have been studied. One of the reasons for this may be that companies are afraid of publishing data that reveal organizational secrets or solutions. Finally, studies of medical processes taking place during job interventions have only just begun.

CONCLUSION

In conclusion, there are both medical and physiological arguments for improved work organization. There is a need in modern working life for improved authority over decisions, intellectual discretion, social support and a reasonable psychological demand level. These goals are achievable, primarily through changes in work organization. The change process itself can be evaluated in many ways. Physiological and medical observations could be of help in evaluating both the process itself and the outcome. Some research has been published, with promising results, but more studies are needed.

REFERENCES

Alfredsson, L., Spetz, C.-L. and Theorell, T. (1985) Type of occupation and near-future hospitalization for myocardial infarction and some other diagnoses. *Int. J. Epidemiol.* **14**, 378–388.

Arnetz, B. B. (1983) Psychophysiological effects of understimulation in old age. Academic thesis. Department of Stress Research, Karolinska Institute, Stockholm.

Arnetz, B. B., Theorell, T., Levi, L., Kallner, A. and Eneroth, P. (1983) An experimental study of social isolation of elderly people—psychoendocrine and metabolic effects. *Psychosomatic Med.*, **45**, 395–405.

Berg, I. (1970) *Education and Jobs.* New York: Praeger.

Broadbent, D. E. (1985) The clinical impact of job design. *Brit. J. Clin. Psychol.*, **24**, 75–84.

Chapman, A., Mandryk, J. A., Frommer, M. S., Edye, B. V. and Ferguson, D. A. (1990) Chronic perceived work stress and blood pressure among Australian government employees. *Scand. J. Work Env. Health*, **16**, 258–269.

Conway, T. L., Vickers, R. R., Ward, H. W. and Rahe, R. H. (1981) Occupational stress and variation in cigarette, coffee and alcohol consumption. *J. Health Soc. Behav.*, **22**, 155–165.

Cooper, C. L. and Marshall, J. (1976) Occupational sources of stress: A review of the literature relating to coronary heart disease and mental ill health. *J. Occ. Psychol.*, **49**, 11–28.

Cooper, C. L. and Payne, R. (1978) *Stress at Work*. New York: Wiley.

Edgren, B. (1986) Sick leave as 'coping'—a way of achieving relief (Swedish). *Arbete, människa, miljö*, Nr. 1, 25–32.

Edgren, B. (1991) Personal communication. Royal Technological College, Stockholm.

Eriksson, I., Orth-Gomér, K., Moser, V. and Theorell, T. (1991) *KRU-stress*. Stockholm: Statshälsan.

de Faire, U. and Theorell, T. (1984) *Life Stress and Coronary Heart Disease*. St Louis: Warren G. Green.

Fielding, J. E. (1989) Work site stress management: National survey results. *J. Occ. Med.*, **31**, 990–995.

Forster, C., Rönnberg, M., Skanse, M. and Svensson, L. (1991) A study of work schedule, organization and work content change in seven communities in Sweden (Swedish). Report number 2, Örebro College, Örebro, Sweden.

Frankenhaeuser, M. (1991) A biopsychosocial approach to work life issues. In J. V. Johnsson and G. Johansson (eds), *The Psychosocial Work Environment: Work Organization, Democratization and Health*. Amityville, NY: Baywood.

Gardell, B. (1982) Worker participation and autonomy: A multilevel approach to democracy at the workplace. *Int. J. Health Services*, **12**, 527–558.

Gardell, B. and Svensson, L. (1981) *Medbestämmande och Självstyre: En Lokal Facklig Strategi för Demokratisering av Arbetsplatsen*. Stockholm: Prisma.

Green, K. (1988) Job characteristics and health-related behaviors among chemical plant workers. Academic thesis. School of Public Health, Johns Hopkins University, Baltimore, MD, USA.

House, J. S. (1981) *Work Stress and Social Support*. Reading: Mass.: Addison-Wesley.

House, J. S., Strecher, V., Metzner, H. L. and Robbins, C. (1986) Occupational stress and health among men and women in the Tecumseh Community Health Study. *J. Health and Soc. Behav.*, **27**, 62–77.

Härenstam, A. (1989) Prison personnel—working conditions, stress and health. A study of 2000 prison employees in Sweden. Academic thesis. Department of Stress research, Karolinska Institute, Stockholm.

Härenstam, A., Palm, . B. and Theorell, T. (1988) Stress and health and the working environment of Swedish prison staff. *Work and Stress*, **2**, 281–290.

Jackson, S. (1983) Participation in decision making as a strategy for reducing job related strain. *J. Appl. Psychol.*, **68**, 3–19.

Johnson, J. V. (1985) The effects of control and social support on work-related strain and adverse health outcomes. Research report 39, Department of Psychology, University of Stockholm.

Johnson, J. V. (1991) Collective control: Strategies for survival in the workplace. In J. V. Johnson and G. Johansson (eds), *The Psychosocial Work Environment: Work Organization, Democratization and Health*. Amityville, NY: Baywood.

Johnson, J. V. and Hall, E. (1988) Job strain, workplace social support and cardiovascular disease: A cross-sectional study of a random sample of the Swedish working population. *Am. J. Public Health*, **78**, 1336–1342.

Johnson, J. V., Hall, E. and Theorell, T. (1989) The combined effects of work strain and social isolation on prevalence and mortality in cardiovascular disease. *Scand. J. Work, Env. Health*, 15, 271–279.

Kahn, R. (1974) Conflict, ambiguity and overload: Three elements in job stress. In A. McLean (ed.), *Occupational Stress*. Springfield, Ill.: Charles Thomas.

Kahn, R., Wolfe, D., Quinn, R., Snoek, J. and Rosenthal, R. (1964) *Organizational Stress: Studies in Role Conflict and Ambiguity*. New York: Wiley.

Karasek, R. A. (1979) Job demands, job decision latitude and mental strain: Implications for job redesign. *Adm. Sci. Qu.*, 24, 284–307.

Karasek, R. A. (1990) Lower health risk with increased job control among white-collar workers. *J. Occ. Behav.*, 11, 171–185.

Karasek, R. A. (1991) The political implications of psychosocial work redesign: A model of the psychosocial class structure. In J. V. Johnson and G. Johansson (eds), *The Psychosocial Work Environment: Work Organization, Democratization and Health*. Amityville, NY,: Baywood.

Karasek, R. A. and Theorell, T. (1990) *Healthy Work. Stress, Productivity and the Reconstruction of Working Life*. New York: Basic Books.

Katz, D. and Kahn, R. (1966) *Social Psychology of Organizations*. New York: Wiley.

Kawakami, N. S., Hayashi, T. and Matsumoto, T. (1989) Relationship between perceived job-stress and glycosylated hemoglobin in white-collar workers. *Ind. Health*, 27, 149–154.

Kilbom, A. (1988) Intervention programmes for work-related neck and upper limb disorder: strategies and evaluation. *Ergonomics*, 31, 735–747.

Kopelman, R. E. (1985) Job redesign and productivity: A review of the evidence. *Nat. Product Rev.* (Summer), 237–255.

Kristensen, T. S. (1989) Cardiovascular disease and the work environment. *Scand. J. Work, Environ, Health*, 15, 165–179.

Kristensen, T. S. (1991) Sickness absence and work strain among Danish slaughterhouse workers: An analysis of absence from work regarded as coping behaviour. *Soc. Sci. Med.*, 32, 15–27.

La Croix, A. Z. (1984) Occupational exposure to high demand/low control work and coronary heart disease incidence in the Framingham cohort. PhD dissertation, Department of Epidemiology, Univ of North Carolina, Chapel Hill.

Lazes, P. (1978) Health workers and decision making. *Urban Health* (April), 34–55.

Lazes, P., Wasilewski, Y. and Redd, J. D. (1977) Improving outpatient care through participation: The Newark experiment in staff and patient involvement. *J. Health Educ.*, 20, 61–68.

Lundberg, U., Fredrikson, M., Wallin, L., Melin, B. and Frankenhaeuser, M. (1989) Blood lipids as related to cardiovascular and neroendocrine functions under different conditions in healthy males and females. *Pharmacology, Biochemistry and Behavior*, 33, 381–386.

Markowe, H. L., Marmot, M. G., Shipley, M. J., Bulpitt, C. H., Meade, T. W. and Stirling, Y. (1985) Fibrinogen; A possible link between social class and coronary heart disease. *Br. Med J.*, 9, 291–300.

Möller, L. and Kristensen, T. S. (1991) Plasma fibrinogen and ischemic heart disease risk factors. *Arteriosclerosis*, 11, 344–350.

Netterström, B. and Sjöl, A. (1991) Glycated haemoglobin (Hb A1C) as an indicator of job strain. *Stress Med.*, 7, 113–118.

Nyhrén, O. (1985) Non-ulcer dyspepsia. Studies on epidemiology, pathophysiology and therapy. Academic thesis. Department of Surgery, Uppsala University, Uppsala, Sweden.

Reed, D. M., La Croix, A. Z., Karasek, R. A., Miller, D. and McLean, C. A. (1989)

Occupational strain and the incidence of coronary heart disease. *Am J Epidemiol.*, **129**, 495–502.

Schnall, P., Pieper, C., Karasek, R. A., Schwartz, J., Schlussel, Y., Devereux, R. B., Ganau, A., Alderman, M., Warren, K. and Pickering, T. (1990) The relationship between job strain, workplace diastolic blood pressure and left ventricular mass index: Results of a case-control study. *JAMA*, **263**, 1929–1935.

Siegrist, J., Matschinger, M., Cremer, P. and Seidel, D. (1988) Atherogenic risk in men suffering from occupational stress. *Atherosclerosis*, **69**, 211–218.

Siegrist, J., Peter, R., Junge, A., Cremer, P. and Seidel, D. (1990) Low status control, high effort at work and ischemic heart disease: Prospective evidence from blue-collar men. *Soc. Sci. Med.*, **31**, 1127–1134.

Svensson, L. (1991) A democratic strategy for organizational change. In J. V. Johnson and G. Johansson (eds). *The Psychosocial Work Environment: Work Organization, Democratization and Health*. Amityville NY: Baywood.

Tagliacozzo, R. and Vaughn, S. (1982) Stress and smoking in hospital nurses. *Am. J. Public Health*, **72**, 441–446.

Theorell, T. (1989) Personal control at work and health: A review of epidemiological studies in Sweden. In A. Steptoe and A. Appels (eds), *Stress, Personal Control and Health*. New York: Wiley.

Theorell, T. (1990a) Family history of hypertension—an individual trait interacting with spontaneously occuring job stressors. *Scand. J. Work. Env. Health*, **16** (suppl), 74–79.

Theorell, T. (1990b) Social support at work (Swedish). *Socialmed. Tidskrift*, **67**, 27–31.

Theorell, T. (1992) Prolactin—a hormone that mirrors passiveness in crisis situations. *Integrative Physiological and Behavioral Science* (in press).

Theorell, T., Harms-Ringdahl, K., Ahlberg-Hulten, G. and Westin, B. (1991c) Psychosocial factors and symptoms from the locomotor system—a multicausal analysis. *Scand. J. Rehab. Med.*, **23**, 165–173.

Theorell, T., de Faire, U., Johnson, J. V., Hall, E., Perski, A. and Stewart, W. (1991a) Job strain and ambulatory blood pressure profiles. *Scand. J. Work. Env. Health*, **17**, 380–385.

Theorell, T., Karasek, R. A. and Eneroth, P. (1990) Job strain variations in relation to plasma testosterone fluctuations in working men—a longitudinal study. *J. Int. Med.*, **227**, 31–36.

Theorell, T., Knox, S., Svensson, J. and Waller, D. (1985) Blood pressure variations during a working day at age 28: Effects of different types of work and blood pressure level at age 18. *J. Human Stress*, **11**, 36–41.

Theorell, T., Moser, V., Orth-Gomér, K., Undén, A.-L. and Eriksson, I. (1992) Endocrine plasma markers during a job intervention. Manuscript, National Institute of Psychosocial Factors and Health, Stockholm.

Theorell, T., Perski, A., Åkerstedt, T., Sigala, F., Ahlberg-Hulten, G., Svensson, J. and Eneroth, P. (1988) Changes in job strain in relation to changes in physiological states: A longitudinal study. *Scand. J. Work. Env. Health*, **14**, 189–96.

Theorell, T., Perski, A., Orth-Gomér, K., Hamsten, A. and de Faire, U. (1991b) The effects of the strain of returning to work on the risk of cardiac death after a first myocardial infarction before the age of 45. *Int J. Cardiol.* **30**, 61–67.

Undén, A.-L. and Orth-Gomér, K. (1991) Cardiovascular effects of social support in the work place: Twenty-four-hour ECG monitoring of men and women. *Psychosom. Med.*, **53**, 50–60.

Wahlstedt, K. G. I. and Edling, C. (1992) Organizational changes at a postal sorting terminal—its effect upon work satisfaction, psychosomatic complaints and sick-leave. Manuscript, Dept. of Occupational Medicine, Uppsala University, Uppsala, Sweden.

Wallin, L. and Wright, I. (1986) Psychosocial aspects of the work environment: A group approach. *J Occ Med* **28**, 384–393.
Winkleby, M. A., Ragland, D. R. and Syme, S. L. (1988) Self-reported stressors and hypertension: Evidence of an inverse association. *Am. J. Epidemiol.*, **127**, 124–134.

Chapter 6

GOAL ORIENTATION AND ACTION CONTROL THEORY: IMPLICATIONS FOR INDUSTRIAL AND ORGANIZATIONAL PSYCHOLOGY

James L. Farr, David A. Hofmann and Kathleen L. Ringenbach
The Pennsylvania State University, USA

A number of recent approaches to understanding motivated behavior in work (and more general) settings have stressed the important role that *self-regulation* plays in such behavior. Self-regulation refers to the cognitive processes related to the allocation of time and effort to the various overt and covert activities directed toward goal or outcome attainment (Kanfer, 1990b). Included here would be, as examples, goal-setting theory (Locke & Latham, 1990), control theory (Carver & Scheier, 1981; Lord & Hanges, 1987; Lord & Maher, 1989; Klein, 1989), social cognitive theory (Bandura, 1986), and the integrated information processing/resource allocation framework of Kanfer and Ackerman (Kanfer, 1987; Kanfer & Ackerman, 1989). Although these approaches differ in terms of the mechanisms used to explain motivated behavior in work settings, they share the perspective that the goals of the individual serve an important function in regulating the allocation of time and effort to various activities (Kanfer, 1990b).

Taken together, the published research studies related to these several approaches offer strong support for the impact of goals on work behavior and performance. However, each approach separately, and the set of approaches collectively, must acknowledge the role of individual differences in goal–performance relationships. Specific delineation of what constitutes these individual differences is not as well developed as other aspects of these theories and represents a theoretical and empirical shortcoming of the extant literature.

Over the past decade two theoretical frameworks, each buttressed with considerable empirical data, have been developed outside the domain of industrial and organizational psychology that have promise for enhanced

International Review of Industrial and Organizational Psychology 1993 Volume 8
Edited by C. L. Cooper and I. T. Robertson. © 1993 John Wiley & Sons Ltd.

understanding of work motivation. Each suggests an individual difference variable that may moderate the relationships among goals, feedback, behavior, and performance outcomes. These approaches are learning versus performance goal orientation (Dweck, 1986, 1989; Dweck & Leggett, 1988; Elliott & Dweck, 1981) and action control theory (Kuhl, 1985, 1992, in press a).

The purposes of this chapter are to describe in some detail the elements of the learning versus performance goal orientation framework and action control theory; to note some ways in which these two approaches complement each other; and to suggest implications that these approaches have for some selected topics of interest to industrial and organizational psychologists. That these approaches are not well integrated at present into the I/O literature is demonstrated by a single reference to each in a recent special issue on theories of cognitive self-regulation published in *Organizational Behavior and Human Decision Processes* (Ajzen, 1991; Bandura, 1991; Binswanger, 1991; Latham & Locke, 1991; Locke, 1991a, b). We believe that I/O psychology theory and research would be well served by consideration of these constructs.

Note: After this chapter was written, an issue of *Applied Psychology: An International Review* (1992, **41**, Issue 2), appeared which included a lead article by Kuhl (which we had had in preprint form), six commentary articles by various researchers on self-regulation, and a rejoinder by Kuhl. Interested readers are referred to these articles for additional material on action control theory.

GOAL ORIENTATION: A SUMMARY OF THEORY AND RESEARCH

The effectiveness and influence of goal setting on subsequent performance has been well documented (Locke & Latham, 1990). The majority of the goal-setting research, however, has been primarily concerned with an individual's *performance* on a specific task. For example, some of the earliest research on the effectiveness of goal setting concerned increasing the performance of logging crews (Latham & Kinne, 1974). The dependent variables in these situations were increases in the amount of wood harvested in a given period of time and employee absenteeism. In addition, each 'sawhand' was given a counter in order to record the number of trees felled (see also Latham & Baldes, 1975). More recent goal-setting investigations have asked subjects to process company invoices and track inventory (Kernan & Lord, 1990), to build a tower using blocks (Mitchell & Silver, 1990), to play a word strategy game (Mathieu, in press), and to input randomly generated numbers (Tubbs & Dahl, 1991), just to name a few.

In most goal-setting research situations, the investigations are centered upon the performance differences between individuals who had been assigned, or who had set their own, differing levels of goals. In achievement situations, however, Dweck and her colleagues (Dweck, 1986, 1989; Dweck & Leggett, 1988) have discussed and demonstrated that the way in which individuals approach a task can influence their behavior in a number of respects. These influences include, but are not limited to, the types of tasks chosen, persistence, reaction to failure, effort, and performance expectations (Dweck, 1989).

While this chapter does not allow for a thorough review of the rather voluminous research conducted by Dweck and her associates, the underlying rationale, theories, and findings are summarized below. Dweck (1989) has recently reviewed many of the findings of this research and the following summary will draw heavily from her review.

Learning versus Performance Goal Orientation

In essence, individuals can approach an achievement task with a number of different goals in mind. The two orientations investigated by Dweck are *learning* and *performance* goal orientations. When approaching a task from a learning goal perspective, the individual's main objective is to increase his or her level of competence on a given task. Often this notion is referred to as a 'mastery' orientation; that is, the individual's objective is to master the particular task. Alternatively, when a task is approached from a performance goal orientation, individuals are primarily concerned with demonstrating their competency either to themselves or to others via their present level of task performance (Dweck, 1989).

Although Dweck refers to these two different approaches as learning and performance goals, others have discussed individuals who are 'task-involved' and 'ego-involved' (e.g. see Jagacinski, 1992; Nicholls, 1984). Task-involved individuals try to demonstrate their ability by learning or mastering the task. Alternatively, ego-involved individuals are primarily concerned with performing better than their peers (Jagacinski, 1992; Nicholls, 1984). One of the implications of the task versus ego-involved orientations is how individuals assess their competence. Specifically, task-involved individuals tend to evaluate their competence from a 'self-referenced' perspective, where competence is based on the degree of improvement (through effort). Ego-involved individuals, however, are more concerned with outperforming others, and, therefore, evaluate their competence in relation to others' performance (Jagacinski, 1992).

In her review, Dweck (1989) focuses on two components of goal-directed behavior: goal value and goal expectancy. Her central interest is how goal value and goal expectancy influence persistence in the face of obstacles, greater effort, and the choice of personally challenging tasks (Dweck, 1989).

Goal Value

The main focus of Dweck's research has been on achievement situations. Although the situation itself may seem to encourage achievement-related cognitions and performance, achievement situations occur only when the *individual* adopts an achievement orientation. Within these achievement situations, however, an individual may adopt one of the two goal orientations discussed above (i.e. learning or performance). The adoption of one of these two goal orientations influences other goal-related variables, specifically, the evaluative standards adopted, goal expectancies, perceived control, task choice, task pursuit, outcome attribution and satisfaction, and task interest (Dweck, 1989). Each of these variables will be discussed briefly below.

Evaluative standards

These are the standards adopted by individuals to gauge their success. Performance goals tend to lead to the adoption of normative standards, while learning goals tend to encourage personal standards. Ames and Ames (1991) have demonstrated that adopting personal standards, as opposed to normative standards, assists in sustaining the benefits of previous success even in the face of failures.

Expectancies

As the difference in evaluative standards would suggest, individuals who adopt a performance goal orientation base their expectations of success on perceptions of their ability *relative* to others. The expectations of learning goal-oriented individuals, alternatively, are related more to the perceived degree of effort required to accomplish the goal. Bandura and Dweck (1981) discovered that these task expectancies can influence the choice of the task; specifically, since the expectations of learning goal individuals are not dependent on the perceived ability of others, they are more likely to choose subjectively difficult and challenging tasks. Performance-oriented individuals tend to focus on their perceived normative ability, and, therefore, are less likely to choose subjectively difficult tasks that might, provided difficulties are encountered during performance, threaten their perceived level of normative competence.

Perceived control

Although the notion of expectancies deals with the expected outcomes, perceived control deals with not only the outcomes but also the relationship between the outcome and one's behavior (Dweck, 1989). This notion of perceived control is analogous to 'instrumentality' perceptions in valence–instrumentality–expectancy (VIE) motivation theory (Vroom, 1964). Several issues become particularly salient for performance goal-oriented individuals regarding their perceived control. As mentioned previously, performance goal-oriented individuals evaluate their success using a normative standard. As a result of this normative reference, the perceived control of performance-oriented individuals should be less because they do not have control over the performance of their referent group.

The assessment of outcomes for learning goal-oriented individuals, as mentioned above, is more dependent on a personal, as opposed to a normative, referent. Given this, the instrumentality perceptions should be stronger. For example, for individuals whose measure of success is their own previous performance, the effort–performance linkage should be stronger (i.e. a more direct link between effort and performance).

Task choice

Since individuals with a performance goal orientation are concerned with obtaining positive evaluations of their performance, they are more likely to choose tasks for which success is guaranteed. In fact, Dweck (1989) stated that 'even individuals with high expectancies of success may sacrifice a potentially fruitful learning opportunity that involves risk of errors for an opportunity to look smart' (p. 101) (see also Elliott & Dweck, 1981). Nicholls (1984) proposed that individuals who are task-involved (or have a learning goal orientation in Dweck's terms) are more likely than ego-involved individuals to choose a task with moderate personal challenge or difficulty, regardless of their expectations of success. In other words, individuals with a learning goal orientation, whose evaluation standards are more self-determined, are free to choose challenging tasks because their performance only needs to improve in order to be considered successful. Ego-involved or performance-oriented individuals, alternatively, base their measure of success on external referents, which means that they are more likely to choose tasks on which they will be able to perform well in a normative sense.

Task pursuit

Goal orientation not only involves the choice of the task, but also the amount of persistence one demonstrates while performing a particular task. Specifically, performance-oriented individuals may sabotage their performance by either developing excuses for their performance or simply 'not trying' (Dweck, 1989; see also Berglas & Jones, 1978). Also, performance goal-oriented individuals are less likely to persist in the face of failure (Bandura & Schunk, 1981; Elliot & Dweck, 1981). In summary, Dweck (1989) states that 'with performance goals, low or shaky expectancies of success may lead one to shun the very tasks that foster learning and mastery experiences, or to pursue them in ineffective ways' (p. 101).

Outcome attribution and satisfaction

Another difference between learning and performance goal orientations involves the attributions and reactions of individuals to their performance. Specifically, learning goal-oriented individuals are less likely to attribute failure to lack of ability, demonstrate negative affect, or show performance disruptions (Elliott & Dweck, 1981). Bandura and Dweck (1981) also demonstrated that attributions following high effort differ for learning and performance-oriented individuals. Specifically, learning goal individuals reported they 'felt smarter' following a high-effort mastery experience. These same individuals were more likely to describe low-effort mastery experiences using words such as 'bored' or 'disappointed' (Bandura & Dweck, 1981; Dweck, 1989). Alternatively, performance-oriented individuals devalue high-effort mastery experiences.

The attribution pattern of learning goal-oriented individuals makes conceptual sense. These individuals use their own previous performance as their evaluative standard and, because additional effort most likely results in increasing performance, high effort would lead to positive attributions. On the other hand, performance goal-oriented individuals view task performance as a way in which to demonstrate their performance and, as a result, high-effort mastery experiences would lead to less positive attributions. In other words, if such individuals have to exert a high degree of effort, then they would attribute the high effort to a lack of ability.

Task interest

Learning situations also foster a greater degree of task interest (Dweck, 1989). Specifically, individuals in a learning situation are less likely to experience negative affect when obstacles are encountered (Bandura & Dweck, 1981; Elliott & Dweck, 1981). Furthermore, high-effort mastery experiences are more likely to produce pleasurable experiences for learning-oriented individuals as well as feelings of pride in one's work (Dweck, 1989). Dweck (1989) also noted that learning type situations are more likely to engender intrinsic motivation and, thus, a greater feeling of personal control.

While the effects of adopting different goal orientations have been briefly outlined above, an individual difference variable has been shown to influence the type of goal orientation adopted by the individuals. Specifically, Dweck and associates (Bandura & Dweck, 1981; Dweck, Tenney, & Dinces, 1982; Dweck, 1989) have discovered that one's *theory of intelligence* can influence the type of goal orientation adopted. For example, Bandura and Dweck (1981) found that children who perceived intelligence as incremental (i.e. can be increased; is malleable), as opposed to fixed (i.e. 'you have it or you don't'), were more likely to adopt a learning goal orientation. Dweck (1989) summarized the results of Bandura and Dweck (1981) and Dweck, Tenney and Dinces (1982) in the following way: 'Thus, children's ideas about intelligence (whether naturally occurring or experimentally induced) appear to be related to whether they view tasks as learning opportunities or competence judgments' (p. 103).

Although the individual difference variable regarding whether one perceives ability as fixed or incremental does influence the degree to which the individual adopts a learning or performance goal, it is not the only influence. Specifically, one must look not only at individual differences with respect to the adoption of a goal orientation, but also at situational influences. For example, Ames, Ames, and Felker (1977) found that competitive reward structures can influence the way in which individuals react to failures as well as their perceptions of their ability. More recently, Ames and Archer (1988) have demonstrated that students who perceived an emphasis on mastery (learning) goals within a classroom exhibited more numerous strategies, demonstrated a preference for challenging tasks, felt more positive towards the class, and also perceived that success in the class was a result of one's effort. Students who perceived their class to have a performance goal orientation were more concerned with their ability, rated their ability as lower and also as the cause of failure. Additionally, Jagacinski and Nicholls (1987) found that social comparison information influenced the self-evaluations of students who were ego-involved (performance-oriented) but not the self-evaluations of students who were task-involved (learning-oriented). Butler (1987) also investigated different types of feedback and how they related to motivational perceptions, interest, and performance. She found that different types of feedback (i.e. comments, praise, and grades) could influence an individual's attributions and performance. Specifically, praise and grades tended to shift individuals into a more ego-involved state (performance-oriented), whereas individualized comments encouraged task-involved (learning-oriented) behaviors (see also Butler, 1988).

The existence of situational influences on goal orientation, in addition to the influence of one's belief about the fixed or malleable nature of intelligence or ability, raises the question of how to characterize goal orientation, that is, is it a person variable, a situational variable, or some hybrid? Dweck appears to treat it generally as an individual difference variable of some stability, but one which can be changed by situational characteristics. We will often discuss the implications of goal orientation as if it were a trait of individuals, but at other times we will note how organizational conditions make one orientation more likely than the other.

A related issue is the dimensionality of goal orientation. Dweck makes little reference to this issue, but generally her writings suggest a single continuum with strong performance goal orientation at one end and strong learning goal orientation at the other. Recent empirical attempts to measure goal orientation in adults have found that two separate dimensions (i.e. one representing strong to weak learning goal orientation and another representing strong to weak performance goal orientation) appear to exist (Farr, 1992; Hofmann, 1992; Zajac, 1991). In the following sections, this should be recalled. We have generally used the terms 'stronger learning goal orientation' and 'stronger performance goal orientation' to describe individuals; these are used in recognition of the fact that someone could be high or low on both dimensions.

Goal Expectancy

The previous section was primarily concerned with the two different types of goal orientation (i.e. learning and performance) and how these different approaches to task performance influence other variables such as choice of task, effort, and reactions to failure. This section takes the notion of goal orientation one step further by looking at the expectancy attributions by the individual regarding task performance. In essence, this section looks at the interrelationships among competence, confidence, and attributions about past and future performance.

One of the more curious discoveries of Dweck and her colleagues was that often the individual with the greatest competence did not possess the greatest amount of confidence (Bandura & Dweck, 1981). For example, Dweck (1989) stated 'there does not seem to be as close or consistent a link as one would expect between children's ability to perform well at a task . . . and their expectancy that they will perform well at the task' (p. 107). In fact, Bandura and Dweck (1981) found that children with low confidence actually had higher achievement on the task. Dweck (1989), interpreting the findings of Bandura and Dweck (1981), concluded that even though the low-confidence children seemed aware of their high ability (i.e. they accurately perceived their relative rank in the class), they still approached the upcoming task with low expectancies of performance.

These results and interpretation beg the question of why individuals who have high ability, and who have had past success, still approach tasks with low performance expectancies. Conversely, one must also ask why some low-ability individuals would have consistently high expectancies of performance. Although a more detailed treatment of expectancy formation has been espoused elsewhere (Dweck & Elliott, 1983), Dweck (1989) chose to focus only on three aspects of this development in her review. We will consider these same three aspects of expectancy: task analysis, standards for success, and processing of outcomes.

Task analysis

One of the consistent findings by Dweck and others is that a 'think strategy' approach to task performance leads to higher expectancies of performance (Anderson & Jennings, 1980; Diener & Dweck, 1978). Individuals who adopt a think strategy tend to focus on strategies and task analysis when confronted with difficulty. Other individuals, instead of focusing on the task and developing effective strategies, tend to focus more of their attention toward thoughts regarding task difficulty and ability. Specifically, Dweck (1989) stated that performance goal-oriented individuals tend to focus their attention on task difficulty and ability, no doubt developing attributions regarding their ability, while learning goal-oriented individuals may tend to focus on identifying the appropriate strategies in order to successfully master the task. Further evidence has demonstrated that individuals who are highly anxious, while they may demonstrate effective strategy development in a non-evaluative situation, quickly shift their focus to ability inadequacies, task-unrelated thoughts, and other types of non-strategy-related task cognitions under conditions of evaluation (see e.g. Meichenbaum & Butler, 1978; Sarason, 1975, 1984; Sarason, Sarason, Keefe, Hayes, & Shearin, 1986; Sarason & Stoops, 1978).

Another variable may also influence an individual's analysis of the task and, subsequently, their assessment of performance expectancy. Specifically, an individual might conceive of two possible types of knowledge required to perform a task adequately: specific skills and knowledge—often referred to as domain knowledge (e.g. see Chi, Glaser, & Farr, 1988)—or more general problem-solving skills—a perspective that would accompany an incremental theory of ability (see above; Dweck, 1989). In other words, individuals may use different models to estimate their task performance expectancies. Some individuals may focus on whether they could perform the task given their current knowledge, skills, and abilities, while others may count on more general strategy and learning skills to come into play and help them 'figure things out'. Dweck (1989) proposes that these different models for developing expectancy attributions may explain why some individuals more easily 'attribute failure to low ability when their ability should have been more than amply validated by past performance' (p. 113).

Standards

Standards, in the Dweck (1989) motivational paradigm, refer to the level of performance or learning that one must obtain to feel successful. As mentioned in the task- and ego-involved literature cited previously (e.g. Jagacinski, 1992; Nicholls, 1984), one can adopt two types of standards: normative or personal. We mentioned earlier that learning goals lead to the adoption of more personally referent standards (e.g. Is my performance better now than it was earlier?). Performance goals, alternatively, tend to encourage the adoption of normative standards (e.g. Is my performance better than others?). Furthermore, there is some evidence that certain children may overevaluate the performance of their referent group (Diener & Dweck, 1980). The standards adopted, whether normative or more personally referenced, would influence an individual's future expectancies of performance.

Processing outcomes

There is a large body of research that suggests that attributions moderate the changes in expectancies and performance following success and failure (e.g. see Dweck, 1989). Gradually, this literature suggests that attributing failure to a lack of ability leads to lower future expectancies, a low level of persistence, and more disruptions in the face of difficulty (Dweck, 1989). Attributing failure to low effort, poor strategies, or bad luck leads to the maintenance of high expectancies, a high level of persistence, and effective performance under failure (Dweck, 1989; also see Dweck & Goetz, 1978). Interestingly, individuals who are learning- (mastery-) oriented may bypass the process of making attributions about difficulties altogether and simply proceed with a search for more effective strategies (Dweck, 1989).

The goal orientation adopted by individuals may also influence the saliency of different outcomes. For example, since performance-oriented individuals are particularly concerned with normative standards and have been shown to have aversive reactions to failures, failure situations might be particularly salient to these individuals (Diener & Dweck, 1980). Learning-oriented individuals, alternatively, seem to focus more on the successful aspects of past performance. Clearly, this differential importance of outcomes for performance- versus learning-oriented individuals would influence their expectancies regarding future performance.

Whether individuals perceive ability as fixed or incremental can influence the way in which they diagnose their ability. Perceptions of intelligence, however, are of particular concern for performance-oriented individuals. As mentioned above, individuals can envision expectancies either related to currently existing domain specific knowledge or based more on general problem-solving skills (Dweck, 1989). The implications of these approaches to diagnosing one's ability are twofold: (i) past success might only lead to estimates of domain specific knowledge and, therefore, may not positively influence future expectancies on different, although possibly related, tasks; and (ii) success through high effort may lead to lower perceptions of intelligence (e.g. 'If I had to work hard to accomplish the task, then I must not have very much ability').

In summary, from the evidence reviewed above and cited in Dweck (1989), it appears as though the following conclusion is warranted:

> Although much research remains to be done, the evidence thus far indicates that generating a learning framework, providing experience with mastering difficulty or coping with failure within that framework, and giving explicit attention to cognitive-motivational mediators [and moderators] can create the conditions for building both abilities and confidence in those abilities. (Dweck, 1989: p. 119)

We agree that much research needs to be conducted, but we also believe that the results and evidence from Dweck's work with children suggest that goal orientation could well be a very influential construct in organizational settings. It should be noted that Kanfer (1990a) has suggested that in adults the effects of the individual's goal orientation and its related theory of intelligence may indirectly affect performance through their effects on the individual's self-efficacy. Such indirect effects, in conjunction with the perhaps separate dimensions of learning and performance goal orientations already mentioned, are likely to produce more complex interactive effects than the ones discussed herein. The reader should be alert to the possibility that our hypotheses should be thought of as starting points for more detailed analysis and conceptualization.

We now turn to the implications of the goal orientation research for organizational settings. In the following section we discuss those implications which are most salient for our own interests. We know that our coverage is not exhaustive and suspect that the reader will be able to add others of personal relevance.

IMPLICATIONS OF GOAL ORIENTATION FOR I/O PSYCHOLOGY

For purposes of exposition we divide the implications of the work of Dweck and her colleagues into several content domains that have received theoretical and empirical attention within I/O psychology. Sometimes such divisions are not completely clear-cut (e.g. separating goal setting and feedback), but we find that understanding is generally better served by the distinctions than by combining related discussions. We attempt to note when topics are related to others.

Goal Setting

One of the most widely studied areas of research in I/O psychology over the past 20 years has been goal setting (see, for example, Locke & Latham, 1990; Locke & Henne, 1986). Robust findings concerning the effects of goals support the general propositions that specific, difficult goals that *are accepted* by the individual lead to higher levels of performance than no goals or more vague or less difficult goals. The emphasis placed on goal acceptance in the previous sentence points to one broad implication of goal orientation for goal-setting theory. The acceptance of difficult goals is likely to be affected by whether the individual is more strongly oriented toward learning or performance goals. More specifically, those with stronger learning goal orientations should be more accepting of difficult goals than those with stronger performance goal orientations, especially if the difficult goals are framed within the context of presenting a challenge or mastery-building opportunity for the individual (Dweck, 1989).

Goal acceptance implies that goals are established by an outside agent (e.g. the manager in a work setting) and then communicated to the individual who reaches some level of acceptance or commitment to these goals. A variant of this would be mutually determined goals established by the manager and employee in some form of joint decision-making. Locke and Latham (1990) discuss goal acceptance as a subset of goal commitment. Goal commitment refers to one's determination to reach the goal, regardless of its origin. The goal may be assigned by a manager, set more jointly, or self-set. Regarding self-set goals, Locke and Latham (1990) argue that goals are often spontaneously set by individuals to guide task behavior and level of effort.

Indeed, we could hypothesize that goal orientation, as a factor internal to the individual, is likely to be more important with regard to self-set goals than to those with an external component. Goal orientation may affect both the difficulty of the goal and the referent of the goal, that is, whether the goal is framed in terms of an internal or external standard. Learning goal-oriented individuals should be more likely to frame a self-set goal in terms of an internal comparison, for example, 'doing better than I did last week on this task'. An individual with a performance orientation should be more likely to use an external referent, for example, 'doing better than most of my co-workers on this task'. Thus, it might be useful to modify the implication stated above in the following way: Those individuals with stronger learning goal orientations should be more accepting of, or more likely to self-set, difficult goals with an internal referent than individuals with a stronger performance goal orientation.

Dweck (1986) would further argue that the main effect of goal orientation on the setting and acceptance of difficult goals for those with a stronger performance goal orientation is affected by the individual's level of confidence in one's ability to perform the task or job. If an individual with a strong performance goal orientation is confident, then difficult goals (especially those with an external or normative referent) are likely to be set or accepted. If such a person is not confident, then relatively easy goals are likely to be set or difficult goals rejected due to concern for being able to demonstate effective task performance to others. For those with learning goal orientations, confidence in one's ability does not affect goal setting or acceptance; rather, moderately difficult goals are likely to be set or accepted since the underlying concern is to improve. Confidence in task ability, as used by Dweck, seems much like self-efficacy, discussed extensively by Bandura (e.g. 1986). Self-efficacy has been researched in connection to goal-setting theory in a number of studies (see Locke & Latham, 1990, Ch. 5, for a review). Locke and Latham (1990) report an average correlation of 0.38 between self-efficacy and level of goal chosen (or normative goal difficulty). Goal orientation theory suggests that the correlation between self-efficacy and self-selected goal should be low for those with learning goal orientations, but strongly positive for those with performance goal orientations. The moderate average correlation (0.38) between self-efficacy and chosen goals reported by Locke and Latham could reflect the mixture of the two goal orientations in the subject samples of the research studies, an interpretation supported by recent data in a laboratory study conducted by Zajac (1991). Kanfer (1990a) has suggested that in adults beliefs about the malleability of intelligence may affect self-efficacy rather than goal orientation, which would result in a different relationship among these variables than would be derived from Dweck's analysis.

A general issue that arises from a consideration of goal orientation is whether the goals typically assigned or self-set by individuals in organizations encourage learning or performance goal orientations. It is our view that most goals assigned to employees tend to be normative in nature, that is, make comparisons between the individual and others in the organization doing similar work. These goals should encourage the development of a performance goal orientation. This could lead to less commitment to difficult goals, increased employee negotiation directed toward lowering goal difficulty, external blame placing for failure to reach goals and other defensive reactions, such as less effective analytic strategies for complex tasks (cf. Amabile, 1988; Wood & Bandura, 1989). Ryer (1991) recently found that normative goals adversely affected task performance, especially for performance goal-oriented individuals. A comparison of the effects of learning versus performance goals appears to be a useful line of future goal-setting research.

Performance Feedback

Goal orientation appears to be linked to a number of issues that can be subsumed under the general heading of performance feedback. Included here are (i) reactions to performance appraisals or feedback; (ii) feedback seeking; (iii) feedback giving; and (iv) the content of feedback messages.

Reactions to performance feedback

Considerable research attention has been given to the reactions that individuals have to performance feedback. Such reactions can be affective (e.g. becoming angry), cognitive (e.g. discounting the message due to its perceived lack of accuracy), or behavioral (e.g. working late at night to meet a task deadline). Much of the literature has addressed affective and cognitive reactions to feedback resulting from a formal performance appraisal process, that is, feedback occurring as a result of a semi-annual or annual evaluation of performance. Dickinson (in press) has reviewed the research in this area. Reactions to more informal feedback, such as occurs during day-to-day interactions between a manager and an employee, have been less studied but are also of interest (cf. Farr, in press).

One of the more consistent findings concerning reactions to feedback is that the sign of the feedback (whether the feedback is primarily positive or negative in tone) is an important determinant of the individual's reaction (Ilgen, Fisher,

206 INTERNATIONAL REVIEW OF INDUSTRIAL AND ORGANIZATIONAL PSYCHOLOGY 1993

& Taylor, 1979). In particular, negative feedback is more likely to be inaccurately perceived and recalled and to be rejected as an accurate portrayal of performance, suggesting a self-serving bias or ego-defensiveness (Ilgen, Fisher & Taylor, 1979). Goal orientation may, however, be an individual difference variable that moderates the individual's reaction to negative feedback. Goal orientation has not been directly examined as such a moderator, although Ilgen, Fisher and Taylor (1979) do argue that individual differences play an important role in such reactions.

The individual with a stronger learning goal orientation is predicted by Dweck to view errors or negative feedback as *information* concerning how to develop task mastery, whereas the individual with a stronger performance goal orientation views negative feedback as (unfavorable) *evaluations* concerning one's competence. Again, the locus of the standards for the feedback (personal or normative) is likely to be important. Thus, the general findings regarding feedback sign reported by Ilgen, Fisher and Taylor (1979) should be even more pronounced for those with a performance goal orientation receiving normative feedback, but non-existent for individuals with learning goal orientations receiving feedback with a personal referent.

Why, then, is the general finding of unfavorable reactions to negative feedback obtained so consistently? We expect that most organizational settings in which feedback research has been conducted encourage performance goal orientations. Certainly, US organizations have been critized for too great a focus on current financial performance. Such attention to short-term profits develops a culture in which current performance is primary and long-term development of competence is less valued by the appraisal and reward systems. More organization members with performance goal orientations than with learning goal orientations would be a predicted by-product of such cultures. A strong current performance climate in an organization would tend to shift initially learning goal-oriented individuals toward a performance goal orientation. Indeed, the defensive nature of performance goal-oriented individuals might be one factor to explain cover-ups as responses to mistakes in organizations and to explain the negative response to whistleblowers in most organizations (e.g. Near & Miceli, 1987).

Goal orientation suggests also that individuals with different orientations may interpret similar feedback in quite variant ways. For example, Dweck (1989) notes that learning goal-oriented individuals interpret the expenditure of much effort in the completion of a task in a positive way, as indicative of their ability to master the task; such individuals find that tasks accomplished with little effort are boring. Performance goal-oriented individuals, however, interpret the requirement of considerable effort as an indication of low ability, whereas accomplishing a task with little effort means the possession of high ability. Thus, an employee's reaction to the manager's comment, 'You've really been working hard lately', could vary considerably!

Feedback seeking

Ashford and Cummings (1983) suggest that individuals are proactive in obtaining performance feedback, that is, they seek feedback about their performance. Feedback may be sought through inquiry (direct requests by the individual for feedback information from another person, typically one's manager or co-worker) or monitoring (observing the work environment and others in it for performance-relevant cues).

Ashford and Cummings argue that feedback can be considered as a resource for the individual to the extent that it provides information about organizational and individual goals. Goal orientation may provide a means for specifying what kinds of performance information an individual may seek, an issue presently addressed in the feedback-seeking literature only in general terms. For example, Ashford and Cummings suggest that the individual's goals form standards used to make sense out of the large amount of information available in the work environment. They further note that important goals for individuals include such things as uncertainty reduction, error correction, ego defense, and mastery motivation. However, they make no attempt to predict whether certain of these goals will be more important than others for various individuals. Nor do Ashford and Cummings address the mode of feedback seeking that may be preferred by various individuals.

Inquiry has high potential costs to the feedback seeker due to the direct, face-to-face interaction that is likely to be associated with it. One important cost is the possibility that the resulting feedback will be negative. Individuals with strong performance goal orientations would find this cost to be extremely aversive and would be motivated to avoid negative feedback. Further, if such an individual were low in confidence or self-efficacy concerning task ability, negative feedback would be perceived as a likely event. Thus, performance goal-oriented individuals with low task self-efficacy should use the monitoring mode of feedback and not the inquiry mode. Highly confident individuals with a performance goal orientation and those individuals with a learning goal orientation would be predicted to use inquiry in addition to monitoring.

Individuals with a learning goal orientation are likely to value mastery motivation more than those with a performance goal orientation and, thus, seek feedback information they view as relevant for mastery. The content of such desired feedback would include various types of information and evaluation concerning the individual's current competence versus past competence, such as improvement over time or the likelihood of assignment to further challenging tasks. Those with a performance goal orientation would seek information concerning present performance, error avoidance, performance compared to that of others, and so on.

As White (1959) has noted, relatively novel tasks and situations provide more information regarding one's competence or mastery over the environment than do familiar tasks. Those with a stronger learning goal orientation might seek feedback with a strategy termed innovation by Farr (1991). Innovation here refers to the introduction of change into the work role by the work performer. The individual may perform a task using new or atypical methods, introduce new tasks into the role set, or alter the priorities for task accomplishment in order to obtain information related to role behavior. Feedback obtained via the innovation strategy should be particularly salient to those concerned with achieving learning goals.

Feedback giving and the content of feedback

Relatively little has been written concerning the factors that are associated with an individual's decision to provide performance information to another. Larson (1984, 1989) has developed conceptual models of this process that include factors that may be affected by the feedback provider's goal orientation. Foremost among these may be implicit theories that feedback providers have about the likely effects of feedback on the recipient's behavior (Larson, 1984). For example, the manager who believes that employees rarely attend to feedback is not likely to provide it.

Larson's writings on implicit theories are focused on the likelihood that feedback is provided or the amount of feedback that may be provided. Goal orientation may serve as an influence on the type of feedback that is provided as well as the amount. Managers may be likely to provide feedback that is consistent with their own goal orientations. This may not be a conscious process, but rather a more subtle influence related to the personal salience of the information that they decide to provide to their employees. Thus, the manager with a strong peformance goal orientation is more likely to inform employees about their current task performance compared to that of others, while the manager with a learning goal orientation is more likely to discuss developmental aspects of the job and strategies for task improvement.

We can speculate that the typical implementation of many personnel practices advocated by behavioral scientists may have unintended negative side-effects when we view them from the perspective of goal orientation. As examples, the establishment of a reward system that provides strong links between the individual's compensation (and other extrinsic outcomes) and current job performance is likely to foster a performance goal orientation; strengthened performance goal orientation may also be a consequence of specific, difficult performance goals when individual or small group performance levels are known publicly.

A performance goal orientation is not necessarily bad in an organizational context, because individuals must be concerned about meeting performance standards. If there is not also a learning goal orientation, however, strong performance goal orientation can be maladaptive (Dweck, 1986). In contexts where there are systems and policies in place that may encourage performance goal orientations, then managers should be especially careful to provide feedback that promotes a learning goal orientation.

Training and Development

Goal orientation suggests several implications for the general area of training and development in organizations. These include trainee motivation, the role of errors or mistakes in the training environment, training for self-management, and skill and knowledge updating.

Trainee motivation

The individual with a strong learning goal orientation is likely to be intrinsically motivated to learn in an organizational training program if the program is perceived as enhancing competence. The performance goal-oriented employee will require clear links between training content and immediate application on the job in order to be highly motivated. Since it is likely that most training classes will include some individuals with stronger performance goal orientations and some with stronger learning goal orientations, the instructional system should make some attempt to provide both forms of motivating conditions.

It is likely at present that most organizational training programs place too much emphasis on performance goals, perhaps unintentionally. The common use of objectively scored, achievement tests (with pass and fail designations) during such programs or as an outcome measure is but one way that performance goals among trainees are encouraged. This is unfortunate, because if one has an imbalance between the two forms of goals in training, it would be preferable to have a stronger emphasis on learning goals.

As noted by Dweck and Leggett (1988), situational factors may override dispositional goal preferences to some extent. It is likely that a stronger emphasis on learning goals for all participants in a training program would promote a better learning climate. Performance goals tend to foster defensive behavior in a training setting because trainees are likely to be concerned that their relatively low level of current knowledge or skill will lead to negative evaluations from others (Farr & Middlebrooks, 1990). Learning goals, however, encourage individuals to expend effort in order to attain greater skill and knowledge; satisfaction becomes a function of effort directed toward learning rather than a function of present capability.

Employees with strong performance goal orientations may also interpret training assignments or opportunities in ways that may decrease their motivation to attend training. Such employees may infer that being sent to a training program means that management believes that their performance is below standard. This inference would be consistent with the idea, discussed earlier, that performance goal-oriented individuals would be primarily interested in feedback salient for how others evaluate their current performance and, therefore, would so interpret any cues they observed during monitoring of the work environment (in this case, the assignement to training).

Role of errors in training

Many training programs are directed toward minimizing the number of errors that trainees make during learning. At its extreme this approach is exemplified with the 'small steps' logic of programmed instruction in which learning is broken down into such small units that the typical trainee makes no, or very few, errors in the course of learning the requisite material. In less extreme examples, learning is based on a tutorial model in which the trainee progresses through a carefully planned series of learning activities. These activities attempt to anticipate where errors might occur and prevent such errors through the presentation of sufficient information to the trainee as well as the provision of practice opportunities. The implicit, if not explicit, message to the trainees is that the commission of errors during training is bad and should be avoided. A further message may be that, since considerable resources have been devoted to the development of the learning activities and system, any errors that are made are clearly the fault of the trainee. This can be thought of as a form of training that is quite consistent with a performance goal model.

There is another approach to the function that errors can play in training that is more consistent with a learning goal model. Recent research in Germany on the training of computer skills (e.g. Frese, Brodbeck, Heinbokel, Mooser, Schleiffenbaum, & Thiemann, 1991; Greif & Keller, 1990) has been based on the proposition that training errors can lead to more effective learning in training due to successful adaptation to, and prevention of, emotional frustration and to the effective development of well-organized mental models of the computer system.

For example, in Frese et al. (1991) instructions provided to trainees in the error-training conditions emphasized that the making of errors was natural when learning a new software system and that errors were opportunities for learning. Basic system instructions and heuristics designed to counter the emotional and frustrating aspects of errors and to reinforce general problem-solving strategies were also provided to these subjects. Subjects were given opportunities to correct their own mistakes, although an instructor would provide assistance if a self-correction did not occur after several minutes. An error-avoidant condition used step-by-step tutorials that minimized the likelihood that errors would be committed by the trainee but which did not give specific explanations for how the commands in each step functioned. Instructors in this condition intervened after the commission of an error to correct the mistake and return the trainee to the tutorial sequence.

The error-avoidant group showed increased frustration across the six-hour training session, but the error-training group's frustration level remained constant. The error-training group was also better at solving difficult tasks under non-speeded conditions than the error-avoidant group. These results suggest that, consistent with a learning goal orientation prediction, the error-training group adapted better to the occurrence of errors and demonstrated better task mastery.

Self-management training

Self-management training (e.g. Kanfer, 1980; Karoly & Kanfer, 1982) attempts to teach people how to regulate their own behavior through the development of self-observation skills, the establishment of personal goals for improved behavior, the identification of environmental factors that may hinder or facilitate such goal attainment, and the development of self-reward and punishment contingent on goal attainment or lack of attainment, respectively. There have been several recent applications of self-management training reported in the I/O psychology research literature (e.g. Frayne & Latham, 1987; Latham & Frayne, 1989; Gist, Bavetta, & Stevens, 1990) that have demonstrated the usefulness of such training.

Frayne and Latham (1987) suggested that Bandura's (1986) concept of self-efficacy is a key factor in explaining how such training can lead to behavioral improvement. Individuals with strong self-efficacy are likely to focus their attention and energy on task and situational demands and to increase effort level when confronted with obstacles. In their research Frayne and Latham (1987; Latham & Frayne, 1989) found significant positive correlations between the self-efficacy of workers who had attended self-management training concerned with decreasing absenteeism and subsequent work attendance.

Another way to view self-management training is from the framework of Dweck's goal-orientation model. Self-management training focuses much attention on increasing the individual's mastery of his or her environment, that is, it is very much oriented toward developing learning goals, to use Dweck's terminology. Self-efficacy can be thought of as a measure of perceived mastery. Thus, Latham and Frayne's results suggest that to the extent that individuals develop mastery or competence beliefs, their targeted behaviors show improvement.

One could argue that the use of specific target goals for some behavior (such as attendance at work) represents a performance goal orientation in self-management training. However, it is important to note that progress toward such goals is measured and rewarded/punished by the individual and *not* by some other person in the work setting. This minimizes the external evaluation that contributes to a performance goal orientation.

It would be interesting to measure initial levels of goal orientation of individuals who would then be given self-management training to contrast the training outcomes of those with learning goal orientation and those with performance goal orientation. In addition, individuals with learning goal orientations might be expected to apply self-management strategies to behavior domains beyond those explicitly addressed in the training since self-management skills represent a way to master situational constraints. Performance goal-oriented individuals would not be expected to generalize across domains.

Skill and knowledge updating

An expanding knowledge base and rapid technological change serve to place the current skills and knowledge of professional and technical employees in danger of becoming obsolete. Many organizations face the challenge of maintaining a competent workforce for tomorrow's competition, while still attending sufficiently to today's efficient production of goods or services in order to survive financially (Willis & Dubin, 1990).

The tension between working on today's tasks while preparing for tomorrow's affects individual employees also. Farr and Middlebrooks (1990) noted that having the time to update technical skills and knowledge is a major constraint identified by professionals. Employees with strong learning goal orientations are likely to be proactive in terms of self-development and technical updating. Many organizations place a large burden on the individual employee to structure and support personal updating activities. Such a strategy may be adequate in cases where there are relatively large proportions of learning goal-oriented employees in the critical job groups, but may fail to be effective when there are not.

Concern that seeking updating may signal inadequate current performance could deter performance goal-oriented individuals from self-initiated development opportunities. The organization will need to promote more vigorously updating opportunities for those with performance goal orientations, including attempts to assure that no 'poor performer' stigma is attached to those who seek such development activities.

Individual Work Role Innovation and Continuous Improvement

Individual work role innovation has been defined as 'the intentional introduction within one's work role of new and useful ideas, processes, products, or procedures' (Farr & Ford, 1990: p. 63). Continuous improvement refers to the view that any task or job can be performed better than it is currently being performed and that an important component of any job incumbent's job is to develop better ways of performing the job. Thus, continuous improvement makes individual work role innovation a part of the role set of any organizational position or job, rather than the sole purview of certain parts of the organization, for example, the research and development department.

Currently, continuous improvement or total quality methods are being advocated as organizational 'cultures' that make organizations more competitive. While the evaluation of such models is currently incomplete, the logic of fostering a concern in every organizational member to improve his or her part of the organization seems sufficiently compelling to warrant consideration of how such models might be better implemented and accepted by such individuals. Goal orientation has been suggested as one individual difference variable with promise of better understanding the acceptance or rejection of work role innovation by work performers (Farr, 1990).

Individual work role innovation is more likely to be accepted by individuals with strong learning goal orientations than by those with strong performance goal orientations. The individual with a learning goal orientation is concerned with increasing personal competence, and role innovation is a useful means to attain such a goal. The implementation of change (or some innovation) into one's job is typically seen as a challenge which can foster learning. Thus, we would expect that learning goal-oriented employees would be work role innovators, but this has not been directly assessed, to our knowledge.

How can performance goal-oriented individuals be motivated to greater levels of role innovation? One way that the value of learning goals for such a person may be increased is by the reinforcement of such goals through verbal statements and actions of the work group manager. The manager, through both formal and informal feedback, can note favorably those work activities of the individual that demonstrate work role innovation or new competencies. The manager can also stress the importance of every organization member becoming more skilled and knowledgeable. Consistent with the error training of Frese et al. (1991), already noted, the manager should indicate that most learning takes place in the performance of new and challenging tasks, or in new ways of doing current tasks, and that errors are natural and opportunities for additional learning. It is especially important that the manager does not punish errors that occur during innovation attempts. Finally, the manager should communicate to the employee a developmental perspective that downplays immediate performance and stresses the importance of a longer term increase in competence.

Amabile (1988) has described a number of organizational conditions that inhibit innovation, several of which are readily interpretable from a goal-orientation framework. Included here are an evaluation environment focused on criticism and external evaluation, severe time pressures for task accomplishment, and competition within work groups (Amabile, 1988). All of these are likely to foster performance goals among organization members.

The methods that were suggested previously for a manager to enhance the learning goal orientation of an employee, so as to increase the likelihood of introducing work role innovations, do indicate a caveat that should be noted. While continuous improvement and work role innovation generally receive only 'positive press', there are some potential negative outcomes associated with such changes that should be recognized (Farr & Ford, 1990). These include the danger of the introduction of change for change's sake, large resource requirements of the change, the introduction of an innovation at a time when the organization is already undergoing substantial change, and unexpected effects on interdependent organizational functions or people.

In addition, there are some organizational settings in which highly reliable performance is the most important goal, for example, the operation of a nuclear power plant. While continuous improvement at an organizational level is still a worthy goal for such an organization, high performance reliability requirements dictate that such improvements be centrally managed. Individual work role innovation is to be encouraged in terms of idea generation, but controlled centrally at the implementation stage. Indeed, in such organizations, performance goal-oriented employees may be quite valued and contribute substantially to the reliable performance of the organization.

At the same time, one must recognize that highly reliable performance can be misleading (Weick, 1987) in the context of a very complex system. Reliability should be construed as a dynamic process; highly reliable current performance does not guarantee reliable future performance because system components will change over time. Performance goal-oriented employees may be more likely to interpret effective current performance as indicating that the system will continue to be reliable, whereas learning goal-oriented individuals may enact searches for subtle indicators of the beginnings of a potential system error.

The work of Dweck and her colleagues is very important to the advancement of understanding individuals in achievement situations. However, Dweck's theory primarily addresses the failure or success of individuals in situations in which a relatively narrow set of goal and task alternatives exist. We know that individuals operate in very complex environments with many task options and many different motivations. Individuals are continually faced with decisions concerning which tasks to initiate, continue with, or terminate. Kuhl and his colleagues have addressed such behaviors from the perspective of action control theory.

ACTION CONTROL THEORY: A SUMMARY OF THEORY AND RESEARCH

Kuhl (1985) points out that many psychologists study only a single behavioral domain in relation to motivation. Yet, in the real world, individuals have multiple motivations for any given behavior and the choice of many different behaviors. Most motivation theories state that individuals are constantly evaluating the consequences of actions, in terms of the various action alternatives and the probability of obtaining the desired consequence. Traditional motivation theory would assume that individuals select the action with the highest (subjective) utility. However, this traditional approach to motivation does not take into account competing actions and consequences of similar motivational strengths. In this scenario of competing actions, it would be rare for the individual to complete a task before another action becomes more dominant. However, we know that individuals do often proceed in a goal-directed fashion and do complete tasks. This indicates that there may be other processes that prevent alternative tasks from becoming dominant before the first action is completed. These control functions have been referred to as volition, ego strength, will power, and self-regulation (Kuhl, in press a).

Self-regulation theories also attempt to explain why individuals do not always act in ways congruent with their intentions, for example, persist in a non-productive or unwanted behavior, even though they have decided to perform another activity. Examples of these behaviors include watching a boring television program instead of turning it off, having difficulty sitting down and initiating paperwork, or having trouble concentrating on reading a textbook, even when there is a desire to study the topic. Kuhl (in press a) says that there are three conditions that must be met in order for individuals to be self-regulating: (i) an individual's positive belief in the ability to successfully control actions (self-efficacy); (ii) positive self-related emotions (self-esteem); and (iii) clear-cut distinctions between the self and others (individuation). He states that self-efficacy is important for self-control because it is a motivational mediator between knowledge and action (Bandura, 1982). Positive self-esteem impacts self-control because it facilitates the initiation and maintenance of behavioral intentions (Arnold, 1984). Individuation is the process of being able to distinguish between self and non-self beliefs, desires, expectations, and attributes. There is a conflict if a state is not distinguished as self-induced or other-induced, and therefore creates a lack of self-monitoring (Kuhl, in press a). For example, an employee attributes wanting to do well on a performance appraisal to the supervisor's wishes, rather than to his or her own desires. The desire to do well on the job is not fully integrated into the self. Therefore, the work activities of the employee most likely will not be supported efficiently by self-regulatory skills (Kuhl, 1992).

There are both rational and non-rational determinants of various behaviors and intentions. Kuhl (1992) states that non-rational explanations of behavior can impact self-esteem, self-efficacy, and individuation, which impacts self-regulation. An important component of Kuhl's self-regulatory theory is the construct of action versus state orientation. Kuhl (1992) states that this construct explains why some individuals allow other mental activities to dissociate with current goals or intentions and reduce the ability of individuals to be self-regulating.

Action orientation is the ability to facilitate the enactment of context-appropriate intentions by means of self-regulatory strategies (Kuhl, in press a). *State orientation* refers to difficulties in enacting such intentions.

Kuhl (1985) indicates that there are at least two factors or antecedents that determine whether an individual is action- or state-oriented. First, the degree of incongruence between any two pieces of information creates a situation in which the individual becomes action- or state-oriented. Relatively small discrepancies lead to action orientations, while relatively large discrepancies result in state orientations. Second, an individual's orientation is also determined by degenerated intentions, or cognitive representations that are due to weakly formed, poorly activated, or unspecified intentions.

Antecedents of state and action orientations can be either proximal or distal. Proximal antecedents include unrealistic intentions, fear of failure, loss of control, false attribution of other's expectations, negative mood, overmotivation, extrinsic motivation, interruptions, time pressure, analytic modes of processing, boredom, and monotony. Irrational beliefs (Ellis, 1973) are often the basis for unrealistic intentions, because they cause the individual to focus attention on some other state and away from the current intention. Some unrealistic intention usually creates the state orientation that is produced by lack of control, fear of failure, overmotivation, and extrinsic motivation. Lack of control (Kuhl, 1981), fear of failure (Atkinson & Feather, 1966; Heckhausen, Schmalt & Schneider, 1985), overmotivation (Atkinson, 1974), and extrinsic motivation (Deci, 1975; Heckhausen, 1989) all cause the individual to become preoccupied with other thoughts, thereby reducing performance capabilities.

Distal antecedents include supererogation, parental attitudes toward overachievement, obedience, and consistency, chronic frustration of basic needs, traumatic experiences, and underachievement. Humbert (1981) found that parents who interrupted their children frequently, and did not let them finish tasks, or who constantly reminded their children of past failures, had children with significantly higher state orientation scores. Kuhl (in press a) says that social standards, such as authoritarian educational styles, overemphasis on orderliness, and expectations of obedience, achievement, and behavioral consistency, also increase the likelihood of a state orientation.

According to Kuhl (1985), there are six different self-regulatory strategies that can be used to activate a current intention. These six processes aid the individual in maintaining the current intention and protecting it from competing action tendencies. First, active *attentional selectivity* facilitates the processing of information supportive to the current intention and blocks the processing of information that is not applicable. For example, employees who are oriented toward working overtime may not even consider going out for dinner with friends. Second, *encoding control* facilitates the protective function of volition by screening only the applicable components of the stimulus that are supportive of the current action. The employee who is working may not even encode that friends are going out for the evening. Third, *emotion control* prevents emotional states from undermining the maintenance of an intention. This strategy would come into play if the employee were very frustrated about working overtime and depressed about not being able to enjoy an evening out with friends. Fourth, *motivation control* comes into play when the current intention is not as strong as a competing intention. The current intention is then strengthened. For example, an employee could increase the subjective value of working overtime by increasing the subjective value of a potential promotion. Fifth, *environmental control* is a more basic strategy in which the environment is manipulated in order to maintain emotional or motivational control. The employee can control the environment by publicly telling the boss and friends that he or she is working overtime. Sixth, *parsimony of information processing* helps the individual to determine when to stop processing information. For example, the employee can control the processing of information by re-directing attention to work and forgetting about having a good time with friends.

The way in which individuals process antecedents and use self-regulatory strategies determines whether they will be action- or state-oriented. According to Kuhl (1985), action-oriented individuals must have the development of declarative representations. A very important aspect of the action-oriented individuals is that they have a metastatic control mode, in which they are able to induce changes in their own intentions. Non-intentional modes, such as wishes, values, norms, and expectations, are transformed into the intentional structure. Therefore, no attentional resources are given to the non-intentional components while the action-oriented individual is engaged in a current intention. Kuhl (1992) states that action-oriented individuals are also able to distinguish between their own beliefs and those of others. Action-oriented individuals are flexible, and are context sensitive when creating a balance between the maintenance of and disengagement from intentions. For example, an action-oriented employee would be able to juggle multiple taskings, work in a goal-directed fashion, shift attention back and forth between tasks while completing tasks along the way, and would need little supervision.

On the other hand, state-oriented individuals are impacted by non-self-related values, beliefs, goals, and expectations. State-oriented individuals often have false externalizations, where they have intentions to achieve based on external factors, such as pleasing someone else, or getting some kind of reward. These individuals also have false internalizations, in which other's beliefs are supported by self-regulatory functions because they are misperceived as being self-defining. State-oriented individuals are often context insensitive, and follow rules imposed by others. Kuhl (in press a) says that individuals with a state orientation symbolically represent a goal in order to reduce anxiety and employ sequential processing in order to reduce the probability of failure. This strategy leads to peformance decrements because the individual cannot simultaneously process several criteria, such as goal adequacy, speed, accuracy, satisfaction of one's needs, and satisfaction of other's goals. In addition, Kuhl (1985) indicates that state-oriented individuals have a catastatic mode of control, which prevents the individual from changing intentions without some external prompt. Further, individuals who are in a metastatic mode are more likely to become action-oriented than those in a catastatic mode, or a change-preventing framework. For example, a state-oriented individual in the workplace would have difficulty dealing with multiple tasks and multiple stresses. The individual would not be a very good independent worker, would require close supervision and direction, would need plenty of time to accomplish tasks, and would need to have tasks split into small manageable pieces.

Kuhl has done empirical work to test his theory of state versus action orientation. A more comprehensive review of his empirical work can be found in Kuhl (1985; in press a). He has developed a set of scales to measure three components of action or state orientations, labeled *preoccupation*, *hesitation*, and *volatility* (Kuhl, in press b). Preoccupation refers to an intrusion of thoughts about past experiences, often failures, that prevent the individual from developing action plans for future goal attainment. Hesitation refers to difficulties in the initiation of a desired course of action. Volatility refers to the tendency to switch impulsively from current activities, even pleasant ones, before they are completed. The state-oriented individual receives high scores on all three scales.

A typical item from the preoccupation scale is (the respondent chooses one of the alternatives for each item): 'When I have lost something that is very valuable to me and I can't find it anywhere: (A) I have a hard time concentrating on something else, (B) I put it out of my mind.' An example of an item from the hesitation scale is: 'When I know I must finish something soon: (A) I have to push myself to get started, (B) I find it easy to get it done and over with.' A typical item from the volatility scale is: 'When I have learned a new and interesting game: (A) I quickly get tired of it and do something else, (B) I can really get into it for a long time.' (For each of these three items, response A indicates state orientation and B indicates action orientation.)

In several experiments Kuhl developed various methods for inducing an action or state orientation. He induced state orientation by introducing unexpected and uncontrollable failures (Kuhl, 1981; Kuhl & Wassiljew, 1985; Kuhl & Weiss, 1983), by asking individuals to write an essay on feelings and attributions of past failures (Kuhl, 1981), and by inducing a degenerated intention (Kuhl & Helle, 1986). Action orientation was also induced by asking subjects to verbalize hypotheses when doing a problem solving-task (Kuhl, 1981; Kuhl & Weiss, 1983), and by having hospital patients record activities on the hospital ward (Kuhl, 1983b).

Kuhl has conducted a series of experiments to test the assumption that metastatic and catastatic modes of control are related to action and state orientations. He tested to see whether motives were congruent with behavior, and found that motive-congruent behavior was associated with action-oriented individuals (Kuhl & Geiger, in press). In another study, Kuhl (1982) examined whether action- or state-oriented individuals were more likely to carry out their intentions. Results from the study showed that action-oriented children had higher correlations of their intention to carry out free-choice activity and the amount of time performing that activity. This pattern of results was reversed for highly routinized activities, in which the correlations for intention-behavior for state-oriented children was higher. This is most likely caused by state-oriented individuals being more likely to follow external demands because of their low self-regulatory skills.

Another series of studies involved the manipulation of failure in order to test the relationship of action versus state orientation to learned helplessness. A good example of this research is reported in Kuhl (1981). Kuhl believed that generalized performance decrements were due to functional helplessness, in which deteriorated cognitions increase state orientations. He found that individuals showed debilitated performance only when encouraged to engage in state-oriented activities.

Kuhl and Koch (1984) found that failure (or negative) feedback caused state-oriented individuals to question why they failed, to have emotional responses to failure, and to have threatened self-esteem, even although the individuals appeared to be intent on completing the task. These results suggest that state-oriented individuals are concerned with unconscious goals, even when consciously performing a task and expressing task-relevant goals. Further, the results suggest that 'performance may be affected by a higher-level control, which involves motivational standards' (Kuhl & Koch, 1984; p. 151).

In addition to studying various aspects of self-regulatory theory, Kuhl has investigated the ways that action- and state-oriented individuals differ in the self-regulatory strategies that are used. Kuhl (1983a) found that there are individual differences in selective attention. Results of the study showed that action-oriented individuals attended to less irrelevant information than state-oriented subjects. In a study conducted by Kuhl and Beckmann (1983), state-oriented individuals used a much more complex decision system, which indicated that action-oriented subjects were more parsimonious in their processing of information, using that which was directly task-relevant.

Kuhl and Kazen-Saad (1990) indicated that state-oriented individuals are much more self-focused and evaluate events and actions in comparison to their own standards, experiences, and long-term goals. They found differences in how action- and state-oriented individuals perceive tasks and goals. Kuhl and Kazen-Saad asked subjects to list as many short-term goals, long-term goals, and intentions as possible. State-oriented individuals listed significantly more long-term goals than the action-oriented subjects. The results from the study also found that state-oriented individuals perceive many more intentions as being very important. These importance attributions and long-term goals create additional intentions that interfere with the current intention.

Beckmann and Kuhl (1984) did a study to test motivation control in which college students were asked to rate the attractiveness of apartments on a list. They were asked to tentatively choose which apartments they would prefer. Action-oriented students showed an increase in the attractiveness of the apartments tentatively chosen when asked to rate the attractiveness for a second time. This suggests that action-oriented individuals selectively attend to incentive-based information, thus increasing the subjective value of the chosen alternative.

Kuhl (1983b) asked individuals who had undergone surgery to rate their pain and to answer questions about ward daily activities in order to study the impact of emotion control. Results indicated that state-oriented patients were more likely to feel greater amounts of pain and to use more analgesics. State-oriented patients tended to focus on their current situation; whereas action-oriented patients were actively making plans to get ready to leave the hospital.

The research findings and associated theory of Kuhl and his colleagues offer interesting explanations for various aspects of motivated human behavior. Next, we will address some of the implications of Kuhl's action control theory for research in work settings.

IMPLICATIONS OF ACTION CONTROL THEORY FOR I/O PSYCHOLOGY

Similar to the approach taken in the discussion of the implications of goal orientation, we have divided the implications of action control theory into several content domains of I/O psychology.

Goal-Setting Theory

Relation of goals and intentions to behavior

Locke and Latham (1990) have discussed in some detail distinctions that can be made between goals and intentions. We will combine these two terms here as our purpose is merely to show that the link between some cognitive representation about future desired actions or end-states and actual behavior is not typically a simple one-to-one relationship. Locke and Latham (1990; Latham & Locke, 1991), in reviewing the large amount of literature on the effect of goals on performance or behavior, note considerable support for the basic tenets of goal-setting theory. However, it is also clear from such reviews that goals do not perfectly predict performance level.

In a related but largely non-overlapping body of research literature, Ajzen (1991) has summarized a number of studies that examined the relation between intentions and behavior from the perspective of his theory of planned behavior. The median correlation between intentions and actual behavior was about 0.40. The addition of other variables from his theory (e.g. perceived behavioral control—a variable not unlike self-efficacy; and subjective norms) increased the median multiple correlation with behavior to about 0.70–0.75 (or the percentage of explained variance to about 50–55%). Thus, the prediction of behavior from theory components, while impressive, is not so accurate that we should not search for other variables that may affect or moderate the link between intentions and behavior.

Action control theory (Kuhl, 1985; in press a) suggests that the distinction between action and state orientation may help to further explain the relationship between goals or intentions and behavior beyond that possible by goal-setting (Locke & Latham, 1990; Latham & Locke, 1991) and planned behavior (Ajzen, 1991) theories in their present formulations. Kuhl (1985) has used the term *enactment* in his discussion of the consistency between intentions and behavior. Inconsistency in an intention–behavior relationship is related to the difficulty of enactment, that is, how hard it is for the individual to carry out or enact the desired intention.

State-oriented individuals have more difficulty in many situations enacting intentions because their self-regulatory strategies (see the earlier description of Kuhl's theory for a listing of these) are less likely to be engaged than those of action-oriented individuals. The focus of the action-oriented individual is on the task and this elicits the self-regulatory processes necessary to maintain goal-directed behavior. The focus on cognitive or emotional states characteristic of the state-oriented individual makes the elicitation of appropriate self-regulatory processes less probable. The state-oriented individual can be characterized as showing (i) preoccupation with past or present events, often failure experiences, and (ii) hesitation in the initiation of intended actions (Kulh, in press a). State-oriented individuals may also be characterized by volatility, the tendency to change activities impulsively, even pleasurable ones, prematurely to alternative ones (Kuhl, in press a). All of these factors would lead to a decrease in the goal–behavior relationship for state-oriented individuals in comparison to action-oriented individuals.

Effects of goals in complex tasks

Wood and his colleagues (1986; Wood & Bailey, 1985; Wood & Locke, 1990; Wood, Mento, & Locke, 1987) have been concerned with how complex tasks are affected by goal-setting processes. They have concluded that the magnitude of goal effects on performance decreases as task complexity increases. Wood and Locke (1990) have noted that more complex tasks require plans or strategies for effective task performance that are less dependent on 'universal' tasks plans (such as increase effort level, persist longer, attend more to the task) and more dependent on problem solving and the development of task-specific plans.

Action control theory may be able to contribute to the understanding of the goal–task complexity relationship. Individuals with a state orientation are described by Kuhl as being context-insensitive and likely to stick with an original intention or plan even when there is a discrepancy between that intention and performance outcomes. Such individuals may persist with one or more of the universal strategies noted above and fail to adapt to a more task-specific strategy, leading to lowered performance. Action-oriented individuals are more context-sensitive and adapt their strategies to emerging performance discrepancies. Such discrepancies would be more likely in complex tasks. Since state- and action-oriented individuals may hold and be committed to similar goals on average, the ineffective strategies of the state-oriented performers result in a lower impact of goals on performance when assessed across samples including both action- and state-oriented individuals.

For example, Kuhl (1982) obtained an interaction between the nature of the task to be performed and action versus state orientation with regard to whether the individual's intentions were achieved. Individuals with an action orientation were found to have a stronger relationship between intentions and behavior when the task was intrinsically satisfying, but state-oriented individuals were better able to enact their intentions when the task was routinized (Kuhl, 1982). Action-oriented individuals may have more consistent links between their intentions and behavior with intrinsically satisfying tasks (which are likely to be novel, challenging, and broad in scope) because they are more flexible with regard to situational or contextual factors that affect whether maintenance or disengagement from original strategies for implementing intentions is more efficacious (Kuhl, 1992). Individuals with a state orientation are effective at following external demands so that their tendency to stick with an original strategy for implementing an intention may lead to performance more consistent with their intentions with a routine or simple task (that is likely immersed in a context with external controls and rewards).

Multiple goals

In situations where there are competing goals (e.g. finish a book chapter versus watch the Olympics on television), Kuhl has generally found that action-oriented individuals are better at maintaining a current intention and protecting it from competing alternatives. This is a point related to the earlier argument that action-oriented individuals are likely to show stronger links between goals and behavior than those with a state orientation. Much of the logic discussed there holds here as well. The existence of explicit competing goals, however, extends the argument to *directional* effects of state orientation, in addition to the commitment to a single goal discussed above. That is, state-oriented individuals are more likely than action-oriented individuals to change their goal *qualitatively*, not just to make a quantitative adjustment in an existing goal or fail to achieve performance at the original standard.

Reactions to Negative Feedback

State-oriented individuals are more likely than action-oriented individuals to ruminate about failure (Kuhl, in press a). This may contribute to maladaptive responses to negative feedback. It is possible that state-oriented individuals would become fixed on old, ineffective strategies for task performance, particularly for complex tasks. Kanfer and Ackerman (1989) would further suggest that such individuals would have fewer cognitive resources to devote to the search for novel approaches to task performance.

Kuhl (1985) suggested that extreme discrepancies between one's performance and one's goals or intentions give rise to state orientation, whereas small discrepancies give rise to action orientations. This suggests that it may be better to give relatively mild or moderate negative feedback when such is necessary so that the adaptive development of new strategies is more likely to take place. It should be remembered that what is perceived as mild versus moderate versus severe levels of negative feedback may be a function of the dispositional tendency of the individual toward action or state.

Training and Development

Malleability of action and state orientations

Kuhl (in press a) has posited both distal and proximal antecedents of action and state orientations (see the earlier discussion of his theory for details). The existence of distal antecedents implies a relatively stable individual characteristic or trait. However, the existence of proximal antecedents suggests that state and action orientations may be modified by training or variations in situational conditions. Indeed, Kuhl (1992) has recently noted that the dispositional stability and generality of action versus state orientation should be considered an empirical question, and that the validity of action control theory is not soley determined by the answer to this question, that is, action control theory does not require that this orientation be a strong, stable trait.

Given that Kuhl and his associates have shown in various studies that the manipulation of situational variables can induce either state- or action-oriented behavior, it seems reasonable to presume that these orientations are malleable, at least to some extent. For individuals who experience difficulty in implementing behavioral intentions (i.e. a state orientation), training in self-regulation that focuses on an action orientation may be useful. Such training in self-management (see also the earlier section on self-management in the goal-orientation portion of this chapter) could use the six self-regulatory processes noted by Kuhl (1985) and described earlier in this chapter.

Stages in acquisition or training

The imposition of difficult goals or a strong focus on the expected end results of training in terms of level of performance at or near the beginning of the training program is likely to induce a state orientation in employees. This would result from the large discrepancy between the trainee's skill and knowledge level at the onset of training versus the final criterion levels expected from individuals at the end of the training program. Once basic competency has been achieved, such goals should encourage an action orientation directed at achieving the final criterion goal levels. In partial support for this idea, Kanfer and Ackerman (1989) found that persons assigned performance goals early in acquisition reported more emotion-related thoughts than those not assigned explicit goals at that point. Kuhl would suggest that such thoughts are intrusive in terms of goal-directed behavior, are probably related to difficulty or failure, and are symptomatic of a state orientation.

Work Role Innovation

Most discussions of innovation in organizations suggest that an important part of the innovative process is the implementation of the innovation (e.g. Kanter, 1988; Amabile, 1988). Kanter has argued the need to be flexible when attempting to innovate within an organization. Particularly when facing the reality of multiple stakeholders with various vested interests, one cannot cling too long or too rigidly to original goals and plans. This suggests a need to be sensitive to contextual cues, a characteristic of the action-oriented individual (Kuhl, in press a). Amabile (1988) has noted that individual barriers to creativity in organizational settings include inflexibility and responding primarily to the goals of others, characteristics consistent with state-oriented persons (Kuhl, 1992). The many barriers to innovation present in most organizations (Kanter, 1988) would also suggest that the state-oriented individual, likely to ruminate about setbacks along the way, is less likely to bring an innovation to final fruition.

Additional Comments on Action versus State Orientation

Kuhl (in press a) has noted that much of the discussion of action versus state orientation seems to imply that state orientation is totally a negative condition, but that such an interpretation is not his intention. Rather, he argues for an assessment of the 'fit' of the individual's orientation to the work environment. He suggests that a state-oriented person may be effective in relatively structured organizations and as part of teams making high-risk decisions in which deliberate decision-making is required. In the latter case, the state-oriented members of a team were noted as more effective decision-makers, whereas the action-oriented members were better at implementation of the decisions. It should be noted that Kuhl's observations concerning state versus action orientation with regard to decision-making have been made within the context of training workshops for managers and not in research settings. It is not clear whether systematic data concerning decision-making are available. Nonetheless, these are interesting questions for future research.

SOME THOUGHTS ON RELATIONSHIPS BETWEEN GOAL ORIENTATION AND ACTION CONTROL THEORY

When the work of Dweck and her associates is considered in conjunction with that of Kuhl and his associates, a number of similarities can be observed. For example, both discuss (i) behaviors and cognitions in achievement-oriented situations; (ii) reactions to negative feedback or failures; and (iii) persistence following failures. The two approaches, however, differ with respect to the context in which the theories have been developed. Specifically, the majority of Dweck's work has been focused on how individuals perform on a particular task; that is, the individuals are either told to perform a task or have actively selected a task to perform. In either case, Dweck's theories regarding both task performance and cognitions begin after the task has been chosen (with the exception of the task-choice studies where subjects chose between a limited number of alternatives). Kuhl's work, on the other hand, has been primarily concerned with how individuals choose among various alternative tasks and/or motivations. Specifically, Kuhl's theory is concerned with how individuals regulate their behavior in a task-rich environment, that is, how individuals move from one task to another.

It is easy to consider, given the above distinction, how the theories developed by Dweck and Kuhl may interrelate. One may envision, for example, that Kuhl's action control theory of self-regulation may easily subsume Dweck's notions of learning versus performance goal orientation. For example, first consider state-oriented individuals. Kuhl found, in essence, two distinguishing features of a state orientation. First, these individuals have difficulty enacting self-regulatory mechanisms which enable them to switch appropriately from one task to another. In other words, state-oriented individuals often need some external motivator to, in actuality, 'force' them to change tasks. Second, Kuhl found that state-oriented individuals also experience more task-irrelevant cognitions during task performance, have negative reactions to failure, and are more likely to attribute failure to ability deficits.

The experience of state-oriented individuals during task performance is similar to findings reported by Dweck for performance-oriented individuals. Specifically, Dweck found that performance goal-oriented individuals have negative reactions to failure and are more likely to attribute failure to lack of ability. In a similar vein, Kanfer and Ackerman (1989) have recently reported that goal setting is dysfunctional during early task performance. Furthermore, individuals in the early goal-setting condition also reported more task-irrelevant thoughts during task performance. Although the performance orientation of the early goal condition subjects was not assessed in the Kanfer and Ackerman (1989) study, it is easy to envision that external goal setting could shift one into a performance orientation. Given this assumption, the greater task-irrelevant cognitions seem to fit Kuhl's findings regarding state-oriented individuals.

Kuhl has also found two defining characteristics of action-oriented individuals: first, these individuals can more easily invoke self-regulatory systems to shift appropriately from task to task; and, second, these individuals are better able to shut out task-irrelevant cognitions and concentrate on the task during performance. In Dweck's paradigm, learning goal individuals seem to be able to focus more of their attention on task performance. For example, remember that performance-oriented individuals are trying to demonstrate their competence to others, while learning-oriented individuals are more interested in learning that task and developing mastery. It is very likely that, since learning goal-oriented individuals are less concerned with external judgments (e.g. less likely to think, 'I'm going to look stupid if I can't figure this out'), they may be able to focus better on the task. In addition, from an information processing perspective (e.g. Norman & Bobrow, 1975), the extraneous thoughts encountered by performance- and state-oriented individuals would reduce the cognitive resources available for task performance, thereby reducing, perhaps, task performance and the search for alternative strategies. Some initial evidence for this notion was found by Diener and Dweck (1978, 1980) who discovered that learning-oriented individuals used better strategies in task performance.

In summary, then, it might be the case that Dweck's theories actually mediate the relationship between the state/action orientation and task performance. Specifically, state-oriented individuals may be more likely to adopt a performance goal orientation which would then lead to the observations of Dweck during task performance. Alternatively, action-oriented individuals may be better suited to learning goals which lead to different reactions to task performance. Although the interrelationships between Dweck and Kuhl's paradigms described above seem intuitively appealing, to our knowledge none of the proposed relationships has been empirically tested. The testing of these notions is something that we must leave to future research.

CONCLUDING COMMENTS

Clearly, we believe that the goal orientation and action control theory constructs should be examined closely by theorists and researchers concerned with individual behavior and attitudes in work settings. We trust that we have been sufficiently persuasive in our arguments that others will undertake such examinations. Before we close this chapter, we do want to reiterate one point alluded to several times in earlier sections.

Much of our discussion regarding both Kuhl's and Dweck's theories has been positioned at the level of individual differences or dispositional tendencies. However, one must not discount the potential effects of contextual influences on individuals. Specifically, it should be recalled that the majority of the research conducted by Dweck and her associates has induced goal orientation (learning or performance) by the manipulation of an experimental situation.

Much of the Kuhl research has adopted similar strategies with regard to action and state orientation.

We have noted in the two sections of this chapter dealing with the implications of goal orientation and action control theory that the nature of 'typical' organizations and the work environment itself may influence an individual's goal orientation and/or self-regulatory mechanisms. In particular, we have suggested that many current organizational systems and characteristics may induce performance goal orientations or state orientations. These include normative-based performance appraisal systems, reward structures focused on short-term results, and training and development programs with strong performance evaluation components. The design of organizational systems to encourage learning goal and action orientations would appear to be a worthy topic for immediate research and appropriate application.

ACKNOWLEDGEMENTS

We should like to thank David Day, Carolyn Jagacinski, Ruth Kanfer, and John Mathieu for their comments on an earlier version of this chapter.

REFERENCES

Ajzen, I. (1991) The theory of planned behavior. *Organizational Behavior and Human Decision Processes*, **50**, 179–211.

Amabile, T. M. (1988) A model of creativity and innovation in organizations. In B. M. Staw & L. L. Cummings (eds), *Research in Organizational Behavior*, vol. 10. Greenwich, CT: JAI Press.

Ames, C., & Ames, R. (1981) Competitive versus individualistic goal structures: The salience of past performance information for causal attributions and affect. *Journal of Educational Psychology*, **73**, 411–418.

Ames, C., Ames, R., & Felker, D. (1977) Effects of competitive reward structure and valence of outcome on children's achievement attributions. *Journal of Educational Psychology*, **69**, 1–8.

Ames, C., & Archer, J. (1988) Achievement goals in the classroom: Students' learning strategies and motivation processes. *Journal of Educational Psychology*, **80**, 260–267.

Anderson, C. A., & Jennings, D. L. (1980) When experiences of failure promote expectations of success: The impact of attributing failure to ineffective strategies. *Journal of Personality*, **48**, 393–407.

Arnold, M. (1984) *Memory and the Brain*. Hillsdale, NJ: Erlbaum.

Ashford, S. J., & Cummings, L. L. (1983) Feedback as an individual resource: Personal strategies for creating information. *Organizational Behavior and Human Performance*, **32**, 370–389.

Atkinson, J. W. (1974) Strength of motivation and efficiency of performance. In J. W. Atkinson & J. O. Raynor (eds), *Motivation and Achievement*. Washington DC: Winston.

Atkinson, J. W., & Feather, E. T. (1966) *A Theory of Achievement Motivation*. New York: Wiley.

Bandura, A. (1982) Self-efficacy mechanism in human agency. *American Psychologist*, **37**, 122–147.

Bandura, A. (1986) *Social Foundations of Thought and Action: A Social-cognitive View.* Englewood Cliffs, NJ: Prentice-Hall.

Bandura, A. (1991) Social cognitive theory of self-regulation. *Organizational Behavior and Human Decision Processes*, **50**, 248–287.

Bandura, A., & Schunk, D. H. (1981) Cultivating competence, self-efficacy, and intrinsic interest through proximal self-motivation. *Journal of Personality and Social Psychology*, **41**, 586–598.

Bandura, M., & Dweck, C. S. (1981) Children's theories of intelligence as predictors of achievement goals. Unpublished manuscript, Harvard University.

Beckmann, J., & Kuhl, J. (1984) Altering information to gain action control: Functional aspects of human information-processing in decison-making. *Journal of Research in Personality*, **18**, 224–237.

Berglas, S., & Jones, E. E. (1978) Drug choice as a self-handicapping strategy in response to noncontingent success. *Journal of Personality and Social Psychology*, **36**, 405–417.

Binswanger, H. (1991) Volition as cognitive self-regulation. *Organizational Behavior and Human Decision Processes*, **50**, 154–178.

Butler, R. (1987) Task-involving and ego-involving properties of evaluation: Effects of different feedback conditions on motivational perceptions, interest, and performance. *Journal of Educational Psychology*, **79**, 474–482.

Butler, R. (1988) Enhancing and undermining intrinsic motivation: The effects of task-involving and ego-involving evaluation on interest and performance. *British Journal of Educational Psychology*, **58**, 1–14.

Carver, C. S., & Scheier, M. F. (1981) *Attention and Self-regulation: A Control-theory Approach to Human Behavior.* New York: Springer-Verlag.

Chi, M. T. H., Glaser, R., & Farr, M. J. (eds) (1988) *The Nature of Expertise.* Hillsdale, NJ: Erlbaum.

Deci, E. L. (1975) *Intrinsic Motivation.* New York: Plenum Press.

Dickinson, T. L. (in press) Reactions to performance appraisals. In H. Schuler, J. L. Farr, & M. Smith (eds), *Personnel Selection and Assessment: Individual and Organizational Perspectives.* Hillsdale, NJ: Erlbaum.

Diener, C. I., & Dweck, C. S. (1978) An analysis of learned helplessness: Continuous changes in performance, strategy, and achievement cognitions following failure. *Journal of Personality and Social Psychology*, **36**, 451–462.

Diener, C. I., & Dweck, C. S. (1980) An analysis of learned helplessness: II. The processing of success. *Journal Personality and Social Psychology*, **39**, 940–952.

Dweck, C. S. (1986) Motivational processes affecting learning. *American Psychologist*, **41**, 1040–1048.

Dweck, C. S. (1989) Motivation. In A. Lesgold & R. Glaser (eds), *Foundations for a Psychology of Education.* Hillsdale, NJ: Erlbaum.

Dweck, C. S., & Elliott, E. S. (1983) Achievement motivation. In P. Mussen (gen. ed.), E. M. Hetherington (vol. ed.), *Handbook of Child Psychology*, vol. 4. New York: Wiley.

Dweck, C. S., & Goetz, T. E. (1978) Attributions and learned helplessness. In J. H. Harvey, W. Ickes, & R. F. Kidd (eds), *New Directions in Attribution Research* (vol. 2). Hillsdale, NJ: Erlbaum.

Dweck, C. S., & Leggett, E. L. (1988) A social-cognitive approach to motivation and personality. *Psychological Review*, **95**, 256–273.

Dweck, C. S., Tenney, Y., & Dinces, N. (1982) [Implicit theories of intelligence as determinants of achievement goal choice] Unpublished data, Harvard University.

Elliott, E. S., & Dweck, C. S. (1981) Children's achievment goals as determinants of learned helplessness and mastery-oriented achievement patterns: An experimental analysis. Unpublished manuscript, Harvard University.

Ellis, A. (1973) *Humanistic Psychotherapy: The Rational Emotive Approach.* New York: McGraw-Hill.

Farr, J. L. (1990) Facilitating individual role innovation. In M. A. West & J. L. Farr (eds), *Innovation and Creativity at Work.* Chichester, UK: Wiley.

Farr, J. L. (1991) Leitsungfeedback und Arbeitsverhalten. In H. Schuler (ed.), *Beurteilung und Froderung beruflicher Leistung.* Stuttgart: Verlagfur Angewandte Psychologie.

Farr, J. L. (1992) [Goal orientation and feedback seeking]. Unpublished raw data.

Farr, J. L. (in press) Informal performance feedback: Seeking and giving. In H. Schuler, J. L. Farr, & M. Smith (eds), *Personnel Selection and Assessment: Individual and Organizational Perspectives.* Hillsdale, NJ: Erlbaum.

Farr, J. L., & Ford, C. M. (1990) Individual innovation. In M. A. West & J. L. Farr (eds), *Innovation and Creativity at Work.* Chichester, UK: Wiley.

Farr, J. L., & Middlebrooks, C. L. (1990) Enhancing motivation to participate in professional development. In S. L. Willis & S. S. Dubin (eds), *Maintaining Professional Competence.* San Francisco: Jossey-Bass.

Frayne, C. A., & Latham, G. P. (1987) Application of social learning theory to employee self-management of attendance. *Journal of Applied Psychology,* 72, 387–392.

Frese, M., Brodbeck, F., Heinbokel, T., Mooser, C., Schleiffenbaum, E., & Thiemann, P. (1991) Errors in training computer skills: On the positive function of errors. *Human-Computer Interaction,* 6, 77–93.

Gist, M. E., Bavetta, A. G., & Stevens, C. K. (1990) Transfer training method: Its influence on skill generation, skill repetition, and performance level. *Personnel Psychology,* 43, 501–523.

Greif, S., & Keller, H. (1990) Innovation and the design of work and learning environments: The concept of exploration in human-computer interaction. In M. A. West & J. L. Farr (eds), *Innovation and Creativity at Work.* Chichester, UK: Wiley.

Heckhausen, H. (1989) *Motivation und Handeln.* Heidelberg: Springer.

Heckhausen, H., Schmalt, H. D., & Schneider, K. (1985) *Achievement Motivation in Perspective.* New York: Academic Press.

Hofmann, D. A. (1992) Task performance and transfer: An assessment of inter-individual differences in intra-individual change. Unpublished doctoral dissertation, The Pennsylvania State University, University Park, PA.

Humbert, C. (1981) Schwierigkeitswahl und leistung nach erfolg und misserfolg als funktion von lageorientierung und standardsetzung. Unpublished diploma thesis, Ruhr-University Bochum.

Ilgen, D. R., Fisher, C. D., & Taylor, M. S. (1979) Consequences of individual feedback on behavior in organizations. *Journal of Applied Psychology,* 64, 349–371.

Jagacinski, C. M. (1992) The effects of task involvement and ego involvement on achievement-related cognitions and behaviors. In D. H. Schunk & J. L. Meece (eds), *Student Perceptions in the Classroom: Causes and Consequences.* Hillsdale, NJ: Erlbaum, 1992.

Jagacinksi, C. M., & Nicholls, J. G. (1987) Competence and affect in task involvement and ego involvement: The impact of social comparison information. *Journal of Educational Psychology,* 79, 107–114.

Kanfer, F. (1980) Self-management methods. In F. Kanfer & A. Goldstein (eds), *Helping People Change: A Textbook of Methods.* New York: Pergamon Press.

Kanfer, R. (1987) Task-specific motivation: An integrative approach to issues of measurement, mechanisms, processes, and determinants. *Journal of Social and Clinical Psychology,* 5, 251–278.

Kanfer, R. (1990a) Motivation and individual differences in learning: An integration of developmental, differential and cognitive perspectives. *Learning and Individual Differences*, **2**, 221–239.

Kanfer, R. (1990b) Motivation theory and industrial and organizational psychology. In M. D. Dunnette & L. M. Hough (eds), *Handbook of Industrial and Organizational Psychology*, 2nd edition, vol. 1. Palo Alto, CA: Consulting Psychologists Press.

Kanfer, R., & Ackerman, P. L. (1989) Motivation and cognitive abilities: An integrative/adaptive-treatment interaction approach to skill acquisition. *Journal of Applied Psychology*, **74**, 657–690.

Kanter, R. M. (1988) When a thousand flowers bloom: Structural, collective, and social conditions for innovation in organizations. In B. M. Staw & L. L. Cummings (eds), *Research in Organizational Behavior*, vol. 10. Greenwich, CT: JAI Press.

Karoly, P., & Kanfer, F. (1982) *Self-management and Behavior Change: From Theory to Practice*. New York: Pergamon Press.

Kernan, M. C., & Lord, R. G. (1990) Effects of valence, expectancies, and goal-performance discrepancies in single and multiple goal environments. *Journal of Applied Psychology*, **75**, 194–203.

Klein, H. (1989) An integrated control theory model of work motivation. *Academy of Management Review*, **14**, 150–172.

Kuhl, J. (1981) Motivational and functional helplessness: The moderating effect of state versus action orientation. *Journal of Personality and Social Psychology*, **40**, 155–170.

Kuhl, J. (1982) Handlungskontrolle als metakognitiver vermittler zwischen intention and handeln: Freizeitaktivitaten bei hauptschulern. *Zeitschrift für Entwicklungspsychologie und padagogische psychologie*, **14**, 141–148.

Kuhl, J. (1983a) *Motivation, Konflikt und Handslungkontrolle*. Heidelberg, FRG: Springer.

Kuhl, J. (1983b) Motivationstheoretische aspekte der depressionsgenese: Der einfuss von lageorienteirung auf schmerzempfinden, medikamentenkonsum und handlungskontrolle. In M. Wolfersdorf, R. Straub, & G. Hole (eds), *Der Depressiv Kranke in der Psychiatrischen Klinik: Theorie und Praxis der Diagnostik und Therapie*. Regensburg: Roderer.

Kuhl, J. (1985) Volitional mediators of cognition-behavior consistency: Self-regulatory processes and action versus state orientation. In J. Kuhl & J. Beckmann (eds), *Action Control: From Cognition to Behavior*. New York: Springer-Verlag.

Kuhl, J. (1992) A theory of self-regulation: Action versus state orientation, self-discrimination, and some applications. *Applied Psychology: An International Review*, **41** (Issue 2), 97–129.

Kuhl, J. (in press a) A theory of action and state orientation. In J. Kuhl & J. Beckmann (eds), *Volition and Personality: Action versus State Orientation*. Toronto/Göttingen: Hogrefe.

Kuhl, J. (in press b) Action versus state orientation: Psychometric properties of the Action Control Scale (ACS-90). In J. Kuhl & J. Beckmann (eds), *Volition and Personality: Action versus State Orientation*. Toronto/Göttingen: Hogrefe.

Kuhl, J., & Beckmann, J. (1983) Handlungskontrolle und umfang der informationsverarbeitung: Wahl einer vereinfachten (nicht optimalen) entscheidungsregel zugunsten rascher handlungsbereitschaft. *Zeitschrift für Sozialpsychologie*, **14**, 241–250.

Kuhl, J., & Geiger, E. (in press) The dynamic theory of the anxiety–behavior relation: A study on resistance and time allocation. In J. Kuhl & J. W. Atkinson (eds), *Motivation, Thought, and Action*. New York: Praeger.

Kuhl, J., & Helle, P. (1986) Motivational and volitional determinants of depression: The degenerated-intention hypothesis. *Journal of Abnormal Psychology*, **95**, 247–251.

Kuhl, J., & Kazen-Saad, M. (1990) Volition and self-regulation: Memory mechanisms mediating the maintenance of intentions. In W. A. Herschberger (ed.), *Volitional Action*. Amsterdam: Elsevier, Science Publishers.

Kuhl, J., & Koch, B. (1984) Motivational determinants of motor performance: The second hidden task. *Psychological Research*, 46, 143–153.

Kuhl, J., & Wassiljew, I. (1985) An information processing perspective on motivation: Intrinsic task-involvement, problem solving, and the complexity of action plans. In G. D'Ydewalle (ed.), *Cognition, Information Processing, and Motivation*, vol. 3. Amsterdam: North Holland Publishing Co.

Kuhl, J., & Weiss, M. (1983) Performance deficits following uncontrollable failure: Impaired action control or global attributions and generalized expectancy deficits? Max Planck Institute for Psychology Research, Munich, FRG.

Larson, J. R., Jr (1984) The performance feedback process: A preliminary model. *Organizational Behavior and Human Performance*, 32, 42–76.

Larson, J. R., Jr (1989) The dynamic interplay between employees' feedback-seeking strategies and supervisors' delivery of performance feedback. *Academy of Management Review*, 14, 408–421.

Latham, G. P., & Baldes, J. J. (1975) The 'practical significance' of Locke's theory of goal setting. *Journal of Applied Psychology*, 60, 122–124.

Latham, G. P., & Frayne, C. A. (1989) Self-management training for increasing job attendance: A follow-up and a replication. *Journal of Applied Psychology*, 74, 411–416.

Latham, G. P., & Kinne, S. B. (1974) Improving job performance through training in goal setting. *Journal of Applied Psychology*, 59, 187–191.

Latham, G. P., & Locke, E. A. (1991) Self-regulation through goal setting. *Organizational Behavior and Human Decision Processes*, 50, 212–247.

Locke, E. A. (1991a) Introduction to special issue. *Organizational Behavior and Human Decision Processes*, 50, 151–153.

Locke, E. A. (1991b) The motivation sequence, the motivation hub, and the motivation core. *Organizational Behavior and Human Decision Processes*, 50, 288–299.

Locke, E. A., & Henne, D. (1986) Work motivation theories. In C. Cooper & I. T. Robertson (eds), *International Review of Industrial and Organizational Psychology*, vol. 1. Chichester, UK: Wiley.

Locke, E. A., Latham, G. P. (1990) *A Theory of Goal Setting and Task Performance*. Englewood Cliffs, NJ: Prentice-Hall.

Lord, R. G., & Hanges, P. J. (1987) A control systems model of organizational motivation: Theoretical development and applied implications. *Behavioral Science*, 32, 161–178.

Lord, R. G., & Maher, K. J. (1989) Cognitive processes in industrial and organizational psychology. In C. Cooper & I. T. Robertson (eds), *International Review of Industrial and Organizational Psychology*, vol. 4. Chichester, UK: Wiley.

Mathieu, J. E. (in press) The influence of commitment to assigned goals and performance on subsequent self-set goals and performance. *Journal of Applied Social Psychology*.

Meichenbaum, D., & Butler, L. (1978) Toward a conceptual model for the treatment of test anxiety: Implications for research and treatment. In I. G. Sarason (ed.), *Test of Anxiety, Theory, Research, and Applications*. Hillsdale, NJ: Erlbaum.

Mitchell, T. R., & Silver, W. S. (1990) Individual and group goals when workers are interdependent: Effects on task strategies and performance. *Journal of Applied Psychology*, 75, 185–193.

Near, J. P., & Miceli, M. P. (1987) Whistle-blowers in organizations: Dissidents or reformers? In L. L. Cummings & B. M. Staw (eds), *Research in Organizational Behavior*, vol. 9. Greenwich, CT: JAI Press.

Nicholls, J. G. (1984) Achievement motivation: Conceptions of ability, subjective experience, task choice, and performance. *Psychological Review*, 91, 328–346.

Norman, D. A., & Bobrow, D. G. (1975) On data-limited and resource-limited processes. *Cognitive Psychology*, 7, 44–64.

Ryer, J. A. (1991) Interactive effects of implicit theories of intelligence and achievement goals on performance following failure. Paper presented at the 3rd annual convention of the American Psychological Society, Washington, DC.

Sarason, I. G. (1975) Anxiety and self-preoccupation. In I. G. Sarason & C. D. Spielberger (eds), *Stress and Anxiety*, vol. 2. Washington, DC: Hemisphere.

Sarason, I. G. (1984) Stress, anxiety, and cognitive interference: Reactions to tests. *Journal of Personality and Social Psychology*, **46**, 929–938.

Sarason, I. G., & Stoops, R. (1978) Test anxiety and the passage of time. *Journal of Consulting and Clinical Psychology*, **46**, 102–109.

Sarason, I. G., Sarason, B. R., Keefe, D. E., Hayes, B. E., & Shearin, E. N. (1986) Cognitive interference: Situational determinants and traitlike characteristiscs. *Journal of Personality and Social Psychology*, **51**, 215–226.

Tubbs, M. E., & Dahl, J. G. (1991) An empirical comparison of self-report and discrepancy measures of goal commitment. *Journal of Applied Psychology*, **76**, 709–716.

Vroom, V. H. (1964) *Work and Motivation*. New York: Wiley.

Weick, K. E. (1987) Organizational culture as a source of high reliability. *California Management Review*, **29**, 112–127.

White, R. W. (1959) Motivation reconsidered: The concept of competence. *Psychological Review*, **66**, 297–333.

Willis, S. L., & Dubin, S. S. (1990) Competence versus obsolescence: Understanding the challenge facing today's professionals. In S. L. Willis & S. S. Dubin (eds), *Maintaining Professional Competence*. San Francisco: Jossey-Bass.

Wood, R. E. (1986) Task complexity: Definition of the construct. *Organizational Behavior and Human Decision Processes*, **37**, 60–82.

Wood. R. E., & Bailey, T. C. (1985) Some unanswered questions about goal effects: A recommended change in research methods. *Australian Journal of Management*, **10**, 61–73.

Wood, R., & Bandura, A. (1989) Impact of conceptions of ability of self-regulatory mechanisms and complex decision making. *Journal of Personality and Social Psychology*, **56**, 407–415.

Wood, R. E., & Locke, E. A. (1990) Goal setting and strategy effects on complex tasks. In B. M. Staw & L. L. Cummings (eds), *Research in Organizational Behavior*, vol. 12. Greenwich, CT: JAI Press.

Wood, R. E., Mento, A. J., & Locke, E. A. (1987) Task complexity as a moderator of goal effects: A meta-analysis. *Journal of Applied Psychology*, **72**, 416–425.

Zajac, D. M. (1991) The interactive effects of self-efficacy and implicit theory of ability on goal setting and performance. Unpublished doctoral dissertation, The Pennsylvania State University, University Park, PA.

Chapter 7

CORPORATE CULTURE: DEFINITION, DIAGNOSIS AND CHANGE

Adrian Furnham and Barrie Gunter
University College, London, UK

Corporate culture has dominated much management thinking for the past decade. Numerous publications, both popular and academic, have explored the cultural perspective on a wide range of management and organizational issues. Some of these writings have proved to be considerably influential among practising managers, most notably perhaps William Ouchi's (1981) *Theory Z*, Pascale and Athos's (1981) *Art of Japanese Management*, Deal and Kennedy's (1982) *Corporate Cultures*, Schein's (1985) *Organizational Culture and Leadership*, Hofstede's (1980) *Culture's Consequences*, and most of all, Peters and Waterman's (1982) *In Search of Excellence*. Furthermore, sophisticated discussion and debate on corporate culture is certainly not restricted to English speakers. Some of the most interesting European ideas are in French (Gauthey, Ratiu, Rodgers & Xardel, 1988) and German (Sackmann, 1989).

These works have created a growing awareness of 'cultural issues' in all sorts of organizations. The significance of the 'culture' concept has been enhanced in particular through the relationship it is often assumed to hold with organizational performance. A well-developed and business-specific culture into which management and staff are thoroughly socialized has been thought, at various times, to underpin stronger organizational commitment, higher morale, more efficient performance, and generally higher productivity (Hampden-Turner, 1990; Graves, 1986; Deal & Kennedy, 1982).

The recent successes of Japanese corporations are frequently held up as testimony to the impact of strongly developed and highly appropriate corporate cultures, which have been carefully nurtured and to which continued reinforcement is tended. The shared corporate values among management and workforce in such companies are identified as important critical features underlying a highly motivated approach to achieving well-defined and clearly understood organizational goals, although the nature of the evidence upon which this is based is uncertain.

International Review of Industrial and Organizational Psychology 1993 Volume 8
Edited by C. L. Cooper and I. T. Robertson. © 1993 John Wiley & Sons Ltd.

Western observers of this 'Japanese' phenomenon who have tried to list the characteristics of successful companies have repeatedly focused on the concept of corporate culture, on the strength and pervasiveness of core values, beliefs and assumptions to which the organizational workforce completely adheres. These 'cultural' attributes have increasingly been linked with corporate success. They are, of course, not the only factors identified as 'causes' of Japanese success, nor is it very clear why they all deserve to be categorized as cultural. Nevertheless, in the eyes of many managers and some academics the concept of corporate culture is parsimonious, powerful, all-pervading and explanatory of success. Smircich and Calas (1987) posed the question why (corporate) culture is an important topic at this particular time. They offer three explanations: a shift in the perspective of business from rational strategic to cultural issues; shifts in organizational and communication theory to more subjective, social constructionist perspectives; and changes in the human sciences moving away from positivism to interpretivism. These practical and epistemological changes supposedly account for the observed interest in corporate culture although there may well be other reasons.

What many of these books on corporate culture fail to provide, despite ostensibly being labelled as handbooks for the practising manager, is detailed information on how culture works or can be shaped, changed, and otherwise managed in practice. Neither do they provide a consistent definition of what culture actually is (Williams, Dobson & Walters, 1989). Thus for many observers the term is overused, overinclusive, but underdefined (Furnham & Gunter, 1993).

While a proper theoretical analysis of culture is essential to understanding what it is and how it works, practitioners also need to know how to make the step from theory to the day-to-day running of an organization. A major problem here is that an anthropological concept has been borrowed and adapted. Hence the confusing and even contradictory perspectives taken by different disciplines such as anthropology, management science and psychology, let alone those of managers and practitioners themselves. Therefore, throughout the literature different paradigms, frameworks and perspectives are found (Smircich & Calas, 1987). In this chapter, we explore the meaning, assessment and manipulation of culture in organizations. In so doing, we hope to provide some shape to a diverse and rapidly growing body of organizational research literature.

THE GENESIS OF A CORPORATE CULTURE

How does a corporate culture begin to develop? How (if at all) do the different individuals employed within an organization come to share common beliefs, attitudes and values related to the work that they do? If corporate culture (however understood and observed) is a dynamic phenomenon and the product of history, it becomes important to know, if one is to create or indeed change culture, how it develops. Various untested but sensible hypotheses have been made with regard to this.

First, an organization's culture can often be traced to its founders (Deal & Kennedy, 1982). These people often possess dynamic personalities, strong values, and a clear vision of what the organization should look like, how it should operate and where it is going. Since they are on the scene first, they play a key role in initial hiring of staff, and their ideas and values are readily transmitted to new employees. These views then become accepted within the organization and persist as long as the founders are on the scene, or even longer (particularly if the founder plays a strong role in the idea of succession).

Second, corporate culture often develops out of an organization's experience with the external environment. Every organization must find a niche, a market, a product and an image for itself in its industry and in the marketplace in which it operates. As it struggles to do so, it may find that some values and practices work better for it than others. For example, an organization may gradually acquire a deep, shared commitment to high quality or speed of delivery. Another company may find that selling products of moderate quality but at attractive prices, works best for it. The result is that a dominant value centring around a price or service emerges, which shapes all the beliefs and behaviours of the employees in that organization.

Third, culture also develops from the need to maintain effective working relationships among organization members (Furnham & Gunter, 1993). Depending on the nature of the organization's business, and the characteristics of the types of people it must hire, different expectations and values may develop. Thus, if a company needs rapid and open communication between its employees, informal working relationships and open expressions of viewpoint will probably come to be valued within it. In contrast, very different values and styles of communication may develop in other organizations working in other industries with different types of personnel.

Beliefs, attitudes and values—regarded by some writers as the key manifestations of culture—which are held by members of an organization are shaped by external and internal forces. Internal shapers include procedures for selection and recruitment of personnel, management and decision-making style, and social and technical systems within the organization. Externally, social, political, legislative, economic and technological systems constitute forces impinging upon the organization, placing constraints upon its activities or motivating and directing the way it conducts its business. While culture is itself influenced by these environmental forces, it also conditions the organization's response to them. Thus, corporate culture is both an input and an output variable; both a cause and consequence. As such, it may be resistant to change.

Culture has historical roots which are usually developed from the original assumptions, strategies and structures made by their founders. As such, culture tends to embody commonly held beliefs, attitudes and values regarding organizational goals, functions and procedures. Williams, Dobson and Walters (1989) distinguish this conception of culture from the idea that it comprises *shared* beliefs, attitudes and values. Culture may not be shared by everyone in the organization regarding how to respond in any given situation. However, there might be a general tendency for individuals to adopt similar styles of appearance, modes of conduct, and perceptions of how the organization does, or should, function, which have a broad commonality across the organization.

Commonalities of belief, attitude and value can occur within the individual's immediate work group in his/her department or division, across the organization, and even more widely in the society or part of society from which the organization's membership is drawn. Culture is thus heterogeneous. Beliefs, attitudes and values regarding work, the workplace or the organization can vary among different groups in an organization. While the dominant culture might prevail throughout, there could be variations in the way it is expressed or manifests itself. However, the point at which one can distinguish different cultures within an organization is unclear, although this is critical for the concept.

Most organizations are characterized by subcultures which form around different roles, functions and levels (Hampden-Turner, 1990) and probably very few beliefs, attitudes or values are common to all members. The typical medium to large organization is characterized by head office, branch, factory, production, sales, union and accounts subcultures. Organizations may contain an executive culture, a management culture and a staff culture. These subcultures can assume varying degrees of significance within the organization, and can be beneficial if they adopt a common sense of purpose but problems arise where they have different priorities and agendas. Then subcultures can clash with each other or with the overall corporate culture, impeding organizational functioning and performance.

For Schein (1990), culture is created through two main factors. First, there is norm formation around critical incidents—particularly where mistakes have occurred. Such critical incidents, which get described in corporate myth, are powerful learning experiences whose effect may be long-lasting. The second factor is identification with leaders and especially with what leaders pay attention to, measure and control: how leaders react to critical incidents and organizational crises; deliberate role modelling and coaching; operational criteria for the allocation of rewards and status; operational criteria for recruitment and selection, promotion, retirement and expulsion.

What these speculations imply is that corporate culture is the product of historical behaviour patterns. It cannot therefore be instantly created or changed. Furthermore, it is both a cause and a consequence of organizational success and failure. While few would disagree with this description, it remains important to specify why the concept of *culture* is necessary. That is, in what sense do other concepts such as norms and roles which are used extensively by psychologists and sociologists become redundant, out-of-favour or simply jettisoned in favour of something more powerfully explanatory?

DEFINING CORPORATE CULTURE

We commence by asking the basic (but difficult) question: what is corporate culture? Before we can begin to understand its significance, how it works and how it can be changed, we need to know what it is we are dealing with. Definitions of culture abound. For over a decade academics from different disciplines and persuasions have attempted to answer this seemingly simple question. Indeed, the journal *International Studies of Management and Organization* has published numerous articles on this topic for 15 years (Evan, 1979; Jamieson, 1980; Hofstede, 1981). One early contribution offered 164 different definitions of culture (Kroeber & Kluckhohn, 1952). 'Culture', in the organization context, was identified as patterns of behaviour transmitted through symbol systems (principally language) embodying the artifacts, attributes and achievements of a group which also comprise value and belief systems about the way the world is conceived to work and how things should be done.

In general, definitions of culture tend to deal primarily either with the way people act or the way they think (Williams, Dobson & Walters, 1989). Culture has been defined as 'the way we do things around here' (Deal & Kennedy, 1982), 'the way we think about things around here', or 'the fabrics of meaning with which human beings interpret their experience and guide their actions' (Geertz, 1973). Other writers have chosen to define culture in terms of both commitment *and* behaviour. Thus, for Margulies and Raia (1978), culture represents 'the commonly shared beliefs, values and characteristic patterns of behaviour that exist within an organization'.

In attempting to arrive at a useful, workable definition some writers have focused on the *dimensions* of corporate culture (Schein, 1990; Hampden-Turner, 1990) and others have examined the *functions* of culture (Williams, Dobson & Walters, 1989; Graves, 1986), while yet others have attempted succinct *definitions* of it (Gonzalez, 1987; Bower, 1966). We return to a discussion of dimensions and functions of corporate culture later in the chapter. Suffice it to say that there still remains no consensus about definition.

According to Deal and Kennedy (1982), corporate culture has a number of specific elements: a widely shared philosophy in the business environment, shared values, specific rites and rituals, and clear, albeit informal, lines of communication. Meek (1988) suggested that corporate culture has much to do with internalizing shared beliefs and behavioural norms. He observed that corporate culture is different from corporate structure but the two are nevertheless related, being interdependent.

Gonzalez (1987) argued that culture is a set of symbols and meanings people use to organize their ideas, interpret their experiences, make decisions, and ultimately guide their actions. Culture often has a 'taken for granted' aspect in that it embodies shared assumptions about how work is done and how people relate to one another. Culture is a pattern of assumptions that a given group has invented, discovered or developed which is learned by its members and which governs the way they behave at work. Thus, culture is important because it can have a direct impact on motivation, work satisfaction and organizational morale.

Hampden-Turner (1990), on the other hand, preferred to list a dozen characteristics of corporate culture:

- Individuals make up the culture.
- Cultures can be rewarders of excellence.
- Culture is a set of affirmations.
- Cultural affirmations tend to fulfil themselves.
- Cultures make sense and have coherent points of view.
- Cultures provide their members with continuity and identity.
- A culture is a state of balance between reciprocal values.
- A corporate culture is a cybernetic system.
- Cultures are a pattern.
- Cultures are about communication.
- Cultures are more or less synergistic.
- Only cultures can learn—and organizations must learn.

This list, for that is all it is, comprises a series of well-known assertions about culture, but does not seem to help either in the description or the understanding of corporate culture. While all the factors may be true, it remains difficult to see how a culture comes about, how it influences behaviour or change.

Williams, Dobson and Walters (1989) provided the following working definition of culture: 'Culture is the commonly held and relatively stable beliefs, attitudes, and values that exist within the organization' (p. 11). These writers envisaged corporate culture as comprising both the conscious and unconscious elements of an organization's thinking and behaviour, although the word, indeed the concept, of 'unconscious' may be anathema to many. Later they note: 'Culture provides the decision-making and problem-solving processes of the organization. It influences the goals, means, and manner of action. It is a source of motivation and demotivation, of satisfaction and dissatisfaction. In short, culture underlies much of the human activity in an organization' (p. 12). Clearly this definition sees culture as a powerful cause, rather than a consequence, or organizational behaviour.

For Schein (1990), however, the nature of corporate culture is more unconscious than conscious. Although the kinds of meanings referred to by other writers might reflect elements of corporate culture, none of them fully represented the essence of culture. According to Schein, 'the term "culture"

Table 7.1 Definitions and meanings of corporate culture

- *Observed behavioural regularities* when people interact, such as the language used and the rituals around deference and demeanour (Goffman, 1959)
- The *norms* that evolve in working groups, such as the particular norms of a 'fair day's work for a fair day's pay' that evolved in the Bank Wiring Room in the Hawthorne studies (Homans, 1950)
- The *dominant* values espoused by an organization, such as 'product quality' or 'price leadership' (Deal & Kennedy, 1982)
- The *philosophy* that guides an organization's policy toward employees and/or customers (Ouchi, 1981; Pascale & Athos, 1981)
- The *rules* of the game for getting along in the organization, 'the ropes' that a newcomer must learn in order to become an accepted member (Ritti & Funkhouser, 1982)
- The *feeling* or *climate* that is conveyed in an organization by the physical layout and the way in which members of the organization interact with customers or other outsiders (Taguiri & Litwin, 1968)

---

should be reserved for the deeper level of *basic assumptions* and *beliefs* that are shared by members of an organization, that operate unconsciously, and that define in a basic "taken-for-granted" fashion an organization's view of itself and its environment' (1990, p. 6).

For Schein, these assumptions and beliefs are *learned* responses to a group's problems of *survival* in its external environment and its problems of internal integration. This deeper level of assumptions is to be distinguished from the 'artifacts' and 'values' that are manifestations or surface levels, but not the essence, of the culture (Schein, 1985; Dyer, 1982). Culture is therefore a *learned product of group experience* and is to be found only where there is a definable group with a significant history. If culture is indeed unconscious, or at least beyond the immediate awareness of its members, it implies that it may be extremely difficult to describe and change. It could be that only external trained observers can really describe it, or that members of the culture might articulate perceptions and beliefs, and manifest behaviour from which the culture can be inferred by an expert.

But what are multinational culture and corporate culture? Schneider (1987) has considered the problems of multinational corporations that are frequently interested in promoting a strong and coherent culture (to improve control coordination and integration of their subsidiaries in different global regions) within local national cultures, where the underlying basic assumptions about work and organizational employment may vary. Culture-specific assumptions include views of the relationship between the organization and the world, and considerations of human nature. Assumptions about the world can reflect several dimensions: (i) control over the environment; (ii) activity versus passivity or doing versus being; (iii) attitudes towards uncertainty; (iv) notions of time; (v) attitudes towards change; and (vi) what determines 'truth'. There is a rich but scattered literature on some of the major psychological and behavioural areas where ethnic rather than corporate culture has important impact (Furnham & Bochner, 1986).

Views about the nature of human relationships include: (i) the importance of the task versus relationships; (ii) the importance of hierarchy; (iii) the importance of individual versus group, and many others (Furnham, Johnson & Rawles, 1985). For instance, some national cultures, often Western ones, view nature as something that can be harnessed and exploited to meet man's needs; time, change and uncertainty can be actively managed. 'Truth' is determined by facts and measurement. Other cultures, most notably Eastern ones, view man as subservient to or in harmony with nature. Time, change and uncertainty are accepted as given. 'Truth' is determined by spiritual and philosophical principles. This attitude is often referred to as 'fatalistic' or 'adaptive'. Many other observations have been made about such things as understanding of deadlines, the role of the individual in a group, the value of equality over equity and so on (Furnham & Bochner, 1986; Furnham & Gunter, 1993).

Others have noted that the term culture tends to be used quite differently by separate disciplines. There is frequently a problem when one discipline (i.e. psychology, management science) borrows a concept from a neighbouring discipline (i.e. anthropology) and attempts to translate it into its own terminology. Sackmann (1989) contrasted the use of the term 'culture' by anthropologists, organizational behaviour theorists and working managers. Comparing anthropologists and managers, for example, she found that the former conceived of culture as more stable, longer term and unconditional in its membership than did the latter. She argued that the use of culture as a variable is based on three major assumptions: (i) culture is one of several organizational variables; (ii) it consists of a finite and patterned set of components which are visible and manifest in artifacts as well as collective behaviour and, in fact, culture consists of these artifacts; and (iii) it serves several functions which contribute to the success of organizations. We shall return to the components and functions of culture in more detail later.

There has been no shortage of definitions of corporate culture. The absence of a firm consensus about what culture represents within the corporate context does little to help us understand how it functions. Even if we find an acceptable (operationalizable) definition which we are prepared to accept for research or practical purposes, in order to understand culture we must go beyond that definition and analyse the characteristics of culture before testing some of the many hypotheses in this area.

Some take an even more radical position, denying the existence of the phenomenon. Thus, looking at a related area, that of climate, Payne (1990) argued that the concept of organizational climite is invalid because people in different parts of the organization have radically different perceptions of the organization (hence these perceptions are not shared) and that where perceptions are consensually shared in small groups, they are not representative of the climate of the whole organization. Thus for Payne (1990) it is possible to have departmental (or subdepartmental) but not organizational climate. The idea that culture is not pervasive or consistent across an organization can of course be empirically tested and may account for considerable organizational style. Indeed it may be that only small or very homogeneous workforces (in terms of employees, product, market) have an organization-wide definable and influencing culture.

THE DIMENSIONS OF CULTURE

Exploration of the facets of culture has led different writers to define the various components of culture or to attempt to produce a dimensional framework within which culture can be elaborated. The componential approach seems much more based on anthropological theories and observational methods, while the dimensional approach seems based more on psychological theories and experimental methods. 'Culture' itself has been conceived by some observers to be composed of subproducts such as artifact, symbols, and collective verbal and non-verbal behaviour. Other products include myths, saga, language systems, metaphors, symbols, ceremonies, rituals, value systems, and norms of conduct (Shrivastava, 1985). More concrete and recognizable examples of artifacts are the logo of a firm, the architecture of its buildings, existing technologies and machinery or tools, the interior design and the use of a work setting, the style of its documentation, and its end products, the organization chart, the typical and expected clothing of employees, and existing status symbols such as company cars, reserved parking or furniture. Verbal examples can be seen in language in general, and speeches, jargon, humorous stories, sagas, legends or myths in particular. Non-verbal behaviours include interpersonal behaviours such as the typical way of approaching each other (e.g. shaking hands), gestures, and dress codes as well as existing forms and functions of rites, rituals and ceremonies such as personal birthday wishes from the boss, congratulations for long tenure, celebration of company anniversaries or the Christmas party.

These components together form the product of culture whose major importance is seen in its attributed functions. It is assumed that culture serves predominantly two functions which can either contribute to organizational success or prevent it. These functions are (i) internal integration and (ii) coordination of activities and creation of a 'we feeling' of strong company identification. Organizational culture thus offers a shared system of meanings, which is the basis for communications between individuals who are members of it, and mutual understanding among them. If these two functions are not fulfilled in a satisfactory way, the culture may significantly reduce the efficiency of an organization. One recent study approach outlined six key features, rather than the dimension of organization culture (Williams, Dobson and Walters, 1989). According to this analysis, culture is learnt, is both an input and an output, is partly conscious, is historically based, is commonly held rather than shared, and is heterogeneous.

Other writers have attempted to describe the dimensional distinctions of corporate cultures. Schein (1990) listed seven dimensions, arguing that these dimensions provide the basis for an interview procedure which can reveal some of the more hidden, implicit facets of corporate culture. These dimensions and the questions they raise are listed in Table 7.2.

The model developed by Schein (1985) helps to organize the pieces of the culture puzzle. According to Schein's model, culture is represented at three levels:

(1) Behaviours and artifacts.
(2) Beliefs and values.
(3) Underlying assumptions.

Table 7.2 Seven dimensions of corporate culture

Dimension	Questions to be answered
1. The organization's relations to its environment	Does the organization perceive itself to be dominant, submissive, harmonizing, searching out a niche?
2. The nature of human activity	Is the 'correct' way for humans to behave to be dominant/proactive, harmonizing, or passive/fatalistic?
3. The nature of reality and truth	How do we define what is not true and how is truth ultimately determined in both the physical and social worlds?
4. The nature of time	What is our basic orientation in terms of past, present and future, and what kinds of time units are most relevant for the conduct of daily life?
5. The nature of human nature	Are humans basically good, neutral or evil, and is human nature perfectible or fixed?
6. The nature of human relationsips	What is the 'correct' way for people to relate to each other, to distribute power and affection? Is life competitive or cooperative? Is the best way to organize society on the basis of individualism or groupism? Is the best authority system autocratic/paternalistic or collegiate/participative?
7. Homogeneity versus diversity	Is the group best off if it is highly diverse or if it is highly homogeneous, and should individuals in a group be encouraged to innovate or conform?

These levels are arranged according to their visibility such that behaviour and artifacts are the easiest to observe, while the underlying assumptions need to be inferred. While the behaviour and artifacts may be observable and beliefs and values can be articulated, their meaning may not be readily comprehensible. To understand what the behaviour or beliefs actually mean to the organization's employees, the underlying assumptions have to be brought to the surface or made manifest. This operation can prove to be extremely difficult to achieve, since this level of corporate culture tends to be taken for granted, and is generally outside the usual awareness of most organization members.

Recently, Schein (1990) has observed that any definable group with a shared history can have a culture, and that within an organization there can therefore be many subcultures. If the organization as a whole has had shared experiences, there will also be a total organizational culture. Within any given unit, the tendency for integration and consistency will be assumed to be present, but it is perfectly possible for co-existing units of a large system to have cultures that are independent and even in conflict with each other.

Despite various theoretical analyses and attempts at both componential and dimensional analyses there still remains no consensus on the definition of corporate culture; whether it is cause, consequence, moderator or epiphenomenon associated with performance; or how, if at all, it can be measured. For some it has been a little like the search for the Holy Grail: long-standing, full of myths and legends, largely unsuccessful, even a pointless exercise.

TYPES OF ORGANIZATION CULTURE

Even if the attempt at definition has not met with success, some researchers have put considerable effort into attempting to categorize different cultures. They appear to believe that developing taxonomies precedes explanation. Organizational cultures vary according to the nature of the beliefs, attitudes and values that are commonly held; they also reflect the dominant value systems of the societies in which they are based. Thus, organizations from different countries will display varied cultural profiles.

The cultures or organizations are also likely to reflect differences in their history, and the function of the organization. Differences may exist between cultural characteristics of organizations in the public and private sectors; between organizations in the service or manufacturing industries, and so on. Attempts have been made by some scholars to produce taxonomies or classifications of corporate culture as a means of comparing and contrasting them. As an exercise this has been found to have a number of advantages and disadvantages (Table 7.3).

Hofstede (1980) undertook a large study into the impact of *national* culture on a single multinational organization. On the basis of this study and a series of smaller projects, he identified four dimensions on which national cultures

Table 7.3 Classifying corporate culture

Advantages
- One is able to compare and contrast cultures so as to be able to predict (and control) areas of misunderstanding/friction before they occur.
- Empirical data of culture groups, clusters, or types may yield counter-intuitive findings that simple guesswork would not show. In other words, there may be good reasons why two superficially similar types do not 'fit' together at a particular level.
- It may be useful to prepare a behavioural culture atlas for a traveller from one organization to another. Only a scheme or category system could facilitate this.
- Theories of classification can be tested by gathering empirical data. In this sense they can be discarded, revised or maintained.
- It specifies the areas of training that become necessary for the culture traveller within and across organizations and cultures. Like the periodic table for the chemist or the map for the explorer, a typology of culture allows more interesting and important work to be done.

Disadvantages
- Classification systems are only as good as the evidence/data upon which they are based and that is frequently poor: hence the taxonomics are weak, commonsensical or wrong.
- Different statistical techniques yield different dimensions and it is not certain which is most useful. There is no agreement upon which particular ways of treating the data are best, yet each can reveal a rather different problem.
- Very 'broad brush' approaches (which offer a small number of distinguishable types) can be insensitive, missing out on the really interesting and important dimensions. In fact, such an approach may be dangerous, giving the illusion of knowledge while often being incomplete or incorrect.
- Classifying cultures does not tell you either the consequences of differences or similarities among them, or what such knowledge signifies in practical terms.

appear to vary (Table 7.4). He was able to plot 40 different nationalities against this typology. More significantly in the current context, he showed that within one multinational organization, there were marked differences culturally based on the prevailing national norms. Hofstede's types can be elaborated as follows:

(1) *Power distance.* The extent to which the less powerful members of institutions and organizations accept that power is distributed *unequally.*
(2) *Uncertainty avoidance.* The extent to which people feel threatened by ambiguous situations and have created beliefs and institutions that try to avoid these.
(3) *Individualism/Collectivism.* This reflects an ethical position of the culture in which people are supposed to look after themselves and their immediate family, or a situation in which people belong to in-groups or collectives which are supposed to look after them in exchange for loyalty.
(4) *Masculinity/Femininity.* A situation in which the dominant values in

Table 7.4 Four dimensions on which national cultures appear to vary

---

The Power Distance Dimension (POW)

Low	*High*
(Australia, Israel, Denmark, Sweden)	(Philippines, Mexico, Venezuela, India, Brazil)
• Less centralization	• Greater centralization
• Flatter organization pyramids	• Tall organization pyramids
• Smaller wage differentials	• More supervisory personnel
• Structure in which manual and clerical work are equal jobs	• Structure in which white-collar jobs are valued more than blue-collared jobs

---

The Masculine-Femininity Dimension (MAS)

Low	*High*
(Sweden, Denmark, Thailand, Finland, Yugoslavia)	(Japan, Australia, Venezuela, Italy, Mexico)
• Sex roles are minimized	• Sex roles are clearly differentiated
• Organizations do not interfere with people's private lives	• Organizations may interfere to protect their interests
• More women in more qualified jobs	• Fewer women are in qualified jobs
• Soft, yielding, intuitive skills are rewarded	• Aggression, competition, and justice are rewarded
• Social rewards are valued	• Work is valued as a central life interest

---

The Individualism-Collectivism Dimension (IND)

Low	*High*
(Venezuela, Columbia, Taiwan, Mexico, Greece)	(United States, Australia, Great Britain, Canada, The Netherlands
• Organization as 'family'	• Organization is more impersonal
• Organization defends employee interests	• Employees defend their own self-interests
• Practices are based on loyalty, sense of duty and group participation	• Practices encourage individual initiative

---

The Uncertainty Avoidance Dimension (UNC)

Low	*High*
(Denmark, Sweden, Great Britain, United States, India)	(Greece, Portugal, Japan, Peru, France)
• Less structuring activities	• More structuring activities
• Fewer written rules	• More written rules
• More generalists	• More specialists
• Variability	• Standardization
• Greater willingness to take risks	• Less willingness to take risks
• Less ritualistic behaviour	• More realistic behaviour

---

society are success, money and things. A situation in which the dominant values in society are caring for others and the quality of life.

More importantly these national characteristics can be applied to organizations, so that a $2 \times 2 \times 2 \times 2$ typology could be formed. Hofstede's work has attracted considerable attention in the psychological literature and enthusiasts have somewhat uncritically, applied his dimensions to corporate cultures. Indeed, various software packages now exist to help managers to categorize their own organization in terms of this system although little hypothesis testing work appears to have been done on the system to conclude whether the categorization is correct or useful. However, the idea that corporate culture can be assessed along these four simple, but important, and unrelated dimensions is interesting. To what extent a particular culture could be described as optimal, ideal or appropriate for an organization has yet to be established.

The taxonomists appear to show considerable agreement as to how to classify corporate culture, although most have been less concerned to describe how these cultures originate or function. Table 7.5 lists some classifications which have been arranged to show the similarities. The fact that there is such similarity between some of the typologies could be a good sign, indicating that they all appear to be tapping into some actual structure that exists. On the other hand, they could all be forms of plagiarism from some early ideas on the subject. However, the underlying dimensions on which many are based do indeed appear consistently in the I/O literature and may, therefore, be a source of confidence to the researcher. Yet despite the attraction of these fourfold typologies there appears to be very little evidence demonstrating the veracity, as opposed to the simplificatory, appeal of these different systems. More importantly, perhaps, few taxonomists offer more than a simple but clear description of the different types of culture. Rarely do they explain how and why these originate or are maintained; their effects on various facets of organizational life and how they change and decay. In short, they offer little in the way of process or mechanism, preferring to remain at the level of description. Yet other researchers have come up with rather different systems. Thus, Cooke and Lafferty (1983) attempt to measure 12 cultural styles (Table 7.6), which cluster into people, tasks and satisfaction styles.

Despite the overall similarity in these disparate systems there remains no overall agreement as to what are the basic categories of culture. These first attempts to describe the major types are no more than interesting intuitions which might or might not be validated. Few of these theorists have attempted the more interesting questions of how these cultures arise, how they are maintained, or how they affect or are affected by performance and wider environmental factors. Despite this there are a surprising number of diagnostic tests on the market which supposedly measure corporate culture (Cooke & Rousseau, 1988; Rousseau, 1991). Clearly what is needed is some attempt to

Table 7.5 Alternative typologies

1. *Tough Guy Culture* Risk-taking Individualistic	1. *Power Culture* Entrepreneurial Ability values	1. *Barbarian* Ego-driven Workaholic	1. *Power-oriented* Competitive Responsibility to personality rather than expertise
2. *Work/Play Hard* Persistent Sociable	2. *Achievement* Personal Intrinsic	2. *Presidential* Democratic Hierarchical	2. *People-oriented* Consensual Rejects management control
3. *Bet your Company* Ponderous Unpressurized	3. *Support Culture* Mutuality Trust	3. *Monarchical* Loyalty Doggedness	3. *Task-oriented* Competency Dynamic
4. *Process Culture* Bureaucratic Protective	4. *Role Culture* Order Dependable	4. *Pharoanic* Ritualized Changeless	4. *Role-oriented* Legality Legitimacy Pure bureaucracy
Authors			
Deal & Kennedy (1982)	Schein (1985)	Graves (1986)	Harrison (1972) Handy (1979) Williams, Dobson & Walter (1989)
Dimensions			
Amount of risk (High/Low) Speed of feedback (Slow/Fast)	Individualistic- Collectivistic	Bureaucratic-Anti- bureaucratic Managerial-Ego drive	Formalization (High/Low) Centralization (High/Low)

evaluate, compare and contrast, and criticize these various measures. Rousseau (1991) has in fact attempted a review of the quantitative methods in culture research (as well as a consideration of qualitative measures). She notes various standard objections to the use of these questionnaires: telling more than you know; organizational uniqueness and non-comparability; an anti-positivist epistemology and ethical issues. In short, opposition to the quantitative assessment of corporate culture maintains that:

(1) Corporate culture is a highly subjective social construction that cannot be studied by researcher-constructed categories and scales with unchanging calibration across field sites.

(2) *A priori* categorization of constructs by researchers doing field research misrepresents the experience of respondents, and is thus invalid.

(3) The use of researcher-derived categories is a distortion of the respondent's perspective and is thus unethical.

Table 7.6 Cultural styles

1. A *Humanistic-Helpful culture* characterizes organizations that are managed in a participative and person-centred way. Members are expected to be supportive, constructive and open to influence in their dealings with one another. (Helping others to grow and develop; taking time with people)

2. An *Affiliative culture* characterizes organizations that place a high priority on constructive interpersonal relationships. Members are expected to be friendly, open and sensitive to the satisfaction of their work group. (Dealing with others in a friendly way; sharing feelings and thoughts)

3. An *Approval culture* describes organizations in which conflicts are avoided and interpersonal relationships are pleasant—at least superficially. Members feel that they should agree with, gain the approval of, and be liked by others. (Making sure people accept you; 'going along' with others)

4. A *Conventional culture* is descriptive of organizations that are conservative, traditional, and bureaucratically controlled. Members are expected to conform, follow the rules, and make a good impression. (Always following policies and practices; fitting into 'the mould')

5. A *Dependent culture* is descriptive of organizations that are hierarchically controlled and non-participative. Centralized decision-making in such organizations leads members to do only what they are told and to clear all decisions with superiors. (Pleasing those in position of authority; doing what is expected)

6. An *Avoidance culture* characterizes organizations that fail to reward success but nevertheless punish mistakes. This negative reward system leads members to shift responsibilities to others and avoid any possibility of being blamed for a mistake. (Waiting for others to act first; taking few chances)

7. An *Oppositional culture* describes organizations in which confrontation prevails and negativism is rewarded. Members gain status and influence by being critical and thus are reinforced to oppose the ideas of others and to make safe (but ineffectual) decisions. (Pointing out flaws; being hard to impress)

8. A *Power culture* is descriptive of non-participative organizations structured on the basis of the authority inherent in members' positions. Members believe they will be rewarded for taking charge, controlling subordinates and, at the same time, being responsive to the demands of superiors. (Building up one's power base; motivating others any way necessary)

9. A *Competitive culture* is one in which winning is valued and members are rewarded for outperforming one another. People in such organizations operate in a 'win-lose' framework and believe they must work against (rather than win over) their peers to be noticed. (Turning the job into a contest; never appearing to lose)

10. A *Competence/Perfectionistic culture* characterizes organizations in which perfectionists, persistence and hard work are valued. Members feel they must avoid all mistakes, keep track of everything, and work long hours to attain narrowly-defined objectives. (Doing things perfectly; keeping on top of everything)

11. An *Achievement culture* characterizes organizations that do things well and value members who set and accomplish their own goals. Members of these organizations set challenging but realistic goals, establish plans to reach these goals, and pursue them with enthusiasm. (Pursuing a standard of excellence; openly showing enthusiasm)

12. A *Self-Actualization culture* characterizes organizations that value creativity, quality over quantity, and both task accomplishment and individual growth. Members of these organizations are encouraged to gain enjoyment from their work, develop themselves, and take on new and interesting activities. (Thinking in unique and independent ways; doing even simple tasks well)

In other words the old ETIC–EMIC debate is alive and well, and thriving on the issues of corporate culture.

However, Rousseau (1991) does actually list and consider various quantitative measures of culture. These include:

(1) *The Norms Diagnostic Index* (Allen & Dyer, 1980)
   This measure attempts to assess seven dimensions of behavioural norms: performance facilitation, job involvement, training, leader–subordinate interaction, policies and procedures, confrontation and supportive climate. No reliability or validity information is reported.

(2) *Kilmann–Saxton Culture-Gap Survey* (Kilmann & Saxton, 1993)
   This questionnaire supposedly measures actual operating norms and those that should be operating if performance, job satisfaction, and morale are to be increased. It has four scales: task support, task innovation, social relationships, and personal freedom. There is some modest evidence of reliability.

(3) *Organizational Culture Profile* (O'Reilly, Chatman & Caldwell, 1988)
   This 54-item inventory supposedly measures nine categories of values regarding what is important, how to behave, and what attitudes are appropriate. Some attempts at ascertaining reliability (but not validity) have been made.

(4) *Organizational Beliefs Questionnaire* (Sashkin, 1984)
   This measure attempts to ascertain ten values shared by the organization, such as innovating or taking risks, attending to details, managing 'hands on'. No evidence of either reliability or validity is mentioned.

(5) *Corporate Culture Survey* (Glaser, 1983)
   This measure attempts to measure the strength and type of culture based on Deal and Kennedy's (1982) four types. However, as yet there appears to be little evidence of the psychometric validity of such a measure.

(6) *Organizational Culture Inventory* (Cooke & Lafferty, 1989)
   This 120-item measure attempts to ascertain scores on 12 scales reflecting a circumplicial model. Individual responses are aggregated to work group and organizational levels. There is evidence of the measure's reliability as well as construct and criterion-related validity (Roberts, Rousseau & La Porte, 1989).

(7) *Organizational Values Congruence Scale* (Enz, 1986)
   This 22-item measure looks at the congruence between employee and management values. A single score is obtained from a summary over the items. Whilst there appears evidence of reliability, none exists for validity.

Despite the proliferation in the number of questionnaire measures to describe or evaluate corporate culture, there appears to be little psychometric validation of these measures, particularly of their dimensional structure, and their construct or predictive validity. Until that has been established thoroughly it seems unwise to use such measures in research or management decisions. However, the usefulness of such measures has been established in the study of specific types of culture (Rousseau, 1989), or more interestingly, when organizations with very different cultures are involved in mergers (Buono, Bowditch & Lewis, 1985).

CHANGING OR MANAGING CORPORATE CULTURE

Not all theorists believe that cultures can be managed. For those who see culture as a metaphor for organizations and take a social constructionist view (Weick, 1979), culture is a context, not a variable, and cannot be moulded or managed. For others, organizations have cultural aspects but are cultures themselves at the same time (Sackmann, 1983). Each employee is not only a carrier of corporate culture but equally a potential source of variation, mutation and development. Hence those who see culture from this perspective recommend attempts at cultural awareness rather than culture moulding.

However, probably the majority of management science and psychologist researchers do take the view that culture can be changed through restructuring and reinforcement. The aim is usually to create the best fit between product, strategy and culture. Hence some have recommended a culture-risk-analysis which aims to determine the probability for successful implementation of an intended strategy in relation to the existing culture (Schwartz & Davis, 1981).

Deshpande and Parasuraman (1986) have proposed a less strategy-determined contingency model of 'strategic culture planning'. They suggest that this approach helps to prevent a culture discrepancy when organizations undertake strategic changes or when they enter a new range in their life-cycle. In their model, the authors combine the strategic marketing planning model of the Boston Consulting Group with a product and business life-cycle model, and with Deal and Kennedy's typology of culture (Deal and Kennedy, 1982). The authors recommend a 'tough-guy/macho culture' when a new product is launched and when the product does not yield much profit. A 'bet-your-company culture' is best suited in a stage of increasing market share and when the introduced product becomes a 'star'. A 'work-hard-play-hard' culture is recommended when the product becomes a 'cash-cow' and the market share is large but hardly growing. A 'process culture' is indicated when the share is small in a growing market and when the product turns out to be a flop.

Such a prescriptive procedure is based on an 'etic' approach, in which external experts determine the 'right' culture type. Bourgeois and Jemison (1984), on the other hand, describe a process in which organization members have first to characterize the existing culture, while the environmental analysis helps to identify consistent and discrepant cultural elements. The culture analysis becomes part of the strategy assessment and the search for a realistic implementation. In the effort to identify existing culture, holders of the variable conception of culture usually use typologies, profile or dimensions (Deal & Kennedy, 1982; Handy, 1979; Harrison, 1972).

In order to change the culture of an organization, some writers recommend that mechanisms are needed which are directed at changing common beliefs, attitudes and values that exist within the organization. Williams, Dobson and Walters (1989) identified six principal mechanisms of culture modification from their study of public and private sector organizations in the United Kingdom. These were: changing the people in the organization; changing people's positions in the organization; changing beliefs, attitudes and values directly; changing behaviour; changing the systems and structures; and changing the corporage image.

Personnel changes can result in shifts in dominant attitudes and beliefs, as new people bring fresh ideas and viewpoints into the organization. This mechanism of change is implemented through recruitment, selection and outplacement policies. If an organization does not want to change its personnel, it can use the alternative strategy of changing their position in the organization. Moving employees around from one department to another can expose them to new experiences which in turn could produce value shifts.

Direct action upon people's beliefs, attitudes and values without any staff movement can be achieved via several techniques which include role modelling, participative group methods (such as circles or briefing groups), role playing, counselling, management education, and formal lines of communication. Rather than trying to alter people's beliefs, attitudes and values, culture change can be achieved through modifications to their behaviour patterns via a newly introduced system of rewards and punishments. Training in new skills may also produce shifts in people's perceptions of their capabilities, and of their view of the organization and their position in it.

Some organizations have implemented alterations of structure which bring about changes to the corporate culture (whether deliberately or not). Structural changes influence the way work is carried out through modifying the functional grouping within the organization. However, the effect of such changes upon culture can be unpredictable. A better technique is to use processes which can be linked more directly with employee behaviour such as reward systems, appraisal and other control mechanisms, such as a fully thought-out and implemented management system (Stringfield & Furnham, 1989).

Corporate image change has been attempted by organizations in the hope of a consequent shift in corporate culture. Developing a corporate image (or a new image) for a company can act upon employees' perceptions of it and of the way it conducts its business. This mechanism may result in changes in certain beliefs about the organization and not in others, although there is very little clear evidence for this.

THE PROCESS OF CULTURE CHANGE

Changing corporate culture takes time and can prove to be difficult to achieve with any degree of success. Mature cultures can be very resistant to change since they are inherently stable and self-reinforcing. Any attempts by outside agents to interfere with the predominant belief or value systems can be met with stubborn resistance. Knowing which corporate mechanism to utilize in the service of a culture-change programme, however, although necessary, is not sufficient by itself to ensure an effective change process. Culture change has to be carefully 'choreographed'.

The *process* of corporate culture change is dynamic. The mechanisms of change have to be integrated within a totally planned change framework. A number of models have been put forward which encapsulate the stages through which an effective culture change programme should pass. One framework, a decision-making model for organizations, outlines a logical chain of key stages which direct an organization's management through the definition of the purpose or 'mission' of the change process: diagnosis of any problems or reasons underlying the need for change; formulation of possible course of action or solutions, together with evaluation of alternatives; and planning how to put the chosen solution or action steps into effect (with adjustments to plans in the light of feedback information) (Williams, Dobson & Walters, 1989).

A similar five-step model put forward by Gonzalez (1987) begins by requiring the organization to clarify for itself why a change in culture is needed. Part of this initial operation is defining what type of culture the organization already has. There should be a rationale for change and once this is established it is important that change is seen to be driven from within because organization members believe it is necessary. The second stage is to define the change in objectives. What is the desired aim of change? What kind of culture does the organization wish to end up with? This stage should involve as many organization members as possible and should identify which organizational beliefs and values need to be changed, how change can be operationally defined in terms of measurable indicators of beliefs and values, and what work norms, structural aspects, and corporate systems and procedures will also need to be altered to accommodate and facilitate culture change.

The third stage involves planning the means to achieve the previously defined objectives. How will the gap between the present and desired cultures be bridged? How will the organizations move from one cultural position to another? Thought will need to be given to how new corporate values can be inculcated among organization members, which work group norms will be modified, and which corporate structures and systems will be changed to produce a work environment conducive to the new behaviours which it is hoped the culture change will bring about. The fourth stage consists of implementing the change plans. This stage involves considering the various mechanics or modes through which the culture change process can be implemented, and how these different change components and channels can best be integrated to generate the desired change. Finally, the change process needs to be evaluated. Feedback on progress that has been made should be supplied to organization members, and indicators of change should be monitored to measure the extent to which the programme has been a success and has met its initially stated objectives.

Another model is the force-field model deriving from the work of Lewin (1951). This model conceptualizes change as the product of two sets of forces: the driving forces and the restraining forces. Accordingly, culture change is brought about by disturbing the equilibrium between these two sets of forces, either by strengthening the driving forces or weakening the restraining forces. The model requires the change agent to identify the different forces impinging upon the organization and to define the relative strengths of these forces. It is essential that both sets of forces are given full attention. Concentrating on one only can bring about undue stress in the force-field system, resulting in undesirable consequences for the organization.

According to the model culture change is produced through a three-stage process. The first stage is to unfreeze existing forces, a step which may be achieved by demonstrating the inadequacies of current belief or value systems in the light of the prevailing business environment. The second stage introduces change aimed at re-establishing equilibrium between forces, either by strengtheninig or weakening the influence of certain existing forces, or by introducing new forces. This stage involves a refreezing process which ensures that the changes brought about by the introduction of new processes or other influences upon organization membership beliefs, values and behaviour are long-lasting rather than transient. This means ensuring that the conditions underlying culture change continue to operate systematically within the organization in a routine fashion.

These three 'models' are commonsensical steps in the process of change. They are not mutually contradictory but simply focus on different aspects of culture, although each has different change strategies, not specifically relevant to culture.

RESISTANCE TO CHANGE

Cultural change within organizations is not easy to achieve; frequently any attempt at corporate culture modification may be met with resistance from individuals or groups within the organization. The need for change may not always be recognized by those who will be affected by it. Culture change brings considerable uncertainty, with employees feeling that their job security or status is under threat. The fault may sometimes lie with the change strategy itself, however, which might fail to take fully into account the way people have been socialized or are accustomed to behaving within an organization. Wholesale change cannot be introduced overnight.

Thus a successful corporate culture change programme must operate through a series of carefully worked out stages. It must begin laying the groundwork by developing the need for change. People in an organization must themselves be convinced that change is necessary. This might involve making them aware of changing market circumstances or of the fact that their way of doing things is simply not effective any more. The change must be 'sold' as something which is designed to operate in their interests and not to undermine their position or security. However, because culture change involves values, beliefs and behaviours, it will often involve the rejection of well-established, deeply entrenched beliefs, and this will not happen unless something better is offered in their place.

Reducing uncertainty is of fundamental importance. Uncertainty breeds resistance and uncooperative tendencies. The organization's membership must be on the side of change and must want it to happen before it can be successfully introduced and implemented. The culture change programme must bring with it a supportive environment which provides opportunities for employees to gain new knowledge and skills, to improve their position, or, at the very least, to increase the probability that their situation could improve. This ought to prove an attractive option compared with the existing scenario in which it is made clear to them that their position will only (inevitably) get worse.

Once change has begun, the new behaviour patterns need to be reinforced. This will inevitably involve both training and changes in management style and practice. Changes among the lower ranks will work only if beliefs and behaviours are first of all successfully changed at the top of the hierarchy.

Culture management and changing culture present numerous problems (Sackmann, 1989). These include:

(1) The location of culture. If the important features of culture are not directly observed (i.e. values, norms) and are not operating at many different levels and also in part unconsciously it is by definition very difficult to manage.
(2) Culture is pervasive. Indeed, it may be the culture of the organization that culture management is impossible, which is, therefore, a self-fulfilling prophesy.
(3) Culture is implicit. It may require an outsider to understand and observe a corporate culture, because insiders are too imbued with it and are unable to be objective.
(4) Culture is a historical product. Because corporate culture develops over time it becomes deeply rooted in individuals through their long-term learning history.

(5) Culture is a political issue. Which dominant coalition in an organization can or should impose its new culture on it?

(6) Culture is pluralistic, being made up of various subcultures. Thus one may manage one or many subcultures but not the organization as a whole.

Culture management is ethnically, culturally and empirically a problematic exercise.

THE MAJOR IMPACT OF CORPORATE CULTURE ON ORGANIZATIONS

Clearly, corporate culture generates strong but subtle pressures to think and act in a particular way. Thus, if an organization's culture stresses such values as services to customers, participative decision making, and a paternalistic attitude towards employees, individuals within the company will tend to adopt these values in their own behaviour. If, by contrast, an organization's culture involves maximizing output, centralized decision making, and 'going by the book', individuals' actions will often reflect these attitudes and values.

Corporate culture also actually relates to performance although many argue that there is no compelling evidence for a clear link between culture and performance (Sackmann, 1989). One view is that in order to influence performance, organizational culture must be strong (basic aspects of the culture are strongly accepted by most employees), and must also possess certain key traits (e.g. humanistic values, concern about quality and innovativeness of products).

But according to Baron and Greenberg (1990) there are three reasons why this relationship is far from clear. First, much of the research on this issue has erroneously assumed that organizations possess a single, unitary culture. Therefore the findings reported may apply only to some groups of employees (often top management in the companies studied). Second, serious questions remain about the measure of cultural strength (qualitative and quantitative) used in these projects. Various researchers have adopted different definitions and therefore it is not clear that the same variable was being assessed in all cases. Third, none of the studies conducted to date have included appropriate comparison or control groups. To demonstrate that possession of certain types of culture contributes to corporate success, it is necessary to show that such cultures are indeed characteristic of highly productive organizations, but not of less successful ones. To date no clear data have been reported on this issue. Certainly there are various ways of measuring the impact of culture on organizations and individuals.

One learns about corporate culture through the process of organizational socialization. Looking at the bombed House of Commons, Churchill said, 'We shape our buildings and afterwards they shape us', thereby implying a sort of reciprocal determinism. The same may be true of corporate culture. Organizations develop or build a culture which afterwards shapes how people 'learn the ropes', 'speak the language' and adapt values in an organization.

For Schein (1990) it is more interesting to understand how culture is *preserved* through socialization. For him there are seven dimensions among which organizational culture socialization processes vary:

(1) Group versus individual: the degree to which the organization processes recruits in batches, as in boot camp, or individually, as in professional offices. This may be partly associated with the size of the organization.
(2) Formal versus informal: the degree to which the process is institutionalized and formalized, as in set training programmes, or is handled informally through apprenticeships, individual coaching by the immediate superior, or the like.
(3) Self-destructive and reconstructing versus self-enhancing: the degree to which the process destroys aspects of the self and replaces them, as in boot camp, or enhances aspects of the self, as in professional development programmes. Clearly few organizations attempt the dramatic strategy of the army, but some do attempt a fairly radical change policy whereby the induction process attempts to shake individuals into a new approach.
(4) Serial versus random: the degree to which role models are provided, as in apprenticeships or monitoring programmes, or are deliberately withheld, as in sink-or-swim kinds of initiations in which the recruit is expected to figure out his/her own solutions.
(5) Sequential versus disjunctive: the degree to which the process consists of guiding the recruit through a series of discrete steps and roles versus being open-ended and never letting the recruit predict what organizational role will come next. Few organizations presumably aim to be disjunctive but it does occur by chance.
(6) Fixed versus variable: the degree to which stages of the training process have fixed timetables for each stage, as in military academies, or rotational training programmes, or are open-ended, as in typical promotional systems where one is not advanced to the next stage until one is 'ready'. The latter is, of course, more demanding and may be part of a secondary selection procedure.
(7) Tournament versus contest: the degree to which each stage is an 'elimination tournament' where one is out of the organization if one fails, or a 'contest' in which one builds up a track record batting average.

But the clearest way to examine the effect of culture on an organization is to see what occurs when two cultures collide in a merger. Buono, Bowditch and Lewis (1985) examined two banks before and after a merger and the resultant culture. Using in-depth interviews, observations and archival data they built up a picture of the subjective and managerial culture of the two banks. The authors also did a climate survey before and after the merger looking at such things as organizational commitment management and supervision practice, job security and so on. The merger led to some interesting solutions such as to which personnel and what aspects to retain from each bank, and to what extent new hybrid factors/cultures needed to be invented. The post-merger survey indicated that bank B employees felt significantly less alienated and less negative after the merger than did former bank A employees.

> This paper has attempted to outline some of the issues involved in the study of organizational cultures and the problems that emerge when two cultures are forced together by a merger. The objective and subjective aspects of a given culture greatly influence the behaviours, satisfaction, and expectations of organizational members. Although individuals may not fully realise this influence during 'normal' organizational functioning, when the culture is threatened it becomes quite salient in people's minds. Since subjective culture evolves over time as a product of shared experience when attempting to merge two firms, the greater the number of these shared experiences that can be reproduced within a period of time, the faster a repertoire of symbols and shared meanings will develop with which the merged group of members can begin to identify, and a new culture can begin to take hold. There is a clear need for those involved with mergers or acquisitions to explicitly consider the central facets of organizational culture much more fully. (p. 498)

The issue of culture management is, of course, particularly important for multinationals where ethnic and corporate cultures may clash. Research done by Laurent showed that senior- to middle-level executives of different nationalities have differing preferences for organizational structure (Laurent, 1983). The statement for which he found the most variance said 'it is important for managers to have at hand precise answers to most of the questions that his subordinates may raise about their work'. The results ranged from 10% agreement for Swedish managers to 66% agreement for Italian managers. If these are typical responses, then there are clear indications about the kind of organizational structures each nationality would prefer. The Italian end of the spectrum would probably assume a more hierarchical structure with less room for flexibility and delegation than the Swedish.

Laurent (1983) also showed that within one multinational, managers tended to become three times more nationalistic at the attitudinal level, although they learnt to blend behaviourally with the corporate norms. One feature of both Laurent's and Hofstede's studies was that in neither case was the questionnaire developed with the idea of eliciting the dimensions and organizational types that were later drawn out. The result is that, in all but two categories, the dimensions against which different nationalities are being compared are the result of grouping only three or four seemingly related questions together. In both studies the questions were of a general nature, and therefore possibly more prone to generating cultural differences.

The particular issues that Schneider (1987) sees leading to the possibility of a clash between national and corporate culture include planning and staffing, career management, appraisal and compensation, selection and socialization.

Over 15 years ago Evan (1978), attempting to ascertain the impact of culture on organizations, was highly critical of the current literature. The points he made remain valid. Hence he set out a seven-point programme for future research. *First*, a multidimensional or, better still, a multicultural team is necessary to eliminate as many unconscious cultural assumptions and biases as possible on the part of the researchers themselves. *Second*, a multidisciplinary team is essential in order to measure how much of the variance in structure and performance of organizational systems is attributable to cultural variables as compared to other variables, such as psychological, structural, inter-organizational and societal. *Third*, one of the principal problems confronting a research team would be to adapt or construct research instruments, which will tap cultural variances with a high level of reliability and validity. *Fourth*, the research instruments measuring cultural variables would be used on (i) a representative sample of the population of a society and (ii) a representative sample of the members of one or more organizations in order to measure 'societal culture' as well as 'organizational subculture'. *Fifth*, in designing sample surveys at least two modes of cross-societal comparisons would be used: (i) intra-systematic comparisons, that is, matching domestic or national firms with those of foreign subsidiaries, distinguishing wholly owned subsidiaries from joint ventures, and controlling for various structural and industrial characteristics; and (ii) intra-organizational comparisons, that is, subsidiaries of the same company and of comparable size, function and technology in different societies. *Sixth*, in addition to sample surveys, at least two other complementary research methods would be desirable: laboratory and field experiments in order to test major causal hypotheses suggested to support the sample surveys and also to test the impact of cultural values on organizational behaviour and organizational system performance. *Finally*, Berrien's (1970) nine principles, which he labels 'A Super-Ego-for-Cross-Cultural Research', should guide the entire research process. They deserve to be quoted:

> The best cross-cultural research is that which: (1) engages the collaborative efforts of two or more investigators of different countries, each of who is (2) strongly encouraged and supported by institutions in their respective countries to (3) address researchable problems of a common concern not only to . . . science . . . but (4) relevant to the social problem of our times. Such collaborative enterprise would begin with (5) the joint definition of the problems, (6) employ comparable methods, (7) pool data that would be 'owned' jointly by the collaborative, who are free to (8) report their own interpretations to their own constituents but (9) obligated to strive for interpretations acceptable to the world community of scholars. (Berrien, 1970: pp. 107–109)

The corporate culture concept, issue, debate is here with us for some time to come. While it will no doubt lose its popular appeal as it gets replaced by yet another popular 'solution' to all management problems, its has uncovered enough of a hornets' nest among academics from different disciplines and epistemological perspectives to provide arguments and research for many years to come.

REFERENCES

Allen, R., & Dyer, F. (1980) A total for tapping the organizational unconscious. *Personnel Journal*, March, 192–199.

Baron, R., & Greenberg, J. (1990) *Behaviour in Organizations*. Boston: Allyn & Bacon.

Berrien, F. (1970) A superego for cross-cultural research. *International Journal of Psychology*, 5, 33–39.

Bourgeois, L., & Jemison, D. (1984) Die analyse der Unterdimens?—'Kultur'. *Gdi-Impals*, 1, 55–62.

Bower, M. (1966) Cited in T. Deal & A. Kennedy, *Corporate Cultures*, Reading, MA: Addison-Wesley.

Buono, A., Bowditch, J., & Lewis, J. (1985) When cultures collide: The anatomy of a merger. *Human Relations*, 38, 477–500.

Cooke, R., & Lafferty, J. (1989) Level V: Organizational cultural inventory—form I. Plymouth MI: Human Synergistics.

Cooke, R., & Lafferty, J. (1986) Level V: Organizational culture inventory—form III. Plymouth, MI: Human Synergistics.

Cooke, R., & Rousseau, D. (1988) Behavioural norms and expectations: A quantitative approach to the assessment of organizational culture. *Group and Organizational Studies*, 13, 245–273.

Deal, T., & Kennedy, A. (1982) *Corporate Cultures*. Reading, MA: Addison-Wesley.

Deshpande, R., & Parasuraman, A. (1986) Linking corporate culture to strategic planning. *Business Horizons*, 3, 28–37.

Dyer, W. (1982) *Cultural Change in Family Firms*. San Francisco: Jossey-Bass.

Enz, C. (1986) *Power and Shared Values in the Corporate Culture*. Ann Arbor: UMI.

Evan, W. (1978) Measuring the impact of culture on organizations. *International Studies of Management and Organization*, 1, 91–112.

Furnham, A., & Bochner, S. (1986) *Culture Shock*. London: Methuen.

Furnham, A., & Gunter, B. (1993) *Corporate Assessment*. London: Routledge.

Furnham, A., Johnson, C., & Rawles, R. (1985) The determinants of beliefs in human nature. *Personality and Individual Differences*, 6, 675–686.

Gauthey, F., Ratiu, I., Rodgers, I., & Xardel, D. (1988) *Leaders san frontiers: Le défi des différences*. Paris: McGraw-Hill.

Geertz, C. (1973) *The Interpretation of Culture*. New York: Basic Books.

Glaser, R. (1983) *The Corporate Culture Survey*. Bryn Mawr: ODD.

Goffman, E. (1959) *The Presentation of Self in Everyday Life*. Edinburgh: Edinburgh University Press.

Gonzalez, R. (1987) *Corporate Culture Modification: A Guide for Managers*. Manila: National Book Inc.

Graves, D. (1986) *Corporate Culture: Diagnosis and Change*. New York: St Martins Press.

Hampden-Turner, C. (1990) *Corporate Culture: From Vicious to Virtuous Circles*. London: Random Century.

Handy, C. (1979) *Understanding Organizations*. Harmondsworth: Penguin.

Harrison, R. (1972) Understanding your organization character. *Harvard Business Review*, 4, 119–128.

Hofstede, G. (1980) *Culture's Consequences: International Differences in Work-Related Values*. Beverly Hills: Sage.

Hofstede, G. (1981) Culture and organizations. *International Studies of Management and Organization*, 4, 15–41.

Homans, G. (1950) *The Human Group*. London: Routledge & Kegan Paul.

Jamieson, I. (1980) The concept of culture and the relevance for an analysis of business enterprise in different societies. *International Studies of Management and Organization*, 3, 71–105.

Kilmann, R., & Saxton, M. (1983) *The Kilman–Saxton Culture-Gap Survey*. Pittsburgh: ODC.

Kroeber, A., & Kluckholm, C. (1952) *Culture: A Critical Review of Concepts and Definitions*. New York: Vintage Books.

Laurent, R. (1983) The cultural diversity of western conceptions of management. *International Studies of Management and Organization*, 13, 75–96.

Lewin, K. (1951) *Field Theory in Social Science*. New York: Harper & Row.

Margulies, N., & Raia, A. (1978) *Conceptual Foundations of Organizational Development*. New York: McGraw-Hill.

Meek, V. (1988) Organizational culture: origins and weaknesses. *Organizational Studies*, 4, 453–473.

O'Reilly, C., Chatham, C., & Caldwell, R. (1988) People, jobs and organizational culture. Working Paper: University of California: Berkeley.

Ouchi, W. (1981) *Theory Z: How American Business can Meet the Japanese Challenge*. Reading, MA: Addison-Wesley.

Pascale, R., & Athos, A. (1981) *The Art of Japanese Management*. New York: Simon & Schuster.

Payne, R. (1990) Madness in our method. *Journal of Organizational Behaviour*, 11, 77–81.

Peters, T., & Waterman, R. (1982) *In Search of Excellence*. New York: Addison-Wesley.

Ritti, R., & Funkhauser, G. (1982) *The Ropes of Skip and the Ropes of Know*. New York: Wiley.

Roberts, K., Rousseau, D., & La Porte, T. (1989) The cultures of high reliability. University of California (Berkeley) Working Paper.

Rousseau, D. (1989) The price of success? Security oriented cultures in high reliability organizations. *Industrial Crisis Quarterly*, 3, 285–302.

Rousseau, D. (1991) Quantitative assessment of organizational culture. In B. Schneider (ed.), *Frontiers in Industrial and Organizational Psychology*. New York: Praeger.

Sackmann, S. (1983) Organizationkultur—de unsichtbare Euflussgrösse. *Gruppendysnamik*, 4, 393–406.

Sackmann, S. (1989) 'Kultur management': Lässt sich Unternelimens kultur machen? *Politische Prozesse in Unternchmen*, 2, 157–184.

Sashkin, M. (1984) *Pillars of Excellence: The Organizational Beliefs Questionnaire*. Bryn Mawr: ODD.

Schein, E. (1985) *Organizational Culture and Leadership*. San Francisco: Jossey-Bass.

Schein, E. (1990) Organizational culture. *American Psychologist*, 45, 109–119.

Schneider, S. (1987) National vs corporate culture: Implications for human resource management. *Human Resource Management*, 27, 231–246.

Schwartz, H., & Davis, S. (1981) Matching corporate culture and business strategy. *Organizational Dynamics*, 10, 30–49.

Shrivastava, P. (1985) Integrating strategy formulation with organizational culture. *Journal of Business Strategy*, **7**, 103–111.

Smircich, L. (1983) Concepts of culture and organizational analysis. *Administrative Science Quarterly*, **28**, 339–358.

Smircich, L., & Calas, M. (1987) Organizational culture: A critical assessment. In K. Roberts & L. Porter (eds), *Handbook of Organizational Communication* (pp. 228–263). Beverly Hills, CA: Sage.

Stringfield, P., & Furnham, A. (1989) Introducing a performance management system. *Human Resources Journal*, **5**, 21–27.

Taguiri, R., & Litwin, G. (eds) (1968) *Organization Climate: Exploration of a Concept.* Boston: Harvard Business School.

van Maanen, J. (1978) People processing: Strategies of organizational socialization. *Organizational Dynamics*, **7**, 18–36.

Weick, K. (1979) *The Social Psychology of Organizing.* Reading, Mass: Addison-Wesley.

Williams, A., Dobson, P., & Walters, M. (1989) *Changing Culture: New Organizational Approaches.* London: IPM.

Chapter 8

ORGANIZATIONAL DOWNSIZING: STRATEGIES, INTERVENTIONS, AND RESEARCH IMPLICATIONS

Steve W. J. Kozlowski, Georgia T. Chao, Eleanor M. Smith
and Jennifer Hedlund
Michigan State University, USA

INTRODUCTION

A number of related yet distinct concepts have become salient over the last decade that address the phenomenon of organizational downsizing. The appearance of new, often oxymoronic, terms in the popular lexicon such as building-down, demassing, deorganization, decruitment, growth-in-reverse, leaning-up, rebalancing, refocusing, and rightsizing (among many others), is indicative of this salience. Indeed, the increasing prevalence and changing nature of downsizing during the 1980s has signalled a fundamental change in organization-environment relations (cf. Terreberry, 1968). This has necessitated a shift in the focus of organizational theory from a preoccupation with organizational growth toward models that incorporate decline, restructuring, and downsizing as integral aspects of organizational lifecycles (Whetten, 1980).

In the early 1980s, organizational downsizing had its primary impact on blue-collar employees and manufacturing organizations. More recently, the scope of downsizing has broadened beyond these traditional targets to affect white-collar employees as well. Downsizing targets increasingly include middle-level managers, professional staff, and even the upper, executive echelons of management. It has also spread beyond manufacturing to encompass service organizations. Moreover, there are indications that both the increasing prevalence and the changing scope of downsizing are international in nature. For practicing managers and organizational theorists, these developments are harbingers of a fundamental and permanent change in the evolution and dynamics of organizational behavior.

International Review of Industrial and Organizational Psychology 1993 Volume 8
Edited by C. L. Cooper and I. T. Robertson. © 1993 John Wiley & Sons Ltd.

Although a substantial literature on downsizing has accumulated over the last decade, this body of literature has several limitations. Downsizing and related phenomena are often not clearly distinguished. The literature is largely descriptive and prescriptive in nature, often in the absence of a sound research foundation. Finally, downsizing theory and research has tended to compartmentalize the phenomenon; it is fragmented by different levels of conceptualization, time-frames, and content areas. There is a need for a more comprehensive perspective on the phenomenon and its effects. The purpose of this chapter is to review the literature on downsizing, identify major limitations, and suggest new directions for theory and research.

The Prevalence and Scope of Downsizing

The number of organizations and jobs affected by downsizing is staggering. Downsizing in the US has increased from an estimated loss of 2 million manufacturing jobs in the early 1980s to 3.2 million jobs lost in the late 1980s (Henkoff, 1990). A survey by the American Management Association indicated that 66% of firms with more than 5000 employees had reduced their workforces in the latter half of the 1980s (Greenberg, 1988). Cases of large-scale downsizing include Citibank cutting 17 000 jobs (Hirsch, 1991), AT&T cutting more than 32 000 jobs (Leana & Feldman, 1988a, b), and General Electric cutting 105 000 jobs during the 1980s (Tomasko, 1990).

Announcements and forecasts of downsizing for the 1990s include continuing impacts on traditional manufacturing firms, such as General Motors' plan to cut 74 000 jobs (Ingrassia & White, 1991), as well as additional cuts in service, high-tech, and government organizations. It has been estimated that 20%, or 300 000 jobs, will be eliminated in the commercial banking industry throughout the 1990s (Hirsch, 1991). The US service sector employs 55 million workers, three times the manufacturing workforce. Although manufacturing productivity has doubled in the last 30 years, service productivity has remained virtually flat, making service more prone to competition and downsizing (Desktop America, 1991). In contrast to its long treasured practice of no layoffs, IBM has announced plans to drastically cut jobs throughout the early 1990s (Verity, 1989). Even the armed forces are not immune. US Public Law 101-510 mandates a reduction of over 30% of military personnel by 1995.

Recent evidence indicates that organizational downsizing has shifted emphasis from blue-collar jobs to white-collar positions. Many observers have noted the large proportion of white-collar employees in US firms, relative to their European and Japanese competitors, and the declines in white-collar productivity (Tomasko, 1990). More than 1 million managerial and professional staff positions have been lost since 1979 (Heenan, 1990), and in the first quarter of 1990, major US corporations cut 110 000 staff positions ('RIF,' 1991). United Airlines cut 25% of its staff and General Motors has plans to do the same (Leana & Feldman, 1988a). In addition, DuPont cut 50% of its executive positions at the Vice-President level and above, and General Electric removed five of its nine layers of management (Milbank, 1991). Between August 1989 and May 1990, of half a million newly unemployed US workers, 65% were managers, professionals, and staff (Mandel, 1990).

The shift from predominantly blue-collar reductions toward the downsizing of white-collar jobs is also evident in Europe. As the European community prepares for a unified market after 1992, the tradition of lifetime employment will end as many organizations restructure for competitive advantage (Melcher & Levine, 1990). In addition, the recent political changes in Central and Eastern Europe have launched ambitious programs to privatize enterprises that were previously state-owned. These changes have already resulted in programs that move away from policies preventing unemployment, toward the downsizing of overstaffed and inefficient organizations.

Chapter Overview

Organizational downsizing through workforce reductions is a complex phenomenon with many contributing factors and related contingencies. It is often used as an adaptive organizational response to environmental pressures that constrain the availability of resources, or it may be used to strategically reposition an organization (Hitt & Keats, 1992). In the former case, situations in which organizations have little or no control in the short term may prompt them to downsize. These situations include eroding market share, international competition, rising labor costs, economic contractions, obsolete technologies or products, and political changes (e.g. as in Europe). Apart from reactions to pressing environmental factors, organizations may also take a more active role in forecasting the future and positioning themselves to meet anticipated challenges. Organizations may create strategies that require restructuring to meet new goals, or a renewed focus on the core strategy may prompt a reassessment of prior acquisitions. Thus, downsizing may also be associated with new acquisitions, mergers, and/or sell-offs of peripheral business. Multiple causes and intended goals may be associated with the decision to downsize.

Much of the theoretical development spawned by the downsizing phenomenon has been directed toward revisions of macro theories addressing organizational evolution. Prior to 1980, models of organizational change and development were generally directed toward stability or growth as base assumptions (Whetten, 1980). Indeed, early organizational lifecycle models did not incorporate processes allowing for shrinkage in size (e.g. Adizes, 1979). As processes of decline became more salient to researchers (e.g. Freeman, 1979; Freeman & Hannan, 1975; Hannan & Freeman, 1978), however, many lifecycle models were developed that addressed dissolution and death as important processes in organizational evolution and change (Cameron & Whetten, 1981; Kimberly & Miles, 1980; Sutton, 1983, 1987; Quinn & Cameron, 1983). Thus, by the 1980s, organizational decline and related processes emerged as important theoretical interests (e.g. Cameron, Kim, & Whetten, 1987; Cameron, Sutton, & Whetten, 1988; Cameron, Whetten, & Kim, 1987; Cameron & Zammuto, 1983; Ferris, Schellenberg, & Zammuto, 1984; Ford, 1980a,b; Gilmore & Hirschhorn, 1983; Greenhalgh, 1983b; Greenhalgh, Lawrence, & Sutton, 1988; Jick & Murry, 1982; McKinley, 1987; Staw, Sandelands, & Dutton, 1981; Sutton & D'Annuo, 1989; Weitzel & Johnson 1989). Although organizational decline processes and downsizing actions are often closely associated, decline and downsizing are not isomorphic (Sutton & D'Aunno, 1989). Downsizing as a unique concept within organizational theory has received relatively little attention (Freeman & Cameron, in press; Kozlowski, Chao, Smith, Hedlund, & Walz, 1991).

The downsizing phenomenon has also generated interest at the more micro level. For example, there is a substantial literature addressing the reactions of terminated individuals to job loss (e.g. Leana & Ivancevich, 1987; Liem & Liem, 1988; Rowley & Feather, 1987) and the reactions of downsizing survivors (e.g. Brockner, 1988; Brockner & Greenberg, 1990; Greenhalgh, 1983a). There is, however, a wide gap in theory and research between downsizing processes considered at the organizational level and individual reactions to workforce reductions. There are numerous theoretical issues that intervene between an organizational decision to downsize, the mechanisms used to accomplish the reduction, individual reactions to the process, and eventual impacts on the organization (e.g. Brockner, 1988; Greenhalgh, 1983a; Staw, Sandelands, & Dutton, 1981). Comprehensive theory that addresses downsizing processes across levels of conceptualization and over time has received relatively little attention in the literature (Kozlowski et al., 1991).

Much of what we know about this emergent phenomenon is based on organizational experiences. Thus, the bulk of our knowledge is descriptive, normative, and prescriptive. We know why downsizing has occurred, how it has been managed, and what its impacts are likely to be. Although there is no shortage of views regarding the nature of downsizing and how it should be accomplished, there is much less theory and even less research to substantiate our knowledge. Moreover, the sheer number of disciplinary perspectives contributing to the downsizing literature has tended to yield conceptual confusion. This has tended to hinder the development of theory and research focused on downsizing.

Give the prevalence, scope, and effects of downsizing, it is appropriate to critically examine this evolving phenomenon. This chapter is designed to accomplish the following objectives. First, our focus is on downsizing as a unique phenomenon distinct from decline and other related factors. Although we may reference related phenomena in our effort to explicate downsizing, they are treated as peripheral issues in the interests of conceptual clarity. Another concern is to distinguish among the separate aspects of the downsizing process as it shifts from the organizational to the individual level. Downsizing targets and strategies (what and how to reduce), transition management (how to manage), and interventions (how to aid) are elaborated. These distinctions provide a framework for the structure of the review.

Second, we review the effects of downsizing. Although in theory downsizing is presumed to have positive outcomes for the organization (e.g. Tomasko, 1990), most of the research literature has addressed its significant negative impacts, especially for individuals. We address the effects of downsizing for terminated personnel and survivors of the process. We examine downsizing effects prior to considering organizational strategies and interventions for the following reason. There is an assumption that the effectiveness of downsizing efforts is ultimately dependent on reactions of survivors to the process (Brockner, 1988); survivor reactions aggregate to impact organizational effectiveness (Kozlowski et al., 1991; Staw, Sandelands, & Dutton, 1981). Thus, the logic underlying the selection of different downsizing strategies or interventions ought to be predicated on minimizing its negative effects on individuals.

The third section addresses the management of the process. This literature, which focuses on downsizing targets and strategies, transition management, and interventions, is largely experience-based. Although this literature is dominated by a prescriptive orientation, it provides a basis for identifying normative mechanisms that are likely to have some value in ameliorating the negative effects of downsizing. Thus, it serves as a representation of practical knowledge regarding management of the downsizing process. In this sense, it provides a foundation for identifying major gaps in our theory and research efforts.

The final section of the chapter considers the limitations in extant research, especially with respect to the development of a more comprehensive perspective. We then propose a theoretically based framework that provides a foundation for more integrative work. We illustrate the utility of the conceptual framework by using it to identify new directions for research. Our primary orientation will be to draw on existing theory or theoretical perspectives that can help elaborate neglected aspects of the downsizing process. The intent is to provide a foundation to guide further development of theory and to promote research on this important phenomenon.

THE NATURE OF ORGANIZATIONAL DOWNSIZING

Downsizing Defined

Downsizing is a deliberate organizational decision to reduce the workforce that is intended to improve organizational performance (Cameron, Freeman, & Mishra, 1991; Freeman & Cameron, in press; Hardy, 1990; Kozlowski et al., 1991). Two key aspects of this definition distinguish downsizing from broader perspectives associated with organizational lifecycles, dissolution, or decline: (i) the decision to downsize is a purposeful organizational response, and (ii) it is designed to improve performance.

Decline takes a broader perspective. It addresses the effects of maladaptation between the organization and its relevant environment. Decline is not a response. It is the result of a failure to respond or an inappropriate response to environmental conditions (Appelbaum, Simpson, & Shariro, 1987; Gilmore & Hirschhorn, 1983; Weitzel & Jonsson, 1989). Thus, voluntary workforce attrition associated with mature organizations that have lost vitality, or with maladapted declining organizations where members may opt for other opportunities, is not evidence of downsizing (Freeman & Cameron, in press). Such shrinkage is not purposeful.

Moreover, the intended purpose of downsizing is regenerative; the response is designed to improve organizational performance (Hitt & Keats, 1992). It is a response that may be used to prevent or reverse decline, but it is not isomorphic with decline. Indeed, this has been a primary source of the conceptual confusion between downsizing and decline. The antecedent environmental factors that create decline conditions (e.g. turbulence, competition, loss of markets, resource constraints, etc.) also signal downsizing as a possible adaptive response. However, downsizing may occur in the absence of overt decline processes. That is, it may be an anticipatory strategic response designed to realign the organization and improve performance in advance of conditions antecedent to decline. Thus, downsizing is not decline (Freeman & Cameron, in press), although downsizing as a response is typically associated with decline conditions (Hitt & Keats, 1992; Kozlowski et al., 1991) and may even be regarded as an indicator of decline (Weitzel & Jonsson, 1989).

The Downsizing Process

To aid clarity as we examine the literature related to downsizing, it is useful to draw distinctions among several aspects of the downsizing process as it proceeds from an organizational level decision to individual level effects. From a normative perspective, this includes such issues as what to target for reduction and which approaches to use, how to implement reductions, and how to manage the impacts on those terminated and those surviving the reductions.

Downsizing targets and strategies

Downsizing as an organizational response may be selected as part of a strategic reorientation or as an incremental effort to ameliorate decline (Freeman & Cameron, 1992). In either instance, the downsizing decision process may be proactive, well-articulated, and designed to support the long-term organizational strategy, or it may be more reactive in nature, with little effort to ensure that the process and its outcomes will be consistent with desired future states (Kozlowski et al., 1991).

Whether downsizing is proactive or reactive in form, at a molar level the initial issues concern what segments of the organization to reduce and how to accomplish the reduction. Targeting refers to those segments slated for reduction and may include combinations of several foci. For example, downsizing may focus on geographic locations such as countries, regions, or specific sites (e.g. corporate headquarters, redundant or obsolete plants). Organizational functions, such as manufacturing, human resources, or research and development, or specific positions representing redundant, superfluous, or obsolete competencies and skills may be targeted. In other instances, downsizing focuses on the reduction of administrative levels in an effort to improve decision making speed and flexibility. This form of targeting is often associated with restructuring and job redesign. It is also possible for downsizing to be essentially untargeted, as in across-the-board personnel cuts.

Downsizing strategies refer to the methods employed to accomplish the reduction, whether precisely targeted or not. In general, downsizing strategies range from those that offer less organizational control, slower reductions, and fewer negative effects on employees (e.g. attrition) to those that are under high control, are quick, and have more negative effects on personnel (e.g. permanent layoffs without assistance; Greenhalgh, Lawrence, & Sutton, 1988). Moreover, although the prescriptive literature on strategy selection is largely oriented toward minimizing the effects of downsizing on terminated personnel, we also address issues relevant to a consideration of impacts on surviving personnel. The collective reactions of survivors to the downsizing process have clear implications for future organizational effectiveness.

Transition management and interventions

Once the downsizing targets and mechanisms have been identified, the process must be implemented and managed. Key issues concern the reduction of uncertainty through extensive communication and the implementation of interventions designed to aid and support both terminated personnel and survivors. Major classes of interventions include outplacement assistance, counseling, and vocational retraining. The primary function of the interventions is to ameliorate the negative effects of the downsizing process. The goal is to help both terminated employees and survivors to accept the process and prepare for new roles. Thus, interventions have direct effects on terminated personnel, survivors, and, via the aggregate reactions of survivors to the process, on the organization itself. Given the presumed impact of downsizing on future effectiveness, we next consider the negative effects that downsizing may have.

THE EFFECTS OF DOWNSIZING

Organizational downsizing can be accomplished using several different strategies or strategy combinations. These strategies will have direct effects on the individuals targeted by the downsizing. For example, individuals who are laid-off or who retire early must deal with the loss of their job and steady source of income. Strategies such as transfers, relocations, work redesign, demotions, and reduced work schedules directly affect the welfare of survivors. However, research indicates that strategies used to accomplish personnel reductions will also influence the behaviors and attitudes of those who survive (Brockner, 1988; Brockner & Greenberg, 1990; Greenhalgh, 1983a). Furthermore, the downsizing process will affect the organization in terms of efficiency and cost savings (Greenhalgh, Lawrence, & Sutton, 1988; Greenhalgh & McKersie, 1980), effectiveness (Freeman & Cameron, in press), and organizational image (Sutton, Eisenhardt, & Jucker, 1985).

Terminated Personnel

The individuals explicitly affected by downsizing are those who lose their jobs; consequently, most research on the impacts of downsizing deal with its effects on terminated personnel. Furthermore, the majority of research highlights the negative outcomes of downsizing for individuals who must leave the organization. The most important effects of downsizing include financial loss, and impacts on well-being, attitudes, and family relationships (Leana & Ivancevich, 1987). This literature includes research on plant closings, national statistics on displaced workers, and general research on the impacts of unemployment and job loss. The literature primarily covers job loss in Australia, the United Kingdom, and the United States.

Financial impacts

Individuals who are laid-off or who must retire early are faced with the immediate prospect of a loss of income. While they may receive severance pay or unemployment insurance, they often fail to find a new job before this income runs out, thus suffering substantial earnings losses (Podgursky & Swaim, 1987). One indicator of the financial impact of job loss is the length of time an individual remains unemployed. For example, Horvath (1987) reported that individuals in the US displaced between January 1981 and January 1986 spent a median duration of 21 weeks unemployed. Buss and Redburn (1987) found that two years after a plant closing, 27% of the affected unretired workforce in that metropolitan area were unemployed; eight years later, 27% of those still in the labor force were unemployed. Cross-sectional research indicates that subjective reports of financial strain are positively related to length of unemployment (Rowley & Feather, 1987; Warr & Jackson, 1984).

Furthermore, individuals may suffer financial losses due to decreased job stability after an initial job loss. Individuals who have lost their jobs may have difficulty finding stable employment, they may hold several jobs with interruptions in employment between each (Buss & Redburn, 1987), or they may only be able to obtain employment in a less attractive position (Burke, 1986). Finally, job loss may interact with the local economy to produce longer periods of unemployment. Burke (1985) reported that a high unemployment rate and poor economy in the area contributed to the large percentage of individuals remaining unemployed 16 months after a plant closing.

Financial losses may continue when reemployment wages and salaries are substantially lower than previous incomes. In a study of a plant closing, Ashton and Iadicola (1989) found that the strongest predictors of income loss included the level of reemployment in terms of full- versus part-time work, and the socio-economic status of the new job. Thus, individuals who are unable to find a full-time job after layoff suffer income loss due to employment in part-time positions. Furthermore, if individuals can only find reemployment in lower paying jobs, they will suffer long-term financial losses that call for living adjustments.

For example, Perrucci, Perrucci, Targ, and Targ (1985) examined a number of adjustments that laid-off employees had to make in their spending habits. Victims of a plant closing reported that they could no longer afford several expenses, including leisure activities, clothing, car expenses, and the replacement of worn-out furniture or household equipment. In addition, over 50% of the sample had cut spending on gifts, entertainment, clothing, food, home upkeep and repair, dental care, and children's expenses other than schooling.

Research on the economic impacts of unemployment suggests certain demographic groups may be especially vulnerable to income loss and difficulty in finding reemployment. However, the research is mixed on the financial impacts of job loss for gender and minority groups. Burke (1985) found that women reemployed after a plant closing received lower salaries than men, and their drop in wages from the previous job was greater than that for men. Yet, it has also been found that job loss is more traumatic for men, since they are traditionally the primary wage earner in the household (Shamir, 1985a). Howland and Peterson (1988) reported that older, poorly educated, minority blue-collar workers experienced large financial losses even when living in the fastest growing Standard Metropolitan Statistical Areas. On the other hand, Hamermesh (1989) could not conclude from examining the plant closing literature that women and minorities suffered greater losses than other workers, although minorities were more likely to be displaced.

Several studies indicate that individuals with longer tenure on the job and individuals in blue-collar jobs experience larger financial losses due to displacement (Hamermesh, 1989; Podgursky & Swaim, 1987; Warr & Payne, 1983). In contrast, Ashton and Iadicola (1989) found that blue-collar workers were likely to experience less income loss than white-collar workers when other predictors such as socio-economic status and educational attainment were controlled. However, because downsizing targeted at white-collar workers is a more recent phenomenon, there is little research examining the experience of job loss for white-collar employees.

Individuals with skills that do not transfer outside of the organization (e.g. Ashton & Iadicola, 1989; Podgursky & Swaim, 1987) and those with less education (e.g. Howland & Peterson, 1988; Podgursky & Swaim, 1987) suffer greater financial losses. In addition, individuals without other personal resources to draw upon will experience greater economic strain (Buss & Redburn, 1987). Further, this financial strain and stress influence the individual's psychological health and well-being (Feather, 1989a; Jackson & Warr, 1984; Leana & Feldman, 1990; Payne & Hartley, 1987).

Well-being

Jahoda (1979) argued that job loss has consequences beyond the loss of a steady source of income. Employment has a number of psychological benefits that are lost when an individual becomes unemployed, which creates stresses and strains. A number of studies report that individuals who lose their jobs suffer physical symptoms caused by the strain of unemployment. Several indicators of the stressful experience of unemployment include the incidence of headaches, stomach problems, high blood pressure and other psychosomatic symptoms, increased drinking, increased smoking, and greater frequency of feeling unwell (Burke, 1984; Kessler, House, & Turner, 1987; Kasl & Cobb, 1979; Kasl, Gore, & Cobb, 1975; Linn, Sandifer, & Stein, 1985; Perrucci et al., 1985; Warr & Payne, 1983). Further, unemployed individuals have shown higher levels of catecholamines compared to employed individuals, indicating greater arousal and stress (Baum, Fleming, & Reddy, 1986). Blood pressure, serum cholesterol, and body weight have been found to be sensitive to changes in employment status experienced by layoff victims; however, it is concluded that these effects do not increase the risk for heart disease, as the effects diminish over time even as unemployment continues (Kasl & Cobb, 1970, 1980).

The strain of unemployment is also manifested in psychological reactions (Dooley & Catalano, 1988). A number of studies indicate that job loss is associated with lower psychological health in general and an increase in psychological symptoms (Dooley & Catalano, 1984a,b; Fineman, 1983; Hepworth, 1980; Iversen & Sabroe, 1988; Liem & Liem, 1988; Stokes & Cochrane, 1984). In addition, research has found that unemployment is positively related to more specific psychological reactions of anxiety (Hamilton, Broman, Hoffman, & Renner, 1990; Kessler, House & Turner, 1987; Kinicki, 1985; Linn, Sandifer, & Stein, 1985; Shamir, 1986; Viney & Tych, 1984; Warr, 1978) and depression (Bolton & Oatley, 1987; Feather, 1989b; Feather

& Barber, 1983; Feather & Davenport, 1981; Hamilton et al., 1990; Kessler, House, & Turner, 1987; Landau, Neal, Meisner, & Prudic, 1980; Linn, Sandifer, & Stein, 1985; Perrucci, Targ, Perrucci, & Targ, 1987; Shamir, 1986; Tiggemann & Winefield, 1984; Viney & Tych, 1984). Those who may be particularly affected include the less educated (Hamilton et al., 1990; Landau et al., 1980), minorities (Hamilton et al., 1990), the unskilled or semi-skilled (Hepworth, 1980), those with a high work orientation (Frohlich, 1983), and those unemployed for longer lengths of time (Hepworth, 1980; Sommer & Lasry, 1984; Warr, 1978).

In addition to effects on general psychological well-being, other research suggests impacts on cognitive functioning and perceptual processes. For example, unemployed individuals have exhibited learned helplessness when attempting to solve puzzles (Baum, Fleming, & Reddy, 1986), as well as cognitive difficulties on tests (Haworth, Chesworth, & Smith, 1990). Furthermore, the self-relevance of a layoff may reduce later perceptions of the foreseeability of the layoff (Mark & Mellor, 1991). Mark and Mellor (1991) found that laid-off individuals reported less hindsight bias (foreseeability of the layoff) than survivors of a layoff; survivors reported less hindsight bias than community members. In order to avoid blame for the layoff, layoff victims may develop a self-serving bias that inhibits hindsight bias. Neither type of bias contributes to learning from the experience of layoff (Mark & Mellor, 1991).

Fortunately, it has been found that the psychological symptoms associated with job loss disappear once an individual becomes reemployed (Warr, Jackson, & Banks, 1988). This is consistent with Jahoda's (1988) assertion that unemployment does not lead to enduring psychiatric disorders; rather it leads to reduced psychological health that can be ameliorated by finding a new job. However, individuals who become reemployed after a long period of unemployment do report that a number of aspects of employment, including job security and pay, have become more important to them (Payne & Jones, 1987). Unfortunately, satisfaction with a new job in terms of pay and benefits may be lower compared to satisfaction with the previous job, at least for older workers (Mallinckrodt, 1990).

Further, the attributions that individuals make in terms of the reasons for job loss (locus and stability) have been found to impact their affective reactions to job loss (satisfaction, self-esteem) and their expectations for reemployment, as well as their actual reemployment 18 months after job loss (Prussia, Kinicki, & Bracker, in press). Thus, unemployment may have long-term effects on the perceptions, attitudes, and choices of unemployed individuals throughout their lives. These longer-term impacts have not been addressed in the literature; short-term effects have received more attention.

Attitudes

A number of researchers have examined the relationship between job loss and several different attitudinal measures. Cohn (1978) and Stokes and Cochrane (1984) report that the unemployed are significantly more dissatisfied with themselves compared to the employed. In addition, Pearlin, Lieberman, Menaghan, and Mullan (1981) found that job loss increased economic strains; these economic strains were negatively related to individual feelings of self-esteem and mastery. Further, these decreases in self-concept were related to increased depression. The self-esteem of unemployed individuals has also been found to be related to social support (Linn, Sandifer, & Stein, 1985; Mallinckrodt & Fretz, 1988), financial concerns (Mallinckrodt & Fretz, 1988) as well as to the length of unemployment (Rowley & Feather, 1987).

On the other hand, Hartley (1980) found that managers who became unemployed did not report decreased self-esteem. In fact, results of interviews with unemployed individuals indicated four categories of self-esteem in response to unemployment. Hartley (1980) suggests that individual differences in reactions to unemployment be considered when studying the impacts of unemployment.

Research has found laid-off workers to report less satisfaction with their lives, their marriages, and their families (Burke, 1984), to be more pessimistic about their economic future, and to report that a factory worker's children have less of a chance to succeed in life than an executive's children (Perrucci et al., 1985). Although Noble (1987) found no radical changes in political attitudes due to job loss in a sample of UK workers, the layoff victims became more isolated and less active, and reported feelings of powerlessness.

In contrast, Little (1976) found that some technical and professional workers had more positive attitudes towards their job loss. A number of them reported that they were still optimistic about the future, that their interests could be expanded, and that job loss provided a challenge or opportunity for them. However, individuals under 30 and over 50, individuals unemployed for longer lengths of time, and individuals unable to keep busy during unemployment were less likely to report positive attitudes. Thus, a positive or negative response to downsizing may depend on the personal resources that can be drawn upon by the displaced worker.

For example, Latack and Dozier (1986) have conceptualized job loss as a career transition. However, for job loss to lead to a positive career change, several factors must be present to moderate the stress of job loss. Several of these factors include: low job involvement and satisfaction, sufficient financial resources, provision of social support and a flexible family structure, well-planned downsizing by the organization, productive job search, and a shorter length of unemployment.

Pliner (1990) reports that individuals who were successful in managing a mid-career transition were more flexible in responding to the circumstances, actively sought information, and exhibited high levels of awareness. In contrast, when testing a stress model of unemployment, Payne and Hartley (1987) found no support for the hypothesis that opportunities and positive experiences due to unemployment improve the health of the unemployed. They suggested that unemployment does not produce enough available opportunities to positively influence the well-being of the unemployed (Payne & Hartley, 1987).

In summary, an individual who has more personal resources may suffer less from the experience of job loss; for example, the individual's family may provide additional sources of income or emotional support during the difficult transition. However, while providing support for the layoff victim, family members will also have to cope with the psychological and financial impacts of job loss on their own lives.

Family relationships

It is clear that the experience of job loss affects not only the displaced employee but the family as well. For example, the loss of income is likely to change the family's standard of living. They may have to make adjustments in their spending (Perrucci et al., 1985), and spouses and children may be pressured to find jobs or work longer hours to support the family (e.g. Elder & Caspi, 1988).

Liem and Liem (1988) found job loss to affect the family in several ways. The husband's emotional response to his job loss later affected his wife's psychological well-being. Job loss also led to a decline in family climate, in terms of decreased family cohesion and increased conflict. In addition, while husbands and wives reported no changes in family norms, husbands did begin performing more tasks traditionally reserved for the wives. Finally, Liem and Liem (1988) found a separation and divorce ratio of 7 to 2 reported between families with unemployed versus employed husbands.

Wilhelm and Ridley (1988) examined the coping responses of couples when the husband was laid-off. Results indicated that financial arguments were positively related to feelings of stress, especially for the wives. In addition, avoidance coping reduced the impact of financial arguments on stress for husbands and wives. While avoiding the reality of the job loss served to decrease the impact of financial arguments on stress, it also served to lessen the impact of saving money on reducing husband's reported stress (Wilhelm & Ridley, 1988).

Atkinson, Liem, and Liem (1986) argue that unemployment stress is experienced not only by the individual, but also by family members and friends. However, there is a lack of research examining the implications of job loss for the long-term functioning of the family unit, or the interaction between job loss and the occurrence of other significant life events.

Demographics

Although research has tended to treat those laid-off as homogeneous, individuals do not appear to react uniformly to job loss (Payne & Hartley, 1987). The impacts of unemployment on demographic groups may be different. It was mentioned previously that unemployment may affect blue- versus white-collar individuals, and men versus women in different ways. With the increase in downsizing of white-collar employees, as well as the increase of women in the workforce, the possibility for differential impact on these groups becomes more important. This section will describe in more detail the effects of unemployment on these individuals, as well as age differences in the reaction to unemployment.

With the increase in layoffs of white-collar employees, research has begun to examine differences in reactions to unemployment from blue- and white-collar workers. It has been reported, for example, that blue-collar workers suffer greater financial strain due to unemployment (Warr & Payne, 1983; Payne, Warr, & Hartley, 1984). On the other hand, it has been suggested that white-collar workers may suffer in more psychological ways because work is more central to their self-definition and social status. However, a study by Payne, Warr, and Hartley (1984) found few differences between the two groups of unemployed workers. Blue- and white-collar workers did not differ in their reactions to unemployment in terms of general health, anxiety, depression, and general psychological distress. Further, there was no significant difference in employment commitment for blue- and white-collar workers. On the other hand, white-collar workers did perceive more career and life-style opportunities as a result of unemployment, while blue-collar workers felt more externally controlled and had problems filling their time (Payne, Warr, & Hartley, 1984). Further research on the different experiences of blue- and white-collar workers during job loss may indicate different interventions that might better assist each of these groups.

It has been suggested that unemployment is a more difficult experience for men because they are traditionally responsible for financially supporting the family. One problem with the research on unemployment is the limited number of studies that include unemployed women in their samples. Therefore, there are only a few studies that can shed some light on any differences in the experience of unemployment for men and women.

For example, in a sample of white-collar, educated, married individuals, men experienced more psychological difficulties than women. However, when the current financial state of the unemployed individual was controlled, the differences between men and women disappeared. 'Thus, the difference between men's and women's reactions to unemployment appears to hinge on varying degrees of financial hardship rather than on differences in the meaning and function of work and family roles' (Shamir, 1985a: p. 76). When women are not responsible for providing for the family, the psychological impact of unemployment may be less.

In a sample of blue-collar workers that included either single women or families needing the second income, men and women experienced similar increases in physical and emotional symptoms due to income loss (Taylor, 1988). Furthermore, Castro, Romero, and Cervantes (1987) found that Latino women reported family, occupational, and economic stress 18 months after a plant closing. Most respondents reported that conditions were difficult for raising a family, that they lacked the skills to find the jobs they wanted, and that there were times when they had no money (Castro, Romero, & Cervantes, 1987). Leana and Feldman (1991) found no significant differences between men and women in their reactions to unemployment in terms of psychological distress, depressive affect, and physiological distress. However, women and men did differ significantly in the ways they coped with job loss; women relied more on symptom-focused activities (e.g. social support) while men relied more on problem-focused activities (e.g. job search).

Snyder and Nowak (1984) found that employed and unemployed blue-collar women did not differ in terms of demoralization, while unemployed men reported significantly more demoralization than employed men. However, reemployed women reported more demoralization than reemployed men. Some women reemployed in fairly high-paying jobs still reported being demoralized; this was due to economic insecurity, fluctuations in household income, greater cutbacks in household spending, and the greater use of their savings (Snyder & Nowak, 1984). Thus, when women hold or share the financial responsibility, they suffer as much as men as a result of unemployment.

In summary, there needs to be additional research on the impact of unemployment for women. With the growing presence of single women in the workforce, the increase in the number of working wives and single-parent families, and the increasing dependency of families on this second source of income, downsizing is likely to show impacts on women that are as severe as those found for men.

There is also some indication that job loss has differential impacts on individuals of various ages. For example, unemployed individuals in different age groups have reported varying levels of factors that might impact the unemployment experience, including financial stress, income change, number of dependents, and a wife who is working (Warr & Jackson, 1984). Further, there is some indication that the experience of job loss is more traumatic for middle-aged individuals compared to individuals new to the workforce or those close to retirement (Frohlich, 1983; Jackson & Warr, 1984; Rowley & Feather, 1987).

While length of unemployment and psychological ill-health have been found to be negatively related for middle-aged individuals, no relationship has been found between the two factors for the young and for those close to retirement

(Jackson & Warr, 1984). Middle-aged individuals may have more difficulties with unemployment because they have a family to support, while young workers do not have families yet and older workers may have already raised their children. Because age is an indicator of an individual's point in their life span, research should be examining how factors associated with life transitions might interact with the experience of job loss.

Coping responses and resources

Individuals may differ in their behavioral reactions to unemployment. Some studies report that individuals who have lost their jobs reduce their activity, withdraw from social contact, avoid threatening events, and become apathetic, cynical, and helpless when they cannot find reemployment (Powell & Driscoll, 1973; Warr, Jackson, & Banks, 1988).

Other research indicates that unemployed individuals spend more time with neighbors and friends, and increase their participation in reading, domestic work, and domestic pastimes. In contrast, they decrease time spent on activities and entertainment that require money (Feather, 1989a; Warr & Payne, 1983). Leana and Feldman (1988a) suggest two broad categories of strategies to cope with job loss: active coping strategies and palliative coping strategies. While active coping strategies focus on eliminating the problem of being unemployed, palliative coping strategies reduce the stress of unemployment by distracting individuals from their problems. An individual's reliance on one of these two categories of coping behaviors may depend on their cognitive appraisal of the job loss and their level of emotional arousal (Leana & Feldman, 1988a). Research suggests that being active and directed in one's activities during unemployment is related to greater psychological health (Brenner & Bartell, 1983; Feather, 1989a; Kilpatrick & Trew, 1985). Keeping active during unemployment may be one way to cope with the stress of unemployment. However, the beneficial effects of activity during unemployment may depend on individual differences of the unemployed. For example, individuals with a high Protestant work ethic and high work involvement may engage in more nonwork activities during unemployment (Shamir, 1985b). In fact, involvement in nonwork activities was found to be positively associated with psychological well-being for individuals with high work ethic and involvement (Shamir, 1985b).

On the other hand, Kinicki and Latack (1990) found that blaming oneself for job loss was positively related to distancing oneself from the job loss and negatively related to proactive job search behavior and nonwork organization. Self-esteem was found to be positively associated with proactive job search and positive self-assessment (Kinicki & Latack, 1990). Interestingly, previous layoff experience was not related to any coping strategy examined; this finding may indicate that individuals experience similar life events differently at different stages in their lives (Kinicki & Latack, 1990).

In addition, individual differences on two factors, sociotropy (social dependency) and autonomy, may produce different vulnerabilities to unemployment (Reynolds & Gilbert, 1991). Reynolds and Gilbert (1991) found an interaction between autonomy and activity, in that highly autonomous individuals who were very active during unemployment reported less depression than less active individuals. In contrast, higher levels of activity are related to greater depression among individuals who are highly sociotropic (Reynolds & Gilbert, 1991).

Another factor that may assist individuals in dealing with unemployment is social support. Although research is mixed in terms of whether social support has a direct or buffering (interactive) impact on reactions to job loss, results indicate generally that social support reduces the negative psychological effects of unemployment (Atkinson, Liem, & Liem, 1986; Brenner & Bartell, 1983; Gore, 1978; Kessler, Turner, & House, 1988; Liem & Liem, 1979; Mallinckrodt & Fretz, 1988; Mallinckrodt & Bennett, in press). Jackson (1988) found that unemployed individuals depend on a small network of family and friends who provide mainly expressive support; in addition, he found that the network of friends decreases and instrumental support increases over time. Further, emotional and instrumental social support have been reported to be positively related to the coping strategy of positive self-assessment (Kinicki & Latack, 1990).

However, individuals may differ in their opportunities for acquiring social support from family and friends. For example, blue-collar workers may have more frequent social contacts and higher levels of emotional support compared to white-collar workers (Atkinson, Liem, & Liem, 1986). In addition, women may have more sources of support than men (Mallinckrodt & Fretz, 1988; Taylor, 1988). Research also suggests that social support is not stable and is affected by the unemployment experience (Atkinson, Liem, & Liem, 1986). Furthermore, social support may be detrimental to individuals who are high on autonomy; high levels of social support may threaten their feelings of independence and achievement (Reynolds & Gilbert, 1991).

While increased activity and social support may serve to mitigate the negative impacts of unemployment, the relationships observed must be tempered by the fact that individuals experience other positive and negative life events along with their unemployment experience. Thus, the experience of unemployment should be examined within the larger scope of events occurring in an individual's life (Dooley & Catalano, 1980; Dooley, Catalona, & Rook, 1988; Dooley, Rook, & Catalano, 1987; Kessler, Price, & Wortman, 1985). For example, Pearlin and Lieberman (1979) found that job loss was related to greater levels of persistent household financial problems, occupational problems, and marital problems. When these role problems were taken into account, the association between the job loss event and psychological distress was diminished.

To cope with job loss, individuals may change other aspects of their lives. Individuals who expect or are forewarned about job loss may cope with this possibility by reducing the frequency of other stressful life events (Kinicki, 1985). Further, research indicates that the coping strategies used by displaced workers change over time (Kinicki & Latack, 1990). In summary, additional research examining job loss in relation to other life events and life transitions is necessary to understand the broader impacts of unemployment on individual lives.

Surviving Personnel

While downsizing has more direct implications for the individuals who lose their jobs, employees who remain with the organization will also be affected by downsizing strategies intended to improve organizational flexibility, increase employee responsibility, and streamline operations. For example, employees may respond with reduced trust and organizational commitment when the organization breaks its 'psychological contract' with them (Buch & Aldridge, 1991). The reactions of these survivors to the downsizing process, as well as their reactions to the organization's treatment of terminated employees, may impact future organizational effectiveness and adaptability.

When jobs are redesigned or employees are retrained as part of the downsizing process, the intention is to increase the responsibilities of employees in order to improve organizational efficiency. The job redesign literature suggests that enriching an employee's job by providing variety or additional responsibilities may make that individual's work more motivating, rewarding and satisfying (Hackman & Oldham, 1980). One can differentiate between job enrichment, in which employees are given more discretion and decision-making responsibility, and job enlargement, in which the amount of work performed is simply increased. The job redesign literature indicates that enriching a job, rather than simply enlarging it, will produce increased work motivation (Hackman & Oldham, 1980).

Downsizing can result in either job enrichment, which is perceived by employees as greater personal control over the job (Greenberger & Strasser, 1986; Osborne, 1990), or job enlargement, which leads to employees feeling overburdened (Byrne, 1988a). In fact, case studies indicate that job redesign and retraining are often poorly planned when used to support downsizing. For example, an employee may be given the responsibilities formerly held by three or four people (Byrne, 1988b). In an empirical study of downsizing survivors, Tombaugh and White (1990) found that, while management expected individuals to handle increased responsibility and decision-making, employees reported significant increases in role conflict, role ambiguity, and role overload, and a decrease in positive feedback following downsizing. Further, satisfied and dissatisfied survivors differed in their levels of role ambiguity, role conflict, and positive feedback, and survivors who intended to leave the organization reported greater increases in role ambiguity and role conflict (Tombaugh & White, 1990).

Ashford (1988) examined the impact of company restructuring on surviving employee feelings of stress, as well as the role of several coping resources and responses in buffering the negative impacts. First, it was found that the uncertainty and disruption associated with the restructuring was positively related to employee feelings of stress. Further, two coping resources, personal control and tolerance for ambiguity, as well as one coping response, sharing emotions, buffered the impact of uncertainty and disruption on feelings of stress before and after the transition. In contrast, individuals who avoided thinking about the restructuring as a coping response reported increased stress, and individuals who asked for feedback before the transition reported greater levels of stress after the transition (Ashford, 1988).

Job transfers and relocations pose a different set of problems for employees experiencing downsizing. A number of organizational, personal, social, and familial factors have been theorized to affect an individual's judgment of the threat of relocation (Luo & Cooper, 1990). Several of these factors include job characteristics such as the quantity, novelty, and discretion of the work, and personal factors such as locus of control and hardiness (Luo & Cooper, 1990). Furthermore, concerns about disruption of the family may set employee opinions against a relocation (Zedeck & Mosier, 1990). For example, individuals with children were less likely to leave an organization to joint a newly created firm (Miller & Labovitz, 1973). Thus, individuals with fewer family ties or responsibilities may be more receptive to the transition.

In addition, when family attitudes towards a transfer are positive or when highly-esteemed coworkers, information contacts, or friends decide to transfer, individuals may be more likely to transfer to a new location (Fox & Krausz, 1987; Miller & Labovitz, 1973). In fact, for British and American individuals who have transferred, coworker interpersonal support has been found to be beneficial in terms of greater job involvement, career satisfaction, and overall work satisfaction, and a decreased intent to leave (Gerpott, 1990). However, these results were not found for a similar group of West German transferees.

Finally, transfers may be especially difficult for women. Due to their traditional role of caring for the children, they may be concerned about the distance of a new job from home (Fox, 1979). In addition, with the increase in dual income families, the decision to relocate will affect both spouses' career plans and opportunities (Luo & Cooper, 1990; Zedeck & Mosier, 1990).

The use of demotions as part of a reduction strategy has a number of negative influences on employees. In order to remain with an organization, individuals may have to accept jobs several levels below their former position (e.g. Byrne, 1988b). This may be accompanied by a salary reduction as well. Along with the financial difficulties of a reduced income, individuals may experience negative self-attitudes and decreased commitment to the organization

(Peters & Lubin, 1989). For example, Schlenker and Gutek (1987) found that demoted employees reported lower self-esteem, lower job satisfaction, and higher intention to leave the organization compared to their nondemoted colleagues.

Several other downsizing strategies targeted at reducing costs include work sharing, part-time schedules, and reduced hours. Although affected employees would experience a reduction in income, the experience may be less painful than being laid-off. Further, these strategies may be a way to spread the pain of reductions across levels in the organization, rather than resorting to layoffs of lower level employees (Watford, 1986). However, individuals who must reduce their work schedules experience similar financial impacts as layoff victims who can only find lower-paying reemployment.

A limitation of the present literature on organizational downsizing is the lack of research on how the role changes for employees who remain in the organization affect their attitudes, behavior, performance, and commitment to the organization. For example, it is suggested that organizational change and role changes are especially stressful for mid-career workers (Davis & Rodela, 1990; Matteson & Ivancevich, 1990). Further, survivor reactions to organizational change may depend on whether these changes result in power and opportunity gains or losses (Gaertner, 1989). However, research has not yet addressed these issues. On the other hand, there is a growing body of research examining how surviving employees react to layoffs of their fellow employees.

Survivor reactions to layoffs

Surviving employees who see their fellow workers and friends being laid-off may experience decreased morale and commitment to the organization. For example, survivors of Atari's downsizing reacted very negatively to the callous manner in which employees were laid-off (Sutton, Eisenhardt, & Jucker, 1985). Survivors observed that greater numbers of lower level relative to upper level employees were being terminated, that employees received no advance notice of their layoff, and that management was not keeping them informed about the downsizing process. Employees responded with decreased morale and strong intentions to leave Atari as soon as possible (Sutton, Eisenhardt, & Jucker, 1985).

Greenhalgh (1983a,b; Greenhalgh & Rosenblatt, 1984) conceptualizes an organizational decline–job insecurity cycle that details several unintended consequences of a workforce reduction. When employees observe an organization's downsizing efforts, they assess the continuity of their own work situations. Employees who observe their organization in decline respond with feelings of job insecurity which impair their productivity, engender resistance to change, and lead to turnover. These responses ultimately affect the organization's adaptability and may lead to further organizational decline

(Greenhalgh, 1983a). In an empirical study of two hospitals to be merged, Greenhalgh (1982) found that survivors of the merger reported greater job insecurity than employees in a control hospital. Survivors experienced this insecurity even though only seven employees were laid-off and the two hospitals were not merged due to community pressures (Greenhalgh, 1982).

Brockner and his associates have performed a series of studies on survivor reactions to layoffs (Brockner, Davy, & Carter, 1985; Brockner, DeWitt, Grover, & Reed, 1990; Brockner, Greenberg, Brocker, Bortz, Davy, & Carter, 1986; Brockner, Grover, & Blonder, 1988; Brockner, Grover, Reed, DeWitt, & O'Malley, 1987). Brockner (1988) has developed a conceptual model of factors that moderate an individual's reactions to layoffs of fellow workers. A number of survivor attitudes and behaviours may be affected by layoffs, including productivity, organizational commitment, and attitudes towards coworkers. This conceptualization is based on justice theory (Brockner & Greenberg, 1990), in which the survivor examines whether the laid-off employees are treated fairly by the organization. For example, survivors may question whether the layoff was a necessary response to an economic downturn, whether layoff victims are adequately forewarned, whether the rules used to choose those to be laid-off are fair, and whether or not the organization provides any 'caretaking activities' to help individuals adjust to the layoff.

Research indicates that survivors can react positively or negatively to the layoff, depending on the perceived fairness of the layoff procedure. For example, in a lab study, Brockner, Davy, and Carter (1985) found survivors to feel positive inequity and guilt when a fellow worker was laid-off, resulting in increased productivity, especially for low-esteem survivors. Similarly, Brockner et al. (1986) reported that survivors increased their quantity of work more when victims were randomly laid-off rather than laid-off based on merit.

In contrast, Brockner et al. (1987) found survivors to react negatively to a layoff when they felt the victim was uncompensated for the layoff and they highly identified with the victim. They found a negative impact on productivity for participants in a laboratory study, while survivors in a field study reported decreased organizational commitment in response to the layoffs (Brockner et al., 1987). In a study of four organizations implementing layoffs, Brockner, Grover, and Blonder (1988) found job involvement to be greater when layoffs were mild rather than severe.

Survivors also report a greater decline in organizational commitment when layoff victims are included in their 'scope of justice,' when the organization does little to explain the layoff situation, and when the survivors perceive that little 'caretaking' is provided for layoff victims (Brockner, 1990). Further, Brockner, Grover, Reed, and DeWitt (1992) found an inverted-U relationship between job insecurity (in terms of perceived threat and perceived control) and survivor work effort, after controlling for the perceived fairness of the layoff. Work effort was greater at moderate levels of job insecurity, compared to low or high levels of job insecurity. In addition, the survivor's economic need to work moderated this relationship, in that the inverted-U relationship was pronounced for survivors with a high economic need to work, but almost nonexistent for those with a low economic need to work.

Finally, Brockner and his associates have also examined the effects of prior organizational commitment (Brockner, Tyler, & Cooper-Schneider, 1991), social influence (Brockner, Wiesenfeld, Stephan, Grover, Reed, DeWitt, & Hurley, 1991), job content and context (Brockner, Wiesenfeld, Reed, Grover, & Martin, 1991), and procedural justice and outcome negativity (Brockner, Konovsky, Cooper-Schneider, & Folger, 1991) on survivor reactions to layoff.

Davy, Kinicki, and Scheck (1991) examined the procedural justice aspect of Brockner and Greenberg's (1990) conceptual model in a longitudinal study of survivor reactions to layoff. They found support for a model linking global process control (general perceptions of the fairness of organizational decisions) before layoff to the perceived fairness of the layoff and job satisfaction (measured 3 months later). In addition, perceived fairness of the layoff was positively related to job satisfaction, and job satisfaction was positively related to organizational commitment. Organizational commitment was negatively related to behavioral intentions to withdraw. Finally, job security, measured one month prior to layoff, was positively related to job satisfaction and behavioral intentions to withdraw.

In addition to impacts on survivors at the individual level, several researchers posit that downsizing will affect functioning at the group level as well. Krantz (1985) describes the tendency for groups to engage in defensive behavior to relieve the stress of downsizing. For example, their social defenses may become rigid and group members may be unable to accommodate the flexible demands of task performance. Staw, Sandelands, and Dutton (1981) also describe the tendency for work groups to become more cohesive and resistant to change in response to environmental threats. Thus, when the organization is most in need of flexible decision making and innovation, survivor reactions may prevent the organization from adapting to its new environmental contingencies and subsequent turbulence.

In summary, research on survivor reactions to downsizing indicates a number of negative impacts that occur in the short term. The prevalence, scope, and continued presence of downsizing as a salient feature of the work environment may make job insecurity a primary concern of employees. The evolution of the downsizing phenomenon is reflected in the shift from research on job loss alone, to research on the job insecurity experienced by survivors of downsizing (e.g. Hartley, Jacobson, Klandermans, & Van Vuuren, 1991). The next step is to examine how downsizing might affect long-term decision making and behavior of employees, including performance, career choices and plans, and future organizational commitment.

DOWNSIZING TARGETS, STRATEGIES, AND TRANSITIONAL INTERVENTION PROCESSES

Given the many negative effects of downsizing and their implications for organizations, a substantial literature has developed that addresses various aspects of the downsizing process. This literature is predominantly experience based. It is descriptive of the normative mechanisms that organizations have used to downsize, and prescriptive as to how reductions should be accomplished (e.g. McKersie & McKersie, 1982; National Alliance of Business, 1983, 1984; National Technical Information Service, 1986; Nelson, 1988; Portela & Zaks, 1989; Price & D'Aunno, 1983; Sweet, 1975). From a conceptual perspective, the relevant components of the downsizing process include target identification, strategy selection, and management of the transition through interventions. Targets refer to the segments of the organization that will absorb downsizing. Strategies represent the specific mechanisms used to operationalize the reduction. Transition management involves implementing interventions such as outplacement, psychological counseling, and vocational training to assist individuals who are affected by the downsizing process.

Downsizing Targets

Organizational decisions regarding target identification range from haphazard and essentially unmanaged reductions to intentional selection of specific segments of the organization to be downsized. For example, an organization may not carefully target areas for reduction, instead making uniform cuts throughout as in across-the-board downsizing. This approach is often based on the need to achieve immediate cost savings. In contrast, an organization may target specific segments (e.g. levels, functions, departments, or positions) in accordance with strategic objectives and related criteria, such as inefficiency, redundancy, or obsolescence.

Across-the-board

Across-the-board reductions are generally made in a uniform fashion, without specific targeting. The organization's objective is to perform the same functions with fewer personnel. Short-term interests in cost savings and time constraints may lead to reductions that are implemented rapidly and dictated by poorly articulated criteria (Gibson, 1985; Kolcum, 1988). For instance, across-the-board cuts are usually based on seniority using a 'last-in/first-out' approach (Kanfer & Hulin, 1985). Across-the-board downsizing has often been used by government units as a method to spread cutbacks across the organization (Carney, 1987). This may be regarded as a means of maintaining a sense of equity among employees (Brockner, 1988). A major problem with this approach is that key personnel competencies or critical functional capabilities may be lost (General Accounting Office, 1978, 1983; Levine, 1984).

Target locations

Downsizing may involve targeting geographic locations. Locations can include countries or regions (Fox & Krausz, 1987) or specific sites such as plants or corporate headquarters (Gibson, Hibbs, & Pitman, 1986; Heenan, 1989). Most of the available literature addresses plant closings. Plants are closed for a variety of reasons including high maintenance costs and technological obsolescence (Perrucci et al., 1985; Perrucci, Perrucci, Targ, & Targ, 1988; Taber, Walsh, & Cooke, 1979); decreased demand and competition (Ashton & Iadicola, 1989; Buss & Redburn, 1987; Cortes-Comerer, 1986; Debow, 1987; Franzem, 1987); and mergers or acquisitions that result in redundancies (Hirsch, 1987; Matte, 1988; Mitchell, 1988). Regional constraints, including high tax rates or highly dispersed divisions, often lead to the targeting of particular locations (Byrne, 1988a,b; Howland, 1988). Particular industries experience high rates of plant closings as part of continuous environmental shifts or long-term industrial decline (Hill & Negrey, 1987). For example, the steel, automotive, and appliance industries are areas that have suffered from competition, environmental turbulence, and generally poor economic conditions (Buss & Redburn, 1987; Cortes-Comerer, 1986; Debow, 1987; Feldman, 1988a,b; Taber, Walsh, & Cooke, 1979). Although locations may be targeted through the use of complex decision criteria, in practice they are often selected in an effort to generate immediate cost savings with little consideration of the long-term implications for the organization (Hardy, 1987, 1990).

Target segments

The identification of specific levels, functions, departments, or positions is assumed to be associated with more careful planning and evaluation. An organization with long-term objectives and well-articulated decision criteria is likely to be more judicious in its selection of downsizing targets (Halcrow, 1985; Mullaney, 1989; Schlenker & Gutek, 1987). The selection of particular segments may reflect the environmental conditions that initiated downsizing (Garry & Votapka, 1990; Greenhalgh, McKersie, & Gilkey, 1985; Zammuto & Cameron, 1985). Particular segments may become redundant or obsolete due to the introduction of advanced technologies, often with significant impacts on blue-collar employees (Chao & Kozlowski, 1986; Cornfield, 1983; Hattrup & Kozlowski, in press), although technological change can also make professional skills obsolete (Kaufman, 1982; Kozlowski, 1987; Kozlowski & Farr, 1988; Kozlowski & Hults, 1987). Organizational restructuring removes layers of administration and reorganizes departmental units (Benson, 1990a; Feldman, 1989; Sheridan, 1988). This process yields reductions that cut superfluous or less critical functions and positions (Cornfield, 1983; Mullaney, 1989). Middle managers, professional staff, and executives are increasingly targeted as part of restructuring (Benson, 1990b; Byrne, 1988b; Imberman, 1989; Mitchell, 1988; Nelson, 1988). Although the targeting of specific segments is often considered to be associated with more careful planning, this need not be the case. Segments may be targeted for simple cost considerations.

Summary

The literature often uses target identification as a substitute for more detailed consideration of the rationale employed during downsizing decisions. Thus, unsubstantiated assumptions have been associated with target selection; that across-the-board downsizing represents a lack of clearly articulated criteria (e.g. Kolcum, 1988), plant closings represent obsolescence or industrial decline (e.g. Perrucci et al., 1985), and target functions or levels represent well-planned changes in structure or strategic mission (e.g. Mullaney, 1989; Sheridan, 1988). In fact, all targets may represent more or less articulated rationales (Garry & Votapka, 1990). For example, across-the-board cuts may represent efforts to maintain equity and preserve survivor sentiments (Carney, 1987) or functions may be targeted as a quick way to cut costs, but without any clear consideration of the long-term effects (Sutton, Eisenhardt, & Jucker, 1985).

The difficulty with focusing on targets alone is that without information about the environmental factors, the nature of the decision process, and the means by which downsizing is accomplished, target information is of little diagnostic value. Targets provide information concerning the scope of downsizing; not why downsizing is initiated, how it is implemented, or how it effects displaced employees, survivors, and the organization.

Strategies for Implementing Downsizing

In association with target identification, an organization also determines how to accomplish reductions. There are a number of methods or strategies that are used to achieve workforce reductions. These strategies range from methods that minimize the impacts on employees (e.g. attrition) to more drastic methods that have significant negative effects on both displaced personnel and survivors (e.g. permanent involuntary layoffs). Strategy selection is not independent of target identification; attrition, for instance, will not be an effective mechanism to accomplish a plant shutdown. As with target identification, strategies may be selected according to well-developed, multidimensional criteria (Kozlowski et al., 1991), or to simple criteria based on narrowly considered economic issues (Hardy, 1987).

Hierarchy of downsizing strategies

Some research has indicated that layoffs are the primary strategy used to accomplish downsizing. Indeed, a large percentage of firms rarely consider other alternatives (McCune, Beatty, & Montagno, 1988). Greenhalgh, Lawrence, and Sutton (1988) proposed that the various downsizing strategies could be arranged in a hierarchy to reflect trade-offs between maintaining employee well-being and maximizing short-term cost savings for the organization. *Natural attrition* offers the greatest preservation of employee well-being and the least short-term savings. It involves the natural process of employee flows entering and exiting the organization. This process can be haphazard in its effects, as when a total hiring freeze does not specify what skills or competencies need to be maintained (General Accounting Office, 1978, 1983), or more selective, as when some areas are frozen and others are allowed replacement or even growth (Greenhalgh, McKersie, & Gilkey, 1985).

Under *induced redeployment*, employees are encouraged to comply voluntarily. This often necessitates incentives to achieve compliance with downsizing efforts. For example, financial incentives help to promote voluntary separation (Cornfield, 1983; Feldman, 1989) or transfer to different jobs or locations (Fox & Krausz, 1987; Greenhalgh, McKersie, & Gilkey, 1985). Senior employees are offered incentives to facilitate early retirement decisions (Kuzmits & Sussman, 1988; Seibert & Seibert, 1989). Other voluntary strategies include curtailed advancement opportunities, optional part-time or short-week schedules, work sharing, and leave-without-pay (Hansen, 1985; Kerachsky, Nicholson, Carvin, & Hershey, 1986).

As one moves down the hierarchy, the strategies become more focused on short-term cost savings. *Involuntary redeployment* includes those strategies listed under induced redeployment, but now employees are required to participate. In addition, demotion or job downgrading (e.g. Mullaney, 1989) is considered an involuntary downsizing strategy. For example, professional employees may be demoted to administrative positions (Schlenker & Gutek, 1987). Reduced work schedules (Bureau of National Affairs, 1982; Watford, 1986), furloughs (General Accounting Office, 1983), and transfers (Franzem, 1987; Sheridan, 1988) may also be implemented without voluntary agreement by employees.

The last two strategies in the hierarchy involve layoffs. Employees may be laid-off, but offered assistance in adjusting to the termination (Patterson & Flanagan, 1983). Assistance may include advanced notification (Perkins, 1987; Rohan, 1985), severance pay (Grier, 1990; Matte, 1988), continuation of benefits (Franzem, 1987; Mullaney, 1989), outplacement (Brammer & Humberger, 1984; Schlossberg & Leibowitz, 1980), psychological counseling (Rundle & DeBlassie, 1981; Valencia, 1985), and vocational retraining (Warr & Lovatt, 1977). The most drastic method of downsizing is layoff without any assistance.

Several observers have noted that a focus on short-term economic criteria often entails hidden costs for the organization that are rarely considered within the context of downsizing strategy selection. These unfactored costs include unemployment insurance taxes, severance payments, and legal expenses (Dean & Prior, 1986; Greenhalgh & McKersie, 1980; Greenhalgh, McKersie, & Gilkey, 1985; Perry, 1985). In addition, severe downsizing strategies may have unintended effects on survivors, including decreased morale and commitment and increased stress and turnover (Dean & Prior, 1986; Hansen, 1985, 1988; Hardy, 1987, 1990).

Decision criteria and constraints

The primary focus on economic criteria is due to the fact that many organizations miss the environmental signals indicating a need for adjustment (Weitzel & Jonsson, 1989). They are then forced into crisis situations which necessitate immediate personnel cut-backs to generate savings (Murray & Jick, 1985). These downsizing efforts are poorly planned and often ineffective. Many instances can be cited in which organizations inadvertently lost essential capabilities and skills through ill-planned downsizing (e.g. Greenhalgh & McKersie, 1980; General Accounting Office, 1978, 1983).

In an effort to improve understanding of the process of target and strategy selection, many researchers have identified internal criteria that ought to guide the decision process. Kozlowski et al. (1991), for example, have suggested that downsizing decision processes may be characterized as proactive or reactive in form. Proactive decisions view downsizing as a long-term process that incorporates a variety of downsizing strategies (Heenan, 1989; Jacobs, 1988; Perry, 1985), is linked to long-range strategic (business) objectives (Greenhalgh, McKersie, & Gilkey, 1985; Halcrow, 1985; Levine, 1984), preserves distinctive and critical competencies (Hitt & Keats, 1992), and is carefully monitored through human resource management (HRM) interventions (Ferris, Schellenberg, & Zammuto, 1984). In contrast, reactive downsizing decisions are poorly articulated with respect to these criteria. The time-frame is compressed, criteria are simplistic, strategically relevant competencies are not considered, and the process is unmanaged. Factors that may determine whether organizational downsizing decisions are proactive or reactive in nature have not received much attention in the literature.

Other researchers (Freeman & Cameron, in press) have suggested that downsizing targets and strategies are determined by the form of organizational adaptation. They have proposed that organizations maintaining the same mission, but attempting to improve efficiency (convergent orientation) downsize incrementally with an emphasis on long-term approaches that minimize negative impacts on personnel. Firms that shift their business strategies to pursue a new mission focus on effectiveness (reorientation). This approach necessitates revolutionary restructuring, shifts in power, and job redesign. Downsizing is likely to be more drastic and severe in its impacts, but is intended to help transform the firm. Inherent in this model is the assumption that the organization has engaged in proactive planning.

Finally, there are a number of external constraints, including the environmental sector, unions, and regulation that may affect downsizing strategies (Bureau of National Affairs, 1982; Greenhalgh, Lawrence, & Sutton, 1988; Hunsicker, 1990; Office of Personnel Management 1981; Phay, 1980; Thompson, Hauserman, & Jordan, 1986). For example, whether the organization is in the public or private sector may constrain its choice of strategy. Greenhalgh, Lawrence, and Sutton (1988) suggest that public agencies are less likely to adopt severe strategies, but recent trends indicate that many government and public service jobs have been eliminated because of budget cuts and poor economic conditions (Carney, 1987; Mullaney, 1989).

The use of particular downsizing strategies may be constrained by labor agreements. Union contracts often specify policies regarding terminations (Smith, 1989; Wolkinson, Chelst, & Shepard, 1985). For example, contracts may stipulate that employees with the least seniority should be targeted first, or that the organization must evaluate alternatives to reductions prior to initiating a layoff (Bureau of National Affairs, 1982; Imberman, 1989). Some unions have attempted to block downsizing plans, and employees have filed suits for breach of contract (Gibson, Hibbs, & Pitman, 1986; Hardy, 1987; Kolcom, 1988; Murphy, Barlow, & Hatch, 1985). In other instances, joint labor–management committees have offered assistance in closing plants, training displaced workers, and helping them find new jobs (Batt, 1983; Chell, 1985; Feldman, 1988a,b; Franzem, 1987; National Alliance of Business, 1984; Newman & Gardner, 1987; Patton, & Patton, 1984).

Organizations must also consider the legal implications of downsizing strategies; regulations exist in Canada, Sweden, the United Kingdom, and the United States (Batt, 1983; Bureau of National Affairs, 1982; Perrucci et al., 1988; Greenhalgh, Lawrence, & Sutton, 1988; Hardy, 1987, 1990; Hunsicker, 1990; Office of Personnel Management, 1981). In the US, terminating certain groups of employees often affects legally protected groups disproportionately (e.g. minorities, women, or older employees). Several pieces of legislation must be considered, including the Civil Rights Acts of 1964, 1972, and 1991, the Age Discrimination in Employment Act of 1972, and the Americans with Disabilities Act of 1990 (Feldacker, 1990; Office of Personnel Management, 1981). Additionally, the Worker Adjustment and Retraining Act (WARN), which went into effect in 1989, requires organizations in the US to give 60 days advance notification to employees affected by plant closings or major layoffs (Colosi, 1989).

Summary

Organizations often downsize reactively, with little consideration of the long-term costs and implications for future effectiveness (Cameron, Mishra, &

Freeman, 1992; Gilmore & Hirschhorn, 1983; Hardy, 1987, 1990; McCune, Beatty, & Montagno, 1988) Proactive downsizing is more complex, involving the use of multiple decision criteria in the selection and configuration of downsizing strategies. Greenhalgh, Lawrence, and Sutton (1988) suggest some of these criteria, and consider the impacts of strategies on employees. Freeman and Cameron (in press) have developed a model of the downsizing process based on the nature of organizational change. Kozlowski et al. (1991) have specified criteria that may determine whether downsizing decisions are proactive and well-articulated or reactive and poorly planned. We address how these perspectives can be integrated to better understand the downsizing decision process, and the selection of targets and strategies, when we consider new directions for theory and research. At this point, however, the review considers how the effects of downsizing decisions on terminated personnel and survivors may be managed.

Transition Management and Intervention Processes

From a practical perspective, even when downsizing strategies have been judiciously selected to maintain employee welfare, displacement with its attendant negative effects will still occur. Thus, as the downsizing process shifts from consideration of organizational level issues toward the individuals affected by the process, efforts to manage the transition and alleviate the impacts on personnel come into focus. Transition management and intervention processes focus on the individual level issues associated with downsizing.

Transition management

Models that address transition management issues generally indicate two primary goals of the process (e.g. Appelbaum, Simpson, & Shapiro, 1987; Bridges, 1986; Brown, 1990). The first goal is to provide support for the personnel most directly affected by downsizing. Displaced personnel need to be informed about the process, financial incentives and benefits need to be provided, and more direct interventions designed to aid coping need to be implemented. The second goal concerns survivors. The organization needs to regain the confidence, trust, and commitment of its employees, and rebuild a positive image (Appelbaum, Simpson, & Shapiro, 1987). The following discussion focuses on two general issues that are important in managing this transition process, communications and financial incentives.

The uncertainty associated with downsizing is often cited as a primary source of anxiety both for survivors and for those who will be displaced (Ashford, 1988; Curtis, 1989; Swinburne, 1981; Zahniser, Ashley, & Inks, 1985). Thus, a vital part of the downsizing process is concerned with keeping all parties informed. This often takes the form of advanced warning of downsizing plans, including discussion with unions, employee associations, and employees. It may also include the provision of information to the media. The main goal of the communication process is to ensure that all constituencies, including terminated personnel, survivors, unions, and the local community, receive necessary information concerning the time-frame involved, the expected impact on the organization and its employees, and the reasons for downsizing.

The provision of honest and accurate information is believed to help reduce uncertainty (Hunsaker & Coombs, 1988) and the spread of rumors (Colvard, 1986; Modic, 1987), while helping to improve morale (Jacobs, 1988; Kiechel, 1985) and to increase survivor loyalty and commitment (Grosman, 1989). The criteria used to make selection decisions should be clearly communicated to terminated employees and survivors to avoid feelings of inequity (Brockner et al., 1987; Chell, 1985; Schweiger & DeNisi, 1991; Smallwood & Jacobsen, 1987). In addition, reassurances of job security need to be communicated to survivors (Hansen, 1985). Managers also need accurate information regarding the downsizing process to ensure effective administration of retrenchment activities (Rohan, 1985). Finally, organizations can use the media to ensure clear communication of their objectives, and their concern for the interests of employees (Matte, 1988).

Although honest, accurate, and timely information is encouraged by the literature, organizations are often required to provide some minimum information to their workforce. In the US, the WARN Act and other legal doctrines (e.g. union contracts), require organizations to notify employees in advance of impending terminations (Rhine, 1986). Few US employers provided advance notice prior to the enactment of the WARN legislation (Ruhm, 1990). If the workforce is unionized, the employer must notify the union in advance and involve the union in the development of the downsizing plan (Colosi, 1989). Canadian organizations are required to establish a Joint Consultative Committee consisting of equal numbers of employer and employee representatives. The committee promotes communication, cooperation, and understanding among employers, employees, and unions (Newman & Gardner, 1987).

Open communication leads to positive outcomes for individuals and the organization (Colvard, 1986; Greenhalgh, McKersie, & Gilkey, 1985). Terminated employees reduce their length of unemployment following downsizing (Addison & Portugal, 1987; Staudohar, 1989; Swaim & Podgursky, 1990), and survivors benefit through reduced uncertainty and reassured job security (Feldman & Leana, 1989). For example, Schweiger and DeNisi (1991) compared employees in a plant receiving advanced communication regarding an anticipated merger with a plant where employees received limited information. The advanced communication helped reduce uncertainty and other dysfunctional outcomes such as stress, low commitment, and diminished productivity. Moreover, advanced communication does not appear to lead to increased absenteeism or decreased productivity (Hershey, 1972).

When the reasons for downsizing and selection criteria are made clear, an organization reduces the likelihood of lawsuits for unfair dismissal (Dickens,

1985; Portela & Zaks, 1989). Effective communication with a union can result in an easier and more efficient implementation of downsizing. A plan to downsize can be made difficult, or even impossible, if an organizaiton fails to gain the cooperation of the union involved (Kolcum, 1988; Perrucci et al., 1987). Finally, by informing the media and its personnel, an organization helps maintain a positive public image (Ehrenberg & Jakubson, 1989), and the loyalty and commitment of its employees (Grosman, 1989).

As part of its downsizing strategy, an organization usually develops an incentive system to induce voluntary dismissal of targeted employees. Incentives include separation bonuses, pension fund distributions, and early retirement options (Barbee, 1989; Ellig, 1983; Steele, 1986; Seibert & Seibert, 1989). Involuntarily dismissed employees may be offered separation packages, often in the form of a number of weeks of severance pay, or extended benefits, to help alleviate the immediate financial concerns resulting from job loss. This descreases the need for an individual to grab the first available job, or to seek out government assistance (Leane & Feldman, 1989). In regard to survivors, Ellig (1983) stressed the importance of being equitable in providing severance pay and early retirement incentives in order to promote a sense of fairness across all employees.

Intervention processes

In addition to communication and financial support, specific interventions directly address the needs of terminated and surviving employees. Outplacement refers to activities which assist terminated personnel in obtaining reemployment. It includes job search assistance, career planning, resume development, and interview training. Counseling helps employees in their adjustment to the psychological and social impacts of downsizing. Counseling is often provided to surviving, as well as terminated, personnel. Training involves assisting employees to acquire new skills and knowledge that will enable them to obtain reemployment or to fill other positions or roles within the organization.

The main goal of outplacement is to help terminated personnel obtain new employment. There are many possible components of outplacement assistance. These include resume preparation, job search workshops, interview training, the provision of job market information, relocation assistance, skills and interests assessment, career planning, and clerical support (Barkhaus & Meek, 1982; Batt, 1983; Brammer & Humberger, 1984; Debow, 1987; Fulmer & Fryman, 1985; Parkhouse, 1988; Patton & Patton, 1984; Perkins, 1990; Quartararo, 1988). Comprehensive outplacement programs may also incorporate psychological counseling and financial planning. Outplacement may also involve helping individuals to relocate to new geographic locations where greater demand for their skills exists (Patton & Patton, 1984). Inplacement has been conceptually linked to outplacement (Latack, 1990). However, it is defined as a strategy to retain employees within the organization and avoid terminations

(Latack, 1990). In this sense it is distinct from outplacement, which is an intervention designed to assist employees who have been displaced.

Outplacement can be provided by the downsizing organization or external agencies to which employees are referred. Outplacement has been conducted through centers, workshops, classroom formats, and on an individual basis (Matte, 1988; Patterson & Flanagan, 1983; Schlossberg & Leibowitz, 1980). Organizational personnel may use contacts to identify possible job openings for those terminated (Schlossberg & Leibowitz, 1980), classes can be designed to deal with different aspects of job loss ranging from financial planning to information about the job market (Patterson & Flanagan, 1983), and external consultants can be brought in to help implement outplacement programs (Debow, 1987; Matte, 1988).

Unions and government agencies are often involved in downsizing activities to ensure that outplacement is provided (Feldman, 1988a,b; Leana & Ivancevich, 1987; Newman & Gardner, 1987). This can take the form of joint committees or ventures to help plan and provide outplacement services (Adams, 1985; Batt, 1983; Forbes, 1987; General Accounting Office, 1989; Newman & Gardner, 1987).

Outplacement alone does not deal with the psychological factors that are associated with job loss (Kanfer & Hulin, 1985). Unemployment due to job loss has been found to relate to depression (Feather & Barber, 1983; Feather & Davenport, 1981), decreased satisfaction with life (Feather & O'Brien, 1986), lower self-esteem (Tiggemann & Winefield, 1984), and stress symptoms (Kessler, Price, & Wortman, 1985; Liem & Liem, 1979). In addition, downsizing may result in conflict, scapegoating, and low morale among survivors (Brockner, 1988; Cameron, Whetten, & Kim, 1987). Counseling may be necessary to reduce some of the psychological effects of job loss and job insecurity.

Psychological counseling is designed to help employees vent their feelings, rebuild their self-esteem, and constructively deal with stress. Rundle and DeBlassie (1981) suggest that displaced workers experience a number of problems upon layoff, including affective problems, stress-related illnesses, financial concerns, training needs, and career insecurities. Counseling can help displaced workers to cope with the trauma of job loss and encourage them to continue job search behaviors (Caplan, Vinokur, Price, & van Ryn, 1989). Some counseling programs focus on reestablishing workers' sense of personal control, rebuilding their self-esteem, and validating of their anger (Schore, 1984). Counseling may also help individuals to attribute their unemployment to uncontrollable, external causes, while stressing that success in obtaining reemployment will be due to internal and controllable factors (Young, 1986). Finally, counselors may encourage employees to rely on the social support of their families and friends to help them adapt to unemployment (Valencia, 1985).

A number of coping mechanisms exist to help terminated employees adjust to the stress associated with job loss (Kessler, Price, & Wortman, 1985; Latack, 1986; Leana & Feldman, 1988a, 1990). Gore (1978) suggested that social support plays a role in how people react to stressful situations. Social support is predicted to buffer the impact of a stressor (e.g. job loss) on an individual's psychological well-being (Carver, Scheier, & Weintraub, 1989; Dooley, Rook, & Catalano, 1987; Ganster, Fusilier, & Mayes, 1986; Kinicki & Latack, 1990; LaRocco, House, & French, 1980; Vinokur & Caplan, 1987). The existence of social support may also increase job seeking behaviors (Mallinckrodt & Fretz, 1988).

An issue that has not received much attention in the literature involves the effect of losing social support networks that revolve around the workplace. Jones (1989) suggests that job loss results in a reduction in the number of social contacts a person has available. Maintaining this form of support may be an objective of intervention programs. Social support can be provided through counselors (Janis, 1983) or group counseling programs (e.g. Mallinckrodt, 1990; Mallinckrodt & Bennet, in press).

Survivors in a downsized organization often need counseling to cope with feelings of guilt, to adjust to additional job responsibilities, or to improve their morale (Gall, 1986). Problems of low productivity, high absenteeism, and high turnover have been identified as resulting from workforce reductions (Brown, 1990; Feldman, 1989). Even when employees leave voluntarily, survivors becomes less satisfied and committed to their jobs (Mowday, 1981).

Some organizations attempt to maintain morale and productivity through simple reassurances of job security (Byrne, 1988b). Employees at different career stages, however, have different concerns (Isabella, 1989). For example, entry level personnel are concerned about the growth opportunities available within the organization, while middle or late career employees focus on long-term job security (Isabella, 1989).

In addition to counseling and outplacement, terminated and surviving employees often require training to take on new jobs or new responsibilities. When a mass layoff or plant closing occurs, the market is flooded with individuals possessing similar skills (Langerman, Byerly, & Root, 1982). Many of these skills are no longer in demand locally or even nationally, thus reducing the likelihood of obtaining reemployment without retraining.

Vocational training may be provided by the downsizing organization or by publicly funded programs. Public assistance of training occurs at local, state, and federal levels (Hansen, 1988). At a local level, adult education and vocational skills courses are offered (Langerman, Byerly, & Root, 1982). At the state level, jointly funded programs with firms have been developed that make referrals and register individuals for training classes (Schore, 1984). In the US, federal assistance is available through the Job Training Partnership Act (JTPA) to provide training interventions (National Alliance of Business, 1983). The National Alliance of Business provides government subsidies to firms hiring and training hard-to-employ individuals, and the JTPA provides assistance to firms involved in efforts to reemploy displaced workers (Leana & Ivancevich, 1987). In Canada, workers receive training assistance through the Manpower Adjustment Committee (Batt, 1983; Newman & Gardner, 1987).

Organizations may offer training programs directly to terminated employees. Training interventions range from simply alerting employees about educational opportunities available to them (Matte, 1988), to providing specific skills training (Warr & Lovatt, 1977). Some organizations encourage employees to seek training, others offer tuition assistance (Feldman & Leana, 1989). Career development centers are occasionally established for aptitude and interest assessment (Langerman, Byerly, & Root, 1982). Training programs have taught employees how to start their own small businesses (Mangum, Tansky, & Keyton, 1988).

Survivors of downsizing may need to be retrained to take on additional responsibilities or to fill new positions within the organization (Byrne, 1988a,b; Sebrell, 1990; Yates, 1985). When an organization uses transfers, demotions, or job redesign as part of its downsizing strategy, employees at all levels may require assistance to cope with job changes (Bridges, 1986; Cochran, Hinckle, & Dusenberry, 1987; Cortes-Comerer, 1986; Greenhalgh, 1982; Imberman, 1989). For example, employees may be retrained to replace those that leave (Yates, 1985), or managers may be trained to function in a newly structured environment (Imberman, 1989). In Japan, retraining is used to keep workers employed within the organization (Hoerr & Zellner, 1990).

Intervention outcomes

Numerous case studies, and an occasional experimental evaluation, point to the positive outcomes of outplacement, counseling, and training interventions. Interventions can provide confidence in adjusting to a difficult situation (Schlossberg & Leibowitz, 1980), encouragement to begin job searches (Patterson & Flanagan, 1983), and the skills necessary to fulfill new positions (Yates, 1985).

The primary outcome of outplacement efforts is the successful placement of displaced personnel into new employment. Vinokur, van Ryn, Gramlich, and Price (1991) and Vinokur, Price, and Caplan (1991) reported better employment outcomes in terms of earnings and job satisfaction, as well as less depression and anxiety for employees who participated in an outplacement program. Additionally, employees perceive these programs as providing them with a sense of direction and encouragement (Parkhouse, 1988). Outplacement can also result in career growth opportunities (Benson, 1990b; Leana & Feldman, 1989); some displaced personnel even start their own businesses or consulting firms (Mangum, Tansky, & Keyton, 1988). However, mismatches may occur between a person's skills, abilities, and interests and job placement due to an unfamiliarity with the worker or a poorly developed outplacement program (Bearak, 1982; Heery, 1989). Outplacement programs should be tailored to individual needs (Benson, 1990b). Hoban (1987) adds that employees at different levels require different types of outplacement assistance. For example, middle and upper level managers are concerned with trying to match their current job characteristics and salary, while lower level employees need to focus on resume writing and interviewing skills (Hoban, 1987).

Counseling, in particular, helps to improve the mental health of those individuals affected by job changes. Studies have shown that more extensive counseling programs have more beneficial outcomes than simple self-help guides. For example, Caplan et al. (1989) found higher perceived self-efficacy and job seeking motivation in individuals who participated in an eight session counseling course than those who engaged in a self-help group. Furthermore, participation in these courses was significantly linked to greater success at reemployment. Other research indicates that without adequate and effective counseling, displaced workers actually become discouraged and reduce job seeking efforts (Powell & Driscoll, 1973).

Survivors also benefit from outplacement and counseling efforts. Intervention efforts indicate to survivors that the organization cares about its employees and, therefore, helps to maintain the morale and productivity of those remaining (Debow, 1987; Franzem, 1987; Perkins, 1987). When an organization chooses to do nothing to help dismissed employees, a negative signal is sent to survivors that may translate into decreased loyalty and productivity (Sutton, Eisenhardt, & Jucker, 1985).

The intended outcome of training is to increase the rate of reemployment for displaced workers. Other positive outcomes associated with training include providing structure to one's day and a sense of work-related identity (Leana & Feldman, 1989). Preliminary evidence suggests that training has beneficial effects (Warr & Lovatt, 1977). However, researchers have conducted few evaluations in which participants and nonparticipants are compared in terms of reemployment success. Low participation has often been identified as a problem in training programs (Buss & Redburn, 1987; Hansen, 1988; Schore, 1984), which makes training evaluation difficult.

Some negative outcomes have been associated with training. If the quality of reemployment is lower than what employees expect they will receive, they feel misled or discouraged (Leana & Feldman, 1989). Training programs should ensure that marketable skills are taught, otherwise reemployment will be difficult (Ashton & Iadicola, 1989; McKersie & McKersie, 1982). Additionally, if displaced workers receive training that will allow them to obtain better jobs, survivors may experience feelings of inequity, which can lead to lowered morale, commitment and productivity (Murray, 1987).

Unfortunately, solid evaluation of these programs is limited. If conducted at all, it is usually in the form of employee opinions (Barkaus & Meek, 1982). The general consensus is that these interventions help to increase rates of reemployment for displaced workers (Matte, 1988), improve employee well-being (Caplan et al., 1989), and increase the morale and commitment of survivors (Feldman, 1989; Gall, 1986). Due to the lack of empirical research, there is little knowledge of what key features of outplacement, counseling, and training programs lead to successful outcomes. In addition, there is little examination of how individual differences interact with these programs.

Outcomes for the organization

Intervention programs are expected to have somewhat indirect, but meaningful, effects on the organization. An organization's image as an employer and its reputation are affected as a result of downsizing. Poor management of a workforce reduction damages an organization's reputation in the business community (Sutton, Eisenhardt, & Jucker, 1985) and unfavorable publicity may hamper downsizing efforts (Gibson, Hibbs, & Pitman, 1986; Hardy, 1987). However, when the process is managed well, and an organization exhibits concern for its employees' well-being, it may receive favorable attitudes from survivors, terminated employees, and the community (Forbes, 1987; Greenhalgh, McKersie, & Gilkey, 1985; Matte, 1988). The organization benefits by maintaining a good public image (Matte, 1988), reducing the likelihood of legal problems (Piccolino, 1988), and increasing the timeliness of the organizational changes (Hayslip & VanZandt, 1985; Mirabile, 1985).

A CONCEPTUAL FRAMEWORK FOR DOWNSIZING THEORY AND RESEARCH

Limitations and the Need for a More Integrative Approach

By definition, organizational downsizing is intended to improve efficiency or effectiveness (Freeman & Cameron, in press). The promises of downsizing include quicker decision making, flexibility, and improvements in quality and productivity (e.g. Tomasko, 1990). Although some organizations have reported substantial savings and performance improvements as a result of downsizing (Bearak, 1988; Byrne, 1988b; Hoban, 1987; Kuzmits & Sussman, 1988; Tomasko, 1990), its potential has generally not been realized in practice (Bennett, 1991; Cameron, Mishra, & Freeman, 1992; Greenhalgh & McKersie, 1980; Heenan, 1989; Kozlowski et al., 1991; Kuzmits & Sussman, 1988; General Accounting Office, 1978, 1983). The amount of available prescriptive advice regarding downsizing and the general lack of empirical support for its effectiveness highlights several limitations in the downsizing literature.

The broad range of literature that has been used to conduct this review required the imposition of an organizational structure to distinguish conceptually distinct issues. This is due in part to the evolution of our understanding of downsizing as it has emerged as a salient phenomenon over the last decade.

Moreover, downsizing has been a source of interest to multiple disciplines, each offering a variety of perspectives, methodologies, and terminology. For example, the literature cited in the preceding review includes material drawn from sociology, labor economics, organizational theory, organizational psychology, psychological counseling and mental health, and management practice. On the one hand, this provides a very rich literature on downsizing related issues. On the other hand, however, it has resulted in the lack of a common language, imprecise constructs, and conceptual overlap. Thus, there is a clear need for organizational scholars to identify the bounds of the phenomena of interest and to develop consensus on key factors, processes, and outcomes. We need a common framework.

A broad examination of the material drawn from more organizationally oriented sources reveals a strong focus on description and prescription. Most of this literature is practice oriented, and is based on perceptions of in-process downsizing experiences or recollections of past processes (Kozlowski et al., 1991). This is certainly an appropriate approach for developing a basic understanding, particularly for an emergent phenomenon. Indeed, this material has served as a foundation for the development of several normative models that address different aspects relevant to the downsizing process (e.g. Appelbaum, Simpson, & Shapiro, 1987; Cameron, Kim, & Whetten, 1987; Greenhalgh, Lawrence, & Sutton, 1988; Sutton & D'Aunno, 1989; Weitzel & Jonsson, 1989).

Given the wide range of potential antecedents of downsizing, the different forms of the process (i.e. convergence versus reorientation), and the different degrees of articulation for decisions regarding the process (i.e. proaction versus reaction), normative models are an insufficient basis for developing solid understanding. They may, however, serve as a foundation for more sophisticated models that are sensitive to the contingencies and temporal processes that relate to downsizing. Indeed, existing theories that address the effects of and adaptation to change at the macro and micro levels may be used to elaborate the processes suggested by normative models of downsizing.

Within organizational science, the little theory and research on downsizing has tended to follow along the traditional distinctions between macro and micro orientations. As Freeman and Cameron (in press) noted, much of the interest at the macro level has addressed theoretical issues relevant to organizational decline. Indeed, downsizing has been treated as a surrogate of decline even though downsizing and decline are not isomorphic. At the macro level, there is a need to address downsizing as an intentional action distinct from decline. Although there are signs of change in this regard (Cameron, Freeman, & Mishra, 1991; Cameron, Mishra, & Freeman, 1992; Freeman & Cameron, in press), downsizing theory and research have not yet addressed the factors that affect the nature of intentions.

At the micro level, the bulk of the empirical research has examined the effects of job loss. This is a traditional research area that is not unique to the emergence of downsizing, although downsizing has spurred new interest. It is safe to conclude that job loss has many serious negative consequences for individuals, families, and communities (e.g. Kasl, Gore, & Cobb, 1975; Kessler, House, & Turner, 1987; Liem & Liem, 1988; Payne, Warr, & Hartley, 1984; Perrucci et al., 1985; Rowley & Feather, 1987). From a downsizing perspective, however, the issue is not the effects *per se*, but how those effects can be ameliorated through the use of various interventions (e.g. outplacement, counseling, and training). Here again, there is a good descriptive, prescriptive, and normative literature, but little sound empirical research on the critical features of these interventions or even on their effectiveness. In addition, the nature of downsizing requires attention to the effects on survivors of the process. The maintenance of motivation and sentiments are key concerns. Moreoever, experience suggests that downsizing is not a one-time event, but a continuing process. Thus, the prolonged effects of job insecurity are also of concern. Although there has been some research and theory addressing survivor effects (e.g. Brockner et al., 1987; Brockner, 1988; Staw, Sandelands, & Dutton, 1981), relative to the amount of research on job loss, this problem has received far less attention.

Finally, we explicitly conceptualize downsizing as a process that proceeds from organizational level considerations to individual level impacts (Kozlowski et al., 1991). Although this is an assumption that is generally inherent in theory addressing downsizing strategies or the effects of downsizing on individuals, it is typically not explicitly specified in either the macro or micro oriented research. We also explicitly conceptualize the effects of downsizing processes on survivors as a critical factor in future organizational effectiveness. Although this assumption is represented in some theory (e.g. Greenhalgh, 1983a; Staw, Sandelands, & Dutton, 1981), it is not addressed in micro level research and is not well represented in macro level theory or research. We believe that by its very nature, the downsizing process incorporates cross-level and multi-level effects (Rousseau, 1985) which are emergent over time (Roberts, Hulin, & Rousseau, 1978). These theoretically based issues can provide a foundation for a more integrative perspective on downsizing.

A Conceptual Framework

Our characterization of the major limitations in the downsizing literature noted previously suggests three theoretically based themes that may provide a foundation for a more integrative conceptualization of downsizing related phenomena. These themes include: (i) a clarification of levels of conceptualization and explicit consideration of cross-level and multi-level effects; (ii) a sensitivity to downsizing as a process with explicit consideration of its temporal implications; and (iii) a clear distinction among different aspects of the downsizing process and the use of existing theory to further elaborate the nature of the phenomenon.

We have applied these themes to the central issues identified in the review to develop a conceptual framework of the downsizing process. We do not view the framework as a theory *per se*. Rather it is an heuristic designed to identify and organize relevant content issues, make salient critical theoretical processes, and provide a structure for integrating existing theoretical perspectives with issues of relevance to downsizing. Where possible, we draw upon the growing theory relevant to downsizing and related phenomena. However, we also draw upon broader theories and frameworks from psychology, sociology, and organizational behavior to elaborate neglected aspects of the process. Thus, the purpose of the framework is to stimulate and guide theoretical development and research that will have common conceptual underpinnings. We explicate the framework by first presenting an overview of the major processes conceptualized in the model. We then illustrate its utility by identifying new research directions.

The heuristic is illustrated in Figure 8.1. It begins at the organizational level with a focus on environmental sensing, intentional decision processes, and their implications. Sensing and interpretation of relevant environmental antecedents activates the decision process with respect to downsizing. Although the environment is composed of objective features and constraints that influence adaptation, sensing is regarded as a perceptual process.

Depending on the nature of the perceived environment, the organization

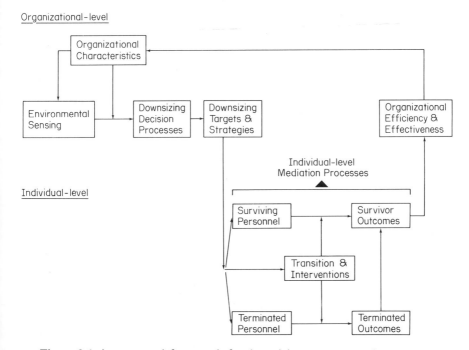

Figure 8.1 A conceptual framework for downsizing processes and outcomes

may refine or redefine its mission. This aspect of the downsizing decision has implications for the intensity of the process and the emphasis placed on workforce reduction versus work restructuring and redesign (Freeman & Cameron, in press). Independent of intensity and emphasis, the decision process may be represented by proactive, highly articulated planning or it may be reactive in form with little evidence for the use of carefully specified decision criteria (Kozlowski et al., 1991).

The framework indicates that the degree of articulation of the downsizing decision process is influenced by characteristics of the organization. Characteristics such as strategic leadership, HRM sophistication, and cultural values enable or support proactive decision processes. In their absence, decisions are more likely to be reactive in nature. The nature of the decision process leads directly to the selection of targets and strategies as described in the review. Continuing at the organizational level, target and strategy selection determines the effectiveness of the downsizing adaptation, given relevant environmental constraints.

We recognize, however, the critical importance of processes that occur at the group and especially the individual levels. The framework illustrates that the relationship between downsizing strategies and effectiveness at the organizational level is mediated by complex psychological processes at lower levels of conceptualization. The configuration of downsizing targets and strategies, their sequence over time, and the nature of their implementation (transition management issues), not only serve to create categories of 'survivors' and 'terminated personnel,' but also affect their perceptions, interpretations, and reactions. For terminated personnel and their families, the negative effects of job loss are well-documented. Many would insist that questions of organizational values and ethics ought to guide the treatment afforded to displaced employees. However, from a purely instrumental perspective, the ways in which an organization supports downsized personnel and the effects of job loss on displaced employees are meaningful vicarious information to downsizing survivors. Survivor reactions of fear, rigidity, loss of commitment, loss of motivation, and failure to innovate may occur at the very time when the organization is most in need of employee support.

Transition management decisions affect the provision and nature of interventions such as outplacement, counseling, and vocational training that are designed to ameliorate the negative effects of downsizing on individuals. The provision and perceived effectiveness of interventions for terminated personnel may affect survivors. Interventions for survivors may also attempt to facilitate their adjustment. Survivor reactions aggregate to influence group and organizational effectiveness. Thus, the position inherent in the framework is that we cannot comprehend the effects of variations in organizational downsizing without attention to processes that have their primary effects at the individual level and unfold over time.

Collective responses and firm performance effectiveness exhibit feedback linkages to organizational characteristics, which may change by virtue of the downsizing effort, and which ultimately affect the firm's adaptation to (perceived) environmental contingencies. The effects of downsizing unfold over time with relatively enduring impacts on the organization and on the individual lives affected by the downsizing process.

Directions for Theory and Research

The utility of this framework can be illustrated by using it to better integrate existing theory on downsizing, to incorporate new or alternative perspectives, and to suggest new or neglected research areas. The primary purpose here is to be broadly integrative, although specific directions for theory elaboration and research are suggested. We begin with a consideration of issues relevant to the organizational level and then address the transition to the individual level.

Environmental variation and the downsizing decision process

Antecedents of organizational change and adaptation accomplished through downsizing are assumed to be properties of the organizational environment (e.g. Weitzel & Jonsson, 1989). Although we assume that relevant environmental features such as economic conditions, competitor actions, and market demand are objective in nature, we take the position that environmental sensing and interpretation are perceptual processes with inherent cognitive biases (e.g. Downey & Slocum, 1975). Thus, the detection of environmental change and its meaning are internal phenomena; variation in detection and interpretation across organizations is anticipated. Some firms may anticipate the antecedents of change in advance of more normative detection, whereas others may lag well after others in the industry have attended to significant change (Weitzel & Jonsson, 1989). Moreover, the meaning of detected features is open to multiple interpretations, especially when the information is equivocal, as it often is (Terreberry, 1968). Thus, detected environmental antecedents are regarded as perceived conditions that provoke refinements of existing business strategy or its redefinition.

Although the literature review identified a broad array of downsizing antecedents, theory has suggested a smaller set of underlying dimensions of environmental variation that are relevant to sensing and interpretation. Zammuto and Cameron (1985), for example, developed a model based on a population ecology perspective of environmental change and organizational adaptation. Although this is a model of organizational decline that focuses on the carrying capacity of environmental niches, it provides a useful framework to represent the nature of perceived environmental turbulence that has relevance for downsizing decisions.

To summarize, Zammuto and Cameron (1985) propose two dimensions that characterize environmental variation, with different patterns of environmental variation related to appropriate forms of domain (i.e. business) strategy. One dimension refers to changes in niche size versus niche shape. The second dimension addresses whether the environmental variation is continuous versus discontinuous in nature (e.g. Tushman & Romanelli, 1985). Reductions in niche size indicate declining resources, reduced demand, or increased competition that require a lower level of organizational activities. Changes in niche shape indicate shifting preferences of external constituencies (society, clients, customers) such that existing organizational activities are no longer supported. Niche shape may evolve to support a modified set of organizational activities or the niche may cease to exist. Changes in size and shape may be incremental and continuous, with clear trends and indications of the change. Discontinuous change is a sudden, qualitative shift that is typically unpredictable.

Zammuto and Cameron (1985) combine these two dimensions of environmental variation into a fourfold typology with each cell representing a unique type of change—erosion, contraction, dissolution, and collapse. Adaptive domain strategies—offense, consolidation, creation, and substitution—are matched respectively to each type of decline. *Erosion* represents continuous changes in niche size that are best addressed with an offensive strategy. The idea is that the organization should focus on doing the same things, but better. This requires expanding markets, introducing new products, and working more efficiently. Doing so requires recruiting new skilled personnel and training existing personnel to improve skills. The workforce may or may not shrink over the long-term time-frame of this process. *Contraction* represents discontinuous changes in niche size that are addressed through a consolidation strategy. This requires increasing efficiency by scaling back operations that are peripheral, although the basic direction of the organization remains unchanged. Downsizing and workforce reductions will be evident in this domain strategy over the short term. *Dissolution* represents continuous changes in niche shape that fit a domain creation strategy. The organization must evolve to fit the changing niche through innovation. This requires an infusion of new competencies, skills, and knowledge and a reconfiguration of organizational structure, power, and jobs. *Collapse* represents discontinuous changes in niche shape that require a domain substitution strategy. The organization must enact a new niche, and quickly. This may be accomplished through mergers and acquisitions as the organization attempts to move into new areas of activity. In addition, existing assets representing the previous niche may be sold-off or written-off as the organization abandons the niche.

Although the model does not explicitly consider downsizing effects, the likely effects can be extrapolated (Ferris, Schellenberg, & Zammuto, 1984). Downsizing related processes that are inherent in the domain strategies are most evident under contraction and collapse. This is undoubtedly because conditions of discontinuous change shorten the time-frame and require more drastic and salient adaptive responses. However, the other forms of environmental variation, erosion and dissolution, may also require downsizing of personnel. Their associated domain strategies require the development of new organizational competencies and an infusion of new individual skills. To the extent that existing personnel cannot be retrained, they are likely to be replaced. Thus, some individuals may be affected by downsizing even when the organization as a whole does not shrink.

How does environmental variation affect the downsizing decision process? Interestingly, theory has not explicitly linked environmental change to the downsizing process. However, Freeman and Cameron (in press) have formulated a model of the downsizing decision process that is predicated on the distinction between two types of organizational change which they label convergence and reorientation, and which is based on the same theory of change (Tushman & Romanelli, 1985) incorporated in the decline model described above. In this instance the focus is on the form of the downsizing processes. Although not explicitly addressed in their downsizing model, the common underpinnings of the two models provide a basis for integration.

Convergence refers to incremental, evolutionary adaptation that is designed to improve performance efficiency as the organization pursues the same basic mission. It is a long-term process that is focused on improved consistency among internal activities and is mediated by middle management. With respect to downsizing, convergent adaptation is more likely to be associated with incrementalism, less drastic forms of workforce reduction, and emphasis on less complex revisions in work, technology, and structure.

In contrast, reorientation refers to radical or metamorphic adaptation that is intended to improve effectiveness through the pursuit of new strategies and goals. It is a short-term revolutionary shift in strategy, power, and control mediated by top management. In this context, downsizing is predicted to be discontinuous, more severe, and more complex. Under reorientation forms of downsizing, efforts to reconfigure the organization and redesign roles determine the nature of downsizing targets and strategies.

We suggest that changes in niche size are more likely to be related to convergent forms of downsizing, whereas changes in niche shape are more likely to be associated with downsizing via reorientation. Zammuto and Cameron (1985) suggest that changes in niche size are associated with forms of adjustment that focus on pursuing the same basic mission, but more efficiently. The time-frame associated with changes in niche size, determined by whether the change is continuous or discontinuous, affects the salience and severity of the downsizing process. Firms engaged in a domain offense strategy due to erosion may not shrink in aggregate, although selective downsizing may be used in the effort to enhance competencies. Organizations under conditions of contraction attempt to consolidate their domains. Thus, as these firms sell-off peripheral businesses, close obsolete and inefficient plants, and reduce surplus personnel, downsizing will be very much in evidence (Ferris, Schellenberg, & Zammuto, 1984).

In contrast, changes in niche shape imply domain strategies designed to shift the organization–environment niche. As the organization adapts to better fit an evolving (dissolution) or different (collapse) niche, it must modify its internal structure and mechanisms to maintain alignment. This internal adjustment process requires a reconfiguration of structure, power, and jobs. This is conceptually related to Freeman and Cameron's (in press) notion of downsizing via reorientation. The time-frame of environmental change is likely to affect the severity of downsizing as a mechanism to accomplish the shift in domain strategy. When engaged in a domain creation strategy due to environmental dissolution, reconfiguration efforts are more extended in time. Downsizing is likely to be more precisely targeted as part of the effort to infuse the firm with new competencies (Ferris, Schellenberg, & Zammuto, 1984) and may not even be apparent in aggregate. Under conditions of environmental collapse, the firm engages in domain substitution strategies designed to enact a new environment. The resulting mergers, acquisitions, and sell-offs will yield drastic and highly salient downsizing processes in the midst of major efforts of restructuring and redesign.

The role of organizational characteristics

A major conceptual issue with respect to downsizing decisions concerns whether the process is proactive or reactive in nature. Downsizing targets and strategies, transition management, and interventions represent choices that have implications for the outcomes of the overall process. Proactivity implies the judicious use of appropriate criteria at each stage of the process. The goal is to ensure that both stages of the process and its outcomes are consistent with the configuration of core competencies, individual capabilities, and sentiments needed to fulfill the organizational mission. Proactive downsizing means targeting superfluous organizational competencies, using strategies to minimize negative impacts while meeting organizational requirements, selecting individuals in such a manner as to preserve superior skills and yet maintain equity, and providing support and assistance for those who are terminated and those who remain. The careful planning that is reflected throughout this process will not only have direct effects on retained competencies and skills, it will also affect the psychological commitment of those who remain to fulfill the mission.

In contrast, reactive downsizing is conducted without concern for process and outcome consistency with business strategy, mission, and goals, or with requisite organizational culture and values. It is more typically associated with immediate efforts at cost containment. This may be prompted by decline pressures where the organization has failed to sense change, has failed to respond, or has responded inappropriately. Or it may reflect the absence of an explicit business strategy. In any case, reactive downsizing is generally associated with little effort to maintain critical competencies, the use of more drastic methods to accomplish downsizing, and more negative impacts on personnel. This is expected to have negative consequences for future organizational states (Kozlowski et al., 1991).

The integration of the Zammuto and Cameron (1985) and Freeman and Cameron (in press) models outlined above, while useful as a way to link environmental variation to forms of downsizing, is limited by its inherent determinism. Moreover, although the convergence and reorientation model of downsizing helps to resolve some of the inherent contradictions in the downsizing process (e.g. the simultaneous combination of downsizing and growth that may occur with the domain offense and domain creation strategies), some assumptions inherent in the model may not be tenable. The formulation assumes a relatively high degree of proaction and articulation among business strategy, downsizing decisions, and desired outcomes. Although this makes sense theoretically, the literature review indicates strongly that organizations often fail to undertake downsizing with any degree of articulated planning; they downsize reactively (McCune, Beatty, & Montagno, 1988). Indeed, empirical data collected by Cameron and his associates (Cameron, Freeman, & Mishra, 1991; Cameron, Mishra, & Freeman, 1992) indicates that reactive, poorly planned downsizing is the norm. In addition, interviews conducted with over 100 major corporate executives in the US indicate that proaction is the rare exception rather than the rule in downsizing (Harback & Craft, 1991). Nevertheless, the literature review also indicates that firms under similar environmental contingencies do not necessarily approach downsizing decisions in the same way. Clearly, some other factors influence whether organizations are proactive versus reactive in their downsizing decisions. This is a critical issue for the effectiveness of downsizing processes that has been neglected in both theory and research.

Our framework suggests that these factors are characteristics of the organization. The perspective taken here is that articulated downsizing decision processes require certain enabling features. When these features are present, downsizing is more likely to conform to the well-planned linkages suggested by theory. In the absence of one or more of these features, downsizing decisions are more likely to conform to the reactive forms of downsizing that are most frequently observed. We propose three characteristics that may serve in this capacity: the strategic leadership of the firm, HRM system sophistication, and organizational culture. We believe that these characteristics are likely to be the most relevant, although we do not propose that this list is exhaustive.

Strategic leadership pertains to the clarity and salience of the vision for the organization developed by top leaders (Hitt & Keats, 1992). Strategies imply planned future states as well as the tactics that are designed to move the firm in the desired direction. In the absence of a clear vision, firm responses are likely to be determined by short-term criteria that have no direct bearing on future states. Developing an effective strategy and adapting the strategy in response to environmental variation requires appropriate environmental sensing mechanisms. In the absence of sensing mechanisms, firms are likely to ignore or misperceive environmental variation. When their responses finally occur, often in the later stages of decline, they are more likely to be reactive in form (Weitzel & Jonsson, 1989). A clear strategic vision also provides evaluative criteria that may be used to preserve the distinctive competencies of the firm (Hitt & Keats, 1992). As a firm develops responses to address conditions of decline, the strategic vision provides a foundation for maintaining the critical leadership skills, technical skills, and less tangible values and sentiments that are consistent with its projected future.

If the strategic vision serves as a criterion, the HRM system serves as the operational mechanism for developing and managing a highly articulated downsizing process. First, the HRM function must be regarded as a strategic asset that is well integrated into high-level decision making within the firm (Jackson & Schuler, 1990). Second, the information potential of the HRM system must be sophisticated to enable precise targeting of surplus competencies and less effective individuals for downsizing and the preservation of necessary skills and high performers (Kozlowski, 1987). Third, the HRM system must have the operational capabilities to track inflows and outflows, retrain and upgrade skills, and manage the transition process (Ferris, Schellenberg, & Zammuto, 1984).

From a macro perspective, organizational culture is a property of the system. Micro perspectives, however, regard culture as a property inherent in the symbolic interactions and perceptions of organizational members; it provides a basis for collective response tendencies (Reichers & Schneider, 1990). Because downsizing is a highly salient symbolic event, it may have a dramatic impact on perceptions of culture. It may reinforce the prevailing culture and symbolize an adherence by the firm to the preservation of pivotal values. This is illustrated by the prior efforts of IBM to maintain its long-standing tradition of no layoffs and respect for the individual (Greenhalgh, McKersie, & Gilkey, 1985). However, downsizing may also symbolize a major shift in the prevailing culture when pivotal values are sacrificed. IBM's recent indications that the no-layoff tradition has ended signal a fundamental change in the nature of the organization. This has implications for the selection of downsizing targets and strategies at the organizational level, and for the collective reactions of organizational members.

When these enabling organizational characteristics are present, the organization is more likely to select downsizing targets and strategies that are proactive, regardless of whether downsizing is convergent or reorientating in form. This framework asserts that proactivity represents an effort to preserve or create requisite competencies and sentiments through the judicious selection of downsizing targets and strategies. From an applied research and theoretical perspective, we believe that the proposed moderators of proactive decision making represent the most pressing research need in the macro area of downsizing. The decision making process affects target and strategy selection with direct linkages to transition management. Thus, these issues bear directly on the individual level impacts on survivors and terminated personnel.

For terminated personnel, the interventions available to help people cope with job loss can significantly affect outcomes such as financial security, mental health, and the ability to find reemployment. Similarly, surviving organizational members benefit from interventions designed to ensure smooth transition and to minimize their fears of future downsizing. For survivors, the ability to cope with downsizing is not only influenced by the kinds of interventions designed to help them, but also by their perceptions of the adjustment of terminated personnel to job loss (Davy, Kinicki, & Scheck, 1991). How the organization treats terminated personnel serves as a forecast of the future if current survivors later become victims of downsizing. The survivors' personal outcomes from downsizing, and their perceptions of how the organization manages terminated personnel, can shape their motivation and job performance. In turn, the collective motivation and performance of survivors will affect the ability of the organization to address the environmental conditions that prompted downsizing.

At the individual level, more comprehensive research on downsizing can build on several existing theoretical perspectives. Despite the maturity of some micro research (e.g. job loss reactions; Eisenberg & Larzarsfeld, 1938), our view is that research at the individual level has been somewhat narrow. We need more research that considers the impacts of downsizing on long-term adjustment and career development, more fully examines the role of individual differences in adjustment, and better integrates this work with existing theoretical perspectives. With these issues in mind, we shift focus to the individual level. Three theoretical approaches are utilized to raise issues for future research; the life course, psychological adjustment, and work adjustment perspectives. To conclude, we consider changes in our conceptualization of organizational career success, and identify some unexplored international issues, raised by downsizing.

Life course theory

By nature, downsizing is a longitudinal phenomenon. In order to understand how downsizing is planned, implemented, and integrated into a repertoire of actions toward organizational improvement, we can approach it as a developmental process. One theoretical approach that explicitly embodies a time perspective is life course theory. Gade (1991) and Elder (1991) postulate that personal and historical life experiences will shape an individual's development. The life course represents a pattern of events that positions an individual for future opportunities or constraints. Historical events, family position, and the individual's personal place in time shape the life course to maintain a steady rate of development, or to redirect the life course along a new trajectory. Although life course theory is not a common framework for existing downsizing research, several studies have incorporated the theory's basic concepts. Brockner & Greenberg (1990) illustrate how survivors are influenced by the perceived justice of fairness of layoff decisions. Gaertner (1989) has examined how downsizing prompted a firm to reorganize and develop a new business strategy, which, in turn, shifted power and opportunities among functional units. Survivors' support for the new strategy depended on how they interpreted the change as being consistent with organizational history and traditional values. Thus, historical events are shown to influence survivor attitudes and behaviors. For individuals who lose jobs, the motivation to continue seeking reemployment may be determined by prior successes and setbacks (Caplan et al., 1989) or individual differences (Kinicki, 1989). In some instances, job loss may represent a positive career transition (Latack & Dozier, 1986). In directing future research, the life course perspective can be utilized to better understand downsizing effects on an individual's short- and long-term financial adjustment, psychological well-being, and family relationships.

An individual's previous financial history may influence how a current income loss or reduction is perceived. The financial adjustment for someone who has been terminated, transferred, or demoted may be easier if the individual has an erratic history of significant income gains and losses in contrast to someone who has experienced only steady income growth. Previous experiences with crises may help the individual to develop effective coping strategies (Kinicki & Latack, 1990). Conversely, an individual may interpret and react to similar crises in different ways depending on the particular life stage the person occupies during a crisis period (Schlossberg, 1984). The life course perspective provides a theoretical framework for understanding individual adjustment to successive changes in financial situations.

A second line of research can examine financial adjustment issues from a household perspective. If the individual's income represents most or all of the family/household income, adjustment may be more salient and encompassing than if the lost/reduced income was not critical to household functioning. Cohn (1978) and Shamir (1985a) have found greater adjustment problems for people who were primary breadwinners, although future research should extend their findings to determine how the relative size of the affected income and the stability of the income impact on the types of coping strategies employed. Elder and Caspi (1988) have demonstrated significant long-term effects of Great Depression job loss on the development history of the affected households.

Financial adjustments resulting from downsizing may also affect an individual's overall well-being. Although researchers such as Jahoda (1979) and Hamilton et al. (1990) have documented the effects of job loss on psychological well-being, life course theory can identify how historical events may influence reactions to downsizing. The increasing prevalence of downsizing may allow individuals to make more external attributions for their job loss. Thus, if the dismissal occurred during a period of massive and widespread downsizing, involuntarily terminated people may be able to support one another and find more government, organization, and personal resources to help them cope with job loss. This may be contrasted with initial downsizing cases when involuntary terminations were unique and fewer support systems were in place. Partial support for this relationship is found in the study by Cohn (1978), where internal attributions for job loss were associated with low local unemployment rates. However, an opposing proposition is that the larger number of involuntarily terminated people exacerbates the unemployment crisis and compounds the problems and stress of those looking for reemployment (Langerman, Byerly, & Root, 1982).

Not only can current business trends affect how individuals adjust to downsizing, but past historical events may also influence this adjustment. Jackson and Warr (1984) and Rowley and Feather (1987) found that the adjustment to job loss was hardest for those people in mid-career. However, it is unclear if the adjustment problems are tied to the middle-career stage, or if the problems are associated with the middle-age cohort of people who are now in mid-career. These individuals developed their careers from the 1950s through the 1990s; an age of prosperity. However, economic forecasters are predicting for the first time that the next generation of Americans will not enjoy a lifestyle that is better than the previous generation (Levy & Michel, 1991). Future mid-career people who experience economic adversity might be able to cope with downsizing better than today's mid-career cohort. The life course perspective can help researchers to separate the effects of historical events and career stages on the adjustment to downsizing. Practical applications of this research could utilize career stages, age cohort experiences, or a combination of both to identify downsizing interventions that would be appropriate for specific groups of people.

In addition to the individual's well-being, the life course perspective is easily extended to research family relationships. Young parents with small children have childcare responsibilities that may encumber the couple's attempts to recover from downsizing. In contrast, more established couples with teenage or adult children may be able to take advantage of their children's abilities to curtail expenses and generate their own incomes. From an applied perspective, research is needed to determine which interventions are most desirable for people in a particular family stage. For example, parents with small children may be most interested in extended health care benefits, whereas parents of college students may prefer supplemental unemployment compensation.

An individual's stage of family development may predict how well the family will adjust to downsizing and may highlight the need for different interventions to aid in the coping process. In addition, life course theory can also explain how downsizing may amplify or trigger life events. Major life events such as marriage, divorce, and even suicide can result from changes in an individual's well-being that are profoundly influenced by downsizing (Elder & Caspi, 1988). The prolonged effects of unemployment or job insecurity impact psychological stages and behaviors such as domestic violence and alcohol/drug abuse (Feather, 1990).

Our review indicated that the critical features of intervention programs are not well specified. Research directed by the life course perspective would emphasize the interactions between work and nonwork events and their impact on individual adjustment and future development. The practical implications would be the identification of intervention features appropriate for individuals with particular needs at different stages of the life course.

Psychological adjustment perspective

Theories of psychological adjustment have focused on how unemployed individuals cope with job loss. Although most of the current research examines reactions or coping outcomes of terminated personnel, research ought also to examine negative reactions of survivors and the role of individual differences. News of impending downsizing could cause a slow-down in work pace, sabotage of work output, or higher incidences of absenteeism, tardiness, and employee theft (Isabella, 1989). Thus, emotional reactions to downsizing strategies could trigger negative expressions of behavior as well as positive coping mechanisms.

- Survivor reactions are probably influenced by the extent to which downsizing directly affects them. Survivors personally affected by downsizing might have stronger reactions than survivors who are protected. Individuals who are potential candidates for termination, or who have to take proactive measures to protect their jobs, are likely to experience more job insecurity, uncertainty, and negative consequences than organizational members who are nonparticipating spectators of the downsizing process. However, the rationale for protecting certain jobs may influence vicarious learning by downsizing spectators. Individuals whose jobs are protected because they are personally indispensable to the organization would perceive more job security than individuals whose jobs are protected because of impersonal reasons, such as sparing a targeted plant from closure. To date, we know of no research examining the effects of downsizing on survivors who differ in their depths of involvement with specific downsizing strategies.

Reactions to downsizing strategies are influenced by the attributions people make about their situations (Mowday, 1981). For individuals who are involuntarily terminated, attribution theory predicts more difficult adjustments for those making internal attributions rather than external attributions to explain their job loss (Prussia, Kinicki, & Bracker, in press). For example, if the individual believes his/her effort or performance level is not high enough to merit retention, efforts to find reemployment may be discouraged. Attributions regarding downsizing decisions also affect the achievement motivation and work attitudes of survivors. The theory predicts harder adjustments for survivors making external attributions about layoff decisions. For example, if the individual attributes his/her survivor status to luck or chance factors, there may be little motivation to work hard for an organization that does not recognize individual merit.

In addition to the attributions people make about downsizing decisions, distinct downsizing targets may react differently to similar decisions. Since 1950, the ratio of blue- and white-collar workers has shifted to represent an increasing proportion of white-collar workers. Recently, downsizing has focused more on the white-collar group, in an attempt to restore a more efficient ratio of production to nonproduction personnel. Thus, the reduction of white-collar jobs reflects a permanent shift back to smaller staffs of nonproduction workers (Tomasko, 1990). Under these circumstances, the likelihood of regaining similar employment may be significantly lower for laid-off white-collar workers than for their blue-collar counterparts. Furthermore, even under conditions of economic growth, organizations may be more willing to hire back production personnel before they expand nonproduction personnel.

The effects of downsizing may differ on other demographic dimensions. Women and minorities generally have less work experience than white males and may be more likely to face uncertainty and stress during downsizing. London and Greller (1991) document how these groups are growing in their proportional share of the labor force, yet most of the research has been conducted on samples of white males (Leana & Feldman, 1991). Currently, there is some evidence to suggest that women are more likely to accept part-time work and job-sharing alternatives; however, antecedents to these decisions are unclear. Furthermore, reasons that explain why women work (e.g. primary breadwinner, supplemental income, or interest in work itself) may be more predictive of acceptable reemployment options rather than gender itself.

In addition to research examining gender and race differences, cultural backgrounds could affect adjustment to job loss or income reduction. For example, cultural expectations that a man should provide for his family could intensify psychological adjustment problems for men and their families. Societal expectations based on old rules may make the adjustment to new roles more difficult. The expectations of friends and family may make it difficult for an individual to adjust to an unemployed status or to a degraded work role. Bennett (1990) describes how one individual maintained for his family an illusion of employment by dressing professionally and leaving and returning home according to the former work schedule. Other cases illustrate the difficult adjustment to new work roles when they are significantly inferior to previous jobs (Schlenker & Gutek, 1987). Identifying individual differences that affect coping behaviors is a critical step in understanding which interventions can be most useful. In addition, the manner by which organizations redesign jobs and revise work expectations will also affect coping behaviors of survivors and potential future strategies of downsizing.

Work adjustment perspective

Research on job design can be applied to downsizing situations. Hackman and Oldham (1980) illustrate how individuals with high growth need strength can respond positively to enriched jobs. Downsizing strategies that remove layers of management have the potential to enrich prevailing jobs by increasing the span of control for surviving managers and empowering more employees with decision-making authority (Greenberger & Strasser, 1986). These changes may enhance a survivor's position in the organization and allow the individual to broaden his/her influence on other organizational levels and functions.

Conversely, changes that do not enrich current jobs or that overload survivors are likely to result in negative consequences. The job enlargement literature documents how role overload or increases in similar duties may result in stress and dissatisfaction (Herzberg, 1982). When survivors are required to maintain high performance levels and to take on the workloads of laid-off coworkers, the results can be negative for both the survivors and the organization (Byrne, 1988a,b; Tombaugh & White, 1990). From a job enrichment or enlargement perspective, research examining the adjustment to work redesign begins at the level of individual interpretation, progresses to the work group reaction level, and aggregates to encompass organizational effectiveness.

In addition to the way organizations restructure jobs, research should examine how survivors redesign their own jobs. Individuals often expand their organizational role beyond formal job requirements in order to enhance their positions (Ilgen & Hollenbeck, 1991). After downsizing, survivors could change their roles in order to protect themselves from future layoffs. These changes may not serve organizational goals, but represent proactive career plans to protect one's job security and maximize opportunities for advancement. Examples of these behaviors include setting easy goals to establish a record of success, increasing specialization to become an indispensable expert, failing to document actions or procedures in order to become an essential resource, and refusing to cooperate with others in order to protect one's area of control (Hall & Mansfield, 1971). These examples illustrate how individual career goals and organizational goals may become less compatible under downsizing.

Although the examples above have negative implications for the organization, some qualitative research has shown how survivor and organizational goals may be more congruent. Bennett (1990) describes some survivors who enjoyed more responsibility and less supervision after downsizing. The consolidation/decentralization of functions can empower survivors to break down traditional management practices and to encourage communication among different organizational units in order to achieve superordinate goals

(Tomasko, 1990). Furthermore, surviving organizational members may be more accountable for larger work tasks. The added responsibility motivates some survivors to seek appropriate training or help in order to ensure that their performance meets expectations.

Research on work adjustment has been focused at the individual level. However, a larger systems perspective is needed to understand how downsizing decisions are linked to job redesign and how performance in these redesigned jobs impacts organizational effectiveness. At the macro level, proactive versus reactive decision making and convergence versus reorientation forms of downsizing influence the extent to which the organization formally redesigns jobs, using enrichment or enlargement. Furthermore, these downsizing decision processes are likely to facilitate or block individual attempts to enrich work roles and behaviors to protect job security.

Changing conceptions of jobs and careers

Apart from the three general research perspectives, theory and research should begin to explore changing conceptualizations of jobs and how they relate to broader career systems. Davis and Wacker (1988) posit that modern job design should consider how formal job contents define interacting roles that satisfy organizational productivity needs as well as individual career needs. Successful job design would meet both organizational and individual needs and allow flexibility to adapt to changing environments.

The prevalence of organizational downsizing and the repeated use of downsizing strategies may force a change in our concepts of work and job security. Downsizing, especially involuntary terminations, breaks employee expectations of lifelong employment or expectations that good performance will always be rewarded. This trend may finalize the death of the 'organization man' concept and force recognition of a multiorganizational career as the new norm (Bennett, 1990). In addition, the growing number of downsizing organizations and those with zero or low growth projections may dramatically increase the number of people experiencing career plateaus (Chao, 1990). This trend may force a reconceptualization of the definition of career success apart from advancement up the organizational hierarchy. If more people are able to define career success without the traditional advancement standard, new definitions could have a profound impact on how future career goals are identified, how motivation is determined, and how people derive satisfaction from their jobs and careers. Drucker (1986) argues for a shift away from a hierarchical chain-of-command focus to a new structure that emphasizes knowlege and competence. Thus, career success would not be based on promotions, but on what the individual knows and can accomplish. Such a change would relegate the managerial hierarchy to a support function for knowledge workers. This would require fundamental changes in organizational values, job responsibilities, and rewards.

Proposals such as Drucker's clearly illustrate the linkage between individual perceptions and reactions to work and their effects on the organization's design of jobs, career paths, and organizational reward systems. The pervasive impact of downsizing on organizations and its implications for our conceptions of career success may be among the most profound legacies of the phenomenon.

International perspective

Beyond the heuristic presented in Figure 8.1, future research should also examine downsizing in other cultures. Most of the current research on organizational downsizing has been conducted in US companies, and most of the research on job loss has been conducted in the UK, the US, and Australia. Clearly, more research is needed to understand the phenomenon in other countries, particularly those without Western European origins. Cultural differences may identify different downsizing strategies and targets than those found in the US. For example, countries such as Germany and Czechoslovakia have previously encouraged the immigration of foreign workers from countries such as Turkey and North Vietnam. Current privatization efforts have downsized many organizations, and an initial strategy to repatriate foreign workers is planned before citizens are involuntarily terminated (D. Maletic, personal communication, 18 June, 1991). In Japan, large corporations have close ties with their supplier companies. This relationship has allowed these corporations to 'transfer' excess personnel to jobs within the supplier firms. In addition, young single women constitute a flexible labor supply; Japanese society typically expects women to marry and resign from the workforce around the age of 25 (Carney & O'Kelly, 1987). Finally, Canada's government interventions specify joint labor–management councils for outplacement purposes (Batt, 1983). Thus, government, organizational, and societal customs in other countries recognize downsizing strategies that are not feasible in the US.

In addition to researching how other countries develop strategies and interventions that differ from the US, more research is needed to understand how US strategies and downsizing targets may be inapplicable in foreign venues. For example, the surge toward privatization in Central Europe occurs in a setting where governments and businesses have very limited financial resources. Thus, the common US strategy of buying-out personnel, or offering generous early retirement packages, is not possible because there are no funds for this strategy. In addition, early retirements may be difficult in Asian countries that show a great deal of respect and reverence for older citizens.

SUMMARY

A review of the organizational literature was conducted to compile current research and applied knowledge relevant to organizational downsizing. Our conceptualization of organizational downsizing defines it as a managerial action designed to increase the organization's efficiency and productivity by reducing human resources in targeted functions or locations. The reviewed literature focuses on the effects of downsizing on both terminated and surviving personnel, as well as on specific strategies and interventions associated with the downsizing process. In addition, a heuristic for future research recognizes both organizational and individual levels that can be used to examine downsizing. Suggested directions for future research were proposed to address limitations identified in the review and to extend theoretical models of downsizing. Finally, we emphasize that individual and organizational levels should be integrated and studied within a longitudinal perspective in order to fully capture the antecedents, processes, and outcomes of organizational downsizing.

ACKNOWLEDGMENT

We gratefully acknowledge the financial support provided for this project by the US Army Research Institute for the Social and Behavioral Sciences (Battelle Scientific Services Contract No. DAAL03-86-D-0001). The views contained in this chapter are those of the authors and should not be construed as an official Department of the Army position, policy, or decision unless so designated by other documentation.

Correspondence concerning this chapter should be directed to Steve W. J. Kozlowski, Department of Psychology, Michigan State University, East Lansing, MI 48824-1117, USA.

REFERENCES

Adams, R. J. (1985) Should works councils be used as industrial relations policy? *Monthly Labor Review*, July, pp. 25–29.

Adizes, I. (1979) Organizational passages: Diagnosing and treating life cycle problems in organizations. *Organizational Dynamics*, 7(2), 3–24.

Addison, J. T., & Portugal, P. (1987) The effect of advance notification of plant closings on unemployment. *Industrial and Labor Relations Review*, 41, 3–16.

Appelbaum, S. H., Simpson, R., & Shapiro, B. T. (1987) The tough test of downsizing. *Organizational Dynamics* 16(2), 68–79.

Ashford, S. J. (1988) Individual strategies for coping with stress during organizational transitions. *Journal of Applied Behavioral Science*, 24, 19–36.

Ashton, P. J., & Iadicola, P. (1989) The differential impact of a plant closing on the reemployment and income patterns of displaced blue- and white-collar employees. *Sociological Focus*, 22(2), 119–142.

Atkinson, T., Liem, R., & Liem, J. H. (1986) The social costs of unemployment: Implications for social support. *Journal of Health and Social Behavior*, 27, 317–331.

Barbee, G. E. (1989) How, when to tell employees they don't have a job for life. *Pension World*, October, pp. 33–34.

Barkhaus, R. S., & Meek, C. L. (1982) A practical view of outplacement counseling. *Personnel Administrator*, March, pp. 77–81.

Batt, W. L., Jr. (1983) Canada's good example with displaced workers. *Harvard Business Review*, July, pp. 6–11, 20, 22.

Baum, A., Fleming, R., & Reddy, D. M. (1986) Unemployment stress: Loss of control, reactance and learned helplessness. *Social Science Medicine*, 22, 509–516.

Bearak, J. A. (1982) Termination made easier: Is outplacement really the answer? *Personnel Administrator*, April, pp. 63–71, 99.

Bennett, A. (1990) *The Death of the Organization Man.* New York: Simon & Schuster.

Bennett, A. (1991) Downsizing doesn't necessarily bring an upswing in corporate profiability. *Wall Street Journal* 6 June, p. B1.

Benson, T. E. (1990a) Executives get a second wind. *Industry Week*, 2 July, pp. 11–18.

Benson, T. E. (1990b) Outplacement does an about-face. *Industry Week*, 4 June, pp. 15–18.

Bolton, W., & Oatley, K. (1987) A longitudinal study of social support and depression in unemployed men. *Psychological Medicine*, 17, 453–460.

Brammer, L. M., & Humberger, F. E. (1984) *Outplacement and Inplacement Counseling.* Englewood Cliffs, NJ: Prentice-Hall.

Brenner, S. O., & Bartell, R. (1983) The psychological impact of unemployment: A structural analysis of cross-sectional data. *Journal of Occupational Psychology*, 56, 129–136.

Bridges, W. (1986) Managing organizational transitions. *Organizational Dynamics*, 15(1), 24–33.

Brockner, J. (1988) The effects of work layoffs on survivors: Research, theory, and practice. *Research in Organizational Behavior*, 10, 213–255.

Brockner, J. (1990) Scope of justice in the workplace: How survivors react to co-worker layoffs. *Journal of Social Issues*, 46, 95–106.

Brockner, J., Davy, J., & Carter, C. (1985) Layoffs, self-esteem, and survivor guilt: Motivational, affective and attitudinal consequences. *Organizational Behavior and Human Decision Processes*, 36, 229–244.

Brockner, J., DeWitt, R. L., Grover, S., & Reed, T. (1990) When it is especially important to explain why: Factors affecting the relationship between managers' explanations of a layoff and survivors' reactions to the layoff. *Journal of Experimental Social Psychology*, 26, 389–407.

Brockner, J., & Greenberg, J. (1990) The impact of layoffs on survivors: An organizational justice perspective. In J. Carroll (ed.), *Applied Social Psychology and Organizational Settings* (pp. 45–75). Hillsdale, NJ: Erlbaum.

Brockner, J., Greenberg, J., Brockner, A., Bortz, J., Davy, J., & Carter, C. (1986) Layoffs, equity theory, and work performance: Further evidence of the impact of survivor guilt. *Academy of Management Journal*, 29, 373–384.

Brockner, J., Grover, S. L., & Blonder, M. D. (1988) Predictors of survivor's job involvement following layoffs: A field study. *Journal of Applied Psychology*, 73, 436–442.

Brockner, J., Grover, S., Reed, T. F., & DeWitt, R. L. (1992) Layoffs, job insecurity, and survivor's work effort: Evidence of an inverted-U relationship. *Academy of Management Journal*, 35, 413–425.

Brockner, J., Grover, S., Reed, T., DeWitt, R., & O'Malley, M. (1987) Survivors' reactions to layoffs: We get by with a little help from our friends. *Administrative Science Quarterly*, 32, 526–541.

Brockner, J., Konovsky, M., Cooper-Schneider, R., & Folger, R. (1991) The interactive effects of procedural justice and outcome negativity on victims and survivors of job loss. Manuscript submitted for publication.

Brockner, J., Tyler, T. R., & Cooper-Schneider, R. (1991) The influence of prior commitment to an institution on reactions to perceived unfairness: The higher they are, the harder they fall. Manuscript submitted for publication.

Brockner, J., Wiesenfeld, B. M., Reed, T., Grover, S., & Martin, C. (1991) The interactive effects of job content and context on the reactions of layoff survivors. Manuscript submitted for publication.

Brockner, J., Wiesenfeld, B., Stephan, J., Grover, S., Reed, T. F., DeWitt, R. L., & Hurley, R. (1991) A social influence analysis of survivors' reactions to layoffs: Evidence from the laboratory and the field. Manuscript submitted for publication.

Brown, J. M. (1990) Transition management: A micro perspective and practice issues. Paper presented at the Fifth Annual Conference of Society for Industrial and Organizational Psychology, Miami, FL, April.

Buch, K., & Aldridge, J. (1991) O.D. under conditions of organization decline. *Organization Development Journal*, **9**(1), 1–5.

Bureau of National Affairs (1982) *Layoffs, RIFs, and EEO in the public sector.* Washington, DC: Author.

Burke, R. J. (1984) The closing at Canadian Admiral: Correlates of individual well-being sixteen months after shutdown. *Psychological Reports*, **55**, 91–98.

Burke, R. J. (1985) Comparison of experiences of men and women following a plant shutdown. *Psychological Reports*, **57**, 59–66.

Burke, R. J. (1986) Reemployment on a poorer job after a plant closing. *Psychological Reports*, **58**, 559–570.

Buss, T. F., & Redburn, F. S. (1987) Plant closings: Impacts and responses. *Economic Development Quarterly*, **1**, 170–177.

Byrne, J. A. (1988a) Caught in the middle. *Business Week*, 12 September, pp. 80–88.

Byrne, J. A. (1988b) The rebel shaking up Exxon. *Business Week*, 18 July, pp. 104–107, 110–111.

Cameron, K. S., Freeman, S. J., & Mishra, A. K. (1991) Best practices in white-collar downsizing: Managing contradictions. *Academy of Management Executive*, **5**(3), 57–73.

Cameron, K. S., Mishra, A. K., & Freeman, S. J. (1992) Organizational downsizing. In G. P. Huber & W. H. Glick (eds), *Organizational Change and Redesign.* New York: Oxford University Press.

Cameron, K. S., Kim, M. U., & Whetten, D. A. (1987) Organizational effects of decline and turbulence. *Administrative Science Quarterly*, **32**, 222–240.

Cameron, K. S., Sutton, R. I., & Whetten, D. A. (1988) *Readings in Organizational Decline: Frameworks, Research, and Prescriptions.* Boston, MA: Ballinger.

Cameron, K. S., & Whetten, D. A. (1981) Perceptions of organizational effectiveness over organizational life cycles. *Administrative Science Quarterly*, **26**, 525–544.

Cameron, K. S., Whetten, D. A., & Kim, M. U. (1987) Organizational dysfunctions of decline. *Academy of Management Journal*, **30**, 126–138.

Cameron, K. S., & Zammuto, R. (1983) Matching managerial strategies to conditions of decline. *Human Resource Management*, **22**, 359–375.

Caplan, R. D., Vinokur, A. D., Price, R. H. & van Ryn, M. (1989) Job seeking, reemployment, and mental health: A randomized field experiment in coping with job loss. *Journal of Applied Psychology*, **74**, 759–769.

Carney, J. D. (1987) Downsizing government: Iowa's challenge. *Journal of State Government*, July, pp. 183–190.

Carney, L. S., & O'Kelly, C. G. (1987) Barriers and constraints to the recruitment and mobility of female managers in the Japanese labor force. *Human Resources Management*, **26**, 193–216.

Carver, C. S., Scheier, M. F., & Weintraub, J. K. (1989) Assessing coping strategies:

A theoretically based approach. *Journal of Personality and Social Psychology*, **56**, 267–283.

Castro, F. G., Romero, G. J., & Cervantes, R. C. (1987) Long-term stress among Latino women after a plant closure. *Sociology and Social Research*, **71**, 85–88.

Chao, G. T. (1990) Exploration of the conceptualization and measurement of career plateau: A comparative analysis. *Journal of Management*, **16**, 181–193.

Chao, G. T., & Kozlowski, S. W. J. (1986) Employee perceptions on the implementation of robotic manufacturing technology. *Journal of Applied Psychology*, **71**, 70–76.

Chell, E. (1985) Handling redundancy situations—an exploratory survey. *Employment Relations*, **7**, 22–26.

Cochran, D. S., Hinckle, T. W., & Dusenberry, D. (1987) Designing a developmental assessment center in a government agency: A case study. *Public Personnel Management*, **16**, 145–152.

Cohn, R. M. (1978) The effect of employment status change on self-attitudes. *Social Psychology*, **41**(2), 81–93.

Colosi, M. L. (1989) WARN: Hazardous to HR health? *Personnel*, April, pp. 59–67.

Colvard, J. E. (1986) Cut out: The ultimate cutback management. *The Bureaucrat*, Spring, pp. 6–8.

Cornfield, D. B. (1983) Chances of layoff in a corporation: A case study. *Administrative Science Quarterly*, **28**, 503–520.

Cortes-Comerer, N. (1986) A venerable giant sharpens its claws. *IEEE Spectrum*, February, pp. 54–65.

Curtis, R. L., Jr. (1989) Cutbacks, management and human relations: Meanings for organizational theory and research. *Human Relations*, **42**, 671–689.

Davis, J., & Rodela, E. S., Jr. (1990) Mid-career transition. *Prevention in Human Services*, **8**, 205–218.

Davis, L. E., & Wacker, G. J. (1988) Job design. In S. Gael (ed.) *The Job Analysis Handbook for Business, Industry, and Government*, Vol. I (pp. 157–172). New York: Wiley.

Davy, J. A., Kinicki, A. J., & Scheck, C. L. (1991) Developing and testing a model of survivor responses to layoffs. *Journal of Vocational Behavior*, **38**, 302–317.

Dean, R., & Prior, D. W. (1986) Your company could benefit from a no-layoff policy. *Training and Development Journal*, August, pp. 38–41.

Debow, Y. (1987) GE: Easing the pain of layoffs. *Management Review*, **76**, 15–18.

Desktop America (1991) *The Economist*, 2 February, p. 66.

Dickens, L. (1985) Industrial tribunals—The people's courts? *Employee Relations*, **7**(1), 27–32.

Dooley, D., & Catalano, R. (1980) Economic change as a cause of behavioral disorder, *Psychological Bulletin*, **87**, 450–468.

Dooley, D., & Catalano, R. (1984a) The epidemiology of economic stress. *American Journal of Community Psychology*, **12**, 387–409.

Dooley, D., & Catalano, R. (1984b) Why the economy predicts help-seeking: A test of competing explanations. *Journal of Health and Social Behavior*, **25**, 160–176.

Dooley, D., & Catalano, R. (1988) Recent research on the psychological effects of UE. *Journal of Social Issues*, **44**, 1–12.

Dooley, D., Catalano, R., & Rook, K. S. (1988) Personal and aggregate unemployment and psychological symptoms. *Journal of Social Issues*, **44**, 107–123.

Dooley, D., Rook, K., & Catalano, R. (1987) Job and non-job stressors and their moderators. *Journal of Occupational Psychology*, **60**, 115–132.

Downey, K. H., & Slocum, J. W. (1975) Uncertainty: Measures, research and sources of variation. *Academy of Management Journal*, **18**, 562–578.

Drucker, P. (1986) Good bye to the old personnel department. *Wall Street Journal*, 22 May, p. A30.

Ehrenberg, R. G., & Jakubson, G. H. (1989) Advance notification of plant closing: Does it matter? *Industrial Relations*, 28, 60–71.

Eisenberg, P., & Lazarsfeld, P. F. (1938) The psychological effects of unemployment. *Psychological Bulletin*, 35, 358–390.

Elder, G. H., Jr (1991) Life course. In E. F. Borgatta & M. L., Borgatta (eds), *The Encyclopedia of Sociology*. New York: Macmillan.

Elder, G. H., & Caspi, A. (1988) Economic stress in lives: Developmental perspectives. *Journal of Social Issues*, 44, 25–45.

Ellig, B. R. (1983) Pay policies while downsizing the organization: A systematic approach. *Personnel*, May–June, pp. 26–35.

Feather, N. T. (1989a) The effects of unemployment on work values and motivation. In U. W. Klienbeck, H. H. Quast, H. Thierry, & H. Hacker (eds), *Work Motivation* (pp. 201–227). Hillsdale, NJ: Erlbaum.

Feather, N. T. (1989b) Reported changes in behaviour after job loss in a sample of older unemployed men. *Australian Journal of Psychology*, 41, 175–185.

Feather, N. T. (1990) *The Psychological Impact of Unemployment*. New York: Springer-Verlag.

Feather, N. T., & Barber, J. G. (1983) Depressive reactions and unemployment. *Journal of Abnormal Psychology*, 92, 185–195.

Feather, N. T., & Davenport, P. R. (1981) Unemployment and depressive affect: A motivational and attributional analysis. *Journal of Personality and Social Psychology*, 41, 422–436.

Feather, N. T., & O'Brien, G. E. (1986) A longitudinal study of the effects of employment and unemployment on school-leavers. *Journal of Occupational Psychology*, 59, 121–144.

Feldacker, B. (1990) *Labor Guide to Labor Law* (3rd edn). Englewood Cliffs, NJ: Prentice-Hall.

Feldman, D. C. (1988a) Helping displaced workers: The UAW–GM human resource center. *Personnel*, March, pp. 34–36.

Feldman, D. C. (1988b) Hope for displaced workers when a plant closes. *Management Review*, 77, April, 16–18.

Feldman, D. C., & Leana, C. R. (1989) Managing layoffs: Experience at the Challenger disaster site and the Pittsburgh steel mills. *Organizational Dynamics*, pp. 52–64.

Feldman, L. (1989) Duracell's first aid for downsizing survivors. *Personnel Journal*, August, pp. 91–94.

Ferris, G. R., Schellenberg, D. A., & Zammuto, R. F. (1984) Human resource management strategies in declining industries. *Human Resource Management*, 23, 381–394.

Fineman, S. (1983) *White Collar Unemployment: Impact and Stress*. Chichester: Wiley.

Forbes, D. (1987) A consensus on helping idled workers. *Business Month*, March, pp. 54–56.

Ford, J. D. (1980a) The administrative component in growing and declining organizations: A longitudinal analysis. *Academy of Management Journal*, 23, 615–630.

Ford, J. D. (1980b) The occurrence of structural hysteresis in declining organizations. *Academy of Management Review*, 5, 589–598.

Fox, S. (1979) Workers' apprehensions due to plant relocation. *Psychological Reports*, 45, 327–332.

Fox, S., & Krausz, M. (1987) Correlates of relocation intention and emotional responses to an Israeli plant relocation. *Journal of Occupational Behaviour*, 8, 325–338.

Franzem, J. J. (1987) Easing the pain. *Personnel Administrator*, January, pp. 48–55.

Freeman, J. (1979) Going to the well: School district administrative intensity and environmental constraint. *Administrative Science Quarterly*, **24**, 119–133.

Freeman, J., & Hannan, M. T. (1975) Growth and decline processes in organizations. *American Sociological Review*, **40**, 215–228.

Freeman, S. J., & Cameron, K. S. (in press) Organizational downsizing: A convergence and reorientation framework. *Organizational Science*.

Frohlich, D. (1983) Economic deprivation, work orientation and health: Conceptual ideas and some empirical findings. In J. John, D. Schwefel, & H. Zollner (eds), *Influence of Economic Instability on Health* (pp. 293–320). Berlin: Springer-Verlag.

Fulmer, W. E., & Fryman, C. (1985) A managerial guide to outplacement services. *SAM Advanced Management Journal*, **50**, 10–12.

Gade, P. A. (1991) Military service and the life-course perspective: A turning point for military personnel research. *Military Psychology*, **3**(4), 187–199.

Gaertner, K. N. (1989) Winning and losing: Understanding managers' reactions to strategic change. *Human Relations*, **42**, 527–546.

Gall, A. L. (1986) What is the role of HRD in a merger? *Training and Development Journal*, April, pp. 18–23.

Ganster, D. C., Fusilier, M. R., & Mayes, B. T. (1986) Role of social support in the experience of stress at work. *Journal of Applied Psychology*, **71**, 102–110.

Garry, G., & Votapka, T. (1990) Oki cuts U.S. staff, closes four offices. *Electronic Buyer's News*, 3 December, pp. 1, 41.

General Accounting Office. (1978) *Personnel Restrictions and Cutbacks in Executive Agencies: Need for Caution*. Washington, DC: Author. (NTIS No. PB78276701).

General Accounting Office. (1983) *Retrenchment and Redirection at the Office of Personnel Management*. Washington, DC: Author. (NTIS No. PB83257493).

General Accounting Office. (1989) *Dislocated Workers: Labor–Management Committees Enhance Reemployment Assistance*. Report to the Committee on Education and Labor, House of Representatives. Washington, DC: Author. (NTIS No. PB89223485).

Gerpott, T. J. (1990) Intracompany job transfers: An exploratory two-sample study of the buffering effects of interpersonal support. *Prevention in Human Services*, **8**, 113–137.

Gibson, W. D. (1985) Union Carbide: Restructuring under stress. *Chemical Week*, 27 November, pp. 94–97.

Gibson, W. D., Hibbs, M., & Pitman, F. (1986) A labor union wields 'PR' weapons. *Chemical Week*, 22 January, p. 57.

Gilmore, T., & Hirschhorn, L. (1983) Management challenges under conditions of retrenchment. *Human Resource Management*, **22**, 341–357.

Gore, S. (1978) The effect of social support in moderating the health consequences of unemployment. *Journal of Health and Social Behavior*, **19**, 157–165.

Greenberg, E. R. (1988) Downsizing and worker assistance: Latest AMA survey results. *Personnel*, November, pp. 49–53.

Greenberger, D. B., & Strasser, S. (1986) Development and application of a model of personal control in organizations. *Academy of Management Review*, **11**, 164–177.

Greenhalgh, L. (1982) Maintaining organizational effectiveness during organizational retrenchment. *Journal of Applied Behavioral Science*, **18**, 155–170.

Greenhalgh, L. (1983a) Managing the job insecurity crisis. *Human Resource Management*, **22**, 431–444.

Greenhalgh, L. (1983b) Organizational decline. In S. B. Bacharach (ed.), *Research in the Sociology of Organizations*, vol. 2. Greenwich, CT: JAI Press.

Greenhalgh, L., & Jick, T. D. (1989) Survivor sense making and reactions to organizational decline. *Management Communication Quarterly*, **2**, 305–327.

Greenhalgh, L., Lawrence, A. T., & Sutton, R. I. (1988) Determinants of workforce reduction strategies in declining organizations. *Academy of Management Review*, **13**, 241–254.

Greenhalgh, L., & McKersie, R. B. (1980) Cost-effectiveness of alternative strategies for cut-back management. *Public Administration Review*, **40**, 575–584.

Greenhalgh, L., McKersie, R. B., & Gilkey, R. W. (1985) Rebalancing the workforce at IBM: A case study of redeployment and revitalization. *Organizational Dynamics*, **14**(4), 30–47.

Greenhalgh, L., & Rosenblatt, Z. (1984) Job insecurity: Toward conceptual clarity. *Academy of Management Review*, **9**, 438–448.

Grier, P. (1990) Shaving the force. *Government Executive*, April, pp. 36–39.

Grosman, B. A. (1989) Corporate loyalty, does it have a future? *Journal of Business Ethics*, **8**, 565–568.

Hackman, J. R., & Oldham, G. R. (1980) *Work Redesign*. Reading, MA: Addison-Wesley.

Halcrow, A. (ed). (1985) For your information: A tale of three companies. *Personnel Journal*, September, pp. 14, 19.

Hall, D. T., & Mansfield, R. (1971) Organizational and individual response to external stress. *Administrative Science Quarterly*, **16**, 533–546.

Hamermesh, D. S. (1989) What do we know about worker displacement in the U.S.? *Industrial Relations*, **28**, 51–59.

Hamilton, V. L., Broman, C. L., Hoffman, W. S., & Renner, D. S. (1990) Hard times and vulnerable people: Initial effects of plant closing on autoworkers' mental health. *Journal of Health and Social Behavior*, **31**, 123–140.

Hannan, M. T., & Freeman, J. (1978) Internal politics of growth and decline. In M. W. Meyer & Associates (eds), *Environment and Organizations* (pp. 177–199). San Francisco, CA: Jossey-Bass.

Hansen, G. B. (1985) Preventing layoffs: Developing an effective job security and economic adjustment program. *Employee Relations Law Journal*, **11**, 239–268.

Hansen, G. B. (1988) Layoffs, plant closings, and worker displacement in America: Serious problems that need a national solution. *Journal of Social Issues*, **44**, 153–171.

Harback, H., & Craft, D. (1991) Strategic leadership and organizational downsizing. Workshop sponsored by the US Army War College, Strategic Studies Institute, hosted by Southern Methodist University, Dallas, TX, November.

Hardy, C. (1987) Investing in retrenchment: Avoiding the hidden costs. *California Management Review*, **29**(4), 111–125.

Hardy, C. (1990) *Strategies for Retrenchment and Turnaround: The Politics of Survival*. Berlin, NY: W. De Gruyter.

Hartley, J. F. (1980) The impact of unemployment upon the self-esteem of managers. *Journal of Occupational Psychology*, **53**, 147–155.

Hartley, J., Jacobson, D., Klandermans, B., & Van Vuuren, T. (1991) *Job Insecurity: Coping with Jobs at Risk*. London: Sage.

Hattrup, K., & Kozlowksi, S. W. J. (in press) An across-organization analysis of the implementation of advanced manufacturing technologies. *Journal of High Technology Management Research*.

Haworth, J. T., Chesworth, P., & Smith, P. (1990) Research note: Cognitive difficulties in samples of unemployed, middle-aged men. *Leisure Studies*, **9**, 253–257.

Hayslip, J. B., & VanZandt, C. E. (1985) Dealing with reduction in force: Career guidance for state employees. *The Vocational Guidance Quarterly*, **33**, 256–261.

Heenan, D. A. (1989) The downside of downsizing. *The Journal of Business Strategy*, November, pp. 18–23.

Heenan, D. A. (1990) The downside of downsizing. *Across the Board*, May, pp. 17–19.

Heery, W. J. (1989) Outplacement through specialization. *Personnel Administrator*, June, pp. 151–155.

Henkoff, R. (1990) Cost cutting: How to do it right. *Fortune*, 9 April, pp. 40–46.

Hepworth, S. J. (1980) Moderating factors of the psychological impact of unemployment. *Journal of Occupational Psychology*, **53**, 139–145.

Hershey, R. (1972) Effects of anticipated job loss on employee behavior. *Journal of Applied Psychology*, **56**, 273–275.

Herzberg, F. (1982) *The Managerial Choice: To be Efficient and to be Human* (2nd edn). Salt Lake City, UT: Olympus Publishing.

Hill, R. C., & Negrey, C. (1987) Deindustrialization in the Great Lakes. *Urban Affairs Quarterly*, **22**, 580–597.

Hirsch, J. S. (1991) Many bankers lose their safe havens. *The Wall Street Journal*, 25 July, pp. B1, B5.

Hirsch, P. (1987) *Pack your own Parachute: How to Survive Mergers, Takeovers, and other Corporate Disasters*. Reading, MA: Addison-Wesley.

Hitt, M. A., & Keats, B. W. (1992) Strategic leadership and restructuring: A reciprocal interdependence. In R. L. Phillips & J. G. Hunt (eds), *Leadership: A Multiorganizational-level Perspective*. New York: Quorum Books.

Hoban, R. (1987) The outplacement option: Everybody wins! *Personnel Administrator*, June, pp. 184–193.

Hoerr, J., & Zellner, W. (1990) A Japanese import that's not selling. *Business Week*, 26 February, pp. 86–87.

Horvath, F. W. (1987) The pulse of economic change: Displaced workers of 1981–85. *Monthly Labor Review*, June, pp. 3–12.

Howland, M. (1988) Plant closures and local economic conditions. *Regional Studies*, **22**, 193–207.

Howland, M., & Peterson, G. E. (1988) Labor market conditions and the reemployment of displaced workers. *Industrial and Labor Relations Review*, **41**, 109–122.

Hunsaker, P. L., & Coombs, M. W. (1988) Mergers and acquisitions: Managing the emotional issues. *Personnel*, March, pp. 56–63.

Hunsicker, J. F., Jr. (1990) The ADA covers discernible as well as unrecognizable disabilities. *Personnel Journal*, August, pp. 81–86.

Ilgen, D. R., & Hollenbeck, J. R. (1991) The structure of work: Job design and roles. In M. D. Dunnette & L. M. Hough (eds), *Handbook of Industrial and Organizational Psychology* (2nd edn). Palo Alto, CA: Consulting Psychologists Press.

Imberman, W. (1989) Managers and downsizing. *Business Horizons*, September, pp. 28–33.

Ingrassia, P., & White, J. B. (1991) GM plans to close 21 more factories, cut 74 000 jobs, slash capital spending. *The Wall Street Journal*, 19 December, pp. A3–A4.

Isabella, L. A. (1989) Downsizing: Survivors' assessments. *Business Horizons*, May, pp. 35–41.

Iversen, L., & Sabroe, S. (1988) Psychological well-being among unemployed and employed people after a company closedown: A longitudinal study. *Journal of Social Issues*, **44**(4), 141–152.

Jackson, P. R. (1988) Personal networks, support mobilization and unemployment. *Psychological Medicine*, **18**, 397–404.

Jackson, P. R., & Warr, P. B. (1984) Unemployment and psychological ill-health: The moderating role of duration and age. *Psychological Medicine*, **14**, 605–614.

Jackson, S. E., & Schuler, R. A. (1990) Human resource planning: Challenges for industrial/organizational psychologists. *American Psychologist*, **45**, 223–239.

Jacobs, D. (1988) Maintaining morale during and after downsizing. *Management Solutions*, April, pp. 5–13.

Jahoda, M. (1979) The impact of unemployment in 1930s and the 1970s. *Bulletin of The British Psychological Society*, **32**, 309–314.

Jahoda, M. (1988) Economic recession and mental health: Some conceptual issues. *Journal of Social Issues*, **44**, 13–23.

Janis, I. L. (1983) The role of social support in adherence to stressful decisions. *American Psychologist*, **38**, 143–160.

Jick, T. D., & Murray, V. V. (1982) The management of hard times: Budget cutbacks in public sector organizations. *Organization Studies*, **3**, 141–169.

Jones, L. (1989) Comparing the effects of two types of unemployment on network status and the incidence of depressive symptoms. *Journal of Applied Social Sciences*, **14**, 117–149.

Kanfer, R., & Hulin, C. L. (1985) Individual differences in successful job searches following a lay-off. *Personnel Psychology*, **38**, 835–847.

Kasl, S. V., & Cobb, S. (1970) Blood pressure changes in men undergoing job loss: A preliminary report. *Psychosomatic Medicine*, **32**, 19–38.

Kasl, S. V., & Cobb, S. (1979) Some mental health consequences of plant closing and job loss. In L. Ferman & J. Gordus (eds), *Mental Health and the Economy* (pp. 255–346). Kalamazoo, MI: W. E. Upjohn Institute for Employment Research.

Kasl, S. V., & Cobb, S. (1980) The experience of losing a job: Some effects on cardiovascular functioning. *Psychotherapy and Psychosomatics*, **34**, 88–109.

Kasl, S. V., Gore, S., & Cobb, S. (1975) The experience of losing a job: Reported changes in health, symptoms and illness behavior. *Psychosomatic Medicine*, **37**, 106–122.

Kaufman, H. G. (1982) *Professionals in Search of Work: Coping with the Stress of Job Loss and Underemployment*. New York, Wiley.

Kerachsky, S., Nicholson, W., Carvin, E., & Hershey, A. (1986) Work sharing programs: An evaluation of their use. *Monthly Labor Review*, May, pp. 31–33.

Kessler, R. C., House, J. S., & Turner, J. B. (1987) Unemployment and health in a community sample. *Journal of Health and Social Behavior*, **28**, 51–59.

Kessler, R. C., Price, R. H., & Wortman, C. B. (1985) Social factors in psychopathology: Stress, social support, and coping processes. *Annual Review of Psychology*, **36**, 531–572.

Kessler, R. C., Turner, J. B., & House, J. S. (1988) Effects of unemployment on health in a community survey: Main, modifying, and mediating effects. *Journal of Social Issues*, **44**, 69–85.

Kiechel, W., III. (1985) Managing a downsized operation. *Fortune*, 22 July, pp. 155–157.

Kilpatrick, R., & Trew, K. (1985) Life-styles and psychological well-being among unemployed men in Northern Ireland. *Journal of Occupational Psychology*, **58**, 207–216.

Kimberly, J. R., & Miles, R. H. (1980) *The Organizational Life Cycle: New Perspectives for Organizational Theory and Research*. San Francisco, CA: Jossey-Bass.

Kinicki, A. J. (1985) Personal consequences of plant closings: A model and prelimary test. *Human Relations*, **38**, 197–212.

Kinicki, A. J. (1989) Predicting occupational role choices after involuntary job loss. *Journal of Vocational Behavior*, **35**, 204–218.

Kinicki, A. J., & Latack, J. C. (1990) Explication of the construct of coping with involuntary job loss. *Journal of Vocational Behavior*, **36**, 339–360.

Kolcum, E. H. (1988) Eastern cuts size by 12% in move to erase losses. *Aviation Week & Space Technology*, 1 August, pp. 84–85.

Kozlowski, S. W. J. (1987) Technological innovation and strategic human resource management: Facing the challenge of change. *Human Resource Planning*, **10**, 69–79.

Kozlowksi, S. W. J., Chao, G. T., Smith, E., Hedlund, J., & Walz, P.

(1991) Organizational downsizing: Individual and organizational implications and recommendations for action (Technical Report 929). Arlington, VA: US Army Research Institute for the Behavioral and Social Sciences.

Kozlowski, S. W. J., & Farr, J. L. (1988) An integrative model of updating and performance. *Human Performance*, **1**, 5–29.

Kozlowski, S. W. J., & Hults, B. M. (1987) An exploration of climates for technical updating and performance. *Personnel Psychology*, **40**, 539–563.

Krantz, J. (1985) Group process under conditions of organizational decline. *Journal of Applied Behavioral Science*, **21**, 1–17.

Kuzmits, F. E., & Sussman, L. (1988) Early retirement or forced resignation: Policy issues for downsizing human resources. *SAM Advanced Management Journal*, **53**, 28–32.

Landau, S. G., Neal, D. L., Meisner, M., & Prudic, J. (1980) Depressive symptomatology among laid-off workers. *Journal of Psychiatric Treatment and Evaluation*, **2**, 5–12.

Langerman, P. D., & Byerly, R. L., & Root, K. A. (1982) *Plant Closings and Layoffs: Problems Facing Urban and Rural Communities*. Des Moines, IA: Drake University, College for Continuing Education.

LaRocco, J. M., House, J. S., & French, J. R., Jr. (1980) Social support, occupational stress, and health. *Journal of Health and Social Behavior*, **21**, 202–218.

Latack, J. C. (1986) Coping with job stress: Measures and future directions for scale development. *Journal of Applied Psychology*, **71**, 377–385.

Latack, J. C. (1990) Organizational restructuring and career management: From outplacement and survival to inplacement. *Research in Personnel and Human Resources Management*, **8**, 109–139.

Latack, J. C., & Dozier, J. B. (1986) After the axe falls: Job loss as a career transition. *Academy of Management Review*, **11**, 375–392.

Leana, C. R., & Feldman, D. C. (1988a) Individual responses to job loss: Perceptions, reactions, and coping behaviors. *Journal of Management*, **14**, 375–389.

Leana, C. R., & Feldman, D. C. (1988b) Layoffs: How employees and companies cope. *Personnel Journal*, September, pp. 31–34.

Leana, C. R., & Feldman, D. C. (1989) When mergers force layoffs: Some lessons about managing the human resource problems. *Human Resource Planning*, **12**, 123–140.

Leana, C. R., & Feldman, D. C. (1990) Individual responses to job loss: Empirical findings from two field studies. *Human Relations*, **43**, 1155–1181.

Leana, C. R., & Feldman, D. C. (1991) Gender differences in responses to unemployment. *Journal of Vocational Behavior*, **38**, 65–77.

Leana, C. R., & Ivancevich, J. M. (1987) Involuntary job loss: Institutional interventions and a research agenda. *Academy of Management Review*, **12**, 301–312.

Levine, C. H. (1984) Retrenchment, human resource erosion, and the role of the personnel manager. *Public Personnel Management Journal*, Fall, pp. 249–263.

Levy, F., & Michel, R. C. (1991) *The Economic Future of American Families*. Washington, DC: Urban Institute Press.

Liem, R., & Liem, J. (1979) Social support and stress: Some general issues and their application to the problem of unemployment. In L. Ferman & J. Gordus (eds), *Mental Health and the Economy* (pp. 347–378). Kalamazoo, MI: W. E. Upjohn Institute for Employment Research.

Liem, R., & Liem, J. H. (1988) Psychological effects of unemployment on workers and their families. *Journal of Social Issues*, **44**, 87–105.

Linn, M. W., Sandifer, R., & Stein, S. (1985) Effects of unemployment on mental and physical health. *American Journal of Public Health*, **75**, 502–506.

Little, C. B. (1976) Technical-professional unemployment: Middle-class adaptability to personal crisis. *Sociological Quarterly*, 17, 262–274.

London, M., & Greller, M. M. (1991) Demographic trends and vocational behavior: A twenty year retrospective and agenda for the 1990s. *Journal of Vocational Behavior*, 38, 125–164.

Luo, L., & Cooper, C. L. (1990) Stress of job relocation: Progress and prospect. *Work & Stress*, 4, 121–128.

Mallinckrodt, B. (1990) Satisfaction with a new job after unemployment: Consequences of job loss for older professionals. *Journal of Counseling Psychology*, 37, 149–152.

Mallinckrodt, B., & Bennett, J. (in press) Social support and the impact of job loss in dislocated blue-collar workers. *Journal of Counseling Psychology*.

Mallinckrodt, B., & Fretz, B. R. (1988) Social support and the impact of job loss on older professionals. *Journal of Counseling Psychology*, 35, 281–286.

Mandel, M. J. (1990) This time, the downturn is dressed in pinstrips. *Business Week*, October, pp. 130–131.

Mangum, S. L., Tansky, J., & Keyton, J. (1988) Small business training as a strategy to assist displaced workers: An Ohio pilot project. *Journal of Small Business Management*, October, pp. 14–21.

Mark, M. M., & Mellor, S. (1991) Effect of self-relevance of an event on hindsight bias: The foreseeability of a layoff. *Journal of Applied Psychology*, 76, 569–577.

Matte, H. (1988) Cheese plant closing opens new doors. *Personnel Administrator*, January, pp. 52–55.

Matteson, M. T., & Ivancevich, J. M. (1990) Merger and acquisition stress: Fear and uncertainty at mid-career. *Prevention in Human Services*, 8, 139–158.

McCune, J. T., Beatty, R. W., & Montagno, R. V. (1988) Downsizing: Practices in manufacturing firms. *Human Resource Management Journal*, 27, 145–161.

McKersie, R. B., & McKersie, W. S. (1982) *Plant Closings: What can be Learned for Best Practice*. Washington DC: US Department of Labor.

McKinley, W. (1987) Complexity and administrative intensity: The case of declining organizations. *Administrative Science Quarterly*, 32, 87–105.

Melcher, R. A., & Levine, J. B. (1990) Fired. New Europe is singing the white-collar blues. *Business Week*, 26 November, pp. 70–71.

Milbank, D. (1991) Changes at Alcoa point up challenges and benefits of decentralized authority. *The Wall Street Journal*, 7 November, p. B1.

Miller, J., & Labovitz, S. (1973) Individual reactions to organization conflict and change. *Sociological Quarterly*, 14, 556–575.

Mirabile, R. J. (1985) Outplacement as transition counseling. *Journal of Employment Counseling*, 22, 39–45.

Mitchell, R. (1988) After Harry Gray: Reshaping United Technologies. *Business Week*, January, pp. 46–48.

Modic, S. J. (1987) Is anyone loyal anymore? *Industry Week*, 7 September, pp. 75–82.

Mowday, R. T. (1981) Viewing turnover from the perspective of those who remain: The relationship of job attitudes to attributions of the causes of turnover. *Journal of Applied Psychology*, 66, 120–123.

Mullaney, A. D. (1989) Downsizing: How one hospital responded to decreasing demand. *Health Care Management Review*, 14, 41–48.

Murphy, B. S., Barlow, W. E., & Hatch, D. D. (1985) Plant Closings: Cases. *Personnel Journal*, November, pp. 22, 25.

Murray, T. J. (1987) Bitter survivors. *Business Month*, May, pp. 28–33.

Murray, V. V., & Jick, T. D. (1985) Taking stock of organizational decline management: Some issues and illustrations from an empirical study. *Journal of Management*, 11, 111–123.

National Alliance of Business. (1983) *Planning for Worker Re-adjustment: A Technical Assistance Guide for States.* Washington, DC: Author.

National Alliance of Business. (1984) *Planning for Workforce Reductions: A Technical Assistance Guide for Employers.* Washington, DC: Author.

National Technical Information Service. (1986) *Citations from the Management Contents Database: Plant Closings and Relocations.* Springfield, VA: National Technical Information Service (PB86872199).

Nelson, R. E. (1988) Common sense staff reduction. *Personnel Journal,* August, pp. 50–57.

Newman, D. G., & Gardner, W. (1987) *Business Closings and Worker Readjustment: The Canadian Approach.* Washington, DC: The National Center on Occupational Readjustment.

Noble, I. (1987) Unemployment after redundancy and political attitudes: Some empirical evidence. In R. M. Lee (ed.), *Redundancy, Layoffs, and Plant Closures: Their Character, Causes and Consequences* (pp. 280–302). London: Croom Helm.

Office of Personnel Management. (1981) *A Survey of Reduction in Force Provisions in Federal Law Agreements.* Washington, DC: Author (NTIS No. PB81202665).

Osborne, J. E. (1990) Combatting the consequences of cutbacks. *Supervisory Management,* July, p. 3.

Parkhouse, G. C. (1988) Inside outplacement—My search for a job. *Harvard Business Review,* January, pp. 66–73.

Patterson, J. L., & Flanagan, J. P. (1983) 'Making the best of a bad situation' for RIF casualties at the Oak Ridge National Laboratory (Tech. Rep. 1983 No. ORNL/TM-8592). Oak Ridge, TN: Oak Ridge National Laboratory.

Patton, H. M., & Patton, J. W. (1984) *The Displaced Worker and Community Response: Case Study of Portsmouth, Scioto County, Ohio.* Lexington: KY: State Research Associates.

Payne, R., & Hartley, J. (1987) A test of a model for explaining the affective experience of unemployed men. *Journal of Occupational Psychology,* **60**, 31–47.

Payne, R., & Jones, J. G. (1987) The effects of long-term unemployment on attitudes to employment. *Journal of Occupational Behavior,* **8**, 351–358.

Payne, R., Warr, P., & Hartley, J. (1984) Social class and psychological ill-health during unemployment. *Sociology of Health and Illness,* **6**, 153–174.

Pearlin, L. I., & Lieberman, M. A. (1979) Social sources of emotional distress. *Research in Community and Mental Health,* **1**, 217–248.

Pearlin, L. I., Lieberman, M. A., Menaghan, E. G., & Mullan, J. T. (1981) The stress process. *Journal of Health and Social Behaviour,* **22**, 337–356.

Perkins, B. (1990) Outplacement from the inside. *Personnel Management,* April, pp. 32–33.

Perkins, D. S. (1987) Whan can CEOs do for displaced workers? *Harvard Business Review,* November, pp. 90–93.

Perrucci, C. C., Perrucci, R., Targ, D. B., & Targ, H. R. (1985) Impact of a plant closing on workers and the community. *Research in the Sociology of Work,* **3**, 231–260.

Perrucci, C. C., Perrucci, R., Targ, D. B., & Targ, H. R. (1988) *Plant Closings: International Context and Social Costs.* Hawthorne, NY: Aldine de Gruyter.

Perrucci, C. C., Targ, D. B., Perrucci, R., & Targ, H. R. (1987) Plant closing: A comparison of effects on women and men workers. In R. M. Lee (ed.), *Redundancy, Layoffs an Plant Closures: Their Character, Causes and Consequences* (pp. 181–207). London, England: Croom Helm.

Perry, L. T. (1985) Least-cost alternatives to layoffs in declining industries. *Organization Dynamics,* **14**(4), 48–61.

Peters, D. L., & Lubin, B. (1989) Stages of 'undeserved' career downturns. *Organization Development Journal*, 7, 79–84.

Phay, R. E. (1980) *Reduction in Force: Legal Issues and Recommended Policy*. Topeka, KS: National Organization on Legal Problems of Education.

Piccolino, E. B. (1988) Outplacement: The view from HR. *Personnel*, March, pp. 24–27.

Pliner, J. (1990) Staying with or leaving the organization. *Prevention in Human Services*, 8, 159–177.

Podgursky, M., & Swaim, P. (1987) Job displacement and earnings loss: Evidence from the displaced worker survey. *Industrial and Labor Relations Review*, 41, 17–29.

Portela, G. M., & Zaks, R. K. (1989) Reductions in force: A practical approach. *Employment Relations Today*, Autumn, pp. 219–225.

Powell, D. H., & Driscoll, P. F. (1973) Middle-class professionals face unemployment. *Society*, January–February, pp. 18–26.

Price, R. H., & D'Aunno, T. (1983) Managing work force reduction. *Human Resource Management*, 22, 413–430.

Prussia, G. E., Kinicki, A. J., & Bracker, J. S. (in press) Psychological and behavioral consequences of job loss: A covariance structure analysis using Weiner's attribution model. *Journal of Applied Psychology*.

Quartararo, R. P. (1988) The human side of merger mania. *Business and Society Review*, Summer, pp. 45–48.

Quinn, R. E., & Cameron, K. S. (1983) Organizational life cycles and shifting criteria of effectiveness: Some preliminary evidence. *Management Science*, 29, 33–51.

Reichers, A. E., & Schneider, B. (1990) Climate and culture: An evolution of constructs. In B. Schneider (ed.), *Organizational Climate and Culture*. San Francisco, CA: Jossey-Bass.

Reynolds, S., & Gilbert, P. (1991) Psychological impact of unemployment: Interactive effects of vulnerability and protective factors on depression. *Journal of Counseling Psychology*, 38, 76–84.

Rhine, B. (1986) Business closing and their effects on employees—adaptation of the tort of wrongful discharge. *Industrial Relations Law Journal*, 3, 362–400.

RIF: An HR challenge (1991) *HR Update*, 2(4), 1.

Roberts, K. H., Hulin, C. L., & Rousseau, D. M. (1978) *Developing an Interdisciplinary Science of Organizations*. San Francisco, CA: Jossey-Bass.

Rohan, T. M. (1985) Motivating the 'lame-duck' manager. *Industry Week*, 24 June, pp. 55–56.

Rousseau, D. M. (1985) Issues of level in organizational research: Multi-level and cross-level perspectives. *Research in Organizational Behavior*, 7, 1–37.

Rowley, K. M., & Feather, N. T. (1987) The impact of unemployment in relation to age and length of unemployment. *Journal of Occupational Psychology*, 60, 323–332.

Ruhm, C. J. (1990) *The Impact of Advance Notice Provisions on Post Displacement Outcomes*. Washington, DC: Department of Labor (NTIS No. PB90218652).

Rundle, J., & DeBlassie, R. R. (1981) Unemployment in the postindustrial age: Counseling redundant workers. *Journal of Employment Counseling*, December, pp. 183–189.

Schlenker, J. A., & Gutek, B. A. (1987) Effects of role loss on work-related attitudes. *Journal of Applied Psychology*, 72, 287–293.

Schlossberg, N. (1984) *Counseling Adults in Transitions*. New York: Springer.

Schlossberg, N. K., & Leibowitz, Z. (1980) Organizational support systems as buffers to job loss. *Journal of Vocational Behavior*, 17, 204–217.

Schore, L. (1984) The Fremont experience: A counseling program for dislocated workers. *International Journal of Mental Health*, 13, 154–168.

Schweiger, D. M., & DeNisi, A. S. (1991) Communication with employees following a merger: A longitudinal field experiment. *Academy of Management Journal*, **34**, 110–135.

Sebrell, W. (1990) The dangers of downsizing. *Computerworld*, 7 May, pp. 109.

Seibert, E. H., & Seibert, J. (1989) Benefits: Look into window alternatives. *Personnel Journal*, May, pp. 80–87.

Shamir, B. (1985a) Sex differences in psychological adjustment to unemployment and reemployment: A question of commitment, alternatives or finance? *Social Problems*, **33**, 67–79.

Shamir, B. (1985b) Unemployment and 'free time'—the role of Protestant work ethic and work involvement. *Leisure Studies*, **4**, 333–345.

Shamir, B. (1986) Protestant work ethic, work involvement and the psychological impact of unemployment. *Journal of Occupational Behaviour*, **7**, 25–38.

Sheridan, J. H. (1988) Sizing up corporate staffs. *Industry Week*, 21 November, pp. 46–48, 52.

Smallwood, W. N., & Jacobsen, E. (1987) Is there life after downsizing? *Personnel*, December, pp. 42–46.

Smith, S. K. (1989) The teacher union contract: A constraint on 'downsizing' the public school? *Journal of Collective Bargaining*, **18**, 229–239.

Snyder, K. A., & Nowak, T. C. (1984) Job loss and demoralization: Do women fare better than men? *International Journal of Mental Health*, **13**, 92–106.

Sommer, D., & Lasry, J. C. (1984) Personality and reactions to stressful life events. *Canada's Mental Health*, **32**, 19–20, 32.

Staudohar, P. D. (1989) New plant closing law aids workers in transition. *Personnel Journal*, January, pp. 87–90.

Staw, B. M., Sandelands, L. E., & Dutton, J. E. (1981) Threat-rigidity effects in organizational behavior: A multilevel analysis. *Administrative Science Quarterly*, **26**, 501–524.

Steele, M. T. (1986) The executive separation package: Handle with care. *Personnel Journal*, October, pp. 42–50.

Stokes, G., & Cochrane, R. (1984) A study of the psychological effects of redundancy and unemployment. *Journal of Occupational Psychology*, **57**, 309–322.

Sutton, R. I. (1983) Managing organizational death. *Human Resource Management*, **22**(2), 391–412.

Sutton, R. I. (1987) The process of organizational death: Disbanding and reconnecting. *Administrative Science Quarterly*, **32**, 542–569.

Sutton, R. I., & D'Aunno, T. D. (1989) Decreasing organizational size: Untangling the effects of money and people. *Academy of Management Review*, **14**, 194–212.

Sutton, R. I., Eisenhardt, K. M., & Jucker, J. V. (1985) Managing organizational decline: Lessons from Atari. *Organizational Dynamics*, **14**, 17–29.

Swaim, P., & Podgursky, M. (1990) Advance notice and job search: The value of an early start. *The Journal of Human Resources*, **25**(2), 147–178.

Sweet, D. H. (1975) *Decruitment: A Guide for Managers*. Reading, MA: Addison-Wesley.

Swinburne, P. (1981) The psychological impact of unemployment on managers and professional staff. *Journal of Occupational Psychology*, **54**, 47–64.

Taber, T. D., Walsh, J. T., & Cooke, R. A. (1979) Developing a community-based program for reducing the social impact of a plant closing. *Journal of Applied Behavioral Science*, **17**, 133–155.

Taylor, M. (1988) A gender-based analysis of the consequences of employment reductions on well-being: Plant workers in two Newfoundland fishing outports. *Canadian Journal of Community Mental Health*, **7**(1), 67–79.

Terreberry, S. (1968) The evolution of organizational environments. *Administrative Science Quarterly*, **12**, 590–613.

Thompson, D. E., Hauserman, N. R., & Jordan, J. L. (1986) Age discrimination in reduction-in-force: The metamorphosis of McDonnell Douglas continues. *Industrial Relations Law Journal*, **8**, 46–67.

Tiggemann, M., & Winefield, A. H. (1984) The effects of unemployment on the mood, self-esteem, locus of control, and depressive affect of school-leavers. *Journal of Occupational Psychology*, **57**, 33–42.

Tomasko, R. M. (1990) *Downsizing: Reshaping the Corporation for the Future*. New York: AMACOM.

Tombaugh, J. R., & White, L. P. (1990) Downsizing: An empirical assessment of survivors' perceptions in a postlayoff environment. *Organization Development Journal*, **8**, 32–43.

Tushman, M. L., & Romanelli, E. (1985) Organizational evolution: A metamorphosis model of convergence and reorientation. *Research in Organizational Behavior*, **7**, 177–222.

US Public Law 101–510 (1990) *National Defense Authorization Act for Fiscal Year 1991*. Washington, DC: US Government Printing Office.

Valencia, M. (1985) Redundancy counselling for manual workers. *Employee Relations* **7**(2), 12–16.

Verity, J. (1989) A bold move in mainframes. *Business Week*, 27 May, pp. 72–78.

Viney, L. L., & Tych, A. M. (1984) To work or not to work? An enquiry of men experiencing unemployment, promotion and retirement. *Psychology & Human Development*, **2**, 57–66.

Vinokur, A., & Caplan, R. D. (1987) Attitudes and social support: Determinants of job-seeking behavior and well-being among the unemployed. *Journal of Applied Social Psychology*, **17**, 1007–1024.

Vinokur, A. D., Price, R. H., & Caplan, R. D. (1991) From field experiments to program implementation: Assessing the potential outcomes of an experimental intervention program for unemployed persons. *American Journal of Community Psychology*, **19**, 543–562.

Vinokur, A. D., van Ryn, M., Gramlich, E. M., & Price, R. H. (1991) Long-term follow-up and benefit-cost analysis of the Jobs program: A preventive intervention for the unemployed. *Journal of Applied Psychology*, **76**, 213–219.

Warr, P. (1978) A study of psychological well-being. *British Journal of Psychology*, **69**, 111–121.

Warr, P., & Jackson, P. (1984) Men without jobs: Some correlates of age and length of unemployment. *Journal of Occupational Psychology*, **57**, 77–85.

Warr, P., Jackson, P., & Banks, M. (1988) Unemployment and mental health: Some British studies. *Journal of Social Issues*, **44**, 47–68.

Warr, P. & Lovatt, J. (1977) Retraining and other factors associated with job finding after redundancy. *Journal of Occupational Psychology*, **50**, 67–84.

Warr, P., & Payne, R. (1983) Social class and reported changes in behavior after job loss. *Journal of Applied Social Psychology*, **13**, 206–222.

Watford, K. (1986) Shorter workweeks: An alternative to layoffs. *Business Week*, April, pp. 77–78.

Weitzel, W., & Jonsson, E. (1989) Decline in organizations: A literature integration and extension. *Administrative Science Quarterly*, **34**, 91–109.

Whetten, D. A. (1980) Organizational decline: A neglected topic in organizational science. *Academy of Management Review*, **5**, 577–588.

Wilhelm, M. S., & Ridley, C. A. (1988) Stress and unemployment in rural nonfarm couples: A study of hardships and coping resources. *Family Relations*, **37**, 50–54.

Wolkinson, B. W., Chelst, K., & Shepard, L. A. (1985) Arbitration issues in the consolidation of police and fire bargaining units. *Arbitration Journal*, **40**, 43–54.

Yates, A. B. (1985) Another aspect of downsizing. *Optimum*, **16**, 35–41.

Young, R. A. (1986) Counseling the unemployed: Attributional issues. *Journal of Counseling and Development*, **64**, 374–378.

Zahniser, G., Ashley, W. L., & Inks, L. W. (1985) *Helping the Dislocated Workers: Employer and Employee Perceptions* (Research and Development Series No. 243D). Columbus, OH: The Ohio State University, The National Center for Research in Vocational Education.

Zammuto, R.F, & Cameron, K.S. (1985) Environmental decline and organizational response. *Research in Organizational Behavior*, **7**, 223–262.

Zedeck, S., & Mosier, K. L. (1990) Work in the family and employing organization. *American Psychologist*, **45**, 240–251.

Chapter 9

GROUP PROCESSES IN ORGANIZATIONS: CONTINUITY AND CHANGE

Linda Argote
Carnegie Mellon University, Pittsburgh, USA
Joseph E. McGrath
University of Illinois, Champaign, USA

This chapter is about how group processes operate and change over time. We begin by presenting some of the issues that arise in organizations when they are viewed as open systems, then present a conceptualization of how groups operate within such organizations (Part I). That latter conceptualization lays out four major sets of group processses, which provide the organizing framework for our review of recent empirical and theoretical literature about groups in organizations (Part II). We end the chapter with some comments about the state of research in this field (Part III).

I INTRODUCTION: A CONCEPTUAL FRAMEWORK REGARDING GROUP PROCESSES IN ORGANIZATIONS

The Nature of Organizations

Organizations as open systems

We begin by assuming that organizations and the groups within them are open systems in the sense discussed by Katz and Kahn (1978). The focal units of potential interest to social and behavioral scientists constitute a subset of the many levels of partially nested open systems that make up the human endeavor (individuals, groups, organizations, communities, cells, organs, social institutions, neural processes, and so on). Moreover, any given focal system at any given level is in dynamic interaction with its environment(s)—that is, with embedding systems at higher levels or organization—and those environments

International Review of Industrial and Organizational Psychology 1993 Volume 8
Edited by C. L. Cooper and I. T. Robertson. © 1993 John Wiley & Sons Ltd.

themselves are changing. Furthermore, any given focal system is composed of sets of subsystems and processes that are in dynamic interaction with one another and with the focal system itself. Finally, we assume that the process of entropy—the 'running down' of the entity, toward less pattern and more randomness—is inherent in social systems as well as in physical systems. The need to stave off entropy gives each focal system an inherent drive toward 'growth'. In order to store up energy and resources against an uncertain future, each focal system must realize a net 'gain' from its interactions (i.e. its input–process–output transactions) with its environment or embedding context, and/or with its component parts or subsystems.

There are multiple criteria of 'success' by which to judge an organization and groups and individuals within it. These include such concepts as effectiveness, productivity, profitability, efficiency (both cost efficiency and process or time efficiency), customer or client satisfaction, employee satisfaction, quality of product, contribution to embedding systems (e.g. to community, to nation state). Those criteria are related to one another in complex and sometimes conflicting ways, and the relative importance given to each of them differs markedly depending on which constituency's perspective is adopted.

Some inherent conflicts in organizations

At noted above, we have assumed that both organizations and groups within them exist as partially nested open systems within an entropy-driven finite universe. If so, then each focal system (and its parts and embedding systems too) must somehow gain more than it spends (in energy and resources) in its interactions with other systems. This need for net gain applies to its relation to the higher level systems within which it is embedded, and to its component parts that it embeds, even though the focal system is usually regarded as not being in competition with those embedding and embedded systems. This same net gain relation applies, of course, to its interactions with the many systems at its own system level—with which it may be explicitly in competition. In a finite universe, such a net gain for all systems is impossible.

That logical impossibility is at the core of a series of *conflicts of interest* among the system, its parts and its embedding systems. For example, it is often the case in complex human organizations that what is good for an organization is adverse to the self-interest of the individuals who are its members, and vice versa. High system effectiveness of a work organization, for example, may be purchased at a serious cost in system well-being of the individuals who make up that organization. Safety violations, or environmental risks, or simply task overloads, may be imposed in the service of a key organizational effectiveness criterion—productivity.

This is more than just a matter of individual versus organization. These conflicts occur at a variety of system levels. For example, these conflicts are sometimes discussed in terms of 'development' versus 'exploitation' of the physical environment, or in terms of disputes between labor and management. They are sometimes translated into underlying questions of distributive justice and discussed in terms of equity versus equality versus need. They can arise, as well, in interpersonal systems, such as a family. A choice that is good for the family might be detrimental to one of its members, and vice versa. These conflicts often get played out as ongoing struggles within individual humans, in forms such as the undesirable side-effects of needed medications, or psychologically satisfying actions that are detrimental to the heart or liver.

These conflicts of interest are inherent in open systems (at least given the definitions and assumptions used here). They do not derive from meanness or greed or stupidity on the part of system managers or members. But they get played out within concrete systems in a number of forms that give social, economic, technological, political and moral content to them.

The system needs to carry out its tasks both effectively and efficiently. The potential difficulty and complexity of system task requirements drives a process of differentiation and specialization of parts. This in turn drives a countervailing process of coordination and integration of function. This creates a need for balance between differentiation and autonomy of parts on the one hand and coordination and centralization of control of system operation on the other.

These conflicts of control are also inherent in open systems, and get expressed in forms that involve social, economic, technological, political and moral content. For example, these conflicts sometimes get discussed in work organizations in terms of decentralization versus centralization of management, or autonomy of workers or of departments. They sometimes get talked about in terms of specialization of roles, and teamwork, and inefficiencies in task performance. They sometimes get discussed within families in terms of independence versus parental control. They sometimes involve individuals' ability to integrate multiple activities and interests effectively, to 'get it all together'.

The ambiguity associated with the environment, coupled with the system's interdependence with that environment, gives rise to a third set of conflicting desiderata. Because the focal system is thoroughly dependent on the environment for the resources it needs for inputs, for system-building, and for distribution of outptuts, high uncertainty with regard to current and future states of the environment constitutes a powerful force affecting system actions. There is a tendency for systems to try to adapt to the environment, hence a need to generate information about current and future conditions. There is a conflicting tendency for systems to try to assimilate the environment, or the parts of it that are crucial sources of system resources and opportunities. Both *adaptation and assimilation* with respect to the environment constitute forms of system change, forms that probably are to some degree in conflict. But there are also powerful forces counteracting any force for change. Social systems at all levels tend to be overdetermined, making it hard to bring about substantial changes in them.

Such *conflict between forces for change and for stability* is also inherent in open systems. The conflicts get played out, in concrete instances, in forms that given them social, economic, technological, political and moral content. Such conflicts, for example, get involved in discussions of monopolies and mergers, of rigidity and adaptability, of old guard and young Turks, of progress and deterioration in institutions, enterprises, marriages, skill acquisition, health care and other service systems, and so forth. They also get involved in matters of lifecycle change within families, and of many kinds of changes for individuals.

To summarize: The entropy and growth processes generate a series of conflicts of interest, the differentiation and integration processes generate a set of conflicts of control, while the uncertainty, adaptation and assimilation processes, plus system maintenance forces, generate a set of conflicts involving stability and change of the system itself. Each of these three sets of conflicts involves a series of conflicting desiderata, not all of which can be maximized simultaneously. Choices on issues involving these conflicting desiderata pose dilemmas for those who are inhabiting and/or managing the systems.

Some organizational dilemmas

These features of open systems, and the inherent conflicts (of interests, of control, and of stability/change) to which they give rise, imply several important dilemmas for anyone making choices at any given system level.

The diversity/consensus dilemma. Task requirements often place conflicting demands on group and organization composition. To carry out their projects effectively, organizations (and work groups within them) must select and achieve consensus on an effective set of goals, strategies, and plans of action, and must carry out these strategies and plans effectively. To do this, they need both: (i) to solve technical problems involved in their task performances; and (ii) to resolve conflicting viewpoints among members and groups regarding goals, strategies, and plans of action. To do the former (i.e. solve technical problems) they need a diversity of personnel with a wide range of talents, information, skills, and knowledge. To do the latter (i.e. resolve conflicting viewpoints) they need a set of personnel who are homogeneous in values, beliefs, and cultural styles.

The efficiency/effectiveness dilemma. Effective coordination requires a proper balance of standardization and adaptability. For efficient performance, work groups (and organizations) need to develop standardized procedures and norms governing behavior, so that individuals (and groups) who must coordinate their work can anticipate where, when, and what others with whom they must coordinate will do. Furthermore, specialization of function in the service of efficiency leads to a differentiation of activities and roles. But such differentiation in turn requires increased integrative activity in the service of an adequate level of coordination—thus lowering 'efficiency'.

At the same time, for effective performance, work groups (and organizations) often have to deal with instances that do not fit the routine pattern; and they must deal with instances in which unanticipated factors (e.g. such as environmental events, or substandard materials) modify the anticipated where-when-what of others' performances. Hence they must be prepared to modify, set aside or disregard standard operating procedures in order to handle those special cases flexibly. Thus, effectiveness requires a balance of standardization versus flexibility of task performance, and a balance of specialized task roles versus generalized and integrative roles.

The autonomy/control dilemma. Efficient performance of complex tasks requires predictability which in turn requires some degree of centralization of control. At the same time, high levels of performance effectiveness require high motivation which in turn requires some degree of autonomy. Therefore, groups and organizations need a proper balance of control and autonomy at each level of operation. However, an increase in control at a given system level (e.g. the organization) implies a decrease in autonomy at lower levels; and an increase in autonomy at a given level implies a decrease in control at higher levels.

There are both economies and diseconomies of scale; and there are advantages and disadvantages to both centralization and decentralization of functions. What is needed is a balance between autonomy and decentralization of power on the one hand, for the sake of both motivation and flexibility, and centralized control on the other hand, for the sake of coordination and predictability.

The information/meaning dilemma. We assume, further, that information is strategic for modern organizations, and this gives rise to a further dilemma. Information acquisition capabilities of organizations have grown tremendously in recent decades. This makes it possible for most organizations to gain rapid access to an enormous amount of information about the environment, to process that information extensively and efficiently, and to transmit it to all parts of the organization virtually instantaneously. But to do so raises the specter of information overload throughout the organization. Furthermore, it raises the possibility of swamping the system with 'junk information' (analogous to junk mail).

Daft and colleagues (e.g. Daft and Lengel, 1986) have drawn an important distinction between environmental uncertainty or ambiguity, on the one hand, and equivocality on the other. The former, they argue, refers to lack of information and can be remedied by acquiring appropriate additional information. The latter, they aver, refers to multiple and/or unclear meanings. Equivocality cannot be altered by information acquisition, but rather requires interpretation and the imposition of meanings on information already available. This dilemma gets played out in a number of venues in organizational affairs. Daft and colleagues relate it to choice among communication media because media differ in the 'richness' of the information they can transmit. Besides richness of information transmission, however, information systems also differ in quality and load of the information they yield because of constraints they place on both information acquisition and information processing. Constraints on information acquisition are limitations on amount of information available; constraints on information processing are impositions of meanings. Again, an appropriate balance of information and interpretation is required.

The Nature of Groups

A general schema about groups

Underlying our presentation here is a general schema or theory about groups (called Time, Interaction and Performance or TIP theory; see McGrath, 1990). That theory regards groups as continuously and simultaneously engaged in three major functions: production, member support, and group well-being. These functions represent, respectively, contributions of the group to its embedding organization, contributions of the group to its participating members, and contributions of the group to its own continued functioning as an intact social unit.

Groups carry out those functions by means of activities in one or another of four modes. The general forms of the modes are: I inception of a project (goal choice); II solution of technical issues (means choice); III resolution of conflict (i.e. of political rather than technical issues); and IV execution of the performance requirements of the project.

These modes transcend the three functions. There are parallel but distinguishable forms of the modes within each of the functions. Furthermore, the modes are not a fixed sequence of phases, but rather are four potential forms of activity by which each of the functions can be pursued in relation to any given project. Groups carry out their projects by means of time/activity paths that consist of mode/function sequences. Every (completed) project involves at least the first and fourth modes for the production function (i.e. the group gets a project and executes it). Any given case may or may not involve modes II and III for the production function (i.e. attempts to solve technical issues or resolve political issues). It also may involve some or all modes of activity with respect to the member support and group well-being functions (e.g. a redistribution of task roles, a reallocation of status or payoff relations, recruitment and socialization of a new member).

In TIP theory, natural groups are involved in a complex set of activities. At any given time, any given natural group is likely to be engaged in more than one project, and to be pursuing each of those projects by means of some sequences of modes of activity with respect to each of the three functions. Study of natural groups thus requires a complex set of observational and conceptual tools.

The performance of a given group in an organization is contingent on a number of sets of factors having to do with: attributes of the group's members; the group's composition, structure, and patterns of interaction, as well as its developmental history; the group's assigned or selected tasks, projects, or objectives; the tools and procedures by which the group will carry out those tasks; and a number of features of the group's organizational, physical, and temporal environment. TIP theory is a general theory of groups. For our present purpose, a detailed analysis of processes in work groups within organizational contexts, we will present a more micro-level model of processes in work groups.

A model of work group processes in organizational contexts

We distinguish between *acting groups*—sets of people who are engaged in interdependent activities (e.g. a planning committee in session; a construction team at work)—and *standing groups*—sets of people who are designated as a unit for identification purposes but who are not carrying out interdependent activities (e.g. all secretarial staff of a firm; workers in the Fifth Street plant). Here, we will deal only with the former: *Acting groups in organizational context.*

All acting groups in organizational contexts are composed of *selected and organized* sets of three components: *people, tools, and purposes*. The term *tools*, here, is intended to include 'tools, rules, and resources'; they are the basic ingredients of *technology* (using that term broadly, as anthropologists do). The term *purposes*, here, refers to *intentions*. Intentions are related to goals and tasks; they are the basic ingredients of *projects*. People are the human component of task forces, teams, work crews, and other forms of work groups in organizational contexts.

Organizations create and use three kinds of groups, which differ in terms of whether the people, the tools, or the purposes have center stage at the time of its establishment: *different people for different tasks*

(1) Sometimes an organization has a specific project. It assigns people to that project—that is, it establishes a *task force* (or a committee). The task force then acquires the tools (technology) it will use to do the project. (For example: a task force organized to develop a plan for cutting operating costs in a certain part of the organization.)

(2) Sometimes the organization recruits a set of people with a particular combination of skills and abilities, and provides them with an appropriate technology, thereby forming a *team* (or work crew), which will then be assigned projects of a given class as those arise in the organization. (For example: an inspection and repair team for a certain type of company product.)

(3) Sometimes the organization acquires a complex set of tools, intended to serve a class of projects/purposes, and then recruits people to be a *crew*

for that technology. (For example: a crew to operate a computerized system for storage and retrieval of supplies in a warehouse.) Steps in formation of these three kinds of groups are shown in Figure 9.1.

Four major sets of processes describe how work groups in organizations come into existence, develop and maintain themselves; do their work; have an impact on (i.e. change) themselves and the rest of the organization and environment; and stay connected to the organization of which they are a part (see Figure 9.2).

A. *Construction processes*: Construction processes refer to the group as an entity, not to the task/projects that the group is or will be performing. These processes include activities in the initial establishment of an (acting) group in organizational context, of one of the three kinds just listed. They subsume activities involving acquisition (of people, tools, and purposes), and aspects of the processes by which groups adapt what they draw from the external environment to their own needs (which Poole and others call adaptive structuration). The construction processes thus involve recruitment and socialization (training) of people;

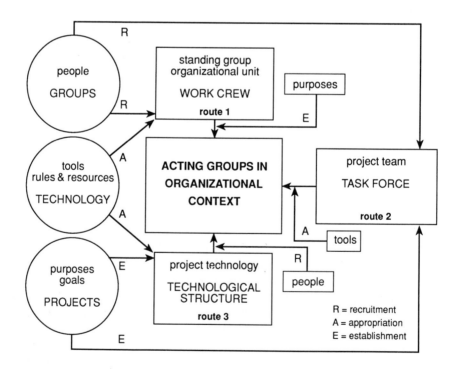

Figure 9.1 Three routes for forming work groups

acquisition and adaptation of tools/technology; and the establishment and elaboration of purposes.

B. *Operations processes*: These processes refer to the operation of the group as it carries out its purposes or projects. Operations processes potentially involve three of TIP theory's modes of activity—technical problem solving, conflict resolution, and, especially, execution. Operations processes may involve not only execution of the project-as-given, but also aspects of adaptive structuration noted above, modifying the project and/or the tools and division of labor, and potentially modifying the group's intentions. Operations processes also include monitoring and managing group activity (i.e. internal leadership).

C. *Reconstruction processes*:These processes refer to how the group uses its own project-execution activities as a basis for *modifying itself*. We distinguish here between modifications of the people, tools, and purposes as they are acquired from the embedding context, *in order to do the project(s)* properly, on the one hand, and modifications of the people, tools, and purposes *as a consequence of having done the project*, on the other. The former kinds of modifications have already been noted in relation to the Construction processes; the latter kinds of modifications have to do with the Reconstruction processes considered here. The reconstruction processes include what has been referred to as 'organizational learning' (Argote and Epple, 1990) and 'group learning' (Hinsz, 1990) and what we will here call 'embedding knowlege'. It involves embedding knowledge in people, in tools (hardware and software) and in purposes, plans, or procedures.

D. *External relations processes*: These processes refer to how the acting-group-in-organizational-context monitors and manages its relations to the organizational and environmental context within which it is embedded. This involves monitoring the external environment with respect to people, tools, and purposes, and managing potential changes in relations between the group and those aspects of that environment— that is assessing their potential value to and threat to the group. Supervisory relations between the organization and the group—the monitoring and managing of the group by the organization—can be regarded as the flip side of this process. External relations refer to the group's reaching out to external sources; supervisory relations involve external sources (the organization) reaching into the group. From the point of view of the larger organization, such supervisory processes are part of its Operations processes.

CORE: Major Processes in Groups

Construction processes

Establishing an acting group in an organizational context (AGinOC) involves selecting, organizing, and fitting together some people, some tools, and some purposes from the embedding context (i.e. from the organizational environment). As already noted, this can be done in three ways, leading to three kinds of acting groups: task forces, teams, and crews.

The process by which *people* are incorporated into AGinOC of any one of the three kinds can be called *recruitment*. People are recruited into task forces (along with purposes), or are recruited into teams or organizational units (along with technology), or are recruited directly to be a crew for a technological system.

The process by which *purposes* are incorporated into AGinOC of any one of the three kinds can be called *establishment*. Purposes or projects are selected along with people to establish task forces, or are selected along with tools to establish technological systems that require crews, or are selected directly as projects for existing teams.

The process by which *tools/technology* are incorporated into AGinOC of any one of the three kinds can be called *appropriation*. Tools/technology are

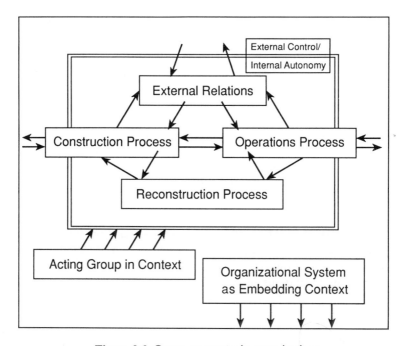

Figure 9.2 Group processes in organizations

appropriated (along with people) into teams, or are appropriated (along with purposes) into technological systems that require crews, or are appropriated directly into existing task forces.

Besides these 'acquisition' considerations by which work groups become established in organizational contexts, the Construction process also subsumes some aspects of what Poole and colleagues (e.g. Poole, Siebold, and McPhee, 1985; Poole and Roth, 1988a,b) call *adaptive structuration*. Adaptive structuration refers to the process by which the social unit in question brings about changes in the people, tools, and purposes of which it is composed, in the process of selecting and organizing those people to use those tools to attain those purposes. As was the case for the acquisition process, we can consider three aspects of adaptive structuration:

> *Socialization* of the people so that they can apply the tools for those purposes. This is sometimes thought of as training, but much of it is less formalized than that.
>
> *Adaptation* of the tools so that the people can apply them to carry out those purposes.
>
> *Elaboration* of the purpose(s) or project(s), (that is, laying out, scheduling, and assigning tasks and steps) so that the people can accomplish the project(s) with the tools. This can also be thought of as formulating a 'project-execution-template' or a project plan; but keep in mind that all of it is not at a deliberate or explicit level. Much of this elaboration is tacit planning, just as much of socialization is tacit.

Operations processes

The adaptive structuration aspects of 'construction' blend into what we are here calling the Operations processes. Included within operations also are two other familiar processes: internal control (i.e. supervision/leadership) and task execution.

Internal control involves *monitoring and managing* of group activity. This is sometimes done by some member(s) of the group and sometimes by someone 'outside' it. This process has been much studied—under labels such as leadership, supervision, control. Those processes include:

> Monitoring coordination and conflict among the people and evaluating their individual and collective performances.
>
> Monitoring the quality of the products in relation to the established project/purposes.
>
> Monitoring the application, usefulness, and cost of the technology, in relation to potential alternatives.

The execution processes by which AGinOC actually carry out their work and generate products has not been studied much in basic research on groups, and has only been studied by very indirect means (e.g. by examining production records and/or profits; or by obtaining evaluations by supervisors) for much organizational research. Direct execution of major projects has been given considerable attention by researchers studying military units, however. Much of that has involved motor tasks, but there are usually major cognitive components embedded within such tasks. Again, it is possible to view execution in relation to the three components here emphasized: the unit members' skills, capabilities and performances; the unit's mission, strategy, and tactics; and the unit's tools and technology (e.g. weapons, transportation, communication equipment). The execution process is at the heart of AGinOC.

Reconstruction processes

The third major set of processes refer to what we term *Knowledge Embedding*. This process involves modifications of the system *as a consequence of doing the project*—in contrast to the adaptive structuration part of the construction process, which refers to modifications of the components (the people, tools, and purposes) *in order to do the project*.

This Knowledge Embedding or system modification process is a form of system change. It, too, involves three sets of subprocesses:

Knowlege changes: Accumulation (or loss!) of tacit and explicit knowledge and skills by group members as a function of doing the project in context (accrual/decrements of skills and knowledge). This is 'embedding knowledge by changing the people'.

Technology changes: Changes in the technology (changes in hardware, software, rules and procedures) as a function of its being used to do the project, and documentation of those changes. This is 'embedding knowledge by changing the technology'.

Project-template changes: Changes in the project-plan (i.e. the differentiation of steps and tasks, division of labor, scheduling and so on) as a function of its being carried out (changes in the project-plan or project-template). This is 'embedding knowledge by changing the project plan or procedures'.

These Embedding processes have not been studied very much, nor have they been incorporated in most conceptualizations of groups—for a very good reason: They do not show up until one is dealing with *a group that has some meaningful history*, some continuation over time. Most group research and theory—even that done in field settings rather than the laboratory—has dealt with groups essentially on a 'one shot' and very short-term basis.

External relations processes

Along with the monitoring and managing of internal processes, there is also a need for someone in the group to keep track of what is going on external to the group—both in its immediate embedding organizational context, and in its broader (e.g. 'industry', community, national, cultural) environment. Group performance and success are affected by its extra-group relations with many key individuals and groups both inside and outside the organization. These extra-group relations are carried out by one or more members of the focal group, and can involve one or more of several functional roles.

We can view these processes, too, as having three subprocesses, one for each of the kinds of 'entities' that get acquired from the embedding context:

Monitoring and managing relations between the AGinOC and other groups and individuals in the embedding system that could potentially provide resources/obstacles for the AGinOC.

Monitoring and managing relations between the AGinOC and tools, rules, and resources (i.e. technology) that exist in the embedding system and are potentially available to be appropriated by the AGinOC.

Monitoring and managing relations between the AGinOC and purposes (goals, tasks, projects) in the embedding system that pose potential changes in opportunities/demands for the AGinOC.

Group processes and types of change

The four major sets of processes imply four major types of change in groups and organizations:

Group development: Because groups and organizations are open systems, akin to organisms, groups and organizations change over time in the course of their 'normal' developmental cycles or patterns. Such developmental change is related to the Constructions processes.

Task attainments: Because completion of the group's projects represents attainment of its production goals, task execution can be regarded as a 'transformation of inputs into outputs', and a change in the relation of the group to its embedding organization and its environmental context. Such task *execution* is related to the Operations processes.

Learning: Because groups and organizations, as well as individuals, usually improve in their effectiveness and efficiency on a given task with practice, they can be said to 'learn'. They do this by 'embedding' knowledge, in the people (group members); by embedding knowledge in the tools/technology used; and by embedding knowledge in the planning templates or project plans by which they carry out their task/purposes. This learning is related to the Reconstruction processes.

Adaptation/assimilation: Because groups and organizations live in a continually changing environment, over time there likely will be changes in some of the conditions upon which group and organizational performance is contingent—in membership, in tasks/purposes, in technology, in operating conditions. Hence there will be changes in group and organizational performance over and above changes due to group (organizational) development, task completion, and group (organizational) learning. This type of adaptation/assimilation is related to the External Relations processes.

II RESEARCH ON GROUP PROCESSES IN ORGANIZATIONS

In this part of the chapter we review the literature on the four sets of group processes discussed in the previous section. Our focus is on groups. Therefore, we concentrate on studies at the group level of analysis. Many of the same processes occur in organizations as in groups, however, so we also include relevant theories and findings from the organizational literature. In some ways, we use the most recent *Annual Review of Psychology* chapter on groups (Levine and Moreland, 1990) as a touchstone on which to build. So we focus our review on literature that has appeared subsequent to their coverage; but some earlier publications that we regard as crucial to our presentation are also included. Several additional reviews of research on groups that may be useful to the reader are Bettenhausen (1991), Goodman, Ravlin, and Argote (1986), Hackman (1992), Hackman and Morris (1975), McGrath and Kravitz (1982), and Sundstrom, DeMeuse, and Futrell (1990) (see Note at end of chapter). Payne and Cooper (1981) and Hackman (1990) provide rich descriptions of groups in organizations. Cartwright and Zander (1968) provide a discussion of the origins of the field of group dynamics as well as a collection of important early papers in the field. Thibaut and Kelly (1959) is another example of an influential early work on groups.

Construction Processes: The Formation and Development of Groups

The consruction process has received considerable attention in the research literature, under a variety of topical headings including: the acquistion, socialization, and training of group members (e.g. see Dyer, 1985; Feldman, 1989; McCallum, Oser, Morgan, and Salas, 1989; Moreland and Levine, 1982; Salas, Blaiwes, Reynolds, Glickman, and Morgan, 1985; Van Maanen, 1978), group composition effects (see Moreland and Levine, in press, for a review); the setting of group goals and the establishment of purposes (e.g. see Weldon, Jehn, and Pradhan, 1991); planning and the development of routines (Gersick and Hackman, 1990; Hackman, Brousseau, and Weiss, 1976); the introduction and adaptation of technology (e.g. see Barley, 1986; Finholt, Sproull, and Kiesler, 1990; Finholt and Sproull, 1989; Hollingshead and McGrath, in press; Kiesler and Sproull, in press; Kiesler, Zubrow, Moses, and Geller, 1985;

McGrath, 1990; McGrath and Hollingshead, 1992; Sproull and Kiesler, 1986); adaptive structuration (e.g. see Poole, Seibold, and McPhee, 1985; Poole and Roth, 1988a,b); and the effect of technology on organizational structure (see Fry, 1982, for a review).

Socialization and training

Moreland and Levine (1982) propose a model of group socialization that deals with three basic processes and several stages or phases of development. Both processes and phases apply dually to the member and to the group. The processes are evaluation, commitment and role transition. Evaluation refers to efforts by groups and individuals to evaluate and change each other's reward value. Commitment is based on the group's and the individual's assessment of the past, present and future reward value of the relationship relative to alternative relationships. Role transition occurs when commitment rises or falls significantly and involves relabeling the individual's relationship with the group (i.e. transition from one phase to another).

For Moreland and Levine (1982), several stages or phases characterize the passage of an individual through a group. The first phase is investigation, in which the individual and the group assess the potential value of forming a relationship with one another. The next phase is socialization; when a new member enters the group, the group attempts to teach the individual appropriate attitudes and behaviors while the individual may try to alter the group. During the next phase, maintenance, the group and the individual negotiate role expectations. If negotiation is unsuccessful, the group and the individual will attempt to resocialize each other (the resocialization phase). If the individual leaves the group, the group and the individual enter the remembrance phase, during which each party may engage in reminiscence about the relationship.

The social unit level at which socialization is done may be important. Van Maanen (1978) identifies seven dimensions that underlie the strategies for organizational socialization, the most important of them being the degree to which individuals are socialized individually or collectively. Feldman (1989) argues for an integration of research on socialization and research on training. He notes that training has typically been focused at the individual level of analysis and concerned with individual learning and its effect on work-related behavior (see Campbell, 1971, and Goldstein, 1980, for reviews of the training literature). By contrast, socialization has been more concerned with how new employees learn 'appropriate' attitudes, values, and behavior.

The interplay between individual training and group socialization is nicely illustrated by a study of socialization of hospital employees. Feldman (1977) found that acceptance by the group was necessary for individuals to feel competent. Newcomers could not find out crucial information they needed to perform their jobs, such as information about preferences of supervisors and about administrative procedures, until they were trusted by coworkers.

Levine and Moreland (1991) argue that work on socialization and training has placed too much emphasis on the specific task knowledge that workers need to perform their individual jobs and on the formal mechanisms used to transmit such knowledge while too little attention has been devoted to the social knowledge that workers need and to informal transmission mechanisms. Those authors identify several kinds of knowledge individuals need to be effective group members: knowledge about the group, including information about group culture, structure, and norms; knowledge about each other, including who is good at what; and knowledge acquired about the kind of work the group performs. (To the extent that this knowledge is acquired through executing the task, it would fit under our reconstruction process.)

The arguments advanced by Feldman (1989) and Levine and Moreland (1991) suggest that group training may be more effective than individual training—at least for certain tasks. In a review of the earlier empirical literature concerning the effectiveness of group versus individual training, Campbell (1971) concluded that team training was better than individual training for tasks requiring interaction, but that its superiority depended on the stimulus fidelity of the task and on the mixture of group and individual reinforcements. Dyer (1985) conducted a more recent review of the team-training literature, with special emphasis on training military teams. She concluded that team training was typically more important for mission success than individual proficiency. The benefits of team training include: greater similarity to the conditions under which units face combat; practice in leader/group interaction and group coordination; opportunities for poorer performers to learn from better performers; and opportunities to build morale and team cohesion. Dyer (1985) emphasized that team training is especially important for tasks involving coordination (cf. Campbell, 1971).

Similarly, Salas and his colleagues emphasize the importance of team training. McCallum et al. (1989) compared behaviors of more effective and less effective teams. Effective teams displayed a higher frequency of behaviors involving asking/giving assistance, identifying errors and reinforcing the identification of these errors than did less effective teams. Effective and less effective teams did not differ in 'morale-building' activities. Leaders of effective teams initiated a smaller percentage of team behavior than those of ineffective teams.

Group composition

Whatever the outcomes of group socialization and training processes the result is a work group composed of members who may exhibit homogeneity or heterogeneity on any of a variety of dimensions. Considerable research has been conducted on the effect of group composition on various performance outcomes. Research in this tradition examines, for example, the effect of group size on group performance, and whether groups that are composed of members who are similar with respect to educational background, ability, beliefs, age and so on perform better than groups composed of members dissimilar on those factors. Moreland and Levine (in press) provide an excellent recent review of the group composition literature.

Some organizational researchers have studied group composition effects under the topic of organizational demography. In his review of the demography literature, Bettenhausen (1991) concluded that most studies have found that homogeneous groups composed of similar members performed better than those composed of dissimilar members. The results of some more recent studies are consistent with that finding. For example, Murnighan and Conlon (1991) found that string quartets that were composed of members who were similar with respect to gender, age, and school backgrounds performed better than those composed of dissimilar members. Jackson, Brett, Sessa, Cooper, Julin, and Peyronnin (1991) found that heterogeneity with respect to age and experience outside the industry was positively related to turnover rates in a study of top management teams in bank holding companies.

In general, we expect that the effect of heterogeneity on group outcomes is likely to depend on the nature of the task, the particular outcome measure(s) studied, and the time span of measurement—as well as on the specific attributes in terms of which heterogeneity-homogeneity is assessed. Recall that, earlier, we identified an organizational dilemma regarding homogeneity (for the sake of consensus) versus diversity (for the sake of a range of skills and abilities) of organizational (or group) personnel. Much of the demography research begs this question, because it focuses on characteristics that may underlie the attainment of value consensus (e.g. age, organizational experience) but ignores the degree of heterogeneity among organizational members in the range of skills and abilities they make use of in their jobs.

One dimension of group demography that has received particular attention lately is tenure—how long individual members have worked in a group or organization. Katz (1982) found that average group tenure was related to the performance of R&D teams in the form of an inverted-U: increases in group tenure or longevity were associated with increases in performance until about 2–4 years, and thereafter were associated with decreases in performance. Finkelstein and Hambrick (1990) found that managerial teams with high (average) tenure followed more persistent strategies that conformed to norms of the industry and performed at levels corresponding to the industry average. O'Reilly, Caldwell and Barnett (1989) found that variation in group tenure among the members of a work group was negatively associated with that group's degree of social integration, which, in turn, was negatively related to group member turnover rates. Goodman and associates found that group familiarity, measured by the number of time a given worker had worked on the same section or job and with the same crew, was positively associated with productivity (Goodman and Leyden, 1991) and negatively associated with accident rates (Goodman and Garber, 1988) in underground coal mines.

High group tenure is the flip side of changes in group membership. Studies have investigated the effect of changes in membership on outcomes such as leadership and the persistence of norms (see also our discussion of turnover and group/organizational learning under the reconstruction process). Insko and his colleagues found that turnover affected the perception of leadership: the most senior (remaining) member in a group was perceived as the leader (Insko, Thibaut, Moehle, Wilson, Diamond, Gilmore, Solomon, and Lipsitz, 1980; Insko, Gilmore, Moehle, Lipsitz, Drenan, and Thibaut, 1982). Trow (1960) found that turnover of group members did not have a negative effect on performance when replacements had previous experience with the task and were at least as able as their predecessors, and when the team had previous experience with the same rate of turnover. On the other hand, Mueller and Price (1989) found that the turnover rate had a negative effect on instrumental communication (i.e. the formal transmission of job information among employees) and behavioral commitment to remain in the organization.

Development of strategies, plans, and procedures

Several researchers have investigated the persistence of group strategy norms in the face of group member turnover, and the transmission of those norms to new 'generations' of group members (e.g. see Jacobs and Campbell, 1961; Weick and Gilfallan, 1971). For example, Weick and Gilfallan (1971) found that groups that were given an arbitrarily chosen, easy strategy in the first generation perpetuated the strategy for the remaining generations of the experiment; whereas groups given an arbitrarily chosen, difficult strategy at the outset abandoned it by the fourth generation–which was the first generation that had no group members present at the start of the study, when the arbitrary, difficult strategy had been imposed. The latter groups adopted a variety of less difficult strategies and these group-chosen strategies persisted for remaining generations. Zucker (1977) found that norms that were institutionalized (that is, norms that were associated with an office and a position rather than with a person) were more likely to persist and be transmitted to new group members than norms that were not institutionalized.

If left to their own devices, groups rarely explicitly plan or develop performance strategies (Hackman, Brousseau, and Weiss, 1976; Weingart, in press). Those that do, however, are likely to perform better, especially under conditions where the appropriate performance strategy is not 'obvious' (Hackman, Brousseau, and Weiss, 1976). Shure, Rogers, Larsen, and Tassone (1962) found that groups that were permitted to plan between periods of task completion performed better than those who could plan only during periods of task completion or who did not have opportunities to discuss and develop plans. Similarly, Weingart (in press) distinguishes between preplanning before performing the task and in-process planning during task performance. She found that groups working toward a difficult goal engaged in less preplanning than those working toward an easy goal.

Assigned group goals

Research has shown that specific and challenging goals can improve performance (cf. Locke, Shaw, Saari, and Latham, 1981). Weldon and her colleagues have developed a theoretical analysis of the processes that mediate that empirically robust relationship (Weldon and Weingart, in press) and have examined some of them empirically (e.g. Weldon, Jehn, and Pradhan, 1991; Weingart, in press). Among the mediating mechanisms that they identify are changes in effort, group planning, changes in individual and group performance plans, and reduced concern for quality. Weingart (in press) found, further, that group goal difficulty influenced group performance through effort, task complexity influenced performance through planning and effort, and the quality of planning also influenced group performance.

In contrast to these studies, Mitchell and Silver (1990) found that people in an individual goal condition performed worse than those in a condition with no specific goal, a group goal condition, and an individual plus group goal condition. They suggest that task strategies mediated the relationship between goal setting and performance, and in particular, that people in the individual goal condition tended to be more competitive and less cooperative than those in the other three conditions.

Technology and structure

Researchers have examined how characteristics of technology affect the structure and performance of groups and organizational units. Much of this work has been carried out in a 'contingency theory' tradition, which argues that the best way to organize depends on characteristics of the environment and the technology. The technological contingency that has received the most attention in the empirical literature is uncertainty or unpredictability. Uncertainty has been examined in relation to dimensions of structure, such as the degree of centralization or formalization of the group. For example, a long tradition of communication studies performed in the laboratory found that centralized structures such as the 'wheel' were more efficient and made fewer errors than decentralized structures for simple tasks (Guetzkow and Simon, 1955; Leavitt, 1951). For complex and uncertain tasks, however, decentralized structures were more efficient and yielded fewer errors (Heise and Miller, 1951; Hutte, 1965; Macy, Christie, and Luce, 1953; Shaw, 1954, 1958, 1964). Furthermore, Faucheaux and Mackenzie (1966) found that groups performing simple tasks evolved toward a centralized structure while those performing complex tasks did not.

Research conducted in the field has also generally provided support for a relationship between (environmental and technological) uncertainty and less formalized, more decentralized structures (Argote, 1982; Becker and Baloff, 1969; Burns and Stalker, 1961; David, Pearce, and Randolph, 1989; Duncan, 1973; Fry and Slocum, 1984; Lawrence and Lorsch, 1967; Schoonhoven, 1981; Van de Ven, Delbecq, and Koenig, 1976). There are some exceptions, however, to this pattern (Bourgeois, McAllister, and Mitchell, 1978; Huber, O'Connell, and Cummings, 1975; Pennings, 1975).

Fry (1982) reviewed a large portion of the literature on technology and structure and found several consistent relationships. First, the largest span of control and the greatest differentiation were found for large batch processing and mass production technologies. Second, the less routine and more uncertain the technology, the more the subunits were likely to adopt less formalized and less centralized structures. Third, the strongest effects of technology on structure were found at the organizational subunit level of analysis (cf. Scott, 1990). The latter finding is not surprising because subunits are more likely to have homogeneous technology than, for example, entire organizations.

Scott (1990) concluded that, although a relationship between technology and structure has been consistently found in the literature, that relationship is not particularly strong. Structure is affected by many other variables such as power, expertise (cf. Barley, 1986), culture (cf. Lincoln, Hanada, and McBride, 1986), personality of the leader (cf. Miller and Droge, 1986), the environment (Duncan, 1973; Lawrence and Lorsch, 1967), and the time of founding (Stinchcombe, 1965). Even though most of this work is at the more macro organizational levels, these multiple contingencies are worth taking into account when examining structural features at a work-group level. A study by Gresov (1989) is a nice example of use of such a multiple-contingency approach to study structure.

Kiesler, Sproull and their colleagues have conducted an extensive program of research on the effects of the introduction of new communication technologies on group and organizational processes (see Kiesler and Sproull, in press, for a review). Their work is characterized by an effective balance of laboratory and field methods. Kiesler and Sproull (in press) conclude that the research evidence shows that, relative to face-to-face meetings, computer-mediated discussions tend to lead to more delays, greater advocacy, 'flaming', more equal participation among group members, and more extreme or risky decisions. The researchers note that technological enhancements in organizational communication systems can lead to outcomes not evident in the laboratory, such as redistributions of work time, relative advantages in participation for peripheral workers, and increases in complexity of group organization.

Adaptive structuration and the socio-technical approach

The idea that structure is multiply determined, rather than being shaped primarily by technology (viewed as a 'given') is carried several steps further in the adaptive structuration tradition. That tradition holds that both organizational (and group) structure and the technology itself are products of an active adaptation process, in which the technology is shaped by the organization or its subunits, as well as being a factor in shaping that organization. For example: Barley (1986) performed an in-depth study of the introduction of a new technology, CT scanners, in two hospitals, working in that adaptive structuration tradition. He found that the introduction of CT scanners increased uncertainty and upset the distribution of expertise and the division of labor in the hospital units. Consistent with findings from studies conducted in the contingency theory tradition, both hospital units became more decentralized with the introduction of the CT scanners and the associated increase in uncertainty. One hospital, however, became more decentralized than the other, and Barley emphasizes this difference between units in the degree of decentralization occasioned by the introduction of the CT scanners.

Poole and his colleagues have also conducted important work in adaptive structuration (e.g. Poole, Seibold, and McPhee, 1985; Poole and Roth, 1988a,b) at the group level, and have introduced the adaptive structuration paradigm as a model for examining the effects of use of electronic media in group decision support systems (e.g. Poole and DeSanctis, 1989, 1990). Some of that work identifies a complex set of alternative group task performance phase sequences, each of them involving an intricate interaction of features of the technology, attributes of the group and its members (including their task performance history), and features of the task at hand. Related work by Bikson, Gutek and colleagues (Bikson and Gutek, 1983; Bikson and Eveland, 1990) has stressed such adaptation in their studies of the importance of the implementation stage when organizations adopt new technology.

In a related area, and working primarily at an organizational level, Daft and his colleagues (Daft and Lengel, 1984; Daft, Lengel, and Trevino, 1987) have examined the relationship between various technologies for communication within groups and organizations on the one hand, and the varying needs for relatively rich media of communication that arise in differing tasks and work settings. These researchers argue that many organizational situations contain high levels of equivocality (i.e. are subject to multiple interpretations) as well as of uncertainty (i.e. a lack of information). They stress the importance of reduction of equivocality, not just reduction of uncertainty. They postulate a continuum of richness of media (with face-to-face communication being at the relatively rich end, and formal written messages such as memos being at the relatively 'lean' or modality-constricted end). They argue that organizational situations vary in degree of equivocality, hence in the need for relatively rich communication. They hypothesize (and find evidence for) a matching of the richness requirements of the situation and the richness of the communication media that successful managers use in those situations.

Closely related to these ideas and with a long history in both group and organizational studies is the socio-technical systems approach, which emphasizes that organizational effectiveness is a joint function of the technical and the social system (Emery and Trist, 1973; Trist and Bamforth, 1951). Many of the early studies in that tradition documented the negative effects of introducing technical arrangements that were incompatible with the needs of the social system (e.g. Trist and Bamforth, 1951).

More recent work growing in part out of that socio-technical approach is the body of research on autonomous work groups and self-managing teams. Core features of autonomous work groups include providing the group with all the resources it needs to do the task, enlarging individual roles, increasing worker participation in decisions, and changing the technical arrangements so that they support those autonomous work groups. A recent empirical study of autonomous work groups in a mineral-processing plant found both positive and negative effects from using such groups. Employees in autonomous work groups had more favorable work attitudes but also higher absenteeism and turnover rates than their counterparts in traditionally designed jobs (Cordery, Mueller, and Smith, 1991). Goodman, Devadas, and Hughson (1988) provide a useful review of the effect of autonomous work groups on outcomes such as productivity, flexibility, job satisfaction and turnover.

Earlier, we noted a dilemma involving, on the one hand, a need for autonomy of work units, for the sake of high motivation of their members, and on the other hand, a need for control by the unit at the next higher level of organization, for the sake of coordinated action (cf. Walton and Hackman, 1986). As we noted in an earlier comment, regarding homogeneity versus diversity of personel, much of the research on autonomous and self-managing work groups seems to beg the other half of the question—what effects does increased autonomy at a given organizational level have on coordination at the next higher organizational level?

Operations Processes: Doing What the Group Does

The operations processes involve a group performing its tasks—whether those be making a decision, laying out a plan, manufacturing a product or providing a service. Typically, as groups perform their tasks, a group activity must be monitored and managed, and conflicts that arise need to be resolved, in order to effect coordination and to meet goals and deadlines. Each of these aspects of group and organizational operations has been given some attention in the research literature.

Task performance processes

Most group and organizational researchers would agree that group task performance processes depend on the nature of the task. Yet there has been relatively little work, theoretical or empirical, to explore those task differences and, especially, to develop a usable conceptual framework or taxonomy for classification of group tasks. McGrath (1984) has provided one such task classification schema; we will use it here, to lay out the different kinds of task performance functions that may be encountered in work groups.

A task classification. McGrath (1984) argues that group tasks can be classified in terms of four underlying performance functions—generating alternatives, choosing among alternatives, resolving conflicts, and executing the (overt, behavioral) performance requirements of a task. Each of these functions subsumes two task types—generating: ideas or plans; choosing: a correct answer or a preferred answer; resolving: conflicts of viewpoint or conflicts of interests; and execution: of performance tasks whose outcomes are to be assessed against external standards or of contests between opposing social units.

McGrath arrays those four performance functions, and the eight task types they subsume, in a two-dimensional circumplex pattern. The two axes of the circumplex reflect the relations of the task types to one another. One axis has to do with the nature of the interdependencies among members of the group. At one end of that axis are tasks on which member performances are relatively independent of one another. Generate tasks, as in the classical brainstorming or creativity tasks, are an exemplar. At the other end of that axis are tasks on which the group's members are in competition—what has been called contrient interdependence—exemplified by negotiation, bargaining, social dilemma, and coalition formation tasks. Those two kinds of tasks will be discussed below, under the headings of 'Groups generating ideas,' and 'Conflict resolution', respectively.

Tasks in the middle of that interdependence axis are the ones characterized by high levels of cooperative interdependence between members. Those tasks are spread along the second axis of the circumplex which has to do with the cognitive versus behavioral requirements of the task. Tasks in the Choose quadrant—problem solving and decision making—are mainly cognitive; tasks in the Execute quadrant are primarily motor performances. Both Choose and Execute tasks often require extensive and intricate coordination among members of the group—but the nature of coordination differs starkly between the cognitive and the motoric domains. They share the label of coordination but may have little else in common.

Group performance of cognitive tasks requires coordination of activities involving information acquisition, processing, and sharing, so as to maximize information in the group, minimize redundancy, avoid overload, and attain a consensus regarding the meanings of that information (i.e. reduce equivocality). Group performance of motor tasks, on the one hand, requires both within-member and between-member synchronization (temporal coordination) of activities involving the processing of materials or the direct application of services. For those tasks, it is often very critical to be able to execute interdependent actions that are temporally synchronized and substantively

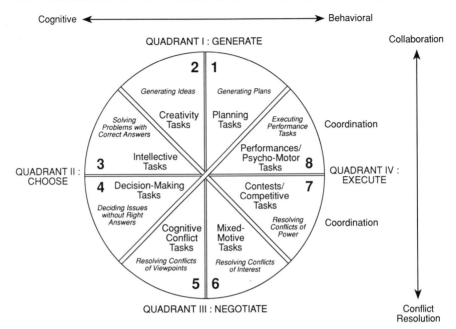

Figure 9.3 Task circumplex: a task classification scheme (adapted from McGrath, 1984)

coordinated within micro-temporal tolerance levels—that is, split second timing.

Most of the theory and research on coordination in groups and organizations has dealt with cognitive tasks rather than motor performances. Exceptions are some of the work on military crews (see McCallum et al., 1989; Dyer, 1985) and some of the work by Goodman on underground coal mining (Goodman and Leyden, 1991). These matters will be discussed further under the headings 'Group performance of cognitive tasks', and 'Coordination in task performance', below.

Some major empirical findings and the ideas of process losses. Three apparently robust empirical findings have shaped much of the empirical and theoretical work on group task performance in the past, namely: (i) that groups are likely to be less effective at solving certain kinds of intellective problems than the group's 'best member' would have been—that is, that 'truth supported', rather than 'truth', wins (see discussion of Laughlin's work under intellective tasks); (ii) that groups of size *n* will produce more, but far less than *n* times more, when given the task of generating ideas or some concrete product; and (iii) that groups engaged in finding a preferred solution to tasks that do not have a single best answer (that is, groups making decisions or judgments rather than solving problems) sometimes experience difficulties in reaching consensus (because of disputes among internal factions) and sometimes reach consensus on the basis of conformity pressures rather than the available information (as in 'groupthink'). There is a long history of work on how group members combine their skills, abilities, and attitudes into a group 'solution' (see McGrath, 1984, for a review). Much of that work has involved the development of combinatorial models—which make a number of assumptions about both member and group processes, and about the nature of the tasks being performed—and then a comparison of actual group performances to the performances predicted by those models.

Steiner (1972) reviewed much of that work and summarized its implications in the concept of 'process losses'. When groups perform less well than has been predicted from some model of how individual members' skills and abilities ought to be combined (e.g. the difference between intellective task performance of the best member and of the interacting groups), they are said to suffer process losses (Steiner, 1972). Process losses are reductions in effectiveness that come about because of coordination and motivational problems associated with increasing group size (from individual to dyad to larger groups).

Various decision aids and techniques (e.g. the Delphi technique and the Nominal Group technique), and more recently, computer mediation by means of electronic group support systems, have been proposed as methods for minimizing process losses and improving both group performance on intellective problems (with correct answers) and group decision making on tasks for which there is no correct answer. Rao and Jarvinpaa (1991) provide a recent review of the literature on group decision support systems (see also reviews by Hollingshead and McGrath, in press, and McGrath and Hollingshead, 1993).

It should be noted that the idea of process losses—when assessed by comparison of group performance with prediction of a combinatorial model—makes a number of assumptions about groups that likely do not hold even in laboratory groups and certainly do not hold for many work groups. First, it assumes that the experimenter knows the correct or best solution, and the optimal path for arriving at it. Second, it assumes that the acting group is not (or at least should not) be doing anything else except the specific task the experimenter has in mind. All other behavior, relating to the task, to the group's process, or whatever, is to be regarded as error, as process losses. In contrast, the group theory laid out in the first section of this chapter (McGrath, 1990) regards acting groups as engaged in multiple projects, often simultaneously; as concerned with three major functions, production, group well-being, and member support, also simultaneously, and as carrying out their work through complex task/activity paths rather than via a fixed sequence of phases or stages of activity. In that view, much of what has been regarded as 'process losses'—somehow reflecting flaws and limitations in those groups—are, rather, to be regarded as evidence that the group is engaged in a more complex production path than the researcher's model anticipated, or is engaged in one of the other functions, or is engaged in one or more projects other than or in addition to the one the researcher had been focusing on. From that perspective, the object of the game is to figure out what the group is doing, and why—rather than to try to identify its 'errors' in the group's process, and then institute interventions (such as Delphi, NGT) to 'fix' it.

As will be evident in the review below, the idea of process losses, and the issues related to group task performance, differ for various kinds of tasks.

Groups generating ideas

The findings regarding the inferiority of groups in rate of generation of ideas, noted above, came about by attempts to test the efficacy of group brainstorming and other related techniques (see McGrath, 1984, for a review). More recently, Diehl and Stroebe (1991) have reopened those issues, presenting both a new conceptualization of the problem and a series of experiments testing that conceptualization. Their work hinges around the idea that group brainstorming—which may well reduce some of the evaluation concerns of members working in groups without the brainstorming rules—nevertheless may prevent higher group production by two essentially artifactual features of that method as implemented. First, groups suffer from 'production blocking'— reduction in amount of time and opportunity per member for putting ideas on the table. Second, groups suffer from various distractions—they cannot think, let alone talk, while they are listening to others present their ideas. Further explorations of these and other features of group performance on tasks requiring generation of ideas are certainly called for.

Group performance of cognitive tasks

McGrath's task categorization in part follows Laughlin's earlier distinction between intellective and judgment or decision tasks—the former having to do with solving a problem that presumably has a correct answer (or correct method of solution), and the latter having to do with developing group consensus on issues that do not have correct answers.

Intellective tasks. Laughlin and his colleagues have conducted an impressive program of research on group performance on problems with a correct answer (e.g. see Laughlin, 1980; Laughlin and Adamopoulos, 1982). Their results indicate strongly that the model that fits the data best is generally a 'truth supported wins' model; that is, if two group members have the right answer, the group will choose the right alternative. For Eureka-type problems in which the right answer is very compelling, the best-fitting model is 'truth wins'.

Groups are almost always more accurate than their average member but they seldom do as well as their best members or as well as predicted by combinatorial rules based on a 'truth wins' model (see Hill, 1982, for a review). On the other hand, groups are considerably better than individuals at identifying and eliminating errors, at rejecting nonplausible alternatives in induction tasks, and at recognizing correct answers once they have been proffered.

Judgment and decision tasks. Two streams of research have dominated the research literature on tasks requiring groups to develop consensus on issues that do not have a correct answer (see McGrath, 1984, for a review). One stream of research in this tradition is the risky shift or group polarization literature (see Dion, Baron, and Miller, 1970, and Myers and Lamm, 1976, for reviews). Another stream of research is the work on jury decision making (see Bray and Kerr, 1981, and Penrod and Hastie, 1979, for reviews). In the latter, Davis' Social Decision Scheme theory (Davis, 1973) examines how group member inputs (e.g. a juror's initial judgments) get combined into a single group output (e.g. a verdict). Results suggest that the mock juries in the studies seem to use a 'two-thirds majority wins' rule (Davis, Bray, and Holt, 1977).

Recent trends. More recently research in this area has begun to deal with a number of additional features of those cognitive tasks, with several lines of promising research. First, Laughlin and colleagues (Hollingshead, 1991; Laughlin, 1988; Laughlin and Shippy, 1983; Laughlin and Sweeney, 1977; Laughlin, Vander Stoep, and Hollingshead, 1991) have extended their work on intellective problems (tasks with correct answers) to deal with group and individual induction, and with group learning and transfer effects. (This work is also relevant to our discussion of group learning under Reconstruction processes, below.) Second, Sniezek and her colleagues (Sniezek, 1992; Sniezek and Buckley, in preparation; Sniezek and Henry, 1989; Sniezek, Paese, and Switzer, in press) have begun to study effects of levels of individual and group confidence on group judgment processes, and to explore the operation of various structural patterns (e.g. 'advisor-judge' models) by which work groups can carry out their decision-making processes. Third, several sets of researchers (e.g. Davis, Kameda, Parks, Stasson, and Zimmerman, 1989; Hinsz, 1990; Stasser, Taylor, and Hanna, 1989; Stasser and Titus, 1985, 1987; Tindale, 1989) have expanded their work to examine a number of aspects of groups as information-processing systems, including such issues as distribution of information, group remembering, informational and social influence processes, and the like. Several other sets of researchers are examining how groups amplify or attentuate cognitive biases found at the individual level of analysis (Argote, Seabright, and Dyer, 1986; Argote, Devadas, and Melone, 1990; Nagao, Tindale, Hinsz, and Davis, 1985; Neale, Bazerman, Northcraft, and Alperson, 1986) and other aspects of groups as information-processing systems (Harmon and Rohrbaugh, 1990; Lazega, 1990). These new lines of work make this an exciting area with high potential for aiding our understanding of task performance processes in work groups.

Coordination in task performance

While coordination has been regarded as an important variable in theoretical work on groups and in organization theory (March and Simon, 1958; Thompson, 1967; Malone, 1986, 1988; Steiner, 1972) it has received little empirical attention. Exceptions at the organization level include work by Georgopoulos and Mann (1962), Georgopoulos (1972), Van de Ven, Delbecq, and Koenig (1976) and Argote (1982). Van de Ven, Delbecq, and Koenig (1976) found that as uncertainty increased, organizational use of programs and rules to achieve coordination decreased and reliance on personal, horizontal channels of communication increased. Argote (1982) found that uncertainty about patient inputs moderated the relationship between means of coordination and measures of organizational effectiveness. When uncertainty was low, programmed means of coordination were more strongly related to effectiveness. When uncertainty was high, nonprogrammed means of coordination were most effective. Malone (1986, 1988) suggests that technology and task differences make different forms of coordination (e.g. hierarchies versus markets) more effective. Komacki, Desselles, and Bowman (1989) add team coordination to their operant model of effective supervision. Coordination—for both cognitive and motoric tasks—is a critical area that would benefit from additional research at the group level.

Conflict resolution

Conflict occurs when group members believe that their goals cannot be achieved simultaneously. The resolution of conflict is an important part of the operations process. Levine and Moreland (1990) provide an excellent review of the literature on conflict in groups. They review several bodies of literature related to conflict including social dilemmas, bargaining, coalition formation and majority and minority influence. Carnevale and Pruitt (1992) review the literature on negotiation and mediation, procedures for resolving conflict.

One type of conflict that occurs in groups has been termed a social dilemma. An example of a social dilemma arises in the shared use of an exhaustible resource. While an individual may be better off taking as much of the resource as possible, the group would be worse off if all individuals did this since the resource would be eliminated. Reviews of the research on social dilemmas can be found in Messick and Brewer (1983) and Orbell and Dawes (1981).

Mannix (1991) conducted a recent study in the social dilemma paradigm. She compared groups who believed that the value of their resources depreciated at a fast rate (high-discount groups) to groups believing that their resources depreciated at a slow rate (low-discount groups). The former were more likely to form coalitions that distributed funding to only a subset of group members. Furthermore, as a result of forming more coalitions, high-discount groups had significantly lower group outcomes than low-discount groups.

Researchers are beginning to extend work on bargaining and negotiation beyond the case of two contending parties to multi-party cases (Bazerman, Mannix, Sondak, and Thompson, 1989; Bazerman, Mannix, and Thompson, 1988; Kramer, 1991). Mannix, Thompson, and Bazerman (1989) argue that the development of integrative solutions is more difficult among multiple parties than in the two-party case: because groups have increased information-processing demands, decision rules must be developed to determine when an agreement has been reached, and interpersonal relationships are more complex and involve the potential for coalitions. Those authors found significant main and interaction effects, for sequential versus package agendas, majority versus unanimous decision rules, and equal versus unequal distribution of power among the parties, on the decision-making structure and outcomes on a mixed-motive negotiation task. In another vein, Brett (1991) draws on recent negotiation research to prescribe effective techniques for transforming conflict within groups into high quality decisions by those groups. Nunamaker, Dennis, Valacich, and Vogel (1991) and Poole, Holmes, and DeSanctis (1991) describe the results of empirical studies of group decision support systems designed to influence conflict management and negotiation in groups.

It is notable that most of the research on conflict and conflict resolution, in groups and organizations, deals with conflict in relatively formal 'confrontational' situations—where two or more parties (such as labor and management) are recognized as having different and partially conflicting interests, and where activities involve formal agreements that can ameliorate conflict among the contending parties. Much of the conflict within actual work groups, however, is of a more informal kind—discontents of particular members with their assigned role responsibilities, and/or with their rewards; personal animosities between group members who are assigned to work interdependently; disagreements about how the task can best be done and who should make the micro-decisions involved in its execution. Conflicts of these informal kinds are highlighted in TIP theory, discussed earlier in this chapter, but have not played a very big part in the empirical research of this field. See Robey, Farrow, and Franz (1989) for an exception.

Leadership

Leadership has received much attention in the research literature for both group and organizational levels (see Levine and Moreland, 1990, and Yago, 1982 for reviews). Some of the perspectives on leadership that have had an impact on past group research and theory include: the human relations approach (Likert, 1961); the Ohio State studies on consideration and initiating structure (Fleishman, 1973); Fiedler's contingency theory (Fiedler, 1967); Vroom and Yetton's decision-making model (Vroom and Yetton, 1973); path-goal theories (House and Mitchell, 1974); Graen's vertical dyad linkage model (Graen and Cashman, 1975); theories of transformational or charismatic leadership (House, 1977); Kerr and Jermier's work on substitutes for leadership (Kerr and Jermier, 1978); work on the social construction of leadership (Chen and Meindl, 1991); and new research on trait-based approaches to leadership (Zaccaro, Foti, and Kenny, 1991).

Two recent approaches to leadership focus explicitly on leadership phenomena in work groups. Hackman and Walton (1986) take a functional approach to leadership, arguing that leaders are effective to the extent that they ensure that all functions critical to task accomplishment and group maintenance are performed. Building on an earlier conceptualization by McGrath (1962), as well as on their own earlier work (e.g. Hackman and Morris, 1975), Hackman and Walton (1986) develop a matrix in which a list of critical leadership functions is related to sets of conditions that foster group effectiveness. The two general leadership functions are monitoring (obtaining and interpreting data) and taking action to create or maintain favorable performance conditions, and these can be directed to information or conditions either internal or external to the group. The conditions that promote group effectiveness are: (i) clear and engaging direction; (ii) a 'facilitative' group structure, including a well-structured task, and appropriately composed group, and appropriate norms; (iii) a supportive organizational context, including reward, training and information systems; (iv) expert coaching; and (v) adequate material resources. Hackman and Walton (1986) point out that the focus of leader actions will be internal to the group at times (e.g. coordinating the activities of group members) and external to the group at other times (e.g. negotiating with superiors for more resources). The external orientation of some leader activities is relevant for our discussion of the external relations processes, later in this chapter.

Komaki, Desselles, and Bowman (1989) take a very different approach to team leadership. They extend an operant model of effective supervision to teams and identify what leaders should do to optimize team performance. They tested their model in a study of sailboat racing, and found two leader behaviors that differentiated successful from unsuccessful race teams: monitoring performance; and providing feedback about consequences to subordinates.

Temporal processes

McGrath and his colleagues have called attention to an important aspect of group life—its temporal dimension (Kelly, 1988; Kelly, Futuran, and McGrath, 1990; Kelly and McGrath, 1985; McGrath, 1988, 1991; McGrath and Kelly, 1986, 1992; McGrath, Kelly, and Machatka, 1984). At the core of their empirical work is the concept of entrainment, which refers to the synchronization or temporal coordination of two or more processes (McGrath, 1991). These authors argue that much group behavior involves both the mutual entrainment of endogenous performance rhythms among group members, and the subsequent entrainment of those bundles of activities to external pacers, such as deadlines or work schedules.

In an early experiment in their program (McGrath, Kelly, and Machatka, 1984), they investigated the effect of 'task load' (20, 40, or 80 anagrams to solve), 'time limit' (5, 10, or 20 minutes to solve), and group size (1, 2, or 4 persons) on performance. Each group had three work periods. The task load remained the same for all periods for any given group, but the time interval either increased, decreased or remained constant. Results regarding initial trials supported several prior findings from the group research literature: groups of any size and for any given time interval solved more anagrams per member-minute the higher the assigned task load; groups of any size and for any given task load solved more anagrams per member-minute the shorter the time limit; and for any given load and time limit, productivity was higher the smaller the size of the group. Thus, the more the work load per member-minute, the more work got done.

Of more interest here, groups seemed to become entrained to the initial amount of time they had to perform the task. For example, dyads in the 5-, 10-, 20-minute trial sequence solved more anagrams in each time period than did subjects in the comparable time periods when they had the sequence: 20-, 10-, and 5-minute trials, for the same task load; and dyads who had a 10-minute period for all three trials scored in between the groups with increasing or decreasing time limit sequences. The second trials were 10 minutes long for all conditions. The second trial performance rates varied as a function of what time interval groups had experienced on the prior trial (Trial 1). These results suggest that groups synchronize their rates of work to fit the temporal conditions of the work situation, and that the initial time limit established a temporal patterning for task performance that persisted even when surrounding temporal conditions had changed.

In other studies (e.g. Kelly and McGrath, 1985; Kelly, Futoran, and McGrath, 1990), those researchers have shown that not only group performance rates but group communications and interaction patterns, and some aspects of product quality, are also susceptible to entrainment processes. For example: short time limits on an initial task seem to induce groups to spend more time on task-oriented behaviors and less time on interpersonal interaction; whereas groups with a longer time period for their initial task engage in more interpersonal interactions. These patterns, too, carry over into later trials even when the initial time conditions no longer hold on those trials.

In subsequent work, Kelly, Futoran, and McGrath (1990) have identified two different temporal patterns for entrainment of task performance that arise as a function of different task conditions on the initial work period. One pattern comes about when the group's experience on initial trials leads to problems of capacity (i.e. not enough time to do all of the required tasks, although each task is easy enough to do). The other pattern comes about when the group's experience on initial trials leads to problems of capability (i.e. the task is difficult to do even though there is plenty of time to do it in). The former (capacity problem) leads to a faster rate of task activity on subsequent trials regardless of the actual time limits set for those later trials; the latter (capability problem) leads to more extensive processing of information, hence to a slower rate of production on subsequent trials, regardless of the actual time limits set for those later trials.

Gersick (1988, 1989) has also done important work on temporal issues in work groups. She has studied the effects of deadlines on group development and performance. In a study of the development of eight naturally occurring task forces (i.e. groups created to carry out a specific project), Gersick (1988) found that groups did not progress on their tasks through a given standard sequence of activities. Rather, each group showed a distinctive pattern of performance strategies, interaction styles, and external relationships. The initial approach of the group persisted for the first half of the group's allotted time. Then, every group underwent a major transition: Old approaches were dropped, new patterns were adopted and significant progress was made. Each group experienced its transition almost exactly halfway (in clock and calendar time) between its first meeting and its deadline for completion of the project, even though the amount of time different groups had to do their projects varied from 7 days to 6 months. Gersick (1989) replicated these field study findings in a laboratory experiment.

Both Gersick, and McGrath and colleagues, suggest that group interaction and task performance are characterized by many such forms of temporal patterning, and that these affect work group activity and its outcomes in a number of ways. They urge more study of temporal processes in this and other areas of social and behavioral sciences. We would endorse that recommendation.

Reconstruction Processes: The Embedding of New Knowledge

As groups gain experience in executing their tasks, they acquire knowledge. The Reconstruction processes entail changes in the system (groups, organizations) resulting from the embedding of knowledge acquired through execution of the task. This knowledge can be preserved by being embedded in the people, in the technology, and/or in the purposes, plans, and procedures of the group. Such preservation typically, although not always, leads to improved group performance.

This important set of group processes, ignored for many years, has been receiving increasing attention in the recent research literature—more at the organizational than at the group level. If, where, and how knowledge is embedded has important implications both for the performance of the system (its task effectiveness in subsequent cycles) and for its impact on the system itself (i.e. changes in people, in technology, and in system purposes).

The group and organizational learning literature is especially relevant for the reconstruction processes; see Huber (1991) for an excellent recent review of the organizational learning literature. Other streams of relevant work concern transactive memory and collective remembering (Wegner, 1986; Clark and Stephenson, 1989), and some of the adaptive structuration literature discussed earlier (e.g. see Barley, 1986; Poole, Siebold, and McPhee, 1986).

Organizational learning

The organizational learning literature focuses on how organizations acquire knowledge as they gain experience, how this knowledge is embedded in organizations, and what the effect of such changes in knowledge is on later performance (cf. Cyert and March, 1963; Argyris and Schon, 1978; Levitt and March, 1988; Walsh and Ungson, 1991). Much past literature on organizational learning consisted of conceptual/theoretical pieces that emphasize the acquisition of knowlege (Duncan and Weiss, 1979; Fiol and Lyles, 1985; Hedberg, 1981) and the development of organizational routines and standard operating procedures (Cyert and March, 1963; Levitt and March, 1988) as organizations gain experience. Gersick and Hackman (1990) discuss the functional and dysfunctional aspects of routines in task-performing groups.

However, there is a growing body of empirical literature on organizational learning curves, which is a special case of the more general literature on organizational learning. This literature examines the relationship between changes in organizational experience and changes in level of performance (see Yelle, 1979, and Dutton and Thomas, 1984, for reviews). Early work focused on changes in productivity associated with increasing organizational experience. Researchers found that as organizations gained experience in production, the unit cost of production typically decreased at a decreasing rate (e.g. see Wright, 1936; Alchian, 1963; Rapping, 1965). This pattern has been found to characterize a wide range of production activities in both the manufacturing and service sectors (Argote and Epple, 1990). There is consdierable variation across organizations, however, in the rate at which productivity grows with increasing experience (Dutton and Thomas, 1984; Hayes and Clark, 1986).

While early work on organizational learning curves focused on the relationship between experience and the unit cost of production, recent work looks at a broader set of outcome measures such as industrial accidents per unit of output (Greenberg, 1971), defects per unit of output (Argote, in press), and late deliveries per unit of output (Darr and Argote, 1991).

Researchers are also investigating the factors responsible for organizational learning curves in order to account for the large observed variation among firms in rates of productivity gains (Hayes and Clark, 1986; Argote and Epple, 1990). Lieberman (1984) found that research and development expenditures accelerated the rate of productivity gains in chemical-processing industries. Surprisingly, both Hayes and Clark (1986) and Galbraith (1990) found that investment in training had a negative effect on productivity gains. The researchers suggested that the negative relationship may have been found either because training was used as a corrective device after productivity problems had already developed, or because the measures of training used in these studies reflected training time but not the quality of training. Adler and Clark (1991) found mixed evidence about the effects of training (and of engineering change orders) on productivity gains.

Argote, Beckman, and Epple (1990) found that turnover of direct production workers was not related to productivity gains in shipyards. Jobs of production workers were standardized and designed to be relatively low in skill requirements (Lane, 1951). The formalized structures of the shipyards may have buffered the organizations from the disruptive effects of turnover.

Devadas and Argote (1990) tested the hypothesis that the effect of turnover on productivity gains depended on whether knowledge is embedded in the work group and its structures, roles and procedures, or in the skills and knowledge of individual workers. They reasoned that in highly structured groups—where roles are elaborated and procedures exist—knowledge is embedded in the group's structure, and therefore group performance ought not be affected very much by the turnover of individual members. In contrast, for groups lacking such structure knowledge can only be embedded in individuals. In these groups, performance ought to be affected by the departure of individual members. Their empirical results supported those expectations.

The results of simulations of the effect of turnover performed by Carley (1992) are consistent with the empirical results of Devadas and Argote (1990). Carley (1992) compared the effect of turnover on teams and hierarchies. She found that while teams in general learn faster and better than hierarchies, hierarchies are less affected by turnover.

Argote, Epple, Devadas, and Murphy (1990) examined the effect of turnover on productivity gains in truck production. They found that the effect of turnover depended on the skill of the departing members: Turnover of highly skilled production workers had a significant negative effect on productivity gains, whereas other types of turnover did not.

Other researchers have examined whether knowledge acquired through learning by doing persists over time, or whether it depreciates. In the conventional formulation of the learning curve, cumulative output is used as a proxy for knowledge acquired through production. This formulation assumes that knowledge is cumulative and that it persists through time. Recent evidence, however, suggests that knowledge may depreciate. That depreciation is evidenced by findings indicating that recent output rates may be a more important predictor of current production than are cumulative output rates spanning a long period of the past (Argote, Beckman, and Epple, 1990).

Why should such knowledge depreciate? Turnover could contribute to the depreciation and loss of organizational knowledge (Simon, 1991). This seems especially likely when organizations do not have procedures and formalized structures (cf. Devadas and Argote, 1990) and when organizational knowledge is embedded in the cognitive and skill apparati of highly skilled workers (cf. Argote et al., 1990). Depreciation could also be caused by changes in the purpose, product or process that render previous knowledge obsolete, or because it is difficult to access organizational records or prior work routines in which the knowledge had been embedded.

Argote (in press) draws on Lenehan's (1982) description of the Steinway piano company to illustrate where and how knowledge can be embedded in organizations. When Steinway's New York facility decided to put a discontinued piano back into production, it discovered that it did not have any records or blueprints about how to make the piano. In order to learn how to make the piano, an engineer who owned one of the models tore it apart and made drawings of its design. He also located records of the piano manufacturing process at Steinway's facility in Germany, and a retired foreman who had valuable notes about how to make the piano. This illustrates how knowledge can be embedded in individuals, in products and purposes, in records, and in the structure of relationships (i.e. the piano itself as a model of its own manufacturing process).

The Steinway example is consistent with theoretical treatments of where knowledge can be embedded in systems. Levitt and March (1988) discuss how knowledge can be embedded in 'documents, accounts, files, standard operating procedures and rule books, in the social and physical geography of organizational structures and relationships, in standards of good professional practice, in the culture of organizational stories, and in shared perceptions of the way things are done around here' (p. 13). Walsh and Ungson (1991) describe how organizational knowledge is distributed across various 'retention facilities' in the organization. These 'retention facilities' include the individuals who work for the organization; the organization's culture; standard operating procedures and practices; roles and organizational structures; and the physical structure of the workplace.

There seems to be agreement that knowledge acquired through executing the task can be embedded in group norms and culture. But while there has been much theorizing about how norms and culture develop (e.g. see Feldman, 1984; Schein, 1990), there is little empirical evidence on the issue. An exception to this is the work of Bettenhausen and Murnighan (1985, 1991). Bettenhausen and Murnighan (1991) found that pairs of individuals who, while bargaining, had continuous cooperative experiences, formed cooperative norms; whereas pairs that had had competitive experiences formed competitive norms. Interpersonal challenges questioning the appropriateness of the group's norms were more successful when they were cooperative. Structural challenges, advocating changes in the task or environment, were more successful when they were competitive. These latter challenges are relevant for the external relations process to be discussed shortly.

Argote (1989) found that agreement about norms was positively associated with the effectiveness of 30 hospital emergency units, but cautioned that the relationship might very well not hold in special cases where the content of the norm was against effectiveness (as was the case for many of the early studies of this topic; cf. Berkowitz, 1954; Schachter, Ellertson, McBride, and Gregory, 1951; Seashore, 1954).

Further research is needed to understand the conditions under which knowledge is stored in various 'retention facilities' within the organization, and to examine the implications that various locations of stored knowledge may have for the persistence or decay of that knowledge, the ease with which it can be brought into play when useful, and the extent to which it transfers across groups and organizations. (The latter, the transfer of knowledge across groups, is discussed under our review of the process of managing external relations.)

Transactive memory and group learning

Related research at the group level focuses on transactive memory and group learning. Transactive memory is concerned with how groups structure and process information collectively (Wegner, 1986; Wegner, Erber, and Raymond, 1991). A transactive memory system is 'a set of individual memory systems in combination with the communication that takes place between individuals' (Wegner, 1986; p. 186). The transactive memory perspective emphasizes that other individuals can be locations of external storage for a given individual. As groups execute a task, individual members learn who is expert about what and rely on these other individuals for expertise in their particular areas. This expands the information available to a particular individual since he or she can rely on the expertise of other group members. Wegner (1986) notes, however, that the connections to other memory systems can create the potential for errors. Furthermore, transactive memory may be very sensitive to effects of turnover. The concept of transactive memory seems promising. Research is needed to determine how groups form transactive memories, the consequences of various memory structures for group outcomes, and the consequences of various changes in group membership, tasks, and conditions, for these transactive memory processses.

In a closely related area, Clark and Stephenson (1989) have examined group or collaborative remembering (see also Hartwick, Sheppard, and Davis, 1982; Hinsz, 1990). Clark and Stephenson (1989) define collaborative remembering as the negotiation of a joint account of a past mutual experience with others. In their review of the literature, Clark and Stephenson identify several empirical regularities about collaborative remembering. Groups generally recall a greater quantity of material than individuals. Collaborative remembering not only extends the volume, and therefore the range of content, of individual remembering, it also yields greater accuracy of recall. It particularly helps in reducing type I, or reconstructive errors—the inclusion of material in recall that is consistent with, but did not actually appear in, the original material.

Such reconstructive errors are less frequent in collaborative than in individual remembering.

Watson, Michaelson, and Sharp (1991) examined the extent to which increased experience in working in a group would affect group versus individual problem solving. Groups worked together over the course of a semester for approximately 30 hours. Two of the three performance measures used in the study indicate that with increased experience, groups were better able to utilize their members' knowledge in making decisions.

Concluding comments

The literatures on group learning and remembering, on transactive memory, and on organizational learning have progressed in parallel with little cross-fertilization. We suspect that each line of work would benefit from information acquired in the other. For example, building on more micro work on group learning and transactive memory should help us understand why organizations sometimes 'learn' inappropriate or maladaptive responses. Conversely, the work on organizational learning could help to elucidate the consequences of effective or ineffective transactive memory systems for performance outcomes.

External Relations Processes: Monitoring and Managing the Group's Relations to its Embedding Systems

Several lines of work are relevant for understanding the processes through which groups manage their external relations. One stream is the work of Ancona and her colleagues which emphasizes how groups acquire knowledge about the environment and how they manage external relations with it (e.g. see Ancona, 1990; Ancona and Caldwell, 1988). Another stream of work is on knowledge transfer—how organizations learn from the experience of others and import knowledge into their system from the external environment (e.g. see Argote and Epple, 1990; Levitt and March, 1988). A third line of work emphasizes how groups respond to environmental threat and uncertainty, including crises (e.g. see Staw, Sandelands, and Dutton, 1981). Those various lines of work draw on several general theoretical perspectives: resource dependence theory (Pfeffer and Salancik, 1978), institutional theory (DiMaggio and Powell, 1983; Meyer and Rowan, 1977; Scott, 1987), contingency theory (Burns and Stalker, 1961), and socio-technical systems theory (Trist and Bamforth, 1951; Emery and Trist, 1973).

Managing external relations

The work of Ancona and her colleagues takes an external perspective to understanding groups. The findings of her study of 100 sales teams (Gladstein, 1984) underscore the importance of the external context in understanding group performance. She found that, although variation between groups in their self-reported measures of group effectiveness could be accounted for by internal factors (e.g. intragroup processes, leadership, training, and organizational tenure), variation among these groups in sales revenue was not related to those factors. Instead, sales revenue was positively correlated with market growth (an external factor) and with organizational experience.

Ancona and her colleagues have also examined the strategies by which groups deal with their external environments. In a study of new product development teams, Ancona and Caldwell (1988) identified three strategies: initiating transactions to either import or export information, resources or support; responding to the initiatives of those outside the groups; and changing the definitions of who is part of the group. Similarly, Ancona (1990) identified three strategies that teams adopt vis-à-vis their environments: informing, parading, and probing. Informing teams remain isolated from their environment. Parading teams passively observe their environments. Probing teams revise their knowledge of the environment through external contact, initiate programs with outsiders, and promote their team's achievements. Probing teams were rated as the best performers among the five consulting teams studied. Member cohesiveness and satisfaction on teams using the probing strategy, however, suffered in the short run.

The literature on intergroup relations is also relevant for understanding how a focal group relates to other groups. Messick and Mackie (1989) provide a recent review of that literature. Brett and Rognes (1986) focus on identifying factors that lead to effective intergroup relations in organizations and on identifying techniques for managing intergroup relations.

The resource-dependence perspective emphasizes that knowledge of the environment is critical for understanding the behavior of organizations. According to resource-dependence theory, organizational effectiveness depends on managing the demands of interest groups and obtaining critical resources (Pfeffer and Salanick, 1978). Organizations are most influenced by those who control important and critical resources for which there are few, if any, alternative sources. Pfeffer and Salancik (1978) discuss various means of changing dependence patterns, such as mergers, vertical and horizontal integration, diversification, growth, joint ventures, the use of interlocking boards of directors, and the formation of associations. Some of these strategies are also available to groups and can be used by them to manage their external relations. The socio-technical systems approach described earlier in our discussion of the construction process also emphasizes that organizations are open to their environments (Emery and Trist, 1973) and draw both information and material resources from them.

Transfer of knowledge

Levitt and March (1988) note that not only do organizations learn from their own direct experience, they also learn from the experience of others. Thus, groups can learn by importing or transferring knowledge from the external environment. The transfer can occur through a variety of mechanisms including: importing personnel with relevant knowledge, observing and/or communicating with other groups, obtaining access to other groups' records and documentation, attending conferences and educational programs, and obtaining technology and products of other groups that have critical knowledge embedded in them (cf. the Steinway example).

Knowledge imported from outside the group is difficult to measure. One approach to measuring this knowledge, which comes out of the learning-curve framework, involves aggregating cumulative output across all groups or organizations in the environment that produce the same product. Just as cumulative output serves as a proxy variable for knowledge acquired by a particular group or organization through experience (see earlier discussion), so cumulative output aggregated across all firms in the environment serves as a proxy variable for knowledge acquired through experience by the industry. In this line of analysis, it is assumed that when cumulative output aggregated across all firms in the environment shows a significant association with the productivity of a particular firm over time, then transfer of learning has occurred. That is, it is assumed that rises in productivity of the focal firm occurred because it benefited from knowledge acquired by other firms in the environment. When using this approach, it is important, of course, to control for other factors besides transfer that affect productivity. Most researchers have studied transfer of knowledge using such a multi-factor approach. Some of those are discussed next.

Using this approach, Zimmerman (1982) examined the transfer of construction knowledge across 10 nuclear reactors built from 1953 to 1963. Construction experience was separated into individual plant experience and aggregate industry experience. While individual plant experience was a more important predictor of construction costs, aggregate industry experience accounted for a significant portion of variance in plant cost. Thus transfer of learning seemed to occur across these organizations, since individual firms benefited from knowledge acquired in the environment.

Transfer is selective. Joskow and Rose (1985) examined transfer across over 400 coal-burning, steam-electric-generating units built from 1960 to 1980. Experience was separated into firm-specific experience, architect-engineer experience, and industry experience. Results indicated that firm-specific and architect/engineer experience accounted for significant portions of variance in unit costs. That is, transfer occurred within firms, and across firms built by the same architect-engineer but not across other firms in the industry.

Darr and Argote (1991) found evidence of transfer in the production of pizzas in 35 fast food franchises in a Midwestern standard metropolitan statistical area. The researchers examined the effect on productivity of store experience, of experience aggregated across all stores in the same franchise, and of experience aggregated across all stores in the area. Results indicated that store experience and franchise experience were significant predictors of productivity, but not the experience of all stores in the area. Thus, such transfer from outside is selective: transfer occurred across stores that were part of the same franchise.

Epple, Argote, and Devadas (1991) examined transfer of productivity gains across shifts within a truck plant. The researchers found that experience with truck production was carried forward when the plant made the transition from one to two shifts. The transfer was not complete, however, since not all of the knowledge possessed by the first shift was transferred to the second.

While there have been many studies of individual's perceptions about how to transfer knowledge across organizations, few studies have examined the relationship between the use of transfer mechanisms and the performance of 'recipient' organizations. An exception is a recent study by Galbraith (1990). Galbraith (1990) found that it was difficult to transfer technologies that are complex and in the early phases of development. Conversely, experience with previous technology transfers and a greater financial stake in the new technology facilitated technology transfer.

Argote, Beckman, and Epple (1990) found that shipyards which began production later were more productive than those with earlier start dates. Once shipyards began production, however, they did not benefit further from production experience at other yards. Kelsey, Mullin, Detre, Mitchell, Cowley, Gruentzig, and Kent (1984) found similar results in their study of angioplasty surgery success rates. These researchers assumed that calendar time was an adequate proxy variable for knowledge acquired in the general environment. The researchers found that calendar time was a significant predictor of surgical success rates only for the first 20 or so operations performed by a surgeon. The researchers suggested that surgeons were most likely to learn from the experience of others when they first began to perform the procedure. Thus, there is evidence that transfer may occur across organizations, but that it seems particularly likely to occur in the early phases of production.

Knowledge transfer and the institutional approach

Institutional theory deals with the process by which organizations adopt institutionalized structures from the environment (DiMaggio and Powell, 1983; Meyer and Rowan, 1977; Tolbert and Zucker, 1983). Rather than emphasizing that organizations adopt practices that increase their productivity (as in the transfer of knowledge work), however, the institutional approach emphasizes that organizations adopt practices that increase their legitimacy (Meyer and Rowan, 1977). According to Meyer and Rowan (1977), the institutional perspective applies more in contexts where it is difficult to measure outputs, such as schools. For example, schools may adopt a succession of practices, ranging from open classrooms to computer technology, in order to be 'up to date' and gain legitimacy—even though there may not be any evidence that the practices improve performance.

DiMaggio and Powell (1983) describe three mechanisms through which organizations adopt practices of other organizations and become similar or 'isomorphic' to them: coercive, mimetic and normative. In coercive isomorphism, organizations adopt structures or practices because they are forced to do so (as when an organization forces a particular organizational structure on its component parts). In mimetic isomorphism, organizations faced with uncertainty imitate what similar organizations are doing. In normative isomorphism, norms that have developed for practices in a particular field are transmitted by professionals as they communicate with professionals in other firms or move across firms.

Scott (1987) elaborates a larger set of such mechanisms through which organizations adopt institutionalized structures, a list that subsumes and extends the DiMaggio and Powell list: the imposition of organizational structure, through coercive isomorphism and legitimate authority; the approval and authorization of organizational structure, for example, by a professional group; the inducement of organizational structure, for example, through funding; the deliberate imitation of organizational structure; the imprinting of organizational structure at the time the organization is founded; the later incorporation of organizational structure; and the substitution of organizational culture for structure.

Environmental threat and uncertainty

The literature on the effects of threats or crises on groups is also relevant for understanding how groups respond to external conditions. Staw, Sandelands, and Dutton (1981) published a conceptual piece, based on a summary of past research, that examined the effect of threat on individuals, groups and organizations. They argued that threat leads to a restriction in information processing and a constriction of control. They suggest that past research findings support the hypothesis that increasing threat is associated with a reduction in the number of information channels used and with an increase in structural centralization (Dunbar and Goldberg, 1978; Isenberg, 1981; Khandwalla, 1978; Smart and Vertinsky, 1977).

Gladstein and Reilly (1985) build on the Staw, Sandelands, and Dutton (1981) model by examining the relationship between threat and centralization. They did not find a relationship between threat and the centralization of influence over decisions; but they did find the predicted relationship between threat and centralization of the communication structure. Argote, Turner, and Fichman (1989) found that groups who reported the highest level of experienced threat adopted the most centralized communication structure. Interestingly, the researchers' manipulation of uncertainty had a stronger effect on the experience of threat by groups than did the manipulation of 'threat'. Driskell and Salas (1991) offer empirical support for a competing hypothesis: that all group members become more receptive to task information provided by others under stress.

Thus, research has yielded inconsistent results about the relationship between threat and influence structures but fairly consistent results about the relationship between threat and communication structures. As the experience of threat increases, communication structures tend to become more centralized. Further research is needed on the conditions under which the increased centralization of communication leads to increased or decreased performance. Staw, Sandelands, and Dutton (1981) suggest some of the conditions under which increased centralization will lead to improved performance. Turner (1988) found that the degree of centralization, the degree of threat, and the nature of the performance cues affected the speed but not the quality of group performance.

As noted earlier, researchers working in the contingency theory tradition have studied the relationships among characteristics of the environment, organizational structure, and organizational performance (e.g. Burns and Stalker, 1961; Leblebici and Salancik, 1981), with environmental uncertainty receiving the most empirical attention. The results are similar to those described earlier in our discussion of technological uncertainty and structure. Other environmental contingencies that have received attention in the empirical literature include environmental turbulence (Emery and Trist, 1965), degree of concentration (Pfeffer and Salancik, 1978); and environmental munificence (Staw and Szwajkowski, 1975).

Two quite different perspectives have recently been used to conceptualize how work groups relate to their environments, and how they change. Sundstrom, DeMeuse, and Futrell (1990) apply an ecological perspective, and Smith and Gemmill (1991) adopt a 'dissipative structure' perspective, for an analysis of small group change under turbulent environmental conditions. Both emphasize the self-organizing abilities of groups, and the importance of relations at their boundaries. Both the ecological perspective and the dissipative structure perspective represent relatively new but growing bodies of work, whose implications have not yet fully penetrated mainstream research in these areas. Both offer promising alternative paradigms for analysis of group processes amidst complex and changing organizational and environmental contexts.

III GROUP PROCESSES IN ORGANIZATIONS: REPRISE AND PROSPECTS

In their *Annual Review of Psychology* chapter on groups, Levine and Moreland (1990) conclude that research on groups is 'alive and well' but currently being done mainly by organizational rather than social psychologists. We concur with the view that the study of groups is, and will continue to be, a thriving area of inquiry for organizational psychologists.

Part of the impetus and support for research on groups stems from their prevalence in organizations and society. Groups are ubiquitous in modern organizations. Autonomous work groups, labor–management steering committees, new product development teams, executive committees, and the like are examples of the myriad types of groups that nowadays form vital parts of organizational life. Understanding how such groups function and what makes them effective has important theoretical and practical implications.

Of the four processes in our model, more research has been done over the years on the Construction and Operations processes than on the other two. But research on Construction and Operations processes has, for the most part, been done by different people working from different perspectives and focusing on different aspects of the acting group in context. Work on operations processes has focused on the group's task, and on its production function. Work on construction processes has focused on the group as an entity, and on the well-being and member support functions. There has not been close integration of the two bodies of work. We hope this chapter can provide a useful information base for such integrative work.

There has been far less research on the Reconstruction and External Relations processes, but such work is on the rise. We see this as a very promising trend. Concerning reconstruction, researchers are examining how groups acquire knowledge, how this knowledge is embedded in social systems, how it may be lost, and the performance consequences of gains (and losses) in knowledge. This research moves beyond viewing groups in static terms and captures the dynamics of group performance changes over time. New research in the operations area also captures the dynamics of group life by focusing on temporal processes in groups. Most real groups have a past and expect a future. Some aspects of groups remain relatively constant over time while other aspects change as the group gains experience—and sometimes obsolescence. If we are to fully understand groups, we must understand the dynamics of their development.

Researchers are also devoting more attention to studying how groups manage their external relations and adapt to changes in the environment. Work groups do not exist in a vacuum. They are embedded in a context—often an organizational context and always a physical, temporal, and socio-cultural environment. They need to manage relations with their embedding contexts in order to acquire resources, gain legitimacy, understand and meet their performance requirements, coordinate their activities with other groups, and so on. For most groups, their survival depends on their ability to manage, successfully, relations with the contexts in which they are embedded. Thus, research on adaptation and external relations is critical to our understanding of acting groups in context.

Researchers are also devoting more attention to studying how changes in membership, technology, environmental conditions and the like affect group processes, structures and outcomes. We see this work as very promising. Not only does it help us to understand the effect of these changes on groups, it also provides fundamental knowledge about the nature of groups as social systems. For example, studies of the effect of membership change on group performance inform us about the extent to which knowledge (about tasks and about group processes) is embedded uniquely in individual members or redundantly in various aspects of the social system. Analyses of the effects of changes in technology on group structures inform us about the extent to which structure is conditioned by technology versus other factors such as culture, power, or member expertise.

Organizational researchers studying groups use a rich array of research strategies, including laboratory studies, experimental and computer simulations, survey research, case studies and analyses of archival data. This is a very positive characteristic, in our view, because the weaknesses of one strategy can be offset by the strengths of others. This is one of the ways in which group research has been enriched by its 'move' to organizational research venues.

Another positive methodological trend of research on groups is a shift from study of relatively few variables to a more multi-variate approach. Many variables affect the development and performance of work groups. It is crucial that both our theories and our methods of analysis take those critical factors into account. This is especially important in field studies, in which the tools of random assignment of cases and experimental manipulations and controls are not applicable. Failure to measure crucial variables in a field study can not only limit what we learn, but can lead us to 'learn' misleading results— to infer relations between variables that are the spurious result of underlying (but unmeasured) variables.

For example, suppose that we are interested in studying the relationship between the strength of a group's internal culture (e.g. the influence power of its norms) and that group's task effectiveness. And suppose that strength of culture is affected by group size: smaller groups have stronger influence processes than larger groups (other things equal). Suppose further that we find a positive relation between strength of culture and an indicator of group task effectiveness, but we neglect to measure the size of the various groups. The relation implied by our correlation could be misleading; it could be due to the mutual dependence of both strength of culture and group effectiveness on group size. Thus, it is important to include as many relevant variables as possible in our models, and in our studies, of group effectiveness.

What can group researchers do to increase the likelihood that our research will bear fruit? McGrath (1986) has earlier argued for moving beyond simple input-output models to models that incorporate group process. We repeat his admonition here—that group researchers should take group process seriously. We also note that an increasing number of researchers are doing so. Focusing on process can help us understand groups more fully, and reconcile conflicting findings in the literature.

We would also advocate taking a more interdisciplinary approach to the study of groups. As an area of inquiry, group research has long been positioned at the intersection of two fields—psychology and sociology. It has long been the case that our understanding of groups could benefit from more synergy between these two fields. Now, group research has become of research interest to—and can benefit from the perspectives of—a number of other fields as well: communications, anthropology, information systems, production systems, organizational behavior, economics, and political science. Our understanding of work groups and how they develop, function, and change, can be enriched by a better integration of the perspectives of all of these varied disciplines.

FOOTNOTES

We searched recent volumes of the following journals for articles relevant for understanding group processes in organizations: *Academy of Management Journal, Academy of Management Review, Administrative Science Quarterly, American Journal of Sociology, American Psychologist, Basic and Applied Social Psychology, British Journal of Social Psychology, European Journal of Social Psychology, Group and Organization Studies, Human Relations, Journal of Applied Behavioral Science, Journal of Applied Psychology, Journal of Applied Social Psychology, Journal of Experimental Social Psychology, Journal of Organizational Behavior, Journal of Personality and Social Psychology, Management Science, Organizational Behavior and Human Decision Processes, Organization Science, Personality and Social Psychology Bulletin, Psychological Bulletin, Research in Organizational Behavior, Small Group Behavior,* and *Social Psychology Quarterly.*

REFERENCES

Adler, P. S., and Clark, K. B. (1991) Behind the learning curve: A sketch of the learning process. *Management Science*, **37**, 267–281.

Alchian, A. (1963) Reliability of progress curves in airframe production. *Econometrica*, **31**, 679–693.

Ancona, D. G., and Caldwell, D. F. (1988) Beyond task and maintenance: Defining external functions in groups. *Groups and Organization Studies*, **13**, 468–494.

Ancona, D. G. (1990) Outward bound: Strategies for team survival in an organization. *Academy of Management Journal*, **33**, 334–365.

Argote, L. (1982) Input uncertainty and organizational coordination in hospital emergency units. *Administrative Science Quarterly*, **27**, 420–434.

Argote, L. (1989) Agreement about norms and work unit effectiveness. Evidence from the field. *Basic and Applied Social Psychology*, **10**, 131–140.

Argote, L. (in press) Group and organizational learning curves: Individual, system and environmental components. *British Journal of Social Psychology*.

Argote, L., Beckman, S. L., and Epple, D. (1990) The persistence and transfer of learning in industrial settings. *Management Science*, **36**, 140–154.

Argote, L., Devadas, R., and Melone, N. (1990) The base-rate fallacy: Contrasting processes and outcomes of group and individual judgment. *Organizational Behavior and Human Decision Processes*, **46**, 296–310.

Argote, L., and Epple, D. (1990) Learning curves in manufacturing. *Science*, **247**, 920–924.

Argote, L., Epple, D., Devadas, R., and Murphy, K. (1990) The acquisition and depreciation of knowledge in manufacturing: Turnover and the learning curve. Paper presented at ORSA/TIMS, Philadelphia, 1990.

Argote, L., Seabright, M. A., and Dyer, L. (1986) Individual versus group use of base-rate and individuating information. *Organizational Behavior and Human Decision Processes*, **38**, 65–75.

Argote, L., Turner, M., and Fichman, M. (1989) To centralize or not to centralize: The effects of uncertainty and threat on group structure and performance. *Organizational Behavior and Human Decision Processes*, **43**, 58–74.

Argyris, C., and Schon, D. (1978) *Organizational Learning*. Reading, MA: Addison-Wesley.

Barley, S. R. (1986) Technology as an occasion for structuring: Evidence from observations of CT scanners and the social order of Radiology departments. *Administrative Science Quarterly*, **31**, 78–108.

Bazerman, M. H., Mannix, E., Sondak, H., and Thompson, L. (1989). Negotiator behavior and decision processes in dyads, groups, and markets. In J. S. Carroll (ed.), *Advances in Applied Social Psychology*, vol. 4. Beverly Hills: Sage.

Bazerman, M. H., Mannix, E. A., and Thompson, L. L. (1988) Groups as mixed-motive negotiations. In E. J. Lawler and B. Markovsky (eds), *Advances in Group Processes*, **5**, 195–216.

Becker, S. W., and Baloff, N. (1969) Organization structure and complex problem solving. *Administrative Science Quarterly*, **14**, 260–271.

Berkowitz, L. (1954) Group standards, cohesiveness, and productivity. *Human Relations*, **7**, 509–519.

Bettenhausen, K. L. (1991) Five years of groups research: What we have learned and what needs to be addressed. *Journal of Management*, **17**, 345–381.

Bettenhausen, K., and Murnighan, J. K. (1985) The emergence of norms in competitive decision-making groups. *Administrative Science Quarterly*, **30**, 350–372.

Bettenhausen, K. L., and Murnighan, J. K. (1991) The development of an intergroup norm and the effects of interpersonal and structural changes. *Administrative Science Quarterly*, **36**, 20–35.

Bikson, T. K., and Eveland, J. D. (1990) The interplay of work group structures and computer support. In Galegher, J., Kraut, R., and Egido, C. (eds), *Intellectual Teamwork*. Hillsdale, NJ: Erlbaum.

Bikson, T. K., and Gutek, B. A. (1983) Advanced office systems: An empirical look at use and satisfaction. In A. M. Smith and D. B. Medley (eds), *AFTIPS Conference Proceedings*: 1983 National Computer Conference.

Bourgeois, L. J., III, McAllister, D., and Mitchell, T. (1978) The effects of different organizational environments upon decisions about organizational structure. *Academy of Management Journal*, **21**, 508–514.

Bray, R., and Kerr, N. (1981) *The Psychology of the Courtroom*. New York: Academic Press.

Brett, J. M. (1991) Negotiating group decisions. *Negotiation Journal*, **7**, 291–310.

Brett, J. M., and Rognes, J. K. (1986) Intergroup relations in organizations. In P. S. Goodman, *Designing Effective Work Groups*. San Francisco, CA: Jossey-Bass.

Brown, J. S., and Duguid, P. (1991) Organizational learning and communities of practice: Toward a unified view of working, learning and innovation. *Organization Science*, **2**, 40–57.

Burns, T., and Stalker, G. M. (1961) *The Management of Innovation*. London: Tavistock.

Campbell, J. P. (1971) Personnel training and development. *Annual Review of Psychology*, **22**, 565–602.

Carley, K. (1992) Organizational learning and personnel turnover. *Organization Science*, **3**, 20–46.

Carnevale, P. J., and Pruitt, D. G. (1992) Negotiation and mediation. *Annual Review of Psychology*, **43**, 531–582.

Cartwright, D., and Zander, A. (eds) (1968) *Group Dynamics: Research and Theory* (3rd edn). New York: Harper & Row.

Chen, C. C., and Meindl, J. R. (1991) The construction of leadership images in the popular press: The case of Donald Burr and *People Express*. *Administrative Science Quarterly*, **36**, 521–551.

Clark, N. K., and Stephenson, G. M. (1989) Group remembering. In P. B. Paulus (ed.), *Psychology of Group Influence*, 2nd edn (pp. 357–391). Hillsdale, NJ: Erlbaum.

Cordery, J. L., Mueller, W. S., and Smith, L. M. (1991) Attitudinal and behavioral effects of autonomous group working: A longitudinal field study. *Academy of Management Journal*, **34**, 464–476.

Cyert, R. M., and March, J. G. (1963) *A Behavioral Theory of the Firm*. Englewood Cliffs, NJ: Prentice-Hall.

Daft, R. L., and Lengel, R. H. (1986) Organizational information requirements, media richness and structural design. *Management Science*, **32**, 554–571.

Daft, R. L., Lengel, R. H., and Trevino, L. K. (1987) Message equivocality, media selection, and manager performance: Implications for information systems. *MIS Quarterly* 9/87, 354–366.

Darr, E., and Argote, L. (1991) The acquisition and transfer of learning in service organizations: Productivity and timeliness in food franchises. Paper presented at ORSA/TIMS, Anaheim, California.

David, F. R., Pearce, J. A., and Randolph, W. A. (1989) Linking technology and structure to enhance group performance. *Journal of Applied Psychology*, **64**, 233–241.

Davis, J. H. (1973) Group decision and social interaction: A theory of social decision schemes. *Psychological Review*, **80**, 97–125.

Davis, J. H., Bray, R. M., and Holt, R. W. (1977) The empirical study of social decision processes in juries: A critical review. In J. Tapp and F. Levine (eds), *Law, Justice and the Individual in Society: Psychological and Legal Issues*. New York: Holt, Rinehart & Winston.

Davis, J. H., Kameda, T., Parks, C., Stasson, M., and Zimmerman, S. (1989) Some social mechanics of group decision making: The distribution of opinion, polling sequence, and implications for consensus. *Journal of Personality and Social Psychology*, **57**, 1000–1012.

Devadas, R., and Argote, L. (1990) Learning and depreciation in work groups: The effects of turnover and group structure. Paper presented at the meetings of the American Psychological Society, Dallas, June 1990.

Diehl, M., and Stroebe, W. (1987) Productivity loss in brainstorming groups: Toward the solution of a riddle. *Journal of Personality and Social Psychology*, **53**, 487–509.

Diehl, M., and Stroebe, W. (1991) Productivity loss in brainstorming groups: Tracking down the blocking effect. *Journal of Personality and Social Psychology*, **61**, 392–403.

DiMaggio, P. J., and Powell, W. W. (1983) The iron cage revisited: Institutional isomorphism and collective rationality in organizational fields. *American Sociological Review*, **48**, 147–160.

Dion, K. L., Baron, R. S., and Miller, N. (1970) Why do groups make riskier decisions than individuals? In L. Berkowitz (ed.), *Advances in Experimental Social Psychology*, vol. 5. New York: Academic Press.

Driskell, J. E., and Salas, E. (1991) Group decision making under stress. *Journal of Applied Psychology*, **76**, 473–478.

Dunbar, R., and Goldberg, W. (1978) Crisis development and strategic response in European corporations. In C. Smart and W. Stanbury (eds), *Studies in Crisis Management*. Toronto: Institute for Research on Public Policy.

Duncan, R. B. (1973) Multiple decision-making structures in adapting to environmental uncertainty: The impact on organizational effectiveness. *Human Relations*, **26**, 273–291.

Duncan, R. B., and Weiss, A. (1979) Organizational learning: Implications for organizational design. In B. Staw (ed.), *Research in Organizational Behavior* (pp. 75–123). Greenwich, CT: JAI Press.

Dutton, J. M., and Thomas, A. (1984) Treating progress functions as a managerial opportunity. *Academy of Management Review*, **9**, 235–247.

Dyer, J. L. (1985) *Annotated Bibliography and State-of-the-Art Review of the Field of Team Training as it Relates to Military Teams*. Fort Benning: US Army Research Institute for the Behavioral and Social Sciences.

Emery, F. E., and Trist, E. L. (1965) The causal texture of organizational environments. *Human Relations*, **18**, 21–32.

Emery, F. E., and Trist, E. L. (1973) Socio-technical systems. In Baker, F. (ed.), *Organizational Systems: General Systems Approaches to Complex Organizations*. Homewood, IL: Richard D. Irwin.

Epple, D., Argote, L., and Devadas, R. (1991) Organizational learning curves: A method for investigating intra-plant transfer of knowledge acquired through learning by doing. *Organization Science*, **2**, 58–70.

Faucheaux, C., and Mackenzie, K. (1966) Task dependency of organizational centrality: Its behavioral consequences. *Journal of Experimental Social Psychology*, **2**, 361–375.

Feldman, D. C. (1977) The role of initiation activities in socialization. *Human Relations*, **30**, 977–990.

Feldman, D. C. (1984) The development and enforcement of group norms. *Academy of Management Review*, **9**, 47–53.

Feldman, D. C. (1989) Socialization, resocialization, and training. In Goldstein, I. L. (ed.), *Training and Development in Organizations*. San Francisco, CA: Jossey-Bass.

Fiedler, F. (1967) *A Theory of Leadership Effectiveness*. New York: McGraw-Hill.

Finholt, T., and Sproull, L. (1989) Electronic groups at work. *Organization Science*, **1**, 41–64.

Finholt, T., Sproull, L., and Kiesler, S. (1990) Communication and performance in ad hoc groups. In J. Galegher, R. Kraut, and C. Egido, (eds), *Intellectual Teamwork*. Hillsdale, NJ: Erlbaum.

Finkelstein, S., and Hambrick, D. C. (1990) Top-management-team tenure and organizational outcomes: The moderating role of managerial discretion. *Administrative Science Quarterly*, **35**, 484–503.

Fiol, C. M., and Lyles, M. A. (1985) Organizational learning. *Academy of Management Review*, **10**, 803–813.

Fleishman, E. A. (1973) Twenty years of consideration and structure. In L. Berkowitz (ed.), *Advances in Experimental Social Psychology*, vol. 11. Orlando, Florida: Academic Press.

Fry, L. W. (1982) Technology-structure research: Three critical issues. *Academy of Management Journal*, **25**, 532–552.

Fry, L., and Slocum, J. (1984) Technology, structure and workgroup effectiveness: A test of a contingency model. *Academy of Management Journal*, **27**, 221–245.

Galbraith, C. S. (1990) Transferring core manufacturing technologies in high-technology firms. *California Management Review*, **32**, 56–70.

Georgopoulos, B. S. (1972) The hospital as an organization and problem-solving system. In B. S. Georgopoulos (ed.), *Organizational Research on Health Institutions* (pp. 9–48). Ann Arbor, MI: University of Michigan, Institute for Social Research.

Georgopoulos, B. S., and Mann, F. C. (1962) *The Community General Hospital*. New York: Macmillan.

Gersick, C. J. G. (1988) Time and transition in work teams: Toward a new model of group development. *Academy of Management Journal*, **31**, 9–41.

Gersick, C. J. G. (1989) Marking time: Predictable transitions in task groups. *Academy of Management Journal*, **32**, 274–309.

Gersick, C. J. G., and Hackman, J. R. (1990) Habitual routines in task-performing groups. *Organizational Behavior and Human Decision Processes*, **47**, 65–97.

Gladstein, D. (1984) Groups in context: A model of task group effectiveness. *Administrative Science Quarterly*, **29**, 499–517.

Gladstein, D., and Reilly, N. (1985) Group decision making under threat: The tycoon game. *Academy of Management Journal*, **28**, 613–627.

Goldstein, I. L. (1980) Training in work organizations. *Annual Review of Psychology*, **31**, 229–272.

Goodman, P. S., Devadas, R., and Hughson, T. L. (1988) Groups and productivity: Analyzing the effectiveness of self-managing teams. In J. P. Campbell and R. J. Campbell (eds), *Productivity in Organizations*. San Francisco, CA: Jossey-Bass.

Goodman, P. S., and Garber, S. (1988) Absenteeism and accidents in dangerous environments: Empirical analysis of underground coal mines. *Journal of Applied Psychology*, **73**, 81–86.

Goodman, P. S., and Leyden, D. P. (1991) Familiarity and group productivity. *Journal of Applied Psychology*, **76**, 578–586.

Goodman, P. S., Ravlin, E. C., and Argote, L. (1986) Current thinking about groups: Setting the stage for new ideas. In P. S. Goodman, *Designing Effective Work Groups*. San Francisco, CA: Jossey-Bass.

Graen, G., and Cashman, J. (1975) A role-making model of leadership in formal organizations: A developmental approach. In J. G. Hunt and L. L. Larsen (eds), *Leadership Frontiers*, (pp. 143–165). Kent: Kent State University Press.

Greenberg, L. (1971) Why the mine injury picture is out of focus. *Mining Engineering*, **23**, 51–53.

Gresov, C. (1989) Exploring fit and misfit with multiple contingencies. *Administrative Science Quarterly*, **34**, 431–453.

Guetzkow, H., and Simon, H. (1955) The impact of certain communication nets upon organization and performance in task-oriented groups. *Management Science* 1, 233–250.

Hackman, J. R. (1990) *Groups that Work (and Those that Don't)*, San Francisco, CA: Jossey-Bass.

Hackman, J. R. (1992) Group influences on individuals in organizations. In M. D. Dunnette and L. M. Hough (eds), *Handbook of Industrial and Organizational Psychology*, vol. 3. Palo Alto, CA: Consulting Psychologists Press.

Hackman, J. R., Brousseau, K. R., and Weiss, J. A. (1976) The interaction of task design and group performance strategies in determining group effectiveness. *Organizational Behavior and Human Performance*, 16, 350–365.

Hackman, J. R., and Morris, C. G. (1975) Group tasks, group interaction process, and group performance effectiveness: A review and proposed integration. In L. Berkowitz (ed.), *Advances in Experimental Social Psychology*, vol. 8 (pp. 45–99). New York: Academic Press.

Hackman, J. R., and Walton, R. E. (1986) Leading groups in organizations. In P. S. Goodman & Associates (eds). *Designing Effective Work Groups* (pp. 72–119). San Francisco, CA: Jossey-Bass.

Hamblin, R. L. (1958) Leadership and crisis. *Sociometry*, 21, 322–335.

Harmon, J., and Rohrbaugh, J. (1990) Social judgment analysis and small group decision making: Cognitive feedback effects on individual and collective performance. *Organizational Behavior and Human Decision Processes*, 46, 34–54.

Hartwick, J., Sheppard, B. L., and Davis, J. H. (1982) Group remembering: Research and implications. In R. A. Guzzo (ed.), *Improving Group Decision Making in Organizations* (pp. 41–72). London: Academic Press.

Hayes, R. H., and Clark, K. B. (1986) Why some factories are more productive than others. *Harvard Business Review*, Number 5, 66–73.

Hedberg, B. (1981) How organizations learn and unlearn? In P. C. Nystrom and W. H. Starbuck (eds), *Handbook of Organizational Design* (pp. 8–27). London: Oxford University Press.

Heise, G., and Miller, G. (1951) Problem-solving by small groups using various communication nets. *Journal of Abnormal and Social Psychology*, 46, 327–335.

Hill, G. W. (1982) Group versus individual performance: Are N + 1 Heads better than one? *Psychological Bulletin*, 91, 517–539.

Hinsz, V. (1990) Cognitive and consensus processes in group recognition memory performance. *Journal of Personality and Social Psychology*, 59, 705–718.

Hollingshead, A. B. (1991) The effects of previous individual or group performance on subsequent group and individual performance. Unpublished Masters thesis. Urbana, Illinois: Department of Psychology, University of Illinois.

Hollingshead, A. B., and McGrath, J. E. (in press) The whole is less than the sum of the parts: A critical review of research on computer-assisted groups. In R. L. Guzzo and E. Salas (eds), *Team Decision and Team Performance in Organizations*. San Francisco, CA: Jossey-Bass.

House, R. J. (1977) A 1976 theory of charismatic leadership. In J. G. Hunt and L. L. Larson (eds), *Leadership: The Cutting Edge*. Carbondale: Southern Illinois University Press.

House, R. J., and Mitchell, T. R. (1974) Path-goal theory of leadership. *Journal of Contemporary Business*, 3, 81–97.

Huber, G., O'Connell, M., and Cummings, L. (1975) Perceived environmental uncertainty: Effects of information and structure. *Academy of Management Journal*, 18, 725–740.

Huber, G. P. (1991) Organizational learning: The contributing processes and the literatures. *Organizational Science*, 2, 88–115.

Hutte, H. (1965) Decision-making in a management game. *Human Relations*, **18**, 5–20.

Insko, C. A., Gilmore, R., Moehle, D., Lipsitz, A., Drenan, S., and Thibaut, J. W. (1982) Seniority in the generational transition of laboratory groups: The effects of social familiarity and task experience. *Journal of Experimental Social Psychology*, **18**, 557–580.

Insko, C. A., Thibaut, J. W., Moehle, D., Wilson, M., Diamond, W. D., Gilmore, R., Solomon, M. R., and Lipsitz, A. (1980) Social evolution and the emergence of leadership. *Journal of Personality and Social Psychology*, **39**, 431–448.

Isenberg, D. J. (1981) Some effects of time-pressure on vertical structure and decision-making accuracy in small groups. *Organizational Behavior and Human Performance*, **27**, 119–134.

Jackson, S. E., Brett, J. F., Sessa, V. I., Cooper, D. M., Julin, J. A., and Peyronnin, K. (1991) Some differences make a difference: Individual dissimilarity and group heterogeneity as correlates of recruitment, promotions, and turnover. *Journal of Applied Psychology*, **76**, 675–689.

Jacobs, R. C., and Campbell, D. T. (1961) The perpetuation of an arbitrary tradition through several generations of a laboratory microculture. *Journal of Abnormal and Social Psychology*, **62**, 649–659.

Joskow, P. L., and Rose, N. L. (1985) The effects of technological change, experience, and environmental regulation on the construction cost of coal-burning generating units. *Rand Journal of Economics*, **16**, 1–27.

Katz, D., and Kahn, R. L. (1978) *The Social Psychology of Organizations*, 2nd edn. New York: Wiley.

Katz, R. (1982) The effects of group longevity on communication and performance. *Administrative Science Quarterly*, **27**, 81–104.

Kelly, J. R. (1988) Entrainment in individual and group behavior. In J. E. McGrath (ed.), *The Social Psychology of Time: New Perspectives* (pp. 89–110). Newbury Park, CA: Sage.

Kelly, J. R., Futoran, G. C., and McGrath, J. E. (1990) Capacity and capability: Seven studies of entrainment of task performance rates. *Small Group Research*, **21**, 283–314.

Kelly, J. R., and McGrath, J. E. (1985) Effects of time limits and task types on task performance and interaction of four-person groups. *Journal of Personality and Social Psychology*, **49**, 395–407.

Kelsey, S. F., Mullin, S. M., Detre, K. M., Mitchell, H., Cowley, M. J., Gruentzig, A. R., and Kent, K. M. (1984). Effect of investigator experience on percutaneous transluminal coronary angioplasty. *American Journal of Cardiology*, **53**, 56C–64C.

Kerr, S., and Jermier, J. M. (1978) Substitutes for leadership: Their meaning and measurement. *Organizational Behavior and Human Performance*, **22**, 375–403.

Khandwalla, P. (1978) Crisis responses of competing versus noncompeting organizations. In C. Smart and W. Stanbury (eds), *Studies on Crisis Management*. Toronto: Institute for Research on Public Policy.

Kiesler, S., and Sproull, L. (in press) Group decision making and communication technology. *Organizational Behavior and Human Decision Processes*.

Kiesler, S., Zubrow, D., Moses, A., and Geller, V. (1985) Affect in computer-mediated communication: An experiment in synchronous terminal-to-terminal discussion. *Human Computer Interactions*, **1**, 77–104.

Komaki, J. L., Desselles, M. L., and Bowman, E. D. (1989) Definitely not a breeze: Extending an operant model of effective supervision to teams. *Journal of Applied Psychology*, **74**, 522–529.

Kramer, R. M. (1991) The more the merrier? Social psychological aspects of multiparty negotiation in organizations. *Research on Negotiation in Organizations*, **3**, 307–332.

Lane, F. C. (1951) *Ships for Victory: A History of Shipbuilding under the U.S. Maritime Commission in World War II*. Baltimore, MD: Johns Hopkins Press.

Laughlin, P. R. (1980) Social combination processes of cooperative, problem-solving groups on verbal intellective tasks. In M. Fishbein (ed.), *Progress in Social Psychology*, vol. 1. Hillsdale, NJ: Erlbaum.

Laughlin, P. R. (1988) Collective induction: group performance, social combination processes, and mutual majority and minority influence. *Journal of Personality and Social Psychology*, **54**, 254–267.

Laughlin, P. R., and Adamopoulos, J. (1982) Social decision schemes on intellective tasks. In H. Brandstatter, J. H. Davis, and C. Stocker-Kreichgauer (eds), *Group Decision Making*. London, Academic Press.

Laughlin, P. L., and Shippy, T. A. (1983) Collective induction. *Journal of Personality and Social Psychology*, **45**, 94–100.

Laughlin, P. R., and Sweeney, J. D. (1977) Individual-to-group and group-to-individual transfer in problem solving. *Journal of Experimental Psychology: Human Learning and Memory*, **3**, 246–254.

Laughlin, P. L., Vander Stoep, S. W., and Hollingshead, A. B. (1991) Collective vs individual induction: recognition of truth, rejection of error, and collective information processing. *Journal of Personality and Social Psychology*, **61**, 50–67.

Lawrence, P., and Lorsch, J. (1967) Differentiation and integration in complex organizations. *Administrative Science Quarterly*, **12**, 1–47.

Lazega, E. (1990) Internal politics and the interactive elaboration of information in workgroups: An exploratory study. *Human Relations*, **43**, 87–101.

Leavitt, H. (1951) Some effects of certain communication patterns on group performance. *Journal of Abnormal and Social Psychology*, **46**, 38–50.

Leblebici, H., and Salancik, G. (1981) Effects of environmental uncertainty on information and decision processes in banks. *Administrative Science Quarterly*, **26**, 578–596.

Lenehan, M. (1982) The quality of the instrument. *The Atlantic Monthly*, **250**, 32–58.

Levine, J. M., and Moreland, R. L. (1990) Progress in small group research. *Annual Review of Psychology*, **41**, 585–634.

Levine, J. M., and Moreland, R. L. (1991) Culture and socialization in work groups. In L. Resnick, J. Levine, and S. Behrend (eds), *Perspectives on Socially Shared Cognition*. Washington, DC: American Psychological Association.

Levitt, B., and March, J. G. (1988) Organizational learning. *Annual Review of Sociology*, **14**, 319–340.

Lieberman, M. B. (1984) The learning curve and pricing in the chemical processing industries. *Rand Journal of Economics*, **15**, 213–228.

Likert, R. (1961) *New Patterns of Management*. New York: McGraw-Hill.

Lincoln, J. R., Hanada, M., and McBride, K. (1986) Organizational structures in Japanese and U.S. manufacturing. *Administrative Science Quarterly*, **31**, 338–364.

Locke, E. A., Shaw, K. M., Saari, L. M., and Latham, G. P. (1981) Goal setting and task performance: 1969–1980. *Psychological Review*, **90**, 125–152.

McCallum, G. A., Oser, R., Morgan, B. R., and Salas, E. (1989) An investigation of the behavioral components of teamwork. Paper presented at the American Psychological Association Convention, New Orleans.

McGrath, J. E. (1962) *Leadership Behavior: Some Requirements for Leadership Training*. Washington, DC: US Civil Service Commission [Mimeographed].

McGrath, J. E. (1984) *Groups: Interaction and Performance*, Englewood Cliffs, NJ: Prentice-Hall.

McGrath, J. E. (1986) Studying groups at work: Ten critical needs for theory and practice. In P. S. Goodman (ed.), *Designing Effective Work Groups* (pp. 362–391). San Francisco, CA: Jossey-Bass.

McGrath, J. E. (ed.) (1988) *The Social Psychology of Time: New Perspectives.* Newbury Park, CA: Sage.

McGrath, J. E. (1990) Time matters in groups. In J. Galegher, R. Kraut, and C. Egido (eds), *Intellectual Teamwork* (pp. 23–61). Hillsdale, NJ: Erlbaum.

McGrath, J. E. (1991) Time, interaction, and performance (TIP): A theory of groups. *Small Group Research*, 22, 147–174.

McGrath, J. E., and Gruenfeld, D. H. (1993) Toward a dynamic and systemic theory of groups: An integration of six temporally enriched perspectives. In M. Chemers and R. Ayman (eds), *Leadership Theory and Research: Perspectives and Directions.* Orlando, FL: Acadamic Press.

McGrath, J. E., and Hollingshead, A. B. (1993) Putting the 'G' back in GSS: Some theoretical issues about dynamic processes in groups with technological enhancements. In L. M. Jessup and J. E. Valacich (eds), *Group Support Systems: New Perspectives.* New York: Macmillan.

McGrath, J. E., and Kelly, J. R. (1986) *Time and Human Interaction: Toward a Social Psychology of Time.* New York: Guilford.

McGrath, J. E., and Kelly, J. R. (1992) Temporal context and temporal patterning in social psychology. *Time and Society*, 1, 399–420.

McGrath, J. E., Kelly, J. R., and Machatka, D. E. (1984) The social psychology of time: Entrainment of behavior in social and organizational settings. In S. Oskamp (ed.), *Applied Social Psychology Annual*, vol. 5. (pp. 21–44). Beverly Hills, CA: Sage.

McGrath, J. E., and Kravitz, D. A. (1982) Group research. *Annual Review of Psychology*, 33, 195–230.

Macy, J., Jr, Christie, L., and Luce, R. (1953) Coding noise in a task-oriented group. *Journal of Abnormal and Social Psychology*, 48, 401–409.

Malone, T. W. (1986) Organizing information processing systems: Parallels between human organizations and computer systems. In W. Zachery, S. Robertson, and J. Black (eds), *Cognition, Computation, and Cooperation.* Norwood, NJ: Ablex.

Malone, T. W. (1988) What is coordination theory? Alfred P. Sloan School of Management Working Paper (SSM WP #2051-88). [Paper presented at the National Science Foundation Coordination Theory Workshop, MIT, Feb. 1988.]

Mannix, E. A. (1991) Resource dilemmas and discount rates in decision making groups. *Journal of Experimental Social Psychology*, 27, 379–391.

Mannix, E. A., Thompson, L. L., and Bazerman, M. H. (1989) Negotiation in small groups. *Journal of Applied Psychology*, 74, 508–517.

March, J. G., and Simon, H. A. (1958) *Organizations.* New York: Wiley.

Messick, D. M., and Brewer, M. B. (1983) Solving social dilemmas: A review. In L. Wheeler and P. Shaver (eds), *Review of Personality and Social Psychology*, vol. 4 (pp. 11–44). Beverly Hills: Sage.

Messick, D. M., and Mackie, D. M. (1989) Intergroup relations. *Annual Review of Psychology*, 40, 45–81.

Meyer, J. W., and Rowan, B. (1977) Institutionalized organizations: Formal structure as myth and ceremony. *American Journal of Sociology*, 83, 340–363.

Miller, D., and Droge, C. (1986) Psychological and traditional determinants of structure. *Administrative Science Quarterly*, 31, 539–560.

Mitchell, T. R., and Silver, W. S. (1990) Individual and group goals when workers are interdependent: Effects on task strategies and performance. *Journal of Applied Psychology*, 75, 185–193.

Moreland, R. L., and Levine, J. M. (1982) Socialization in small groups: Temporal changes in individual-group relations. In L. Berkowitz (ed.), *Advances in Experimental Social Psychology*, vol. 15 (pp. 137–192). New York: Academic Press.

Moreland, R. L., and Levine, J. M. (in press) The composition of small groups. In E. J. Lawler, B. Markovsky, C. Ridgeway, and H. Walker (eds), *Advances in Group Processes*, vol. 9. Greenwich, CT: JAI Press.

Mueller, C. W., and Price, J. L. (1989) Some consequences of turnover: A work unit analysis. *Human Relations*, **42**, 389–402.

Murnighan, J. K., and Conlon, D. (1991) The dynamics of intense work groups: A study of British string quartets. *Administrative Science Quarterly*, **36**, 165–186.

Myers, D. G., and Lamm, H. (1976) The group polarization phenomenon. *Psychological Bulletin*, **83**, 602–627.

Nagao, D. H., Tindale, R. S., Hinsz, V. B., and Davis, J. H. (1985) Individual and group biases in information processing. Paper presented at the meeting of the American Psychological Association, Los Angeles, CA.

Neale, M. A., Bazerman, M. H., Northcraft, G. B., and Alperson, C. (1986) 'Choice shift' effects in group decisions: A decision bias perspective. *International Journal of Small Group Research*, **2**, 33–42.

Nunamaker, J. F., Dennis, A. R., Valacich, J. S., and Vogel, D. R. (1991) Information technology for negotiating groups: Generating options for mutual gain. *Management Science*, **37**, 1325–1346.

O'Reilly, C. A., Caldwell, D. F., and Barnett, W. P. (1989) Work group demography, social integration, and turnover. *Administrative Science Quarterly*, **34**, 21–37.

Orbell, J., and Dawes, R. (1981) Social dilemmas. In G. M. Stephenson and J. H. Davis (eds), *Progress in Applied Social Psychology*, vol. 1 (pp. 37–65). Chichester, UK: Wiley.

Payne, R., and Cooper, C. L. (1981) *Groups at Work*. Chichester, UK: Wiley.

Pennings, J. (1975) The relevance of the structural contingency model for organizational effectiveness. *Administrative Science Quarterly*, **20**, 395–410.

Penrod, S., and Hastie, R. (1979) Models of jury decision making: A critical review. *Psychological Bulletin*, **86**, 462–492.

Pfeffer, J., and Salancik, G. R. (1978) *The External Control of Organizations: A Resource Dependence Perspective*. New York: Harper & Row.

Poole, M. S., and DeSanctis, G. (1989) Use of group decision support systems as an appropriation process. *In Proceedings of the 22nd Annual Hawaii International Conference on System Sciences*, vol. 4 (pp. 149–157).

Poole, M. S., and DeSanctis, G. (1990) Understanding the use of decision support systems: The theory of adaptive structuration. In J. Fulk and C. Steinfield (eds), *Organizations and Communication Technology* (pp. 175–195). Newbury Park, CA: Sage.

Poole, M. S., Holmes, M., and DeSanctis, G. (1991) Conflict management in a computer-supported meeting environment. *Management Science*, **37**, 926–953.

Poole, M. S., and Roth, J. (1989a) Decision development in small groups IV: A typology of decision paths. *Human Communication Research*, **15**, 323–356.

Poole, M. S., and Roth, J. (1989b) Decision development in small groups V: Test of a contingency model. *Human Communication Research*, **15**, 549–589.

Poole, M. S., Seibold, D. R., and McPhee, R. D. (1985) Group decision making as a structurational process. *Quarterly Journal of Speech*, **71**, 74–102.

Rao, V. S., and Jarvinpaa, S. L. (1991) Computer support of groups: Theory-based models for GDSS research. *Management Science*, **37**, 1347–1362.

Rapping, L. (1965) Learning and World War II production functions. *Review of Economics and Statistics*, **47**, 81–86.

Robey, D., Farrow, D. L., and Franz, D. R. (1989) Group process and conflict in system development. *Management Science*, **35**, 1172–1191.

Salas, E., Blaiwes, A. R., Reynolds, R. E., Glickman, A. S., and Morgan, B. B., Jr (1985) Teamwork from team training: New directions. *Proceedings of the 7th Interservice/Industry Training Equipment Conference and Exhibition*. Orlando, FL: American Defense Preparedness Association.

Schachter, S., Ellertson, N., McBride, D., and Gregory, D. (1951) An experimental study of cohesiveness and productivity. *Human Relations*, **4**, 229–238.

Schein, R. H. (1990) Organizational culture. *American Psychologist*, **45**, 109–119.

Schoonhoven, C. B. (1981) Problems with contingency theory: Testing assumptions hidden within the language of contingency theory. *Administrative Science Quarterly*, **26**, 349–377.

Scott, W. R. (1987) The adolescence of institutional theory. *Administrative Science Quarterly*, **32**, 493–511.

Scott, W. R. (1990) Technology and organization: An organizational level perspective. In P. S. Goodman and L. S. Sproull (eds), *Technology and Organizations*. San Francisco, CA: Jossey-Bass.

Seashore, S. E. (1954) *Group Cohesiveness in the Industrial Work Group*. Ann Arbor, MI: Institute for Social Research.

Shaw, M. E. (1954) Some effects of problem complexity upon problem solution efficiency in different communication nets. *Journal of Experimental Psychology*, **48**, 211–217.

Shaw, M. E. (1958) Some effects of irrelevant information upon problem solving by small groups. *Journal of Social Psychology*, **47**, 33–37.

Shaw, M. E. (1964) Communication networks. In L. Berkowitz (ed.), *Advances in Experimental Social Psychology*, vol. 1 (pp. 111–147). New York: Academic Press.

Shure, G. H., Rogers, M. S., Larsen, I. M., and Tassone, J. (1962) Group planning and task effectiveness. *Sociometry*, **25**, 263–282.

Simon, H. A. (1991) Bounded rationality and organizational learning. *Organization Science*, **2**, 125–132.

Smart, C., and Vertinsky, I. (1977) Designs for crisis decision units. *Administrative Science Quarterly*, **22**, 640–657.

Smith, C., and Gemmill, G. (1991) Change in the small group: A dissipative structure perspective. *Human Relations*, **44**, 697–716.

Sniezek, J. A. (1992) Groups under uncertainty: An examination of confidence in group decision making. *Organizational Behavior and Human Decision Processes*, **52**, 124–155.

Sniezek, J. A., and Buckley, T. (in preparation) Choice accuracy and confidence in a judge-advisor social decision system.

Sniezek, J. A., and Henry, R. A. (1989) Accuracy and confidence in group judgment. *Organizational Behavior and Human Decision Processes*, **43**, 1–28.

Sniezek, J. A., Paese, P. W., and Switzer, F. S. (in press). The effect of choosing on confidence in choice. *Organizational Behavior and Human Decision Processes*.

Sproull, L., and Kiesler, S. (1986). Reducing social context cues: Electronic mail in organization communication. *Management Science*, **32**, 1492–1512.

Stasser, G., Taylor, L., and Hanna, C. (1989) Information sampling in structured and unstructured discussions of three- and six-person groups. *Journal of Personality and Social Psychology*, **57**, 67–78.

Stasser, G., and Titus, W. (1985) Pooling of unshared information in group decision making: Biased information sampling during discussion. *Journal of Personality and Social Psychology*, **48**, 1467–1478.

Stasser, G., and Titus, W. (1987) Effects of information load and percentages of shared information on the dissemination of unshared information during group discussion. *Journal of Personality and Social Psychology*, **53**, 81–93.

Staw, B., Sandelands, L., and Dutton, J. (1981) Threat-rigidity effects in organizational behavior: A multi-level analysis. *Administrative Science Quarterly*, **26**, 501–524.

Staw, B. M., and Szwajowski, E. (1975) The scarcity-munificence component of organizational environments and the commission of illegal acts. *Administrative Science Quarterly*, **20**, 345–354.

Steiner, I. D. (1972) *Group Process and Productivity*, New York: Academic Press.

Stinchcombe, A. L. (1965) Social structure and organizations. In J. G. March (ed.), *Handbook of Organizations* (pp. 142–193). Chicago: Rand McNally.

Sundstrom, E., DeMeuse, K. P., and Futrell, D. (1990) Work teams: Applications and effectiveness. *American Psychologist*, **45**, 120–133.

Thompson, J. D. (1967) *Organizations in Action*. New York: McGraw-Hill.

Thibaut, J. W., and Kelley, H. H. (1959) *The Social Psychology of Groups*. New York: Wiley.

Tindale, R. S. (1989) Group vs individual information processing: The effects of outcome feedback on decision making. *Organizational Behavior and Human Decision Processes*, **44**, 454–471.

Tolbert, P. S., and Zucker, L. G. (1983) Institutional sources of change in the formal structure of organizations: The diffusion of civil service reform, 1880–1935, *Administrative Science Quarterly*, **28**, 22–39.

Trist, E., and Bamforth, D. (1951) Some social and psychological consequences of the longwall method of coal getting. *Human Relations*, **4**, 3–38.

Trow, D. B. (1960) Membership succession and team performance. *Human Relations*, **13**, 259–269.

Turner, M. E. (1988) Threat: Assessments and consequences for work group performance. Unpublished PhD dissertation, Carnegie-Mellon University.

Van de Ven, A., Delbecq, A., and Koenig, R. (1976) Determinants of coordination modes within organizations. *American Sociological Review*, **41**, 322–328.

Van Maanen, J. (1978) People processing: Strategies of organizational socialization. *Organizational Dynamics*, **7**, 18–36.

Vroom, V. H., and Yetton, P. W. (1973) *Leadership and Decision Making*. Pittsburgh: University of Pittsburgh Press.

Walsh, J. P., and Ungson, G. R. (1991) Organizational memory. *Academy of Management Review*, **26**, 57–91.

Walton, R. E., and Hackman, J. R. (1986) Groups under contrasting management strategies. In P. S. Goodman (ed.), *Designing Effective Work Groups* (pp. 168–201). San Francisco, CA: Jossey-Bass.

Watson, W., Michaelson, L. K., and Sharp, W. (1991) Member competence, group interaction, and group decision making: A longitudinal study. *Journal of Applied Psychology*, **76**, 803–809.

Wegner, D. M. (1986) Transactive memory: A contemporary analysis of the group mind. In B. Mullen and George R. Goethals (eds), *Theories of Group Behavior*. New York: Springer-Verlag.

Wegner, D. M., Erber, R., and Raymond, P. (1991) Transactive memory in close relationships. *Journal of Personality and Social Psychology*, **61**, 923–929.

Weick, K. E., and Gilfallan, D. P. (1971) Fate of arbitrary traditions in a laboratory microculture. *Journal of Personality and Social Psychology*, **17**, 179–191.

Weingart, L. R. (in press) The impact of group goals, task component complexity, effort, and planning on group performance. *Journal of Applied Psychology*.

Weldon, E., Jehn, K. A., and Pradhan, P. (1991) Processes that mediate the relationship between a group goal and improved group performance. *Journal of Personality and Social Psychology*, **61**, 555–569.

Weldon, E., and Weingart, L. R. (in press) Group goals and performance. *British Journal of Social Psychology*.

Wright, T. P. (1936) Factors affecting the costs of airplanes. *Journal of the Aeronautical Sciences*, **3**, 122–128.

Yago, A. G. (1982) Leadership: Perspectives in theory and research. *Management Science*, **28**, 315–366.

Yelle, L. E. (1979) The learning curve: Historical review and comprehensive survey. *Decision Sciences*, **10**, 302–328.

Zaccaro, S. J., Foti, R. J., and Kenny, D. A. (1991) Self-monitoring and trait-based variance in leadership: An investigation of leader flexibility across multiple group situations. *Journal of Applied Psychology*, **76**, 308–315.

Zimmerman, M. B. (1982) Learning effects and the commercialization of new energy technologies: The case of nuclear power. *Bell Journal of Economics*, **13**, 297–310.

Zucker, L. G. (1977) The role of institutionalization in cultural persistence. *American Sociological Review*, **42**, 726–743.

INDEX

Index compiled by Caroline Sheard

*International Review of Industrial
and Organizational Psychology*

CONTENTS OF VOLUME 1—1986

*International Review of Industrial
and Organizational Psychology*

CONTENTS OF VOLUME 2—1987

CONTENTS OF VOLUME 3—1988

*International Review of Industrial
and Organizational Psychology*

CONTENTS OF VOLUME 4—1989

*International Review of Industrial
and Organizational Psychology*

CONTENTS OF VOLUME 5—1990

*International Review of Industrial
and Organizational Psychology*

CONTENTS OF VOLUME 6—1991

*International Review of Industrial
and Organizational Psychology*

CONTENTS OF VOLUME 7—1992

SUBSCRIPTION NOTICE

*T*his Wiley product is updated annually to reflect important changes in the subject matter. If you purchased this copy directly from John Wiley & Sons, we will have already recorded your subscription and will inform you of new volumes. If, however, you made your purchase from a bookseller and wish to be notified of future volumes, please complete the information opposite and return to Wiley (address printed overleaf).

WILEY

Publishers Since 1807

COOPER: Volume 8   0471 936340

☐ *Please send further details on*
☐ *Volume 7 1992*
☐ *Volume 6 1991*
☐ *Volume 5 1990*
☐ *Volume 4 1989*
☐ *Volume 3 1988*
☐ *Volume 2 1987*
☐ *Volume 1 1986*

Personal rates available for further details please telephone 0243 770400

NAME: _____

ADDRESS: _____

_____

_____

COUNTRY: _____ ☎ _____

SUBSCRIPTION NOTICE

*T*his Wiley product is updated annually to reflect important changes in the subject matter. If you purchased this copy directly from John Wiley & Sons, we will have already recorded your subscription and will inform you of new volumes. If, however, you made your purchase from a bookseller and wish to be notified of future volumes, please complete the information opposite and return to Wiley (address printed overleaf).

WILEY

Publishers Since 1807

COOPER: Volume 8   0471 936340

☐ *Please send further details on*
☐ *Volume 7 1992*
☐ *Volume 6 1991*
☐ *Volume 5 1990*
☐ *Volume 4 1989*
☐ *Volume 3 1988*
☐ *Volume 2 1987*
☐ *Volume 1 1986*

Personal rates available for further details please telephone 0243 770400

NAME: _____

ADDRESS: _____

_____

_____

COUNTRY: _____ ☎ _____

By air mail
Par avion

IBRS/CCRI NUMBER:
PHQ−D/1204/PO

NE PAS AFFRANCHIR

NO STAMP REQUIRED

REPONSE PAYEE
GRANDE-BRETAGNE

Sarah Stevens (MARKETING)
John Wiley & Sons Ltd.
Baffins Lane
CHICHESTER
West Sussex
GREAT BRITAIN
PO19 1YN